Study & Master
Study Guide 12
Mathematics

Noleen Jakins | Deirdre Yeo

EXAM PRACTICE

Please note that all the tests in this Study Guide provide the type of questions that could be asked in the Grade 12 exams.

Test C always provides questions that follow the breakdown and content of the final exam for the relevant Topic.

CAMBRIDGE
UNIVERSITY PRESS

The Water Club, Beach Road, Granger Bay, Cape Town 8005, South Africa

Cambridge University Press is part of the University of Cambridge.

It furthers the University's mission by disseminating knowledge in the pursuit of education, learning and research at the highest international levels of excellence.

www.cambridge.org
Information on this title: www.cambridge.org/9781107678040

© Cambridge University Press 2013

This publication is in copyright. Subject to statutory exception and to the provisions of relevant collective licensing agreements, no reproduction of any part may take place without the written permission of Cambridge University Press.

First published 2013
7th printing 2015

Printed in South Africa by Creda Communications

ISBN 978-1-107-67804-0 Paperback

Editor: Alison Paulin
Proofreaders: Alison Paulin, Magda de Jager
Typesetter: Maryke Garifallou
Illustrator: Maryke Garifallou
Proj id: 20224

If you want to know more about this book or any other Cambridge University Press publication, phone us at +27 21 4127800, fax us at +27 21 419-8418 or send an e-mail to capetown@cambridge.org

Contents

Topic 1	**Patterns, sequences and series**	**1**
	Arithmetic and geometric sequences	1
	Using general forms and definitions	2
	Calculating arithmetic and geometric means	5
	Using the general form and simultaneous equations (complex procedures)	7
	Series and sigma notation	9
	Using summative formulae and geometric series	10
	Proofs for summative formulae	12
	Using quadratics, summative formulae and inequalities	13
	Using quadratics, summative formulae and inequalities (complex procedures and problem solving)	14
	Tests	20
Topic 2	**Functions and inverses**	**23**
	Formal definition of a function	24
	Ways of representing functions	24
	Domain and range	27
	Increasing and decreasing functions (complex procedures)	27
	Inverses	29
	Average gradient	33
	Types of functions and their properties	35
	Transforming (shifting) of graphs	40
	Exponential functions	41
	The exponential function and its graph	43
	Logarithms	45
	The logarithmic function and its graph	47
	Logarithmic and exponential functions are inverses of one another	48
	Using logs to solve an exponential equation	52
	Tests	53
Topic 3	**Finance: Growth and decay**	**57**
	Revision of Grades 10 and 11 Finance	58
	Present value and future value annuities	61
	Investments, savings and retirement annuities	61
	Sinking funds	64
	Present value: Loans and car finance	67
	Use logarithms to calculate the value of the time period n	69
	Outstanding balance of a loan	70
	Tests	73
Topic 4	**Trigonometry**	**77**
	Compound angle identities	79
	Deriving the compound angle identities (complex procedures)	80
	Deriving and working with double angle identities	81
	Solving equations involving compound angles	84

        Proving identities (complex procedures) 86
        Problems in three dimensions 89
        Proving identities using triangles in two dimensions (complex procedures) 93
        Tests 96

Topic 5   **Polynomial functions** **99**
        The remainder and factor theorems 100
        Solving for x in cubic polynomials 104
        Graphs of cubic polynomials 104
        Tests 107

Topic 6   **Differential calculus** **109**
        What is calculus? 110
        The concept of a limit 110
        Average gradient or rate of change 112
        Using first principles to find the first derivative 115
        Using the rules of differentiation to find derivatives 116
        Finding the equations of tangents and normals to curves 117
        Putting everything together 120
        The concept of a limit (complex procedures) 121
        First principles (complex procedures) 121
        Using the laws for differentiation (complex procedures) 122
        Tangents (complex procedures) 123
        Graphs of cubic functions 124
        Interpreting cubic graphs and problems based on curve sketching 130
        Finding the equation of a cubic function 132
        Graph interpretation (complex procedures) 134
        Using maxima and minima to solve problems 137
        Applications involving the calculus of motion 140
        Complex procedures and problem solving using calculus 143
        Tests 146

Topic 7   **Analytical geometry** **149**
        Review of formulae 150
        Using formulae: revision of Grades 10 and 11 work 151
        Finding the equation of a circle 152
        Determining the centre and the radius of a circle 154
        Finding the equation of a tangent to a circle 155
        Finding points of intersection 156
        Finding the length of a tangent from an external point 157
        Integrated problems involving lines and circles 158
        Intersecting circles 161
        Tests 165

Topic 8   **Euclidean geometry and measurement** **168**
        Proportion 169
        Similar polygons 169
        The midpoint theorem 170
        Similarity 171

	Proving the theorem of Pythagoras using similarity	172
	Preparing for exams	174
	Tests	175

Topic 9	**Statistics: Regression and correlation**	**180**
	The normal distribution	181
	Symmetry and skewed data	184
	Bivariate data: regression and correlation	191

Topic 10	**Counting and probability**	**202**
	Independent events	203
	Dependent events	204
	Mutually exclusive events	204
	Inclusive events	204
	Complementary rule	205
	Counting	206
	Two-way contingency tables	207
	Venn diagrams	209
	Factorial notation and its uses	210
	Tests	211

Solutions		**218**
Topic 1	Patterns, sequences and series	218
Topic 2	Functions and inverses	228
Topic 3	Finance: Growth and decay	242
Topic 4	Trigonometry	256
Topic 5	Polynomial functions	267
Topic 6	Differential calculus	272
Topic 7	Analytical geometry	287
Topic 8	Euclidean geometry and measurement	295
Topic 9	Statistics: Regression and correlation	299
Topic 10	Counting and probability	308

TOPIC 1 Patterns, sequences and series

In Grade 10 you covered linear number patterns, and in Grade 11 you learnt about quadratic number patterns. In this Topic for Grade 12, your knowledge of number patterns is extended. **Arithmetic sequences** and **geometric sequences** are introduced and you will learn about formulae for these. These formulae will be used together with other algebraic techniques to solve a variety of problems that involve number sequences and series.

Knowledge and skills for this Topic

If you struggle with any of the work listed below, revise the relevant work before continuing with this Topic, as lack of this knowledge will hamper your progress:

- a basic understanding of algebra including the manipulation of algebraic expressions, equations and inequalities.
- a working knowledge of simultaneous equations
- a working knowledge of exponential theory and equations
- quadratic equations, solution both by factorisation and formulae.
- a basic working knowledge of logarithms and how to use logs to solve simple equations.

Content of final exam

- Arithmetic, geometric and quadratic sequences and series are examinable. (Quadratic sequences form part of the Grade 11 syllabus.)
- A variety of questions will be asked which will include knowledge and routine procedures, complex procedures and problem solving. Complex procedures and problem solving are indicated in this Study Guide. All other work falls under knowledge and routine procedures.
- Bookwork: Determining the summative formulae is examinable.

Relevant formulae

$$\sum_{i=1}^{n} 1 = n \qquad \sum_{i=1}^{n} i = \frac{n(n+1)}{2} \qquad \sum_{i=1}^{n}(a+(n-1)d) = \frac{n}{2}[2a+(n-1)d]$$

$$\sum_{i=1}^{n} ar^{i-1} = \frac{a(r^n - 1)}{r - 1}; r \neq 1 \qquad \sum_{i=1}^{\infty} ar^{i-1} = \frac{a}{1-r}; -1 < r < 1$$

Arithmetic and geometric sequences

> **Note**
> A sequence may also be called a progression. In this Study Guide, we use the term 'sequence'.

Your success in this Topic will be based on your ability to recognise and to categorise the sequence as arithmetic or geometric, and then to select the correct formulae and algebraic tools to solve the problem. Many learners struggle to recognise what type the number sequence is and then struggle to interpret and to complete the problem. For this reason, this Study Guide often compares arithmetic and geometric sequences.

Arithmetic sequences	Geometric sequences
The general sequence is: $a; a + d; a + 2d; a + 3d; \ldots$ a is the **first term** and d is the **common difference**. By definition: $d = T_2 - T_1 = T_3 - T_2$	**The general sequence is:** $a; ar; ar^2; ar^3; \ldots$ a is the **first term** and r is the **common ratio**. By definition: $r = \dfrac{T_2}{T_1} = \dfrac{T_3}{T_2}$
Examples of arithmetic sequences 2, 4, 6, 8, … $\quad d = 4 - 2 = 6 - 8 = 2$ 4; 1; –2; –5;… $\quad d = 1 - 4 = -2 - 1 = -3$ $\log x; 2\log x; 3\log x; \ldots$ $d = 2\log x - \log x = 3\log x - 3\log x = \log x$.	**Examples of geometric sequences** 2, 4, 8, 16, … $r = \dfrac{4}{2} = \dfrac{8}{4} = 2$ 3; 15; 75; 225; … $r = \dfrac{15}{3} = \dfrac{75}{15} = 5$
The **general form** or **nth term** is given by the formula: $T_n = a + (n-1)d$ where a is the first term, T_1 d is the common difference n is the term number.	The **general form** or **nth term** is given by the formula: $T_n = ar^{n-1}$ where a is the first term, T_1 r is the common difference n is the term number.

Using general forms and definitions

The basic work in this Topic involves the direct interpretation and use of formulae and procedures. Worked examples are often scaffolded, in other words you are led through to the solution by a sequence of steps.

Finding an expression in terms of *n* for a series of numbers

Worked examples

Consider the two sequences given below. Use the relevant formulae to find a general expression for each sequence.

1. 2; 7; 12; 19
2. 2; 6; 18; …

Solutions

1. 2; 7; 12; 19 is arithmetic

   $a = 2$ and $d = 7 - 2 = 12 - 7 = 5$
   Using $T_n = a + (n-1)d$

   $T_n = 2 + (n-1)5$
   $T_n = 2 + 5n - 5$
   $T_n = 5n - 3$

   Identify the type of sequence as arithmetic or geometric. Write down the values for a and d or r.
   Write down the values for a and d or r.
   Select the relevant formula and find the general term by substituting the relevant values.

2. 2; 6; 18; … is geometric

   $a = 2$ and $r = \dfrac{6}{2} = \dfrac{18}{6} = 3$

   Using $T_n = ar^{n-1}$

   $T_n = 2.3^{n-1}$

   Identify the type of sequence as arithmetic or geometric.
   Write down the values for a and d or r.
   Select the relevant formula and find the general term by substituting the relevant values.

Using the general form and the definition of d or r

You will use the general form and the definition of d or r to:
- find the values of a and d or r, OR
- determine the sequence, OR
- find the values for specific terms, e.g. if you are asked 'Find the value of the fiftieth term'.

Worked examples

Find the first three terms for each of the sequences given below, list the values for a and d for 1 and a and r for 2. In each case find the value for the 21st term.

1. $T_n = 17n - 2$
2. $T_n = 3.2^{2-n}$

Solutions

Remember
$a = T_1; d = T_2 - T_1$
$= T_3 - T_2; r = \dfrac{T_2}{T_1} = \dfrac{T_3}{T_2}$

1. $T_n = 17n - 2$ *Use the 'rule' as it is given and substitute for $n = 1, 2$ and 3. List your result as a sequence of numbers.*

   $T_1 = 17(1) - 2 = 15$
   $T_2 = 17(2) - 2 = 34 - 2 = 32$
   $T_3 = 17(3) - 2 = 51 - 2 = 49$

   Number sequence: 15; 32; 49

   $a = 15; d = T_2 - T_1 = 32 - 15 = 17$

   $T_{21} = 17(21) - 2 = 357 - 2 = 355$ *Substitute for n in the general form of the sequence to find the value of a specific term.*

2. $T_n = 3.2^{2-n}$
   $T_1 = 3.2^{2-1} = 3.2^1 = 6$
   $T_2 = 3.2^{2-2} = 3.2^0 = 3.1 = 3$
   $T_3 = 3.2^{2-3} = 3.2^{-1} = \dfrac{3}{2}$

   Number sequence: $6; 3; \dfrac{3}{2}$

   $a = 6$ and $r = \dfrac{T_2}{T_1} = \dfrac{3}{6} = \dfrac{1}{2}$

   $T_{21} = 3.2^{2-21} = 3.2^{-19} = 5.72 \times 10^{-6}$

Using the general form and the definition of d or r to find the value of n

Worked examples

1. Given the sequence $11; 2; -7; \ldots$ find the value of n if $T_n = -169$.

2. Calculate the number of terms in the sequence $\dfrac{3}{2}; -1; \dfrac{2}{3}; \ldots; -\dfrac{16}{81}$.

3. Use a formula to find which term in the arithmetic series $-71; -68; -65; \ldots$ is the first term to exceed 10.

4. Calculate the number of terms in the sequence: $5; 10; 20; \ldots 81\ 920$

You need to know

A solid working knowledge of **linear equations**, **exponents** and **exponential equations** is necessary to solve this type of problem.

Solutions

When the type of sequence is not given, you need to study the sequence to determine whether it is arithmetic or geometric. You can then use the appropriate definition or formula to solve the problem.

1. $a = 11; d = 2 - 11 = -9$

   > $11; 2; -7; \ldots$ is arithmetic. Use $d = T_2 - T_1$.
   > Substitute for T_n, a and d in $T_n = a + (n-1)d$ and solve for n.

   $T_n = -169$
   $-169 = 11 + (n-1)(-9)$
   $-169 = 11 - 9n + 9$
   $9n = 11 + 169 + 9$
   $9n = 189$
   $n = 21$

2. $a = \frac{2}{3}; r = \frac{-1}{\frac{3}{2}} = -\frac{2}{3}$

   > $\frac{3}{2}; -1; \frac{2}{3}; \ldots$ is geometric.
   > Use $r = \frac{T_2}{T_1}$. Substitute for T_n, a and r in $T_n = ar^{n-1}$ and solve for n.

   $T_n = -\frac{16}{81}$

   $-\frac{16}{81} = \frac{3}{2}\left(-\frac{2}{3}\right)^{n-1}$

   $-\frac{16}{81}\left(\frac{3}{2}\right) = \left(-\frac{2}{3}\right)^{n-1}$

   $-\frac{32}{243} = \left(-\frac{2}{3}\right)^{n-1}$

   $-\left(\frac{2}{3}\right)^5 = \left(-\frac{2}{3}\right)^{n-1}$

   $\therefore 5 = n - 1$
   $n = 6$

   Once the bases are equal, equate the exponents and solve for n.

3. $-71; -68; -65; \ldots$
   $a = -71; d = -68 - (-71) = 3$
   $10 < -71 + (n-1)3$

   The sequence is arithmetic.
   Identify a and work out d.
   This problem calls for the general form $T_n = a + (n-1)d$ and an inequality.

   $10 < -71 + 3n - 3$
   $84 < 3n$
   $n > 28$
   $\therefore n = 29$

4. $T_1 = a = 5; r = 2$
   $81\,920 = 5 \cdot 2^{n-1}$

   The sequence is geometric. Identify a and work out r.
   You need to find n. Substitute for a, r and T_n in the general form and solve for n: $T_n = ar^{n-1}$

   $\frac{81\,920}{5} = 2^{n-1}$
   $16\,384 = 2^{n-1}$
   $2^{14} = 2^{n-1}$
   $14 = n - 1$
   $n = 15$

Exercise 1

1. Given the arithmetic sequence 180; 173; 166; ... determine:
   1.1 the values of a and d
   1.2 the value of the 40th term
   1.3 which term of the sequence is equal to 33
   1.4 the general form for the sequence in terms of n.

2. Given the geometric sequence $\frac{1}{8}; \frac{1}{4}; \frac{1}{2}; \ldots$ calculate:
   2.1 the common ratio
   2.2 the value of T_9
   2.3 n if $T_n = 2$
   2.4 the general form for the sequence in terms of n.

3. Given $T_n = \frac{3^n}{15}$:
   3.1 show that this sequence of numbers is geometric
   3.2 find the value of n if $T_n = \frac{729}{15}$
   3.3 calculate the value of the tenth term, correct to one decimal place.

4. Find the general term for the sequence: 9; –6; 4; ...

5. Find the first three terms for each of the sequences given by the general forms listed below. Use this information to show whether each sequence is arithmetic, geometric or neither, and then find the 8th term for each sequence.
   5.1 $T_k = 2.3^{k+1}$
   5.2 $T_k = 2(3k - 1)$
   5.3 $T_k = \frac{k}{k-2}$

Calculating arithmetic and geometric means

Arithmetic means	Geometric means
The formula: $y = \frac{x+z}{2}$ can be used to calculate the arithmetic mean of the arithmetic sequence: $x; y; z; \ldots$: In the arithmetic sequence: $x; y; z; \ldots$: $y - x = z - y$ $2y = x + z$ $\therefore y = \frac{x+z}{2}$	The formula: $y = \pm \sqrt{xz}$ can be used to calculate the geometric mean of the geometric sequence: $x; y; z; \ldots$ In the geometric sequence: $x; y; z; \ldots$: $\frac{y}{x} = \frac{z}{y}$ $y^2 = xz$ $\therefore y = \pm \sqrt{xz}$

Worked examples

1. Find the value of y in the arithmetic sequence: 25; y; 16.

2. Find the value(s) of y in the geometric sequence: 25; y; 1.

3. Given the arithmetic sequence 1; x; y; 10, find the values of x and y.

4. $\frac{1}{3}; y; \frac{3}{4}; \ldots$ is a geometric sequence with $y < 0$. Determine the value(s) of y.

Solutions

1. $y = \frac{25 + 16}{2} = 20{,}5$

   > Given: $x; y; z \ldots$ is arithmetic.
   > Substitute for x and z in $y = \frac{x+z}{2}$ to find the arithmetic mean, y.

2. $y = \pm\sqrt{(25)(1)} = \pm 5$

   > Given: $x; y; z \ldots$ is geometric.
   > Substitute for x and z in $y = \pm\sqrt{xy}$ to find the geometric mean, y.

   Two possible sequences of numbers exist in this case:
   $25; 5; 1 \ldots$ and $25; -5; 1 \ldots$

3. $1; x; y; 10$

   $T_1 = a; T_2 = a + d; T_3 = a + 2d; T_4 = a + 3d$ — Interpret the problem by rewriting the information using relevant formulae.

   $T_4 = a + 3d$
   $10 = 1 + 3d$
   $9 = 3d$
   $\therefore d = 3$

   $T_2 = a + d$

   Study the information and decide which algebraic techniques can be used to solve the problem. In this case use simultaneous equations.

   $x = 1 + 3 = 4$

   $T_3 = a + 2d$
   $y = 1 + 2(3) = 7$

4. $\frac{1}{3}; y; \frac{3}{4}; \ldots$

   $y = -\sqrt{\left(\frac{1}{3}\right)\left(\frac{3}{4}\right)} = -\sqrt{\frac{1}{4}} = -\frac{1}{2}$

   Substitute for x and z in $y = \pm\sqrt{xz}$, and simplify. In this case we are given that $y < 0$, so we use only $y = -\sqrt{\left(\frac{1}{3}\right)\left(\frac{3}{4}\right)} = -\frac{1}{2}$.

Exercise 2

1. Find the value(s) of p such that $\frac{2}{3}; p; \frac{27}{2}$ are in geometric progression.

2. Find both the arithmetic mean and the geometric mean of 4 and 6.

3. Given the arithmetic sequence $2; p; 5; \ldots$:
   - **3.1** Find the value(s) of p.
   - **3.2** Determine the value of the 77th term.
   - **3.3** What term in this sequence is equal to 77?

4. $81; x; 4$ are the first three terms of a geometric sequence, with $x < 0$. Calculate:
   - **4.1** the value of x.
   - **4.2** the 10th term of this sequence.

Using the general form and simultaneous equations (complex procedures)

> **You need to know**
> A solid working knowledge of **simultaneous equations** is necessary to solve this type of problem.

Worked examples

1. The third term of an arithmetic sequence is 8 and the eighth term is 23. Use this information to calculate the value of the first term and the 50th term.

2. The third term of a geometric sequence is 8 and the tenth term is $\frac{1}{16}$. Use this information to calculate the value of the first and the seventh terms.

3. Find the value(s) of x and y in the geometric series $\frac{1}{5}; x; y; \frac{8}{5}; \ldots$

4. Find the value of p, q, and r in the arithmetic sequence $-4; p; q; r; 40$.

Solutions

1. Elimination has been used in this example. It is your choice which method you use.

   > Interpret the given information using $T_n = a + (n-1)d$ to set up two linear equations.

   $T_3 = a + (3-1)d$
   $8 = a + 2d$ [Equation 1]
   $T_8 = a + (8-1)d$
   $23 = a + 7d$ [Equation 2]
   $a + 7d = 23$
   $-a - 2d = -8$ Solve for a and d simultaneously using either elimination or substitution.
   $5d = 15$
   $\therefore d = 3$

   $a + 2d = 8$ Equation 1: Find a by substituting for d into Equation 1.
   $a + 2(3) = 8$
   $\therefore a = T_1 = 8 - 6 = 2$

   $T_n = a + (n-1)d$ Substitute for n, a and d in the general form to find the value of a specific term.

   $T_{50} = 2 + (50 - 1)(3) = 2 + 49(3) = 2 + 147 = 149$

> **You need to know**
> **Simultaneous equations** in a different format are used here.
> Note that it makes your working easier if you arrange your solution with $\frac{ar^9}{ar^2}$ as opposed to $\frac{ar^2}{ar^9}$.
> **Basic exponential theory** is used.

2. Substitute for n, a and d in the general form to find the value of a specific term.
   $T_n = ar^{n-1}$
   $T_3 = ar^{3-1} = ar^2$
   $8 = ar^2$ [Equation 1]
   $T_{10} = ar^{10-1} = ar^9$
   $23 = ar^9 = \frac{1}{16}$ [Equation 2]
   $\frac{ar^9}{ar^2} = \frac{\frac{1}{16}}{8}$
   $r^7 = \frac{1}{16} \div 8 = \frac{1}{128} = \frac{1}{2^7}$ Solve for a and r simultaneously. In this case a is eliminated.
   $\therefore r = \frac{1}{2}$

TOPIC 1   Patterns, sequences and series

$$a\left(\tfrac{1}{2}\right)^2 = 8 \qquad \text{Substitute for } r \text{ in } ar^2 = 8.$$
$$\therefore a = 8 \div \left(\tfrac{1}{2}\right)^2 = 32$$

> Substitute for n, a and r in the general form to find the value of a specific term.
> Substitute for r in $ar^2 = 8$.

$$T_7 = ar^{7-1} = 32\left(\tfrac{1}{2}\right)^{7-1} = 32\left(\tfrac{1}{2}\right)^6 = \tfrac{1}{2}$$

You need to know
Simultaneous equations using substitution

3. By definition: $\dfrac{T_2}{T_1} = \dfrac{T_3}{T_2}$ and $\dfrac{T_3}{T_2} = \dfrac{T_4}{T_3}$ Use $r = \dfrac{T_2}{T_1} = \dfrac{T_3}{T_2}$ to set up two separate equations in terms of x and y.

$\dfrac{x}{\frac{1}{5}} = \dfrac{y}{x}$ and $\dfrac{y}{x} = \dfrac{\frac{8}{5}}{y}$

$5x^2 = y$ [Equation 1]

$y^2 = \dfrac{8x}{5}$ [Equation 2]

$(5x^2)^2 = \dfrac{8x}{5}$ Solve for x and y simultaneously using substitution. Substitute for y in Equation 2.

$25x^4 = \dfrac{8x}{5}$

$\dfrac{x^4}{x} = \dfrac{8}{5 \times 25}$

$x^3 = \dfrac{8}{125} = \left(\dfrac{2}{5}\right)^3$

$\therefore x = \dfrac{2}{5}$ and $y = 5\left(\dfrac{2}{5}\right)^2 = 5\left(\dfrac{4}{25}\right) = \dfrac{4}{5}$

4. $-4;\ p;\ q;\ r;\ 40$ Interpret the given information.
$T_1 = -4 = a$ $T_5 = a + 4d = 40$ Substitute for a and work out d.
$40 = -4 + 4d$
$44 = 4d$
$\therefore d = 11$

$p = -4 + 11 = 7;\ q = 7 + 11 = 18;\ r = 18 + 11 = 29$ Calculate the required values.

Exercise 3 (complex procedures)

1. The sixth term of an arithmetic sequence is 14 and the 14th term is –2. Determine the value of the tenth term.

2. Determine the first term and the constant ratio of a geometric sequence of which the fourth term is 54 and the seventh term is –1 458.

3. $3;\ x;\ y;\ z;\ 19;\ \ldots$ is an arithmetic series of numbers. Find the values of x, y and z.

4. Given that $T_2 = 6$ and $T_7 = 192$, determine the geometric sequence (i.e. the first three terms), and the value of the 21st term.

5. In an arithmetic sequence, $T_3 = x$, and $T_7 = y$, find the value of T_{11} in terms of x and y.

6. If the numbers 42, 32 and 2 are added to the first, second and third terms of a geometric sequence respectively, the three terms will all be equal. Calculate the values for the three terms.

Series and sigma notation

A **sequence** given as $T_n = 2n + 3$ can be written as: 5; 7; 9; 11; ...

A **series** given as $5 + 7 + 9 + 11 + ...$ can be written as $\sum_{n=1}^{n} 2n + 3$.

Remember that the sigma or summative symbol $\sum$ means that we must add a specified number of terms.

For example: $\sum_{n=1}^{6} 2n + 3$ means that the first 6 terms must be added together.

So $\sum_{n=1}^{6} 2n + 3 = 5 + 7 + 9 + 11 + 13 + 15 = 60$.

$\sum_{n=3}^{5} 2n + 3$ means that only the third, fourth and fifth terms must be added together.

So $\sum_{n=3}^{5} 2n + 3 = 9 + 11 + 13 = 33$.

Remember

The number of terms in a sigma series is calculated by subtracting the first digit to be substituted from the last number to be substituted, and adding one.
For example:
$\sum_{n=5}^{13} 3n - 2$
Number of terms
$= (13 - 5) + 1$
$= 9$ terms.

Worked examples

1. Evaluate: $\sum_{n=1}^{4} 3n - 2$

2. Evaluate: $\sum_{k=5}^{8} 4\left(\frac{1}{2}\right)^{k-1}$

3. Express the following series in sigma notation: $3 + 7 + 11 + ... + 83$

Solutions

1. $\sum_{n=1}^{4} 3n - 2 = [3(1) - 2] + [3(2) - 2] + [3(3) - 2] + [3(4) - 2] = 1 + 4 + 7 + 10$
   $= 22$

2. $\sum_{k=5}^{8} 4\left(\frac{1}{2}\right)^{k-1} = 4\left(\frac{1}{2}\right)^{5-1} + 4\left(\frac{1}{2}\right)^{6-1} + 4\left(\frac{1}{2}\right)^{7-1} + 4\left(\frac{1}{2}\right)^{8-1}$
   $= \frac{1}{4} + \frac{1}{8} + \frac{1}{16} + \frac{1}{32} = \frac{15}{32}$

3. Note that this sequence is arithmetic.
   $3 + 7 + 11 + ... + 83$
   $a = 3; d = 4$
   $T_n = a + (n-1)d = 3 + (n-1)4 = 4n - 1$ Find an expression for the series in terms of n.
   $T_n = a + (n-1)d$
   $83 = 4n - 1$ Find the term number of the last term.
   $84 = 4n$
   $\therefore n = 21$

   $\sum_{n=1}^{21} (4n - 1)$ Summarise your results using sigma notation.

TOPIC 1   *Patterns, sequences and series*

Using summative formulae and geometric series

> **The sum of an arithmetic series** $a, a + d; a + 2d; a + 3d; \ldots n$ terms
> is given by the formula $S_n = \frac{n}{2}[2a + (n-1)d]$
> or $S_n = \frac{n}{2}(a + l)$ when the last term l is known.

> **The sum of a geometric series** $a; ar; ar^2; ar^3; \ldots n$ terms
> is given by the formula $S_n = \frac{a(r^n - 1)}{r - 1}; r \neq 1$

> A geometric series is **convergent** if $-1 < r < 1$.
> The sum to infinity of a geometric series is given by the formula $S_\infty = \frac{a}{1-r}$
>
> Note: If $r < -1$ or $r > 1$ the series is **divergent** and **does not have a sum to infinity.**

Worked examples

1. Given the arithmetic sequence 7; 2; –3; … calculate the sum of the first 18 terms.

2. Calculate the value of $\sum_{n=1}^{27} 3n + 4$.

3. Use a formula to find the sum of the first seven terms of the series
$\frac{1}{81} + \frac{1}{27} + \frac{1}{9} + \ldots$

4. Show that the progression $6 - 3 + \frac{3}{2} - \frac{3}{4} + \ldots$ is convergent, and then find the sum to infinity for this progression.

5. Given the geometric series: $1 + (-3) + 9 + \ldots$ find the value of n if $S_n = -182$.

Solutions

1. $a = 7; d = 2 - 7 = -5$ — The sequence is arithmetic. Identify a and work out d.

    $S_n = \frac{n}{2}[2a + (n-1)d]$ — Select the appropriate formula according to the type of sequence. Substitute all values and use your calculator.

    $S_{18} = \frac{18}{2}[2(7) + (18-1)(-5)]$

    $S_n = 9[14 + 17(-5)]$

    $S_n = -639$

2. $a = 3(1) + 4 = 7$ — The sequence is arithmetic. Identify a and work out l because we know that the last term is term number 27.

    $l = 3(27) + 4 = 85$ — Select the appropriate formula according to the type of sequence. Substitute all values and use your calculator.

    $S_n = \frac{n}{2}(a + l)$

    $S_{27} = \frac{27}{2}(7 + 85)$

    $S_{27} = 1\,242$

Remember
If you are not specifically asked to give your answer as a decimal, you can leave it as a fraction.

3. $a = \frac{1}{81}; r = \frac{1}{27} \div \frac{1}{81} = \frac{81}{27} = 3$ — First decide what type of sequence you are working with, then identify a and work out r.

    $S_n = \frac{a(r^n - 1)}{r - 1}$ — Select the appropriate formula according to the type of sequence. Substitute all values and use your calculator.

$$S_7 = \frac{\frac{1}{81}(3^7 - 1)}{3 - 1}$$

$$S_7 = \frac{1093}{81}$$

4. $r = \frac{-3}{6} = \frac{-1}{2}$. *Calculate the value for r and give a reason for convergence.*

    $\therefore$ progression is convergent because $-1 < r < 1$.

    $S_\infty = \frac{a}{1-r}$ *Substitute for a and r in the formula for the sum to infinity.*

    $S_\infty = \frac{6}{1-(-\frac{1}{2})} = 4$

5. $a = 1$; $r = \frac{-3}{1} = -3$ *This sequence is given as geometric. Identify a and work out r.*

    $S_n = \frac{a(r^n - 1)}{r - 1}$ *This problem calls for the summative formula and results in an exponential equation.*

    $-182 = \frac{1[(-3)^n - 1]}{-3 - 1}$

    $728 = (-3)^n - 1$

    $729 = (-3)^n$

    $3^6 = (-3)^n$

    $\therefore n = 6$

You need to know
- exponents
- exponential equations

Remember
While the bases 3 and -3 are not equal, $n = 6$. Raising to an even power will always result in a positive number.

Exercise 4

1. $\sum_{n=1}^{23} (5n - 1)$. Determine:
    1.1 the first term, T_1
    1.2 the last term, T_{23}
    1.3 the sum of this series.

2. $\sum_{n=3}^{7} 2.3^{n-1}$. Determine:
    2.1 the first three terms
    2.2 the sum of this series.
    2.3 Is this series divergent or convergent? Give a reason for your answer.

3. Calculate: $\sum_{k=4}^{85} (5k + 2)$

4. Given: $3; -9; 27; \ldots$
    4.1 Determine the eleventh term.
    4.2 Express the sum of the series to the first 11 terms in sigma notation.
    4.3 Determine the sum of the first eleven terms.

5. Determine n if $\sum_{k=1}^{n} \frac{4}{3}\left(\frac{3}{2}\right)^{k-1} = \frac{665}{24}$.

6. Given that $T_n = 5 - 6n$, determine S_{43}.

7. Given the sequence: $2; 3\frac{1}{2}; 5; \ldots$, determine T_{12} and S_{12}.

8. Consider the set of all natural numbers.
    8.1 Express the sum of the first 89 natural numbers in sigma notation.
    8.2 Use a formula to find the sum of the first 89 natural numbers.

9. Use a formula to find the sum of the first 21 multiples of 2.
10. Given the series: 1,25; 2,5; 3,75; ...; ... 12,5:
    10.1 Find n, when $T_n = 12,5$
    10.2 Find the sum for this series.
11. Calculate: $\sum_{r=5}^{12} (2r - 5)\sqrt{p}$
12. Determine the sum of the infinite series $8 - 3 + \frac{9}{8} - ...$
13. Calculate $\sum_{n=1}^{\infty} 8^{1-n}$ if it exists.
14. Calculate the value of r if $\sum_{n=1}^{\infty} 2r^{n-1} = 12$

Proofs for summative formulae

Deriving the summative formulae is examinable.

> **Bookwork:**
> $S_n = \frac{n}{2}[a + a + (n - 1)d]$

Proving the summative formula for an arithmetic series

> **General method:**
> 1. Write out the sequence to n terms.
> 2. Write the sequence out in reverse order.
> 3. Add the lines together and divide the result by 2.

$$S_n = [a] + [a + d] + [a + 2d] + ... + [a + (n-2)d] + [a + (n-1)d]$$
$$S_n = [a + (n-1)d] + [a + (n-2)d] + [a + (n-3)d] + ... + [a + d] + [a]$$
Add: $2S_n = [2a + (n-1)d] + 2[a + n - 1)d] + 2[a + n - 1)d] + ... + 2[a + (n-1)d] + 2[a + (n-1)d]$

$\therefore 2S_n = n[2a + (n-1)d]$
$\therefore S_n = \frac{n}{2}[2a + (n-1)d]$

If we substitute l for $[a + (n - 1)d]$ (the last of n terms), then
$S_n = \frac{n}{2}[a + a + (n - 1)d]$
$\therefore S_n = \frac{n}{2}[a + (a + (n - 1)d]$
$\therefore S_n = \frac{n}{2}[a + l]$

Proving the summative formula for a geometric series

> **Bookwork:**
> $\therefore S_n = \frac{a(r^n - 1)}{r - 1}, r \neq 1$
>
> **General method:**
> 1. Write out the sequence to n terms.
> 2. Multiply each term by r, and move each term one place to the right as shown below.
> 3. Subtract the two lines from each other.
> 4. Factorise and make S_n the subject of the formula.

> **Note**
> These two formulae are equivalent and both will give the same answer. The first formula is easier to use when $r > 1$ and the second formula is easier to use when $r < 1$.

$$S_n = a + ar + ar^2 + ar^3 + \ldots + ar^{n-2} + ar^{n-1} \quad \text{①}$$
$$r \times S_n = ar + ar^2 + ar^3 + \ldots + ar^{n-2} + ar^{n-1} + ar^n \quad \text{②}$$
$$rS_n - S_n = -a + 0 + 0 + 0 + \ldots + 0 + 0 + ar^n \quad \text{Subtract ① from ②}$$
$$\therefore rS_n - S_n = ar^n - a$$
$$\therefore S_n(r - 1) = a(r^n - 1)$$
$$\therefore S_n = \frac{a(r^n - 1)}{r - 1}, \ r \neq 1$$

OR subtracting ① – ②, i.e. $rS_n - S_n$, gives us the formula $S_n = \frac{a(r^n - 1)}{r - 1}, \ r \neq 1$

Deriving the summative formula for the sum to infinity for geometric series

> $S_\infty \to \frac{a}{1-r}$ as $n \to \infty$

Using the summative formula: $S_n = \frac{a(1 - r^n)}{1 - r} = \frac{a}{1-r} - \frac{ar^n}{1-r}$

As $n \to \infty; \ r^n \to 0$ As n gets bigger and bigger, r^n will get closer and closer to 0. We say that as n approaches infinity, r^n approaches zero.

as $n \to \infty \therefore \frac{ar^n}{1-r} \to 0$ as $n \to \infty$

$\therefore S_\infty \to \frac{a}{1-r}$

Using quadratics, summative formulae and inequalities

Worked examples

1. The sum to n terms of the arithmetic series $4 + 1 + (-2) + (-5) + \ldots = -3\ 621$. Find the value of n.

2. Determine the largest value of n such that $\sum_{x=1}^{n} (3x - 2) < 2\ 000$.

Solutions

> **You need to know**
> quadratic equations: it is often quicker and easier to use the formula to solve a quadratic equation with large numbers

> **Remember**
> The formula used to solve a quadratic equation is $ax^2 + bx + c = 0$.
> $x = \frac{-b \pm \sqrt{b^2 - 4ac}}{2a}$

1. $a = 4; \ d = 1 - 4 = -3$ Identify a and work out d.

   $S_n = \frac{n}{2}[2a + (n-1)d]$ This problem calls for the S_n formula $S_n = \frac{n}{2}[2a + (n-1)d]$ and results in a quadratic equation.

   $-3\ 621 = \frac{n}{2}[2(4) + (n-1)(-3)]$

   $-7\ 242 = n(8 - 3n + 3)$

   $-7\ 242 = n(11 - 3n)$

   $-7\ 242 = 11n - 3n^2$

   $3n^2 - 11n - 7\ 242 = 0$

   $n = \frac{-(-11) \pm \sqrt{(-11)^2 - 4(3)(-7\ 242)}}{2(3)}$

   $n = \frac{-142}{3}$ or $n = 51$ The value of n cannot be negative, and n must be a natural number.

   $\therefore n = 51$

TOPIC 1   Patterns, sequences and series

2. $\sum_{x=1}^{n}(3x-2) < 2\,000$

Determine the first three terms of the sequence. Identify a and work out d.

$T_1 = [3(1) - 2] = 1$; $T_2 = [3(2) - 2] = 4$; $T_3 = [3(3) - 2] = 7$

$\therefore a = 1$ and $d = 3$

$S_n = \frac{n}{2}[2a + (n-1)d] < 2\,000$

This problem calls for the summative formula: $S_n = \frac{n}{2}[2a + (n-1)d]$ and results in a quadratic inequality.

$\frac{n}{2}[2(1) + (n-1)(3)] < 2\,000$

$n(2 + 3n - 3) < 4\,000$

$3n^2 - n < 4\,000$

$3n^2 - n - 4\,000 < 0$

$n = \frac{1 \pm \sqrt{1 - 4(3)(-4\,000)}}{2(3)}$

This equation cannot be factorised. The quadratic formula has been used.

$n = 36{,}68$ OR $n = -36{,}35$

The largest value of n that will make $\sum_{x=1}^{n}(3x-2) < 2\,000$ is 36.

Exercise 5

1. In the sequence 11; 16; 21; …:
   1.1 find the first term that is larger than 200
   1.2 find n if $S_n = 1\,170$
   1.3 find the smallest value for n for which $S_n > 1\,500$.

2. How many terms of the series $12 + 15 + 18 + \ldots$ do we need to find a sum of 255?

3. How many terms of the sequence $7 + 11 + 15 + \ldots$ will give a sum larger than 200?

4. In an arithmetic sequence S_n equals $n^2 + 3n$. Calculate:
   4.1 the first term and the constant difference
   4.2 the sum of the first 8 terms
   4.3 the eighth term
   4.4 the smallest value for p, if $\sum_{n=1}^{p} n^2 + 3n > 880$.

5. Find n if $\sum_{a=3}^{5}(2a + 3n) = 51$.

6. Find the value of p for which $\sum_{x=1}^{p}(22 - 4x) < -160$.

Using quadratics, summative formulae and inequalities (complex procedures and problem solving)

These types of problems rely on a solid understanding and working knowledge of all routine procedures. Problems are more detailed and may involve skills from other sections of work, including quadratics, inequalities, some complex algebra, trigonometry and logs. They may combine both general forms and summative formulae into one problem. Completing these problems successfully relies on your understanding and interpretation of the problem and your application of the basic procedures.

Worked examples

1. $4x - 2$; $x + 1$; and $x - 3$ are the first three terms of a geometric sequence.
   1.1 Determine the value of x if x is an integer, and then, based on your answer, show that the first three terms of the sequence are 18, 6 and 2.
   1.2 Write down the nth term (T_n) of the sequence and determine the value of n if $T_n = \frac{2}{243}$.
   1.3 Determine the sum to infinity of the terms of this sequence.

2. The sixth term of an arithmetic sequence is 17 and the sum of the first 20 terms is 610. Determine:
   2.1 the common difference of the sequence
   2.2 the first term of the sequence
   2.3 the sum of the first 25 terms of the sequence.

3. Convert $2,5\dot{6}$ into a common fraction.

4. Determine the values of a and d if $\sum_{n=1}^{r} [a + (n-1)d] = 2r^2 + r$.

5. What is the greatest value of p for which $\sum_{k=1}^{p} \frac{1}{9}(3)^{k-2} < 4\,000$.

Solutions

1. 1.1 $\frac{x+1}{4x-2} = \frac{x-3}{x+1}$

> Interpret the problem: The first three terms are related by definition: $r = \frac{T_2}{T_1} = \frac{T_3}{T_2}$.
> Use this to set up an algebraic equation.

You need to know
- algebraic fractions
- quadratic equations

$(x + 1)^2 = (4x - 2)(x - 3)$
$x^2 + 2x + 1 = 4x^2 - 14x + 6$
$0 = 3x^2 - 16x + 5$
$0 = (3x - 1)(x - 5)$
$x = \frac{1}{3}$ or $x = 5$

$x = \frac{1}{3}$ is inadmissible since $x \in \mathbb{Z}$; $\therefore x = 5$

$T_1 = 4x - 2 = 4(5) - 2 = 18$
$T_2 = x + 1 = 5 + 1 = 6$
$T_3 = x - 3 = 5 - 3 = 2$

1.2 $T_n = ar^{n-1}$

> Substitute for a and r into the general form to find an algebraic expression for the nth term.

$= 18\left(\frac{1}{3}\right)^{n-1}$
$= 18(3^{-1})^{n-1}$
$= 2.3^2 . 3^{-n+1}$
$T_n = 2.3^{3-n}$

You need to know
- exponents
- exponential equations

$T_n = \frac{2}{243}$ Use the general form and your knowledge of exponents to solve for n.

$2.3^{3-n} = \frac{2}{243}$

$\frac{2.3^3}{3^n} = \frac{2}{243}$

$\frac{1}{3^n} = \frac{2}{243} \cdot \frac{1}{2.27}$

$\frac{1}{3^n} = \frac{1}{3^8}$

$\therefore n = 8$

1.3 $S_\infty = \frac{a}{1-r}$ Substitute for a and r into the formula for the sum to infinity, and calculate using your calculator.

$S_\infty = \frac{18}{1-\frac{1}{3}} = 27$

2. 2.1 Translate the given information into two separate equations using the relevant formulae:

$T_6 = 17$ $\qquad\qquad S_{20} = 610$

$17 = a + 5d$ ....① $\qquad 610 = \frac{20}{2}(2a + 19d)$

$\qquad\qquad\qquad\qquad\qquad \therefore 610 = 10(2a + 19d)$

$\qquad\qquad\qquad\qquad\qquad \therefore 61 = 2a + 19d$ ....②

① × 2 $\qquad 34 = 2a + 10d$ ....③

② − ③ $\qquad 27 = 9d$ Solve for a and d using elimination.

$\therefore d = 3$ (Substitution could also be used.)

2.2 $17 = a + 5(3)$ Substitute for d in any of the two equations, and solve for a.

$17 - 15 = a$

$\therefore a = 2$

2.3 $S_n = \frac{n}{2}[2a + (n-1)d]$

$S_{25} = \frac{25}{2}[2(2) + (25-1)3]$ Substitute for n, a and d in the correct summative formula. Use your calculator.

$S_{25} = \frac{25}{2}[2(2) + (25-1)3]$

$S_{25} = 950$

3. $2{,}56565656\ldots = 2 + \left(\frac{56}{100} + \frac{56}{10\,000} + \frac{56}{1\,000\,000} + \ldots\right)$

> In the brackets is an infinite geometric series.
> The series has a sum to infinity since $-1 < \frac{1}{100} < 1$

$\frac{56}{100} + \frac{56}{10\,000} + \frac{56}{1\,000\,000} + \ldots$ has $a = 0{,}56$ and $r = \frac{1}{100}$

$S_\infty = \frac{a}{1-r} = \frac{0{,}56}{1-\frac{1}{100}} = \frac{56}{99}$

$\therefore 2{,}\dot{5}\dot{6} = 2\frac{56}{99}$

4. $S_r = 2r^2 + r$ The format of this question can be confusing. It is simply letting you know that it is an arithmetic progression.

You need to know

simultaneous equations: elimination has been used in this example; it is your choice which method you use

> **Note**
> $S_1 = a$
> $S_2 = T_1 + T_2$
> $\quad = 2a + d$

$S_1 = 2(1)^2 + (1) = 3 = a$
$S_2 = 2(2)^2 + 2 = 10$
$\therefore 2a + d = 10$
But $a = 3$
$\therefore 2(3) + d = 10$
$\therefore d = 4$

> **You need to know**
> the log laws:
> $\log m^n = n \log m$
> has been used here

5. $\sum_{k=1}^{p} \frac{1}{9}(3)^{k-2} < 4\ 000$, i.e. $S_p < 4\ 000$

$T_1 = \frac{1}{9}.3^{1-2} = \frac{1}{9}.3^{-1} = \frac{1}{27}$

$T_2 = \frac{1}{9}.3^{2-2} = \frac{1}{9}.3^0 = \frac{1}{9}$

$T_3 = \frac{1}{9}.3^{3-2} = \frac{1}{9}.3^1 = \frac{1}{3}$ Find the first three terms. Identify a and calculate r.

$\therefore a = \frac{1}{27}; r = \frac{1}{9} \div \frac{1}{27} = 3$

$S_p < 4\ 000$

$\frac{\frac{1}{27}(3^p - 1)}{3 - 1} < 4\ 000$ Use the summative formula to set up the inequality.

$\frac{1}{54}(3^p - 1) < 4\ 000$

$3^p < 216\ 001$

$\log 3^p < \log 216\ 001$

$p < \frac{\log 216\ 001}{\log 3}$ Logs must be used to solve this exponential inequality.

$p < 11{,}18$

$p = 11$

Worked examples: word problems

Number patterns can be used in everyday situations.

1. Ryan is planning to complete his first Argus cycling tour in 20 weeks' time. His personal trainer suggests that he cycles at least 2 500 km in total, starting with a total of 60 km in his first week of training, and that he increases this total by the same amount every week. How many kilometres will Ryan have to cycle in total in his last week? Give your answer correct to the nearest km.

2. In 2010 in a private game reserve in Limpopo, 102 impala babies were born. Statistics show that the impala population grows at 3,2% per annum. If the game park can only cope with 200 impala babies a year, in which year will the park no longer be able to sustain this growth rate in its impala population.

3. A particular shrub stands 1 metre tall at present. This shrub's growth each year is two thirds of its growth in the previous year. What is the greatest height that this shrub can reach?

Solutions

1. Sequence is arithmetic with:
   $a = 60; n = 20; S_{20} \geq 2\ 500$

> This problem can be solved using the arithmetic formula $S_n = \frac{n}{2}[2a + (n-1)d]$, which will provide a minimum value for d. Then use the general term: $T_n = a + (n-1)d$.

$$S_{20} = \frac{20}{2}[2(60) + (19)d]$$

$$\therefore \frac{20}{2}[2(60) + (19)d] \geq 2\,500$$

$$10(120 + 19d) \geq 2\,500$$

$$1\,200 + 190d \geq 2\,500$$

$$190d \geq 1\,300$$

$$d \geq 6{,}84$$

$T_{20} = 60 + (19 \times 7 \text{ km}) = 193 \text{ km}$

In the last week Ryan must complete 193 km in total.

2. Sequence is geometric with:
$a = 102; r = 1{,}032; T_n > 200$

$$T_n = ar^{n-1} = 102(1{,}032)^{n-1} > 200$$

$$(1{,}032)^{n-1} > \frac{200}{102}$$

$$(n-1)\log(1{,}032) > \log\frac{200}{102}$$

$$(n-1) > \frac{\log\left(\frac{200}{102}\right)}{\log 1{,}032}$$

$$n > 21{,}3769\ldots + 1$$

$$n > 22{,}3769\ldots$$

$$\therefore n = 23$$

To solve this problem, find the first value of n for which $T_n > 200$.

In 23 years' time this park will not be able to sustain its impala baby population.

3. Sequence is geometric with:
$a = 1; r = \frac{2}{3}$

$$S_\infty = \frac{1}{1 - \frac{2}{3}} = 3$$

This sequence is convergent. To solve this problem, use $S_\infty = \frac{a}{1-r}$.

This shrub has a maximum height of 3 metres.

Exercise 6
(complex procedures and problem solving)

1. The first three terms of a geometric sequence are $4(k-2); 2k-6; k-2$.
   1.1 Determine the value of k.
   1.2 Show that this sequence is convergent.
   1.3 Calculate the sum to infinity for this sequence.

2. Evaluate: $\frac{151 + 149 + 147 + \ldots + 101}{99 + 97 + 95 + \ldots + 51}$

3. In an arithmetic series, the sum of the first four terms is 4 and the value of the third term is 6. Calculate the sum of the first 6 terms.

4. The sum of n terms of an arithmetic series is 760. The first term is −5 and the nth term is 100. Calculate n and d.

5. If $x^2 + 3x - 2$; $2x + 3$; $x^2 - 2x - 1$; ... form an arithmetic progression, find the value of x.

6. The second term of an arithmetic progression is -1, and the sum of the first ten terms is 130. If the sum of the first n terms is equal to 400, calculate the value of n.

7. The first term of a geometric progression is 4. The sum of the first and the third terms is equal to $2\frac{1}{20}$ times the second term. Calculate the common ratio.

8. To bore for water costs R100 per metre for the first metre, and then the cost per metre rises by R50 for every metre bored, up to a depth of 100 m. Hereafter the cost rises by R100 per metre. If the total cost of the borehole is R307 450, calculate its depth.

9. Determine the sum of all the multiples of 3 between 300 and 600.

10. Determine the first three terms of the geometric series of which the second term is 4 and the sum to infinity is 18.

11. The sum of the first three terms of a geometric series is 31 and the product of the first three terms is 125. Find these first three terms.

12. Jamila starts working and earns R100 000 per year. Her expenditure during the first year is x rand per year. Her annual increase is R10 000 per year, and her expenses increase by R6 000 per year. If she has saved R350 000 after 10 years, find the value of x.

13. The sum to infinity for a geometric series is $\frac{3}{2}$ and the sum of the first three terms is $\frac{14}{9}$. Find the first three terms of this series.

14. For which values of x will the series $1 + \frac{x}{2x-1} + \left(\frac{x}{2x-1}\right)^2 + \left(\frac{x}{2x-1}\right)^3 + \ldots$ converge?

15. Express $0,34\dot{2}$ as a common fraction.

16. The sum of 3 consecutive terms of an arithmetic series is 27 and their product is 585. Find the first three terms.

Test A: Knowledge and routine procedures

1. Prove that the sum of n of an arithmetic series is given by the formula $S_n = \frac{n}{2}[2a - (n-1)d]$, where a is the first term and d is the common difference. (5)

2.
   - **2.1** State whether the sequence $\sqrt{3}; \sqrt{12}; \sqrt{27}; \ldots$ is arithmetic or geometric, giving the common ratio or the common difference. (2)
   - **2.2** Use a formula to find the sum of the first ten terms, leaving your answer in simplified surd form. (2)

3.
   - **3.1** Find the first three terms for the sequence described by $T_n = 2(-2)^{n-1}$ (3)
   - **3.2** Show that this sequence is geometric. (2)

4. Express $-4 - 1 + 2 + 5 + \ldots + 20$ in sigma notation. (4)

5. The first term of a geometric sequence is 2 and the common ratio is $1\frac{1}{2}$.
   - **5.1** Determine the value of the fifth term. (2)
   - **5.2** Find the sum of the first ten terms, correct to 2 decimal places. (2)

6. Given the sequence: $4; x; 32$:
   - **6.1** find the value of x if the sequence is arithmetic (2)
   - **6.2** find the value of x if the sequence is geometric. (2)

7. Show that the infinite series $8 - 3 + \frac{9}{8} - \ldots$ is convergent, and then show that this series will never exceed 6. (5)

8. Given that $T_k = 5k - 3$:
   - **8.1** show that this sequence is arithmetic (4)
   - **8.2** determine the value of n if $\sum_{k=1}^{n}(5k - 3) = 2\,235$ (6)

9. Determine the value of n if $4 + 2 + 1 + \ldots$ to n terms $= 7\frac{31}{32}$. (6)

10. If $\cos x + \cos^3 x + \cos^5 x + \ldots$ is a convergent geometric series, determine the sum to infinity for this series in the simplest form. (3)

Total: 50

Test B: Complex procedures and problem solving

1. An arithmetic series has ten terms. The sum of the first three terms of this series is 18 while the sum of the last three terms is 81. Find the sum of all ten terms. (8)

2. The sides of an equilateral triangle are 100 cm each. The midpoints of the sides are joined to form a new equilateral triangle. This process continues indefinitely. Calculate the sum of the perimeters of this indefinite series of triangles. (4)

3. 3.1 For which values of x will the infinite geometric series
   $1 + (x^2 - 3) + (x^2 - 3)^2 + \ldots$ be convergent? (6)

   3.2 Calculate the sum to infinity if $x = 1,5$. (3)

4. Three numbers form an arithmetic sequence. Their sum is 24.
   4.1 If a is the first term and d is the common difference, show that $a + d = 8$. (2)
   4.2 If the first number is decreased by 1 and the second number is decreased by 2, the three numbers then form a geometric sequence. Find the numbers. (8)

5. The following sequence is a combination of an arithmetic and a geometric sequence: 3; 3; 9; 6; 15; 12; … Study the sequence and use it to answer the questions that follow:
   5.1 Write down the next two terms. (2)
   5.2 Work out the value for $T_{22} - T_{21}$. (6)
   5.3 Prove that all the numbers in this sequence are divisible by 3. (4)

6. What is the least value of n for which: $\sum_{p=1}^{n} \frac{2}{5}(2)^{2p-1} > 11\,000$. (7)

Total: 50

Test C: Breakdown and content as per final exam

Structured test: full content as examinable in matric exams, including Grade 10 and 11 content.

1. Prove that $a + ar + ar^2 + \ldots + ar^{n-1} = \dfrac{a(r^n - 1)}{r - 1}$ (5)

2. Calculate the 11th term of the sequence $3;\ 3\sqrt{3};\ 9;\ \ldots$ (3)

3. Given that: $\displaystyle\sum_{n=1}^{5} \log x^n$:
   3.1 write down the first three terms of this sequence (1)
   3.2 state whether the series is arithmetic or geometric, and give a reason for your answer. (2)

4. The first three terms of an arithmetic sequence are: $\dfrac{-4}{5};\ \dfrac{-3}{5};\ \dfrac{-2}{5}$.
   Find an algebraic expression for the sum of first n terms. Write your answer in its simplest form. (4)

5. Calculate the value of M if: $M = \displaystyle\sum_{k=3}^{11} 5^{k-4}$ (5)

6. In an arithmetic series the fourth term is -2 and the eighth term is -18. Find the number of terms in the series if its sum is -144. (8)

7. Given the geometric series $6 + p + 3\tfrac{3}{8} + \ldots$ Calculate the values of r (the constant ratio) and p if it is given that $S_\infty = 3\tfrac{3}{7}$. (5)

8. A **quadratic pattern** has a second term of 7, a third term of 19 and a fifth term of 61.
   8.1 Calculate the second difference of the quadratic pattern. (5)
   8.2 Hence, or otherwise, calculate the first term. (2)

9. 9.1 $a;\ b;\ \sqrt{3}$ are three consecutive terms of a geometric sequence. Determine the relationship between a and b. (2)
   9.2 Furthermore, $a;\ b;\ \sqrt{3}$ are also the sides of a right-angled triangle with $a < b < \sqrt{3}$. Determine the relationship between a and b. (2)
   9.3 Then prove that $a = \dfrac{\sqrt{3}(\sqrt{5} - 1)}{2}$. (6)

Total: 50

TOPIC 2 Functions and inverses

In Grades 10 and 11 you learnt that when an input value (or *x*-value) is linked to an output value (or *y*-value) by a rule that creates a set of ordered pairs, this is called a 'relation'.

In Grade 12 a more formal definition of a function is required.

Knowledge and skills for this Topic

For the Grade 12 work in this Topic, you need a good grasp of the following knowledge and skills:
- understand functions
- be able to work with tables, equations, graphs, words and formulae
- recognise the general form of the equation used for straight lines, parabolas, hyperbolae, and exponential, logarithmic and trigonometric graphs
- be able to sketch, find the equations of, and interpret these graphs
- transform the equations of these graphs either by vertical or horizontal translations
- understand the concept of an average gradient between two points
- have a working knowledge of inequalities related to all of these graphs.

Difficulty with this Topic is often the result of not being able to link the correct equation to the given graph.

Content of final exam
- Draw the graphs of the functions taught in Grades 10, 11 and 12 and their inverses.
- Determine the domain and range of these graphs.
- Distinguish between one-to-one relations and many-to-one relations.
- If the inverse is not a function, know how to restrict the domain of the original function such that the inverse is a function.
- Know and apply the exponential laws.
- Understand and use the definition of a logarithm.
- Draw exponential and logarithmic graphs.
- Solve exponential and logarithmic inequalities graphically.
- Find the equation of the graph after it has been reflected in the *x*- and *y*-axes (or in the line $y = x$).

Formal definition of a function
The definition of a function can be given as follows:

> **Formal definition of a function**
> A function is a special relation between a set of *x*-values (input values), and a set of *y*-values (output values) such that for every *x* value there is one and only one *y* value.

This means that when giving this set of ordered pairs of numbers (coordinates), **no *x*-value** may be repeated.

Ways of representing functions
Functions can be represented in the following five different ways.

1. A set of ordered pairs
In a set of ordered pairs, the first number of each pair represents the *x*-value and the second number represents the *y*-value.
- If all *x*-values are different, then the set of ordered pairs represents a function. For example {(0; 2), (1; 3), (2; 4), (3; 5)}.
- If any two *x*-values are the same, then the set of ordered pairs DOES NOT represent a function. For example {(0; 2), (1; 3), (0; 4), (3; 5)}.

2. A table with *x*-values and *y*-values
The same rules that apply to ordered pairs can be used when using a table that gives the *x*-values and *y*-values.

x	0	1	2	3
y	2	3	4	5

3. An equation
Different kinds of equations represent different kinds of graphs. The equations used in algebra in the Grades 10, 11 and Grade 12 curriculum are summarised in the table below.

Equation	Linear $y = mx + c$	Quadratic $y = ax^2 + bx + c$	Hyperbola $y = \frac{k}{x + p} + q$
Example of equation	$y = x + 2$	$y = x^2 - 3x - 2$	$y = \frac{8}{x + 2} + 1$
Graph	line through (−2, 0) and (0, 2)	parabola with roots at −1 and 2, minimum at −2	hyperbola with asymptotes $y = 1$ and $x = -2$, passing through (0, 5) and (−6, 0)
Mapping	one-to-one	many-to-one	one-to-one
Classification	function	function	function

Equation	Exponential $y = a^x + p$	Log $y = \log_a x$	Cubic $y = ax^3 + bx^2 + cx + d$
Example of equation	$y = 2x - 1$	$y = \log_3 x$ **Note:** $x > 0$	$y = x(x-1)(x+2)$ $y = x^3 + x^2 - 2x$
Graph	graph with asymptote $y = -1$	graph through $x = 1$	graph through $-2, 0, 1$
Mapping	one-to-one	one-to-one	many-to-one
Classification	function	function	function

4. Mapping

Mapping is about which x-values (domain) are connected to which y-values (range). Different equations represent different types of mappings. The two types of mapping described below will result in the relationship between the input values (x) and the output values (y) being a function.

Mapping of linear functions

Linear functions are one-to-one mappings. This means that every x-value is connected to only one y-value.

Vertical line test: if $f(x)$ is a function a vertical line will cut the graph once.

Horizontal line test: if the inverse is a function a horizontal line will cut the graph once.

x	y
0	−2
1	−1
2	0
3	1

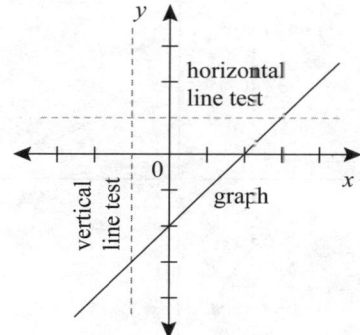

Mapping of quadratic functions

Quadratic functions are many-to-one mappings. This means that every x-value is connected to only one y-value BUT every y-value is connected to two x-values.

Vertical line test: $f(x) = x^2$ is a function because this line cuts the graph once.

Horizontal line test: indicates two properties of this function that are important:
1. The line cuts the graph in two places, so it is a many-to-one mapping.
2. The inverse of the graph will not be a function.

x	y
−2	4
−1	1
0	0
1	
2	

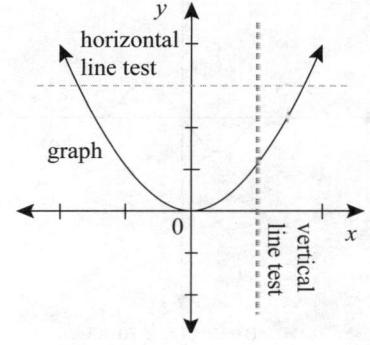

TOPIC 2 *Functions and inverses*

Other mappings
Other mappings that do not represent functions are one-to-many and many-to-many mappings.

5. Graphs
To determine without using mapping whether a graph represents a function or not, do a vertical line test. If this vertical line cuts the graph only once for any x-value selected, the graph is a function.

Worked examples
On each of the following sketch graphs:
1. state the type of mapping
2. determine whether the relationship represented by each graph is a function or not.

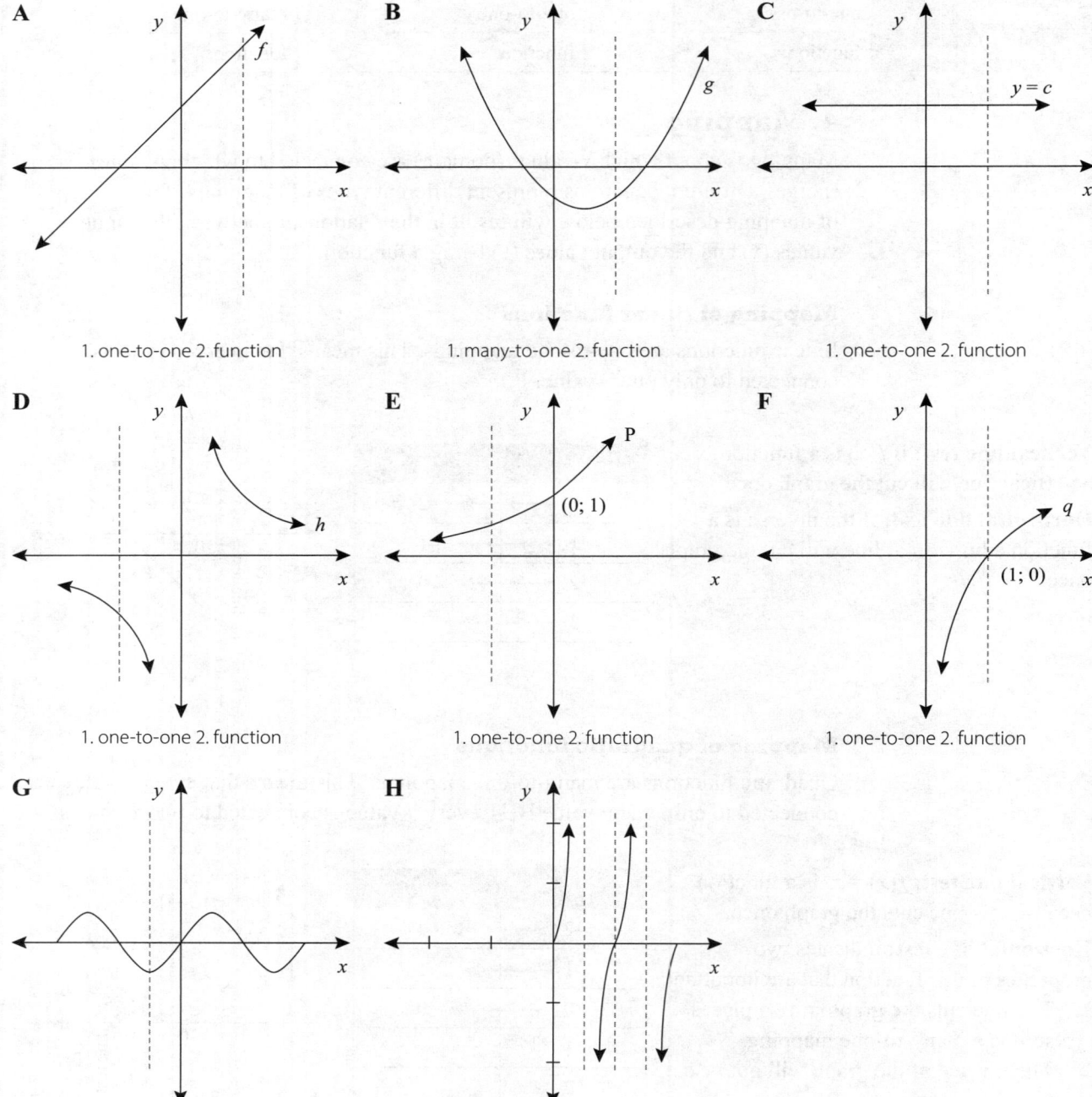

Domain and range

Here are some reminders about the domain and the range of a function.
- The **domain** is made up of the x-values for which the graph is defined, and the x-values are the independent variables.
- The **range** is made up of the y-values for which the graph is defined, and the y-values are the dependent variables, because they depend on the x-values.
- When determining the domain and range, we must be aware of two important facts:
  - When working with fractions, the denominator cannot be zero.
  - Because all functions, even inverses, involve the set of real numbers, there are restrictions when working with square roots (for parabolas, which are addressed later). The square root of a negative number is **not real**: so $\sqrt{p}$ is real if $p \geq 0$, and not real if $p < 0$.
- There is more than one way to express the domain and range of a graph. For example, if the y-values of a graph are defined from negative infinity to the point where $y = 4$, we could write:

Range: $y \leq 4; y \in \mathbb{R}$
OR $y \in (-\infty; 4]$
OR $-\infty < y \leq 4$

Increasing and decreasing functions (complex procedures)

You can work out whether a function is increasing or decreasing as follows:

Increasing function

If the values of y increase as the values of x increase, then this is an increasing function.

Also, if you draw a tangent to the curve of a graph, and this tangent has a positive gradient, then this is an increasing function.

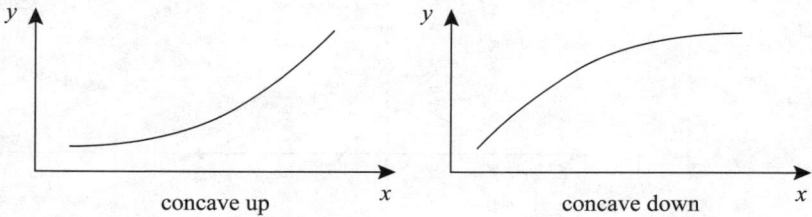

The values of y increase as the values of x increase.

Decreasing function

If the values of y decrease as the values of x increase, then this is a decreasing function.

Also, if you draw a tangent to the curve of a graph, and this tangent has a negative gradient, then this is a decreasing function.

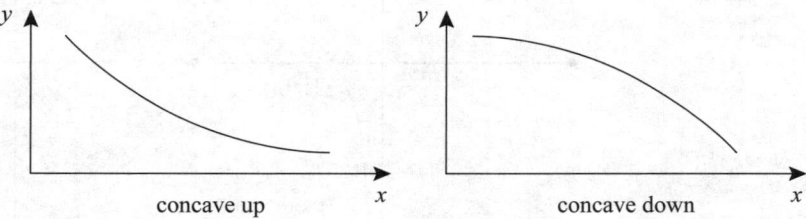

The values of y decrease as the values of x increase.

The gradient of the tangent at any point on a curve is a derivative, which is part of calculus, so this concept is more easily explained using calculus. Refer to the calculus chapter when you revise increasing and decreasing intervals.

Worked examples

1. State the values of x for which $f(x)$ is:
   1.1 increasing
   1.2 decreasing

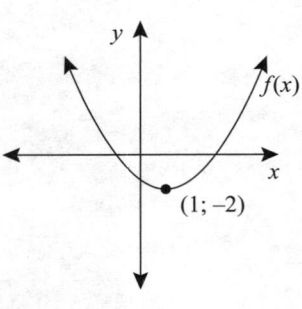

2. State the values of x for which $g(x)$ is:
   2.1 increasing
   2.2 decreasing

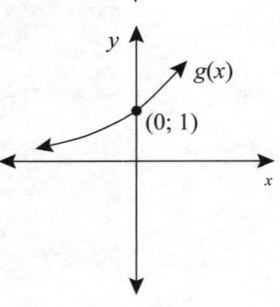

Solutions
1.1 $x > 1$ 1.2 $x < 1$
2.1 $x \in \mathbb{R}$ 2.2 nowhere

Exercise 1

1. Determine the values of x for which the following graphs are increasing.

   1.1
   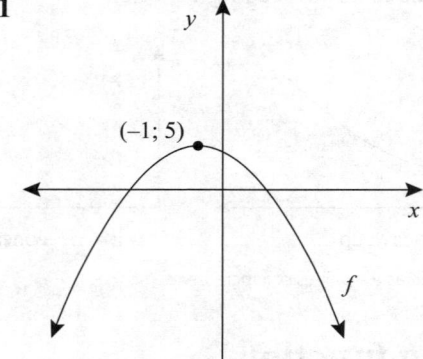

   1.2
   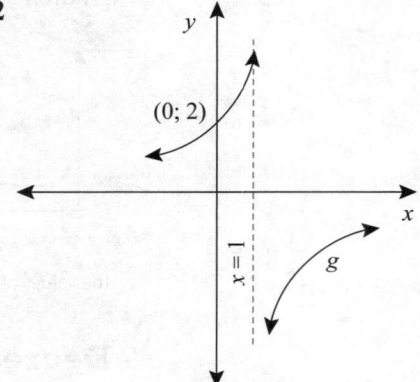

   1.3
   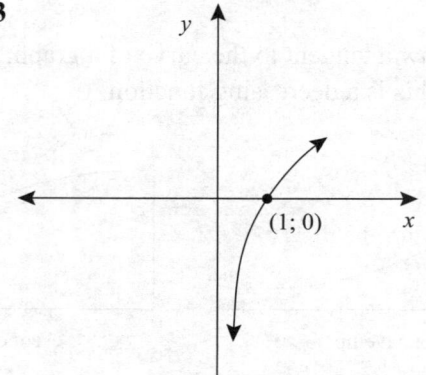

   1.4
   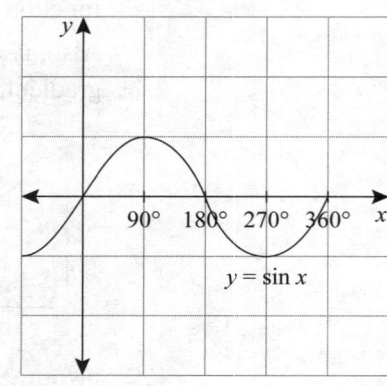

2. For which values of x are the following graphs decreasing?

2.1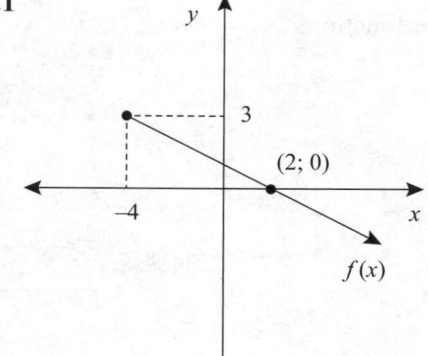

2.2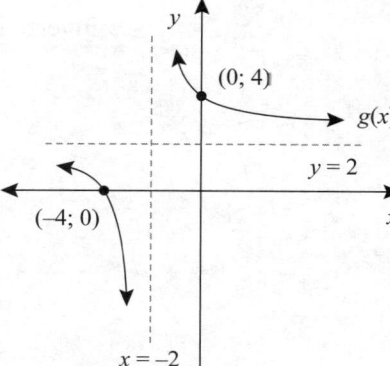

2.3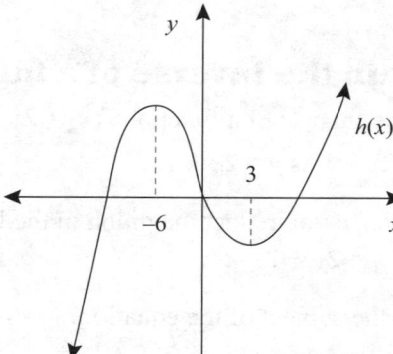

2.4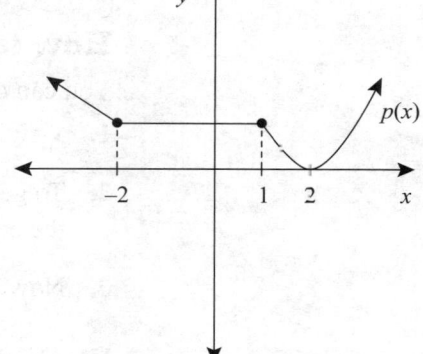

Inverses

Note
Do not confuse $f^{-1}(x)$ with the reciprocal $\frac{1}{f(x)}$.

An inverse is a reflection in the line $y = x$. To obtain the equation of an inverse, the input values (the domain) of f (the function) become the output values, and the output values (the range) of f become the input values. So swop the x and the y in the original function and then make y the subject of the formula.

If the resulting relationship is a function, we can use the notation $f^{-1}(x)$, which indicates that the inverse of the original function is also a function.

Testing whether an inverse is a function or not

To determine whether the inverse is a function, perform a **horizontal** line test on the original function.

A horizontal line cuts the hyperbola $y = \frac{8}{x}$ once, indicating that the inverse is a function.

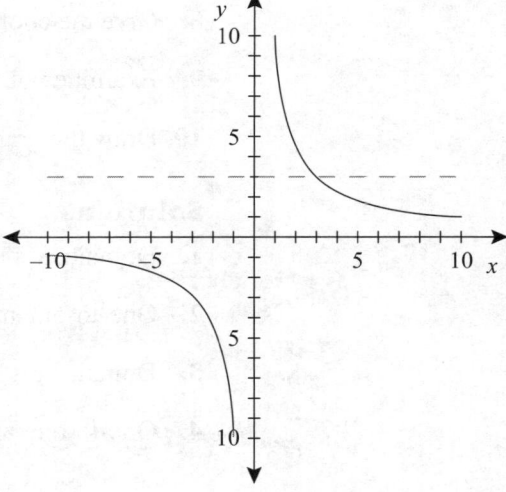

A horizontal line cuts the parabola more than once, indicating that the inverse is NOT a function.

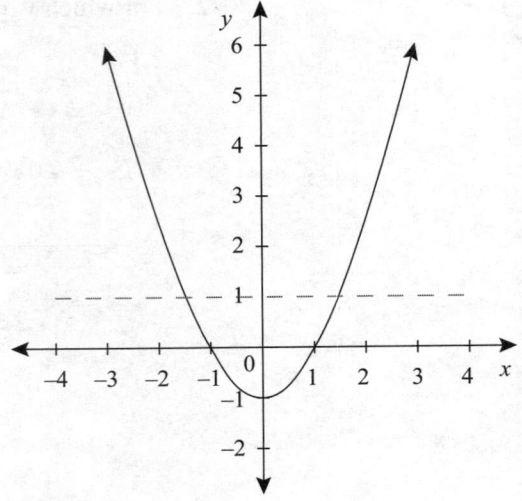

How to obtain the inverse of a function

You can obtain the inverse of a function $f(x) = 2x + 1$ by following these steps:

1. Write $f(x) = 2x + 1$ as $y = 2x + 1$.

2. To get the inverse you reflect the graph in the line $y = x$. So swop the x and y in the equation: $x = 2y + 1$

3. Now make y the subject of the equation: $y = \frac{1}{2}x - \frac{1}{2}$

Worked examples

Use the function $f(x) = 2x + 1$ and the information above to answer the following questions:

1. State the domain and range of $f(x)$.

2. What type of mapping does $f(x)$ represent?

3. State the domain and range of the inverse $f^{-1}(x)$.

4. What type of mapping does this inverse represent?

5. Does this inverse represent a function? Give a reason for your answer.

6. Draw the graphs of $f(x)$ and $f^{-1}(x)$ on the same set of axes.

7. Give the coordinates of the x-intercept and y-intercept of $f(x)$.

8. Give the coordinates of the x-intercept and y-intercept of $f^{-1}(x)$.

9. Examine your answers for 7. and 8. and write down what you notice.

10. Draw the graph of $y = x$ on the same system of axes. What do you notice?

Solutions

1. Domain: $x \in \mathbb{R}$; Range: $y \in \mathbb{R}$

2. One-to-one mapping

3. Domain: $x \in \mathbb{R}$; Range: $y \in \mathbb{R}$

4. One-to-one mapping

5. Yes, there is a one-to-one mapping and every x-value has a unique y-value.

6. and 10. Graphs:

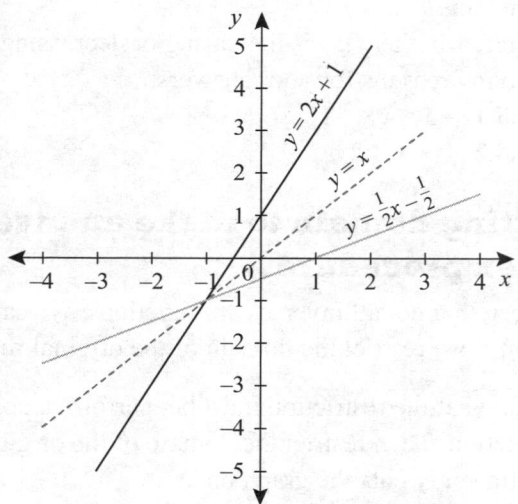

7. x-intercept of $f(x)$ is $\left(-\frac{1}{2}; 0\right)$ and y-intercept is $(0; 1)$

8. x-intercept of $f^{-1}(x)$ is $(1; 0)$ and y-intercept is $\left(0; -\frac{1}{2}\right)$

9. The x-intercept of $f(x)$ becomes the y-intercept of the inverse and the y-intercept of $f(x)$ becomes the x-intercept of the inverse. The points are reflected in the line $y = x$.

10. The two graphs are symmetrical about the line $y = x$. If the point $(0; 1)$ is on f, then the point $(1; 0)$ is on the inverse graph of f.

Exercise 2 (includes complex procedures)

1. Consider the function $f(x) = 2x - 3$, $x \in [-3; 4]$:
    1.1 Write down the domain and range of f.
    1.2 What type of mapping is $f(x)$?
    1.3 Determine the inverse of this function.
    1.4 Can the inverse of the function be labelled $f^{-1}(x)$? Give a reason for your answer.
    1.5 On the same system of axes, sketch the graphs of $f(x)$ and $f^{-1}(x)$, clearly indicating the intercepts with the axes. What do you notice about these intercepts?
    1.6 On the same system of axes, draw the graph of $y = x$. What do you notice about this line?
    1.7 Is $f(x)$ increasing or decreasing on the interval $-3 < x < 4$? Give a reason for your answer.

2. Consider the function $f(x) = x^2 - 1$:
    2.1 Write down the domain and range of $f(x)$.
    2.2 What type of mapping is $f(x)$?
    2.3 Determine the inverse of this function.
    2.4 Can the inverse of the function be labelled $f^{-1}(x)$? Give a reason for your answer.
    2.5 If the inverse of the function $f(x)$ is to be a function itself, what restrictions must be placed on $f(x)$?

2.6 On the same system of axes, sketch the graphs of $f(x)$ and its inverse, clearly indicate the intercepts with the axes. What do you notice?

2.7 On the same system of axes, draw the graph of $y = x$. What happens on this line?

2.8 State whether $f(x)$ is increasing or decreasing on the following intervals, giving reasons for your answers:

2.8.1 $-3 < x < -1$

2.8.2 $0 < x < 2$

Restricting domain to make an inverse a function (complex procedures)

We have seen that not all inverses are functions. We can make sure that an inverse is a function if we restrict the domain of the original function.

To work out what the restriction must be, perform a horizontal line test on the original function. Then restrict the domain of the original function so that this horizontal line only cuts the graph once.

Worked examples

1. Draw the graph of $f(x) = 3x^2$. Is this graph a function? Give a reason for your answer.

2. Determine the equation of the inverse and draw the graph on the same set of axes. Then draw $y = x$. Is this graph a function? Give a reason for your answer.

3. Restrict the domain of $f(x)$ such that $f^{-1}(x)$ is a function.

4. Find the point(s) of intersection of $f(x)$ and $f^{-1}(x)$.

Solutions

1. Yes this graph is a function.
   For every x-value there is only one y-value.

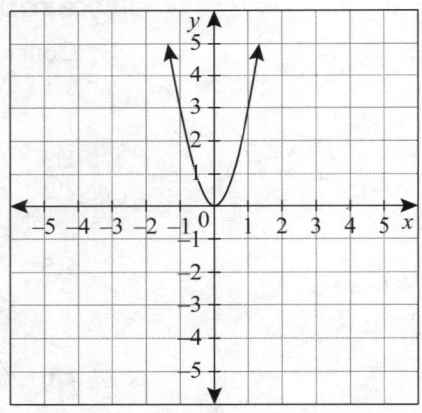

2. $y = 3x^2$

   $x = 3y^2$

   $y^2 = \tfrac{1}{3}x$

   $y = \pm\sqrt{\tfrac{1}{3}x}, x \geq 0$

   No the graph of the inverse is not a function. Each x-value has more than one y-value.

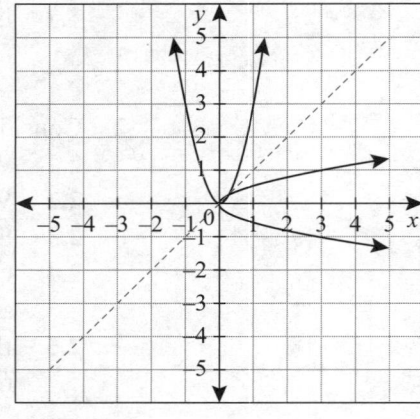

3. Domain of f: $x \leq 0$ or $x \geq 0$ (or you can write: $x \in (-\infty; 0]$ or $x \in (0; \infty]$. On making the restriction, do the horizontal line test.

4. $3x^2 = \pm\sqrt{\frac{1}{3}}$ $\frac{1}{3}x = 0$ OR $27x^3 - 1 = 0$

    $9x^4 = \frac{1}{3}x$ $\therefore x = 0$ $\therefore x^3 = \frac{1}{27}$

    $9x^4 - \frac{1}{3}x = 0$ $\therefore x = \frac{1}{3}$

    $\frac{1}{3}x(27x^3 - 1) = 0$ $\therefore y = 3 \times 0^2 = 0$ OR $y = 3 \times \left(\frac{1}{3}\right)^3 = \frac{1}{3}$

    $x = 0$ or $x = \frac{1}{3}$

The points of intersection of $f(x)$ and $f^{-1}(x)$ are $(0; 0)$ and $\left(\frac{1}{3}; \frac{1}{3}\right)$.

Average gradient

Average gradient $= \frac{\text{change in } y}{\text{change in } x}$

To find the average gradient, which is also called the average rate of change, simply find the gradient between two points on the curve, using the normal gradient formula.

Generally the x-values are given, and you will need to find the y-value for each point and then use $\frac{y_2 - y_1}{x_2 - x_1}$ = average gradient.

> **Exam tip**
> It is strongly suggested that you draw a sketch for this type of question.

Worked example
Find the average gradient as x increases from 0 to 2 on the curve $f(x) = y = \frac{1}{2}x^2$.

Solution
First draw the graph:

When $x = 0$ then $y = f(0) = 0$.
The point is A (0; 0).

When $x = 2$ then $y = f(2) = 2$, so the point is B (2; 2).

Average gradient $= \frac{y_B - y_A}{x_B - x_A} = \frac{2 - 0}{2 - 0} = 1$

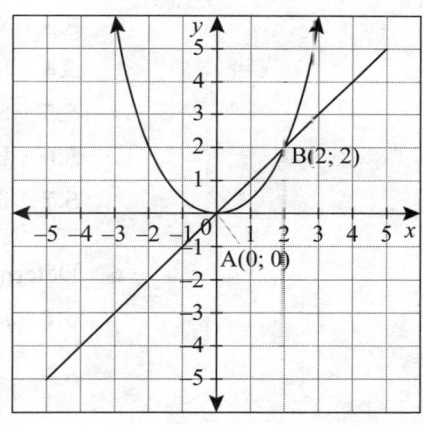

Exercise 3

1. If $f(x) = -x^2 + 2x + 3$, determine the value of the following:
   1.1 $f(0)$ 1.2 $f(3)$ 1.3 $f(x + 1)$
   1.4 $f(-1)$ 1.5 x, if $f(x) = 0$
   1.6 What is being determined in 1.2 and 1.4? Give a reason for your answer.

2. If $f(x) = x^2 - 4$, determine the following:
   2.1 $f(3)$ 2.2 $f(3 + h)$ 2.3 $\frac{f(3+h) - f(3)}{h}$

2.4 Explain what is being determined in 2.1.

2.5 If h in question 2.3 indicates a small change in x, what is being determined in this question?

3. If $s(t) = 2t + t^2$ represents speed (metres per second), determine each of the following.
   3.1 $s(0)$
   3.2 $s(5)$
   3.3 Determine the average rate of change for $s(t)$ as t increases from 1 to 8 seconds.
   3.4 Determine $s(5 + h)$
   3.5 Determine $\frac{s(5 + h) - s(5)}{h}$
   3.6 What is being determined in 3.5?

4. If $p(x) = \frac{2}{x+3} - 1$ determine the following:
   4.1 the domain of $p(x)$
   4.2 y for $p^{-1}(x)$
   4.3 Draw the graph of $p(x)$.
   4.4 Use the graph drawn in 4.3 to determine whether the inverse of $p(x)$ is a function.
   4.5 State the domain and range of $p^{-1}(x)$.
   4.6 Is $p(x)$ increasing or decreasing as x increases from –6 to –4? Explain.
   4.7 Determine the average rate of change of p as x increases from 0 to 2.

5. If $g(x) = \sqrt{3 - x}$ determine the following:
   5.1 What is the domain of $g(x)$?
   5.2 What is the range of $g(x)$?
   5.3 What is the inverse of $g(x)$?
   5.4 Is the inverse of $g(x)$ a function?
   5.5 State the domain and range of $g^{-1}(x)$.
   5.6 Determine the average rate of change of $g(x)$ between $x = -6$ and $x = -1$.
   5.7 Is $g(x)$ increasing or decreasing between $x = -6$ and $x = -1$?

6. Determine the domain and range of the following:
   6.1 $p(x) = \frac{6}{2-x} + 1$ **6.2** $f(x) = -2(x+1)^2 + 3$
   6.3 $t(x) = \sqrt{x^2 - 4}$

7. If $x \in \{-2; -1; 0; 1; 2; 2\}$, determine the value(s) of x for which $\sqrt{\frac{16}{2-x}}$ is:
   7.1 rational   **7.2** undefined
   7.3 not real   **7.4** irrational

8. Determine $f^{-1}(x)$ for each of the following:
   8.1 $f(x) = 5x - 2$ where $x \in [-1; 4]$ **8.2** $h(x) = x^2 - 4$
   8.3 $g(x) = \frac{3}{x-1}$ **8.4** $p(x) = 3^x + 1$

Types of functions and their properties

In this section the following types of functions will be covered:
- linear function
- quadratic function
- hyperbolic function (covered extensively in Grade 11)
- exponential function
- logarithmic function
- cubic function. (this function will be covered in the calculus section of this book).

For each function you need to be able to carry out the following:
- find the domain
- find the range
- determine the type of mapping
- find the inverse and determine whether it is a function or not
- sketch the graph using SCRAM to find the following properties:

S = shape which is generally determined by using the co-efficient of the highest power of x

C = cut(s) on the y-axis, i.e. the y-intercepts, and to find these use $x = 0$ and solve for y

R = roots, i.e. x-intercepts, and to find these let $y = 0$ and solve for x

A = axis of symmetry (which can also be named A/S) or asymptotes, if any

M = maximum and/or minimum values of the function.

Linear functions

The graph of a linear function is a straight line. Linear functions are recognised by the equations $y = mx + c$ OR $ax + by = k$.

Drawing a straight line graph

To draw the graph use SCRAM, as described above. Each letter represents a different property you need to find in order to draw the graph.

S – Shape

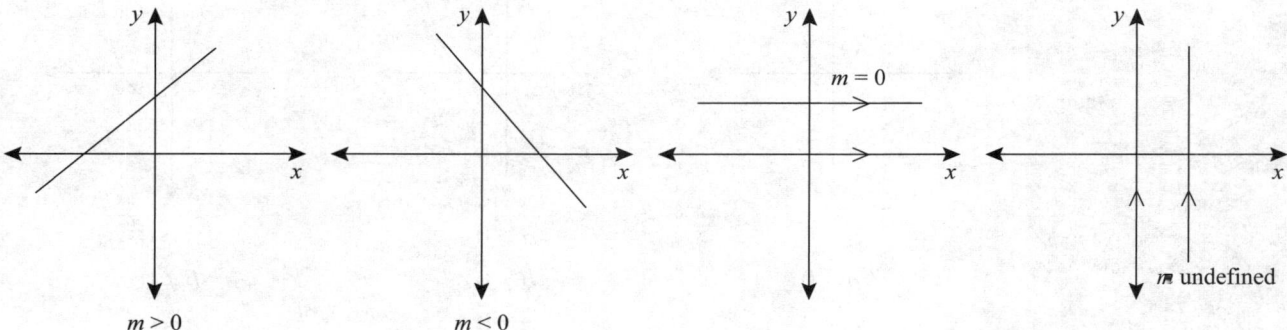

C – Cut(s) on the y-axis i.e. y-intercept: $y = c$ or $y = \frac{k}{b}$.

R – Roots i.e. x-intercept(s): $x = \frac{-c}{m}$ or $c = \frac{k}{a}$.

A – No axis of symmetry needed here.

M – No need to refer to max or min here.

For this function you need to be able to determine the following:
- Domain: $x \in \mathbb{R}$
- Range: $y \in \mathbb{R}$
- Type of mapping: this is always a one-to-one mapping with the exception of a vertical line, which is a one-to-many mapping.
- Inverse and whether it is a function or not:
  For $y = mx + c$ the inverse is $y = \frac{1}{m}x - \frac{c}{m}$
  OR for $ax + by = k$ the inverse is $y = \frac{-b}{a}x - \frac{k}{a}$
  Both of these equations are functions.
- Increasing or decreasing function: if the gradient is positive (slopes UP to the right) this is an increasing function, and if the gradient is negative (slopes DOWN to the right) then it is a decreasing function.

Exercise 4

Draw the following straight line graphs.

1. $y = 3x + 6$
2. $y - 2 = x$
3. $2y - 3x + 6 = 0$
4. $3 + y = 0$
5. $x - 3 = 0$

Quadratic function: parabola

The graph of a quadratic function is a parabola. It can be recognised by the following equations:

$$y = ax^2 + bx + c \quad \text{OR} \quad y = a(x - p)^2 + q$$

Draw the graph using SCRAM.

S – Shape

a > 0 (smiley graphs)

> **Remember**
> - The coordinates of the turning point are $(p; q)$.
> - If $a > 0$ then the graph has a:
>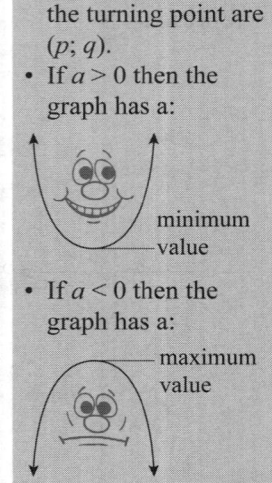
>   minimum value
> - If $a < 0$ then the graph has a:
>   maximum value

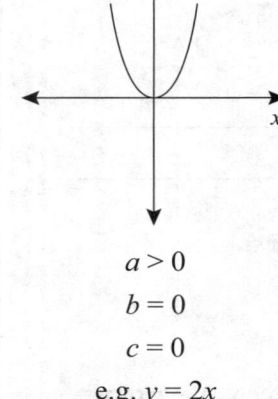

$a > 0$
$b = 0$
$c = 0$
e.g. $y = 2x$

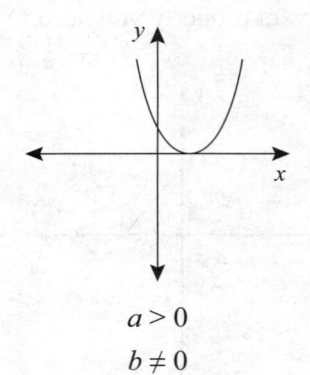

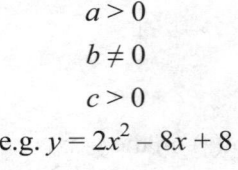

$a > 0$
$b \neq 0$
$c > 0$
e.g. $y = 2x^2 - 8x + 8$

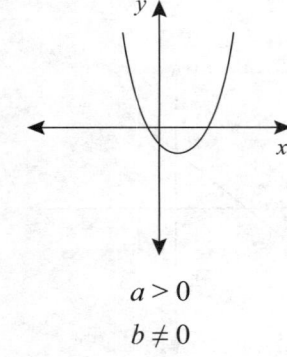

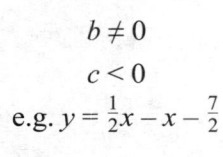

$a > 0$
$b \neq 0$
$c < 0$
e.g. $y = \frac{1}{2}x - x - \frac{7}{2}$

a < 0 (frowny graphs)

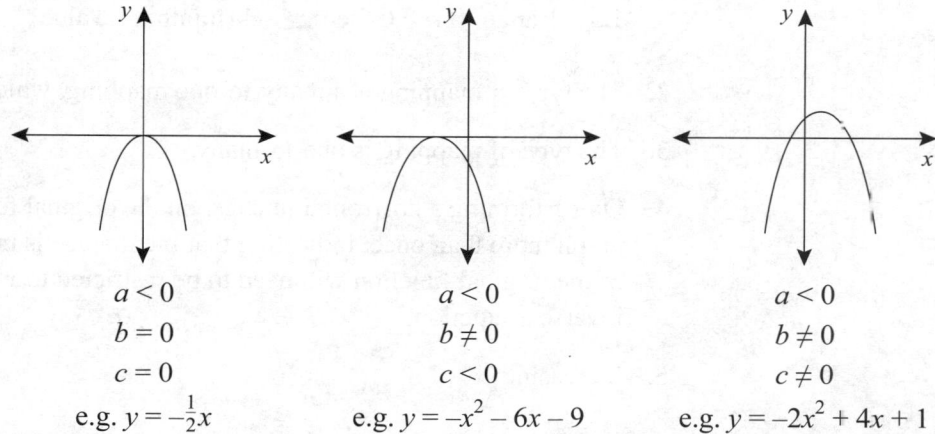

$a < 0$
$b = 0$
$c = 0$
e.g. $y = -\frac{1}{2}x$

$a < 0$
$b \neq 0$
$c < 0$
e.g. $y = -x^2 - 6x - 9$

$a < 0$
$b \neq 0$
$c \neq 0$
e.g. $y = -2x^2 + 4x + 1$

C – Cut(s) on the y-axis, in other words y-intercepts: $y = c$ or $y = ap^2 + q$

R – Roots: these are the x-intercept(s), so let $y = 0$ and solve the quadratic equation.

A – Axis of symmetry:
- For the first form of the equation, $y = ax^2 + bx + c$, the axis of symmetry is $x = -\frac{b}{2a}$. For the second form of the equation, $y = a(x - p)^2 + q$, the axis of symmetry is $x = p$.

M – Maximum or minimum values of y occur at the turning point:
- Substitute the value of x at the turning point into the equation to find the value of y.
- If $a > 0$ the function has a minimum value of y.
- If $a < 0$ the function has a maximum value of y.

In this graph:
- The axis of symmetry is obtained from the formula $x = -\frac{b}{2a}$. This also gives us the x-value at the turning point.
- The minimum or maximum value of the graph is the y-value at the turning point, so substitute the value of x into the equation to find the value of y.

Worked examples

1. Given that $f(x) = x^2 - 2x - 3$, determine the following:
   1.1 the turning point (T.P.) of the parabola
   1.2 the domain of $f(x)$
   1.3 the range of $f(x)$

2. What type of mapping is represented by $f(x)$ and is $f(x)$ a function?

3. What type of mapping is represented by the inverse of $f(x)$?

4. Is the inverse a function? If not, how can the domain of $f(x)$ be restricted so that the inverse becomes a function.

5. State the values of x for which $f(x)$ is increasing.

Solutions

1. 1.1 The x-value at the turning point is the axis of symmetry: $x = -\frac{b}{2a} = \frac{-2}{2} = 1$.
   The y-value at the turning point is the minimum value of the graph:
   $y = (1)^2 - 2(1) - 3 = -4$. So the turning point is at $(1; -4)$.
   (We can also find the turning point using calculus, but this will be covered later.)

1.2 Domain: $x \in \mathbb{R}$

1.3 Range: If $a > 0$ then $y \geq -4$ (minimum value)

2. The type of mapping is a many-to-one mapping, which is a function.

3. The type of mapping is one-to-many.

4. On performing a horizontal line test on the original function, the line cuts the graph more than once, indicating that the inverse is not a function. The domain of the original function will need to be restricted to $x \geq 0$ or $x \leq 0$ to make the inverse a function.

5. Increasing: $x > 1$

Worked example

Draw a sketch graph of $y = x^2 - 5x - 6$

Solution

S – Shape: $a > 0$

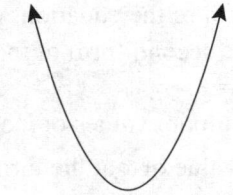

C – Cut on the y-axis: let $x = 0$, then $y = -6$.

R – Roots: the x-intercepts (let $y = 0$):
$$x^2 - 5x - 6 = 0$$
$$(x - 6)(x + 1) = 0$$
$$x = 6 \text{ or } x = -1$$

A – Axis of symmetry: $x = -\frac{b}{2a} = \frac{5}{2} = 2{,}5$

(Or halfway between the two roots i.e. $\frac{6 + (-1)}{2} = \frac{5}{2} = 2{,}5$

M – Minimum valued because $a > 0$.

Minimum value: $y = \frac{-(b^2 - 4ac)}{4a}$

$= \frac{-25 - 4(-6)}{4}$

$= \frac{-49}{4}$

$= -12{,}25$

The turning point is $(2{,}5; -12{,}25)$. To get this, use the values obtained for A and M in SCRAM, OR if you are going to use the simpler way of finding the y-value of the turning point, then substitute this for the minimum value:

$x = 2{,}5$
$y = (2{,}5)^2 - 5(2{,}5) - 6$
$= -12{,}25$

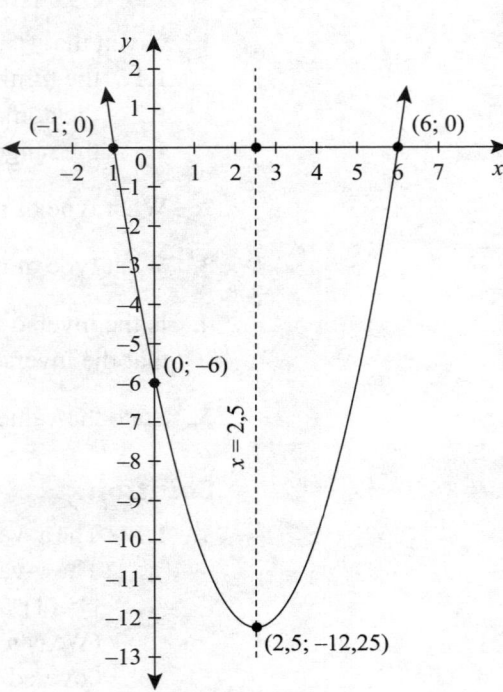

Exercise 5

1. **1.1** Draw the graph of the parabola $y = -x^2 + 3x + 4$ using SCRAM.
   1.2 Using the graph for question 1.1, give the values of x for which the graph is an increasing function.

2. **2.1** Sketch the following graph: $y = 2x^2 + 4x - 6$ using SCRAM.
   2.2 Using your answers in question 2.1, give the values of x for which the graph is a decreasing function.

Exercise 6 (complex procedures)

1. Consider $f(x) = 1 - x^2$.
   1.1 Sketch $f(x)$.
   1.2 What is the range of $f(x)$?
   1.3 On the same system of axes, sketch the graph of the inverse of $f(x)$.
   1.4 Determine the equation of the inverse together with the restrictions on the inverse that ensure that the inverse is a function.
   1.5 State the domain and range of $f^{-1}(x)$.
   1.6 Determine the average rate of change for $f(x)$ between $x = -5$ and $x = -3$.
   1.7 Give two values of x for which $f^{-1}(x)$ is not defined.

2. The diagram alongside represents the graphs of the function $f(x) = 2x^2 - 4x - 6$ with P(–2; 10) an endpoint on $f(x)$.
   Using algebraic methods and graphs, answer the following questions:

   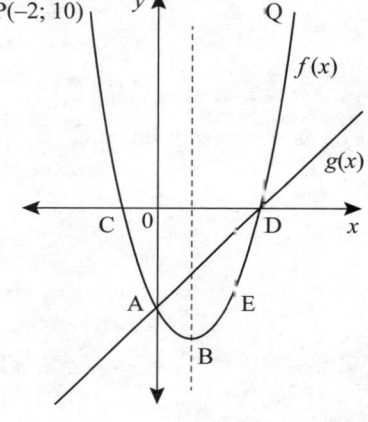

   2.1 Determine the coordinates of the points A, B, C, D, E and Q, where E is symmetrical to A, and Q is symmetrical to P with respect to the axis of symmetry.
   2.2 Determine the equation of the straight line $g(x)$.
   2.3 Write down the domain and range of $f(x)$.
   2.4 How can the domain of $f(x)$ be restricted so that $f^{-1}(x)$ is a function?
   2.5 Using the graph:
   2.5.1 Solve for x in the following inequality: $2x^2 - 4x - 6 > 0$.
   2.5.2 Find the value of p if the roots of $2x^2 - 4x - 6 = 0$ are equal.

3. In the diagram alongside is the graph of $f(x) = a(x - p)^2 + q$.

   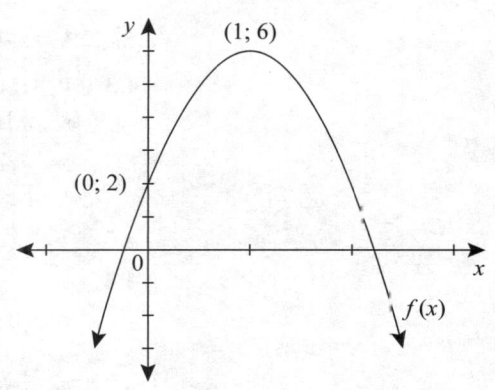

   3.1 Determine the values of a, p and q, writing the equation in the form $f(x) = a(x - p)^2 + q$.
   3.2 Write down the range of $f(x)$.
   3.3 State how the domain of $f(x)$ must be restricted such that the inverse of $f(x)$ is a function.
   3.4 If the graph of $f(x)$ is

reflected in the x-axis to form the graph of $h(x)$, write down the equation of $h(x)$ in the form $h(x) = a(x-p)^2 + q$.

3.5 Determine the value of $f(x) - h(x)$ when $x = 0$.

3.6 For which values of x is $f(x) > h(x)$?

3.7 Explain how the graph of $f(x)$ must be transformed to obtain the graph of $g(x) = x^2$.

Transforming (shifting) of graphs

Here are some guidelines on transforming graphs.

1. **Parabola:** $y = (x-a)^2 - b$
   - Add a onto the x-values to make a horizontal shift (which is counter-intuitive).
   - Subtract b from the y-values to make a vertical shift.

2. **Hyperbola:** $y = \dfrac{k}{x-p} + q$
   - Domain: $x \in \mathbb{R}, x \neq -p$
   - Range: $y \in \mathbb{R}, y \neq +q$
   - Asymptotes are obtained from the restrictions above: $x = -p$ and $y = +q$
   - Horizontal shift to the right of p units.
   - Vertical shift of q units upwards.

3. **Exponential graphs:** $y = a^{x+p} + q$
   - The first term can be written as: $a^p \cdot a^x$, indicating that the y-values are multiplied by the value of a^p.
   - Vertical shift of q units upwards.
   - Reflections of $y = a^x$:
     - In the x-axis: the sign of the y must change $\therefore y = -a^x$
     - In the y-axis: the sign of the x must change $\therefore y = a^{-1x}$
     - In the line $y = x$: swop the x and y values and make y the subject of the formula, so $x = a^y$ and then $y = \log_a x$

4. **Trigonometric graphs**

   4.1 $y = a \sin bx$ or $y = a \cos bx$
   - a increases or decreases the amplitude
   - b changes the period of the graph to $\dfrac{360°}{b}$
   - Reflections: $y = -a \sin -b^x$ or $y = -a \cos -bx$, $-a$ indicates a reflection in the x-axis and $-b$ indicates a reflection in the y-axis.

   4.2 $y = a + \sin(x+b)$ or $y = a + \cos(x+b)$
   - Horizontal shift of b units to the left (remember that this is counter-intuitive).
   - Vertical shift of a units upwards.

   4.3 $y = a \tan bx$
   - All y-values will be multiplied by a.
   - b changes the period of the graph to $\dfrac{180°}{b}$, shifting the asymptotes.
   - Reflections: $y = -a \tan -bx$, $-a$ indicates a reflection in the x-axis and $-b$ indicates a reflection in the y-axis.

   4.4 $y = a + \tan(x+b)$
   - Horizontal shift of b units to the left (remember that this is counter-intuitive).
   - Vertical shift of a units upwards.

Exponential functions

Revision: exponential function and exponential laws

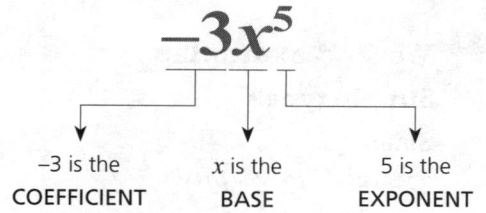

−3 is the COEFFICIENT
x is the BASE
5 is the EXPONENT

Definition
$b^n = b \cdot b \cdot b \ldots n$ times where $b \in \mathbb{R}$ and $n \in \mathbb{N}_0$.

The laws of exponents

Law 1: $b^x \cdot b^a = b^{x+a}$

When the bases are the same and you multiply, write down the base and add the exponents.

Law 2: $\frac{b^x}{b^a} = b^{x-a}$

When the bases are the same and you divide, write down the base and subtract the exponents:

- The exponent $x - a$ will be positive if $x > a$.
- The exponent $x - a$ will be zero if $x = a$.
- The exponent $x - a$ will be negative if $x < a$.

Remember
$b^{-x} = \frac{1}{b^x}$

Law 3: $(b^a)^x = b^{a \cdot x}$

When you raise a power to a power, write down the base and multiply the exponents.

Law 4: $(a \cdot b)^x = a^x \cdot b^x$ AND $\left(\frac{a}{b}\right)^x = \frac{a^x}{b^x}$

When you multiply or divide with the same exponents, raise each exponent to the same power.

Law 5: $\sqrt[x]{b^y} = b^{\frac{y}{x}}$

Surds (roots) give exponents. Get rid of the surd sign first, then divide all exponents that were under the surd sign (in this case y) by the order of the surd (in this case x).

Simplify expressions and solve equations

Exam tip

In the final exam you will be asked to simplify expressions or solve equations that involve exponents. These guidelines will help you:

1. If the expression or equation includes multiply or divide signs, write the bases in terms of **Powers Of Prime** factors, i.e. POP the bases.
2. If the expression or equation includes plus or minus signs, FACTORISE or simplify.
3. ALWAYS change decimals to FRACTIONS.

Remember
For these expressions you must POP the bases.

Expressions that include × or ÷ signs

There are simple and complex types of expressions that include × or ÷ signs, as shown below.

Worked examples

Simple type

Simplify.

$$32^x \cdot 8^{2x} = (2^5)^x \cdot (2^3)^{2x} \qquad \text{POP the bases.}$$
$$= 2^{5x} \cdot 2^{6x}$$
$$= 2^{11x}$$

Complex type (complex procedure)

$$\frac{5^{2n-1} \cdot 125^{n+1}}{5^{-(3n-3)}} = \frac{5^{2n-1} \cdot (5^2)^{-4n} \cdot (5^3)^{n+1}}{5^{-(3n-3)}}$$
$$= \frac{5^{-3n+2}}{5^{-(3n-3)}}$$
$$= 5^{-1} \qquad \text{Exponent laws 4 and 1.}$$
$$= \frac{1}{5} \qquad \text{Write answer with positive exponent.}$$

Exercise 7 (complex procedures)

1. $\left(\dfrac{27x^{-3}}{8\sqrt{x^4}}\right)^{-\frac{4}{3}}$ 2. $\dfrac{2^{2n+3} \cdot 3^{2n-1}}{6^{2n}}$

3. $\dfrac{5^{x+1} \cdot 125^{x-2}}{25^{2(x-1)}}$ 4. $\dfrac{4^x \cdot 15^{x-2}}{6^{x+1} \cdot 10^x}$

5. $\dfrac{50^{-n+1} \cdot 2^{n-1} \cdot 25^{-1}}{9^{n+2} \cdot 225^{-n-1}}$

Expressions with + or − signs

There are two types of expressions that have + or − signs: the common factor type and the trinomial type.

Remember
For these expressions you must factorise or simplify.

Worked examples

Common factor type

Simplify (by taking out a common factor).

$$\frac{2^n + 2^{n+3}}{2^{n-2}} \qquad \text{The bases are the same and have the same variable in the exponent.}$$
$$= \frac{2^n(1 + 2^3)}{2^n \cdot 2^{-2}} \qquad \text{Take out a common factor.}$$
$$= \frac{1 + 8}{\frac{1}{2^2}}$$
$$= 9 \times 4$$
$$= 36$$

Trinomial type

Factorise.

1. $x^{\frac{1}{2}} - x^{\frac{1}{4}} - 6 = \left(x^{\frac{1}{4}} - 3\right)\left(x^{\frac{1}{4}} + 2\right)$ If the exponent of one term is half of the exponent of another term, look for a trinomial.

2. $3^{2x+1} + 5.3^x - 2$
= $3.3^{2x} + 5.3^x - 2$

Disguised trinomial: change the first term so that the exponent is double that of the middle term.

= $(3.3^x - 1)(3^x + 2)$

3. In this expression we will use the k method to factorise the trinomial. To do this we take the base and the exponent of the middle term and make this k.

$2^{2x} - 6.2^x + 5$

Let $2^x = k$: $2^{2x} = 2^x \cdot 2^x = k^2$

$k^2 - 6k + 5$
= $(k-5)(k-1)$
∴ $(2^x - 5)(2^x - 1)$

Exercise 8
Simplify the following:

1. $\dfrac{3^{n+2} - 3^{n+1}}{3^n + 3^{n+2}}$

2. $\dfrac{2^{n+4} - 6.2^{n+1}}{2^{n+2}}$

3. $\dfrac{2.3^x - 9.3^{x+2}}{3^x + 2.3^{x-1}}$

Exercise 9 (complex procedures)
Factorise the following:

1. $x - 8x^{\frac{1}{2}} + 15$

2. $3^{2x} + 3.3^x - 10$

3. $2^{2x+1} - 2^x - 3$

The exponential function and its graph

The graph of the function $y = a^x$ is an exponential graph. We recognise an exponential function when it has x as an exponent.

Use SCRAM to draw the graph:

S – Shape

Examples of usual exponential graphs

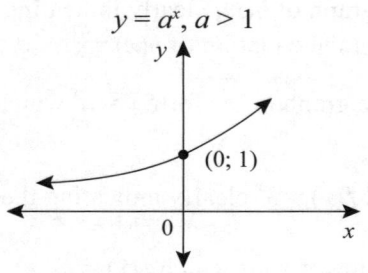
$y = a^x, a > 1$

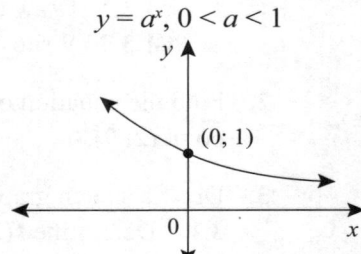
$y = a^x, 0 < a < 1$

Examples of reflections of exponential function in the x- and y-axes

Reflected in the y-axis: $(x; y)$ becomes $(-x; y)$:

Note
$y = 2^{-x}$ is equivalent to $y = \left(\dfrac{1}{2}\right)^x$.
$0 < \dfrac{1}{2} < 1$

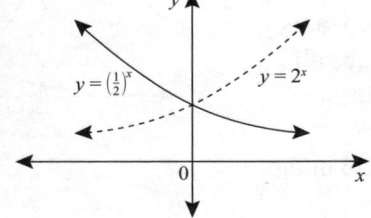

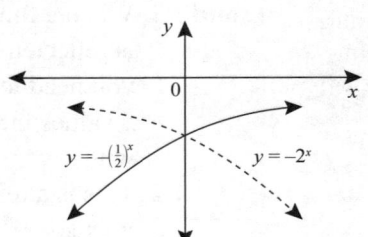

Reflected in the x-axis: $(x; y)$ becomes $(x; -y)$:

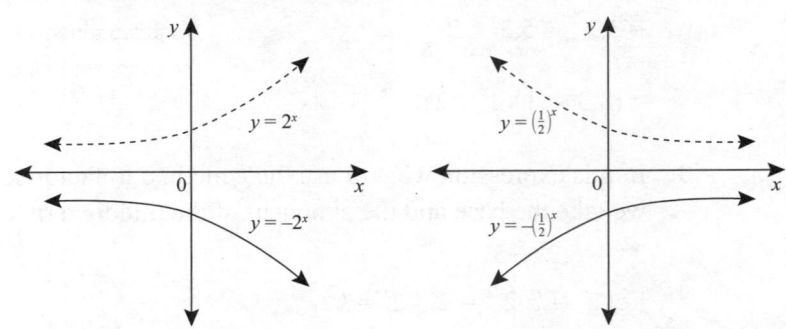

C – Cut(s) on the y-axis i.e. y-intercept will have coordinates $(0; 1)$, unless the graph has been transformed.

R – Roots i.e. x-intercept(s): There are none, unless the graph has undergone a transformation.

A – No axis of symmetry. There is a horizontal asymptote, $y = 0$.

M – No need to refer to max or min here.

For this function you need to be able to determine:
- Domain: $x \in \mathbb{R}$
- Range: $y > 0$
- Type of mapping: this is always a one-to-one mapping, indicating a function.
- Inverse and whether it is a function or not: The inverse is $y = \log_a x$ and this is a function (this will be addressed later).
- Increasing or decreasing: If $a > 1$ the function is increasing. If $0 < a < 1$ the function is decreasing.

Worked examples

1. Draw the sketch graph of $f(x) = 2^x$ clearly indicating intercepts with the axes.
   1.1 Draw the graph of $g(x) = 2^{-x}$ on the same system of axes.
   1.2 Explain the transformation from $f(x)$ to obtain $g(x)$.
   1.3 If $h(x)$ is the graph of $f(x)$ reflected in the x-axis:
      1.3.1 Draw the graph of $h(x)$, clearly indicating intercepts with the axes.
      1.3.2 Write down the equation of $h(x) = \ldots$

2. Find the equation of the graph in the form $y = a^x$ which passes through the point $(2; 9)$.

3. Draw a sketch graph of $f(x) = 3^x$ clearly indicating the intercepts with the axes.
   3.1 Determine $f(2)$.
   3.2 Determine the value of x for which $f(x) = \frac{1}{9}$.
   3.3 Determine the domain and range of $f(x)$

Remember
A note about other reflections i.e. mirror images:
- If a function is reflected in the y-axis, replace all x values in the formula with $-x$.
- If a function is reflected in the x-axis, replace all y values in for formula with $-y$.
- If a graph is reflected in the line $y = x$, replace every x-value in the equation with y, and every y-value with x. (Simply swop all x's and y's in the equation.)

Solutions

1. and 1.1 When a function or graph is reflected in the y-axis, you need to replace all x values in the formula with $-x$.

1.2 This is a reflection in the y-axis.

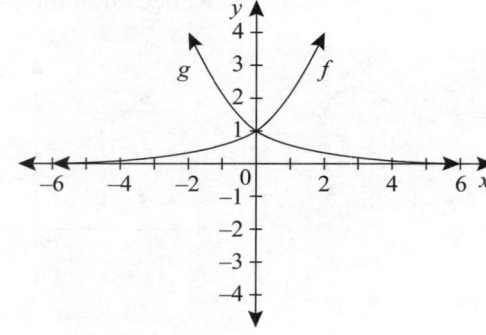

1.3.1 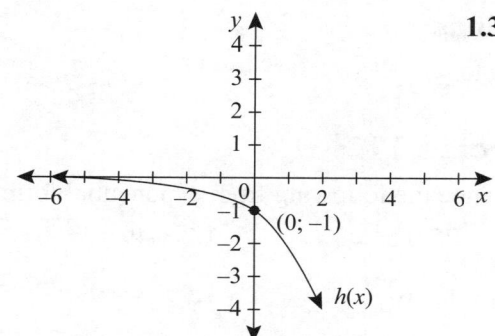 **1.3.2** $-y = 2^x$
$\therefore y = -2^x$
$\therefore h(x) = -2^x$

2. The equation is $y = a^x$. Substitute the point (2; 9) into the equation and solve for a:
$9 = a^2$
$a = (9)^{\frac{1}{2}}$
$a = 3, a > 0 \therefore y = 3^x$

3. 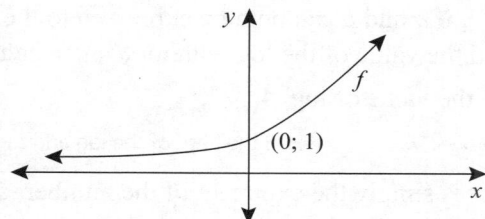   **3.1** $f(2) = 3^2 = 9$
3.2 $f(x) = \frac{1}{9}$
$3^x = \frac{1}{9} = 3^{-2}$
$x = -2$
3.3 Domain $f(x)$: $x \in \mathbb{R}$
Range $f(x)$: $y > 0, y \in \mathbb{R}$

Exercise 10 (includes complex procedures)

1. Find the equation of the graph in the form $f(x) = a^x$, which passes through the points:
   1.1 (3; 8) **1.2** $\left(3; \frac{27}{8}\right)$

2. Draw the sketch graph of $f(x) = 2^x + 1$, and answer the following questions:
   2.1 Determine the value of $f(-3)$ and $f(1)$.
   2.2 Determine the value of x if $f(x) = 17$.
   2.3 State the domain and range of $f(x)$.
   2.4 Is $f(x)$ an increasing or decreasing function on the interval $x \in [-2; 2]$? Give a reason for this answer.
   2.5 Determine the equation of:
      2.5.1 $g(x)$ if $f(x)$ is reflected in the y-axis
      2.5.2 $p(x)$ if $f(x)$ is reflected in the x-axis.

Logarithms

Definition
A logarithm is the power to which the base of a number must be raised to give that number.

If $x = b^y$, then $y = \log_b x$ where $b > 0$ and $b \neq 1$.

Worked examples
1. Change $8 = 2^3$ from index (exponent) form to log form.
2. Change $3 = \log_5 125$ from log form to exponent form.

Solutions
1. $3 = \log_2 8$
2. $125 = 5^3$

Exercise 11

1. Change the following from exponential form to logarithmic form.
   - **1.1** $25 = 5^2$
   - **1.2** $49 = 7^2$
   - **1.3** $32 = 2^5$
   - **1.4** $1 = 6^0$
   - **1.5** $3 = 9^{\frac{1}{2}}$
   - **1.6** $16 = 64^{\frac{2}{3}}$

2. Change the following from logarithmic form to exponential form.
   - **2.1** $\log_3 81$
   - **2.2** $\log_4 64 = 3$
   - **2.3** $\log_5 625 = 4$
   - **2.4** $3\log_8 4 = \frac{2}{3}$
   - **2.5** $3\log_3 3 = 1$
   - **2.6** $3\log_9 243 = \frac{5}{2}$

Finding the value of a log without using a calculator

- In the $\log_a b$, if a and b can both be expressed to the **same prime number base**, we can find the value of the log without using a calculator. Here is an example:

  Determine the value of $\log_8 4$.

  $\log_8 4 = \log_{2^3} 2^2$ POP the base of the log and the number to obtain the **same base**.

  The answer is simply the exponent of the number, divided by the exponent of the base:

  $= \frac{2}{3}$

  Use this method to check the values on the right hand side of 2.1 to 2.6 in Exercise 11 above.

- If a and b **cannot be expressed to the same base**, we use the log law $\log_a b = \frac{\log b}{\log a}$. Here is an example:

  Determine the value of $\log_3 14$.

  $\log_3 14 = \frac{\log 14}{\log 3} \approx 2{,}4$

Exercise 12

Determine the value of the following. (You can check the answers using your calculator.)

1. $\log_8 32$
2. $\log_9 27$
3. $\log_{125} 25$
4. $\log_{16} 64$
5. $\log_{49} 7$
6. $\log_{\frac{1}{2}} 4$

The four log laws you will use in financial maths

The four log laws that you will use to solve real-life problems related to finance, growth and decay, are:

Law 1: $\log_b (AB) = \log_b A + \log_b B$

Law 2: $\log_b \frac{A}{B} = \log_b A - \log_b B$

Law 3: $\log A^n = n \log A$

Law 4: $\log_B A = \frac{\log A}{\log B}$

Exam tip

Manipulation involving the log laws will not be examined. Their application will be covered in the Finance topic of this Study Guide.

The logarithmic function and its graph

You will recognise a logarithmic function by the following equation:

$$y = \log_a x$$

To draw the log graph use SCRAM:

S – Shape

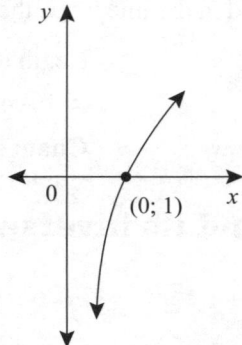

$y = \log_a x$
$a > 1$
increasing function

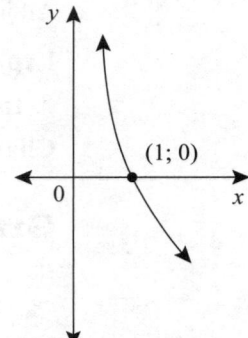

$y = \log_a x$
$0 < a < 1$
decreasing function

Examples of reflections of logarithmic functions in the *x*- and *y*-axes

Reflected in the *y*-axis: $(x; y)$ becomes $(-x; y)$:

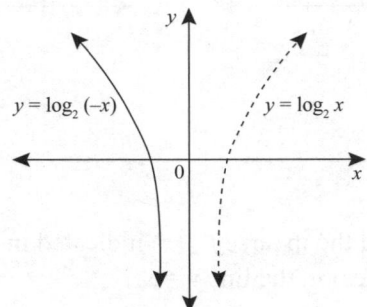
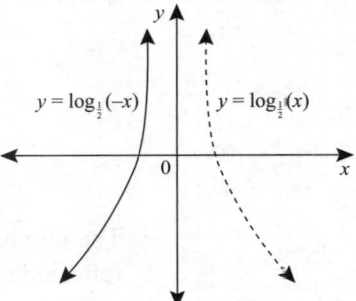

Reflected in the *x*-axis: $(x; y)$ becomes $(x; -y)$:

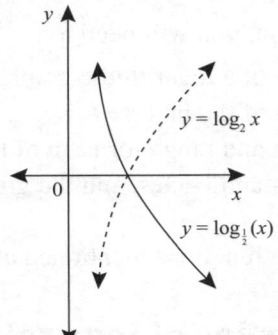
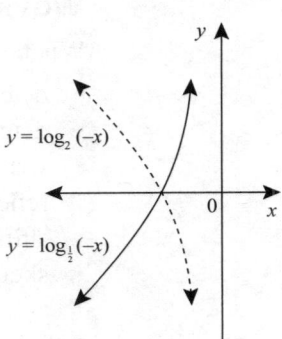

On drawing these graphs we notice that there are some **restrictions**:

C – Cuts: There are no *y*-intercepts because *x* cannot be zero.

R – Roots: The *x*-intercept is always at $(1; 0)$, unless the graph has been transformed.

A – There is no axis of symmetry. There is a vertical asymptote at $x = 0$.

M – There is no need to refer to the maximum or minimum for this function.

For this function you need to find:
- Domain: $x > 0$
- Range: $y \in \mathbb{R}$
- Mapping: this is always a one-to-one mapping, so is always a function.
- Inverse and whether a function or not: $y = a^x$ which is a function.
- Increasing or decreasing: If $a > 1$ the function is increasing. If $0 < a < 1$ the function is decreasing.

Logarithmic and exponential functions are inverses of one another

All inverse graphs are reflected in the line $y = x$, therefore the x and y values will swop.

Exponential: $y = a^x$ **Logarithmic:** $y = \log_a x$

∴ **Inverse:** $x = a^y$ ∴ **Inverse:** $x = \log_a y$

Change to log form: $y = \log_a x$ **Change to exponential form:** $y = a^x$

Graph of $f(x) = a^x$ and its inverse $f^{-1}(x) = \log_a x$

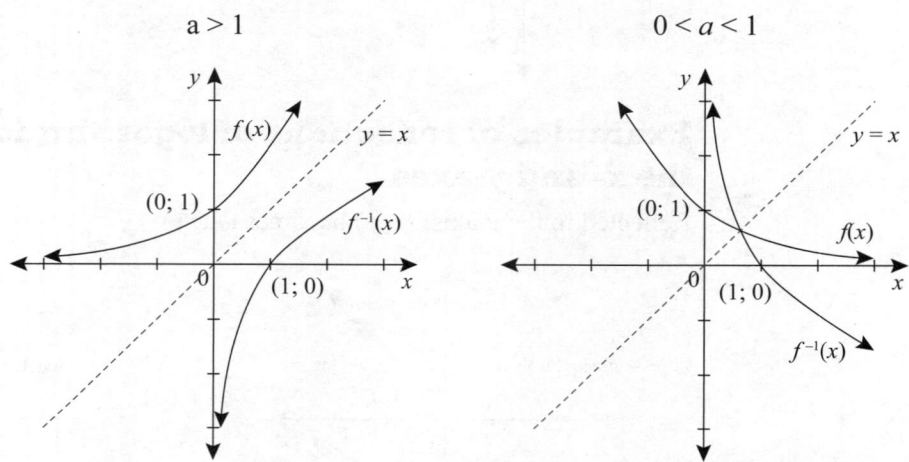

The graphs of $f(x)$ and the inverse $f^{-1}(x)$ indicated in the sketches above are reflected (mirror images) in the line $y = x$.

Working with $f(x) = \log_a x$, $a > 0$, $a \neq 1$

When you use this equation, you will need to:
- determine the equation of a logarithmic graph given the coordinates of a point
- determine the equation of the inverse f^{-1}
- write down the domain and range for each of the following functions: f, f^{-1}, reflections of f in the x- and y-axes, and the graph resulting from a horizontal shift
- sketch graphs of all the functions mentioned above.

Important properties of logs relevant to graphs of logarithmic functions

1. One of the restrictions on $y = \log_a x$ is that x must be positive, therefore write '$x < 0$' next to any equation that has $y = \log_a (-x)$, as this would result in a positive value of x.

2. $-\log_a x$ may be expressed as (a) $\log_{\frac{1}{a}} x$ or (b) $\log_a \frac{1}{x}$.

   For example, when $y = \log_2 x$ is reflected across the x-axis, the equation becomes $y = -\log_2 x$.

   (a) $y = \log_2 x$ OR   (b) $y = \log_2 x$

          $-y = \log_2 x$ $y = -\log_2 x$

          $y = -\log_2 x$ $y = \log_2 x^{-1}$

          which may be written as: $y = \log_2 \frac{1}{x}$

          $y = \log_{\frac{1}{2}} x$

3. Similarly, $y = -\log_2(-x)$ may be written as

   $y = \log_{\frac{1}{2}}(-x); x < 0$ OR $y = \log_2\left(-\frac{1}{x}\right); x < 0$

Worked examples

1. Determine a if the graph of $f(x) = \log_a x$, $a > 0$, $a \neq 1$ goes through the point $(16; 2)$.

2. Determine the equation of the inverse f^{-1}.

3. Write down the domain and range of $f(x)$ and its inverse in the form f^{-1}.

4. Sketch the graph of $f(x)$ and its inverse on the same system of axes.

Solutions

1. $y = \log_a x$ 2. $y = \log_4 x$

       $2 = \log_a 16$ $x = \log_4 y$

       $a^2 = 16$ $y = 4^x$

       $a = 4, a > 0$ $f^{-1}(x) = 4^x$

3. Domain$_f$: $x \in (0; \infty)$, Range$_f$: $y \in \mathbb{R}$
   Domain$_{f^{-1}}$: $x \in \mathbb{R}$, Range$_{f^{-1}}$: $y \in (0; \infty)$

4.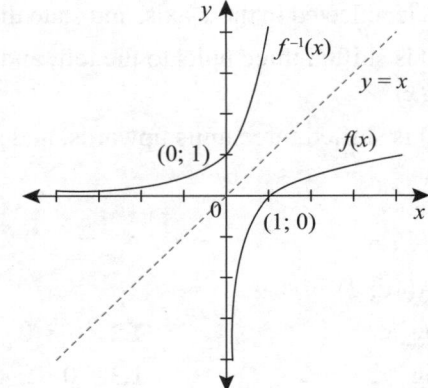

Exercise 13

The graph of $f(x) = \log_a x$, $a > 0$, $a \neq 1$ goes through the point $(81; 4)$.

1. Determine a.

2. Determine the equation of the inverse f^{-1}.

3. Write down the domain and range of $f(x)$ and its inverse in the form f^{-1}.

4. Sketch the graph of $f(x)$ and its inverse on the same system of axes.
5. Show that f is a one-to-one relation.

Working with $f(x) = \log_a x$, $a > 0$, $a \neq 1$ (complex procedures)

The complex procedures you need to be able to carry out when working with this type of equation are listed below:
- For which values of x is $f^{-1}(x) > -1$?
- Determine the function h if the graph of h is the reflection of the graph of f in the y-axis.
- Determine the function k if the graph of k is the reflection of the graph of f in the x-axis.
- Determine the function p if the graph of p is obtained by shifting the graph of f two units to the left. (This is a horizontal translation or shift.)

Worked examples

1. Consider $f(x) = \log_4 x$ which passes through the point A(16; 2).
    1.1 Determine the equation of the inverse f^{-1}.
    1.2 For which value(s) of x is $f^{-1} < 1$?
    1.3 For which value(s) of x is $f < 16$?

2. Determine the following equations:
    2.1 $h(x)$ if $f(x)$ is reflected in the y-axis
    2.2 $p(x)$ if $f(x)$ is reflected in the x-axis
    2.3 $k(x)$ if $f(x)$ is shifted three units to the left
    2.4 $q(x)$ if $f(x)$ is shifted three units upwards.

3. Sketch the graph of $f(x)$ and:
    3.1 $h(x)$ if $f(x)$ is reflected in the y-axis, and state the domain and range of $h(x)$
    3.2 $p(x)$ if $f(x)$ is reflected in the x-axis, and state the domain and range of $p(x)$
    3.3 $k(x)$ if $f(x)$ is shifted three units to the left, and state the domain and range of $k(x)$
    3.4 $q(x)$ if $f(x)$ is shifted three units upwards, and state the domain and range of $q(x)$.

Solutions

1. $f(x) = \log_4(x)$; A(16; 2)
    1.1 $y = \log_4 x$
    $x = \log_4 y$
    $f^{-1}(x) = y = 4^x$

    1.2 $x < 0$

    1.3 $0 < x < 2$

2. 2.1 $h(x) = \log_4(-x)$, $x < 0$

    2.2 $p(x) = -\log_4 x$
    $p(x) = \log_4 x^{-1}$
    $p(x) = -\log_4 \frac{1}{x}$

    2.3 $k(x) = \log_4(x + 3)$

    2.4 $q(x) = 3 + \log_4 x$

3. **3.1** Domain$_h$: $x < 0$; Range$_h$: $y \in \mathbb{R}$ **3.2** Domain$_p$: $x > 0$; Range$_p$: $y \in \mathbb{R}$

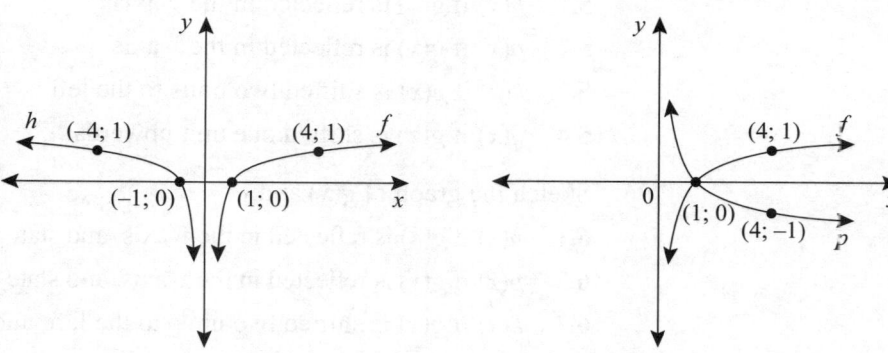

3.3 Domain$_k$: $x > -3$; Range$_k$: $y \in \mathbb{R}$ **3.4** Domain$_q$: $x > 0$; Range$_q$: $y \in \mathbb{R}$

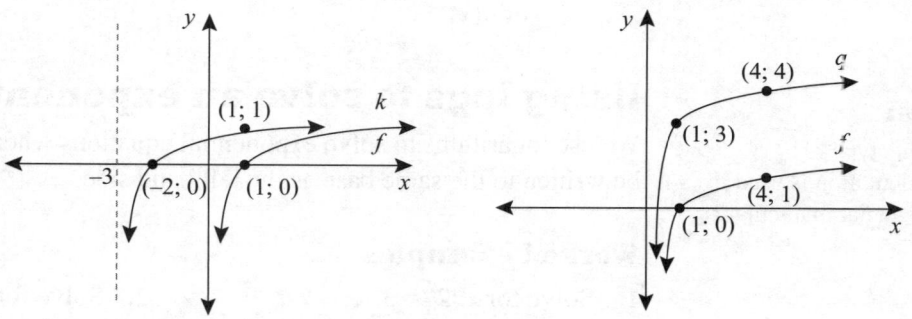

Exercise 14 (complex procedures)

1. Consider $f(x) = \log_2 x$ which passes through the point B(16; 4).
   - **1.1** Determine the equation of the inverse f^{-1}.
   - **1.2** Sketch the graph of $f(x)$ and f^{-1} on the same system of axes.
   - **1.3** For which value(s) of x is $f^{-1}(x) < 1$?
   - **1.4** For which value(s) of x is $f(x) < 16$?

2. Determine the following equations:
   - **2.1** $h(x)$ if $f(x)$ is reflected in the y-axis
   - **2.2** $p(x)$ if $f(x)$ is reflected in the x-axis
   - **2.3** $k(x)$ if $f(x)$ is shifted two units to the right
   - **2.4** $q(x)$ if $f(x)$ is shifted one unit downwards.

3. Sketch the graph of $f(x)$ and:
   - **3.1** $h(x)$ if $f(x)$ is reflected in the y-axis, and state the domain and range of $h(x)$
   - **3.2** $p(x)$ if $f(x)$ is reflected in the x-axis, and state the domain and range of $p(x)$
   - **3.3** $k(x)$ if $f(x)$ is shifted two units to the right, and state the domain and range of $k(x)$
   - **3.4** $q(x)$ if $f(x)$ is shifted one unit downwards, and state the domain and range of $q(x)$.

4. Consider $g(x) = \log_{\frac{1}{2}} x$ which passes through the point C(4; −2).
   - **4.1** Determine the equation of the inverse g^{-1}.
   - **4.2** Sketch the graph of $g(x)$ and g^{-1} on the same system of axes.
   - **4.3** For which value(s) of x is $g^{-1}(x) < 1$?
   - **4.4** For which value(s) of x is $g(x) < -2$?

5. Determine the following equations:
   5.1 $h(x)$ if $g(x)$ is reflected in the y-axis
   5.2 $p(x)$ if $g(x)$ is reflected in the x-axis
   5.3 $k(x)$ if $g(x)$ is shifted two units to the left
   5.4 $q(x)$ if $g(x)$ is shifted one unit upwards.

6. Sketch the graph of $g(x)$ and:
   6.1 $h(x)$ if $g(x)$ is reflected in the y-axis, and state the domain and range of $h(x)$
   6.2 $p(x)$ if $g(x)$ is reflected in the x-axis, and state the domain and range of $p(x)$
   6.3 $k(x)$ if $g(x)$ is shifted two units to the left, and state the domain and range of $k(x)$
   6.4 $q(x)$ if $g(x)$ is shifted two units upwards, and state the domain and range of $q(x)$.

Note
This type of calculation is used in financial mathematics.

Using logs to solve an exponential equation

We use logarithms to solve exponential equations when the right hand side cannot be written to the same base as the left hand side.

Worked examples
1. Solve for x: $2^x = 3$
2. Solve for n: $3{,}12^n = 29$

Solutions
1. $\quad 2x = 3$ — It is not possible to make the bases equal.
   $\log 2^x = \log 3$ — Take the log of both sides.
   $x \log 2 = \log 3$ — Use log law 3.
   $x = \dfrac{\log 3}{\log 2}$ — Divide both sides by log 2.
   $x \approx 1{,}58$

2. $\quad 3{,}12^n = 29$
   $\log (3{,}12)^n = \log 29$
   $n \log 3{,}12 = \log 29$
   $n = \dfrac{\log 29}{\log 3{,}12}$
   $n \approx 2{,}96$

Exercise 15
Solve for n in the following equations:

1. $1{,}05^n = 5{,}6$
2. $\left(1 + \dfrac{0{,}12}{44}\right)^n = 1{,}026$
3. $250(1{,}075)^{n+1} = 5\,076$
4. $10\,000\left(1 + \dfrac{0{,}08}{12}\right)^{n-1} = 15\,000$
5. $85(1{,}05)^{n-2} = 400$

Test A: Knowledge and routine procedures

1. Use the definition of a logarithm to complete the following statement:
   If $p^m = x$, then $m = \ldots$ (1)

2. Using the definition of a logarithm:
   Change the following to logarithmic form:
   2.1 $3^4 = 81$
   2.2 $\left(\frac{1}{2}\right)^3 = \frac{1}{8}$ (2 × 2)

   Change the following to exponential form:
   2.3 $\log_{10} 100 = 2$
   2.4 $\log_2 64 = 6$
   2.5 $\log_a b = k$ (3 × 2)

3. Determine the value of $\log_{25} 125$ without using a calculator. (2)

4. Given $f(x) = -x^2 + 2x + 3$:
   4.1 Determine $f(1)$. (1)
   4.2 For which value(s) of x is:
     4.2.1 $f(x) = 0$? (3)
     4.2.2 $f(x) = 4$ (3)
   4.3 Write down the coordinates of the turning point of $f(x)$. (1)
   4.4 State the range of $f(x)$. (1)
   4.5 Using the information from your answers to the questions above, write the equation of $f(x)$ in the form $y = a(x - p)^2 + q$. (3)

5. The graph below represents $f(x) = a(x - p)^2 + q$ and $g(x) = mx + c$.

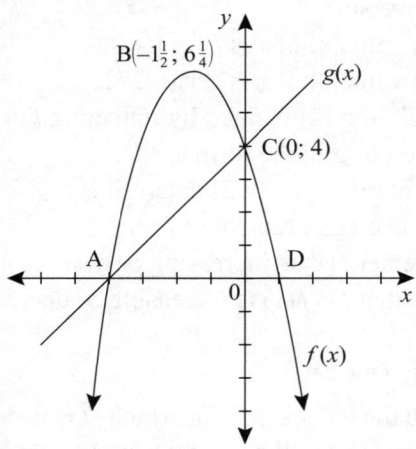

   5.1 Determine the numerical values of a, p and q. (4)
   5.2 **5.2.1** Is $f(x)$ a minimum or maximum valued curve? (1)
       5.2.2 Write down the value of this min/max value of $f(x)$. (1)
   5.3 State the domain and range of $f(x)$. (2)
   5.4 Calculate the value of the average gradient of $f(x)$ between:
     5.4.1 C and D (3)
     5.4.2 A and B. (2)

5.5 What type of mapping is indicated by:
    5.5.1 $f(x)$ (1)
    5.5.2 $g(x)$? (1)
5.6 Determine the equation of $g(x)$. (2)
5.7 Determine the inverse of $g(x)$. (3)
5.8   5.8.1 Sketch the graphs of $f(x)$, its inverse, and the line $y = x$ on the same system of axes. (3)
    5.8.2 How must the domain of $f(x)$ be restricted such that the inverse of $f(x)$ is a function? (2)

Total: 50

Test B: Complex procedures and problem solving

1. Given: the sketch graph of $f(x) = \left(\frac{1}{3}\right)^x$:

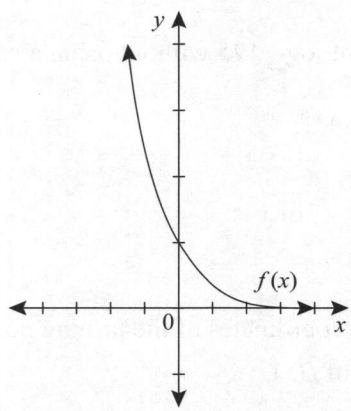

  1.1 Write down the coordinates of the y-intercept and one other point on the graph of f. (2)
  1.2 Determine the equation of the inverse of f, and draw the graphs of f and its inverse. (3)
  1.3 For which value(s) of x is $f^{-1}(x) > 0$? (1)
  1.4 For which value(s) of x is $f(x) < 27$? (2)
  1.5 If the graph of g is obtained by reflecting f in the y-axis, write down the equation of g in the form $y = \ldots$ (2)
  1.6 Over the interval $x \in [0; 2]$ determine:
    1.6.1 the average gradient of $f(x)$ (4)
    1.6.2 whether $f(x)$ is increasing or decreasing (1)
    1.6.3 whether $f^{-1}f(x)$ is increasing or decreasing. (1)

2. Given $f(x) = \log_3(x - 2)$:
  2.1 Determine the values of x for which $f(x)$ is defined. (2)
  2.2 Explain how $f(x)$ will be transformed to obtain $g(x) = \log_3 x$. (2)
  2.3 Draw the graph of $g(x)$ and $f(x)$. Hence determine the value(s) of x for which $\log_3(x - 2) < 0$. (3)
  2.4 Determine the equation of $g^{-1}(x)$ in the form $y = \ldots$. (3)
  2.5 Determine the equation of h if the graph h is obtained by reflecting the graph of f in the x-axis. (3)

3. When earthquakes occur, the Richter scale is used to measure the magnitude (which is the amount of energy released). This scale is a logarithmic scale with a base of 10. This means that an increase of 1 in magnitude results in a factor increase of 10 times more energy being released. An earthquake that measures 7 on the Richter scale is far more destructive than an earthquake measuring 1 on the Richter scale.

   3.1 Earthquakes with magnitude x and y have Richter scale readings of $\log x = 9$ and $\log x = 6$. Determine the ratio of x to y and explain what this indicates. (4)

   3.2 Given that $T_n = 6(5^n)$, which term is the first to exceed 378 000? (4)

4. In the diagram below, the graphs of $f(x) = \log_{\frac{1}{2}} x$ and $g(x) = mx$ are provided. R is the x-intercept of $f(x)$ and the points of intersection of $f(x)$ and $g(x)$ are P$(a; -1)$ and Q$(4; b)$.

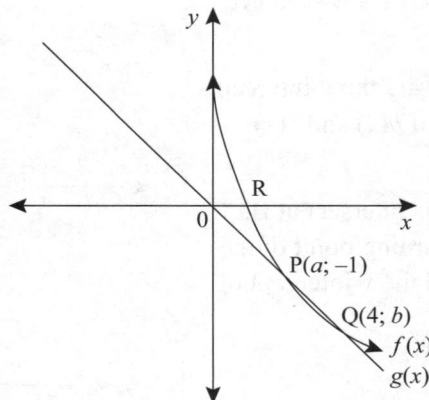

Determine the following:

4.1 the coordinates of R (1)

4.2 whether f is a one-to-one mapping or not, and validate this answer (2)

4.3 the value of a (1)

4.4 the value of b (1)

4.5 the average gradient between points P and Q (2)

4.6 the value(s) of x for which $f(x) \geq g(x)$ (2)

4.7 the equation of $h(x)$ if h is a reflection of f through the x-axis (2)

4.8 the equation of $k(x)$ if k is obtained by shifting the graph of f one unit to the right. (2)

Total: 50

Test C: Breakdown and content as per final exam

1.1 Draw a sketch graph of $f(x) = 2x - 1$. (1)

1.2 Write down the equation and draw a neat sketch graph of each of the following:

1.2.1 $f^{-1}(x)$ (3)

1.2.2 $h(x) = \frac{1}{f(x)}$ (3)

1.2.3 $g(x) = f\left(\frac{1}{x}\right)$ (3)

2. Given $h(x) = \frac{3}{x-2} + 1$:
   2.1 Write down the equations of all the asymptotes of $h(x)$. (2)
   2.2 Determine the coordinates of the x- and y-intercepts of $h(x)$. (4)
   2.3 Draw a sketch graph of $h(x)$. Label all asymptotes and points of intersection with the axes. (4)
   2.4 Determine:
       2.4.1 a if P$(a; -2)$ lies on $h(x)$ (1)
       2.4.2 b if Q$(-1; b)$ lies on $h(x)$ (1)
       2.4.3 the average gradient of $h(x)$ between points P and Q (2)
       2.4.4 whether $h(x)$ is increasing or decreasing on the interval $x \in [a; -1]$. (1)
   2.5 How will $h(x)$ be shifted to obtain $f(x) = \frac{3}{x}$? (2)

3. The graphs of $f(x) = 3^x - 9$ and $h(x) = ax^2 + bx + c$ are sketched alongside.

   A $(0; 4)$ and C are the y-intercepts of the graphs of $h(x)$ and $f(x)$ respectively.

   The two graphs intersect at B, which is the turning point of the graph of h and the x-intercept of both graphs.

   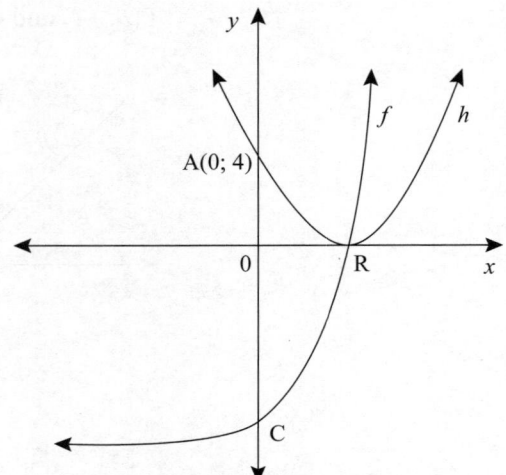

   3.1 Determine the coordinates of B and C. (4)
   3.2 Write down the equation of the asymptote of the graph of f. (1)
   3.3 Determine the equation of $g(x)$ if $g(x) = f(2x) + 6$. (2)
   3.4 Determine the equation of $g(x)$ in the form $y = \ldots$ (2)
   3.5 Write down the equation of p if p is a reflection of f about the x-axis. (2)
   3.6 For which value(s) of x is $g^{-1}(x)$ defined? (2)

4. 4.1 Simplify without using a calculator:
       $\left(\sqrt{3x^2} - 1\right)^2 + \sqrt{12x^2}$. (3)
   4.2 If it is given that $x = 1\,000\,000\,000\,001$, determine the value of $\frac{x^2 - 1}{x + 1}$ without using a calculator. All your working must be shown. (3)
   4.3 Thulani is an engineer and is out in the field needing to do the following calculation without a calculator. Use algebra and assist Thulani in determining the value of:
       $2\,013^2 - 2\,011 \times 2\,015 + 2\,010 \times 2\,016 - 2\,008 \times 2\,018$ (4)

   Total: 50

TOPIC 3   Finance: Growth and decay

In Grade 10 you learnt how to use the formulae for simple interest and compound interest to solve problems involving interest, hire purchase, inflation, population growth and other real life problems. You also worked with the fluctuation of exchange rates.

In Grade 11 the same formulae were used to include straight line depreciation and depreciation on reducing balance, including the graphic representation of these concepts. You also worked with the effect of different periods of compounding growths and decay, including the work on effective and nominal interest rates.

In Grade 12 you will work with the compound increase and decrease formulae to calculate the value of n, which represents the number of compounding periods. You will also learn to apply your knowledge of geometric series to solve annuity and bond repayment problems and critically analyse different loan options.

Knowledge and skills for this Topic

For the Grade 12 work in this Topic, you need a good grasp of the following knowledge and skills:

- understand the meaning of a percentage
- understand simple and compound interest and their formulae, and how to change the subject of the formula
- understand and work with the laws of exponents and logarithms
- know how to work with arithmetic and geometric sequences and apply them to simple interest and compound interest
- know how to work with timelines related to finance.

Content of final exam

- Do simple interest calculations related to hire purchase.
- Use compound interest formulae to perform various calculations on inflation, loan options or investment opportunities.
- Work with straight line depreciation and depreciation on a reducing balance.
- Work with a timeline to perform various financial calculations.
- Solve problems using the present and future value annuity formulae.
- Using logarithms to determine the number of loan payments or investment periods.
- Analyse various loan options.

Revision of Grades 10 and 11 Finance

Depreciation
The formulae and graphs for straight line depreciation and depreciation on a reducing balance are given below.

Straight line depreciation
$$F = P(1 - in)$$

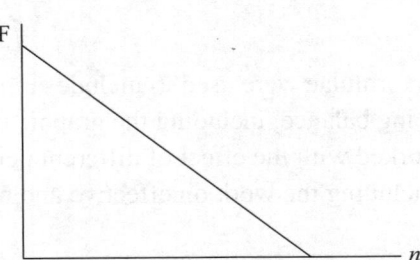

Reducing balance depreciation
$$F = P(1 - i)^n$$

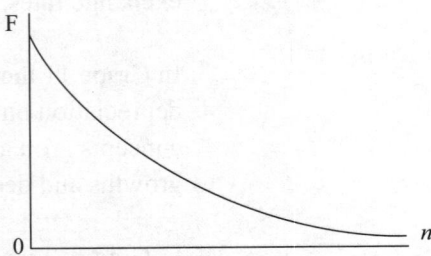

Nominal and effective interest rates
To convert effective interest rate to a nominal interest rate, or vice-versa, use this formula:

$$1 + i_{\text{effective}} = \left(1 + \frac{i_{\text{nominal}}}{m}\right)^m$$

An effective interest rate is the annual rate of interest that takes into account the effect of compounding. Compounding constantly increases the value of the deposit, so an effective interest rate will be greater than a nominal interest rate.

A nominal interest rate is the 'stated' rate of interest, which also states the number of times per year the interest is calculated, e.g. 8% p.a. compounded monthly. That rate is used for i in the Fv formula for both lump sum deposits and annuities:

$$Fv = P\left[\frac{\left(1 + \frac{0{,}08}{12}\right)^{n \times 12}}{\frac{0{,}08}{12}}\right] \text{ and } Fv = x\left[\frac{\left(1 + \frac{0{,}08}{12}\right)^{n \times 12}}{\frac{0{,}08}{12}} - 1\right]$$

The necessity for converting from effective to nominal is dealt with in the section 'Investments, savings and retirement annuities'.

Worked example
Fumane wants to invest R100 000 and is faced with two choices. Bank A is offering an interest rate of 12% p.a. compounded monthly, while Bank B is offering an interest rate of 12,2% p.a. compounded quarterly. Which bank is offering the better deal?

Solution
Bank A:

$1 + i_{\text{effective}} = \left(1 + \frac{i_{\text{nominal}}}{m}\right)^m$

$1 + i_{\text{eff}} = \left(1 + \frac{0{,}12}{12}\right)^{12}$

$i_{\text{eff}} = 0{,}126825$

rate = 12,68% p.a.

Bank B:

$1 + i_{\text{effective}} = \left(1 + \frac{i_{\text{nominal}}}{m}\right)^m$

$1 + i_{\text{eff}} = \left(1 + \frac{0{,}122}{4}\right)^4$

$i_{\text{eff}} = 0{,}127696$

rate = 12,77% p.a.

So Bank B has the better deal.

Exercise 1

1. Convert the following nominal interest rates to the **effective** interest rates per period stated. Give your answer to four decimal places.
   - **1.1** 9% p.a. compounded quarterly
   - **1.2** 8,4% p.a. compounded monthly
   - **1.3** 7,8% p.a. compounded daily
   - **1.4** 8% p.a. compounded semi-annually
   - **1.5** 9,2% p.a. compounded bi-annually
   - **1.6** 8,5% p.a. compounded weekly

2. Using the same rates as in question 1, convert the nominal interest into **annual** effective interest rates.

Exercise 2 (complex procedures)

1. Determine, using the annual effective interest rate, which of the following investments is the better investment:
   - **1.1** A: an investment at 8,4% p.a. compounded daily
     OR B: an investment at 8,5% p.a. compounded weekly
   - **1.2** C: an investment at 8,25% p.a. compounded monthly
     OR D: an investment at 8,3% p.a. compounded quarterly

2. A bank is offering the following interest rates on different fixed deposits:

   A – 7,9% p.a. on funds invested for five years or longer
   B – 7,8% p.a. compounded monthly on money invested for at least three years
   C – 7,75% p.a. compounded weekly on money invested for at least two years

   Kgethang wishes to invest his money for six years. Determine which of the options he should select to obtain the best return on his money.

Exercise 3

1. **1.1** Mhambi invests R56 700 at 7,5% p.a. compounded monthly. Calculate the value of his investment after five years.
   1.2 What is the effective annual interest rate he received for this investment?
   1.3 Jabulile, Mhambi's sister, also invests R56 700 into a fixed deposit earning 7,5% p.a. compounded monthly. But she deposits an additional amount of R10 000 after two years. Calculate the value of her investment after five years.

2. Shafika is saving for an exciting trip to Europe in five years' time. She deposits an initial amount of R12 000 into a savings account at 7,8% p.a. compounded monthly. At the end of the second year she deposits R7 500 into the account and another R5 000 at the end of the third year. Calculate the value of this investment after five years.

3. Convert the following nominal interest rates to effective annual interest rates (to two decimal places).
   - **3.1** 10,5% p.a. compounded monthly
   - **3.2** 9,3% p.a. compounded weekly
   - **3.3** 8,7% p.a. compounded quarterly
   - **3.4** 7,5% p.a. compounded semi-annually

4. Convert an effective interest rate of 9% p.a. to a nominal interest rate per annum compounded monthly.

5. Tebello wins R300 000 on the lottery and invests all the money into a savings account at 8,75% p.a. compounded monthly. After two years she withdraws R158 000 to purchase a car. After another year she deposits R35 000 into this account. Calculate how much money Tebello will have in her investment account after six years.

6. Mthunzi has just started working and is planning to save R65 000 to purchase a motorbike in three years' time. At the beginning of each year he will make three equal deposits into a savings account at 7,8% p.a. compounded quarterly. Calculate the value of these annual deposits.

7. Marcel purchases a new vehicle for R125 000. In five years' time he wishes to buy the same model, the average inflation rate over this five year period is 5,5% p.a., while the same model of car depreciates by 12% p.a.
   7.1 Determine the cost of the new vehicle in five years' time.
   7.2 What will the car be worth at the end of five years using:
      7.2.1 the reducing balance method of depreciation?
      7.2.2 the straight line balance method of depreciation?
   7.3 If Marcel uses his old car as a trade-in after five years, how much will he be required to pay for the new vehicle then, if the reducing balance method of depreciation has been used?

8. Ayanda borrows money from the bank in order to finance a new business. The bank charges her an interest rate of 10,5% p.a. compounded annually. Calculate the present value of the loan (the amount originally borrowed) if she pays off the loan in four years from now with a payment of R 200 000.

9. A swimming pool has been neglected and a certain type of bacteria is developing. At the start of the process, a 2 litre sample is tested and 2 000 bacteria are found. After 20 minutes another 2 litre sample is tested, and the bacteria count has increased to 6 000. It is found that the growth fits the compound interest future value formula.
   9.1 Calculate an estimated growth rate of the bacteria per minute.
   9.2 Using your answer for 9.1, how many bacteria will be present at the end of 1 hour.

10. After the 2011 South African population census, a population of approximately 51,7 million people was recorded. After the 2001 census the approximate population of South Africa was recorded as 44,8 million. Assuming that the population growth rate follows the compound increase formula:
    10.1 calculate the average annual percentage growth rate of the South African population
    10.2 determine the estimated population of South Africa for the year 2021 if the population of South Africa continues to grow at this average rate.

Present value and future value annuities

An annuity is a sequence of equal payments made at regular intervals of time. There are two main types of annuities:
1. annuities where we find a future value – this is where regular payments are being made into a savings or investment account
2. annuities where we find a present value – this is where regular payments are being made to pay off a loan or bond.

The timeline below represents the basic structure of an annuity:

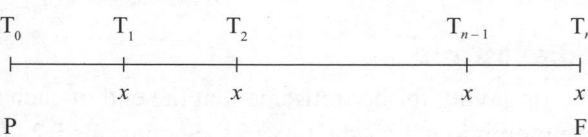

Note
There is no payment at T_0, and there is a payment at T_n.

P (representing the present value) is at the start of the timeline for the basic structure of an annuity and F (representing the future value) is at the end of the timeline. Depending on the context of the question, P and F may appear in other positions, but P will always appear to the left of F.

The x represents monthly payments made and the n represents the total number of payments made.

It is important to note that payments commence at one period after the present value P at T_0 and end after n payment periods at T_n.

Investments, savings and retirement annuities

In these situations a regular payment x is deposited into an account and attracts interest at a stated interest rate i per interest period for n periods.

In most cases, the nominal rate as stated is used in the formula. However, when the deposits are made at a given number of times a year, e.g. quarterly (which is four times a year, i.e. every three months), and the stated interest rate is given at a rate **per annum** (effective rate), then this rate must be converted to the nominal interest rate before calculating the future value.

For example, Jabu deposits R500 **every month** into a savings account that earns 6,5% **per annum**. Calculate how much will be in his account after five years. We need the nominal interest rate for the formula, so it is necessary to convert the effective rate of 6,5% p.a. to the nominal rate.

In order to calculate the future value F of money at T_n we work to the right on the timeline.
- The structure of an annuity starts at T_0, with the first payment occurring at T_1.
- Each payment is treated as the present value of a compound interest investment for the remaining period, each producing a future value. The sum of all these future values is determined using the formula for the future value of an annuity.
- A final payment of x is made immediately before the end of this process.

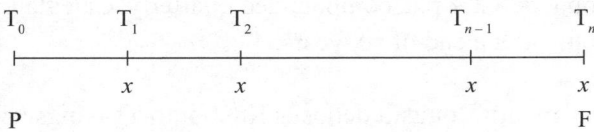

From the timeline we can see that:
$$F = x + x(1+i) + x(1+i)^2 + x(1+i)^3 + \ldots + x(1+i)^{n-1}$$

Formula for future value

The equation above indicates that this is the sum to n terms of a geometric series of which the formula is $S_n = \frac{a(r^n - 1)}{(r - 1)}$ where $r \neq 1$. Substitute the following:

$a = x \qquad r = (1 + i) \qquad n = $ number of payments made:

$$F = \frac{x\left[(1 + i)^n - 1\right]}{1 + i - 1}$$

$$F = \frac{x\left[(1 + i)^n - 1\right]}{i}$$

Worked example

Andrea starts saving for her retirement at the end of each month starting at the end of the month in which she turns 21. She invests R2 000 every month into a retirement annuity (savings account) at 7,5% p.a. compounded monthly, until the end of the month of her 60th birthday. Calculate how much money she will have in this retirement annuity by then.

Solution

$T_0 \qquad T_1 \qquad T_2 \qquad\qquad\qquad T_{(60-21)\times 12}$

Age 21 $\qquad\qquad$ 2 000 $\qquad\qquad\qquad$ Age 60

$$i = \frac{0,075}{12}$$

$F = \frac{x\left[(1 + i)^n - 1\right]}{i}$ where $x = $ R2 000, $n = (60 - 21) \times 12 = 468$ and $i = \frac{0,075}{12}$

$$F = \frac{2\,000\left[\left(1 + \frac{0,075}{12}\right)^{468} - 1\right]}{\frac{0,075}{12}}$$

$F = $ R5 588 919,57

Exercise 4

Use timelines for this exercise on future value annuities.

1. Calculate the accumulated amount of 36 monthly payments immediately after the 36th payment, if the interest is at 8,5% p.a. compounded monthly, and the monthly payments are as follows:
   - **1.1** R500
   - **1.2** R800
   - **1.3** R1 000
   - **1.4** R1 200
   - **1.5** R1 500

2. Find the value of each of 20 quarterly payments if the future value is R85 000 and the interest rates are as follows:
   - **2.1** 8,5% p.a. compounded quarterly
   - **2.2** 8,75% p.a. compounded quarterly
   - **2.3** 9% p.a. compounded quarterly

3. At the end of every month Faranaaz deposits R1 200 into an interest-bearing account at 8,2% p.a. compounded quarterly. Calculate the amount in this account at the end of six years.

4. Every month Bongani deposits R890 into a savings account earning 7,7% per annum. Determine the amount in this account after 48 months.

5. Paballo is planning to purchase a new car in three years' time. The car she really wants will cost approximately R220 000 in 3 years' time. Determine the amount of money she will need to deposit into an interest bearing account at 9,2% p.a. compounded monthly to reach this amount in time.

6. Ahmed is now thirty years old. He decides to make financial plans to retire at the age of 55. He will need a capital amount of R2 000 000. Determine how much he must deposit every month into an investment account at 9% p.a. compounded monthly.

7. Every month Themba deposits R1 200 into a ten-year annuity for his daughter Phumelele's education. Themba starts the payments one month after taking the annuity at interest rate of 7,85% per annum. Calculate the value of the annuity at the end of ten years.

8. Starting at the end of the year in which Daniel turns five, his grandmother deposits R2 500 into a savings account earning 8,3% per annum at the end of every year. Determine the value of this investment at the end of the year in which Daniel turns 21.

9. Zwoluga plans to be a millionaire in 5 years' time. She believes she can obtain an average return of 22% p.a. on the stock market. Determine how much she needs to invest every month to realise her dream.

10. Mulalo makes 48 equal monthly payments of Rx into an account earning 8,8% p.a. compounded monthly. If the value of the account after the 48th payment is R157 531,28, determine the value of x.

Exercise 5 (complex procedures)

Use timelines for this exercise on future value annuities.

1. Starting on her 18th birthday, Miriam deposits R2 000 per month into an account at 8,5% p.a. compounded monthly. On her 28th birthday she stops making these regular payments and allows the interest to accumulate on this money.
    1.1 Determine how much money she will have in this account on her 60th birthday.
    1.2 Miriam is excited about the estimated value of her investment and tells Eva, a friend hers, about this. Eva is the same age as Miriam. Eva however decides to travel first. She only starts depositing R2 000 into an investment earning the same interest, i.e. 8,5% p.a. compounded monthly, starting on her 25th birthday and making a final payment on her 60th birthday. Determine how much money Eva will have in her account on her 60th birthday.
    1.3 Determine the total amount of interest earned by:
        1.3.1 Miriam
        1.3.2 Eva.

2. Joseph has just finished a business degree at university and is very excited about his future. He decides to open an investment account and deposits R2 500 into this account at the end of every month. He has negotiated a good interest rate of 9% p.a. compounded monthly. He also decides that at the end of every year he will deposit an additional R10 000 into this investment account. Determine the amount in this account after ten years.

3. Three friends, Alex, Kayla and Anne-Marie are excitedly planning an island holiday after they finish studying in three years' time. They plan to book a package trip that at present costs R17 500 each. The inflation rate is estimated to be 4,8% per annum.

   3.1 Determine how much they will pay for this same package holiday in three years' time.

   3.2 They all decide to start saving money now. Draw a timeline for each person, indicating all the relevant details on the line, using this information, and answering the questions below:

   3.2.1 Alex deposits the same amount at the end of every month into a savings account that earns interest at 7,6% p.a. compounded monthly. Determine the monthly amount Alex deposits into this savings account.

   3.2.2 Kayla deposits R3 000 semi-annually into a savings account, at 8,2% p.a. compounded semi-annually. Determine whether Kayla, at the end of three years, will have enough money for this trip.

   3.2.3 Anne Marie's aunt will give her a lump sum which she deposits into a savings account earning 8,2% p.a. compounded quarterly. Determine the lump sum of money Anne-Marie's aunt gives to her so that she can invest the money in order to pay for the trip in 3 years' time.

Sinking funds

Sinking funds are set up in order to purchase new or replace old equipment at some time in the future.

Worked examples

1. A sinking fund is set up to purchase a new car in two years' time. It is estimated that the new car will cost R135 000. Determine the amount that needs to be invested monthly into an account at 8,1% p.a. compounded monthly in order to pay cash for the car.

2. A sinking fund for R300 000 is set up by a school to update the computer system in five years' time. The interest rate is 7,5% p.a. Determine the size of the annual payments if:
   2.1 payments start in one year's time
   2.2 payments start immediately.

3. A sinking fund for R1 200 000 at 8% p.a. is set up to replace the buses at a school in ten years' time. Determine the size of ten equal annual payments if:
   3.1 payments start in one year's time
   3.2 payments start immediately.

Solutions

1. Number of months $= 2 \times 12 = 24$

   Interest per month $= \frac{0,081}{12}$

   Future value $=$ R135 000

   $F = x\left[\frac{(1+i)^n - 1}{i}\right]$

$$135\,000 = x\left[\frac{\left(1 + \frac{0{,}081}{12}\right)^{24} - 1}{\frac{0{,}081}{12}}\right]$$

$$x = R5\,200{,}59$$

2. 2.1 $\quad F = x\left[\dfrac{(1+i)^n - 1}{i}\right]$

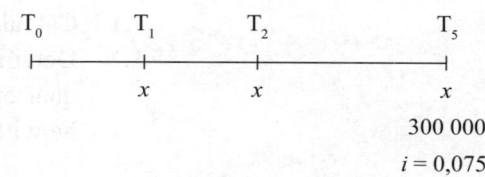

$$x = \frac{300\,000}{\left[\frac{(1 + 0{,}075)^5 - 1}{0{,}075}\right]}$$

$$= R51\,649{,}42$$

2.2

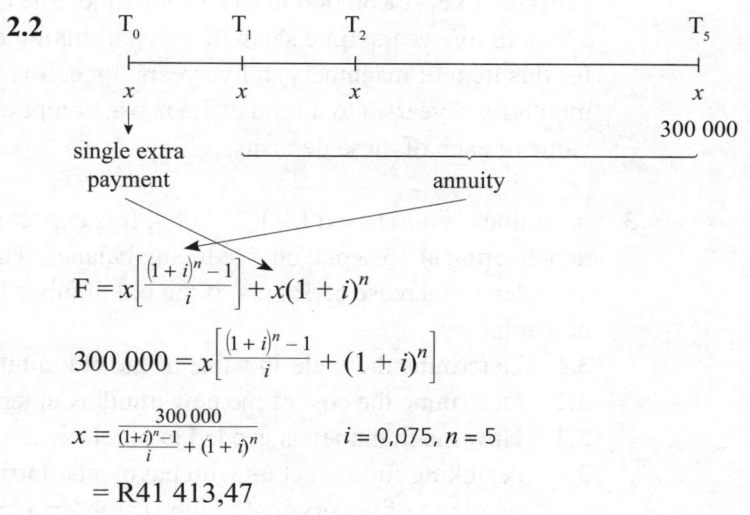

$$F = x\left[\frac{(1+i)^n - 1}{i}\right] + x(1+i)^n$$

$$300\,000 = x\left[\frac{(1+i)^n - 1}{i} + (1+i)^n\right]$$

$$x = \frac{300\,000}{\frac{(1+i)^n - 1}{i} + (1+i)^n} \qquad i = 0{,}075,\ n = 5$$

$$= R41\,413{,}47$$

3. 3.1 $\quad F = x\left[\dfrac{(1+i)^n - 1}{i}\right]$

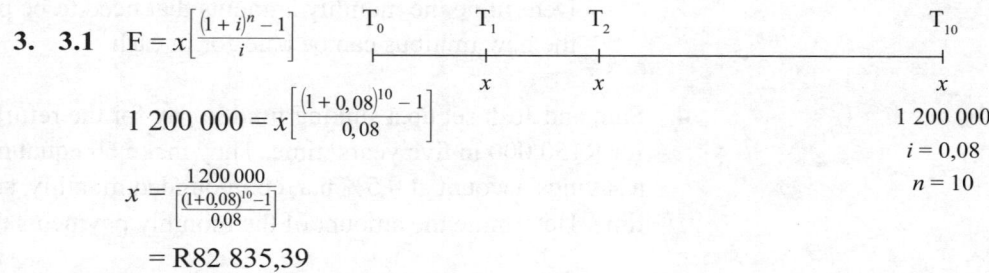

$$1\,200\,000 = x\left[\frac{(1 + 0{,}08)^{10} - 1}{0{,}08}\right]$$

$$x = \frac{1\,200\,000}{\left[\frac{(1+0{,}08)^{10} - 1}{0{,}08}\right]}$$

$$= R82\,835{,}39$$

3.2

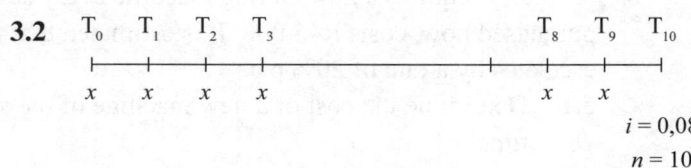

$i = 0{,}08$
$n = 10$

The structure of an annuity to use the formula above has no payment at T_0, but does have a payment at T_{10}. Here we use:

F at T_{10} = (annuity formula) $- x + x(1 + i)^n$ The x come from T_0 on the timeline, and the $x(1+i)^n$ comes from T_{10}.

$$1\,200\,000 = x\left[\frac{(1{,}08)^{10} - 1}{0{,}08}\right] - x + x(1{,}08)^{10}$$

$$1\,200\,000 = x\left[\frac{(1{,}08)^{10} - 1}{0{,}08} - 1 + x(1{,}08)^{10}\right]$$

$$x = \frac{1\,200\,000}{\left[\frac{(1{,}08)^{10} - 1}{0{,}08} - 1 + (1{,}08)^{10}\right]} = R76\,699{,}43$$

Exercise 6

1. Yazeem wishes to purchase a car in three years' time. The car he wants costs R180 000. It is estimated that the value of the car will appreciate at 4,5% per annum.
   1.1 Calculate the value of this car in three years' time.
   1.2 Determine what sum of money Yazeem must invest at the end of every quarter into a savings account at 7,5% p.a. compounded quarterly so that he will have enough money to purchase the car in three years' time.

2. Mantso runs a printing press and calculates that an item of machinery is expected to cost R60 000 in five years' time. She decides that instead of taking a loan in five years' time she will set up a sinking fund so that she can pay cash for this item of machinery in five years' time. She will make deposits every month for 5 years into a fund at 7,5% p.a. compounded monthly. Determine the value of each of these deposits.

3. A minibus is purchased for R250 000. It is expected to last for ten years and is depreciating at 15% p.a. on a reducing balance. The cost of the new minibus is expected to increase at 5% p.a. if the old minibus is used as a trade-in on the new minibus:
   3.1 Determine the trade-in value of the old minibus in ten years' time.
   3.2 Determine the cost of the new minibus in ten years' time.
   3.3 How much money is needed to purchase the new minibus?
   3.4 A sinking fund is set up with payments starting one month after the purchase of the original minibus at 8% p.a. compounded monthly. Determine the monthly amounts that need to be paid into the fund so that the new minibus can be paid for in cash.

4. Sam and Josh set up a sinking fund to pay for the refurbishing of their kitchen for R150 000 in five years' time. They make 60 equal monthly payments into a savings account at 8,5% p.a. compounded monthly, starting in one month's time. Determine the amount of the monthly payments they make.

5. A factory requires a new cutting machine every seven years. The present one, purchased now, costs R45 000. It is estimated that the cost of this machine escalates by a rate of 20% p.a.
   5.1 Determine the cost of a new machine of the same type in seven years' time.
   5.2 This machine depreciates at 12% p.a. on a reducing balance. Calculate the scrap value (depreciated value) of the present machine in seven years' time.
   5.3 The owner of the factory sets up a sinking fund to replace this machine in seven years' time. He makes quarterly payments into an account earning 8% p.a. Payments start three months after the purchase of the original machine and the last payment is made when the new machine is purchased. Determine the quarterly payments which must be made into this sinking fund.

Present value: Loans and car finance

With loans and car financing, the starting amount (the present value) is progressively decreased due to regular payments (x). The outstanding balance attracts interest at an interest rate (i) per period for n periods. The compounding period coincides with the payment period. The formula for the present value and the structure of this annuity is derived as follows:

- The process starts at T_0, with the first payment occurring at T_1.
- Each payment x has its own present value calculated: $P_1; P_2; P_3; \ldots P_n$
- The final payment x completes the process, leaving a zero balance, in other words a fully paid-off loan.

In order to calculate the present value (P) of money at T_0 we work to the left (backwards) on the timeline.

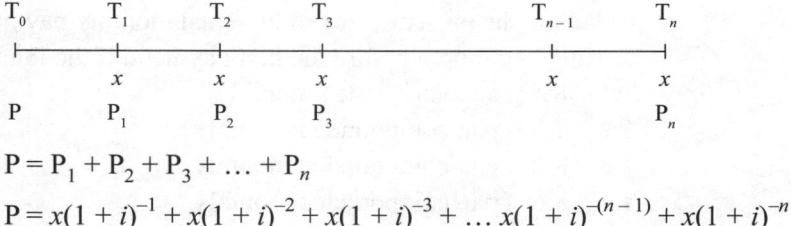

$$P = P_1 + P_2 + P_3 + \ldots + P_n$$
$$P = x(1 + i)^{-1} + x(1 + i)^{-2} + x(1 + i)^{-3} + \ldots x(1 + i)^{-(n-1)} + x(1 + i)^{-n}$$

Formula for present value

The equation above indicates that this is the sum to n terms of a geometric series, for which the formula is $S_n = \frac{a(r^n - 1)}{(1 - r)}$, where $r \neq 1$. Substitute the following:

$a = x(1 + i)^{-1}$ $\quad r = (1 + i)^{-1}$ $\quad n =$ number of payments made

$$P = \frac{x(1 + i)^{-1}[(1 + i)^{-n} - 1]}{(1 + i)^{-1} - 1}$$

$$P = \frac{\frac{x}{1+i}[(1 + i)^{-n} - 1]}{\frac{1}{1+i} - 1}$$

$$P = \frac{x[(1 + i)^{-n} - 1]}{1 - (1 + i)} \qquad \text{Multiply both numerator and denominator by } (1 + i).$$

$$P = \frac{x[1 - (1 + i)^{-n}]}{i}$$

It is important to note that:

- The two annuity formulae $F = \frac{x[(1 + i)^n - 1]}{i}$ and $P = \frac{x[1 - (1 + i)^{-n}]}{i}$ hold only when payment commences one period from the present and ends after n periods.
- Using a timeline to analyse problems is a useful technique.
- In the work above an important principle is assumed. This principle is that the compounding period is equal to the payment period, in other words the effective interest per period must be used.

Worked example

Kayla buys a car, and decides to pay R4 500 per month on a loan offered at 14% p.a. compounded monthly. She pays the loan off in one year. Determine the present value (to the nearest rand) for the loan on the car.

```
T₀   T₁   T₂   T₃           T₁₁  T₁₂
|----|----|----|----...----|----|
P   4 500 4 500 4 500      4 500 4 500
```

Solution

$P = 4\,500(1 + i)^{-1} + 4\,500(1 + i)^{-2} + 4\,500(1 + i)^{-3} + \ldots 4\,500(1 + i)^{-(n-1)}$
$\quad + 4\,500(1 + i)^{-n}$

This is the sum of a geometric series where:

$a = 4\,500(1 + i)^{-1} \qquad r = (1 + i)^{-1} \qquad n = 12 \qquad S_n = a\left(\dfrac{r^n - 1}{r - 1}\right)$

$P = 4\,500(1 + i)^{-1}\left[\dfrac{(1 + i)^{-12} - 1}{(1 + i)^{-1} - 1}\right]$

$P = R50\,119$

Exercise 7

1. Calculate the present value of 20 equal monthly payments of R750 on a loan, starting one month before the first payment, if the interest is:
   1.1 8% p.a. compounded monthly
   1.2 7,8% p.a. compounded monthly
   1.3 8,2% p.a. compounded monthly
   1.4 8,6% p.a. compounded monthly
   1.5 9,8% p.a. compounded monthly
   1.6 16,5% p.a. compounded monthly.

2. Calculate the value of 16 equal quarterly payments, which will repay a loan of R30 000, if the payments begin one quarter after the granting of the loan, if the interest is:
   2.1 8,3% p.a. compounded quarterly
   2.2 9,5% p.a. compounded quarterly
   2.3 11,2% p.a. compounded quarterly
   2.4 14% p.a. compounded quarterly
   2.5 14,2% p.a. compounded quarterly
   2.6 17% p.a. compounded quarterly.

Exercise 8 (complex procedures)

1. Ms van Schalkwyk needs to borrow money to repay a debt. How much can she borrow if she undertakes to repay the loan by making 20 equal monthly payments of R800 each at 9% p.a. compounded monthly? The first payment is made one month after the loan was granted.

2. Bianca obtains a loan of R165 000 at 17,5% p.a. compounded monthly from a bank to purchase a car. Determine the monthly payments if the loan commences one month after it has been granted and is paid off five years later.

3. A young couple take out a 25 year mortgage to purchase a house and can only afford a monthly payment of R1 350. If the annual interest rate is 8,5% p.a. compounded monthly, determine the initial value of the bond the bank is prepared to grant to them.

4. Mr Drinkalot is involved in a car accident, resulting from driving under the influence of alcohol, and has injured a third party. The judgement against him

requires that he pay a monthly amount of R1 650 for six years for injuries sustained by the third party. Determine the amount to be invested in an account at 7,8% p.a. compounded monthly that would meet this financial obligation.

5. Mr and Mrs Luvhome are determined to purchase a new home for R2 200 000. They decide to pay a 40% deposit on this new home. They then apply for a bond to cover the balance. Starting one month after the bond was granted, the period of the bond is 15 years with an interest rate of 8,2% p.a. compounded monthly.
   5.1 Calculate the value of the deposit paid for the new home.
   5.2 Determine the value of the monthly payments.

Use logarithms to calculate the value of the time period n

In $F = P(1 + i)^n$ or $F = P(1 - i)^n$ use logarithms to solve for n:

Method 1
Change from exponent form to log form: $a = b^n$
$\therefore \log_b a = n$
Follow with $\frac{\log a}{\log b} = n$

Method 2
Take log of both sides:
$a = b^n$
$\therefore \log a = \log b^n$
$\log a = n \log b$
$\frac{\log a}{\log b} = n$

Worked examples

1. Solve for n if $5^n = 8$.

2. Lindi invests R12 000 earning 7,5% p.a. compounded monthly. When the value of the investment is R17 500 she decides to cash in the investment. Calculate the period of this investment in years and days.

Solutions

1. $\quad 5^n = 8$

   $\log_5 8 = n$

   $\frac{\log 8}{\log 5} = n$

   $n = 1{,}292$

2. $F = P(1 + i)^n$

   $17\,500 = 12\,000\left(1 + \frac{0{,}075}{12}\right)^n$ where n = number of months.

   $\left(1 + \frac{0{,}075}{12}\right)^n = \frac{17\,500}{12\,000}$

   $n = \log_{\left(1 + \frac{0{,}075}{12}\right)} \frac{17\,500}{12\,000}$

   $n = 60{,}555282$

   $n = 5$ years 17 days

Exercise 9

Solve for n correct to two decimal places.

1. $(1{,}075)^n = 2{,}865$

2. $30\,000(1{,}082)^n = 38\,000$

3. $15\,000(1{,}085)^{-n} = 12\,000$

4. $5\,670\left(\dfrac{1{,}07^n - 1}{0{,}07}\right) = 120\,000$: also explain in words what is being calculated here and indicate your explanation on a timeline.

Exercise 10 (complex procedures)

1. If it earns an interest rate of 8% p.a., determine the number of years (correct to one decimal place) it would take for an investment to:
   1.1 double in value
   1.2 quadruple in value.

2. The price of a loaf of bread was R9,19 during 2012 and increased by 11,7% during the following year. Determine how many years (correct to two decimal places) it will take for the price of a loaf of bread to double.

3. Every month R1 500 is invested into a savings account earning 9% p.a. compounded monthly. Determine how long it will take for the future value of the account to accumulate to at least R100 000. Give your answer in years and days.

4. Steve borrows R14 000 from the bank and agrees to repay the loan with monthly instalments of R800. Payment commences one month after the granting of the loan. The interest rate is 9% p.a. compounded monthly for the entire period of the loan. Determine the number of payments of R800 he will make.

5. Xandi is granted a loan of R800 000 at 8,5% p.a. compounded monthly to purchase a home.
   5.1 Determine the value of the monthly payments on the loan if it is to be repaid after 20 years, starting one month after the loan is granted.
   5.2 Xandi decides she would like to pay the loan off earlier and makes monthly payments of R7 500. Determine how many payments she will make to settle the loan.
   5.3 Calculate how much extra Xandi paid after increasing her monthly payments.
   5.4 By making these extra payments, how much earlier did she settle the loan?

Outstanding balance of a loan

The outstanding balance is the amount owing on the loan at a particular time. An outstanding balance is calculated:
- when there has been a change in the interest rate, or
- if the borrower pays a lump sum into the loan, or
- if the borrower wishes to repay the loan in a shorter or longer period of time, or
- when payments are missed.

The outstanding balance is always calculated immediately after a specific payment is made.

There are two ways to calculate an outstanding balance:
1. If the payments, including the final payment, are equal, then the present value of all payments still to be made is calculated to get the outstanding balance.
2. The outstanding balance = (original loan with interest added) – (payments made with interest added).

Worked examples

1. A loan of R50 000 at 9% p.a. compounded monthly will be fully paid at the end of five years.

   1.1 Determine the value of the equal monthly payments.

   1.2 Determine the outstanding balance (BO) immediately after the 20th payment using both methods of calculating an outstanding balance.

Solutions

1.

$T_0 \quad T_1 \quad\quad\quad T_{20} \quad\quad\quad T_{5 \times 12}$

$x \quad\quad\quad\quad BO$

$-50\,000 \quad\quad\quad\quad\quad\quad\quad i = \frac{0,09}{12}$

1.1 $P = x\left[\dfrac{1-(1+i)^{-n}}{i}\right]$

$x = \dfrac{50\,000}{\left[\dfrac{1-\left(1+\frac{0,09}{12}\right)^{-5 \times 12}}{\frac{0,09}{12}}\right]}$

$= R1\,037,92$

1.2 Balance outstanding at T_{20}
= future value of loan to T_{20} – future value of payments made until T_{20}

$= P(1+i)^{20} - x\left[\dfrac{(1+i)^{20}-1}{i}\right] \quad\quad P = 50\,000,\ i = \frac{0,09}{12},\ x = 1\,037,92$

$= 50\,000\left(1+\frac{0,09}{12}\right)^{20} - 1\,037,92\left[\dfrac{\left(1+\frac{0,09}{12}\right)^{20}-1}{\frac{0,09}{12}}\right]$

$= R35\,753,09$

OR

Balance outstanding at T_{20} = present value of payments yet to be made:

$Pv = BO = x\left[\dfrac{1-(1+i)^{-40}}{i}\right]$

$= 1\,037,92\left[\dfrac{1-\left(1+\frac{0,09}{12}\right)^{-40}}{\frac{0,09}{12}}\right]$

$= R35\,753,09$

Exercise 11

1. Ontitlile and Mogotsi can afford to pay R3 500 monthly for 20 years to purchase their first home. Interest rates on bonds are 9% p.a. compounded monthly.

   1.1 Calculate the value of the house they can afford to purchase.

   1.2 Determine the balance of the loan at the end of:

   1.2.1 4 years **1.2.2** 8 years **1.2.3** 12 years

   1.2.4 16 years **1.2.5** 20 years.

1.3 Use your answers to the questions above to draw a graph indicating the balance of the loan on the vertical axis and the time elapsed on the horizontal axis.

1.4 Over which period of the loan does the balance of the loan decrease the slowest?

2. Harold purchases a minibus for R220 000. He secures vehicle finance at a rate of 9,5% p.a. compounded monthly over a period of five years.
   2.1 Determine his monthly payments.
   2.2 Calculate his outstanding balance on this loan after three years.
   2.3 Determine the total amount of interest Harold will pay on this loan.

3. Nolundi borrows R70 000 to set up a small business. She makes equal annual payments to pay off the loan earning interest at a rate of 7,7% p. a. compounded annually. She will pay off the loan after 6 years.
   3.1 Determine the annual payments.
   3.2 Calculate the outstanding balance at the end of the fourth year.
   3.3 Calculate the total amount of interest Nolundi pays on this loan.

4. Chelan borrows R8 000 from a micro-lender (i.e. loan shark) for emergency expenses. The interest on this loan is 4% per month compounded monthly. The loan is paid off after 6 months.
   4.1 Determine the value of the monthly payments.
   4.2 Determine the balance of the loan after three months.
   4.3 Calculate the total value of the interest paid on the loan.

5. Timothy and Karen purchase a house for R1 200 000. They decide to let the house for R5 000 per month. They are able to raise a 100% bond over 30 years at a rate of 8,6% p.a. compounded monthly.
   5.1 They use the rental to pay the monthly payments. Determine how much extra they will need to pay into the bond every month.
   5.2 Determine the outstanding balance after ten years.
   5.3 If the interest rate changes to 8% p.a. compounded monthly after ten years and the period of the bond remains unchanged, determine the new monthly payments.
   5.4 Timothy and Karen decide to keep paying the original monthly amount. Determine the new period of the loan.

Test A: Knowledge and routine procedures

1. Corina wants to purchase an apartment for R900 000. She is required to pay a 10% deposit and will take a loan for the balance from a bank.
   1.1 Calculate the value of the deposit. (2)
   1.2 The bank loan she obtains is at 8% p.a. compounded monthly. Corina calculates that this loan will have an effective interest rate of 8,3% per annum. Is her calculation correct or not? Justify your answer. (4)
   1.3 Corina takes out a loan on the balance of the purchase price over 20 years. Her payments start one month after the loan is granted. Determine her monthly instalment if interest is charged at 8% p.a. compounded monthly. (4)
   1.4 Corina calculates that she can repay R10 000 every month. Determine how long it will take her to repay the loan amount. (4)

2. Calculate the number of years it will take for an item to depreciate to a quarter of its value at 5% p.a. on a reducing balance. (4)

3. Two nephews Ditiro and Khumo each receive R800 000, which they will invest for five years. They invest the money as follows:
   - Ditiro: 9,5% per annum simple interest. At the end of 5 years he will receive a bonus of 2,5% of the present value of the investment.
   - Khumo: 9% per annum compounded quarterly.

   Determine who will have the largest investment after five years.
   Justify your answer and show all calculations. (6)

4. Li Jing opens a savings account with an initial deposit of R5 000 on 1 May 2013. She then makes 36 monthly payments of R600 into the same savings account at the end of every month. Her first payment of R600 is made on 31 May 2013. The savings account earns interest at 7,5% p.a. compounded monthly.
   4.1 Determine the future value of the savings account after the 36th payment is made. (6)
   4.2 Determine the total amount of interest Li Jing earns on this savings account. (3)

5. R7 565 is invested into an account earning interest at i % p.a. compounded monthly. After 30 months the account has a value of R12 755,35. Determine the value of i. (4)

6. Given: $F = P(1 + ni)$ where P and i are positive constants.
   6.1 State whether the graph of F, as a function of n, is linear, quadratic, exponential or none of these. (1)
   6.2 Draw a possible graph of F, as a function of n. (2)
   6.3 Given: $F = P(1 + i)^n$ where P and i are positive constants:
      6.3.1 State whether the graph of F, as a function of n, is linear, quadratic, exponential or none of these. (1)
      6.3.2 Draw a possible graph of F, as a function of n. (2)

7. Lindiwe's retirement plan is to invest R1 200 each month into an investment account at 8,4% p.a. compounded monthly. She starts paying into this investment account at the end of the month in which she turns 21 years old and will make her final payment on her 55th birthday. Determine the value of the fund on her 55th birthday. (4)

8. Justin makes 60 equal monthly payments of Rx into a savings account earning an interest rate of 7,5% p.a. compounded monthly. If the value of the fund after the 60 payments is R60 000, determine the value of these monthly payments. (3)

Total: 50

Test B: Complex procedures and problem solving

1. A couple want to buy their first house for R900 000. They agree to pay monthly instalments of R9 000 on a 20 year loan at 10% p.a. compounded monthly. The first payment is made one month after the loan is granted.
   1.1 Show that the loan will be paid off after 216 months. (4)
   1.2 The couple encounter unexpected medical expenses and are unable to pay the 100th, 101st and 102nd monthly payments. At the end of the 103rd month they decide to increase their monthly payments so they can still pay the loan off in 216 months. (i.e. 114 equal monthly payments). Determine the value of the new monthly instalments. (7)

2. Milo buys furniture to the value of R15 000. He borrows the money on 1 January 2013 from a financial institution that charges an interest rate of 9% p.a. compounded monthly. Milo agrees to pay monthly instalments of R600. The agreement of the loan allows Milo to start paying these equal monthly instalments from 1 July 2014.
   2.1 Determine the total amount owing to the financial institution on 1 June 2014. (2)
   2.2 How many months will it take Milo to pay back the loan? (4)
   2.3 What is the balance of the loan immediately after Milo has made the 20th payment? (3)

3. Ithumeleng wants to borrow money to purchase a motorbike that costs R75 000 and plans to repay the full amount over a period of 4 years in monthly instalments. There are two options:

   Option 1: A bank calculates what Ithumeleng would owe if she borrowed R75 000 for four years at a simple interest rate of 10,5% p.a. She will then pay that amount back in equal monthly instalments over four years.

   Option 2: Ithumeleng could also borrow R75 000 from the bank. She will pay the bank in equal monthly instalments over four years, the first payment being made at the end of the first month after the loan is granted. Compound interest is charged at 11% p.a. on a reducing balance.
   3.1 If Ithumeleng chooses Option 1, what are her monthly instalments? (4)
   3.2 If Ithumeleng chooses Option 2, what are her monthly instalments? (6)
   3.3 Which option is better for Ithumeleng? (2)
   3.4 What interest rate could 10,5% p.a. in Option 1 be replaced with so that there is no difference between the two options? (3)

4. A debt of R20 000, bearing an interest at 9% p.a. compounded quarterly, is being paid off in quarterly payments of R2 500 each. Determine the outstanding balance after the sixth payment. (10)

5. A man wants to have R50 000 in 12 years' time. His bank manager suggests that he invest by depositing R4 000 immediately, Rx in two years' time, R4 000 after a further three years and a final payment of R2x in ten years' time. The interest rate is 9% p.a. compounded annually for the entire period of the loan. Determine the value of x. (5)

Total: 50

Test C: Breakdown and content as per final exam

1. 1.1 The computer equipment for a small business is valued at R60 000 and depreciates at a rate of 16% p.a. on a reducing balance method. After how many years will the equipment be worth R20 000? (4)
   1.2 Bianca receives a bursary of R120 000 for her studies at university. She invests the money at a rate of 9% p.a. compounded yearly. She decides to withdraw R30 000 at the end of each year for her studies, starting at the end of the first year. For how many full years will this investment finance her studies? (4)

2. Abdul Aziz's annual salary is R180 000 and his annual expenses total R136 000. His salary increases by R18 000 each year while his expenses increase by R22 000 each year. Each year he saves the excess of his income.
   2.1 Represent his total savings as a series. (4)
   2.2 If Abdul Aziz continues to manage his savings in this manner, after how many years will he have nothing left to save? (3)
   2.3 Abdul Aziz calculates that if his expenses increase by x rand every year (instead of R22 000 each year), he will spend as much as he earns in the 25th year. Determine the value of x. (2)

3. A taxi company has just purchased a new minibus for R350 000. It has decided to replace the minibus in five years' time. The minibus is expected to depreciate at 15% per annum and will be used as a trade-in on a new minibus. The replacement cost of a new minibus is expected to increase by 6% per annum.
   3.1 Determine the trade-in value of the present minibus in five years' time. (3)
   3.2 Determine the cost of the replacement minibus in five years' time. (3)
   3.3 How much will the taxi company need to purchase the new minibus in five years' time? (1)
   3.4 The taxi company wants to pay cash for a new minibus in five years' time after trading in the present minibus. The company sets up a fund earning interest at 7,5% p.a. compounded monthly.
   - Rx is deposited into this account every month starting one month after purchasing the present minibus.
   - They make these monthly deposits for 60 months.
   - After 60 months they have the exact amount needed to purchase the new minibus after trading in the present minibus.
   Determine the value of x. (6)

3.5 Suppose that six months after the purchase of the present minibus and every other six months thereafter, the firm withdraws R3 000 from the account to pay for maintenance of the minibus. If it makes ten such withdrawals, what will the new monthly deposit need to be for this account so that the firm has enough money to pay cash for the new minibus? (4)

4. Xholani wants to purchase a car costing R150 000. The car is advertised in the following manner:
- No deposit is necessary.
- The first payment is due three months after the date of purchase.
- The interest rate is quoted at 10% p.a. compounded monthly.
- The period of the loan is five years.

4.1 Calculate the amount owing two months after the purchase date, which is one month before Xholani is due to pay the first instalment. (3)

4.2 Xholani bought this car on 1 May 2014 and made his first payment on 1 August 2014. Thereafter he made 60 equal payments on the first day of every month.
   - **4.2.1** Determine his monthly payments. (3)
   - **4.2.2** Calculate the total of all Xholani's payments. (1)
   - **4.2.3** Determine the amount of interest Xholani has paid over the period of the loan. (2)

4.3 Ifraan has also bought a car for R150 000. He took out car finance for R150 000, at an interest rate of 10% p.a. compounded monthly. He also made 60 equal monthly payments, however, he started payments one month after the loan was granted.
   - **4.3.1** Determine his monthly payments. (3)
   - **4.3.2** Calculate the total of all Ifraan's payments. (1)
   - **4.3.3** Determine the amount of interest Ifraan has paid over the period of the loan. (2)

4.4 Calculate the difference between Xholani's and Ifraan's total repayments. (1)

Total: 50

TOPIC 4 Trigonometry

Grade 12 trigonometry rests firmly upon and extends the topics studied in Grades 10 and 11. If you struggle with any section of trigonometry, revise the relevant sections before continuing.

Compound angle identities are introduced for the first time in Grade 12. You will work with identities and equations that involve compound angle identities and double angle identities.

Knowledge and skills for this Topic

For the Grade 12 work in this Topic, you need a good grasp of the following knowledge and skills:
- derive and use the identities $\sin^2\theta + \cos^2\theta = 1$ and $\tan\theta = \frac{\sin\theta}{\cos\theta}$
- derive and use reduction formulae to simplify expressions, including negative angles
- determine the values of a variable for which an identity holds
- determine the general solutions of trigonometric equations
- determine solutions in specific intervals.

Content of final exam
- Work with and derive compound angle identities.
- Use the general solution to solve more complicated equations involving compound angles.
- Prove identities involving compound angle identities.

Some useful tools for trigonometry are the formulae given below and the trigonometry toolbox given on the next page.

Relevant formulae

$$\sin(\alpha + \beta) = \sin\alpha\cos\beta + \cos\alpha\sin\beta$$

$$\sin(\alpha - \beta) = \sin\alpha\cos\beta - \cos\alpha\sin\beta$$

$$\cos(\alpha + \beta) = \cos\alpha\cos\beta - \sin\alpha\sin\beta$$

$$\cos(\alpha - \beta) = \cos\alpha\cos\beta + \sin\alpha\sin\beta$$

$$\cos 2\alpha \begin{cases} \cos^2\alpha - \sin^2\alpha \\ 1 - 2\sin^2\alpha \\ 2\cos^2\alpha - 1 \end{cases} \qquad \sin 2\alpha = 2\sin\alpha\cos\alpha$$

Trigonometry toolbox

Trigonometric ratios in a right-angled triangle

$\sin \theta = \dfrac{y}{r}$ $\qquad \cos \theta = \dfrac{x}{r} \qquad \tan \theta = \dfrac{y}{x}$

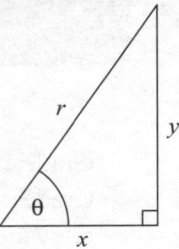

Using special angles to get exact values

From the diagrams:

$\sin 60° = \dfrac{\sqrt{3}}{2} \qquad \sin 30° = \dfrac{1}{2} \qquad \cos 30° = \dfrac{\sqrt{3}}{2}$

$\sin 45° = \dfrac{1}{\sqrt{2}} \qquad \cos 45° = \dfrac{1}{\sqrt{2}} \qquad \tan 45° = \dfrac{1}{1}$

The values that you get from the diagrams are called 'exact values'.

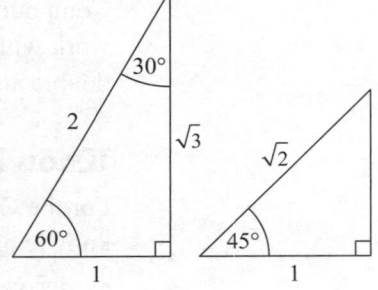

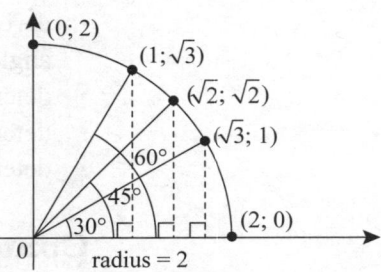

Defining trigonometric ratios for angles between 0° and 360°

Use the diagram alongside to reduce functions of angles greater than 90° to functions of acute angles. Examples:

$\sin(180° - \theta) = +\sin \theta \qquad \cos(180° + \theta) = -\cos \theta$

$\tan(360° - \theta) = -\tan \theta \qquad \sin(180° + \theta) = -\sin \theta$

$\cos(360° - \theta) = +\cos \theta$

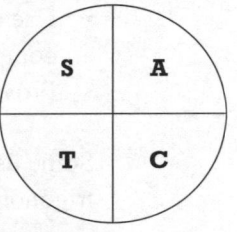

The unit circle

$\sin \theta = \dfrac{y}{1} = y \qquad \cos \theta = \dfrac{x}{1} = 1 \qquad \tan \theta = \dfrac{y}{x}$

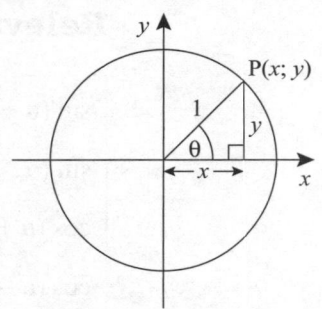

Trigonometric identities

$\tan \theta = \dfrac{\sin \theta}{\cos \theta}$ but $\cos \theta \neq 0 \qquad\qquad \sin^2 \theta + \cos^2 \theta = 1$

Co-ratios

Values for the angles $(90° - \theta)$

$\sin(90° - \theta) = \cos \theta$

$\cos(90° - \theta) = \sin \theta$

Values for the angles $(90° + \theta)$

$\sin(90° + \theta) = \cos \theta$

$\cos(90° + \theta) = -\sin \theta$

Negative values

$\sin(-x) = -\sin x$

$\cos(-x) = \cos x$

$\tan(-x) = -\tan x$

Compound angle identities

The compound angle formulae are given to you in the table below. For the final exam you may be asked to prove this identity:

$$\cos(A - B) = \cos A \cos B + \sin A \sin B$$

In Grade 12 we will work with, derive and prove identities that involve compound angles. We will also use the general solution to solve more complicated equations involving compound angles.

Note
Double angle identities are considered to be a type of compound angle identities.

Compound angle formulae

Compound angle identities	Double angle identities
$\cos(\alpha - \beta) = \cos\alpha\cos\beta + \sin\alpha\sin\beta$	$\sin 2\alpha = 2\sin\alpha\cos\alpha$
$\cos(\alpha + \beta) = \cos\alpha\cos\beta - \sin\alpha\sin\beta$	$\cos 2\alpha = \cos^2\alpha - \sin^2\alpha$
$\sin(\alpha + \beta) = \sin\alpha\cos\beta + \cos\alpha\sin\beta$	$\cos 2\alpha = 2\cos^2\alpha - 1$
$\sin(\alpha - \beta) = \sin\alpha\cos\beta - \cos\alpha\sin\beta$	$\cos 2\alpha = 1 - 2\sin^2\alpha$

Worked examples

1. Without using a calculator, determine the value of:
   $\sin(A + 28°)\cos(17° - A) + \sin(17° - A)\cos(A + 28°)$

2. Determine the value of $\cos 15°$ without using a calculator.

Remember
'Special angles' can be used to solve problems when no calculators are allowed, for example:

For question 1
$\sin 45° = \frac{1}{\sqrt{2}}$
$\cos 45° = \frac{1}{\sqrt{2}}$

For question 2
$\cos 30° = \frac{\sqrt{3}}{2}$

Solutions

1. $\sin(A + 28°)\cos(17° - A) + \sin(17° - A)\cos(A + 28°)$
   $= \sin[(A + 28°) + (17° - A)]$ — Use the relevant compound angles formula to 'squash' the expression into a single trigonometric ratio.
   $= \sin(28° + 17°)$
   $= \sin(45°)$
   $= \frac{1}{\sqrt{2}}$
   $= \frac{\sqrt{2}}{2}$ — Change denominators to rational numbers.

2. $\cos 15° = \cos(45° - 30°)$
   $= \cos 45°\cos 30° + \sin 45°\sin 30°$ — Use the relevant compound angles to EXPAND the expression.
   $= \left(\frac{1}{\sqrt{2}}\right)\left(\frac{\sqrt{3}}{2}\right) + \left(\frac{1}{\sqrt{2}}\right)\left(\frac{1}{2}\right)$
   $= \frac{\sqrt{3}}{2\sqrt{2}} + \frac{1}{2\sqrt{2}}$
   $= \frac{\sqrt{3} + 1}{2\sqrt{2}}$

Deriving compound angle formulae (complex procedures)

To prove an identity, remember that any point in a Cartesian plane can be expressed in terms of the radius (which is that point's distance from the origin) and θ (the angle of rotation from the positive x-axis). This means that the definitions for $\sin\theta$ and $\cos\theta$ can be used to express any point $P(x; y)$ as $P(r\cos\theta; r\sin\theta)$.

TOPIC 4 Trigonometry

$\sin \theta = \frac{y}{r} \therefore y = r \sin \theta$

$\cos \theta = \frac{x}{r} \therefore x = r \cos \theta$

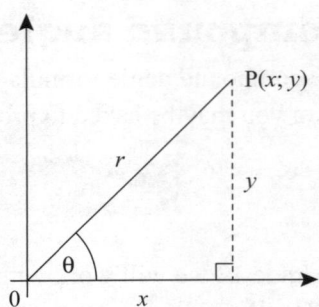

Proving the identity cos (A − B) = cos A cos B + sin A sin B

Given: Points T and Q, OQ = r, TÔX = A, QÔX = B, TÔQ = A − B

Prove using trigonometric ratios

T(r cos A; r sin A) and Q (r cos B; r sin B)

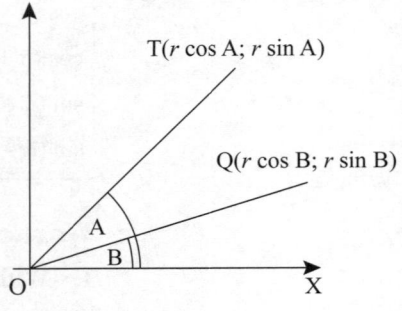

Remember

The distance formula:
Distance = $\sqrt{(x_2 - x_1)^2 + (y_2 - y_1)^2}$

The cosine rule:
In any △ABC:
$a^2 = b^2 + c^2 - 2bc \cos A$

First use the distance formula

$\therefore TQ^2 = (r \cos A - r \cos B)^2 + (r \sin A - r \sin B)^2$
$= r^2 \cos^2 A - 2r^2 \cos A \cos B + r^2 \cos^2 B + r^2 \sin^2 A - 2r^2 \sin A \sin B$
$\quad + r^2 \sin^2 B$
$= r^2 (\cos^2 A + \sin^2 A) + r^2 (\sin^2 B + \cos^2 B) - 2r^2 (\cos A \cos B + \sin A \sin B)$
$= 2r^2 - 2r^2 (\cos A \cos B + \sin A \sin B)$
$= 2r^2 [1 - (\cos A \cos B + \sin A \sin B)]$

Then use the cosine rule in △TOQ

$TQ^2 = r^2 + r^2 - 2r^2 \cos (A - B)$
$= 2r^2 - 2r^2 \cos (A - B)$
$= 2r^2 [1 - \cos (A - B)]$

Prove by putting the two expressions for TQ² equal to each other

$2r^2 [1 - \cos (A - B)] = 2r^2 [1 - (\cos A \cos B + \sin A \sin B)]$
$\quad 1 - \cos (A - B) = 1 - (\cos A \cos B + \sin A \sin B)$
$\quad \cos (A - B) = \cos A \cos B + \sin A \sin B$

Deriving the compound angle identities (complex procedures)

The remaining three compound angle identities can be derived from $\cos (\alpha - \beta) = \cos \alpha \cos \beta + \sin \alpha \sin \beta$. You may be asked to derive any of these identities in a test or an examination. It is worth learning and practising these, which are complex procedures.

Remember

$\cos (-\beta) = \cos \beta$
$\sin (-\beta) = -\sin \beta$
$\cos (90° - \beta) = \sin \beta$
$\sin (90° - \beta) = \cos \beta$

Proofs

1. $\cos (\alpha + \beta) = \cos [\alpha - (-\beta)]$
$= \cos \alpha \cos (-\beta) + \sin \alpha \sin (-\beta)$
$= \cos \alpha \cos \beta - \sin \alpha \sin \beta$

2. $\sin(\alpha - \beta) = \cos[90° - (\alpha - \beta)]$
   $= \cos[(90° - \alpha) + \beta]$
   $= \cos[(90° - \alpha) - (-\beta)]$
   $= \cos(90° - \alpha)\cos(-\beta) + \sin(90° - \alpha)\sin(-\beta)$
   $= \sin\alpha\cos\beta - \cos\alpha\sin\beta$

3. $\sin(\alpha + \beta) = \cos[90° - (\alpha + \beta)]$
   $= \cos[(90° - \alpha) - \beta]$
   $= \cos(90° - \alpha)\cos\beta + \sin(90° - \alpha)\sin\beta$
   $= \sin\alpha\cos\beta + \cos\alpha\sin\beta$

Worked examples

1. Given that $\cos(\alpha - \beta) = \cos\alpha\cos\beta + \sin\alpha\sin\beta$, deduce:
   1.1 $\cos(90° - \alpha) = \sin\alpha$ **1.2** $\sin(90° - \alpha) = \cos\alpha$

Note
For 1.2 you can also use the same method as in 1.1.

Solutions

1.1 $\cos(90° - \alpha) = \cos 90°\cos\alpha + \sin 90°\sin\alpha = 0\cos\alpha + 1\sin\alpha = \sin\alpha$

1.2 $\sin(90° - \alpha) = \cos[90° - (90° - \alpha)] = \cos\alpha$

Deriving and working with double angle identities

Worked examples

1. Given that $\sin(A + B) = \sin A\cos B + \cos A\sin B$:
   1.1 deduce that $\sin 2A = 2\sin A\cos A$
   1.2 deduce that $\cos 2A = 1 - 2\sin^2 A$.

2. Without using a calculator, calculate the value of $\dfrac{\cos 300° \sin 140°}{\sin 45° \sin 290° \sin 160°}$.

3. If $\tan 40° = t$, find the value of $\cos 80°$ in terms of t.

4. If $\tan\theta = \frac{3}{4}$ and $\theta \in [90°; 270°]$ determine, without using a calculator, the value of $\sin 2\theta$.

You need to know
- reduction formulae
- co-ratios

Remember
$-\sin(\beta)$
$= -\cos(90° - \beta)$

Solutions

1. **1.1** $\sin 2A = \sin(A + A)$
   $= \sin A\cos A + \cos A\sin A$
   $= 2\sin A\cos A$

   1.2 $\cos 2A = \cos(A + A)$
   $= \cos A\cos A - \sin A\sin A$
   $= \cos^2 A - \sin^2 A$
   $= 1 - \sin^2 A - \sin^2 A$
   $= 1 - 2\sin^2 A$

2. $= \dfrac{\cos 300° \sin 140°}{\sin 45° \sin 290° \sin 160°}$

   $= \dfrac{\cos(360° - 60°)\sin(180° - 40°)}{\sin 45°(\sin 360° - 70°)\sin(180° - 20°)}$ Simplify to acute angles using reduction formulae.

   $= \dfrac{\cos 60° \sin 40°}{\sin 45°(-\sin 70°)\sin 20°}$ Use co-ratios and double angle formulae to simplify further.

   $= \dfrac{\cos 60° \sin 20° \cdot \cos 20°}{\sin 45°(-\cos 20°)\sin 20°}$

   $= \dfrac{2\cos 60°}{-\sin 45°}$

   $= \dfrac{2\left(\frac{1}{2}\right)}{-\left(\frac{\sqrt{2}}{2}\right)}$ Use special angles to get exact values.

   $= -\sqrt{2}$

TOPIC 4 Trigonometry

3. $\tan 40° = \frac{t}{1}$

By definition $y = t$ and $x = 1$. Use the given information to find the value of r.

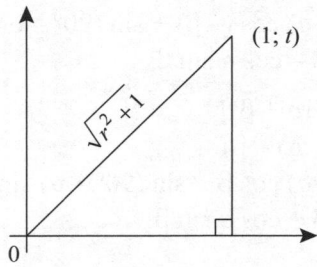

Using Pythagoras: $r = \sqrt{t^2 + 1}$

$\cos 80° = \cos 2(40°)$ Rewrite $\cos 80°$ as $\cos 2(40°)$ and expand using an appropriate double angle identity.

$= \cos^2 40° - \sin^2 40°$

$= \left(\frac{1}{\sqrt{t^2+1}}\right)^2 - \left(\frac{t}{\sqrt{t^2+1}}\right)^2$ Use trig definitions to express each ratio in terms of t, and then simplify fully.

$= \frac{1}{t^2+1} - \frac{t^2}{t^2+1}$

$= \frac{1-t^2}{t^2+1}$

Alternative way to reach solution:

Use $\cos 2\alpha = 2\cos^2 \alpha - 1$ OR $\cos 2\alpha = 1 - 2\sin^2 \alpha$

4. $\tan \theta = \frac{3}{4}$ and $\theta \in [90°; 270°]$

By definition $y = -3$ and $x = -4$

Remember
The tan ratio is positive in quads 1 and 3, but is restricted here to quad 3, so both the x and y values are negative.

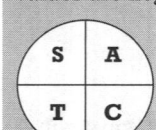

Using Pythagoras:

$r = \sqrt{(-3)^2 + (-4)^2}$ Use trig definitions, the CAST diagram and Pythagoras's theorem to find the value of r.

$= \sqrt{25} = 5$

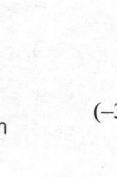
$(-3; -4)$
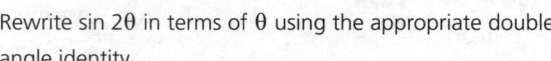

$\sin 2\theta = 2 \sin \theta \cos \theta$ Rewrite $\sin 2\theta$ in terms of θ using the appropriate double angle identity.

$= 2\left(\frac{-3}{5}\right)\left(\frac{-4}{5}\right)$ Use trig definitions to express each ratio as a fraction and simplify fully.

$= \frac{24}{25}$

More complex problems

More complex problems require an integration of trigonometric theory.

Solution paths for these types of problems may not be obvious and often require some thinking and planning before you start your work.

Worked example

If $\sin 61° = \sqrt{t}$, determine the value of $\cos 73° \cos 15° - \sin 73° \sin 15°$ in terms of t.

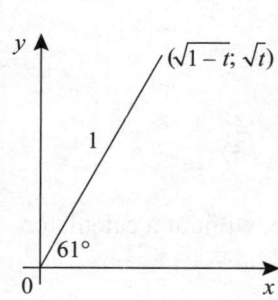

Solution

$\sin 61° = \frac{\sqrt{t}}{1}$

$y = \sqrt{t}, r = 1$ by definition

$x = \sqrt{1 - (\sqrt{t})^2} = \sqrt{1-t}$ Use the trig definition and Pythagoras to work out the value of x in terms of t.

$\cos 73° \cos 15° + \sin 73° \sin 15°$ Use $\cos A \cos B + \sin A \sin B = \cos(A - B)$ to simplify the expression. **Important:** The co-ratio $\cos 58° = \sin 32°$ cannot be used in this case.

$= \cos(73° - 15°)$

$= \cos 58°$

$= \cos 2(29°)$

$= 2\cos^2 29° - 1$ Use $\cos 2A = 2\cos^2 A - 1$ and change the angle to have a more useful value.

$= 2\sin^2 61° - 1$ Use co-ratio to express $\cos 29°$ in terms of t.

$= 2(\sqrt{t})^2 - 1$

$= 2t - 1$

Exercise 1

1. Expand the following using the compound angle formulae, and simplify using special angles where possible:
   - **1.1** $\cos(x - 20°)$
   - **1.2** $\sin(A + 45°)$
   - **1.3** $\cos(2A + 30°)$
   - **1.4** $\sin(2A - 45°)$

2. Determine the value of the following without using a calculator:
   - **2.1** $\sin 35° \cos 25° + \cos 35° \sin 25°$
   - **2.2** $\cos 22,5° \cos 37,5° - \sin 22,5° \sin 37,5°$
   - **2.3** $\cos 20° \cos 40° - \sin 20° \sin 40°$
   - **2.4** $\cos 170° \cos 50° + \sin 170° \sin 50°$
   - **2.5** $\sin(A + 45°)\cos(15° + A) - \cos(A + 45°)\sin(15° + A)$

3. Determine the value of $\sin 75°$ without using a calculator.

4. If $\sin 23° = p$, write down the following in terms of p. DO NOT use a calculator.
   - **4.1** $\cos 23°$
   - **4.2** $\sin 46°$

5. Simplify the following without using a calculator:

   $\dfrac{\tan(-60°)\cos(-156°)\cos 294°}{\sin 492°}$

6. Given: $\sin \alpha = \frac{8}{17}$ where $90° \leq \alpha \leq 270°$. With the aid of a sketch and without using a calculator, calculate:
   - **6.1** $\sin(90° + \alpha)$
   - **6.2** $\cos 2\alpha$

7. If $\sin 33° = \sqrt{\alpha}$, determine the value of the following in terms of α:
   $\cos 48° \cos 15° + \sin 48° \sin 15°$

Exercise 2 (complex procedures)

1. If $\cos x = 2\sin y \cos y$, and $0° \leq y \leq 90°$, show that: $x + 2y = 90°$.

2. If $\tan A = 0,5$ and $\cos A > 0$, determine, without using a calculator and with the aid of a sketch, the value of $2\sin\frac{A}{2}\cos\frac{A}{2}$.

TOPIC 4 *Trigonometry*

3. **3.1** Prove that $\sin(45° + θ)\sin(45° - θ) = \frac{1}{2}\cos 2θ$.

   3.2 Hence determine the value of $\sin 75° \sin 15°$.

4. Without using a calculator, show that $\cos 165° = -\frac{\sqrt{2}}{4}(1 + \sqrt{3})$.

5. Prove that $2\cos^2(x - 45°) - \sin 2x = 1$, and hence deduce, without a calculator, that $\cos^2(-15°) = \frac{1}{2}\left(1 + \frac{\sqrt{3}}{2}\right)$.

Solving equations involving compound angles

The general solution must be used when no interval is given. The general solution is used to find the values of the angles that fall within a given interval.

> **In general solutions:**
> - When $\sin x = 0$, write $x = 0° + n180°$ (NOT $n360°$).
> - When $\cos x = 0$, write $x = 90° + n180°$ (NOT $n360°$).
> - For all other values of $\sin x$ and $\cos x$, add $n360°$ to the solution.
> - For all solutions of $\tan x$, including $\tan x = 0$, add $n180°$.
> - For $\sin x$ and $\cos x$, any value greater than 1 or less than –1 has NO solution for x.
> - When asked to calculate the maximum or minimum value of the LHS of an equation involving $\sin x$ or $\cos x$, substitute 1 (for max) or –1 (for min) into the RHS of the equation.

Solving equations involving double angles using basic factorisation and the general solution

Worked examples

1. Determine the general solution of $\sin 2x + \cos x = 0$.

2. Hence solve for x if $x \in [-90°; 180°]$.

Remember
Reduction formulae:

$180° - θ$	$θ$
$180° + θ$	$360° - θ$

Solutions

1. $\sin 2x + \cos x = 0$ — Expand $\sin 2x$ using compound angle identities.
   $2\sin x \cos x + \cos x = 0$
   $\cos x (2\sin x + 1) = 0$ — Factorise the equation.
   $\cos x = 0$ or $2\sin x + 1 = 0$ — Solve for x in the appropriate quadrants.
   $x = 90° + n180°, n \in \mathbb{Z}$
   OR $\sin x = -\frac{1}{2}$

   Your reference angle is $x = 30°$
   $x = (180° + 30°) + n360°$
   OR $x = (360° - 30°) + n360°$ — Solve for x.

   $x = 210° + n360°$
   OR $x = 330° + n360°, n \in \mathbb{Z}$

2. $x = -90°; 90°; -30°$ — Use the general solution to find the values of the angles that exist within the given interval.

Solving equations involving compound angles

Worked examples
Solve for x in each of the following for $[0°; 360°]$:
1. $\sin x \cos 34° + \cos x \sin 34° = \sin 75°$

2. $\cos x \cos 20° + \sin x \sin 20° = \sin 32°$

Solutions
1. $\sin x \cos 34° + \cos x \sin 34° = \sin 75°$
   $\sin(x + 34°) = \sin 75°$ 'Squash' using the appropriate compound identity.

   Quad 1: $x + 34° = 75° + n360°$
   $x = 41° + n360°, n \in \mathbb{Z}$ Solve for x in both quads 1 and 2.
   OR
   Quad 2: $x + 34° = (180° - 75°) + n360°$
   $x = 71° + n360°, n \in \mathbb{Z}$
   $\therefore x = 41°$ or $x = 71°$

2. $\cos x \cos 20° + \sin x \sin 20° = \sin 32°$
   $\cos(x - 20°) = \sin 32°$ 'Squash' using the appropriate compound identity.

   $\cos(x - 20°) = \cos 58°$ Use co-ratios.

   Quad 1: $x - 20° = 58° + n360°$ Solve for x in both quads 1 and 4.
   $x = 78° + n360°$
   OR
   Quad 4: $x - 20° = (360° - 58°) + n360°$
   $x = 322° + n360°, n \in \mathbb{Z}$
   $\therefore x = 78°$ or $x = 322°$

More complex factorisation when solving equations involving double or compound angle identities

Worked examples
1. Find the general solution for the equation $\sin^2 x + \sin 2x - \sin x - 2\cos x = 0$.
2. Hence solve for x if $x \in [-270°; 90°]$.

Solutions
1. $\sin^2 x + \sin 2x - \sin x - 2\cos x = 0$
   $\sin^2 x + 2\sin x \cos x - \sin x - 2\cos x = 0$
   $\sin x(\sin x + 2\cos x) - 1(\sin x + 2\cos x) = 0$ Factorise the equation.
   $(\sin x + 2\cos x)(\sin x - 1) = 0$
   $\sin x + 2\cos x = 0$ or $\sin x - 1 = 0$ Solve for x in each case, if possible.
   $\sin x = -2\cos x$ $\sin x = 1$
   $\frac{\sin x}{\cos x} = -2$ $x = 90° + n360°, n \in \mathbb{Z}$
   $\tan x = -2$
   $x = 116{,}57° + n180°, n \in \mathbb{Z}$

2. $x = 116{,}57° + n180°$ or $x = 90° + n360°$, $n \in \mathbb{Z}$ — Use the general solution to find the values of the angles that exist within the given interval.

$\therefore x = -63{,}43°; -243{,}43°; 90°; -270°$

Exercise 3

1. Determine the general solution of the following equation: $\sin 2x + 2 \sin x + \cos^2 x + \cos x = 0$. Round your answer off to one decimal place where applicable.

2. Find the general solution of $\cos 2x = 1 - 3 \cos x$.

3. Solve for x if $\sin 2x = \sin x - \cos x + 2\sin^2 x$ and $-90° \leq x < 90°$.

4. Given: $\sin^2 \beta + 2 \sin \beta \cos \beta - \sin^2 \beta - \cos^2 \beta = 0$. Find the general solution for β, correct to one decimal place.

5. Given that $\sin x = \cos 2x - 1$:
   5.1 show that $2 \sin^2 x + \sin x = 0$
   5.2 determine the general solution of the equation: $\sin x = \cos 2x - 1$.

6. Solve for x: $\tan x = \sin 2x$ for $x \in [-90°; 180°]$.

7. Solve for x: $6 \sin^2 x + 2 \sin 2x = 1$ for $x \in [-180°; 200°]$.

8. Solve for x: $\cos 3x \cos x + \sin 3x \sin x = -\frac{1}{\sqrt{2}}$ for $x \in [-90°; 180°]$.

Proving identities (complex procedures)

There are no hard and fast rules for proving identities and more than one 'solution path' often exists. Some guidelines, which may be helpful when proving identities, have been given below.

Guidelines for proving identities

1. Work with ONE SIDE at a time. Indicate clearly which side you are working with. You may then need to work with the other side, until the LHS equals the RHS.
2. Use $\tan \theta = \frac{\sin \theta}{\cos \theta}$ to rewrite all tan ratios in terms of $\sin \theta$ and $\cos \theta$.
3. The identity $\sin^2 \theta + \cos^2 \theta = 1$ can be used to rewrite $\sin^2 \theta + \cos^2 \theta$ as 1, or to expand the number 1 into the ratios $\sin^2 \theta + \cos^2 \theta$.
4. You can use the identity $\sin 2P = 2 \sin P \cos P$ to expand $\sin 2P$ or to simplify $2 \sin P \cos P$.
5. To expand or to simplify expressions, use the identity $\cos 2P = \cos^2 P - \sin^2 P$,
   OR $\cos 2P = 2 \cos^2 P - 1$
   OR $\cos 2P = 1 - 2 \sin^2 P$.
6. Factorisation involving common factors, trinomials, the difference of two squares or grouping can be used to simplify expressions.
7. When working with fractions, set up common denominators.
8. Don't forget to reach your conclusion: $\therefore$ LHS = RHS, or $\therefore$ RHS = LHS, whichever it is you have proved.

You may not move parts of the identity from one side to the other.
An identity is NOT an equation.

Worked examples

1. Prove that $\tan \theta + \frac{\cos \theta}{\sin \theta} = \frac{2}{\sin 2\theta}$.
2. Prove that $\frac{1 + \sin 2x}{\cos 2x} = \frac{\cos x + \sin x}{\cos x - \sin x}$.

Solutions

1. $\tan \theta + \frac{\cos \theta}{\sin \theta} = \frac{2}{\sin 2\theta}$

   LHS: $\tan \theta + \frac{\cos \theta}{\sin \theta}$ Change $\tan \theta$ into $\frac{\sin \theta}{\cos \theta}$.

   $= \frac{\sin \theta}{\cos \theta} + \frac{\cos \theta}{\sin \theta}$

   $= \frac{\sin^2 \theta + \cos^2 \theta}{\cos \theta \sin \theta}$ Simplify using $\sin^2 \theta + \cos^2 \theta = 1$.

   $= \frac{1}{\cos \theta \sin \theta}$

   RHS: $\frac{2}{\sin 2\theta}$ Use $\sin 2\theta = 2 \sin \theta \cos \theta$ to expand $\sin 2\theta$.

   $= \frac{2}{2 \sin \theta \cos \theta}$ Simplify using your knowledge of fractions.

   $= \frac{1}{\sin \theta \cos \theta}$

   $\therefore$ LHS = RHS

> **Note**
> You worked with the LHS first, so you write LHS first in the conclusion.

2. **LHS:** $\frac{1 + \sin 2x}{\cos 2x}$ Use $\sin 2x = 2 \sin x \cos x$ and $\cos 2x = \cos^2 x - \sin^2 x$ to expand $\sin 2x$ and $\cos 2x$.

   $= \frac{1 + 2 \sin x \cos x}{\cos^2 x - \sin^2 x}$

   $= \frac{\cos^2 x + \sin^2 x \cos x}{\cos^2 x - \sin^2 x}$ Use $\sin^2 x + \cos^2 x = 1$ to set up a trinomial expression. Factorise to simplify.

   $= \frac{(\cos x + \sin x)(\cos x + \sin x)}{(\cos x - \sin x)(\cos x + \sin x)}$ Simplify using your knowledge of fractions.

   $= \frac{(\cos x + \sin x)}{(\cos x - \sin x)}$

   $\therefore$ LHS = RHS

Adaptations of the double angle identities

The angle on the RHS becomes half the size of the angle on the LHS:

$\sin A = 2 \sin \tfrac{1}{2}A \cos \tfrac{1}{2}A$ $\cos A = \cos^2 \tfrac{1}{2}A \sin^2 \tfrac{1}{2}A$

$\sin 4A = 2 \sin 2A \cos 2A$ $\cos 4A = 2 \cos^2 2A - 1$

$\sin 6A = 2 \sin 3A \cos 3A$ $\cos 6A = 1 - 2 \sin^2 3A$

Worked example

Sometimes more than one solution path exists, as shown in this example.

Prove the identity $4 \sin \theta \cos^3 \theta - 4 \cos \theta \sin^3 \theta = \sin 4\theta$.

Solution

Method 1: Working with both the LHS and the RHS

RHS: $\sin 4\theta = 2 \sin 2\theta \cos 2\theta$ Use $\sin 2\theta = 2 \sin \theta \cos \theta$ to expand $\sin 2\theta$.

$= 2(2 \sin \theta \cos \theta) \cos 2\theta$

$= 4 \sin \theta \cos \theta \cos 2\theta$

TOPIC 4 Trigonometry

Note
You worked with the RHS first, so you write RHS first in the conclusion.

Remember
$\sin 2\theta = 2 \sin \theta \cos \theta$ may be used to rewrite double angles that are multiples of 2, so:
$\sin 4\theta = 2 \sin 2\theta \cos 2\theta$
$\sin 6\theta = 2 \sin 3\theta \cos 3\theta$
$\sin 10\theta = 2 \sin 5\theta \cos 5\theta$

LHS: $4 \sin \theta \cos^3 \theta - 4 \cos \theta \sin^3 \theta$ Factorise using common factors.
$= 4 \sin \theta \cos \theta (\cos^2 \theta - \sin^2 \theta)$
$= 2(2 \sin \theta \cos \theta)(\cos 2\theta)$ Use $\cos^2 \theta - \sin^2 \theta = \cos 2\theta$ to simplify the expression.
$= 4 \sin \theta \cos \theta \cos 2\theta$
$\therefore$ RHS = LHS

Method 2: Changing ONLY the LHS
LHS: $4 \sin \theta \cos^3 \theta - 4 \cos \theta \sin^3 \theta$
$= 4 \sin \theta \cos \theta (\cos^2 \theta - \sin^2 \theta)$
$= 2(2 \sin \theta \cos \theta) \cos 2\theta$ Use $2 \sin \theta \cos \theta = \sin 2\theta$ to simplify.
$= 2 \sin 2\theta \cos 2\theta$
$= \sin 4\theta$
$\therefore$ LHS = RHS

Complex problems on proving identities

Complex problems on proving identities are often multi-layered and involve identities, equations and general trigonometric principles.

You may be asked to state the values of the angle(s) for which the identity is not defined. To do this, you equate each denominator to 0 and solve for the angle.

Worked examples

1. Prove that $\frac{1 - \cos^2 A + \sin 2A}{\sin A + 2 \cos A} = \sin A$.

2. For what value(s) of A is $\frac{1 - \cos^2 A + \sin 2A}{\sin A + 2 \cos A} = \sin A$ not defined?

Solutions

1. LHS: $\frac{1 - \cos^2 A + \sin 2A}{\sin A + 2 \cos A}$

   $= \frac{\sin^2 A + \sin 2A}{\sin A + 2 \cos A}$

   $= \frac{\sin^2 A + 2 \sin A \cos A}{\sin A + 2 \cos A}$

   $= \frac{\sin A(\sin A + 2 \cos A)}{\sin A + 2 \cos A}$

   $= \sin A$

   $\therefore$ LHS = RHS

2. Not defined for $\sin A + 2 \cos A = 0$.

   $\therefore \sin A = -2 \cos A$

   $\frac{\sin A}{\cos A} = -2$

   $\tan A = -2$

   $A = 116,57° + n180°, n \in \mathbb{Z}$

Exercise 4

1. Simplify: $\frac{1 - \cos 2x - \sin x}{\sin 2x - \cos x}$. Leave your answer as a single trigonometric ratio.

2. Prove that $\frac{\sin \beta - \sin \beta}{\cos 2\beta + \cos \beta} = \frac{\sin \beta}{\cos \beta + 1}$.

3. 3.1 Prove that $\sin 3A = 3 \sin A - 4 \sin^3 A$.

   3.2 Hence write down the minimum value of $\frac{\sin 3A}{\sin A}$.

4. Consider the expression $\sin x + \cos x$.
   4.1 Prove that: $(\sin x + \cos x)^2 = \sin 2x + 1$.
   4.2 Hence determine the maximum value of $\sin x + \cos x$.

5. If $\tan \beta = \frac{1}{a}$ and $0° < \beta < 90°$, prove that $a \cos 2\beta + \sin 2\beta = a$.

Problems in three dimensions

For problems involving three dimensions, use the same method as for problems in two dimensions.

How to solve problems in three dimensions

Step 1 The problem usually involves two triangles with a common side.

Step 2 Often one of the triangles is right-angled. If so, use ratio definitions rather than the sine rule, cosine rule or area rule.

Step 3 Draw a large, neat diagram showing all the given information.

Step 4 In three-dimensional problems right angles often don't look like right angles as they do when drawn in two dimensions. Draw all vertical lines vertical so that a right angle may look like one of these diagrams.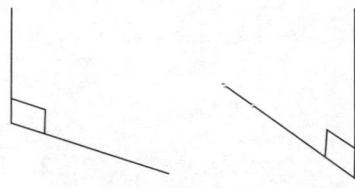

Step 5 Always shade the horizontal plane.

Step 6 Use geometry to obtain additional information, such as exterior angles of triangles, corresponding and alternate angles.

Step 7 Where you encounter problems with three triangles, work from the one with the most information to the second and then the third.

Step 8 Use the cosine formula, the sine formula or trigonometric ratios to solve the problem.

Worked examples

1. Use the diagram and calculate:
   1.1 AB
   1.2 CP

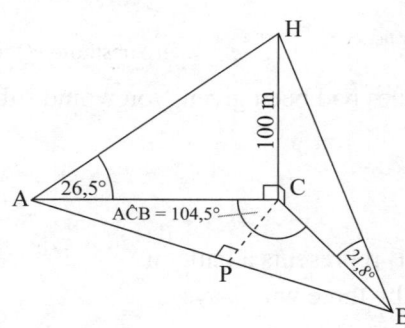

2. P, Q and R are three points in the same horizontal plane, and PS and RT are the two vertical poles. Wires are strung from Q to the tops of the poles. The wire from Q to S forms an angle of $x°$ with the ground. The other wire forms an angle of $y°$ with the horizontal plane. It is t metres long.

   $Q\hat{P}R = \theta$ and $P\hat{R}Q = z$.

   Prove that $PS = \dfrac{t \sin z \tan x \cos y}{\sin \theta}$

Solutions

1. **1.1** In △HAC: $\tan 26{,}5° = \frac{100}{AC}$

    ∴ AC = 200,6 m

    In △HBC: $\tan 21{,}8° = \frac{100}{BC}$

    ∴ BC = 250,0 m

    In △ABC:
    $AB^2 = AC^2 + BC^2 - 2AC \cdot BC \cos 104{,}5°$
    $= 200{,}6^2 + 250^2 - 2(200{,}6)(250)\cos 104{,}5°$
    $= 127\,853{,}47$
    $AB = 357{,}6$ m

    1.2 Area △ABC $= \frac{1}{2} AC \cdot BC \cdot \sin 104{,}5°$
    $= 24\,276{,}3$ m^2

    Area △ABC $= \frac{1}{2} \cdot AB \cdot CP$

    ∴ $\frac{2 \text{ area}}{AB} = CP$

    ∴ 135,8 m = CP

2. In △TQR:

    $\frac{QR}{t} = \cos y$

    ∴ QR = $t \cos y$ .... ①

    In △PQR:

    $\frac{PQ}{\sin Z} = \frac{QR}{\sin \theta}$

    ∴ PQ $= \frac{QR \sin z}{\sin \theta}$

    $= \frac{t \cos y \sin z}{\sin \theta}$ .... ② Substitute QR from ①

    In △PQS:

    $\frac{PS}{PQ} = \tan x$

    ∴ PS = PQ $\tan x$

    $= \frac{t \cos y \sin z \tan x}{\sin \theta}$ Substitute PQ from ②

    If numerical values had been given, you would substitute them now to calculate PS.

Note
Proceed from △TQR to △PQR (link QR) then from △PQR to △PQS (link PQ)

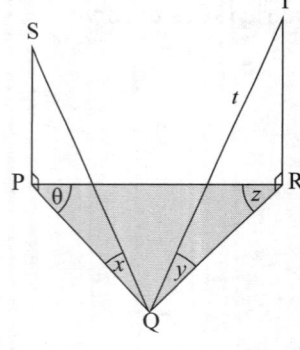

Exercise 5

1. In the diagram, B represents a balloon held in position by three wire stays, PB, BR and BQ.
    BP = BQ.
    QP̂R = 68°, PQ̂R = 42°,
    BP̂Q = 35° and PR = q.

    1.1 Show that PB $= \frac{q \sin 35°}{\sin 42°}$.

    1.2 Calculate q if PB = 54,5 m.

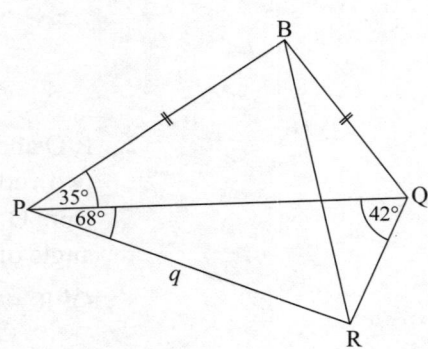

2. In the diagram, B, C and D are three vertices of the floor of a rectangular hall. A is a light on the ceiling so that B, A and D are in the same vertical plane.
The angle of elevation of A from B is 15,6°; BC = 9 m; CD = 40 m and BA = 20 m.
Calculate:
2.1 the height of the light above the floor (AT)
2.2 the length of AD in metres.

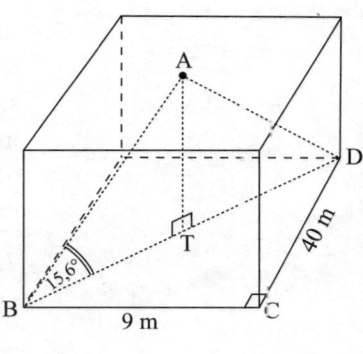

3. A, B and C are three points in the same horizontal plane, with A equidistant from B and C. Â = 60°. I is the centre of the incircle of △ABC and HI is a perpendicular tower. The angle of elevation of the tower from C is α.

3.1 If BC = x m, show that the height of the tower is x tan α tan 30°.

3.2 Calculate the height of the tower if AC = 25,6 m and α = 70,6°.

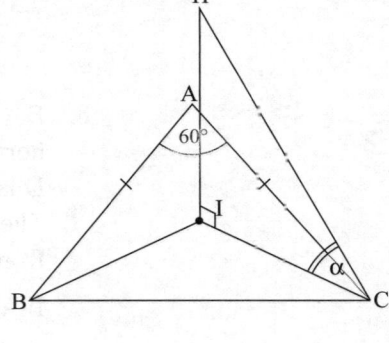

4. Refer to the diagram and prove that
$$AD = \frac{BE \sin z \sin(x + y)}{\cos x \sin y}.$$

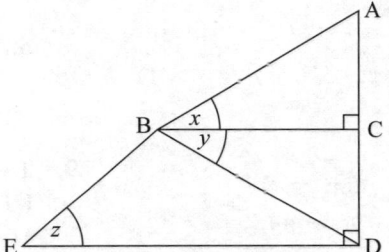

5. In the diagram, ABCD is a trapezium with AD parallel to BC. BÂD is 90° and BĈD is 150°. CD is produced to E, and points A and B are joined to F. The line AD cuts BE at F.
Let EÂD = x and EB̂C = y.

5.1 Show that $BE = \frac{AB \cos x}{\sin(y - x)}$.

5.2 Hence (or otherwise) prove that
$$CE = \frac{2AB \cos x \sin y}{\sin(y - x)}.$$

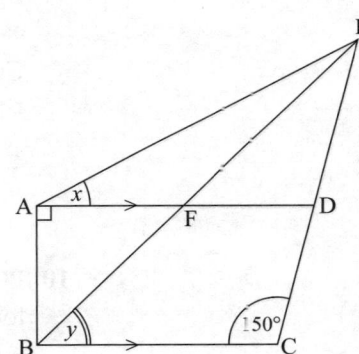

6. In the diagram Q is the foot of a vertical tower PQ, while R and S are two points in the same horizontal plane as Q. The angle of elevation of P, as measured from R, is x. RQ̂S = y, QS = a metres and the area of △RQS = A m².

6.1 Prove that $PQ = \frac{2A \tan x}{a \sin y}$.

6.2 Calculate the value of y if PQ = 77 m, a = 89 m, A = 1 480 m² and x = 46,5°.

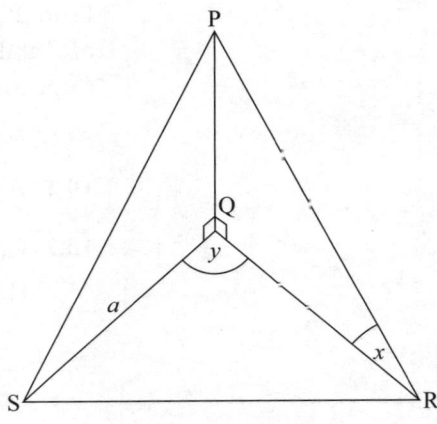

7. In the diagram, AB is a vertical flagpole planted in the middle of two concentric circles in the same horizontal plane. From point C on the inner circle with radius r, the angle of elevation of A is x. From point D on the outer circle, the angle of elevation of A is y.

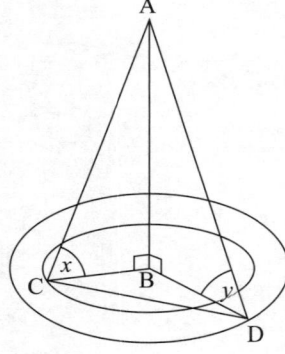

   7.1 Show that the radius of the outer circle is $\frac{r \tan x}{\tan y}$.

   7.2 If $B\hat{D}C = 30°$, show that $\sin B\hat{C}D = \frac{\tan x}{2 \tan y}$.

   7.3 You are also given that $x = 45°$ and $y = 30°$. Show, without using a calculator, that $C\hat{B}D = 90°$.

8. B, C and D are three points in the same horizontal plane. The distance from C to D is x. There is a vertical tower AB at B. The angle of elevation of A as measured from D is α.

   If $A\hat{C}D = \beta$ and $A\hat{D}C = \theta$, prove that:

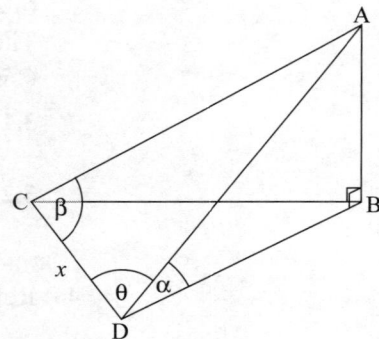

   8.1 $AD = \frac{x \sin \beta}{\sin(\theta + \beta)}$

   8.2 $AB = \frac{x \sin \alpha \sin \beta}{\sin(\theta + \beta)}$

   Then calculate AB if $x = 50$ m, $\alpha = 42°$, $\beta = 63°$ and $\theta = 54°$.

Hint
Draw in LP.

9. Two equal cardboard rectangles KLMN and NMPR, each 10 m by 7 m, are placed at right angles to one another as shown in the diagram. Calculate the angle between LN and NP.

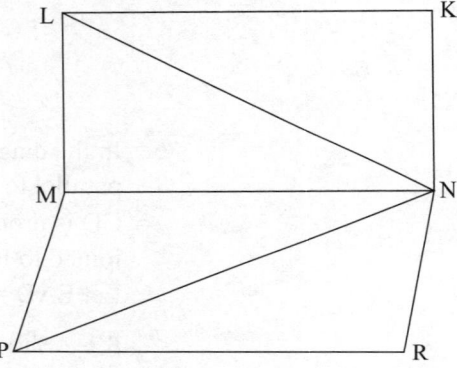

10. PQ and AB are two vertical towers. R is in the same horizontal plane as Q and B. From R, the angles of elevation of P and A are θ and 2θ respectively.

    $A\hat{Q}R = 90° + \theta$ and $A\hat{R}Q = 90° - 2\theta$.

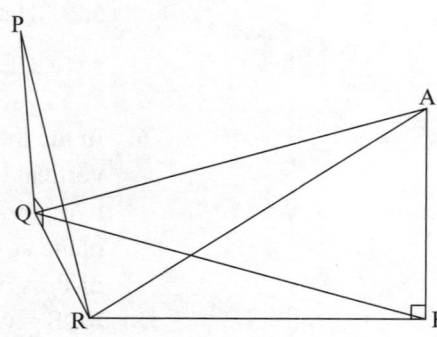

    10.1 If $QR = a$, prove that $\frac{AB}{PQ} = \frac{2 \cos^2 \theta}{\tan \theta}$.

    10.2 Calculate $\frac{AB}{PQ}$ if $\theta = 30°$.
    (Leave your answer in surd form.)

11. In the diagram, SR is a vertical mast. P, Q and R are three points in the same horizontal plane. PS and QS are stay ropes.
PQ = m, QS = k, $P\hat{Q}S = \alpha$

The angle of elevation of S from P is β.

If $k = 2m$, show that
PS = $m\sqrt{5 - 4\cos\alpha}$.

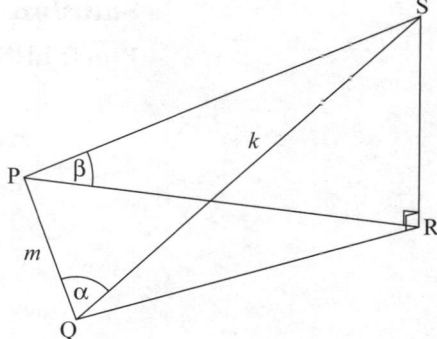

Proving identities using triangles in two dimensions (complex procedures)

Here are some guidelines on proving more complex identities using triangles in two dimensions.

1. Try to express one of the angles in terms of the others by using the sum of angles in a triangle = 180°, and then use the trigonometric ratio that is used in the question.

   OR

2. If that doesn't work, drop a perpendicular from one of the vertices of the triangle, and then use the trigonometric ratio that has been used in the question.

   (a) If the expressions on the left and right of the equals sign contain cosines, use the cosine rule. Get rid of the variable (which is not required) by repeating the cosine rule.

   (b) If the expression contains sines, use the sine rule.

Worked example

RTP: In $\triangle ABC$, AD $\perp$ BC

prove that $a = b \cos C + c \cos B$

where a = BC, b = AC and c = AB.

Remember
RTP stands for required to prove.

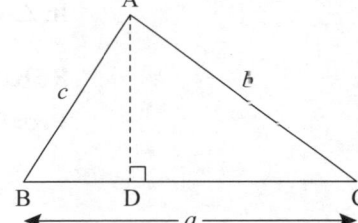

Solution

Proof: RHS = $b \cos C + c \cos B$

$= b\left(\frac{DC}{b}\right) + c\left(\frac{BD}{c}\right)$

$= DC + BD$

$= a$

$\therefore$ RHS = LHS

Exercise 6

1. In $\triangle ABC$, CD $\perp$ AB, prove that $c = a \cos B + b \cos A$.

2. In $\triangle PQR$, PM $\perp$ QR, prove that $p = q \cos R + r \cos Q$.

Identities using the cosine and sine rules

Worked example

In $\triangle ABC$ prove that $\frac{\cos B}{\cos C} = \frac{c - b\cos A}{b - c\cos A}$, $c \neq 90°$.

Solution

Proof: LHS $= \dfrac{\cos B}{\cos C}$ Both sides contain cosines so use the cosine rule.

$= \dfrac{a^2 + c^2 - b^2}{2ac} \div \dfrac{a^2 + b^2 - c^2}{2ac}$ $b^2 = a^2 + c^2 - 2ac \cos B$
$\cos B = \dfrac{a^2 + c^2 - b^2}{2ac}$

$= \dfrac{a^2 + c^2 - b^2}{2ac} \times \dfrac{2ab}{a^2 + b^2 - c^2}$

$= \dfrac{\left[(b^2 + c^2 - 2bc \cos A) + c^2 - b^2\right]b}{c\left[(b^2 + c^2 - 2bc \cos A) + b^2 - c^2\right]}$ The numerator does not contain a. Use the cosine rule again to eliminate a^2.

$= \dfrac{b(2c^2 - 2bc \cos A)}{c(2b^2 - 2bc \cos A)}$

$= \dfrac{2bc(c - b \cos A)}{2bc(b - c \cos A)}$

$= \dfrac{c - b \cos A}{b - c \cos A}$

$\therefore$ LHS = RHS

Exercise 7

1. Prove the following identities in $\triangle ABC$:

   1.1 $\dfrac{\cos B}{\cos A} = \dfrac{a - b \cos C}{b - a \cos C}, \hat{A} \neq 90°$

   1.2 $\dfrac{\cos A}{\cos C} = \dfrac{c - a \cos B}{a - c \cos B}, \hat{C} \neq 90°$

2. Prove the following identity in $\triangle PQR$:

   $\dfrac{\cos P}{\cos R} = \dfrac{r - p \cos Q}{p - r \cos Q}, \hat{R} \neq 90°$

Worked example

In $\triangle ABC$ prove that $\tan A = \dfrac{a \sin C}{b - a \cos C}$

Solution

Proof: LHS $= \tan A$ Use the tan A identity.

$= \dfrac{\sin A}{\cos A}$ The numerator contains sin A and we need sin C. Use the sine rule: $\dfrac{\sin A}{a} = \dfrac{\sin C}{c}$. The denominator contains cos A and we need cos C. Use the cosine rule twice.

$= \dfrac{a \sin C}{c} \div \dfrac{b^2 + c^2 - a^2}{2bc}$

$= \dfrac{a \sin C}{c} \times \dfrac{2bc}{b^2 - a^2 + a^2 + b^2 - 2ab \cos C}$

$= \dfrac{2ab \sin C}{2b^2 - 2ab \cos C}$

$= \dfrac{2ab \sin C}{2b(b - a \cos C)}$

$= \dfrac{a \sin C}{b - a \cos C}$

$\therefore$ LHS = RHS

Worked example

In $\triangle ABC$, prove that $a + b + c = (b + c) \cos A + (c + a) \cos B + (a + b) \cos C$.

Solution

Proof: LHS $= (b + c) \cos A + (c + a) \cos B + (a + b) \cos C$

$$= (b + c)\left(\frac{b^2 + c^2 - a^2}{2bc}\right) + (c + a)\left(\frac{a^2 + c^2 - b^2}{2ac}\right) + (a + b)\left(\frac{a^2 + b^2 - c^2}{2ab}\right)$$

$$= \frac{(ab + ac)(b^2 + c^2 - a^2) + (ab + bc)(a^2 + c^2 - b^2) + (ac + bc)(a^2 + b^2 - c^2)}{2abc}$$

$$= \frac{ab^3 + abc^2 - a^3b + ab^2c + ac^3 - a^3c + a^3b + abc^2 - ab^3 + a^2bc + bc^3 - b^3c + a^3c + ab^2c - ac^3 + a^2bc + b^3c - bc^3}{2abc}$$

$$= \frac{2abc^2 + 2ab^2c + 2a^2bc}{2abc}$$

$$= c + b + a$$

$\therefore$ RHS = LHS

Exercise 8

1. In $\triangle ABC$ prove that $\tan B = \dfrac{b \sin C}{a - b \cos C}$.

Test A: Knowledge and routine procedures

1. Simplify, without using a calculator: $\dfrac{\cos(60°-A)+\cos(60°+A)}{\cos A}$. (4)

2. If $\cos^2 12° - \sin^2 12° = m$, express, without the use of a calculator, the following in terms of m. Answers may be left in surd form.
   - 2.1 $\cos 24°$ (1)
   - 2.2 $\dfrac{\sqrt{3}}{2}\cos 6° + \dfrac{1}{2}\sin 6°$ (4)

3. Find the general solution to $\dfrac{1}{2}(\theta + 10°) = \sin\theta\cos\theta$ without the aid of a calculator. (7)

4. Given: $\dfrac{1-\cos 2\theta}{\sin 2\theta} = \tan\theta$.
   - 4.1 Prove the identity. (5)
   - 4.2 Hence determine the value of $\tan 22{,}5°$ without using a calculator. (4)

5. Given: $\sin A = \dfrac{8}{17}$ and $90° < A < 180°$.
   - 5.1 Find, using a sketch and without a calculator, the value of $\cos A$. (3)
   - 5.2 If it is further given that $\sin B = \dfrac{12}{13}$ and $\hat{B}$ is acute, find without using a calculator the value of $\tan(720° + A + B)$. (4)

6. Given that $\cos(A - B) = \cos A \cos B + \sin A \sin B$, deduce a formula for $\cos(A + B)$. (4)

7. Given that $\sin(A + B) = \sin A \cos B + \cos A \sin B$, deduce a formula for $\sin 2P$. (2)

8. Given: $\sin(A + B) - \sin(A - B) = 2\cos A \sin B$.
   - 8.1 Prove the identity above. (3)
   - 8.2 Use the identity in 8.1 to simplify $\sin 5x - \sin x$. (4)
   - 8.3 Hence, or otherwise, find the general solution for x if $\sin 5x - \sin x = 0$. (5)

Total: 50

Test B: Complex procedures and problem solving

1. If $\sin 36° \cos 12° = p$ and $\cos 36° \sin 12° = q$, determine in terms of p and q the value of:
   1.1 $\sin 48°$ (3)
   1.2 $\sin 24°$ (3)
   1.3 $\cos 24°$ (3)

2. If $4 \tan \theta = 3$ and $180° < \theta < 360°$, determine with the aid of a diagram:
   2.1 $\sin \theta + \cos \theta$ (4)
   2.2 $\tan 2\theta$ (5)

3. Solve for β, correct to one decimal place if necessary: $\sin 2\beta = 1 - 4\cos^2 3$. (6)

4. Show that $\sin^2 20° + \sin^2 40° + \sin^2 80° = \frac{3}{2}$.
   (*Hint:* $40° = 60° - 20°$ and $80° = 60° + 20°$.) (7)

5. D, E and F are on the same horizontal plane. MF = h and is vertical to the horizontal plane. $\hat{B}$ is the angle of elevation from E to M.

   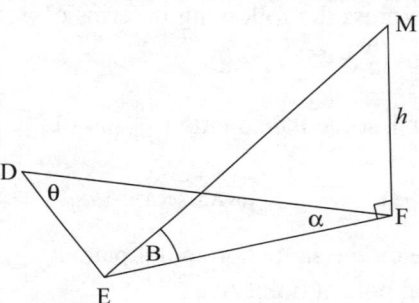

   Prove that DF = $\frac{h \sin(\theta + \alpha)}{\sin \theta \tan \beta}$. (4)

6. 6.1 Prove that $\tan 2x + 2\sin x = \frac{2\sin x(2\cos x - 1)(\cos x + 1)}{\cos 2x}$. (6)

   Hence calculate the values of x if:

   6.2 $\tan 2x + 2 \sin x = 0$ for $x \in [0°; 360°]$ (6)

   6.3 $\tan 2x + 2 \sin x$ is undefined for $x \in [0°; 360°]$ (3)

   Total: 50

Test C: Breakdown and content as per final exam

1. Simplify as far as possible: $\dfrac{\sin(180° - 2x) \cdot \tan(-45°)}{\cos(x - 90°)}$. (4)

2. Given: $\sin 22° \cos 12° = a$ $\sin 12° \cos 22° = b$
   $\cos 22° \cos 12° = c$ $\sin 22° \sin 12° = d$

   Express the following in terms of a, b, c and d:

   2.1 $\sin 34°$ (2)

   2.2 $\cos 10°$ (2)

3. It is known that $13 \sin \alpha - 5 = 0$ and $\tan \beta = -\tfrac{3}{4}$ where $\alpha \in [90°; 270°]$ and $\beta \in [90°; 270°]$. Determine, without using a calculator, the values of the following:

   3.1 $\cos \alpha$ (3)

   3.2 $\cos(\alpha + \beta)$ (5)

4. Prove, without using a calculator, that if $\sin 28° = a$ and $\cos 32° = b$, then $b\sqrt{1-a^2} - a\sqrt{1-b^2} = \tfrac{1}{2}$ (4)

5. If $\cos \beta = m$, express the following in terms of m, without using a calculator:
   $\sin\left(\tfrac{\beta}{2} + 45°\right) \cos\left(\tfrac{\beta}{2} + 45°\right)$. (4)

6. If $\theta \in [0°; 180°]$, solve the equation $\dfrac{\cos 2\theta}{\sin 4\theta} = 1$. (8)

7. Prove that $\tan 2A + \dfrac{1}{\cos 2A} = \dfrac{\sin A + \cos A}{\cos A - \sin A}$. (9)

8. A, B and C are on the same horizontal plane.
   AD is a vertical pole at point A.

   $B\hat{D}A = \alpha$

   $B\hat{A}C = 90° + \alpha$

   $A\hat{C}B = 2\alpha$

   $DB = 10$ units

   8.1 Determine AB in terms of α. (2)

   8.2 Prove that BC = 5 units. (2)

   8.3 Prove that $AC = \dfrac{5 \cos 3\alpha}{\cos \alpha}$. (5)

   Total: 50

TOPIC 5 Polynomial functions

In Grades 10 and 11 you learnt how to manipulate algebraic expressions by multiplying a binomial by a trinomial, factorising trinomials, using the difference of two squares, using the sum and difference of two cubes, and grouping. In addition you learnt how to simplify, add and subtract algebraic fractions.

In Grade 12 you will work with the remainder and factor theorems for polynomials up to the third degree. You will also learn to factorise third degree polynomials using the factor theorem.

Knowledge and skills for this Topic

For the Grade 12 work in this Topic, you need a good grasp of the following knowledge and skills:

- understand and work with factorising trinomials, difference of squares, sum and difference of cubes and grouping
- using the remainder and factor theorems determine which values of x are the zeros of a polynomial
- determine the factor once the zero of the polynomial has been determined
- use any method to factorise a third degree polynomial
- determine the x-intercepts of the third degree polynomial
- given the polynomial, the binomial which can be divided into this polynomial, and the remainder, determine the variable(s) given in the polynomial.

Difficulty with this Topic is often the result of an inability to solve quadratic equations and draw the graphs in a Cartesian plane, or to interpret a given sketch.

Content of final exam

- Factorise any polynomial up to and including a third degree polynomial.
- Apply the theory of the remainder and factor theorems to third degree polynomials.
- Determine remainders.
- Use the remainder to find given variables.
- Solve cubic equations by:
  - finding the first zero of a cubic function
  - then finding the factor
  - then using both of these to divide and find the other factor of a cubic equation.
- Solve for x in cubic equations in order to find the x-intercepts of a cubic graph.

The remainder and factor theorems

The remainder theorem is an invaluable tool to help you factorise polynomials of the third degree. In a polynomial, all the coefficients of a polynomial are real numbers and the exponents are all counting numbers.

The degree of a polynomial is determined by the greatest exponent.
$P(x) = 4x^3 + 2x^2 - 3x + 7$ is a polynomial of the third degree.

If $f(x) = 4x^2 - 5x + 7$
then $f(3) = 4(3)^2 - 5(3) + 7$
$f(a + b) = 4(a + b)^2 - 5(a + b) + 7$, etc.

Note
This example shows the use of function notation.

Knowledge of the factor theorem enables us to factorise a polynomial of a higher degree than two. This theorem is a specific result of the remainder theorem.

The remainder theorem

If any polynomial $f(x)$ is divided by $(ax - b)$, until the remainder does not contain x, then the remainder is equal to $f\left(\frac{b}{a}\right)$.

This means that the value to be substituted always has the opposite sign from the sign in the factor.

Application and proof

If $f(x) = 2x^2 + 5x + 4$ is divided by $2x - 1$, until the remainder does not contain x, the remainder is $f\left(\frac{1}{2}\right)$.

$f(x) = 2x^2 + 5x + 4$
$ = \underset{\underset{\text{divisor}}{\downarrow}}{(2x - 1)}\ \underset{\underset{\text{quotient}}{\downarrow}}{Q(x)} + \underset{\underset{\text{remainder}}{\downarrow}}{R}$

$f\left(\frac{1}{2}\right) = [2\left(\frac{1}{2}\right) - 1]Q(x) + R$
$\phantom{f\left(\frac{1}{2}\right)} = 0 + R$
$\phantom{f\left(\frac{1}{2}\right)} = \text{Remainder}$

$\therefore$ Remainder $= f\left(\frac{1}{2}\right)$
$\phantom{\therefore \text{Remainder}} = 2\left(\frac{1}{2}\right)^2 + 5\left(\frac{1}{2}\right) + 4$
$\phantom{\therefore \text{Remainder}} = 2 \times \frac{1}{4} + \frac{5}{2} + 4$
$\phantom{\therefore \text{Remainder}} = 7$

The factor theorem

If $(x - p)$ is a factor of $f(x)$, then remainder $= f(p) = 0$.

Worked examples

1. Determine the remainder if $2x^3 - 4x^2 + x - 5$ is divided by $x - 2$.

2. $(x - 1)$ and $(x - 2)$ are two factors of the expression $x^3 - 2x^2 - ax + b$. Determine a and b and the other factor.

3. If $x^2 + x - 6$ is a factor of $g(x) = 2x^3 + px^2 - 17x + q$, determine p and q and then factorise the expression.

Remember

It isn't necessary to use long division to find the remainder, because according to the remainder theorem, the remainder $= f(2)$.

Solutions

1. Let $f(x) = 2x^3 - 4x^2 + x - 5$
    Remainder $= f(2)$ $x - b = [x - (-2)]$ ∴ +2 is substituted
    $= 2(2)^3 - 4(2)^2 + 2 - 5$
    $= -3$

2. Let $f(x) = x^3 - 2x^2 - ax + b$

    Simultaneous equations can be solved in three ways:
    1. Use the elimination method
    2. Use the substitution method
    3. Make the coefficient of one variable in each equation the same. Make these terms the subject of each equation, then equate the right hand sides.

    $(x - 1)$ is a factor ∴ Remainder $= f(1) = 0$
    $f(1) = 1 - 2 - a + b = 0$
    ∴ $-a + b = 1$ ……………………… ①

    $(x - 2)$ is a factor ∴ Remainder $= f(2) = 0$
    ∴ $f(2) = 8 - 8 - 2a + b = 0$
    ∴ $-2a + b = 0$ ……………… ②

    ① − ②:
    ∴ $a = 1$
    ∴ $b = 2$
    ∴ $f(x) = x^3 - 2x^2 - x + 2$
    $= (x - 1)(x - 2)(x + p)$
    $= (x^2 - 3x + 2)(x + 1)$ $x^2 \cdot x = x^3$ and $(2)(1) = 2$
    ∴ $(x + 1)$ is the other factor.

3. $x^2 + x - 6 = (x + 3)(x - 2)$
    $(x + 3)$ is a factor
    ∴ Rem $= g(-3) = 0$
    ∴ $-54 + 9p + 51 + q = 0$
    ∴ $9p + q = 3$ ……………… ①

    $(x - 2)$ is a factor
    ∴ Rem $= f(2) = 0$
    ∴ $16 + 4p - 34 + q = 0$
    ∴ $4p + q = 18$ ……………… ②

    ① − ②: $9p + q - 4p - q = 3 - 18$
    ∴ $5p = -15$
    ∴ $p = -3$
    ∴ $q = 30$

    $g(x) = 2x^3 - 3x^2 - 17x + 30$
    $= (x^2 + x - 6)(2x - 5)$ $x^2 \cdot x = x^3$ and $(-6)(-5) = 30$
    $= (x + 3)(x - 2)(2x - 5)$

Factorising cubic polynomials in the form
$f(x) = ax^3 + bx^2 + cx + d$

Step 1 Use the factor theorem to determine the first factor. You already know that if $f(m) = 0$ then $(x - m)$ is a factor. So you need to find a value of m so that $f(m) = 0$, and then $(x - m)$ is a factor of $f(x)$.
Substitute $1, -1, 2, -2, \ldots$ for x until the value of $f(x) = 0$.

The factor must be written with the opposite sign from the sign of the relevant integer.

Step 2 Divide $f(x)$ by $(x - m)$. The quotient will be a quadratic trinomial or binomial, i.e. the first term will be ax^2.

Step 3 Factorise the quadratic expression.

There are several methods besides long division of determining the quotient when the first factor of a cubic expression is known. One method is set out below, and a further two methods will be given in the section on 'Graphs of cubic polynomials'.

Method 1

Factorise $x^3 + 2x^2 - 5x - 6$.

Let $f(x) = x^3 + 2x^2 - 5x - 6$
then $f(2) = 2^3 + 2(2)^2 - 5(2) - 6 = 0$

$\therefore x - 2$ is a factor

$\therefore x^3 + 2x^2 - 5x \times 6 = (x - 2)(x^2 + kx + 3)$ $x \cdot x^2 = x^3$ and $(-2)(3) = -6$

To determine k, carry out the following:

$x^3 + 2x^2 - 5x \times 6 = (x - 2)(x^2 + kx + 3)$

$-2x^2 + kx^2 = 2x^2$ OR $3x - 2kx = -5x$
$\therefore kx^2 = 4x^2$ $\therefore -2kx = -8x$
$\therefore k = 4$ $\therefore k = 4$

$\therefore f(x) = (x - 2)(x^2 + 4x + 3)$
$= (x - 2)(x + 3)(x + 1)$

> **Using the calculator**
> By using the table mode on the calculator, the x-values (roots) that make $f(x) = 0$ can be found.
> 1. Press MODE
> 2. Select table. You are now prompted to enter $f(x)$.
> 3. Enter $f(x)$ and press =.
> 4. Prompt is Start? Select the largest negative factor of the constant term.
> 5. Prompt is End? Select the largest positive factor of the constant term.
> 6. Prompt is Step? Enter 1 or $\frac{1}{2}$.
> 7. Now find x values for which $f(x) = 0$.

Worked examples

1. Factorise $x^3 - 7x^2 - 10x + 16$.
2. Factorise $2x^3 - 3x^2 - 11x + 6$.
3. The expressions $2x^3 - 5x^2 + 2ax + 52$ and $x^3 + 3ax^2 + 11x - 6$ leave the same remainder when divided by $x - 2$. Use the remainder theorem to find the value of a.

Solutions

1. Let $f(x) = x^3 - 7x^2 - 10x + 16$
   Rem $= f(1) = 1 - 7 - 10 + 16 = 0$
   $\therefore (x - 1)$ is a factor
   $f(x) = x^3 - 7x^2 - 10x + 16$
   $= (x - 1)(x^2 - 6x - 16)$
   $= (x - 1)(x - 8)(x + 2)$

2. Let $f(x) = 2x^3 - 3x^2 - 11x + 6$
   Rem $= f(1) = 2 - 3 - 11 + 6 = -6 \therefore (x - 1)$ is not a factor
   Rem $= f(-1) = -2 - 3 + 11 + 6 = 12 \therefore (x + 1)$ is not a factor
   Rem $= f(2) = 16 - 12 - 22 + 6 = -12 \therefore (x - 2)$ is not a factor
   Rem $= f(-2) = -16 - 12 + 22 + 6 = 0 \therefore (x + 2)$ is a factor
   $f(x) = 2x^3 - 3x^2 - 11x + 6$
   $= 2x^3 - 3x^2 - 11x + 6$
   $= (x + 2)(2x^2 - 7x + 3)$
   $= (x + 2)(2x - 1)(x - 3)$

3. Let $f(x) = 2x^3 - 5x^2 + 2ax + 52$
   Rem $= f(2) = 2(2)^3 - 5(2)^2 + 2a(2) + 52$
   $= 4a + 48$
   Let $g(x) = x^3 + 3ax^2 + 11x - 6$
   Rem $= g(2) = (2)^3 + 3a(2)^2 + 11(2) - 6$
   $= 12a + 24$

   $f(2) = g(2)$
   $\therefore 4a + 48 = 12a + 24$
   $\therefore 8a = 24$
   $\therefore a = 3$

Exercise 1

1. Find the remainder if $x^3 + 4x^2 - x + 3$ is divided by $2x + 1$.

2. Given: $f(x) = 2x^3 + x^2 - 5x + 2$. Factorise $f(x)$ by using the factor theorem.

3. Given: $f(x) = 2x^3 + ax^2 + ax - 2$. If $f(x)$ is divided by $2x + 1$, the remainder is b. Determine a in terms of b.

4. Given: $g(x) = x^3 + max^2 + na^2x + 8a^3$, $a \neq 0$. If $(x - a)(x + 2a)$ is a factor of $g(x)$, calculate the values of m and n.

5. Prove that $x + 3$ is a factor of $x^3 - 2x + 3x^2 - 6$.

6. For which value of m will $x - 3$ be a factor of $x^3 + m^2x^2 - 11x - 15m$?

7. If $p^2 + p - 2$ is a factor of $p^4 - ap^3 - 5p^2 + 8p - b$, calculate a and b.

8. Given the expression $2x^3 + m^2x + 81$:
   8.1 for which value of m will $x - m$ be a factor?
   8.2 use this value of m and factorise the expression.

9. Given the expression $m^3 - 3m + 2$:
   - **9.1** factorise the expression
   - **9.2** hence solve the following equation: $(3x - 4)^3 - 3(2x - 5) - (3x + 1) = 0$.

Solving for x in cubic polynomials

In the equation, the cubic polynomial is in the form $ax^3 + bx^2 + cx + d = 0$, and the instruction is 'Solve for x.'

Use the same method as in the previous exercise to factorise the left hand side. Write '= 0' on the right hand side in each step, then write down the values for x.

Example: $(x + 2)(2x^2 - 5x + 3) = 0$
$$(x + 2)(2x - 3)(x - 1) = 0$$
$$x = -2 \text{ or } = \tfrac{3}{2} \text{ or } x = 1$$

Exercise 2

Factorise and then solve for x in the following equations:

1. $x^3 + x^2 - 4x - 4 = 0$
2. $2x^3 - 3x^2 - 2x + 3 = 0$
3. $3x^3 - x^2 + 3x - 1 = 0$

Graphs of cubic polynomials

A cubic function is written in the form $y = ax^3 + bx^2 + cx + d$, $a \neq 0$. There may be one, two or three x-intercepts on the graph.

To represent a cubic function graphically follow these steps:

1. To find the x-intercepts, make $y = 0$.
2. Then use the factor theorem to find the first x-intercept.
3. Using this x-intercept, write down the linear factor.
4. Use one of the optional methods to obtain a quadratic factor.
5. Factorise the quadratic factor and solve for x to determine the other x-intercepts (if they exist).

Dividing a cubic polynomial by a linear factor

Worked example

In this example, a further two methods of finding the quadratic factor are used. If $x - 3$ is a factor of $x^3 - 6x^2 + 5x + 12$, factorise the expression completely. Hence, state the values of the x-intercepts if $y = x^3 - 6x^2 + 5x + 12$.

Solution

Method 2 Algebraic method

$x^3 - 6x^2 + 5x + 12$	Divide the cubic polynomial by $x - 3$.
$= x^2(x - 3) - 3x^2 + 5x + 12$	Start by writing down the factor $(x - 3)$.
$x \times ? = x^3$	Determine the coefficient of the factor $(x - 3)$ by calculating the question mark for x^2.

$$= x^2(x-3) - 3x(x-3) - 4x + 12$$ Now multiply your answer for (2) by the linear factor and determine the remaining terms so that the second line is equal to the first line.

$$= x^2(x-3) - 3x(x-3) - 4(x-3)$$ Keep the first term as is and repeat steps 1 to 3 until division is complete.

$$= (x-3)(x^2 - 3x - 4)$$ $(x-3)$ should now be a common factor.

$$= (x-3)(x-4)(x+1)$$ Factorise the quadratic factor.

$$y = x^3 - 6x^2 + 5x + 12$$ To solve for x, let $y = 0$.

$$x^3 - 6x^2 + 5x + 12 = 0$$

$$(x-3)(x-4)(x+1) = 0$$

$$x = 3 \text{ or } 4 \text{ or } -1$$

Method 3 Division by inspection

Factorise further by trinomial or difference of squares:

$$x^3 - 6x^2 + 5x + 12$$

$$= (x-3)(\ldots)$$ $x - 3$ is one factor, and the other factor is a trinomial.

$$= (x-3)(x^2 + \ldots - 4)$$ $x \cdot x^2 = x^3$ and $(-3)(-4) = 12$

> To obtain the middle term, work with the x^2 terms. The x^2 term in the original polynomial is $-6x^2$. The sum of the products of the arrows indicated must add up to $-6x^2$.

$$= (x-3)(x^2 + \ldots - 4)$$

$$-3x^2 + x(?) = -6x^2$$

$$-3x^2 + x(-3x) = -6x^2$$

$$\therefore \text{middle term} = -3x$$

Worked example

Solve for x: $x^3 + 4x^2 + x - 6 = 0$.

Solution

Let $f(x) = x^3 + 4x^2 + x - 6$ Use the factor theorem

$f(1) = 0 \therefore x - 1$ is a factor

Method 2 Algebraic method

$$x^3 + 4x^2 + x - 6 = 0$$
$$x^2(x-1) + 5x^2 + x - 6 = 0$$
$$x^2(x-1) + 5x(x-1) + 6x - 6 = 0$$
$$x^2(x-1) + 5x(x-1) + 6(x-1) = 0$$
$$(x-1)(x^2 + 5x + 6) = 0$$
$$(x-1)(x+3)(x+2) = 0$$
$$x = 1 \text{ or } -3 \text{ or } -2$$

Method 3 By inspection

OR $\quad x^3 + 4x^2 + x - 6 = 0$

$$(x-1)(x^2 + 5x + 6) = 0$$
$$(x-1)(x+3)(x+2) = 0$$
$$x = 1 \text{ or } -3 \text{ or } -2$$

Exercise 3

Find the x-intercepts, and draw a rough sketch graph indicating the intercepts with the axes of the following equations:

1. $y = 2x^3 + 3x^2 - 3x - 2$
2. $y = 2x^3 - 3x^2 - 11x + 6$
3. $y = 2x^3 - x^2 - 18x + 9$
4. $y = 3x^3 + 8x^2 + 3x - 2$
5. $y = 2x^3 + 9x^2 - 8x - 15$

Test A: Knowledge and routine procedures

1. Given: $f(x) = x^3 + 3x^2 - 2x - 4$:
   1.1 prove that $(x + 1)$ is a factor of $f(x)$ (2)
   1.2 Now solve for x if $f(x) = 0$. (5)

2. If $f(x) = 2x^3 - 26x^2 - 24$:
   2.1 calculate $f(-3)$ and explain the meaning of your answer (3)
   2.2 factorise $f(x)$. (4)

3. Solve for x.
   3.1 $x^3 - x^2 - 8x + 12 = 0$ (6)
   3.2 $8x^3 - 14x^2 - 25x + 42 = 0$ (8)

4. If $(x - 1)$ and $(x + 2)$ are two factors of the expression $x^3 - 2x^2 - ax + b$, find the values of a and b and the other factor(s) of the expression. (7)

Total: 35

Test B: Complex procedures and problem solving

1. For the expression $f(x) = x^3 - 3x^2 + 2$:
   1.1 find the factors (4)
   1.2 hence, solve for x if $f(x) \leq 0$. (3)

2. Determine what must be added to $3x^3 + 4x^2 - 5x + 2$ to make it exactly divisible by $x - 3$. (3)

3. Factorise $f(x) = -x^3 + 6x^2 - 9x + 4$. (6)

4. For the expression $px^3 + qx^2 - 2x - 3$:
   4.1 find the values of p and q if $4x^2 - 1$ is a factor of the expression. (9)
   4.2 hence, find the other factor of $px^3 + qx^2 - 2x - 3$. (2)

5. One of the roots of $2x^3 + x^2 - 5x + 2$ is 1. Determine the other roots. (6)

6. Two factors of $f(x) = x^3 + mx^2 - nx + 8$ are $(x - 1)$ and $(x + 4)$.
   6.1 Find the values of m and n. (8)
   6.2 Hence, solve for x if $f(x) = 0$. (4)

Total: 45

Test C: Breakdown and content as per final exam

1.
   1.1 State the factor theorem. (2)
   1.2 State the remainder theorem. (2)
   1.3 If $f(x) = 5 - 2x^2$ is divided by $x + k$ and the remainder is $9k$ determine the value(s) of k. (5)
   1.4 Consider the function $f(x) = x^3 + 3x^2 - 4$.
       1.4.1 Determine $f(1)$. (2)
       1.4.2 Determine x if $f(x) = 0$. (5)
       1.4.3 Hence or otherwise solve for x if $f(x) \geq 0$. (2)

2. Given that $g(x)$ is a third degree polynomial, and $g(-2) = g(5) = 3$, and $g(0) = 6$, and two of the roots of $g(x)$ are h and p, determine the following:
   2.1 the remainder when $g(x)$ is divided by $(x - 5)$ (2)
   2.2 the degree of Q(x) if $g(x) = (x - h)(x - p)Q(x) + R$, where R is independent of x (1)
   2.3 Explain why $x^2 + 3x + 5 = 0$ has no real roots. (Use $\Delta = b^2 - 4ac$.) (3)

3. The graph of $f(x) = -2x^3 - 7x^2 - x + 10$ is sketched below.

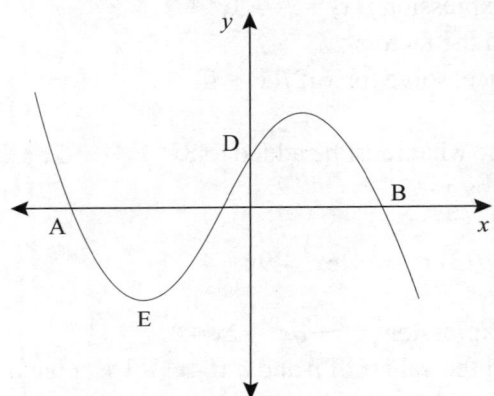

   3.1 Use the factor theorem to show that $(x + 2)$ and $(x - 1)$ are factors of $f(x)$. (4)

   3.2 Determine the third factor of $f(x)$. (3)

   3.3 Write down the coordinates of points A and B, indicated in the sketch. (2)

   3.4 Is the curve increasing or decreasing between points E and D? Give a reason for your answer. (2)

   3.5 For which values of x is $f(x) \leq 0$? (2)

   Total: 37

TOPIC 6 Differential calculus

Calculus is new to you in Grade 12. In this Topic you will use the knowledge you have gained in Grades 10 and 11 on algebra, graph work and exponential theory.

Knowledge and skills for this Topic

For the Grade 12 work in this Topic, you need a good grasp of the following knowledge and skills:

- functional notation, straight lines graphs and parabolas
- algebra and the simplification of algebraic fractions
- factorising binomials, trinomials and cubic equations
- inequalities, both linear and quadratic
- exponents and exponential theory
- the factor and remainder theorem.

Difficulty with this Topic is often the result of poor prerequisite knowledge and the failure to select the correct mathematical tools.

Content of final exam

- Use the concept of a limit to approximate the average gradient (or the rate of change).
- Use the concept of a limit to approximate the gradient at a point.
- Use first principles to find the first derivative.
- Use the rules of differentiation to find derivatives.
- Find the equations of tangents to curves.
- Find the second derivative and use it to determine the concavity of a function.
- Sketch and interpret graphs of cubic functions.
- Solve practical problems involving maximum and minimum values, rates of change, and the calculus of motion.

Relevant formulae

$$x = \frac{-b \pm \sqrt{b^2 - 4ac}}{2a} \qquad f'(x) = \lim_{h \to 0} \frac{f(x+h) - f(x)}{h}$$

What is calculus?

Calculus is probably one of the most powerful and widely used tools in the field of mathematics. Calculus enables you to find the gradient of a function at any point. So far you have only been able to determine the gradient of a straight line, but now you will learn how to find the gradient of a curve at a point, using differential calculus. This is useful information to have when plotting graphs, as it enables you to find turning points (places where the gradient is 0), for example.

The concept of a limit

The concept of a limit is integral to your understanding of calculus. The limit of a function simply asks: 'What does the y-value tend to as the x-value tends to a particular value?'

When you see $x \to 0$, this means 'x tends to 0', or 'x gets nearer to 0'.

Worked examples

1. Find the limit of $f(x) = \frac{3}{4}x + 1$ as the value of x tends to zero.

2. Find $\lim_{x \to -3} (x^2 + 2x + 1)$.

Solutions

1. $\lim_{x \to 0} f(x) = \lim_{x \to 0} \left(\frac{3}{4}x + 1\right) = 1$

   In our minds we substitute 0 for x and remove lim: i.e. $\frac{3}{4}(0) + 1 = 0 + 1 = 1$. We cannot actually show this step as the x-value is not 0, it only tends to 0.

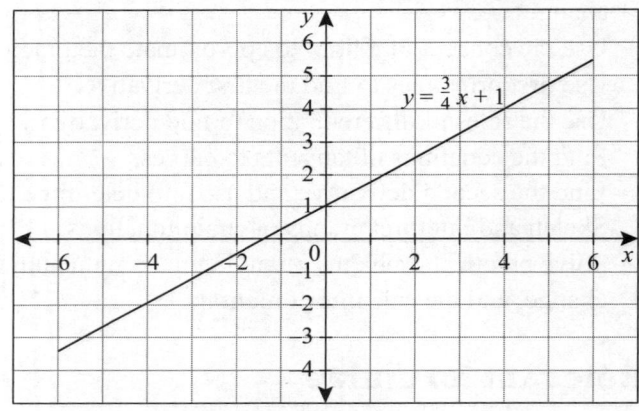

As you can see from the graph, as x tends zero, $f(x)$ tends to 1.

2. $\lim_{x \to -3} (x^2 + 2x + 1)$
   $= 4$

   Substitute –3 for x: $(-3)^2 + 2(-3) + 1$.

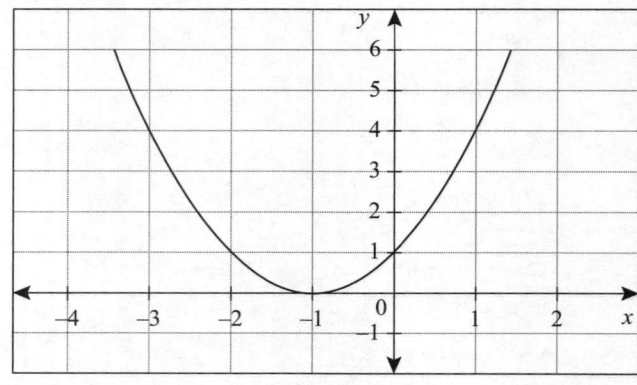

As you can see from the graph, as x approaches -3, y approaches 4.

Working with limits is not always so simple!

Study the examples given below to understand this concept better.

Worked examples

1. Find $\lim\limits_{x \to 0} \frac{4}{x}$
2. Find $\lim\limits_{x \to 3} \frac{3x^2 - 27}{x - 3}$

Solutions

1. As can be seen from the graph, the solution to this problem has two parts:

    As $x \to 0$ for $x > 0$, the y-value of the graph tends to positive infinity.

    As $x \to 0$ for $x < 0$, the y-value of the graph tends to negative infinity.

    Replacing x with 0 will result in $\frac{4}{0}$ which is undefined, and is therefore NOT the correct answer!

    For $x > 0$, $\lim\limits_{x \to 0} \frac{4}{x} \to \infty$

    For $x < 0$, $\lim\limits_{x \to 0} \frac{4}{x} \to -\infty$

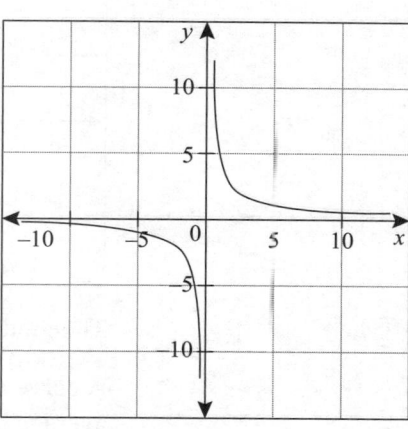

Note
If substituting for the limit gives a zero denominator, factorise and cancel before substituting for the limit.

2. **Incorrect solution**:

    $\lim\limits_{x \to 3} \frac{3x^2 - 27}{x - 3}$

    $= \frac{3(3)^2 - 9}{(3) - 3} = \frac{0}{0}$

    In this case, simply replacing x with 3 is **incorrect**, because division by zero is undefined.

    Correct solution:

    $\lim\limits_{x \to 3} \frac{3x^2 - 27}{x - 3}$

    $= \lim\limits_{x \to 3} \frac{3(x - 3)(x + 3)}{(x - 3)}$

    $= \lim\limits_{x \to 3} 3(x + 3) = 18$

    SIMPLIFY the algebraic fraction before substituting for the value the x tends to.

You need to know
- algebraic fractions
- factorising quadratic and cubic expressions

Exercise 1

Determine the limits of the following:

1. $\lim\limits_{x \to 2} 3x$
2. $\lim\limits_{x \to 2} 4(x - 5)$
3. $\lim\limits_{x \to -4} \frac{2x^2 + 9x - 5}{2x - 1}$
4. $\lim\limits_{x \to 1} \frac{x^3 + 64}{x + 4}$
5. $\lim\limits_{x \to 1\frac{1}{2}} \frac{8x^2 - 8x - 6}{2x - 3}$
6. $\lim\limits_{x \to -3} \frac{x^3 + 3x^2 + x + 3}{x + 3}$

Average gradient or rate of change

The rate of change means how the value of *y* changes as the value of *x* changes. A straight line has a constant gradient, and the **rate of change for the straight line is equal to the gradient of the line**.

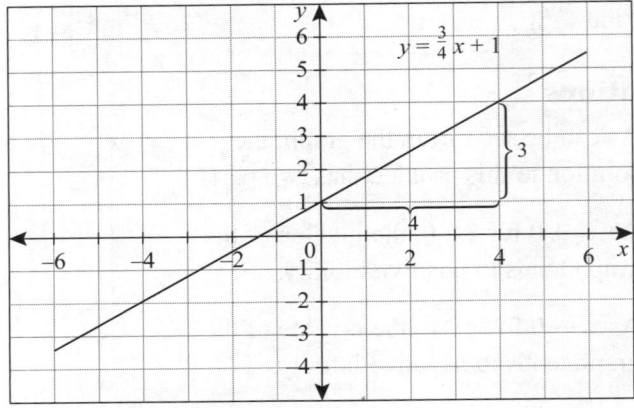

The gradient for $y = \frac{3}{4}x + 1$ is simply $\frac{\Delta y}{\Delta x} = \frac{3}{4}$.

A curve does not have a constant gradient or rate of change, but we can find the average gradient between any two points on any curve. The calculus definition for average gradient is:

$$\text{Average gradient} = \frac{f(x + h) - f(x)}{h}$$

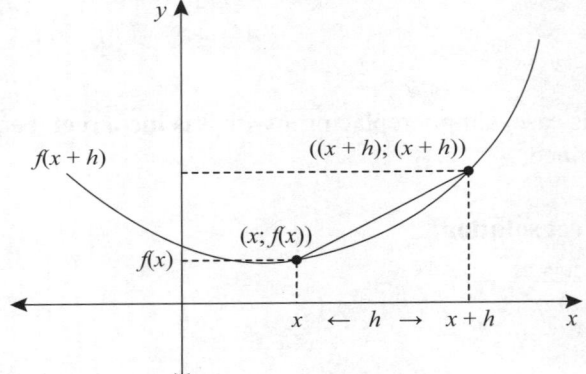

h = number of units x has moved

x = original value of $x(x_1)$

$x + h$ = new value of $x(x_2)$

$f(x) = y$ coordinate of x_1

$f(x + h) = y$ coordinate of x_2

This definition is often confusing.

The more familiar definition for gradient will give the same result: $m = \frac{y_2 - y_1}{x_2 - x_1}$

Worked example

Given the equation $f(x) = x^2$, find the average gradient (or rate of change) between $x = 1$ and $x = 3$.

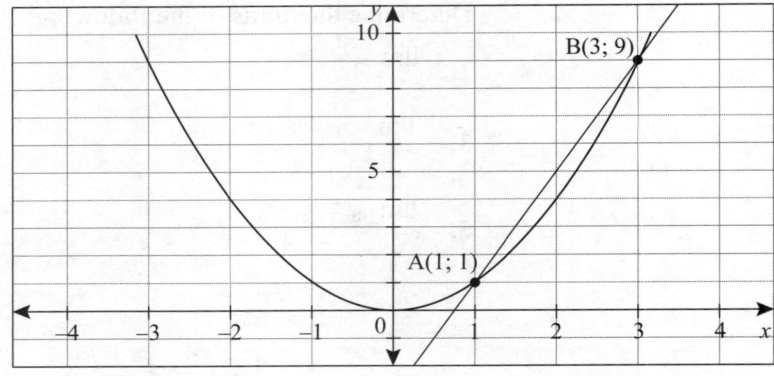

112   STUDY & MASTER MATHEMATICS STUDY GUIDE GRADE 12

Solution

This problem can be completed by using the definition for the gradient or the calculus definition for the average gradient.

At $x = 1, f(1) = 1^2 = 1$

At $x = 3, f(3) = 3^2 = 9$

$\therefore$ A $(1; 1)$ and B$(3; 9)$

$\therefore m_{AB} = \frac{9-1}{3-1} = \frac{8}{2} = 4$

OR Average gradient $= \frac{f(x+h) - f(x)}{h}$

$= \frac{9-1}{2} = \frac{8}{2} = 4 \qquad f(x+h) = 9, f(x) = 1,$ and $h = 3 - 1 = 2$

Using definition for average gradient and gradient at a point

Moving two points on a curve closer and closer until the difference between the x-values is very small, (i.e. $h \to 0$), will give us an **approximation of the gradient at a point** on the curve. This concept is summarised by the definition:

$$\text{Gradient at a point} = \lim_{h \to 0} \frac{f(x+h) - f(x)}{h}$$

Using this definition results in an expression called the **gradient function**. This may be used to find the gradient at **any point** on the given curve.

If you are asked to find the gradient at a **specific point**, you will be given the value of x at that point.

There are two methods of finding the gradient at a point:

Method 1 Substitute the x-value in the definition for 'gradient at a point'. See worked example 1.3 below.

Method 2 Use the formula for 'average gradient' to obtain the gradient function. Place this in the definition for 'gradient at a point'. Then substitute the x-value. See worked examples 2.1 and 2.2.

In both cases we assume that h is so close to 0 that we may mentally substitute 0 for h to obtain the final answer.

Worked examples

1. Given the graph of $f(x) = x^2$, determine:

    1.1 the average gradient of f between $x = 1$ and $x = 4$

    1.2 the average gradient of f between the points $x = -2$ and $x = -2 + h$

    1.3 the gradient of $f(x)$ at $x = -3$, using the definition for gradient at a point.

2. Given that $f(x) = -x^2 + 2$:

    2.1 find the gradient function for $f(x)$

    2.2 hence find the gradient at the point where $x = 5$.

Solutions

1. **1.1** Average gradient: $= \dfrac{f(x+h) - f(x)}{h}$

    $= \dfrac{f(1+3) - f(x)}{3}$

    $= \dfrac{f(4) - f(1)}{3}$

    $= \dfrac{(4)^2 - (1)^2}{3}$

    $= \dfrac{16 - 1}{3} = 5$

    If this format confuses you, you can simply use the analytical definition:
    Gradient $= \dfrac{y_2 - y_1}{x_2 - x_1} = \dfrac{16 - 1}{4 - 1} = \dfrac{15}{3} = 5$

    You need to know
    functional notation

    1.2 Here you have no choice but to use the definition for average gradient:

    Average gradient $= \dfrac{f(x+h) - f(x)}{h}$

    $= \dfrac{f(-2+h) - f(-2)}{h}$

    $= \dfrac{(-2+h)^2 - (-2)^2}{h}$

    $= \dfrac{4 - 4h + h^2 - 4}{h}$

    $= \dfrac{-4h + h^2}{h}$

    $= \dfrac{h(-4 + h)}{h}$

    $= -4 + h$

    Method 1

    1.3 $\lim\limits_{h \to 0} \dfrac{f(x+h) - f(x)}{h}$

    $= \lim\limits_{h \to 0} \dfrac{f(-3+h) - f(-3)}{h}$

    $= \lim\limits_{h \to 0} \dfrac{(-3+h)^2 - (-3)^2}{h}$

    $= \lim\limits_{h \to 0} \dfrac{9 - 6h + h^2 - 9}{h}$

    $= \lim\limits_{h \to 0} \dfrac{h(-6 + h)}{h}$

    $= \lim\limits_{h \to 0} (-6 + h) = -6$

    Remember
    You have to write $\lim\limits_{h \to 0}$ with every step, except the answer, or you will lose marks.

    Method 2

2. **2.1** It is often easier to start by finding $f(x+h)$ and then to substitute for $f(x+h)$ and $f(x)$ in the definition for average gradient:

    $f(x+h) = -(x+h)^2 + 2 = -(x^2 + 2xh + h^2) + 2$

    $= -x^2 - 2xh - h^2 + 2$

    Average gradient $= \dfrac{f(x+h) - f(x)}{h}$

    $= \dfrac{-x^2 - 2xh - h^2 + 2 + x^2 - 2}{h}$

    $= \dfrac{-2xh - h^2}{h}$

    $= \dfrac{h(-2x - h)}{h}$

    $= -2x - h$

    This expression cannot be simplified further. This expression is known as the **gradient function**.

Method 2

2.2 Gradient at a point $= \lim_{h \to 0} \frac{f(x+h) - f(x)}{h}$

$= \lim_{h \to 0} (-2x - h)$

Gradient when $x = 5$: $\lim_{h \to 0} [-2(5) - h] = -10$

Exercise 2

1. Find the average gradient/rate of change as x increases from 1 to 3 on the curve $f(x) = 4x^2 - 3$.

2. Use the definition for average gradient to find the gradient function for $f(x) = 4x^2 - 3$.

3. Find the average rate of change as x increase from -1 to 0 for the curve $f(x) = -x^2 - 1$.

4. Find the gradient function, i.e. the average gradient, for $f(x) = 2x^2 + 3$ and use your result to find the gradient at the points where $x = -3$ and where $x = 9$.

Using first principles to find the first derivative

Definition: The derivative of any function $f(x)$ is the new function $f'(x)$ defined at any value of x by:

$$f'(x) = \lim_{h \to 0} \frac{f(x+h) - f(x)}{h}$$

Using this definition to find the first derivative is known as differentiation by first or by basic principles. Note that this is the same definition used to find the gradient at a point, therefore:

$$f'(x) = \text{gradient at a point}$$

Worked example

Use first principles to find the derivative of $f(x) = x^2 - 4$.

Solution

$f(x) = x^2 - 4$

$f(x+h) = (x+h)^2 - 4$ Start by finding $f(x+h)$.

$\qquad = x^2 + 2xh + h^2 - 4$

$f'(x) = \lim_{h \to 0} \frac{f(x+h) - f(x)}{h}$ Substitute for $f(x+h)$ and $f(x)$ in $f'(x) = \lim_{h \to 0} \frac{f(x+h) - f(x)}{h}$.

$= \lim_{h \to 0} \frac{(x+h)^2 - 4 - (x^2 - 4)}{h}$ Don't forget to distribute correctly across the minus sign!

$= \lim_{h \to 0} \frac{x^2 + 2xh + h^2 - 4 - x^2 + 4}{h}$

$= \lim_{h \to 0} \frac{2xh + h^2}{h}$

$= \lim_{h \to 0} \frac{h(2x + h)}{h}$ Simplify by factorising: take out the common factor h which allows you to cancel out h.

$= \lim_{h \to 0} (2x + h)$ Drop $\lim_{h \to 0}$ only when you mentally substitute 0 for h.

$= 2x$

TOPIC 6 *Differential calculus*

Exercise 3

1. Find the derivative of the function $f(x) = 3x^2$ from first principles.

2. Use the definition of the first derivative to prove that $f'(x) = 5$ given that $f(x) = (5x - 3)$.

3. For the curve $f(x) = -x^2 + 3$ find the first derivative using first principles.

4. Using first principles find $f'(x)$ for the curve $f(x) = 3x^2 + 3x$.

5. Use basic principles and the definition of the derivative to show that the first derivative of $f(x) = mx + c$ is $f'(x) = m$.

Using the rules of differentiation to find derivatives

To find a derivative, use the formula $\frac{d}{dx}(ax^n) = anx^{n-1}$, for any real number, together with the rules:

- $\frac{d}{dx}[f(x) \pm g(x)] = \frac{d}{dx}f(x) \pm \frac{d}{dx}g(x)$
- $\frac{d}{dx}kf(x) = k\frac{d}{dx}f(x)$ (where k is a constant).

Different notations for the derivative

There are various ways of writing derivatives. Take note of how to set out your work in the correct mathematical format, and of the different notations for differentiation, as shown in the examples below for the same expression:

$\frac{d}{dx}3x^4 = 12x^3$

$f'(x) = 12x^3$, if $f(x) = 3x^4$

$D_x(3x^4) = 12x^3$

$\frac{dy}{dx} = 12x^3$, if $y = 3x^4$

Worked examples

Use the differentiation rules to do the following:

1. Determine $f'(x)$ if $f(x) = (3x + 5)^2$.

2. Determine $D_x\left(-6\sqrt{x^2} + \frac{6}{x^3}\right)$.

3. Determine $\frac{dy}{dt}$ if $y = \frac{t^2 - 4}{4t + 8}$.

4. Show that $\frac{d}{dx}(2x - 3)(2x + 3) \neq \frac{d}{dx}(2x - 3) \times \frac{d}{dx}(2x + 3)$.

Solutions

1. $f(x) = (3x + 5)^2$
   $= 9x^2 + 30x + 25$ Simplify algebraic expressions fully before applying the rules of differentiation.

   $f'(x) = 18x + 30$

> **Note**
> - The x in $\frac{d}{dx}$ or $f(x)$ indicates that the derivative is with respect to the variable x.
> - $\frac{dy}{dx}$ means that the equation is in the y form.

> **You need to know**
> algebraic multiplication and simplification

> **You need to know**
> exponential laws and how to use them

> **Remember**
> The derivative of a constant = 0.

> **You need to know**
> simplification of algebraic fractions using factorisation

2. $D_x\left(-6\sqrt{x^2} + \frac{6}{x^3}\right)$
   $= D_x(-6x^{\frac{1}{2}} + 6x^{-3})$ Rewrite terms **without variable denominators or surd signs** before applying the rules of differentiation.
   $= -6\left(\frac{1}{2}\right)x^{-\frac{1}{2}} + 6(-3)x^{-4}$
   $= -3x^{-\frac{1}{2}} - 18x^{-4}$
   $= \frac{-3}{\sqrt{x}} - \frac{18}{x^4}$

3. $y = \frac{t^2 - 4}{4t + 8}$
   $= \frac{(t-2)(t+2)}{4(t+2)}$ Simplify algebraic expressions fully before applying the rules of differentiation.
   $= \frac{(t-2)}{4}$
   $\frac{dy}{dt} = \frac{1}{4}$

4. $\frac{d}{dx}(2x-3)(2x+3) = \frac{d}{dx}4x^2 - 9 = 8x$ Simplify products before applying the rules of differentiation.
   $\frac{d}{dx}(2x-3) \times \frac{d}{dx}(2x+3) = 2 \times 2 = 4$
   $\therefore \frac{d}{dx}(2x-3)(2x+3) \neq \frac{d}{dx}(2x-3) \times \frac{d}{dx}(2x+3)$

Exercise 4

1. Use the rules of differentiation to find the first derivative for each of the expressions given below.

   1.1 $-6x^2$ **1.2** $\frac{-6}{x^3}$

   1.3 $-63\sqrt{x^5}$ **1.4** $\frac{-6x^5 + 3x^2}{x^2}$

   1.5 $\frac{2x^2 - 7x + 3}{2x - 1}$

2. Calculate $f'(x)$ for each of the expressions given below:

   2.1 $f(x) = (2x - 5)^2$ **2.2** $f(x) = \frac{x^4 - 3x^2 + 1}{x^2}$

3. Determine:

   3.1 $D_x\left(2\sqrt{x} - \frac{5}{\sqrt{x}}\right)$ **3.2** $\frac{dy}{dt}$ if $y = \frac{9 - 5t + 3t^{\frac{1}{2}}}{t}$

   3.3 $\frac{dy}{dx}$ if: $3xy = 3x - 9x^2 + 6$

4. $f(x) = \left(6x^2 - \frac{2}{x^2}\right)^2$, find $\frac{df(x)}{dx}$

5. $y = \frac{4x^2 + 5}{3x^3}$, find $\frac{dy}{dx}$

Finding the equations of tangents and normals to curves

A **tangent** to a point on a curve is a straight line that touches the curve at a single point and has the same gradient as the curve at that point.

A **normal** is a line that is perpendicular to a tangent.

To find the gradient of the tangent:

Find the first derivative and substitute the x-coordinate of the point of contact $(a; b)$, i.e. $f'(a) = m_{tangent}$

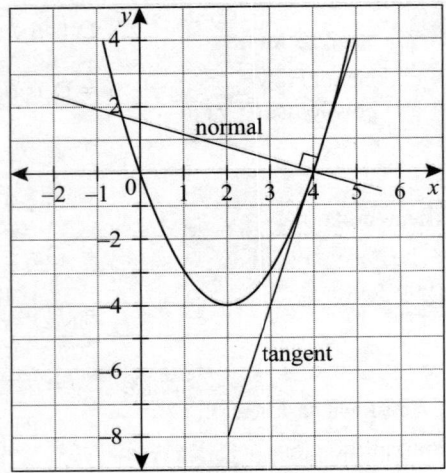

To find the equation of the tangent:

- Substitute both the x and y-coordinates of the point of contact and the gradient in the equation for a straight line.
  Use either $y = mx + c$
  or $y - y_1 = m(x - x_1)$.

To find the equation of the normal to a tangent at a common point of contact:

- A normal is perpendicular to a tangent, so
  $m_{normal} \times m_{tangent} = -1 \therefore m_{normal} = \frac{-1}{m_{tangent}}$

- Substitute both the x- and y-coordinates of the point of contact and the gradient in the equation for a straight line. Use either $y = mx + c$ or $y - y_1 = m(x - x_1)$.

Worked examples

1. Determine the equations of the tangent and the normal to $f(x) = 3x^2 - 8x + 5$ at $x = 2$.

2. Given that $g(x) = -x^2 + 2x - 1$, determine the coordinate point on the curve of g where the gradient of the tangent is -6.

3. The line $y = 22 + 11x$ is a tangent to the curve defined by $h(x) = -x^2 - 5x + 2$. Find the point of contact.

You need to know

how to find the equation of a line

Remember

To find the y-value, substitute the x-value in $f(x)$.

Remember

The equation of a line is given as $y - y_1 = m(x - x_1)$ where m is the gradient and $(x_1; y_1)$ is the point of contact.

Solutions

1. $f(x) = 3x^2 - 8x + 5$

   $f'(x) = 6x - 8$

   $f'(2) = 6(2) - 8 = 4$ The gradient at the point of contact $x = 2$ is given by $f'(2)$.

   The gradient of the tangent at the point of contact $= 4$.

   Point of contact: $(2; f(2))$
   $= (2; 3(2)^2 - 8(2) + 5) = (2; 1)$

Method 1

Equation of the tangent:

$y - y_1 = m(x - x_1)$

$y - 1 = 4(x - 2)$

$y - 1 = 4x - 8$

$y = 4x - 7$

Equation of the normal:

$m_{normal} = -\frac{1}{4}$, point of contact: $(2; 1)$

$y - y_1 = m(x - x_1)$

$y - 1 = -\frac{1}{4}(x - 2)$

$y = -\frac{1}{4}x + \frac{3}{2}$

Method 2

Equation of the tangent:

$y = mx + c$

$y = 4x + c$

$1 = 4(2) + c$ $m = 4$, and (1; 2) is the point of contact

$c = -7$

$\therefore y = 4x - 7$ Don't forget to write the equation in terms of y.

> **Remember**
> The equation of a line is given as $y = mx + c$.

Equation of the normal:

$y = mx + c$

$y = -\frac{1}{4}x + c$

$1 = -\frac{1}{4}(2) + c$

$c = \frac{3}{2}$

$\therefore y = -\frac{1}{4}x + \frac{3}{2}$

2. To find the x-coordinate, find $f'(x)$ and set it equal to the given gradient and solve for x:

   $g(x) = -x^2 + 2x - 1$
   $g'(x) = -2x + 2 = -6$
   $2x = 6 + 2$
   $\therefore x = 4$

   To find the y-coordinate, substitute for x in $f(x)$ and calculate y:
   $g(4) = -(4)^2 + 2(4) - 1 = -9$
   Point of contact: $(4; -9)$

3. To find the x-coordinate, find $f'(x)$, set it equal to gradient of the tangent, and solve for x:

   $h(x) = -x^2 - 5x + 2$
   $h'(x) = -2x - 5$
   $11 = -2x - 5$ $y = 22 + 11x \therefore m_{tangent} = 11$
   $2x = -11 - 5$
   $x = -8$

   To find the y-coordinate, substitute for x in $f(x)$ and calculate y:
   $h(-8) -(-8)^2 - 5(-8) + 2 = -22$
   Point of contact: $(-8; -22)$

Exercise 5

1. Find the equation of the tangent to the curve $f(x) = x^2$ at $x = -3$.

2. Find the equation of the tangent to the curve $g(x) = (x - 2)^2$ at the point where the graph meets the y-axis.

3. The tangent to the curve $h(x) = -2x^2 - x + 4$ is given as $x + y = 3$. Find the coordinates of the point of contact of the tangent and the curve.

4. Find the equation of the tangent and the normal to the curve of $y = \frac{6}{x}$ at the point where $x = -2$.

TOPIC 6   Differential calculus

5. Given: $f(x) = -x^2 + 1$.
   5.1 Find the average gradient of f between the points where $x = -2$ and $x = -2 + h$.
   5.2 Hence, find the gradient of the tangent to f at the point $(-2; -3)$ and work out the equation of the tangent to the curve at this point.
   5.3 At which point on the curve will the gradient be equal to 10?

6. Find the equation of the tangent to $y = -2x^3 + 4x^2 + 3$ at $x = 2$.

7. Find the equation of the tangent to $y = x^2 + x$ at $\left(-\frac{1}{2}; -\frac{1}{4}\right)$.

8. Find the equation of the tangent to $y = -x^2 + 6x$, which is parallel to the line $y - 3 = x$.

Putting everything together

Exercise 6

1. Determine $\lim\limits_{h \to 0} \left(\frac{(5-h)^2 - 25}{h} \right)$.

2. Find:
   2.1 $D_x(4x^{-3})$
   2.2 $D_x\left(\frac{x^2 - 3}{3x}\right)$

3. Given: $y = 5x^2$.
   3.1 Use the definition $\lim\limits_{h \to 0} \frac{f(x+h) - f(x)}{h}$ to find the first derivative for $y = 5x^2$.
   3.2 Describe briefly what $f(x+h) - f(x)$ means.
   3.3 Calculate $\lim\limits_{h \to 0} \frac{f(-2+h) - f(-2)}{h}$.
   3.4 Find the equation of the tangent to this curve at $x = -2$.

4. If $A(1; 2)$ and $B(1+h; 3(1+h)^2 - 1)$ are two points on the graph of $y = 3x^2 - 1$:
   4.1 find the gradient of the line AB
   4.2 find the gradient of AB when $h = 3$.

5. Given: $y = -3x^2$
   5.1 From first principles find the first derivative of this equation.
   5.2 Now determine the gradient of the graph of $y = -3x^2$ at the point when $x = -\frac{1}{6}$.
   5.3 Now find the equation of the tangent at this point.

6. Use the rules of differentiation to determine $f'(x)$ for each of the functions given below:
   6.1 $f(x) = (x+1)(x^2 - 3)$
   6.2 $f(x) = \frac{x^2 - x - 6}{x + 2}$
   6.3 $f(x) = \frac{3}{x}$

7. Given: $f(x) = x^2 - 2$.
   7.1 Calculate: $\frac{f(3) - f(1)}{2}$.
   7.2 What does the answer to 7.1 represent?
   7.3 Determine $f'(x)$ from first principles.
   7.4 Hence or otherwise calculate the coordinates of the point M on the curve where the gradient of the tangent to this curve is 4.

The concept of a limit (complex procedures)

Worked examples

Given that $f(x) = \left(\frac{4}{x-2} + 3\right)$, determine:

1. $\lim_{x \to \infty} \left(\frac{4}{x-2} + 3\right)$
2. $\lim_{x \to -\infty} \left(\frac{4}{x-2} + 3\right)$
3. $\lim_{x \to 0} \left(\frac{4}{x-2} + 3\right)$
4. $\lim_{x \to 2} \left(\frac{4}{x-2} + 3\right)$

5. Sketch the graph of $f(x) = \left(\frac{4}{x-2} + 3\right)$ to verify your solutions.

Solutions

1. $\frac{4}{x-2} \to 0$ as $x \to \infty$ $\therefore \lim_{x \to \infty} \left(\frac{4}{x-2} + 3\right) = 3$

2. $\frac{4}{x-2} \to 0$ as $x \to -\infty$ $\therefore \lim_{x \to \infty} \left(\frac{4}{x-2} + 3\right) = 3$

3. $\frac{4}{x-2} \to \frac{4}{0-2} \to -2$ as $x \to 0$ $\therefore \lim_{x \to 0} \left(\frac{4}{x-2} + 3\right) = 1$

4. $\frac{4}{x-2} \to \frac{4}{2-2} \to 0$ as $x \to 2$

   $\therefore \lim_{x \to 2} \left(\frac{4}{x-2} + 3\right) = \infty$ for $x > 2$ $\therefore \lim_{x \to 2} \left(\frac{4}{x-2} + 3\right) = \infty,$

   $\lim_{x \to 2} \left(\frac{4}{x-2} + 3\right) = -\infty$ for $x < 2$ $\therefore \lim_{x \to 2} \left(\frac{4}{x-2} + 3\right) = -\infty.$

5. The solution to this problem is better understood by examining the graph of $f(x)$.

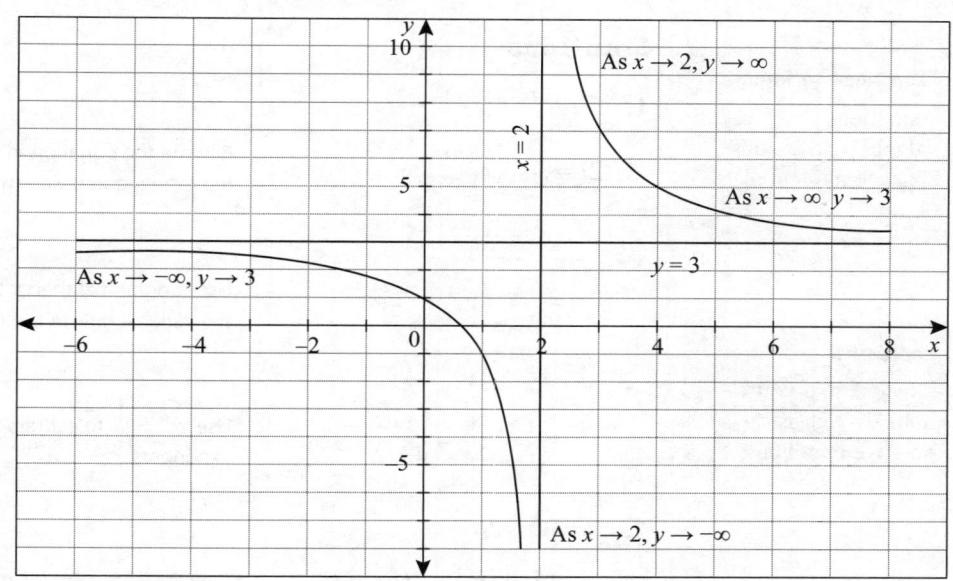

First principles (complex procedures)

Worked example

Use the definition for the derivative (i.e. first principles) to find the derivative of $f(x) = \frac{4}{x}$.

> **You need to know**
> algebraic fractions: common denominators, addition, subtraction, multiplication and division

Solution

$f(x) = \frac{4}{x}$

$f(x+h) = \frac{4}{(x+h)}$ Start by finding $f(x+h)$

$f'(x) = \lim\limits_{h \to 0} \frac{f(x+h) - f(x)}{h}$

$= \lim\limits_{h \to 0} \left(\frac{\frac{4}{x+h} - \frac{4}{x}}{h} \right)$ Substitute for $f(x+h)$ and $f(x)$ in $f'(x) = \lim\limits_{h \to 0} \frac{f(x+h) - f(x)}{h}$

$= \lim\limits_{h \to 0} \left(\frac{\frac{4x - 4(x+h)}{x(x+h)}}{h} \right)$ To add or subtract fractions, find a common denominator.

$= \lim\limits_{h \to 0} \left(\frac{-4h}{x(x+h)} \times \frac{1}{h} \right)$ 'Tip and times' to move h onto the top fraction.

$= \lim\limits_{h \to 0} \frac{-4}{x^2 + xh}$

$= -\frac{4}{x^2}$ **Remember:** Drop $\lim\limits_{h \to 0}$ only in the last step!

Using the laws for differentiation (complex procedures)

Worked examples

1. If $t = \frac{v^3 - 3v + \sqrt{v}}{v^2} - t$, find $\frac{dt}{dv}$, expressing your answer using positive exponents.

2. If $y = p^3 - 2p$ and $p = 5 - 3x$, determine $\frac{dy}{dx}$.

> **You need to know**
> equations
> algebraic fractions
> basic exponential laws

Solutions

1. $t = \frac{v^3 - 3v + \sqrt{v}}{v^2} - t$

    $2t = \frac{v^3 - 3v + \sqrt{v}}{v^2}$ Rewrite the equation in terms of v: move $-t$ onto the right hand side, and divide through by 2.

    $t = \frac{v^3 - 3v + \sqrt{v}}{2v^2}$

    $t = \frac{v}{2} - \frac{3}{2}v^{-1} + \frac{v^{-\frac{3}{2}}}{2}$ Use exponential theory to rewrite the equation to have the variable only in the numerators.

> **Remember**
> Always give your final answer using positive exponents.

    $\frac{dt}{dx} = \frac{1}{2} + \frac{3}{2}v^{-2} - \frac{3}{4}v^{-\frac{5}{2}}$

    $= \frac{1}{2} + \frac{3}{2v^2} - \frac{3}{4v^{\frac{5}{2}}}$ Use $x^{-n} = \frac{1}{x^n}$ to express your answer using positive exponents.

2. $y = p^3 - 2p$

    $y = (5 - 3x)^3 - 2(5 - 3x)$ Substitute $(5 - 3x)$ for p.

    $= (25 - 30x + 9x^2)(5 - 3x) - 2(5 - 3x)$

    $= 125 - 150x + 45x^2 - 75x + 90x^2 - 27x^3 - 10 + 6x$

    $= 115 - 219x + 135x^2 - 27x^3$

    $\frac{dy}{dx} = 219 + 270x - 81x^2$

Tangents (complex procedures)

Worked examples

1. Find the value of x for which the tangent to the curve $f(x) = x^2 - 3x + 1$ is parallel to the tangent to the curve $g(x) = 2x^2 + 5x - 2$.

2. Hence find the equation of the tangent $h(x)$ to $f(x)$ at the x-value found above.

3. Hence find the point(s) of intersection between $h(x)$ and $g(x)$.

Solutions

1. $f(x) = x^2 - 3x + 1$ $\qquad$ $g(x) = 2x^2 + 5x - 2$
   $f'(x) = 2x - 3$ ....Equation ① $\qquad$ $g'(x) = 4x + 5$ ....Equation ②

   $2x - 3 = 4x + 5$ $\qquad$ For the tangents to be parallel, make $f'(x) = g'(x)$ and solve for x.

   $-2x = 8$
   $x = -4$

2. Required gradient: $f'(-4) = 2(-4) - 3 = -11$
   Point of contact: $(-4; (-4)^2 - 3(-4) + 1) = (-4; 29)$
   Equation of tangent:
   $y - 29 = -11(x + 4)$ $\qquad$ To find the required gradient, substitute for x in $f'(x)$ or $g'(x)$.

   $y = -11x - 15$

3. $\qquad h(x) = g(x)$
   $-11x - 15 = 2x^2 + 5x - 2$ $\qquad$ To find the point of intersection, put $h(x) = g(x)$ and solve for x.

   $0 = 2x^2 + 16x + 13$

   $x = \frac{-b \pm \sqrt{b^2 - 4ac}}{2a}$

   $= \frac{-16 \pm \sqrt{16^2 - 4(2)(13)}}{2(2)}$

   $x \approx 0{,}92$ OR $x \approx -7{,}08$
   $y \approx -11(0{,}92) - 15 = -25{,}12$ OR $y \approx -11(-7{,}08) - 15 = 62{,}88$
   Points of contact: $(0{,}92; -25{,}12)$ and $(-7{,}08; 62{,}88)$

Exercise 7 (complex procedures)

1. Use first principles to find the derivative of $f(x) = 2x^3$.

2. Use first principles to show that the derivative of $f(x) = ax^2 + bx + c$ is $2ax + b$.

3. Use the rules of differentiation to do the following:

   3.1 Determine $f'(x)$ if $f(x) = \frac{(x+2)^3}{\sqrt{x}}$.

   3.2 Determine $f'(\beta)$ if $f(\beta) = \left(\beta^{\frac{3}{2}} - 3\beta^{-\frac{1}{2}}\right)^2$.

4. If $y = 6 - 5x$, determine:
   - **4.1** $\frac{dy}{dx}$
   - **4.2** $\frac{dx}{dy}$
   - **4.3** Hence prove that $\frac{dy}{dx} = 1 \div \frac{dx}{dy}$.

5. Find:
   - **5.1** $\frac{d}{d\beta} f(\beta)$, if $f(\beta) = \beta - \beta^{\frac{1}{4}} + \beta^{-2\sqrt{3}}$, giving your answer in positive exponents
   - **5.2** $\frac{d}{dx}\left(\frac{dy}{dx}\right)$ if $y = -3x^4 + 4x^3 + 6x^2 - 22$.

6. If $f(t) = (2t - 1)^2(\sqrt{t} - 1)$, determine $f'(2)$.

7. Determine $D_t\left(\frac{t^2 - 3t^{-2}}{2\sqrt{t^3}}\right)$.

Graphs of cubic functions

General form: $y = ax^3 + bx^2 + cx + d$.

Shape: Basic shape is determined by the value of a.

- If $a > 0$: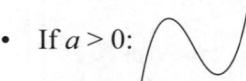

- If $a < 0$: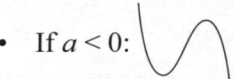

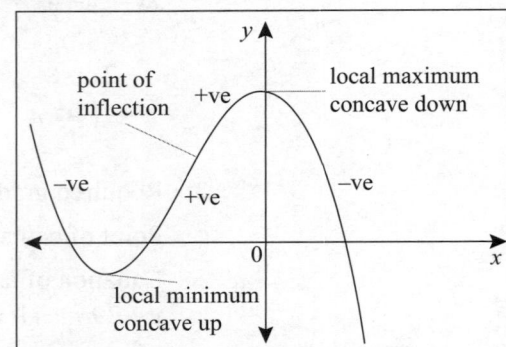

Intercepts:
- To find the *x*-intercept: make $y = 0$ and solve for x.
- To find the *y*-intercept: make $x = 0$ and solve for y.

Stationary points:
- A **local minimum** is found where the gradient changes from negative to positive.
- A **local maximum** is found where the gradient changes from positive to negative.
- The gradient does not change sign at the point of inflection.

To find local minimum and maximum turning points:

Determine $f'(x)$:
- Set $f'(x) = 0$ and solve for the *x*-value(s) of the turning point(s).
- Substitute the value(s) of x in $f(x)$ and calculate the *y*-value(s) of the turning point(s).

To find a point of inflection:

Determine $f''(x)$:
- Set $f''(x) = 0$ and solve for the *x*-value of the point of inflection.
- Substitute the value of x in $f(x)$ and calculate the *y*-value of the point of inflection.

To determine concavity at the respective turning points:

Use the second derivative test, which states that if a function is twice differentiable at the critical point x (i.e. where c is the *x*-value of the turning point) then:
- if $f''(c) < 0$ then f is concave down and has a local maximum at x
- if $f''(c) > 0$ then f is concave up and has a local minimum at x
- if $f''(c) = 0$, the test is inconclusive.

Worked examples

1. $f(x) = x^3 - 4x^2 - 11x + 30$
   1.1 Determine the coordinates of the x- and the y-intercepts.
   1.2 Determine the coordinates of the local turning points.
   1.3 Sketch the graph of $f(x)$.
   1.4 Find the point of inflection.
   1.5 For which value(s) of x is $f(x) > 0$?
   1.6 For which value(s) of x is $f'(x) > 0$?

2. Without sketching the graph of $f(x) = x^3 - x$:
   2.1 determine where f is concave up and where it is concave down
   2.2 determine where f is decreasing.

You need to know
- factor and remainder theorem to factorise cubic equations
- quadratic equations
- functional notation

Solutions

1. $f(x) = x^3 - 4x^2 - 11x + 30$

   1.1 x-intercepts: $0 = x^3 - 4x^2 - 11x + 30$
   $0 = (x - 2)(x - 5)(x + 3)$ To find the x-intercept make $y = 0$ and solve for x.
   $\therefore x = 2$, or $x = 5$ or $x = -3$ To find the y-intercept make $x = 0$ and solve for y.
   y-intercept: $f(0) = (0)^3 - 4(0)^2 - 11(0) + 30$
   $y = 30$

   1.2 $f(x) = x^3 - 4x^2 - 11x + 30$
   $f'(x) = 3x^2 - 8x - 11$
   $0 = (3x - 11)(x + 1)$ To find the stationary points make $f'(x) = 0$ and solve for x.
   $\therefore x = \frac{11}{3}$ or $x = -1$

   $f\left(\frac{11}{3}\right) = \left(\frac{11}{3} - 2\right)\left(\frac{11}{3} - 5\right)\left(\frac{11}{3} + 3\right)$
   $= \frac{-400}{27} \approx -14{,}81$

   $f(-1) = (-1 - 2)(-1 - 5)(-1 + 3) = 36$ Substitute the respective x-values in $f(x)$ to calculate the respective y-values.

   Turning points are found at $\left(\frac{11}{3}; \frac{-400}{27}\right)$ and $(-1; 36)$

   1.3 $\left(\frac{11}{3}; \frac{-400}{27}\right)$ is a local minimum and $(-1; 36)$ a local maximum.

   To sketch the graph:
   The basic shape is determined by the value of a:

   If $a > 0$: ⋎⋏

   If $a < 0$: ⋏⋎

   - Use a suitable scale. Mark off the x and y-intercepts and the local stationary points.
   - Sketch the graph by joining all the points with a smooth curve.
   - Clearly indicate the values for all stationary points.

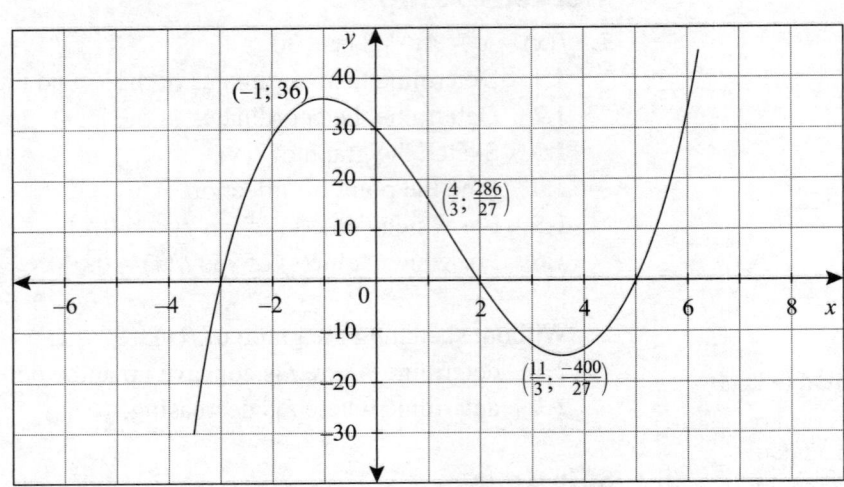

- $f(x) > 0$ is found where the graph lies above the x-axis.
- $f'(x)$ = the gradient, and $f'(x) > 0$ is found where the graph is increasing, i.e. the gradient is positive.

    1.4 $f''(x) = 6x - 8$

           $0 = 6x - 8$ To find a point of inflection, make $f''(x) = 0$ and solve for x. Substitute the x-values in $f(x)$ to calculate the y-values.

        $\therefore x = \frac{8}{6} = \frac{4}{3}$

        $f\left(\frac{4}{3}\right) = \left(\frac{4}{3} - 2\right)\left(\frac{4}{3} - 5\right)\left(\frac{4}{3} + 3\right)$

             $= \frac{286}{27} \approx 10{,}59$

    Point of inflection: $\left(\frac{4}{3}; \frac{286}{27}\right)$

    1.5 $f(x) > 0$ where $(-3; 2) \cup (5; \infty)$ The values for which $f(x) > 0$ and $f'(x) > 0$ can be read directly from the graph.

    or you can write: where $-3 < x < 2$ or $x > 5; x \in \mathbb{R}$

    1.6 $f'(x) > 0$ where $(-\infty; -1) \cup \left(\frac{11}{3}; \infty\right)$

    or you can write: where $x < -1$ or $x > \frac{11}{3}; x \in \mathbb{R}$

2. $f(x) = x^3 - 3x$

    2.1 $f'(x) = 3x^2 - 3$

           $0 = 3x^2 - 3$

           $0 = 3(x^2 - 1)$

           $0 = 3(x - 1)(x + 1)$

Stationary points are found at $x = 1$ and at $x = -1$.

$f''(x) = 6x$

$f''(1) = 6$

$f''(x) > 0$ at $x = 1$, $\therefore f$ is concave up at $x = 1$.

$f''(-1) = -6$

$f''(x) < 0$ at $x = -1$, $\therefore f$ is concave down at $x = -1$.

Remember

When you use $f''(x)$ to determine concavity:
- if $f''(c) < 0$ then f is concave down and has a local maximum at x
- if $f''(c) > 0$ then f is concave up and has a local minimum at x.

2.2 To determine where f is decreasing:

> $f'(x) < 0$ is found where the **graph** of the **gradient** function falls below the x-axis.
> A curve is increasing where $f'(x) > 0$ and decreasing where $f'(x) < 0$.

$f'(x) < 0$
$f'(x) = 3x^2 - 3$
$3x^2 - 3 < 0$
$3(x-1)(x+1) < 0$
f is decreasing where $-1 < x < 1$.

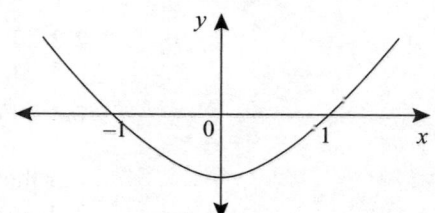

Summary of shapes and characteristics of cubic curves with two stationary points

Graphs with $a > 0$ and TWO stationary points

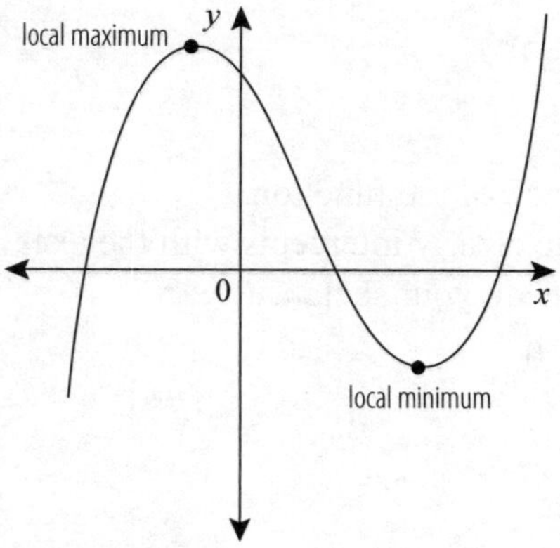

3 x-intercepts 2 turning points	2 x-intercepts 2 turning points	1 x-intercept 2 turning points

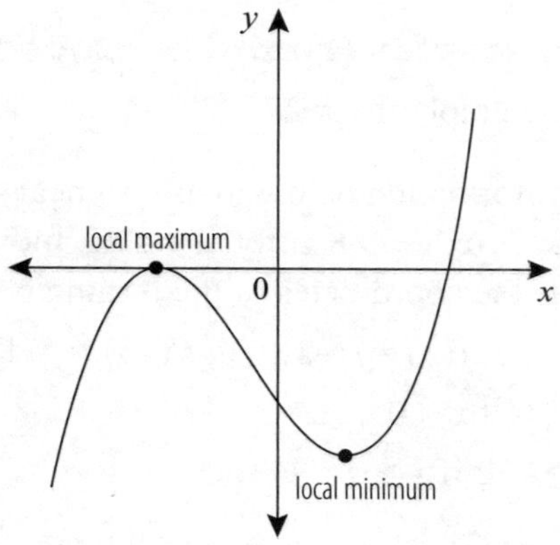

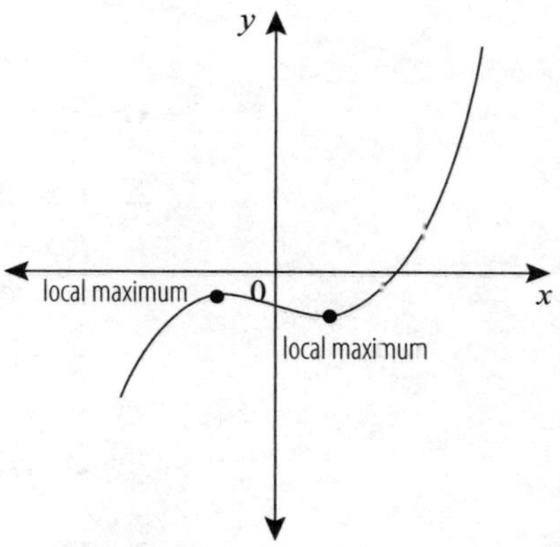

Graphs with $a > 0$ and TWO stationary points

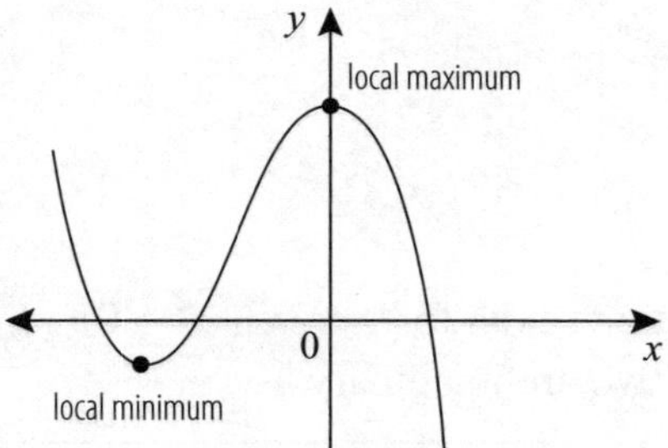

3 x-intercepts 2 turning points	2 x-intercepts 2 turning points	1 x-intercept 2 turning points

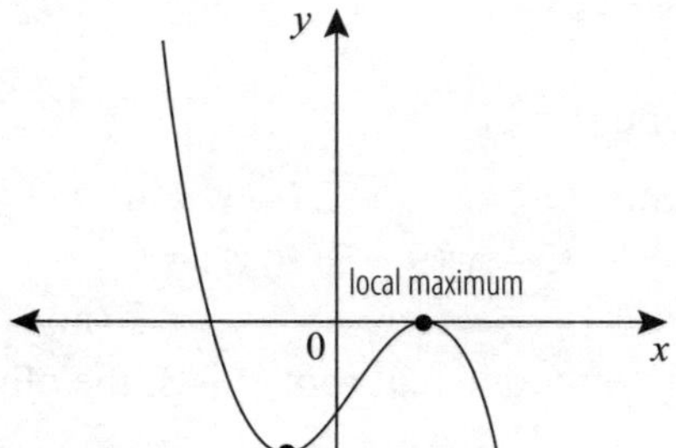

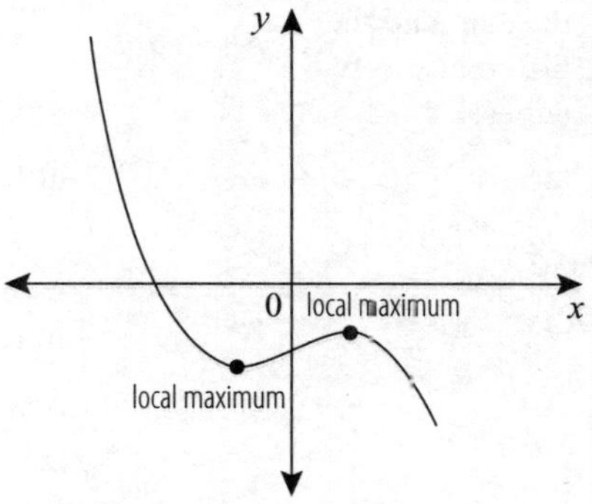

Exercise 8

1. Given: $f(x) = x^3 - x^2 - x + 1$.

    1.1 Prove that $x - 1$ is a factor of $f(x)$. Hence determine the other factors and the values of x for which $f(x) = 0$.

    1.2 Calculate the stationary points for $f(x)$.

    1.3 Use this information to draw a neat sketch graph of f showing all intercepts with the **axes** and the coordinates for the stationary points.

TOPIC 6 Differential calculus

1.4 For which values of x is $f(x) > 0$?

1.5 For which values of x is $f'(x) > 0$?

1.6 Determine the equation of the tangent to the curve when $x = -2$.

2. Given: $y = x^3 + 3x^2 - 9x - 27$.

   2.1 Sketch the graph, indicating the point of inflection.

   2.2 For which values of x is this graph increasing? Set your answer out using interval notation.

   2.3 For which values of x is $f(x) < 0$?

3. For the function defined by $f(x) = 5 + 3x^2 - x^3$, determine the concavity, inflection points, local maximum and minimum points, and the intervals where this function is increasing or decreasing. Sketch the graph of this function.

4. Sketch the graph of $f(x) = -x^3 + 2x^2 + 7x + 4$, clearly showing all intercepts with axes, turning points and their coordinates. Show all working details.

Worked examples (complex procedures)

1. Sketch the graph of $y = 27 - x^3$.

2. Use the information below to draw a neat sketch of the function $f: x \to ax^3 + bx^2 + cx + d$ for $x, y \in \mathbb{R}$. Indicate clearly intercepts with the axes as well as the coordinates of the turning points on your sketch.
   - $f(0) = 27, f(3) = f(-3) = 0, f'(-3) = f'(1) = 0$
   - $f(x) \leq 0$ if $x < 0$
   - $f(x) \geq -32$ if $x > 0$

3. Discuss the concavity for $f(x) = x^4 - 4x^3$.

> **You need to know**
> how to factorise the sum and the difference of two cubes:
> $(x^3 - y^3) = (x - y)$
> $(x^2 + xy + y^2)$
> $(x^3 + y^3) = (x + y)$
> $(x^2 - xy + y^2)$

Solutions

1. $y = 27 - x^3$

   Shape: $a < 0$, ∴

   y-intercept: $y = 27$

   x-intercepts: $\quad 27 - x^3 = 0$
   $$(3 - x)(9 + 3x + x^2) = 0$$
   $$x = 3 \text{ (no solutions exist for } 9 + 3x + x^2 = 0)$$

   Therefore only one real root exists, the other two are imaginary.

   Local maximum and minimum points:
   $f(x) = 27 - x^3$
   $f'(x) = -3x^2$
   $\quad 0 = 3x^2$
   $\therefore x = 0$
   At $x = 0, f(0) = 27$

   Points of inflection: these are found when the **gradient** of the curve **does not change**, in other words it remains **neither** positive nor negative. Because this graph has only one real x-intercept, we must suspect that this stationary point is a point of inflection.

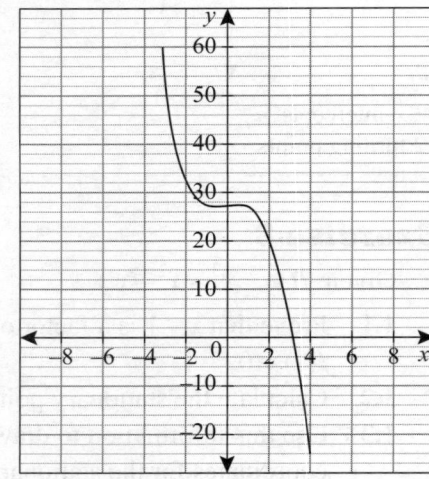

$$f''(x) = 6x$$
$$0 = 6x$$
$$x = \frac{0}{6} = 0$$

At $x = 0, f(0) = 27$ ∴ $(0; 27)$ is a point of inflection.

2. Carefully examine and interpret all the given information:

   $f(0) = 27$: $(0; 27)$ i.e. the y-intercept for this graph is 27

   $f(3) = f(-3) = 0$: $(3; 0)$ and $(-3; 0)$ are x-intercepts

   $f'(-3) = f'(1) = 0$: the turning points for the graph are found at $x = -3$ and $x = 1$

   $f(x) \leq 0$ if $x < 0$: the graph has a local maximum value of 0

   $f(x) \geq -32$ if $x > 0$: the graph has a local minimum value of -32

   The local maximum is found at $(-3; 0)$.

   The local minimum is found at $(1; -32)$.

   Use all the information to sketch the graph.

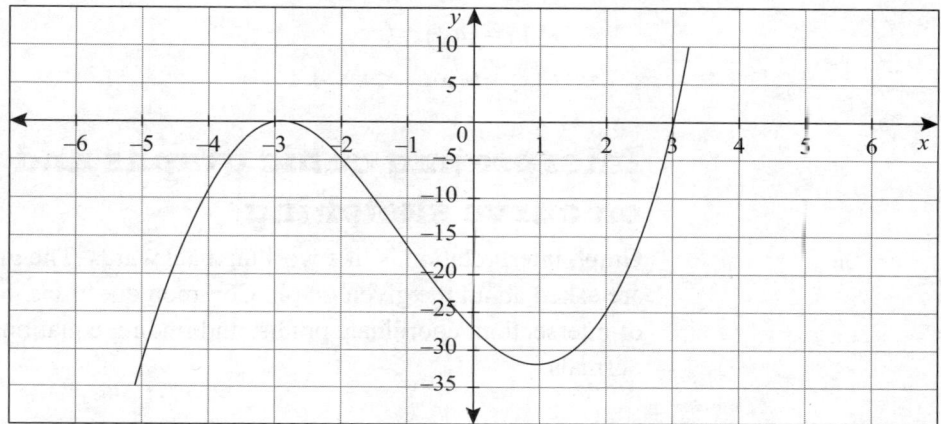

3. $f(x) = x^4 - 4x^3$
   $f'(x) = 4x^3 - 12x^2$
   $0 = 4x^2(x - 3)$
   $x = 0$ or $x = 3$
   $f''(x) = 12x^2 - 24x$
   $f''(3) = 12(3)^2 - 24(3) = 36$

   Use $f''(x)$ to determine concavity:
   - if $f''(c) < 0$ then f is concave down and has a local maximum at x
   - if $f''(c) > 0$ then f is concave up and has a local minimum at x.

   $f''(x) > 0$ at $x = 3$ ∴ f is concave up at $x = 3$.

   $f''(0) = 0$ which is inconclusive.   Results are inconclusive when $f''(0) = 0$. The first derivative must then be used to determine concavity.

   $f'(-1) = 4(-1)^3 - 12(-1)^2$
   $= -16$

   $f'(1) = 4(1)^3 - 12(1)^2$
   $= -8$

   $f'(x)$ is decreasing both to the left and the right of $x = 0$

   ∴ $(0; 0)$ is a point of inflection.

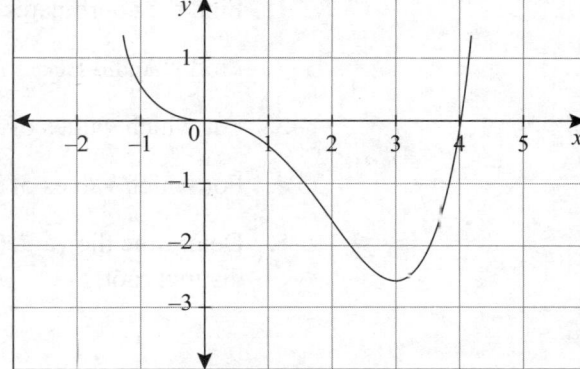

Note
While it is not necessary to draw a graph to discuss concavity, the graph will help you to understand and check solution.

Exercise 9 (complex procedures)

1. Discuss the concavity for $g(x) = x^4 - 6x^2$. Use this information and any other necessary calculations to help you to sketch the graph of $g(x)$.

2. Discuss the concavity of $g(x) = x + \frac{4}{x}$.

3. Given: $f(x) = x^3 - 3x^2 + 3x + 2$.

   3.1 Determine the stationary points, if any.

   3.2 Sketch the graph of f.

   3.3 For what values of x is $f(x) \leq 0$?

   3.4 For what values of x is $f'(x) > 0$?

4. Use the information given below to sketch the graph of $f(x) = ax^3 + bx^2 + cx + d$:
   - $f(1) = f(4) = 0$
   - $f(0) = f(3) = 4$
   - $f'(1) = f'(3) = 0$
   - $f'(x) > 0$ for $1 < x < 4$

Interpreting cubic graphs and problems based on curve sketching

Graph interpretation is like working backwards. The graph is given and questions are asked about the given graph. Common questions involve distances, points of intersection, coordinate points, and finding equations of graphs, tangents and normals.

Worked examples

- The graphs represents the functions $f(x) = x^3 - 2x^2 - 4x + 8$ and $g(x) = 3x + 1$.
- $f(x)$ cuts the x-axis at D and A and the y-axis at B. C and A are turning points for graph f.
- The two graphs meet at F, G and H.
- $g(x)$ cuts the y-axis at E and the x-axis at I.

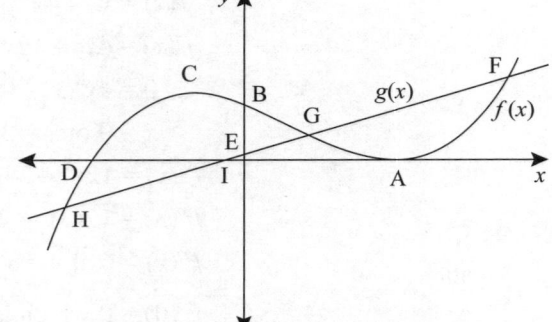

1. Find the coordinates of points A and C.

2. Find DA and EB.

3. For which values of x is $f(x) > 0$?

4. For which values of x is $f(x)$ decreasing?

5. Determine the value(s) of k for which $x^3 - 2x^2 - 4x + 8 = k$ will have three distinct roots.

You need to know
- factorising trinomials
- solving quadratic equations
- using functional notation

Solutions

1. Points A and C are local minimum and maximum points. Use $f'(x) = 0$ to find the x-values for A and C:
$$f(x) = x^3 - 2x^2 - 4x + 8$$
$$f'(x) = 3x^2 - 4x - 4$$
$$0 = 3x^2 - 4x - 4$$
$$0 = (3x + 2)(x - 2)$$
$$x = -\tfrac{2}{3} \text{ or } x = 2$$
$$f\left(-\tfrac{2}{3}\right) = \left(-\tfrac{2}{3}\right)^3 - 2\left(-\tfrac{2}{3}\right)^2 - 4\left(-\tfrac{2}{3}\right) + 8 = \tfrac{256}{27} \approx 9{,}48$$
$$f(2) = (2)^3 - 2(2)^2 - 4(2) + 8 = 0$$
$$\therefore C\left(-\tfrac{2}{3}; \tfrac{256}{27}\right) \text{ and } A(2; 0)$$

Don't forget to find the corresponding y-values. Give your answers in coordinate form.

You need to know
factorisation using grouping

2. $f(x) = x^3 - 2x^2 - 4x + 8$
$$0 = x^2(x - 2) - 4(x - 2)$$

Points D and A are x-intercepts. Make $y = 0$ and solve for x by factorisation.

$$0 = (x - 2)(x^2 - 4)$$
$$0 = (x - 2)(x - 2)(x + 2)$$
$$x = 2 \text{ or } x = -2$$
$\therefore$ D(–2; 0) and A(2; 0)
$\therefore$ DA = 4 units

$$f(0) = 0^3 - 2(0)^2 - 4(0) + 8 = 8$$
$\therefore$ B (0; 8)

Points E and B are y-intercepts. Use $x = 0$ in each case and solve for y.

$$g(0) = 3(0) + 1 = 1$$
$\therefore$ E(0; 1)
$\therefore$ EB = 7 units

You need to know
- set builder notation
- interval notation

3. $f(x) > 0$ when $x > -2$, $x \neq 2$ (set builder notation)
OR $(-2; \infty)$, $x \neq 2$ (interval notation)

4. $f(x) < 0$ when $-\tfrac{2}{3} < x < 2$ (set builder notation)

A graph is decreasing where its gradient is negative.

OR $\left(-\tfrac{2}{3}; 2\right)$ (interval notation)

5. Note that $k = y$. For $x^3 - 2x^2 - 4x + 8$ to have three distinct roots, the graph needs to cut the x-axis anywhere between the maximum and minimum turning points.
i.e. $0 < y < 9\tfrac{13}{27}$
$\therefore 0 < k < 9\tfrac{13}{27}$

TOPIC 6 *Differential calculus*

Finding the equation of a cubic function

The method used to find the equation for a cubic function depends on the type of information given. In worked example 1 below, the x-intercepts are given, and in worked example 2 the turning points are given. In both cases:
- use substitution to set up equations in terms of the unknown values given
- solve the equations simultaneously.

Worked examples

1. The graph alongside is represented by the function $f(x) = ax^3 + bx^2 + cx$. Use the information given to determine the values of a, b and c.

2. Given the graph of $g(x) = 2x^3 + ax^2 + bx - 1$, with turning points $(-2; -5)$ and $(-1; -6)$, determine the values of a and b.

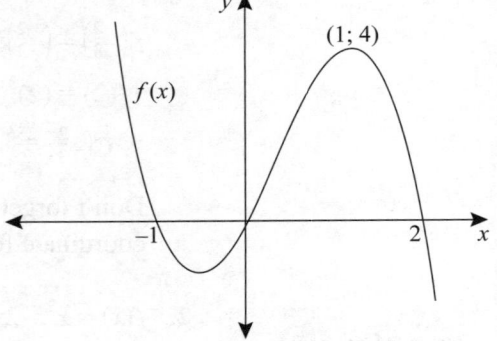

Solutions

You need to know
- functional notation
- solution of basic equations
- algebraic multiplication and simplification

1. Because $x = -1, 0$, and 2 are roots of the equation, we can write $f(x)$ in the form $f(x) = a(x + 1)(x - 0)(x - 2)$. Substitute for x and y using any other given point:
$f(x) = a(x + 1)(x - 0)(x - 2)$
$(1; 4)$ is a point of the graph
$\therefore f(1) = a(1 + 1)(1 + 0)(1 - 2)$
$\quad 4 = a(2)(1)(-1)$
$\quad 4 = -2a$
$\therefore a = -2$

Thus $f(x) = -2x(x + 1)(x - 2)$
$\qquad = -2x^3 + 2x^2 + 4x$
$\therefore a = -2, b = 2, c = 4$

You need to know
simultaneous equations

2. The turning points are given. Find $g'(x)$. Substitute the relevant x-values in $g'(x)$ to set up two equations:
$g(x) = 2x^3 + ax^2 + bx - 1$
$g'(x) = 6x^2 + 2ax + b$
$g'(-2) = 6(-2)^2 + 2a(-2) + b$
$\quad 0 = 24 - 4a + b$
$\therefore b = 4a - 24$ .... ①

$g'(-1) = 6(-1)^2 + 2a(-1) + b$
$\quad 0 = 6 - 2a + b \therefore b = 2a - 6$ .... ②

$4a - 24 = 2a - 6$ \qquad Solve simultaneously for a and b.
$\quad 2a = 18$
$\therefore a = 9, b = 2(9) - 6 = 12$

Exercise 10

1. Use the information given in the graph to find the equation for the graph.

   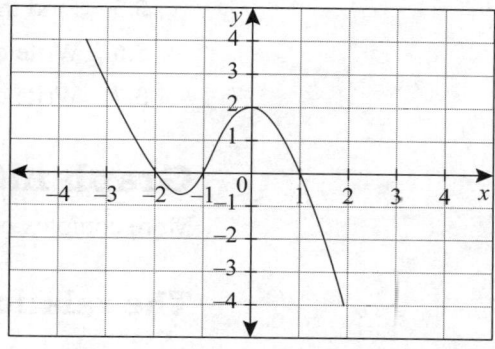

2. Use the information given in the graph to find the equation for the graph.

   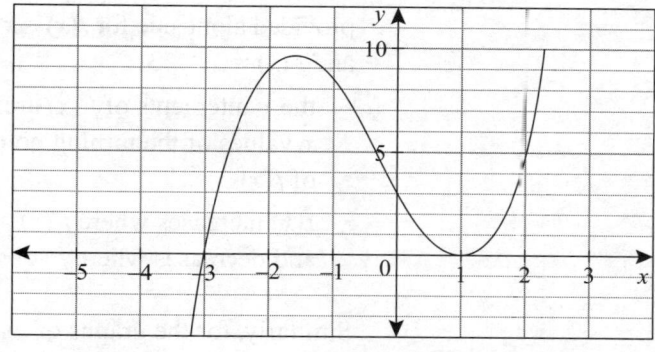

3. Given the graph of $f(x) = x^3 + ax^2 + bx - 4$, with turning points $(1; 0)$ and $(3; -4)$, determine the values of a and b.

4. Sketched below is the graph of
   $g(x) = -2x^3 - 3x^2 + 12x + 20$
   $= -(2x - 5)(x + 2)^2$.

   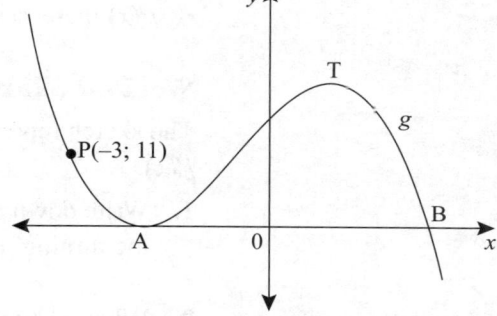

   4.1 Determine the length of AB.

   4.2 Determine the x-coordinate of T.

   4.3 Determine the equation of the tangent to g at $P(-3; 11)$, in the form $y = \ldots$.

   4.4 Determine the value(s) of k for which $-2x^3 - 3x^2 + 12x + 20 = k$ has three distinct roots.

   4.5 Determine the coordinates of the point of inflection.

   4.6 For which value(s) of x is $f(x) < 0$?

   4.7 For which value(s) of x is $f'(x) < 0$?

5. The graph represents the functions f and g with $f(x) = ax^3 - cx - 2$ and $g(x) = x - 2$. A and $(-1; 0)$ are the x-intercepts of f. The graphs of f and g intersect at A and C and at $(0; -2)$.

   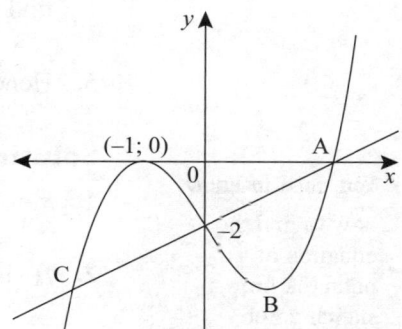

   5.1 Determine the coordinates of A.

   5.2 Show by calculation that $a = 1$ and $c = 3$.

   5.3 Determine the coordinates of B, a turning point of f.

TOPIC 6 Differential calculus

5.4 Show that the line BC is parallel to the *x*-axis.

5.5 Find the equation of the tangent to $f(x)$ at $x = -2$.

5.6 Write down the value(s) of k for which $f(x) = k$ will have only ONE root.

5.7 Write down the values of x for which $f'(x) < 0$.

Graph interpretation (complex procedures)

More complex procedures often involve interpretations from derivatives.

The relationship between $f(x)$, $f'(x)$, and $f''(x)$

As can be seen in the graphs provided alongside for $f(x) = x^3 - 3x$ and $f'(x) = 3x^2 - 3$:

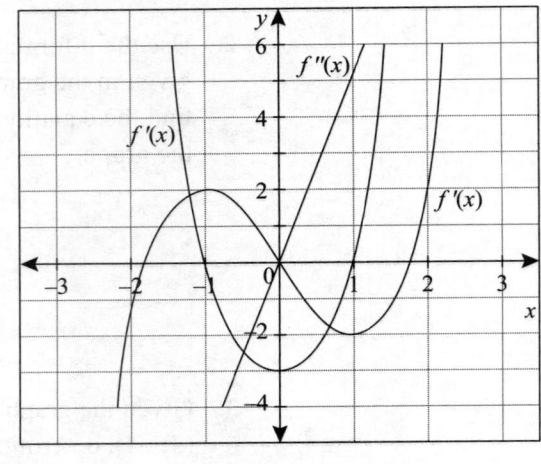

- the *x*-intercepts of $f'(x)$ are the *x*-values of the turning points of $f(x)$
- $f(x)$ increases where $f'(x) > 0$ and decreases where $f'(x) < 0$.

Similarly, for the graphs of $f'(x) = 3x^2 - 3$ and $f''(x) = 6x$:

- the *x*-intercept of $f''(x)$ is the *x*-value of the turning point of $f'(x)$
- $f'(x)$ increases where $f''(x) > 0$ and decreases where $f''(x) < 0$.

Worked examples

The sketch represents the graph of $f'(x)$.

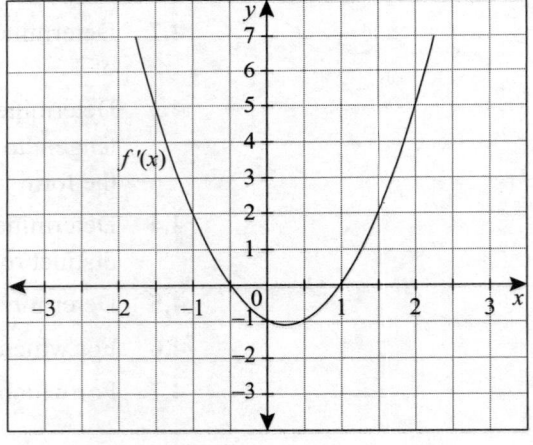

1. Write down the *x*-value(s) of the turning point(s) of $f(x)$.

2. What is the value of the gradient of $f(x)$ at $x = -1$?

3. For what values of x is $f(x)$ increasing?

4. Use the given information to find the equation for $f'(x)$.

5. Hence find the equation for $f(x)$.

> **You need to know**
> how to find the equation of a parabola from a sketch graph

Solutions

1. $x = -0{,}5$ or $x = 1$

2. $f(-1) = 2$

3. $x < -0{,}5$ or $x > 1$ $f(x)$ is increasing where $f'(x) > 0$

4. $y = a(x + 0{,}5)(x - 1)$
    $-1 = a(0{,}5)(-2)$
    $\therefore a = 2$
    $f'(x) = 2(x + 0{,}5)(x - 1)$
    $f'(x) = 2x^2 - x - 1$

    Substitute $(0; -1)$ for x and y.

5. $f(x) = \frac{2}{3}x^3 - \frac{1}{2}x^2 - x + d$

    Work 'backwards' from $f'(x)$ to find $f(x)$ by trial and error. Note that you cannot find the value of the y-intercept d from the given information.

Worked example

Finding the equation of a cubic curve is not always a simple procedure. The information given for the graph below indicates that we set up and use three different equations and solve them simultaneously.

Determine the equation of the cubic function $f(x) = ax^3 + bx^2 + cx + d$, given in the graph below, where $(2; 5)$ and $(1; 4)$ are the local maximum and minimum respectively and -15 is the value of the y-intercept.

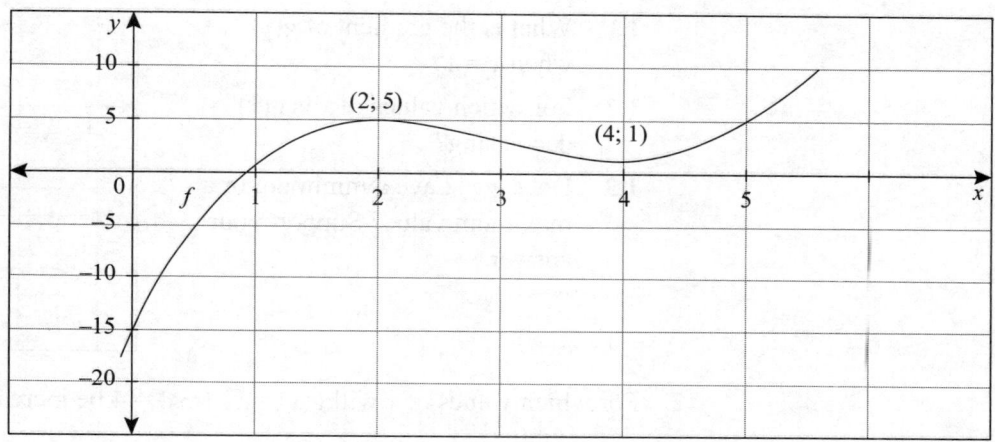

Solution

You need to know
how to use elimination to solve systems of simultaneous equations

Two turning points are found at $f'(x) = 3ax^2 + 2bx + c = 0$

$(2; 5)$ is a turning point: $\therefore f'(2) = 3a(2)^2 + 2b(2) + c$

$0 = 12a + 4b + c$ ....①

$(4; 1)$ is a turning point: $\therefore f'(4) = 3a(4)^2 + 2b(4) + c$

$0 = 48a + 8b + c$ ....②

$f(x) = ax^3 + bx^2 + cx + d$

From the graph: $d = -15$

We have three unknowns, so we need three equations.

$(2; 5)$ is a point on the graph:

$f(2) = a(2)^3 + b(2)^2 + c(2) - 15$

$5 = 8a + 4b + 2c - 15$

$20 = 8a + 4b + 2c$

$10 = 4a + 2b + c$ ....③

① – ②: $0 = 12a + 4b + c$
         $0 = -48a - 8b - c$
         ─────────────────
         $0 = -36a - 4b$

∴ $0 = -9a - b$ ……………………………… ④

① – ③: $0 = 12a + 4b + c$
         $-10 = -4a - 2b - c$
         ─────────────────
         $-10 = +8a + 2b$

∴ $-5 = 4a + b$ ……………………………… ⑤

④ + ⑤: $0 = -9a - b$
         $-5 = 4a + b$
         ─────────────
         $-5 = -5a$

∴ $a = 1, b = -9, c = 24$

∴ $f(x) = x^3 - 9x^2 + 24x - 15$

Exercise 11 (complex procedures and problem solving)

1. The graph of $g'(x)$ is provided.

   1.1 What is the gradient of $g(x)$ when $x = 1$?
   1.2 For which values of x is $g(x)$ decreasing?
   1.3 Does $g(x)$ have a minimum or a maximum value? Support your answer.

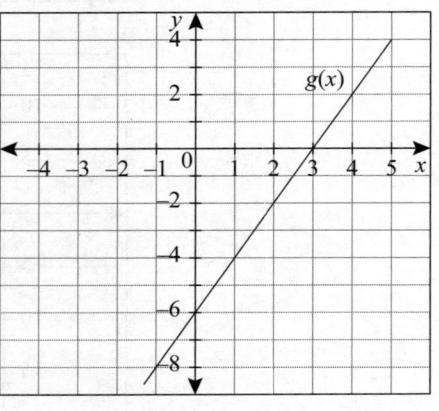

2. For which values of x will $g(x) = x^3 + 3x^2 - 4$ be increasing?

3. Given: $h(x) = 2x^3 + x^2 + x - 4$.

   3.1 Prove that $h(x) = 2x^3 + x^2 + x - 4$ does not have any maximum or minimum values.
   3.2 Find the coordinates of the point of inflection for $h(x)$.

4. Use the graph given alongside to determine the values of x for which:

   4.1 $f(x) \geq 0$
   4.2 $f'(x) \geq 0$
   4.3 $f'(x) > f(x)$
   4.4 $f'(x) \cdot f(x) \leq 0$

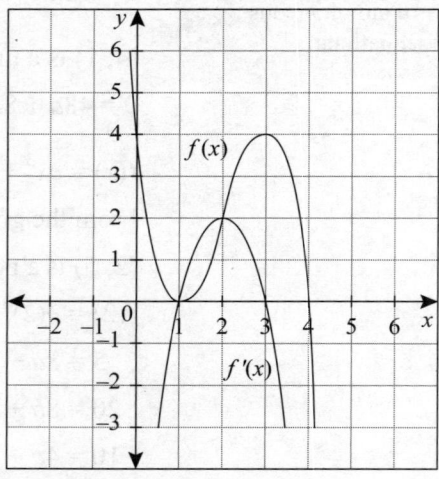

5. Use the information given in the graph alongside to determine the equation of the cubic function shown.

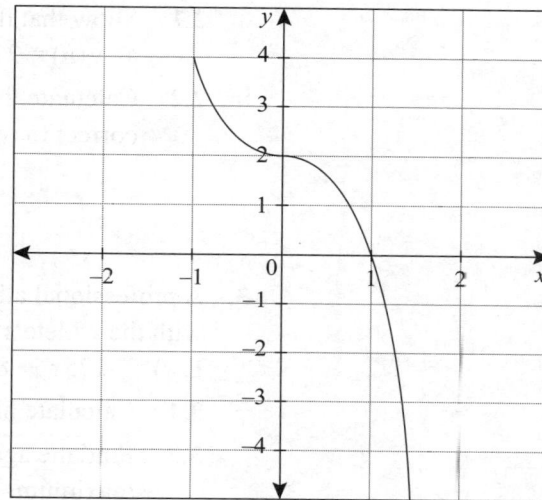

6. Given that $f'(x) = -5x^2 - 7x + 6$:
   6.1 determine the values of x for which $f(x)$ is decreasing
   6.2 if $f(0) = 2$, determine $f(x)$.

Using maxima and minima to solve problems

Calculus can be used to solve problems involving maximum or minimum values in a wide variety of contexts. In each case the derivative must be used to find the maximum or minimum value(s), which can then be used to solve the problem.

An expression can only be derived in terms of one variable. This means that to use calculus all problems must be translated into **an equation written in terms of only one variable**.

> **Steps for using calculus to solve problems involving maxima and minima**
> 1. Set up a diagram if necessary to help you to understand the problem.
> 2. Use what you are given to set up an equation in terms of only ONE variable.
> 3. Determine $f'(x)$.
> 4. Solve for $f'(x) = 0$.
> 5. Tie up all 'loose ends', i.e. reread the problem and make sure you have answered the question, using words where necessary.

You need to know
- formulae for the volume and total surface area for all shapes, including cones, spheres, rectangular prisms, cylinders
- manipulation of equations, both linear and quadratic
- translating words into algebraic equations
- changing the subject of the formula

Worked examples

1. A farmer wants to fence a rectangular field with an area of 441 m². She has a restricted budget and needs to minimise the amount of fencing she uses.
   1.1 Find the minimum perimeter that will enclose this rectangular field.
   1.2 If this farmer decides to use an existing cliff face as one of the longer sides, find the new length and breadth of the field (which will still enclose 441 m²), and the new minimum amount of fencing required.
   1.3 The farmer decides to add a 3 m gate onto the length of this field. Calculate the area of the new cliff-side field that has had a 3 m gate added.

2. The vertical height of the cone shown on the next page is h cm, the slant height is 9 cm and the radius is r cm.

TOPIC 6 *Differential calculus*

2.1 Show that the volume of this cone can be expressed as $V(h) = 27\pi h - \frac{1}{3}\pi h^3$.

2.2 Calculate the maximum volume of this cone, correct to two decimal places.

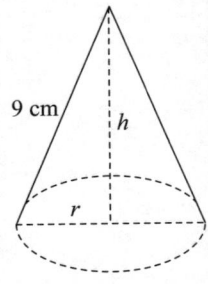

3. A professional athlete's earning ability in rand, E, varies with the athlete's age in years, x, according to the formula $E(x) = -125x^2 + 8\,000x - 4\,650$.

   3.1 Calculate his earnings at age 28.

   3.2 Find the age at which this professional athlete's earnings will be at a maximum.

   3.3 Calculate his maximum earnings.

Solutions

1. 1.1 Let one side be x:

> **You need to know**
> - finding the first derivative using the power rule
> - addition and subtraction of fractions
> - solution of basic equations

Step 1 Set up a diagram to help you to understand the problem.	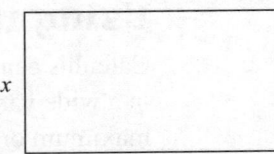

$$\text{Area} = x \times \text{length}$$
$$441 = x \times \text{length}$$
$$\therefore \text{length} = \frac{441}{x}$$

Step 2 Use what you are given to set up an equation in terms of only one variable.

$$\text{Perimeter} = 2l + 2b$$
$$\therefore P(x) = 2x + 2\left(\frac{441}{x}\right)$$
$$= 2x + 882x^{-1}$$

Step 3 Determine $f'(x)$.

$$P'(x) = 2 + 2(-1)(441)x^{-2}$$
$$P'(x) = 2 - \frac{882}{x^2}$$

Step 4 Solve for $f'(x) = 0$.

$$0 = 2 - \frac{882}{x^2}$$
$$0 = 2x^2 - 882$$
$$x^2 = 441$$
$$x = 21 \text{ m}$$

Step 5 Tie up all loose ends, i.e. reread the problem and make sure you have answered the question.

Dimensions of field = 21 m by 21 m
$$\therefore \text{Minimum perimeter} = 2(21 + 21)$$
$$= 84 \text{ m}$$

1.2 $\therefore P(x) = 2x + \left(\frac{441}{x}\right)$

$\therefore P'(x) = 2 - \frac{441}{x^2}$ Farmer now only needs to enclose three sides.

$0 = 2 - \frac{441}{x^2}$

$0 = 2x^2 - 441$

$x^2 = \frac{441}{2}$

$x = 21\frac{21\sqrt{2}}{2} \approx 14{,}85$ m

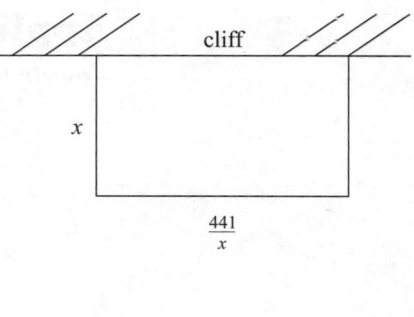

New dimensions: breadth is 14,85 m and length is (441 ÷ 14,85) = 29,70 m
Therefore new minimum amount of fencing is (2 × 14,85) + 29,70 = 59,4 m.

1.3 Breadth = 14,85 m.
Length = 29,7 + 3 = 32,7 m
New area = 14,85 × 32,7 = 485,6 m².

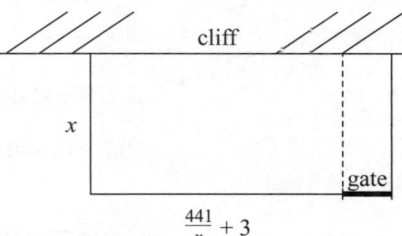

You need to know
- formulae for volume and total surface area of cones, spheres, rectangular prisms, cylinders
- the theorem of Pythagoras

2. Volume $= \frac{1}{3}\pi r^2 h$ formula for volume of a cone

$r^2 = 9^2 - h^2$ Pythagoras

2.1 Volume $= \frac{1}{3}\pi r^2 h$

$V(h) = \frac{1}{3}\pi(9^2 - h^2)h$ Substitute for r to express the volume in terms of h only.

$V(h) = \frac{1}{3}\pi h(81 - h^2)$

$V(h) = 27\pi h - \frac{1}{3}\pi h^3$

2.2 $V'(h) = 27\pi - \pi h^2$ Maximum volume is found when $V'(h) = 0$.

$0 = 27\pi - \pi h^2$

$\pi h^2 = 27\pi$

$h = \sqrt{27} = 3\sqrt{3}$ cm

$\therefore$ Maximum volume $= 27\pi(3\sqrt{3}) - \frac{1}{3}\pi(3\sqrt{3})^3 = 293{,}84$ cm³

3. $E(x) = -125x^2 + 8\,000x - 4\,650$

3.1 $E(x) = -125x^2 + 8\,000x - 4\,650$

$E(28) = -125(28)^2 + 8\,000(28) - 4\,650$ To find earnings at any particular age simply substitute for x.

$= R121\,350$

At age 28 he will earn R121 350.

3.2 $E'(x) = -250x + 8\,000$

$0 = -250x + 8\,000$ Solve $E'(x) = 0$ to find the maximum value for x.

$250x = 8\,000$

$x = 32$

Earnings will be at a maximum when the athlete is 32.

3.3 $E(x) = -125x^2 + 8\,000x - 4\,650$

$E(32) = -125(32)^2 + 8\,000(32) - 4\,650$

$= R123\,350$

Athlete's maximum earnings: R123 350

Applications involving the calculus of motion

You are familiar with the relationship between distance, speed and time.

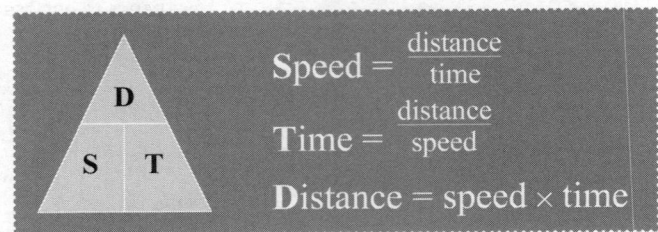

When an equation of motion is represented by a curve, rates of change can be used to calculate velocity (rate of change of distance/displacement with time) and acceleration (rate of change of velocity with time) of a moving object.

First derivative: $\frac{\text{velocity}}{\text{speed}} = \frac{ds}{dt}$

Second derivative: acceleration $= \frac{dv}{dt}$

Worked examples

An arrow is shot vertically into the air. The height it reaches is given by the formula $h(t) = 30t - 3t^2$, where height, h, is measured in metres and time, t, in seconds.

1. How many seconds does it take for the arrow to reach its maximum height, and what is the maximum height?

2. What is the height of the arrow after 3 seconds?

3. How fast is the arrow travelling:
   3.1 after 4 seconds
   3.2 after 7 seconds?

4. How long does it take for the arrow to reach the ground?

5. Calculate the rate of acceleration or deceleration for this arrow.

6. Calculate the initial speed at which this arrow was launched.

7. At what speed did the arrow hit the ground?

Solutions

1. $h(t) = 30t - 3t^2$
   $h'(t) = 30 - 6t$ Maximum height is achieved when $h'(x) = 0$.
   $0 = 30 - 6t$
   $6t = 30$
   $\therefore t = 5$

   It takes 5 seconds for the arrow to reach its maximum height.

   $h(t) = 30t - 3t^2$
   $h(5) = 30(5) - 3(5)^2 = 75$ To find the height reached at a specific point in time, substitute for required time, t, in the original equation $h(t)$.

   The arrow reaches a maximum height of 75 m.

2. $h(t) = 30t - 3t^2$

$h(3) = 30(3) - 3(3)^2 = 63$

To find the height reached at a specific point in time, substitute for required time, t, in the original equation $h(t)$.

The arrow has reached a height of 63 m after 3 seconds.

3. **3.1** $h'(t) = 30 - 6t$

$h'(4) = 30 - 6(4) = 6$ m/s

> Instantaneous speed/velocity of an object is the rate of change of the distance with respect to time, i.e. $\frac{dh}{dt}$, which is the gradient at that specific point in time. To find speed at any point in time, t, substitute for t in $h'(t)$.

Four seconds after it is launched the arrow will be travelling at 6 m/s.

3.2 $h'(t) = 30 - 6t$

$h'(7) = 30 - 6(7) = -12$ m/s

Seven seconds after it is launched the arrow will be travelling at 12 m/s.

4. $h(t) = 30t - 3t^2$

$0 = 30t - 3t^2$

$0 = 3t(10 - t)$

$\therefore t = 0$ or $t = 10$

The arrow leaves the ground and returns to the ground when $h(t) = 0$.

It takes 10 seconds for the arrow to reach the ground.

Note
While it is not necessary to draw the graph representing the flight of the arrow, the graph will help you to understand and interpret calculus of motion.

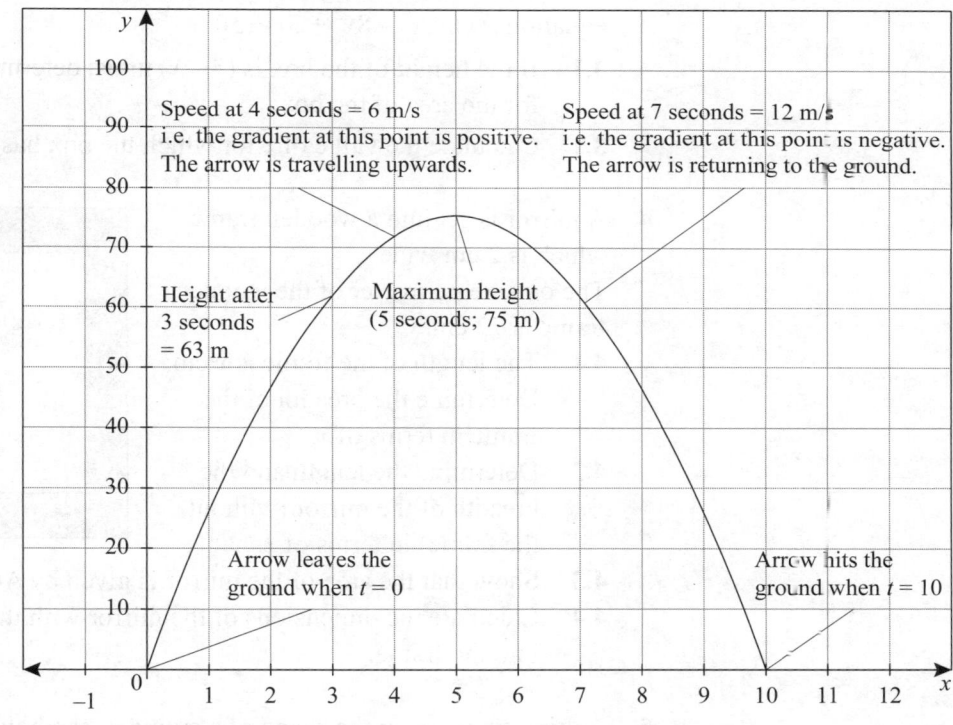

Note
Negative speeds mean that the object is **returning**, or **descending**, not that it is going slower.

Negative accelerations mean that the speed of the object is **decreasing**.

5. $h(t) = 30t - 3t^2$

$h'(t) = 30 - 6t$

$h''(t) = -6$

Acceleration/deceleration, i.e. the change in speed with respect to time, is given by the second derivative, $h''(t)$.

This arrow is decelerating constantly at 6 m/s.

TOPIC 6 *Differential calculus*

6. $h'(t) = 30 - 6t$
   $h'(0) = 30 - 6(0) = 30$ m/s   Initial speed is found at $h'(0)$.
   Arrow is launched at 30 m/s.

7. $h'(t) = 30 - 6t$
   $h'(10) = 30 - 6(10) = -30$ m/s   Speed at which arrow hits the ground is found at $h'(10)$.
   Arrow is travelling at 30 m/s when it hits the ground.

Exercise 12

1. The perimeter of a rectangle, x metres in width, is 106 cm. Calculate the maximum area of the rectangle.

2. A stone is thrown vertically upwards at a velocity of 25 m/s, and its height, h metres above the ground after t seconds, is given by the formula $h = 25t - 5t^2$.
   2.1 Calculate $\frac{dh}{dt}$.
   2.2 Now calculate the velocity of the stone at $t = 1,5$.
   2.3 What is the average velocity between the points (1; 20) and (2,5; 31,25)?
   2.4 After how many seconds does the stone reach its maximum height, and what is its maximum height? How fast is the stone travelling at this point?

3. The volume of a rectangular box, which is open at the top, is given by the equation $f(x) = x^3 - 8x^2 + 5x + 50$.
   3.1 If the height of the box is $(5 - x)$ units, determine an algebraic expression for the area of the box.
   3.2 Calculate the value of x for which the box has a maximum volume.

4. A mirror is set into a wooden frame which is 2 cm wide.
   The outside perimeter of the wooden frame is 72 cm.
   4.1 The length of the frame is x cm. Determine the breadth of the frame in terms of x.
   4.2 Determine the length and the breadth of the mirror (without the frame) in terms of x.
   4.3 Show that the area of the mirror is given by $A(x) = -x^2 + 36x - 128$ cm^2.
   4.4 Calculate the dimensions of the mirror with the largest area that can fit into the frame.

5. A drinking glass, in the shape of a cylinder, can hold 200 ml of liquid when full.
   5.1 Show that the height of the glass, h, can be expressed as $h = \frac{200}{\pi r^2}$.
   5.2 Show that the total surface area of the glass can be expressed as $S(r) = \pi r^2 + \frac{400}{r}$.
   5.3 Hence determine the value of r for which the total surface area of the glass is a minimum.

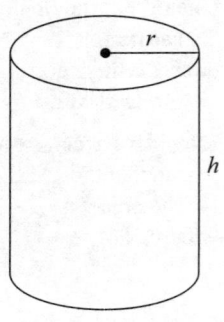

6. A particle moves according to the formula $s = 6t - 24\sqrt{t} + 30$, where s is its distance in millimetres from a fixed point P after t seconds.
   6.1 Determine its distance from P after 9 seconds.
   6.2 The particle reaches its minimum distance from P after t seconds. Determine the value of t.

Complex procedures and problem solving using calculus

Worked example

The diagram shows the graph of $f(x) = -x^2 + 16$.

If $f(x)$ is reflected in the x-axis, find the maximum size of the rectangle PQRS that can be inserted between the two graphs, as shown in the diagram alongside.

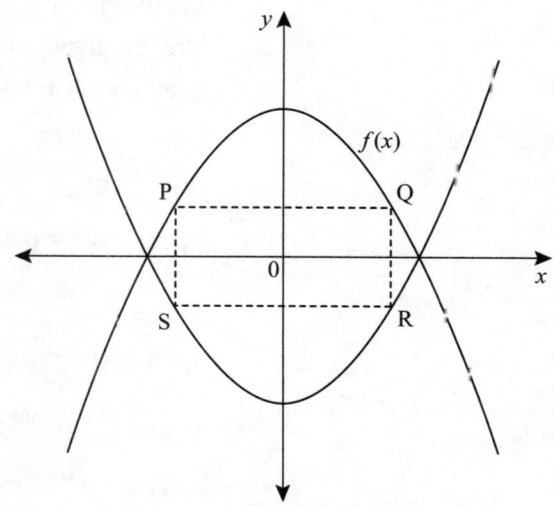

Solution

To find the maximum area we need an expression for the length, PQ, and the breadth, QR, in terms of x.

$PQ = x_Q - x_P$
$ = x_Q - (-x_Q)$ $\qquad x_Q$ and x_P are additive inverses.
$ = 2x_Q = 2x$

$f(x) = -x^2 + 16 \therefore y_Q = -x^2 + 16$

Equation of the reflected graph:
$g(x) = x^2 - 16 \therefore y_R = x^2 - 16$

$QR = y_Q - y_R$
$ = (-x^2 + 16) - (x^2 - 16)$
$ = -2x^2 + 32$

Area PQRS = PQ × QR
$A(x) = 2x(-2x^2 + 32)$
$ = -4x^3 + 64x$
$A'(x) = -12x^2 + 64$
$0 = -4(3x^2 - 16)$ $\qquad$ To maximise, find $f'(x)$ and solve for x in $f'(x) = 0$.
$3x^2 = 16$
$x^2 = \frac{16}{3}$
$x = \frac{3}{4}$ $\qquad x = \pm\sqrt{\frac{16}{3}}$ but a length cannot be negative so we use only the positive value.

$\therefore$ Maximum area $= -4\left(\sqrt{\frac{16}{3}}\right)^3 + 64\left(\frac{16}{3}\right) \approx 292{,}07$

Worked examples

Esasa drives trucks for Express Couriers who pay R225 per hour. Esasa has to deliver a truckload of goods to a nearby town, 150 km away. If she travels at a constant speed of x km/h, fuel costs R12/litre, and the rate at which fuel is consumed per hour has been calculated as $\left(2 + \frac{x^2}{200}\right)$:

1. calculate the most economical speed for the round trip
2. hence calculate the total cost of the trip for Express Couriers.

Solutions

1. Let the speed = x.

   Use the given information to set up equations for the total cost of the trip:

   Total cost = driver's wages + petrol costs

   Driver's wages = time × hourly rate

   $\qquad = \frac{2(150)}{x} \times 225$ \qquad time = $\frac{\text{distance}}{\text{speed}}$

   Petrol costs = time × fuel consumption × cost of fuel/litre

   $\qquad = \frac{2(150)}{x}\left(2 + \frac{x^2}{200}\right) \times 12$

   Total cost = $\frac{2(150)}{x} \times 225 + \frac{2(150)}{x}\left(2 + \frac{x^2}{200}\right) \times 12$

   $C(x) = \frac{dy}{dx} + \frac{3\,600}{x}\left(2 + \frac{x^2}{200}\right)$ \qquad Simplify the information.

   $C(x) = \frac{67\,500}{x} + \frac{7\,200}{x} + 18x$

   $C(x) = \frac{74\,700}{x} + 18x$

   $C'(x) = -74\,700x^{-2} + 18$ \qquad To find the minimum speed, solve for x in $C'(x) = 0$.

   $0 = -74\,700x^{-2} + 18$

   $18x^2 = 74\,700$

   $x \approx 64{,}42$ km/h

   The most economical speed is approximately 64 km/h.

2. Total cost to company for this delivery:

   $C(x) = \frac{74\,700}{x} + 18x$ \qquad To find the actual cost, substitute for x in $C(x)$.

   $C(64{,}42) = \frac{74\,700}{64{,}42} + 18(64{,}2) = 2\,319{,}14$

   Total cost to company for this delivery: R2 319,14

Exercise 13
(complex procedures and problem solving)

1. Prove that $y = x^3 + 2x^2 + 9x + 8$ has no maximum or minimum values.

2. The relationship between the vertical displacement (y) and the horizontal displacement (x) of a rocket that is launched is $y = 8x^2 \sin 60° - x \cos 60°$. Both vertical and horizontal displacements are measured in kilometres. Calculate:

    2.1 the maximum height the projectile can reach, correct to the nearest metre
    2.2 the horizontal displacement the projectile has undergone the moment it strikes the earth, correct to the nearest km
    2.3 the size of the angle at which the projectile is launched.

3. A length of wire, 4 metres long, is cut into two pieces. One piece is bent into the shape of a square and the other into the shape of a circle.

   3.1 If the length of wire that is used to make the circle is x metres, show that the sum of the areas of the circle and the square is given by:
   $f(x) = \left(\frac{1}{16} + \frac{1}{4\pi}\right)x^2 - \frac{x}{2} + 1 \text{ m}^2$.

   3.2 How should the wire be cut so that the sum of the areas of the circle and the square is a minimum?

4. A cylinder with a height of $2x$ units is placed inside a sphere with a radius of $5\sqrt{3}$ units. O is the centre of the sphere.

   4.1 Show that the volume of the cylinder is $V = 150\pi x - 2\pi x^3$.

   4.2 Calculate the height of the cylinder if it is of a maximum volume.

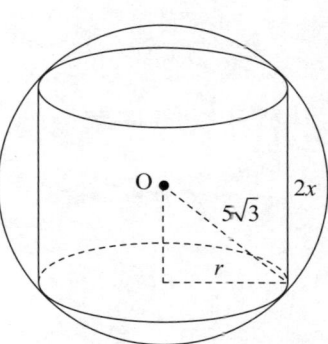

5. Motsumi is making model of a rondavel out of clay for his design project. Motsumi's model has a radius of x cm and a height of h cm. The height of the roof itself (the cone) is $(h - 3)$ cm and the volume of the conic roof is 90 cm³.

   5.1 Show that $h = \frac{270 + 3\pi r^2}{\pi r^2}$.
   (Volume of a cone $= \frac{1}{3}\pi r^2 h$)

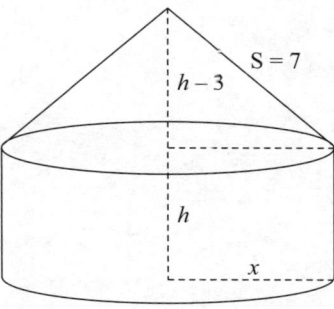

   5.2 Motsumi wants to paint the entire clay model. Determine the maximum surface area for the clay rondavel, without a floor. Leave your answer correct to the nearest cubic cm.
   (Total surface area without base $= \pi rs + 2\pi rh$)

TOPIC 6 Differential calculus

Test A: Knowledge and routine procedures

1. Given: $f(x) = x^3$.
   1.1 Determine $f'(x)$ by first principles. (5)
   1.2 Determine the average gradient of $f'(x)$ between $x = 1$ and $x = -3$. (3)

2. Use differentiation rules to differentiate the following:
   2.1 $y = \dfrac{2}{3\sqrt{x}} - \sqrt[5]{x}$ (4)
   2.2 $y = \dfrac{x^4 + 3x^2 - 5}{x}$ (4)

3. Given: $f(x) = x^3 + x^2 - 5x + 3$.
   3.1 Calculate the x and y intercepts of f. (5)
   3.2 Determine the turning points of f. (5)
   3.3 Determine the coordinates of the point of inflection. (3)
   3.4 Hence sketch the graph of f. Show clearly ALL intercepts with the axes and any turning points. (3)
   3.5 What is the equation of the tangent to $f(x)$ when $x = 2$? (3)
   3.6 What are the x-coordinates of the turning points $f(x-1)$? (2)

4. Find the equation for the graph given below. Use the information given in the sketch to find the equation for the given curve. (6)

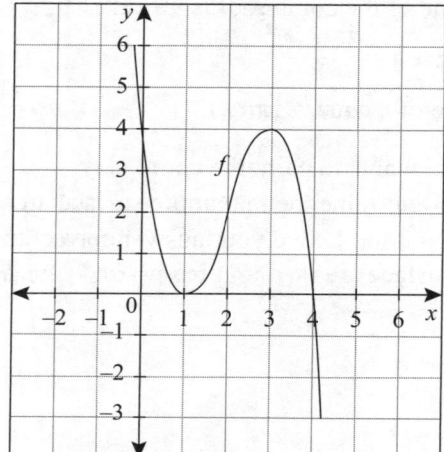

5. Use the information given in the diagram to answer the questions that follow.

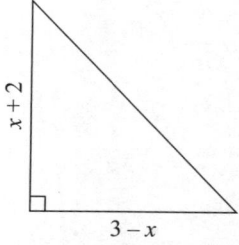

   5.1 Show that the area of the triangle in the diagram above is given by:
   $A(x) = \dfrac{-x^2}{2} + \dfrac{x}{2} + 3$ (2)
   5.2 Calculate the value of x for which the area will be a maximum. (3)
   5.3 Hence calculate the area of the given triangle. (2)

   Total: 50

Test B: Complex procedures and problem solving

1. Given $f(x) = \frac{1}{x^2}$, determine $f'(x)$ from first principles. (5)

2. Determine the concavity of $f(x) = 7x^3 - 3x + 6$. (6)

3. Determine $f'(x)$ if $f(x) = \dfrac{25x^2 - 70x + 49}{x - \frac{7}{5}}$. (5)

4. Given: the curve $y = x^3 - 2x^2 + 3x - 4$.

   4.1 Determine the coordinates of the points on the curve such that the gradient of both tangents is 2. (5)

   4.2 What are the equations of the two tangents at these two points? (5)

5. A mine is discharging waste on a dump that forms a cone shape. The radius of the circular base is r metres, the height is h metres, and the semi-vertical angle is a constant 40° (i.e. BÂC = 40°). The volume of a cone $= \frac{1}{3}\pi r^2 h$.

   5.1 Show that the volume of the dump $= \dfrac{\pi r^3}{3 \tan 40°}$. (3)

   5.2 Find the radius of the base (to the nearest metre) when the volume is 72 000 m³. (3)

   5.3 Find the rate of increase in the radius when the radius has the value calculated in 5.2. (4)

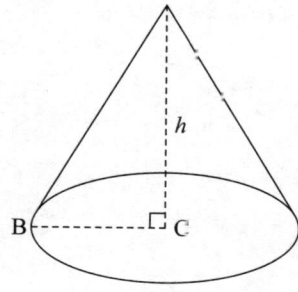

6. If $f(x) = ax^2 - 6$, $y > 0$ and $f^{-1}(2) = f'(4)$, determine the value of a. (8)

7. The straight line in the figure represents $f'(x)$. The x and y-intercepts are -2 and -4 respectively.

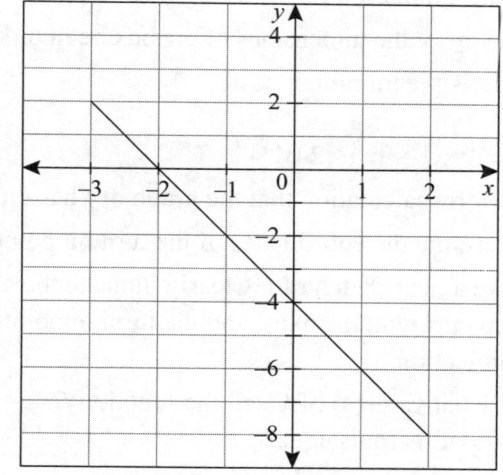

   7.1 Determine the equation for $f'(x)$. (2)

   7.2 $f(x) = ax^2 + bx + c$. $f(x)$ has equal roots.
   Use this information and $f'(x)$ to determine the values for a, b, and c. (4)

   Total: 50

Test C: Breakdown and content as per final exam

1. Given: $f(x) = \frac{x^3}{3}$.
   1.1 Determine $f'(x)$ from first principles. (5)
   1.2 Determine the coordinates of the point of inflection of f. (2)
   1.3 Is it possible to draw a tangent having a negative gradient to the curve of f? Give reasons for your answer. (2)

2. Determine $\lim\limits_{x \to 5} \frac{3x^2 - 13x - 10}{2x^2 - 9x - 5}$ (3)

3. Determine $\frac{dy}{dx}$ if:
   3.1 $y = (x^3 + 1)(x^2 - 2)$ (4)
   3.2 $y = \frac{\sqrt{x} - 4}{\sqrt{x}}$ (4)

4. A rectangular box with a square base and no lid is to have a volume of 500 m³, and is to be made of steel that costs R120/m². Let the length of the base be x.

   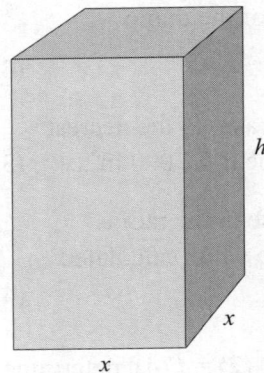

   4.1 Find an expression for h in terms of x. (2)
   4.2 Show that the total surface area of the box, without a lid, can be given by the expression $S(x) = x^2 + \frac{2\,000}{x}$. (2)
   4.3 What must the dimensions of the box be in order to minimise its cost? (4)
   4.4 What is the minimum cost? (2)

5. Given: $f(x) = x^3 - 9x^2 + 24x$.
   5.1 Show by calculation that the graph of f has only one real x-intercept. (4)
   5.2 Determine the coordinates of the turning point of f. (5)
   5.3 Make a neat sketch of f. Clearly indicate the coordinates of all the intercepts with the axes, and the turning points and points of inflection. (3)
   5.4 For what value(s) of k will the function $f(x) = x^3 - 9x^2 + 24x = k$ have TWO of its roots equal? (2)

6. The equation of a tangent to the curve of $f(x) = ax^2 + bx$ is $y - x - 4 = 0$. If the point of contact is $(-1; 3)$, determine the values of a and b. (6)

Total: 50

TOPIC 7 Analytical geometry

Analytical (or coordinate) geometry uses the Cartesian plane to help you to understand and solve geometry problems. In Grades 10 and 11 you studied formulae used to solve problems involving lines and distances. In Grade 12 you studied and solved problems involving both lines and the equations of circles.

Knowledge and skills for this Topic

For the Grade 12 work in this Topic, you need a good grasp of the following knowledge and skills:

- basic algebraic manipulation and factorisation
- quadratic equations, solution by factorisation, and formulae
- simultaneous equations, both linear and quadratic
- squares completion
- basic geometry of circles, and the relationship between tangents and radii
- the theorem of Pythagoras to solve problems in right angled triangles
- all coordinate geometry skills learnt in Grades 10 and 11.

Content of final exam

Questions will require an integration of all skills you learnt in Grades 10, 11 and 12. You will be required to perform routine coordinate geometry procedures and to solve problems in a Cartesian plane using:

- the distance formula
- gradients and the relationships between perpendicular and parallel lines
- midpoints
- the equation of a line through two given points
- the equation of a line through one point and parallel or perpendicular to a given line
- the inclination of a line, where $\tan \theta = m$ is the gradient of the line
- the equation of circles with centre as the origin or anywhere else in the Cartesian plane
- the equation of tangents
- the relationship between tangents to circles and radii.

Relevant formulae

$$y = mx + c \qquad y - y_1 = m(x - x_1) \qquad m = \frac{y_2 - y_1}{x_2 - x_1} \quad \left(\frac{x_1 - x_2}{2} ; \frac{y_1 + y_2}{2} \right)$$

$$x^2 + y^2 = r^2 \qquad (x - a)^2 + (y - b)^2 = r^2 \qquad \text{Distance} = \sqrt{(x_2 - x_1)^2 + (y_2 - y_1)^2}$$

Review of formulae

1. **The distance between two points**
   Take the two points as $A(x_1; y_1)$ and $B(x_2; y_2)$.
   $$AB = \sqrt{(x_2 - x_1)^2 + (y_2 - y_1)^2}$$
   $$\text{or } AB = \sqrt{(x_A - x_B)^2 + (y_A - y_B)^2}$$

2. **The midpoint of a line segment**
   If $A(x_1; y_1)$ and $B(x_2; y_2)$ then the coordinates of $P(x; y)$, the midpoint of AB, is
   $$x = \frac{x_1 + x_2}{2}; y = \frac{y_1 + y_2}{2}$$

3. **Gradient of a line**
   If $A(x_1; y_1)$ and $B(x_2; y_2)$ then the gradient (slope) of $AB(m_{AB})$ is:
   $$m_{AB} = \frac{y_2 - y_1}{x_2 - x_1} \quad \text{or} \quad m_{AB} = \frac{y_1 - y_2}{x_1 - x_2}$$

4. The angle a line makes with the positive x-axis (inclination of the line)
   $$\tan \theta = \frac{y_2 - y_1}{x_2 - x_1} = m$$

   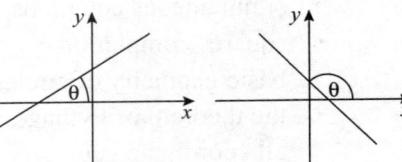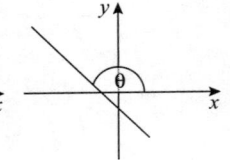

   If $\tan \theta > 0$, then θ is an acute angle.
   If $\tan \theta < 0$, then θ is an obtuse angle.

5. **The equation of a line**
   $$y = mx + c \quad \text{OR} \quad y - y_1 = m(x - x_1) \quad \text{OR} \quad \frac{y - y_1}{x - x_1} = m$$

   To find the equation of a straight line, you need:
   5.1 the gradient (m)
   5.2 the coordinates of one point on the line.

> **Note**
> The formula $m_1 \cdot m_2 = -1$ cannot be applied when one of the lines is parallel to the y-axis.

6. **Perpendicular and parallel lines**
   6.1 The product of the gradients of perpendicular lines is -1:
   $m_1 \cdot m_2 = -1$ and if $m_{AB} \cdot m_{CD} = -1$, then $AB \perp CD$.
   6.2 When two lines are parallel, then $m_1 = m_2$ and if $m_{AB} = m_{CD}$, then $AB \parallel CD$

7. **Points of intersection of straight lines**
   To determine the points of intersection of two straight lines, you solve the two equations of the lines simultaneously.
   7.1 Write the equations of both the lines in the form $y = mx + c$.
   7.2 Let the y-values equal one another.
   7.3 Determine the x-value of the point of intersection.
   7.4 Calculate the corresponding y-value using substitution.

8. **Median of a triangle**
   The median of triangle:
   - bisects the opposite side
   - bisects the area of a triangle.

   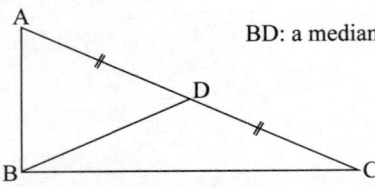

   Equation of a median
   8.1 Determine the coordinates of D using the formula for the midpoint.
   8.2 Use B and D to find the equation.

9. **Altitude of a triangle**

    The altitude of a triangle is perpendicular to the opposite side.

    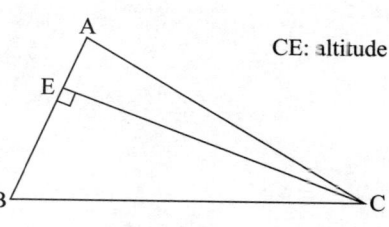
    CE: altitude

    Equation of an altitude
    9.1 Find m_{AB}
    9.2 Determine m_{CE} using $m_{AB} \cdot m_{CE} = -1$.
    9.3 Use m_{CE} and C to find the equation.

10. **Perpendicular bisector of a given line segment (also found in a triangle)**

    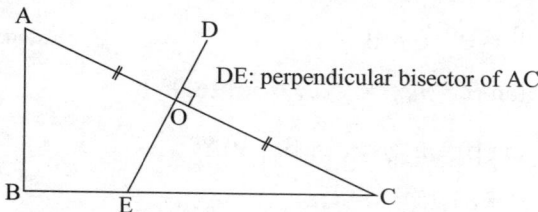
    DE: perpendicular bisector of AC

    Equation of a perpendicular bisector
    10.1 Determine the coordinates of O using the midpoint formula.
    10.2 Find m_{AC}
    10.3 Determine m_{DE} using DE $\perp$ AC.
    10.4 Use O and m_{DE} to find the equation.

Using formulae: revision of Grades 10 and 11 work

Note that Grade 11 content has not been extensively revised in this Study Guide, but has been incorporated into exercise questions.

Worked examples

1. Given: A(–5; 1), B(1; 6), C(7; –2). Determine:

    1.1 the length of AC
    1.2 the equation of the line BC
    1.3 $A\hat{B}C$
    1.4 the midpoint P of AB
    1.5 the equation of the line parallel to AC and that passes through the point (–1; 3)
    1.6 whether AB is perpendicular to $6x + 5y = 18$.

Solutions

1.

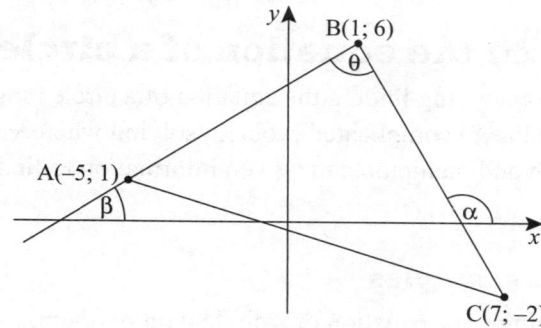

1.1 $AC = \sqrt{(-5-7)^2 + [1-(-2)]^2}$
    $= \sqrt{153}$
    $= 12,4$

1.2 $m_{BC} = \frac{6-(-2)}{1-7} = \frac{8}{-6} = \frac{-4}{3}$

$\therefore$ Equation $_{BC}$ is $\frac{y-y_1}{x-x_1} = m$

$\therefore \frac{y-6}{x-1} = \frac{-4}{3}$

$\therefore 3y - 18 = -4x + 4$

$3y = -4x + 22$

$y = -\frac{4}{3}x + 7\frac{1}{3}$

1.3 $\hat{B} = \theta = \alpha - \beta$ Exterior angle

$\tan \alpha = m_{BC} = \frac{-4}{3} \therefore \alpha = 126{,}9°$

$\tan \beta = m_{AB} = \frac{5}{6} \therefore \beta = 39{,}8°$

$\theta = 87{,}1°$

$\therefore A\hat{B}C = 87{,}1°$

1.4 $P\left(\frac{-5+1}{2}; \frac{1+6}{2}\right)$

$\therefore P\left(-2; \frac{7}{2}\right)$

1.5 $m_{AC} = \frac{-2-1}{7+5}$

$= \frac{-3}{12}$

$= -\frac{1}{4}$; through $(-1; 3)$

Equation: $y - 3 = -\frac{1}{4}(x+1)$

$= -\frac{1}{4}x - \frac{1}{4}$

$\therefore y = -\frac{1}{4}x + 2\frac{3}{4}$

1.6 $m_{AB} = \frac{5}{6}$; $6x + 5y = 18$

$5y = -6x + 18$

$y = -\frac{6}{5}x + 3\frac{3}{5}$

$\therefore m_1 = -\frac{6}{5}$

$\therefore m_{AB} \cdot m_1 = -1$

$\therefore AB \perp 6x + 5y = 18$

Finding the equation of a circle

Problems involving finding the equation of a circle range from simple substitution into formulae to complicated problem solving where you first need to interpret, work with and manipulate the given information to find the circle centre and the radius.

Worked examples

1. Determine the equation of a circle with midpoint $(-1; 2)$ and a radius of $\sqrt{6}$.

2. Determine the equation of a circle that has as its diameter a line segment with endpoints $(5; 3)$ and $(-3; 6)$.

3. Determine the equation of a circle(s) passing through the points $A(-3; 4)$ and $B(4; 5)$, having a radius of 5 units.

Remember

$(a; b)$ are the coordinates for a circle that does not have the origin $(0; 0)$ as its centre. Simply substitute for a, b and r into the formula $(x - a)^2 + (y - b)^2 = r^2$

Remember

The midpoint of the given diameter is the circle centre.
Use $\left(\frac{x_1 + x_2}{2}; \frac{y_1 + y_2}{2}\right)$ to find the midpoint.

You need to know
- how to factorise and to solve quadratic equations
- how to solve both linear and quadratic simultaneous equations

Solutions

1. $\qquad (x - a)^2 + (y - b)^2 = r^2$
   $\qquad [(x - (-1))^2 + (y - 2)]^2 = (\sqrt{6})^2$
   $\qquad (x + 1)^2 + (y - 2)^2 = 6$

Note

You do not need to simplify the equation unless asked to do so.

2. Use the midpoint theorem to find the centre.

   Circle centre: $\left(\frac{x_1 + x_2}{2}; \frac{y_1 + y_2}{2}\right) = \left(\frac{5 + (-3)}{2}; \frac{3 + 6}{2}\right)$

   $\qquad (a; b) = \left(\frac{2}{2}; \frac{9}{2}\right) = \left(1; \frac{9}{2}\right)$

   Use the distance formula to find the radius:

   $\frac{\text{Diameter}}{2} = \text{radius}$

   $\therefore r = \frac{\sqrt{(x_2 - x_1)^2 + (y_2 - y_1)^2}}{2}$

   $\quad = \frac{\sqrt{(-3 - 5)^2 + (6 - 3)^2}}{2}$

   $\quad = \frac{\sqrt{(-8)^2 + (3)^2}}{2}$

   $\quad = \frac{\sqrt{73}}{2}$

   Substitute the values you found for a, b and r into the formula:
   $(x - a)^2 + (y - b)^2 = r^2$
   $(x - 1)^2 + \left(y - \frac{9}{2}\right)^2 = \left(\frac{\sqrt{73}}{2}\right)^2$
   $(x - 1)^2 + \left(y - \frac{9}{2}\right)^2 = \frac{73}{4}$

3. This is a complicated problem. Drawing a rough sketch will help you to understand the given information.

   Notice that two different circles with the same radius can be drawn through the points A$(-3; 4)$ and B$(4; 5)$.

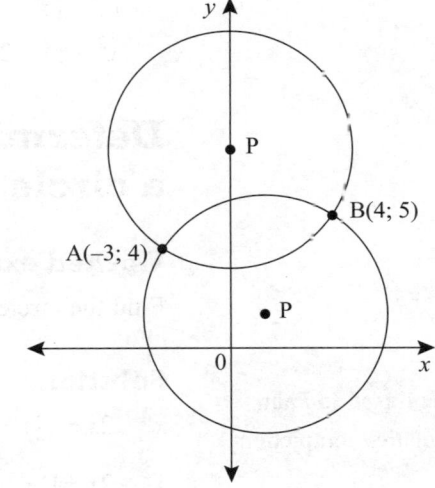

   Let the circle centre be P$(x; y)$
   Then PA = PB = r equal radii
   PA^2 = PB^2 Eliminate the $\sqrt{\ }$ sign by squaring both sides.
   $(x + 3)^2 + (y - 4)^2 = (x - 4)^2 + (y - 5)^2$ Use the distance formula and substitute for P$(x; y)$, A$(-3; 4)$ and B$(4; 5)$ and simplify fully.

$$x^2 + 6x + 9 + y^2 - 8y + 16 = x^2 - 8x + 16 + y^2 - 10y + 25$$
$$6x + 9 - 8y + 16 = -8x + 16 - 10y + 25$$
$$14x + 2y = 16$$
$$7x + y = 8 \quad \text{......①}$$

You now have one equation with two unknown values. Use the information to generate another equation in terms of x and y.

$$PA = r^2$$

Use the distance formula and substitute for P(x; y) and A(–3; 4). Simplify fully.

$$(x + 3)^2 + (y - 4)^2 = 5^2$$
$$x^2 + 6x + 9 + y^2 - 8y + 16 = 25$$
$$x^2 + y^2 + 6x - 8y = 0 \quad \text{......②}$$
$$7x + y = 8 \quad \text{......①}$$

Rewrite equation ① in the y form.

$$\therefore y = 8 - 7x$$
$$x^2 + (8 - 7x)^2 + 6x - 8(8 - 7x) = 0$$
$$x^2 + 64 - 112x + 49x^2 + 6x - 64 + 56x = 0$$

Substitute for y in equation ②.

$$50x^2 - 50x = 0$$

Simplify fully.

$$50x(x - 1) = 0$$

Use factorisation to solve the resultant quadratic equation.

$$\therefore x = 0 \text{ or } x = 1$$

The centres of the two circles are (0; 8) and (1; 1).

Use substitution to find the y coordinates for each point: $y = 8$, $y = 1$.

Equation for circle with centre (0; 8) and a radius of 5:
$$(x - 0)^2 + (y - 8)^2 = 5^2$$

Use $(x - a)^2 + (y - b)^2 = r^2$ to find the equations for each of these circles.

$$x^2 + y^2 - 16y + 39 = 0$$

Simplify.

Equation for circle with centre (1; 1) and a radius of 5:
$$(x - 1)^2 + (y - 1)^2 = 5^2$$
$$x^2 + y^2 - 2x - 2y - 23 = 0$$

Determining the centre and the radius of a circle

Worked example

Find the circle centre and the radius for the circle defined by $x^2 - 2x + y^2 + 4y = 5$.

You need to know
squares completion

Remember
$(x - 1) = 0, \therefore x = 1$
and $(y + 2) = 0$,
$\therefore y = -2$

Solution
$$x^2 - 2x + \left(\tfrac{2}{2}\right)^2 + y^2 + 4y + \left(\tfrac{4}{2}\right)^2 = 5 - \left(\tfrac{2}{2}\right)^2 + \left(\tfrac{4}{2}\right)^2$$
$$x^2 - 2x + 1^2 + y^2 + 4y + 2^2 = 5 - 1^2 + 2^2$$

Complete the square for $x^2 - 2x$ and for $y^2 + 4y$ respectively. Don't forget to "balance" your equation.

$$(x - 1)^2 + (y + 2)^2 = 8$$

Circle centre: (1; –2) Radius: $\sqrt{8} = 2\sqrt{2}$.

Finding the equation of a tangent to a circle

You need to know

A tangent is perpendicular to the radius of the circle at the point of contact.

Given: Point of contact, C, and circle centre, D.

To find the equation of the tangent to this circle, you need to determine m_{DC}, using $m = \frac{y_2 - y_1}{x_2 - x_1}$,

and you need to determine m_{AB},

using $m_{DC} \times m_{AB} = -1$.

You would use m_{AB} and the point of contact, C, to find the equation of the tangent at this point.

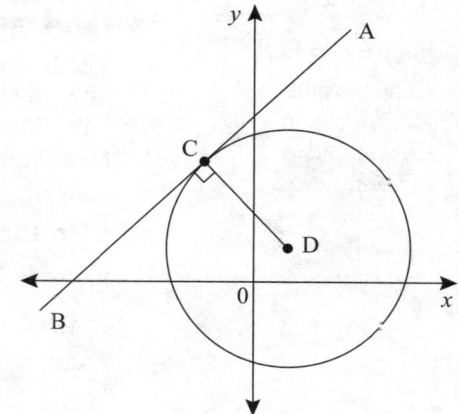

Worked examples

1. Find the equation of the tangent to the circle with centre A(4; −3) at the point of contact B(−2; −1).

2. Determine the equation of the tangent that touches the circle $x^2 + 2x + y^2 - 4y = 20$ at the point P(3; 5).

Solutions

1. $m_{AB} = \frac{y_B - y_A}{x_B - x_A} = \frac{-1 - (-3)}{-2 - 4} = \frac{2}{-6} = -\frac{1}{3}$ Determine the gradient of the radius AB.

   Gradient of tangent: $m = 3$ tangent ⊥ radius
   Determine the gradient of the tangent through B.

   $y - (-1) = 3[x - (-2)]$ Substitute for m and B(−2, −1) into $y - y_1 = m(x - x_1)$ to find the equation of the tangent.

   $y + 1 = 3(x + 2)$
   $y + 1 = 3x + 6$
   $y = 3x + 5$

2. $x^2 + 2x + \left(\frac{2}{2}\right)^2 + y^2 - 4y + \left(\frac{4}{2}\right)^2 = 20 + \left(\frac{2}{2}\right)^2 + \left(\frac{4}{2}\right)^2$ Find the centre by completing the square.

   $x^2 + 2x + (1)^2 + y^2 - 4y + (2)^2 = 20 + (1)^2 + (2)^2$
   $(x + 1)^2 + (y - 2)^2 = 25$

   Circle centre: (−1; 2) Point of contact: (3; 5)

   $m_{radius} = \frac{y_2 - y_1}{x_2 - x_1} = \frac{5 - 2}{3 - (-1)} = \frac{3}{4}$ Find the gradient of the radius.

   $m_{tangent} = -\frac{4}{3}$ tangent ⊥ radius Determine the gradient of the tangent.

   $y - 5 = -\frac{4}{3}(x - 3)$ Substitute for m and P(3; 5) into $y - y_1 = m(x - x_1)$ to find the equation of the tangent.

   $y = -\frac{4}{3}x + 9$

Finding points of intersection

You need to know
- algebra and factorisation
- linear and quadratic equations
- simultaneous equations

Worked examples

1. The line $y = -\frac{x}{2} + 2$ cuts the circle $x^2 + y^2 = 5$ at A and T. Find the coordinates of A and T.

2. Determine the points of intersection of $y = -x + 3$ and $x^2 + y^2 + 6x - 4y - 3 = 0$.

Solutions

1. $y = -\frac{x}{2} + 2$ ....① $x^2 + y^2 = 5$ ....②

   $x^2 + \left(-\frac{x}{2} + 2\right)^2 = 5$ Use ① to substitute for y in ②.

   $x^2 + \frac{x^2}{4} - 2x + 4 = 5$

   $\frac{4x^2 + x^2 - 8x + 16}{4} = \frac{20}{4}$ Simplify using a common denominator.

   $5x^2 - 8x - 4 = 0$

   $(5x + 2)(x - 2) = 0$ Factorise and solve the quadratic equation.

   $x = -\frac{2}{5}$ or $x = 2$

   $y = -\left(-\frac{2}{5}\right) \div 2 + 2$ or $y = -\frac{2}{2} + 2$ Don't forget to substitute for x in ① to find the corresponding y values for each point.

   $y = \frac{11}{5}$ or $y = 1$

   Points of intersection: $A\left(-\frac{2}{5}; \frac{11}{5}\right)$, $T(2; 1)$.

2. $y = -x + 3$ ....①

   $x^2 + y^2 + 6x - 4y - 3 = 0$ ....②

   $x^2 + (-x + 3)^2 + 6x - 4(-x + 3) - 3 = 0$ Substitute for y in ②.

   $x^2 + x^2 - 6x + 9 + 6x + 4x - 12 - 3 = 0$

   $2x^2 + 4x - 6 = 0$

   $(x + 3)(x - 1) = 0$ Factorise and solve the quadratic equation.

   $x = -3$ or $x = 1$

   $y = 6$ or $y = 2$

   Points of intersection: $(-3; 6)$ and $(1; 2)$

Exercise 1

1. Find the equations of the following circles:
   - **1.1** the circle passing through the origin with a radius of $\sqrt{3}$.
   - **1.2** the circle passing through the origin and the point $(-5; 6)$
   - **1.3** the circle with the origin as its centre and that touches the line $2x + y = 5$.

2. The line $2y - x = 5$ intersects the circle $x^2 + y^2 = 10$. Find the coordinates of the point of intersection.

3. The line $5y = -x + 13$ intersects the circle $x^2 + y^2 = 13$ at C and D. Find the length of CD.

4. Find the equation of the tangent to the circle $x^2 + y^2 = 34$ at the point $(-3; 4)$.

5. Find the equation of the circle with centre $(-3; 4)$ and a radius of 2.

6. Find the radius and the centre for each of the circles given below:
   6.1 $x^2 + y^2 - 2x + 4y + 1 = 0$
   6.2 $x^2 + y^2 + 6x - 8y = 11$

7. Determine the points of intersection of the line $y + 1 = 0$ with the circle having its centre at $(-1; 0,5)$ and a radius of 2,5.

8. Find the equation of the tangent to the circle $x^2 + y^2 - 2x + 2y - 11 = 0$ at the point $(-2; 1)$.

Finding the length of a tangent from an external point

You need to know

Theorem of Pythagoras: in any right angled triangle ABC, with $\hat{B} = 90°$, $AC^2 = BC^2 + AB^2$.

Worked examples

1. Write down the length of the tangent from the point $(-4; 8)$ to the circle $x^2 + y^2 = 25$.

2. Write down the length of the tangent from the point $(-4; 8)$ to the circle $x^2 + y^2 - 6x - 4y - 12 = 0$.

Solutions

1. It often helps to draw a diagram to help you to see what you need to do:
   $O\hat{B}P = 90°$ tangent ⊥ radius
   $OB = 5$ radius

   Using the distance formula:
   $PO = \sqrt{[0 - (-4)]^2 + (0 - 8)^2} = \sqrt{80}$

   Length of tangent PB:
   $PB = \sqrt{PO^2 - OB^2}$ Pythagoras
   $PB = \sqrt{(\sqrt{80})^2 - 5^2} = \sqrt{55} = 7{,}416 \approx 7{,}42$

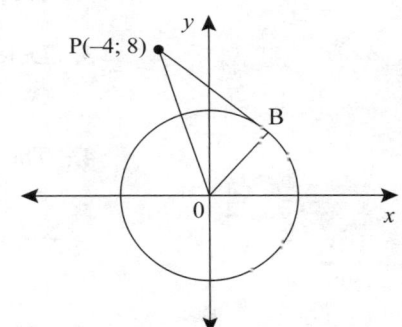

2. Use completion of squares to find the coordinates for the circle centre A:
   $x^2 + y^2 - 6x - 4y - 12 = 0$
   $x^2 - 6x + \left(\frac{6}{2}\right)^2 + y^2 - 4y + \left(\frac{4}{2}\right)^2 = 12 + \left(\frac{6}{2}\right)^2 + \left(\frac{4}{2}\right)^2$
   $(x - 3)^2 + (y - 2)^2 = 25$
   Circle centre: $A(3; 2)$, radius $AB = 5$
   $A\hat{B}P = 90°$ tangent ⊥ radius

   Using the distance formula:
   $PA = \sqrt{(-4 - 3)^2 + (8 - 2)^2} = \sqrt{85}$

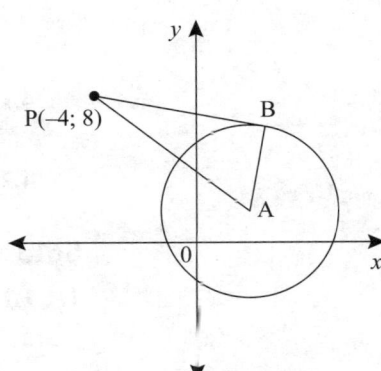

Length of tangent PB:

$PB = \sqrt{PA^2 - AB^2}$ by Pythagoras

$PB = \sqrt{(\sqrt{85})^2 - 5^2} = \sqrt{60} = 7{,}7459 \approx 7{,}75$

Integrated problems involving lines and circles

Worked examples

1. Given A(2; 1), B(–6; 3), C(–2; –3) and F(–4; a). (F is not shown in the diagram.) Determine:
   1.1 the equation of the median AD
   1.2 the equation of the altitude AE
   1.3 the equation of the perpendicular bisector PQ of AC
   1.4 the equation of the circle with centre A and that passes through the origin
   1.5 the value of a if AB ⊥ BF.

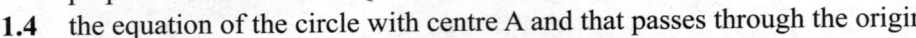

2. A(5; 5), B(–7; 1), C(1; –7) are the vertices of △ABC.
   2.1 Show that △ABC is an isosceles triangle.
   2.2 Determine the equation of the circle with the origin as centre and that passes through point A.
   2.3 Determine the equation of the perpendicular bisector of BC.
   2.4 Determine the equation of the line through A and that is parallel to BC.

3. Determine the equation of the tangent to the circle:
   $(x - 4)^2 + (y - 5)^2 = 10$ at the point A(a; 6).

4. The equation of the circle in the diagram is $x^2 + y^2 - 6x + 2y + t = 0$.
   PA is a tangent and P the point (–2; 0).

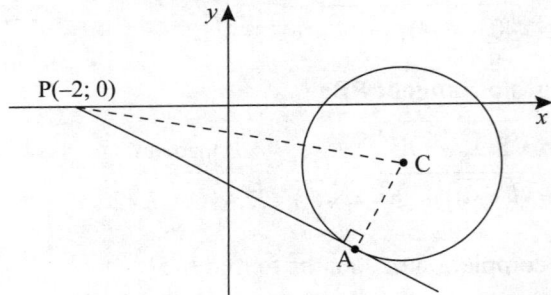

   4.1 Determine the coordinates of the centre of the circle and the radius (in terms of t).
   4.2 If PA = $3\sqrt{2}$, calculate t.

Solutions

1. 1.1 Median: AD

   $D\left(\dfrac{-6-2}{2}; \dfrac{3-3}{2}\right) = D(-4; 0)$

   $m_{AD} = \dfrac{1-0}{2-(-4)} = \dfrac{1}{6}$

   1.2 Altitude: AE

   $m_{BC} = -\dfrac{6}{4} = -\dfrac{3}{2}$

   ∴ $m_{AE} = \dfrac{2}{3}$

∴ Equation $_{AD}$: $y = mx + c$ Equation $_{AE}$: $y = \frac{2}{3}x + c$

$\qquad y = \frac{1}{6}x + c$ $(2; 1): 1 = \frac{2}{3}(2) + c$

$(-4; 0): 0 = \frac{1}{6}(-4) + c$ $\therefore c = -\frac{1}{3}$

$\qquad \frac{2}{3} = c$ $\therefore y = \frac{2}{3}x - \frac{1}{3}$

$\qquad \therefore y = \frac{1}{6}x + \frac{2}{3}$

1.3 Perpendicular bisector: PQ

$S\left(\frac{2-2}{2}; \frac{-3+1}{2}\right)$

$= S(0; -1)$

$m_{AC} = \frac{-4}{-4} = 1$

$\therefore m_{PQ} = -1$

$\therefore$ Equation $_{PQ}$: $y = -x + c$

$S(0; -1): -1 = 0 + c$

$\qquad -1 = c$

$\qquad \therefore y = -x - 1$

1.4 $(x-2)^2 + (y-1)^2 = OA^2$

$\therefore (x-2)^2 + (y-1)^2 = 5$ $\qquad$ $OA = \sqrt{4+1}$

1.5 $m_{AB} = -\frac{2}{8} = -\frac{1}{4}$

$\therefore m_{BF} = 4 = \frac{3-a}{-2}$

$\therefore 3 - a = -8$

$\therefore a = 11$

2. 2.1 $AB = \sqrt{(-7-5)^2 + (1-5)^2}$

$\qquad = \sqrt{160}$

$AC = \sqrt{(1-5)^2 + (-7-5)^2}$

$\qquad = \sqrt{160}$

$\therefore AB = AC$

$\therefore \triangle ABC$ is an isosceles triangle

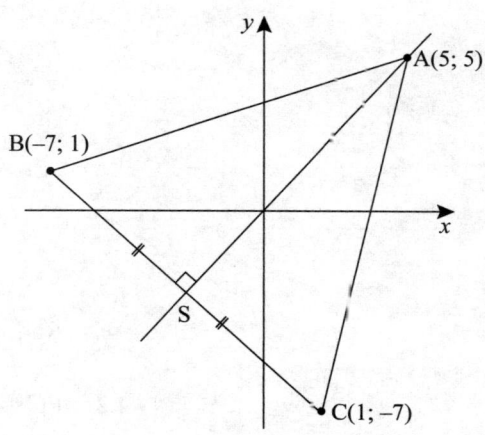

2.2 $\qquad$ Circle: $x^2 + y^2 = r^2$

$\qquad$ Through $(5; 5): 5^2 + 5^2 = r^2$

$\qquad\qquad\qquad \therefore 50 = r^2$

$\therefore x^2 + y^2 = 50$

Note
Perpendicular bisector of BC will pass through A because △ABC is isosceles.

2.3 $S\left(\frac{-7+1}{2}; \frac{1-7}{2}\right)$

∴ $S(-3; -3)$

$m_{BC} = -\frac{8}{8} = -1$

∴ $m_{\text{perp.bisector}} = 1$

Perpendicular bisector: $y = mx + c$
$$y = x + c$$
$$S(-3; -3): -3 = (-3) + c$$
$$0 = c$$
∴ $y = x$

2.4 $m_{BC} = -1$

∴ $m = -1$

∴ $y = -x + c$

Through $A(5; 5)$: $5 = -5 + c$
$$10 = c$$
∴ $y = -x + 10$

3. Substitute $A(a; 6)$ in: $(a - 4)^2 + 1^2 = 10$
$$\therefore (a - 4)^2 = 9$$
$$a - 4 = \pm 3$$
$$a = 7 \text{ or } a = 1$$

Centre of circle: $M(4; 5)$

$A_1(7; 6)$ or $A_2(1; 6)$

∴ $m_{A_1M} = \frac{1}{3}$ $\quad\quad\quad\quad\quad\quad\quad\quad\quad\quad m_{A_2M} = -\frac{1}{3}$

∴ $m_{\text{tangent1}} = -3$ $\quad\quad\quad\quad\quad\quad\quad m_{\text{tangent2}} = 3$

Equation of tangents:

∴ $\frac{y-6}{x-7} = -3$ $\quad\quad\quad\quad\quad\quad\quad\quad\quad \frac{y-6}{x-1} = 3$

∴ $y = -3x + 27$ $\quad\quad\quad\quad\quad\quad\quad\quad y = 3x + 3$

4. 4.1 $\quad\quad\quad\quad\quad x^2 + y^2 - 6x + 2y = -t$

∴ $x^2 - 6x + 9 + y^2 + 2y + 1 = -t + 9 + 1$ Completing the square

∴ $(x - 3)^2 + (y + 1)^2 = -t + 10$

∴ Centre: $C(3; -1)$

Radius: $\sqrt{10 - t}$

4.2 $PC = \sqrt{[3 - (-2)]^2 + (-1 - 0)^2}$
$$= \sqrt{26}$$

$PA = 3\sqrt{2}$

$AC = \sqrt{10 - t}$

$PC^2 = PA^2 + AC^2$ $\quad\quad\quad\quad\quad\quad\quad\quad\quad$ Pythagoras; $P\hat{A}C = 90°$; tangent ⊥ radius

∴ $26 = 18 + 10 - t$

∴ $t = 2$

Intersecting circles

The radius of a circle can be used to solve problems involving the intersection of circles.

Worked examples

1. Show that the circles $x^2 + y^2 - 16x - 20y + 115 = 0$ and $x^2 + y^2 + 8x - 10y + 5 = 0$ have an external point of contact.

2. Show that the circles $x^2 + y^2 + 2x - 6y + 9 = 0$ and $x^2 + y^2 + 8x - 6y + 9 = 0$ have an internal point of contact.

3. Show that the circles $x^2 + y^2 + 6x - 2y - 54 = 0$ and $x^2 + y^2 - 22x - 8y + 112 = 0$ do not intersect.

Conditions for circles to touch each other

Touch externally:
AB = R + r

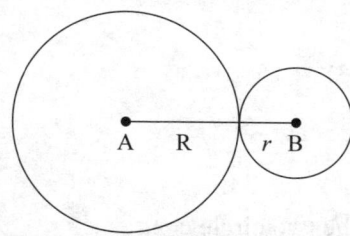

Touch internally:
AB = R − r

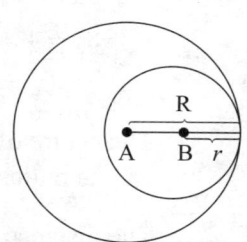

Conditions for circles neither to intersect nor to touch each other

Never touch:
AB > R + r

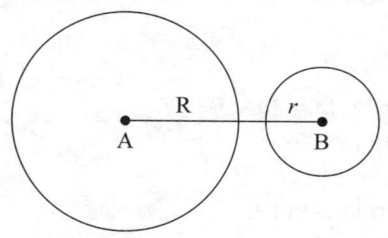

Conditions for circles to intersect each other

Intersect:
AB < R − r

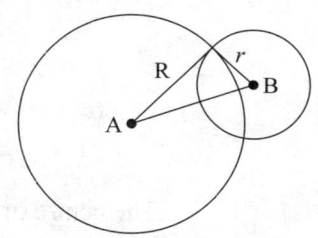

Solutions

1. $x^2 + y^2 - 16x - 20y + 115 = 0$
$x^2 - 16x + 8^2 + y^2 - 20y + 10^2$
$= -115 + 64 + 100$ Complete the square to find the circle centre and the radius for each circle.
$(x - 8)^2 + (y - 10)^2 = 49$

The centre of this circle is at (8; 10) and its radius is 7.

$x^2 + y^2 + 8x - 10y + 5 = 0$
$x^2 + 8x + 4^2 + y^2 - 10y + 5^2$
$= -5 + 16 + 25$
$(x + 4)^2 + (y - 5)^2 = 36$

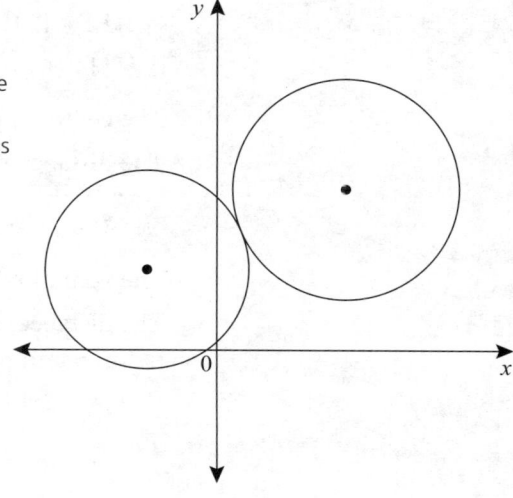

The centre of this circle is at (–4; 5) and its radius is 6.

The sum of radii is 13.

The distance between the two circle centres is: $\sqrt{[8-(-4)]^2 + (10-5)^2}$
$$= \sqrt{169}$$
$$= 13$$

The **sum** of the radii is equal to the distance between the two circle centres, therefore the circles touch externally.

2. $x^2 + y^2 + 2x - 6y + 9 = 0$
$x^2 + 2x + 1^2 + y^2 - 6y + 3^2 = -9 + 1 + 9$ Complete the square to find the circle centre and the radius for each circle.

$(x + 1)^2 + (y - 3)^2 = 1$

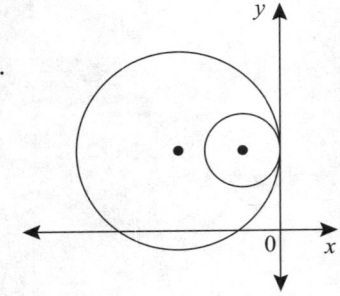

The centre of this circle is at (–1; 3) and its radius is 1.
$x^2 + y^2 + 8x - 6y + 9 = 0$
$x^2 + 8x + 4^2 + y^2 - 6y + 3^2 = -9 + 16 + 9$
$(x + 4)^2 + (y - 3)^2 = 16$

The centre of this circle is at (–4; 3) and its radius is 4.

The distance between the two circle centres is:

$\sqrt{[-1-(-4)]^2 + (3-3)^2} = \sqrt{9} = 3$

The distance between the two circles is equal to the **difference** between the two radii, which means that the two radii are collinear.

These two circles touch each each other internally.

3. $x^2 + y^2 + 6x - 2y - 54 = 0$
$x^2 + 6x + 3^2 + y^2 - 2y + 1^2 = 54 + 9 + 1$
$(x + 3)^2 + (y - 1)^2 = 64$

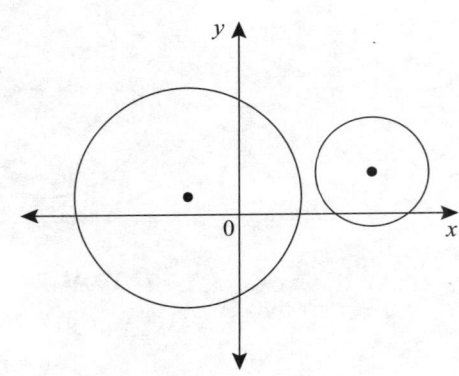

The centre of this circle is at (–3; 1) and its radius is 8.

$x^2 + y^2 - 22x - 8y + 112 = 0$
$x^2 - 22x + 11^2 + y^2 - 8y + 4^2$
$= -112 + 121 + 16$
$(x - 11)^2 + (y - 4)^2 = 25$

The centre of this circle is at (11; 4) and its radius is 5.

The distance between the two circle centres is:

$\sqrt{(-3-11)^2 + (1-4)^2} = \sqrt{205} \approx 14{,}32$

The sum of radii is 13.

The distance between the two circle centres is greater than the sum of their radii, therefore these two circles do not touch or intersect.

Exercise 2

1. In the diagram A(3; –8) and B(9; 10) are two vertices of △ABC.
   The altitude AD cuts the median CM at Q(9; 4).

   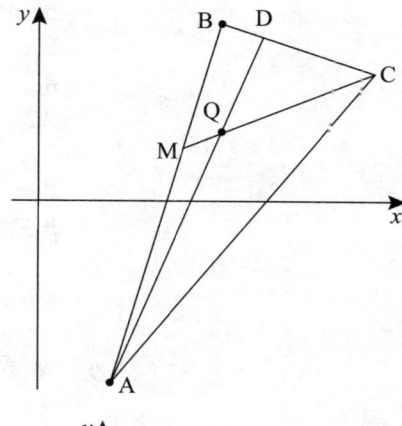

   Determine:
   1.1 the gradient of AQ
   1.2 the equation of BC
   1.3 the equation of CM
   1.4 BÂQ.

2. In the diagram:
   AB: $y = 5x - 17$
   BC: $x + y = 13$
   Calculate the equation of the median BD.

3. Given the circle $x^2 + y^2 - 6x - 2y + 1 = 0$:
   3.1 determine the coordinates of the centre of the circle and the length of the radius
   3.2 calculate t if the length of a tangent from a point A(t; 7) to the point P on the circumference of the circle is $2\sqrt{13}$.

4. The point M(2; 2) is the centre of chord PQ of the circle $x^2 + y^2 - x - 2y - 5 = 0$.
   4.1 Determine the coordinates of the centre of the circle and the radius.
   4.2 Determine the equation of chord PQ.

5. Circle A with centre A and equation $(x - 2)^2 + (y + 2)^2 = 4$ and circle B with centre B and equation $x^2 + y^2 + 4x - 2y + k = 0$ touch externally.
   5.1 Calculate the radius of circle B in terms of k.
   5.2 Calculate the length of AB and the value of k.
   5.3 If the two circles touch in the points T$\left(\frac{2}{5}; -\frac{4}{5}\right)$, determine the equation of the tangent in the form: $ax + by + c = 0$.

6. In the diagram, B(–1; 1) is the centre of the circle. CA is a tangent at A. C is the point (–1; 26); CBA = ARO = θ; CA = 20 units.

   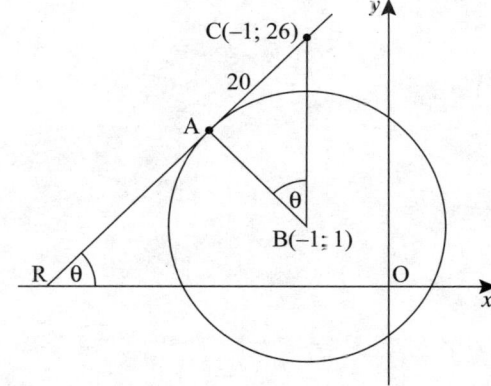

   Calculate:
   6.1 the length of the radius of the circle
   6.2 the equation of the circle
   6.3 the equation of tangent CR
   6.4 the equation of radius AB
   6.5 the coordinates of A.

7. Determine the length of a tangent drawn from point (6; –2) to the circle $x^2 + y^2 - 6x + 2y + 8 = 0$.

8. A circle with centre M(5; 4) and radius 5 cuts the x-axis at A and B, with A the point closest to the origin.
   8.1 Write down the equation of the circle.
   8.2 Find the coordinates of A and B.
   8.3 Determine the equations of the tangents to the circle from point P with points of contact A and B.
   8.4 Determine the coordinates of P.
   8.5 Determine the coordinates of the centre of the circumscribed circle of quadrilateral AMBP.
   8.6 Calculate the size of $A\hat{M}B$.

9. A circle has centre A(–2; 6) and radius $\sqrt{50}$ units.
   9.1 Write down the equation of the circle in the form $x^2 + y^2 + ax + by + c = 0$.
   9.2 If B(4; 9) is the centre of chord PQ, calculate the equation of the chord PQ.
   9.3 Calculate the coordinates of P and Q if P is closer to the y-axis than Q.
   9.4 T is the point (11; 1). Show that T lies outside the circle.
   9.5 If the tangent from T meets the circle at S, calculate the length of TS.

10. Given: $x^2 + y^2 - 6x + 4y = -9$
    10.1 Determine the centre O and the radius of the circle.
    10.2 Determine the equation of the line through (0; –3) and (3; 0).
    10.3 Determine the points of intersection A and B, of the circle and the line in question 10.2.
    10.4 Determine the length of the chord AB.

Test A: Knowledge and routine procedures

1. Given a circle with equation $x^2 + y^2 + 6x - 4y = 23$. Determine the length of the radius of the circle as well as the coordinates of the midpoint of the circle. (6)

2. A(−1; 5) is a point on the circle $(x - 2)^2 + (y - 3)^2 = 13$. The centre of the circle is at M. The line with equation $3y - 2x - 5 = 0$ cuts the circle at B and C.
   - 2.1 Determine the equation of the tangent to the circle at A. (5)
   - 2.2 Calculate the coordinates of B and C. (8)
   - 2.3 Prove that BC is a diameter of the circle. (3)

3. Prove that the straight line $3y - x - 10 = 0$ touches the circle $x^2 + y^2 = 10$. Also determine the point of contact. (5)

4. In the diagram, A is the point (0; 4) and B is the point (4; 12). The straight line TAC has a gradient of $\frac{1}{3}$.
   KAB is a straight line.
   - 4.1 Find $C\hat{T}X$ (2)
   - 4.2 Calculate $B\hat{A}C$ (5)

   Give your answers correct to two decimal places.

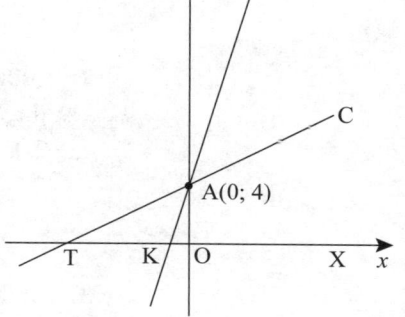

5. In the diagram P(5; 2), Q(1; −1) and R(9; −5) are the vertices of a triangle. PW is an altitude of the triangle with W on QR.

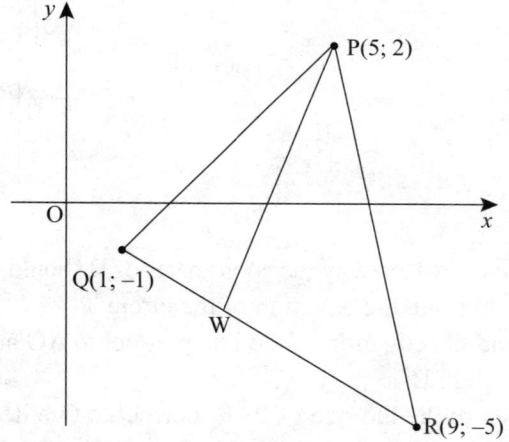

   Calculate:
   - 5.1 the length of QR (leave your answer in simplest surd form) (2)
   - 5.2 the equation of QR (4)
   - 5.3 the equation of the altitude PW (3)
   - 5.4 the coordinates of W (3)
   - 5.5 the area of △PQR (4)

   Total: 50

Test B: Complex procedures and problem solving

1. In the diagram, A(–3; 11) and C(1; 3) are the coordinates of two points on circle ABC with AB a diameter. The equation of AB is $y = 3x + 20$.

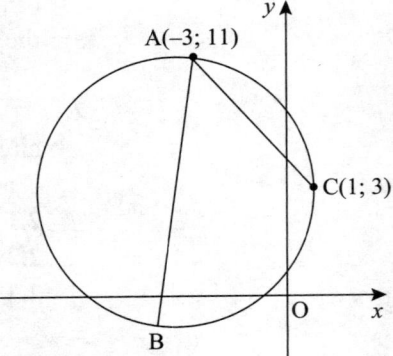

   Calculate:
   1.1 the equation of the perpendicular bisector of AC (6)
   1.2 the equation of circle ABC (6)
   1.3 the length of diameter AB (leave your answer as a simplified surd) (2)
   1.4 the area of triangle ABC. (4)

2. A circle with centre P(m; n) touches the y-axis at point Q and passes through point R(–1; –1). If P is on line $2x + y + 4 = 0$:
   2.1 calculate the possible coordinates of P (10)
   2.2 write down the equation(s) of the circle(s) in the form $(x - a)^2 + (y - b)^2 = r^2$ (4)

3. In the diagram, A(3; 2) lies on the circumference of a circle with centre P. The circle passes through the origin and cuts the x-axis at B.

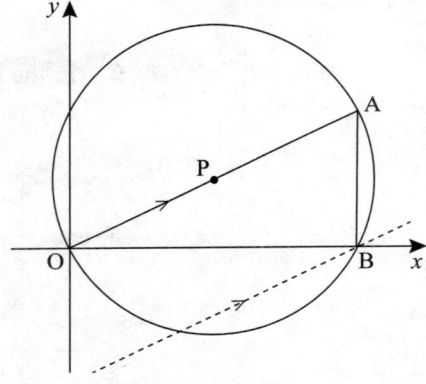

   3.1 Give a reason why the coordinates of B should be (3; 0). (2)
   3.2 Determine the equation of the circle. (4)
   3.3 Find the equation of the line parallel to AO and passing through B. (3)
   3.4 Determine the size of PÂB, correct to two decimal places. (3)
   3.5 If B is transformed by a rotation of 90° anticlockwise about the origin, determine the coordinates of B′. (2)
   3.6 Describe the location of B′ with reference to the circle. (2)
   3.7 Write down the equation of the circle with centre at B and with A on the circumference. (2)

   Total: 50

Test C: Breakdown and content as per final exam

1. The points A(–2; 3), B(–3; -3) and C(4; 0) are given.
   1.1 Calculate the angle that AB makes with the x-axis, correct to one decimal place. (3)
   1.2 Determine the coordinates of M, the midpoint of AC. (2)
   1.3 Determine the perimeter of ΔABC to the nearest whole number. (7)
   1.4 Determine the equation of the line parallel to AB that passes through M. Leave your equation in the form $ay + bx = c$. (4)
   1.5 Find the value of t if points A(–2; 3), B(–3; -3) and D(–1; t) are collinear. (2)

2. The equation of a circle is $x^2 + y^2 - 8x + 6y = 15$.
   2.1 Prove that the point (2; –9) is on the circumference of this circle. (2)
   2.2 Determine an equation of the tangent to the circle at the point (2; –9). (7)

3. Calculate the length of the tangent AB drawn from the point A(6; 4) to the circle with the equation $(x - 3)^2 + (y + 1)^2 = 10$. (5)

4. A circle with centre A and equation $(x - 3)^2 + (y + 2)^2 = 25$ is given in the diagram below. B is the y-intercept of the circle.

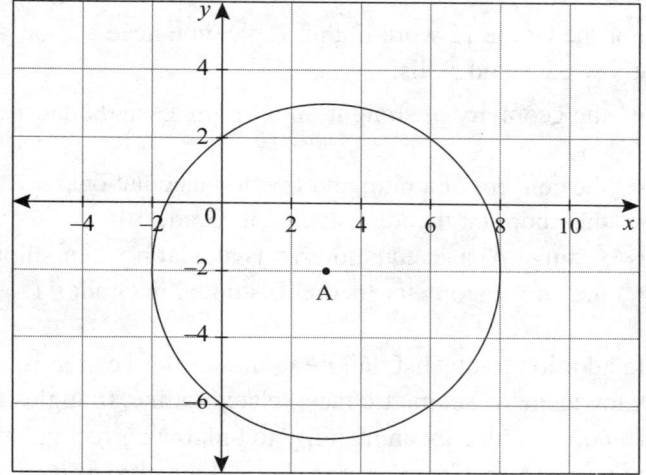

   4.1 Determine the coordinates of point B. (4)
   4.2 The circle is enlarged by a scale factor of $\frac{3}{2}$. Write down the equation of the new circle in the form $(x - a)^2 + (y - b)^2 = r^2$. (3)
   4.3 In addition to the circle with centre A and equation $(x - 3)^2 + (y + 2)^2 = 25$, you are given the circle $(x - 12)^2 + (y - 10)^2 = 100$ with centre B.
      4.3.1 Calculate the distance between the centres A and B. (2)
      4.3.2 At how many points do these two circles intersect? Justify your answer. (2)

5. Determine the equations of the two tangents to the circle defined by the equation $x^2 + y^2 = 20$, given that both tangents are parallel to the line with the equation $y = -2x + 4$. (7)

Total: 50

TOPIC 8 Euclidean geometry and measurement

In Grade 10 you learnt that line segments joining the midpoints of two sides of a triangle are equal to half the length of and parallel to the third side of the triangle. You also investigated special properties of quadrilaterals. The geometry learnt in Grades 8 and 9 can also be used in Grades 10 to 12.

In Grade 11 you investigated and proved the theorems of the geometry of circles, assuming the results from earlier Grades. Properties and proofs related to tangents and cyclic quadrilaterals are also studied in Grade 11. On solving circle geometry problems, you learnt how to give reasons for statements when required.

In Grade 12 you will work with similar geometric figures, revising the necessary and sufficient conditions for polygons to be similar. You will then use these facts and additional theorems and axioms to prove geometry riders, using similar triangles within triangles and circles.

Knowledge and skills for this Topic

For the Grade 12 work in this Topic, you need a good grasp of the following knowledge and skills:

- the geometry of straight lines, triangles and quadrilaterals studied in Grades 8 and 9
- the concept of a ratio and fraction calculations
- the midpoint theorem studied in Grade 10
- setting up basic equations and calculating their solutions
- the circle geometry theorems studied in Grade 11.

In addition to this list, failure to master this section is often the result of a poor knowledge of geometric facts related to line, triangles and quadrilaterals. This can be compounded by an inability to link the correct geometric facts to the geometry of circles and to similar triangles and the ratio of their sides.

Content of final exam

- Use results of proofs established in earlier Grades.
- Use similar triangles to calculate lengths using ratios of the sides of the triangles.
- Use a tangent to a circle perpendicular to the radius, drawn to the point of contact, to solve problems.
- Prove the theorems of the geometry of circles.
- Use the theorems above and their converses to solve geometry riders.

Proportion

A ratio is a comparison of two quantities. A **proportion** is an equation with a ratio on either side of the equation, so you will have 'a ratio = a ratio', e.g. $\frac{1}{3} = \frac{2}{6}$.

When two triangles are similar, the angles of the triangles are equal, so we call the triangles 'equiangular'. Also the lengths of the corresponding sides of the triangles are proportional. This means that proportions can be used to find the unknown sides of similar triangles.

Worked example

Find the value of x using the two similar triangles provided.

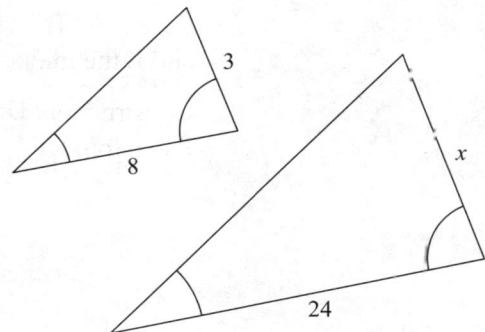

Solution

In these two similar triangles the value of x can be found using ratios that are equal to one another.

1. To do this, first set up a proportion, starting with the length of the unknown, x.

2. The lengths of the sides of the triangle that containing the unknown variable will be on the same side of the proportion, while the lengths of the sides of the other triangle will be on the other side of it.

3. Also write the corresponding sides in the same position in each ratio representing the proportion. So if the value of shorter side of the first triangle is the numerator, and the value of longer side is the denominator, then do the same for the other triangle.

$$\frac{x}{24} = \frac{3}{8}$$
$$8x = 3 \times 24$$
$$x = 9$$

Similar polygons

Any polygon will be similar to another polygon when the corresponding interior angles are equal and the corresponding sides are in the same proportion. An enlargement or a reduction of any polygon will result in a polygon that is similar to the original polygon.

Worked example

If in the two pentagons ABCDE and PQRST:

$\hat{A} = \hat{P}, \hat{B} = \hat{Q}, \hat{C} = \hat{R}, \hat{D} = \hat{S}, \hat{E} = \hat{T}$ and

$\frac{AB}{PQ} = \frac{BC}{QR} = \frac{CD}{RS} = \frac{DE}{ST} = \frac{EA}{TP}$

then polygon ABCDE is similar to polygon PQRST.

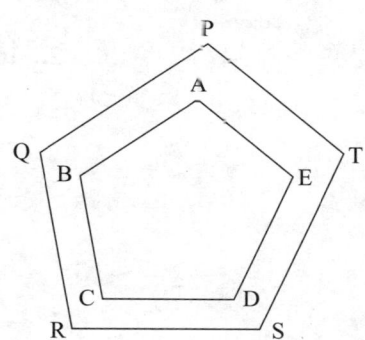

Properties of similar polygons
- Corresponding angles are equal.
- Corresponding sides are in the same proportion.
- Corresponding diagonals are in the same proportion.
- The ratio of the areas of the two polygons is the square of the ratio of the sides.

The midpoint theorem
In any triangle, the line joining the midpoints of two sides in the triangle is parallel to the third side and equal to half the length of the third side.

Given: △ABC with D the midpoint of AB and E the midpoint of AC. DE is joined.

Construction: Draw DE its own length to F and join CF.

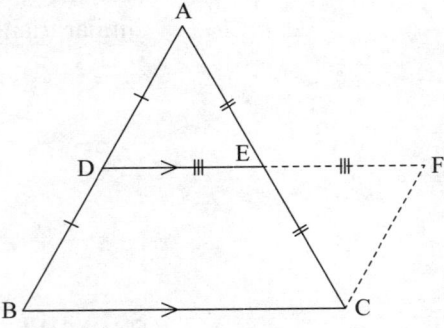

Proof: ADCF is a parallelogram

Remember
RTP means 'required to prove'.

RTP: ADCF is a parallelogram
Diagonals AC and DF bisect one another, ∴ DF ∥ BC.
$$DF = BC$$
and $DE = \frac{1}{2} DF$
∴ $DE = \frac{1}{2} BC$ and DE ∥ BC
∴ ADCF is a parallelogram.

Proof: A line parallel to one side of a triangle divides the other two sides proportionally

1. In △ABC, DE ∥ BC
   ∴ $\frac{AD}{DB} = \frac{AE}{EC}$
   and $\frac{AD}{AB} = \frac{AE}{AC}$
   and $\frac{AB}{DB} = \frac{AC}{EC}$

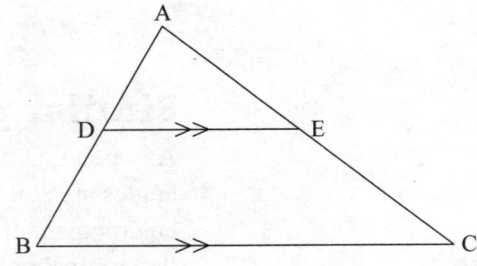

2. In △ATC, if $\frac{AS}{ST} = \frac{AP}{PC}$, then SP ∥ TC.

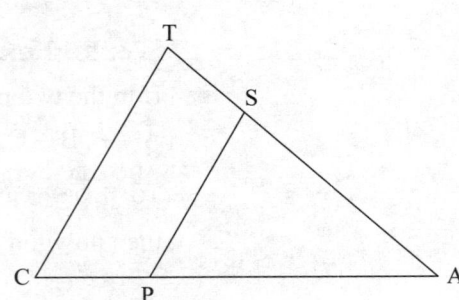

Similarity

Two triangles are said to be similar if and only if their corresponding angles are equal and their corresponding sides are in proportion.

There are three valid methods of proving triangles similar:

1. Two angles in one triangle are equal to two angles in another triangle.

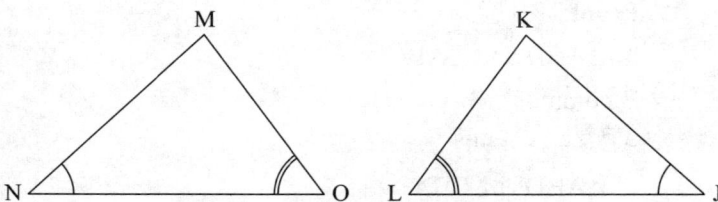

2. Three sides in one triangle are proportional to the three corresponding sides in another triangle.

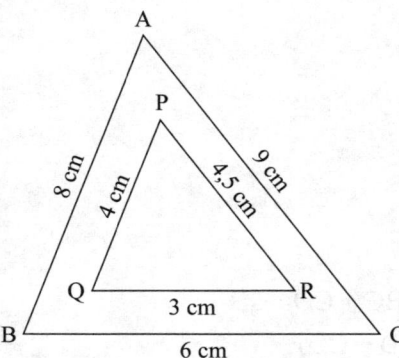

3. One angle in one triangle is equal to an angle in another triangle and the lengths of the sides which include this angle are proportional.

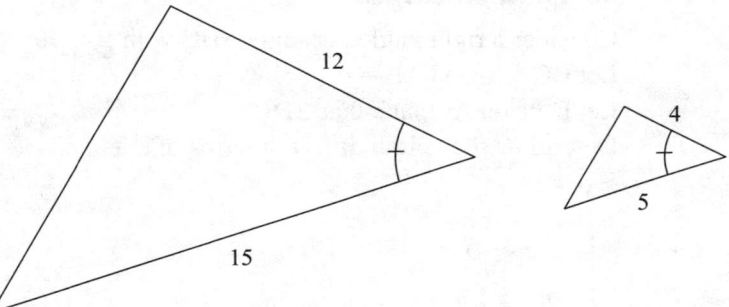

Proof: Equiangular triangles are similar

Remember
||| means 'is similar to'

Prove that
△MNO ||| △KJL.

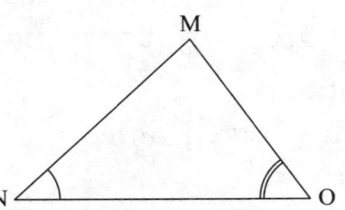
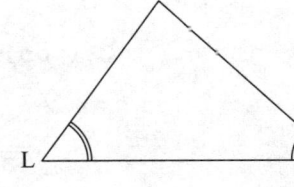

In △s MNO and KJL:

$\hat{N} = \hat{J}$ given

$\hat{O} = \hat{L}$ given

∴ △MNO ||| △KJL   ∠, ∠

∴ $\frac{MN}{KJ} = \frac{NO}{JL} = \frac{MO}{KL}$

Or $\frac{MN}{NO} = \frac{KJ}{JL}$

TOPIC 8 Euclidean geometry and measurement   171

Proving the theorem of Pythagoras using similarity

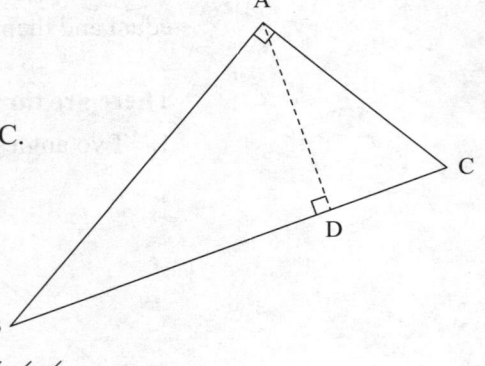

Given: Any $\triangle ABC$ with $\hat{A} = 90°$.
RTP: $BC^2 = AB^2 + AC^2$
Construction: Draw $AD \perp BC$ with D on BC.

Proof:
In $\triangle ABD$ and $\triangle ABC$:
$\hat{B}$ common
$A\hat{D}B = \hat{A} = 90°$
$\therefore \triangle ABD \;|||\; \triangle CBA$ ∠, ∠, ∠
$\therefore \frac{AB}{CB} = \frac{BD}{BA} = \frac{AD}{CA}$
$\therefore AB^2 = BD \cdot BC$

In $\triangle ADC$ and $\triangle ABC$:
$\hat{C}$ common
$A\hat{D}C = \hat{A} = 90°$
$\therefore \triangle CDA \;|||\; \triangle CAB$ ∠, ∠, ∠
$\therefore \frac{CD}{CA} = \frac{AC}{CB} = \frac{AD}{BA}$
$\therefore AC^2 = CD \cdot CB$

$AB^2 + AC^2 = BD \cdot BC + CD \cdot CB$
$\qquad\qquad\quad = BC(BD + CD)$
$\qquad\qquad\quad = BC^2$

Worked example

Consider a right angled triangle ABC with $\hat{B} = 90°$.
Let $BC = a$, and $AB = c$.
Let D be on AC such that $B\hat{D}C$.
Determine the length of BD in terms of a and c.

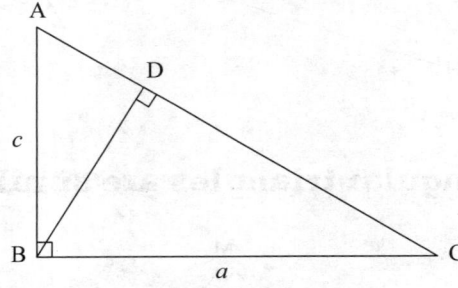

Solution

$\triangle CDB \;|||\; \triangle CBA \;|||\; \triangle BDA$ AA

$\therefore \frac{DB}{BA} = \frac{BC}{AC}$

$DB = \frac{BA \cdot BC}{AC}$

$\quad\;\; = \frac{ca}{AC}$

$\quad\;\; = \frac{ca}{\sqrt{a^2 + c^2}}$

Note

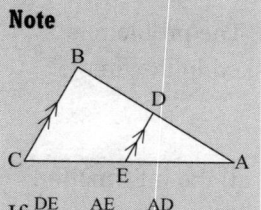

If $\frac{DE}{BC} = \frac{AE}{AC} = \frac{AD}{AB}$

∴ △ADE ||| △ABC

Ways in which similarity can be asked

1. Prove that △ABC ||| △DEF.

2. Prove that $\frac{PQ}{DE} = \frac{QR}{EF}$:
   - First prove: △PQR ||| △DEF.
   - Then deduce the proportion of the sides.

3. Prove that KN · PX = NR · YP.
   - Find two triangles in which KN, PX, NR and YP (or sides equal to these) appear.
   - Thus prove that: △KNR ||| △YPX.
   - Every time you prove triangles similar, write down the ratio of the proportional sides, even if this is not asked, as it will help you with the rest of the question.

Worked examples

In △ABC, P is the midpoint of AC.
RS ∥ BP and $\frac{AR}{AB} = \frac{3}{5}$. CR cuts BP into T.

Determine with reasons the following ratios:
1. $\frac{AS}{SC}$
2. $\frac{RT}{TC}$
3. $\frac{\text{Area } \triangle TPC}{\text{Area } \triangle RSC}$

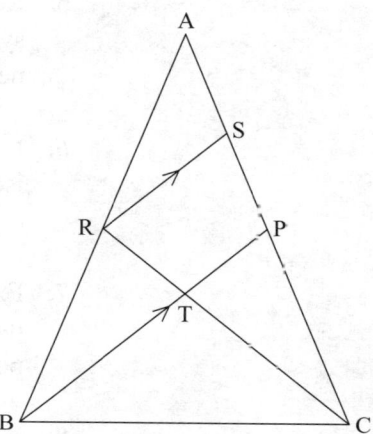

Solutions

1. $\frac{AS}{SP} = \frac{AR}{RB}$ RS ∥ BP

   $= \frac{3}{2}$

   ∴ $\frac{AS}{SC} = \frac{3}{7}$

2. $\frac{RT}{TC} = \frac{SP}{PC}$ RS ∥ TP

   $= \frac{2}{5}$

3. $\frac{\text{Area } \triangle TPC}{\text{Area } \triangle RSC} = \frac{\frac{1}{2} TC \cdot PC \sin T\hat{C}P}{\frac{1}{2} RC \cdot SC \sin R\hat{C}S} = \frac{TC}{RC} \cdot \frac{PC}{SC}$

   $= \frac{5}{7} \cdot \frac{5}{7}$

   $= \frac{25}{49}$

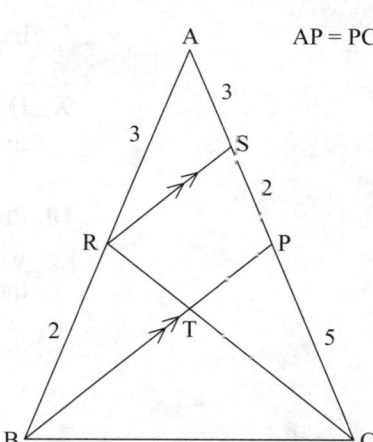

AP = PC

TOPIC 8 *Euclidean geometry and measurement*

Preparing for exams

1. **Know** your **theorems** and basic geometric facts (axioms). The problem is always based on the proof or the statement of the proof asked in the first question.

2. Mark all the given information in pen on the diagram and all the information you work out in pencil.

3. Make sure to indicate circle centres, parallel and perpendicular lines, tangents, radii, diameters and equal chords.

4. Mark equal angles using algebra, i.e. use variables, e.g. x and y, and mark relationships between angles using arcs.

5. Read the statement about what you need to prove, and rephrase it using symbols and = signs. Remember that each question is usually the clue to the next question.

6. Use the special facts stated, e.g. the exterior angle of a triangle, properties of an isosceles triangle, two tangents intersecting from the same circle are equal, and equal chords subtending equal angles.

7. Examine what was given and take note of what information has not yet been used. Any related statements that follow the given facts will be useful at the point at which they are given.

8. Wherever possible, give a reason for a statements you make. When evaluating a reason the examiner will want to know without a doubt which geometric fact has been used in the right place, so **be specific**.

9. **Do not** name points that have not been named for you, and **do not** draw extra lines unless you are asked to.

10. Plan your work first, and then set it out in a logical flow of statements, backed with reasons. Lay your work out neatly, leaving space for clarifying your thoughts further.

Test A: Knowledge and routine procedures

Determine the lengths of the sides with letters.

1. 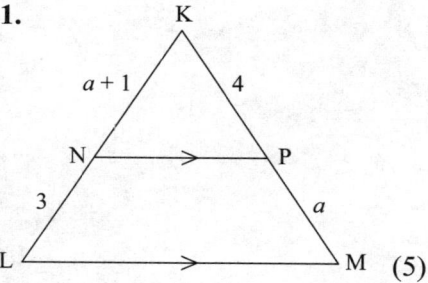 (5)

2. 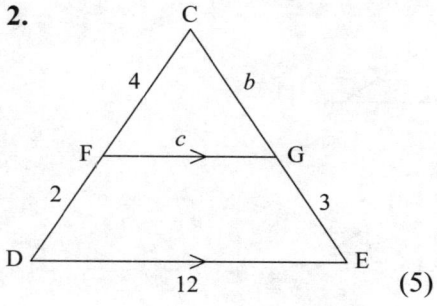 (5)

3. 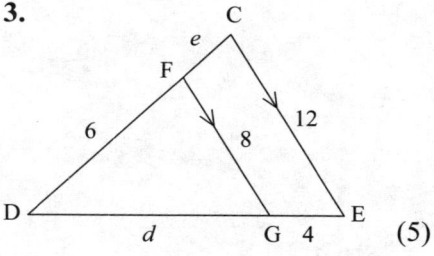 (5)

4. 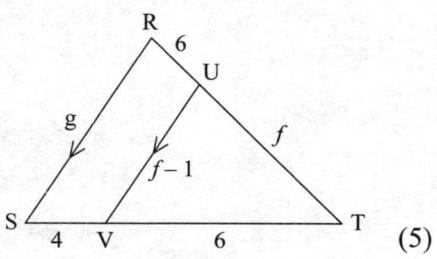 (5)

5. 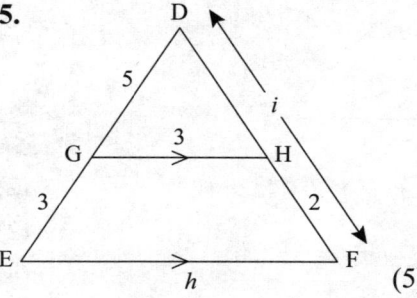 (5)

6. 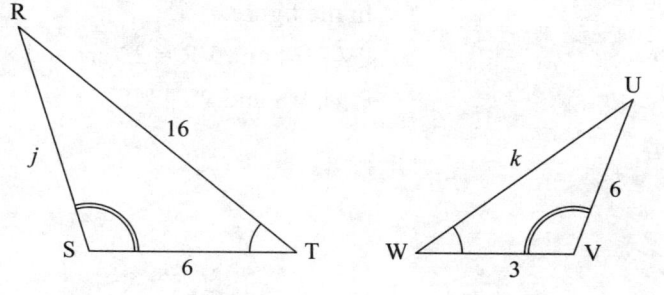 (5)

7. 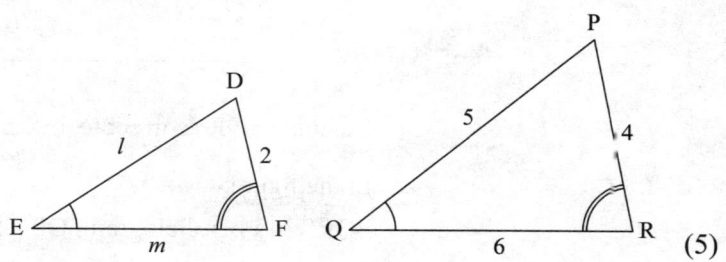 (5)

8. 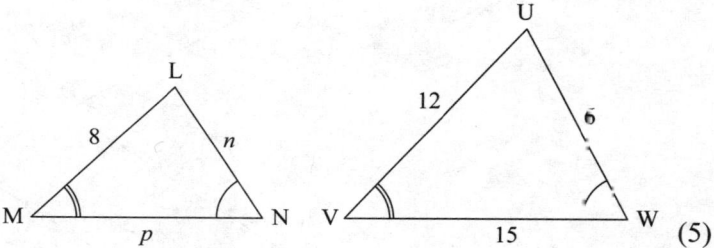 (5)

9. 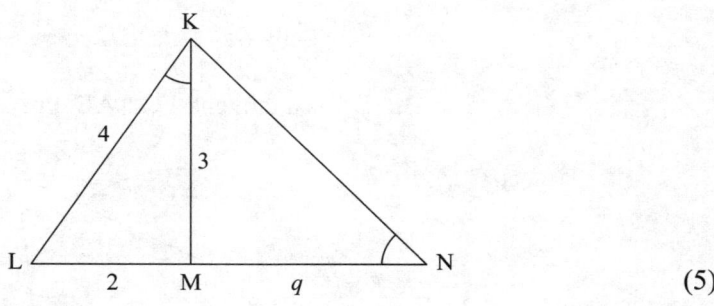 (5)

10. 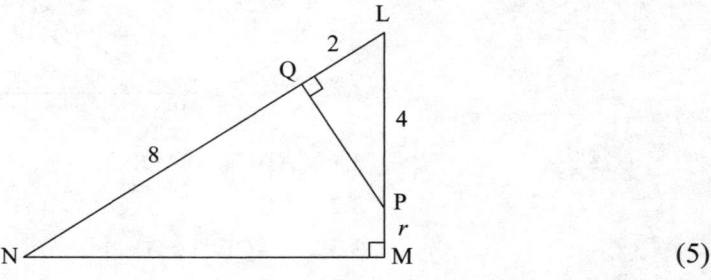 (5)

Total: 50

Test B: Complex procedures and problem solving

1. In the figure:
   PV = 24 cm, VR = 22 cm and ST = 12 cm.
   PQ ∥ VS and PS ∥ VT.

   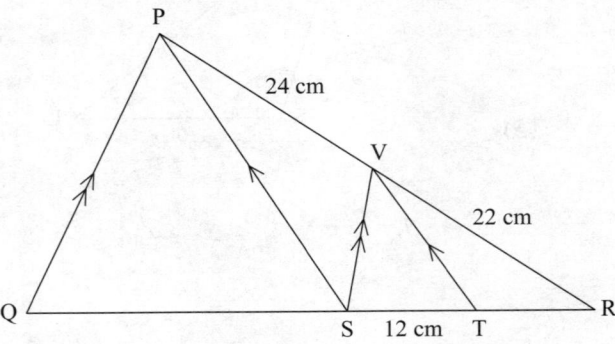

   Calculate: QR (correct to 1 decimal place). (4)

2. In the figure:
   PQRS is a parallelogram. QS ∥ BC and $\frac{QB}{BR} = \frac{2}{3}$.

   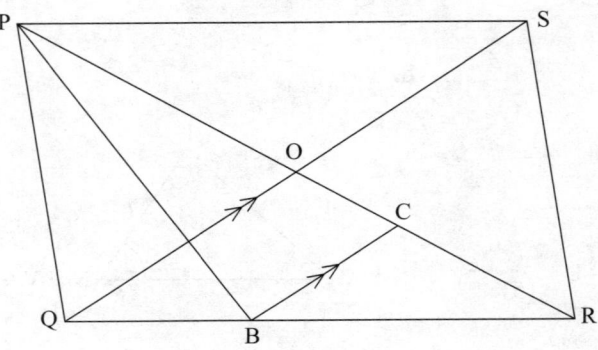

   Calculate $\frac{PO}{OC}$. (3)

3. BA is a tangent. FG ∥ AE. Prove that:

   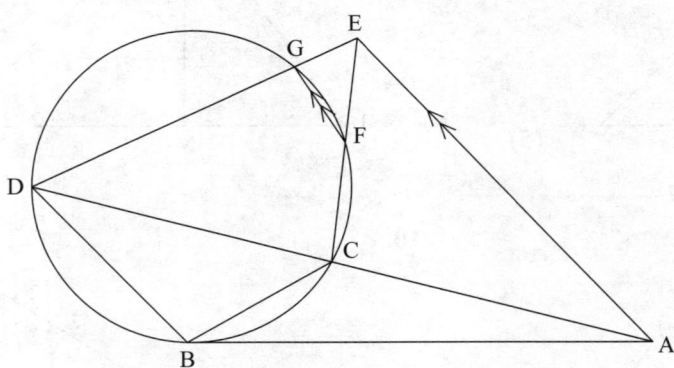

   3.1 △ABC ||| △ADB (2)
   3.2 $AB^2 = AD \cdot AC$ (2)
   3.3 △ACE ||| △AED (4)
   3.4 AB = AE. (4)

4. In the figure, AD and CF are medians of △ABC and they cut one another at point S. Line segment FPQ is parallel to BS and cuts AS at P and AC at Q. Prove that AQ = $\frac{1}{4}$AC. (5)

Remember
Medians are concurrent and the ratio of SD : AS = 12.

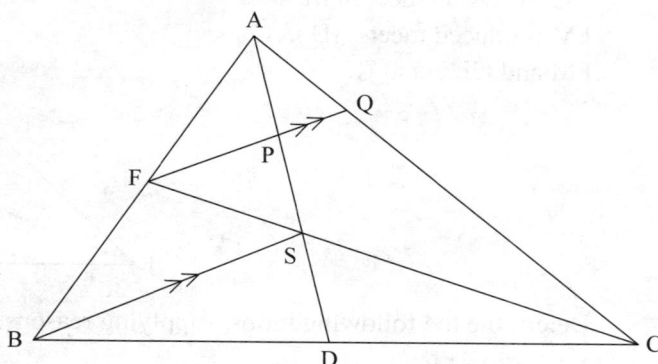

5. In the diagram below, A, B, C and D are points on the circumference of the circle. BD and AC intersect at E.
EB = 8 cm, DC = 8 cm and AE : EC = 4 : 7.

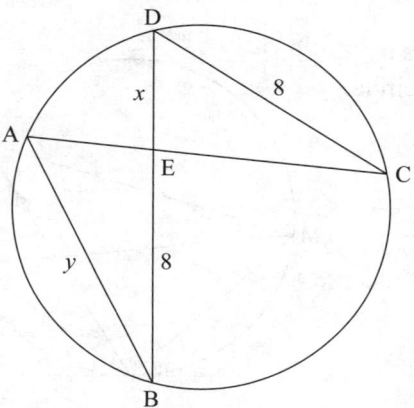

If DE = x units and AB = y units, calculate x and y. (6)

6. In the diagram below, M is the centre of the circle. FEC is a tangent to the circle at E. D is the midpoint of AB.

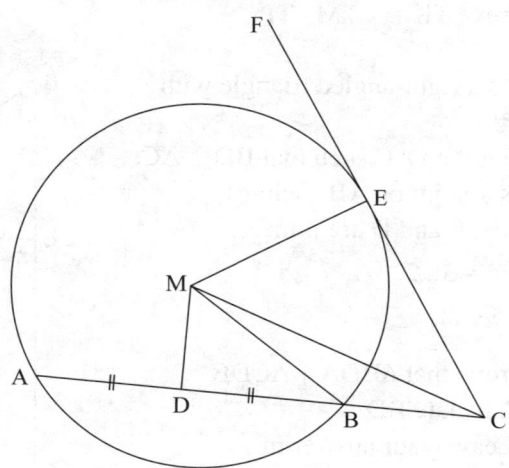

6.1 Prove MDCE is a cyclic quadrilateral. (3)
6.2 Prove that $MC^2 = MB^2 + DC^2 - DB^2$. (3)
6.3 Calculate CE if AB = 60 mm, ME = 40 mm and BC = 20 mm. (4)

Total: 40

Test C: Breakdown and content as per final exam

1. In the figure, the medians AE and DG of △AFD meet in M.
   FM produced meets AD in C.
   FM and GE cut at K.

   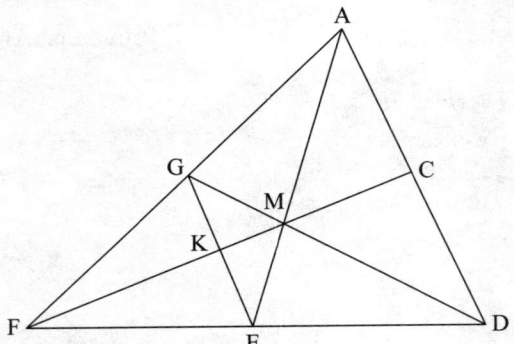

   Determine the following ratios, supplying reasons:
   1.1 FM : MC (1)
   1.2 FK : KC (5)
   1.3 FK : KM (4)
   1.4 Area △GKM : Area △CMD (6)

2. SM = SP. YZ is a tangent to the circle.
   KZ ∥ LS.

   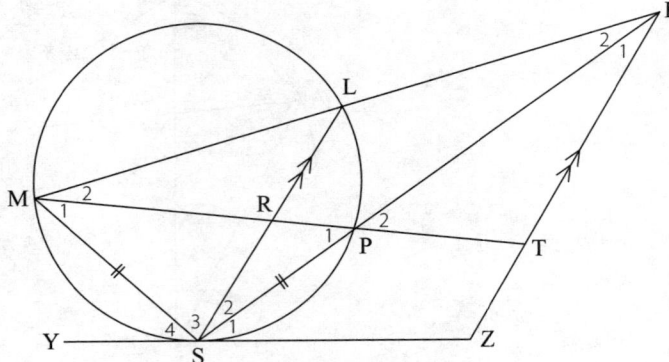

   Prove that:
   2.1 △KZS ||| △SRP (4)
   2.2 KT · KS = KZ · KP (4)
   2.3 TK is tangent to circle KMP (4)
   2.4 Prove TK = $\sqrt{TM \cdot TP}$ (4)

3. △ABC is a right-angled triangle with $\hat{B} = 90°$.
   D is a point on AC such that BD ⊥ AC, and E is a point on AB such that DE ⊥ AB. E and D are joined.
   AD : DC = 3 : 2.
   AD = 15 cm.

   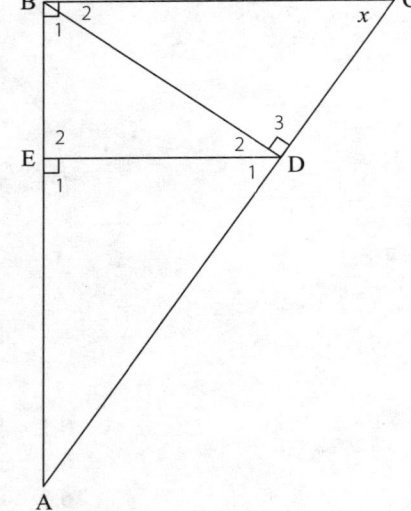

   3.1 Prove that △BDA ||| △CDB. (3)
   3.2 Calculate BD.
        (Leave your answer in surd form.) (3)
   3.3 Calculate AE.
        (Leave your answer in surd form.) (6)

4. In the diagram below, points R, P, A, Q and T lie on a circle. RA bisects $\hat{R}$ and AB = AQ. RA and TQ produced meet at B.

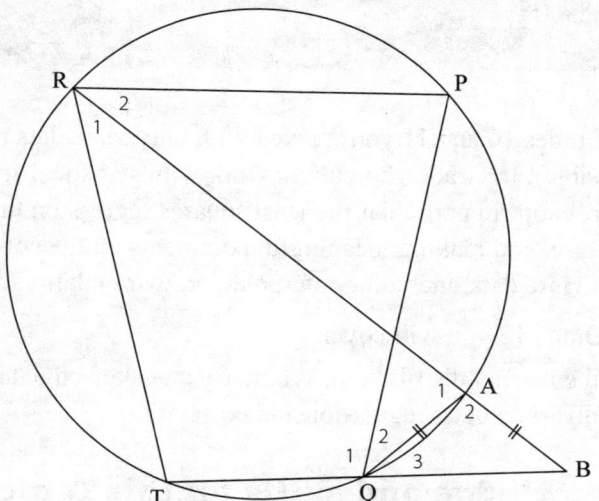

Prove that:

4.1 AQ bisects $P\hat{Q}B$ (3)

4.2 TR = TB (2)

4.3 $\hat{P} = T\hat{R}P$ (3)

Total: 52

TOPIC 9 Statistics: Regression and correlation

In Grades 10 and 11 you worked with univariate data (i.e. data with only one variable). In Grade 12 you will work with statistical summaries, scatter plots, regression (in particular the least squares regression line) and correlation to analyse, and making meaningful comments on the context associated with given **bivariate** data, including interpolation, extrapolation on skewness.

In Grade 12 you will cover:
- the normal distribution, symmetry and skewed data
- bivariate data: regression and correlation.

Knowledge and skills for this Topic

For the Grade 12 work in this Topic, you need to have a good grasp of all the skills you learnt in Grades 10 and 11 as well as the new skills you will learn in Grade 12.

Content of final exam

- Integrated questions involving the use of statistical summaries of both univariate and bivariate data.
- Collect, organise and interpret univariate data in order to determine:
  - measures of central tendency, in both grouped and ungrouped data
  - five-point summary
  - box and whisker diagrams
  - measures of dispersion (mean, modal interval, percentiles, quartiles, IQR and semi-IQR.
- Represent measures of central tendency and dispersion in univariate numerical data by:
  - setting up, interpreting and using stem and leaf plots, bar graphs, line graphs, histograms, frequency polygons and ogives (cumulative frequency curves)
  - manually calculating the variance and standard deviation of sets of data (for small sets of data) and using calculators (for large sets of data) and representing results graphically
  - representing, recognising and interpreting skewed data in box diagrams, whisker diagrams and frequency polygons
  - identifying outliers.
- Represent bivariate numerical data (i.e. data with two variables) as a scatter plot and draw in lines of best fit.
- Suggest intuitively and by simple investigation whether a linear, quadratic or exponential function would best fit the data.
- Use a calculator to calculate the linear regression line that best fits a given set of bivariate numerical data.
- Use a calculator to calculate the correlation coefficient of a set of bivariate numerical data and make relevant deductions.
- Interpolate and extrapolate values from given bivariate data sets.

Relevant formulae

$$\bar{x} = \frac{\sum fx}{n} \qquad \sigma^2 = \frac{\sum_{i=1}^{n}(x_1 - \bar{x})^2}{n} \qquad \hat{y} = a + bx \qquad b = \frac{\sum(x - \bar{x})(y - \bar{y})}{\sum(x - \bar{x})^2}$$

The standard deviation definition is not given on your formula sheet, but is well worth noting:

$$\text{Standard deviation} = \sqrt{\frac{\sum f(x - \bar{x})^2}{n}}$$

The normal distribution

Notes on calculator usage

You will be required to use a calculator to calculate the correlations coefficient and regression lines. You may use your calculator to find the mean and the standard deviation, but you can also be asked to perform these calculations manually on small sets of data.

In Grade 12 you are expected to recognise only one type of distribution: the **normal distribution**. This distribution is a theoretical distribution that we use to help us to carry out calculations and to draw conclusions about data that has been collected. Much of the data we gather can be modelled using the normal distribution. The normal distribution is shaped like a bell, as shown in the diagram.

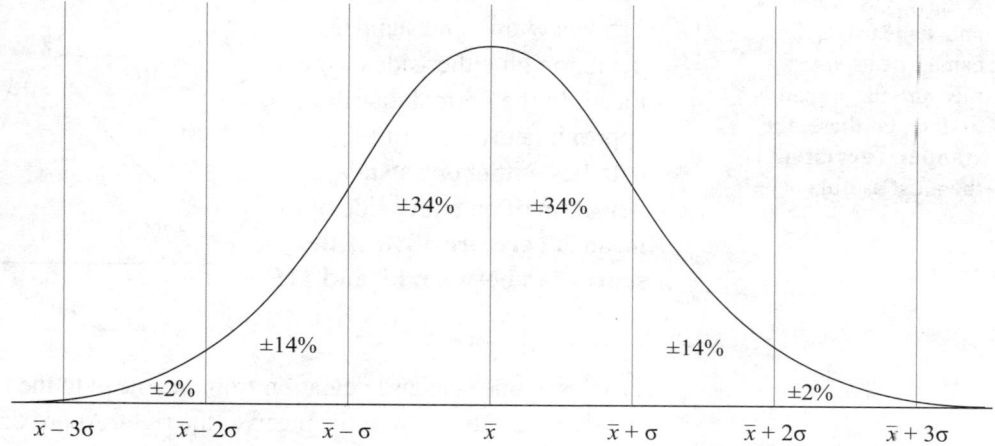

- The normal distribution is perfectly symmetrical about the mean.
- The ends of the bell curve approach, but don't actually touch the x-axis.
- The x-axis is an asymptote to the bell curve.

As you can see, most of the data occurs close to the mean. An important point to remember is that approximately $\frac{2}{3}$ of the data fall within one standard deviation (σ) on either side of the mean. In addition, for a symmetrical distribution, the mean, median and the mode are the same.

In the normal distribution, approximately 99,7% (that's almost 100%) of the data lie under the curve:

- **±68%** of the data lie within one standard deviation on either side of the mean
- **±34%** lie between the mean and one standard deviation to the right of the mean and ±34% lie between the mean and one standard deviation below the mean.
- **±14%** of the data lie between the first and the second deviation from the mean both to the left and to the right of the mean
- **±2%** of the data lie between the second and the third standard deviation on either side of the mean, as summarised in the diagram.

TOPIC 9 Statistics: Regression and correlation

Using the normal distribution and standard deviation to interpret data

Worked examples

The members of a local gym did a fitness test. The performance scores were analysed and found to follow a normal distribution with a mean of 100 and a standard deviation of 15.

1. Approximately what percentage of the scores lie between 85 and 115?

2. If a performance score between 115 and 130 indicates that a member is fit, approximately what percentage of the members falls into this category?

3. If there are 500 members at the local gym, how many of them would you expect to score more than 130?

4. If there are 500 members at the local gym, how many members would be classified as unfit?

> **Note**
> Range, IQR, variance and standard deviation can all be used to measure the spread of data. Of these, the **standard deviation** is the most useful.

Solutions

1. $100 - 15 = 85$ and $100 + 15 = 115$
   The interval between 85 and 115 lies within one standard deviation on either side of the mean. In the normal distribution, approximately 68% of the data lies within one standard deviation of on either side of the mean. **Therefore 68% of the scores lies between 85 and 115.**

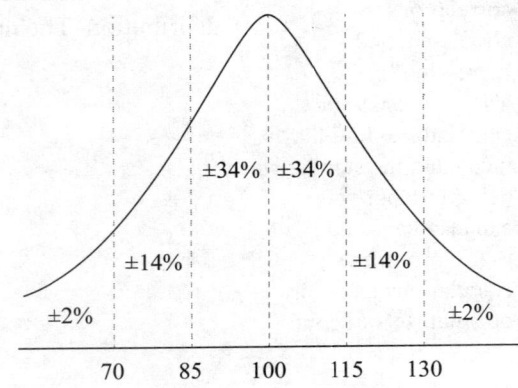

2. $115 + 15 = 130$
   115 lies at one standard deviation from the mean to the right and 130 lies at two standard deviations from the mean to the right. Approximately 14% of the normal distribution lies between one standard deviation and two standard deviations from the mean. **Therefore 14% of the scores lies between 115 and 130.**

3. 130 lies at two standard deviations from the mean to the right. In a normal distribution, 2% of the population lies in the region above the second standard deviation. 2% of 500 = 10, **therefore 10 members would be above 130.**

4. A performance score of between 115 and 130 indicates that a member is fit, therefore all scores below 115 are classified as unfit. 2% + 14% + 34% + 34% = 84%. Therefore 84% of the members will be classified as unfit.
   84% of 500 = 420, **therefore 420 members would be classified as unfit.**

Worked examples

A survey was conducted on the heights of senior high school basket ball and soccer players. The cumulative results for both sporting codes were found to fit into normal distributions with a mean height of 186 cm and a standard deviation of 5 cm for the basket ball players, and a mean height of 176 cm and a standard deviation of 9 cm for the soccer players.

> **Remember**
> Standard deviation tells us about the **spread** of data around the mean. A small standard deviation means that data is tightly clustered around the mean and the bell shape is steep and narrow. A large standard deviation means that data is more widely spread around the mean and the bell shaped curve is relatively flat and wide.

1. Using only the facts and the figure provided, discuss the differences between these two normal distributions. Give reasonable reasons for these differences.

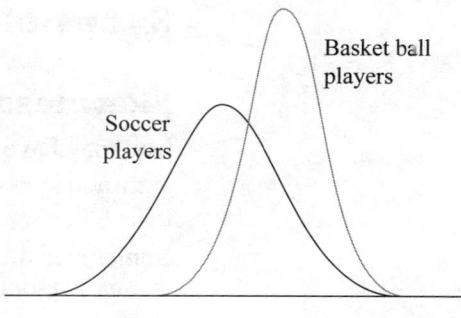

2. 500 soccer players took part in this survey. How many of these players are between 167 cm and 185 cm in height?

3. How many soccer players will be taller than 194 cm?

4. Only 6 basketball players are shorter than 176 cm. How many basketball players were there in the survey?

5. Based on the theory of the normal curve, is the tallest player in this survey a soccer player or a basket ball player?

Solutions

1. The heights of the basketball players are tightly clustered around the mean, while those of the soccer players are more loosely clustered around the mean. Basketball players in general are taller than soccer players. Being taller is an advantage on the basketball court, which accounts for taller learners choosing to play basketball. Height is of little consequence on the soccer field, so this sporting code attracts learners of all heights.

2. 176 cm − 9 cm = 167 cm
   176 cm + 9 cm = 185 cm
   A height of 167 cm lies one standard deviation away from the mean and a height of 185 cm lies one standard deviation above the mean. 68% of the data in a normal distribution lie within these two boundaries. 68% of 500 = 340. 340 soccer players lie within one standard deviation of the mean height for soccer players.

3. 176 cm + 9 cm + 9 cm = 194 cm
   A height of 194 cm lies two standard deviations above the mean height for soccer players. Only 2% of a normal distribution are found above the mean. 2% of 500 = 10. Only 10 soccer players are taller than 194 cm.

4. A height of 176 lies 2 standard deviations from the mean, which accounts for only 2% of the distribution.
   2% = 6 players
   ∴ 1% = 3 players
   100% = 300 players

   The distribution of basketball players consists of 300 players.

5. Theoretically the tallest players in each distribution are found at 3 standard deviations above the mean.
   Tallest soccer player = 176 cm + 9 cm + 9 cm + 9 cm = 203 cm
   Tallest basketball player = 186 cm + 5 cm + 5 cm + 5 cm = 201 cm

   Theoretically the tallest person in this combined survey is a soccer player.

Symmetry and skewed data

Skewness

You may have noticed the shape of the normal distribution. It is an example of a **symmetric distribution**. A symmetric distribution has data that are symmetrically distributed on either side of the mean. Not all distributions are symmetric. Sometimes they are **skewed**. Examples of the different shapes of distributions are shown below.

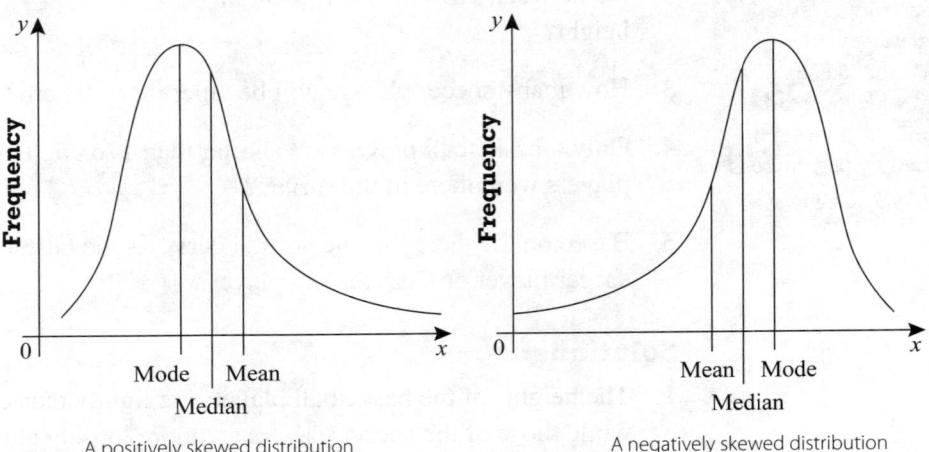

- A positively skewed distribution tails off to the *right*. The median and mode are *lower* than the mean.
- A negatively skewed distribution tails off to the *left*. The median and mode are *higher* than the mean.

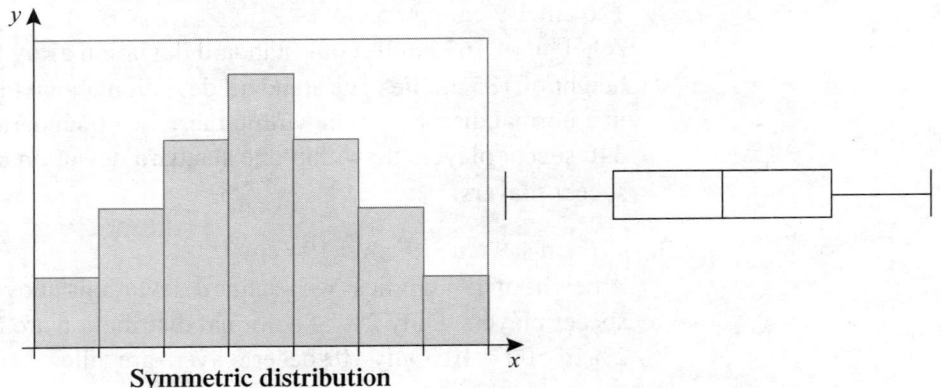

Skewed distributions

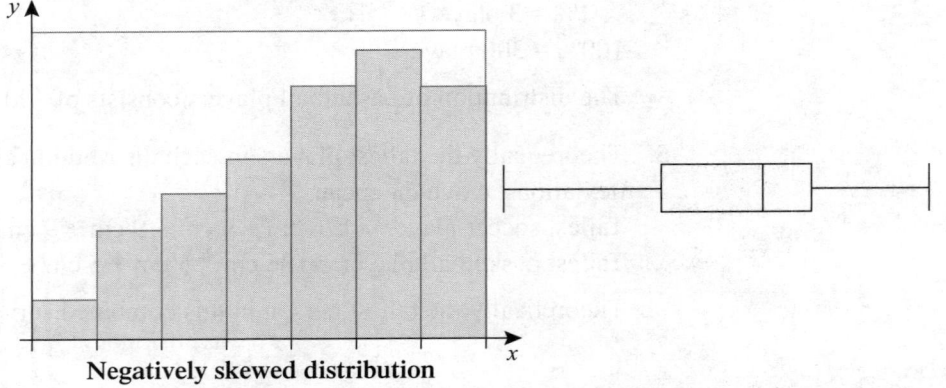

184   STUDY & MASTER MATHEMATICS STUDY GUIDE GRADE 12

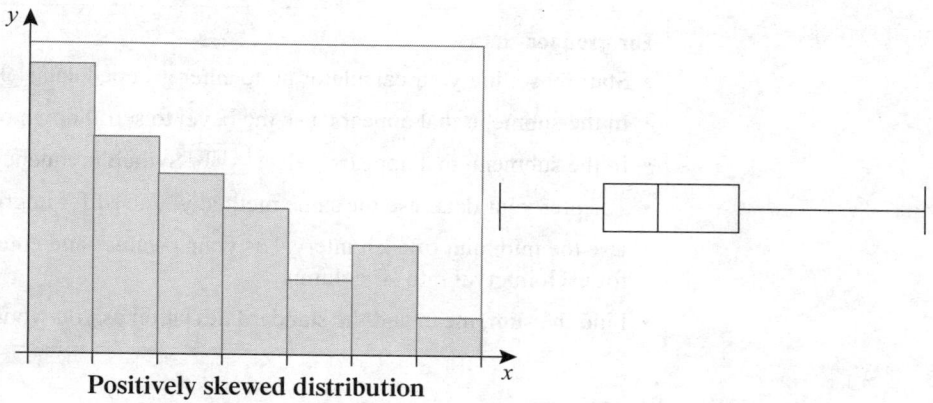

Positively skewed distribution

Bar graphs and box-and-whisker plots for different distributions

'Skewness' can be determined from a general distribution curve, ogives, box and whisker plots, and histograms.

Worked examples

The data below shows the energy levels, in kilocalories per 100 g of 11 different snack foods.

| 440 | 620 | 580 | 690 | 615 | 550 | 620 | 680 | 545 | 490 | 755 |

1. Calculate the mean energy level of the snacks.

2. Calculate the standard deviation.

3. Set up a box and whisker plot to summarise the distribution of the different snack foods. Use this to discuss the skewness of this distribution.

4. If an outlier is defined as a score that lies more than 1,5 times the interquartile range (IQR) away from the box, are there any outliers in this data set?

5. The energy levels, in kilocalories per 100 g, of 10 different breakfast cereals had a mean of 545,7 kilocalories and a standard deviation of 28 kilocalories. Which of the two types of food show greater variation in energy levels? What can you conclude?

You need to know
- how to calculate the mean and the standard deviation
- how to find a five-point summary
- how to use a five-point summary to set up a box and whisker plot.

Using your calculator to find the mean and the standard deviation

Perform manual calculations to find the mean and the standard deviation only when asked to do so. When possible, use your calculator:

- Use the mode button and select the STAT mode form the sub menu.
- Select VAR form the next sub menu.
- Insert the data values into the table that appears, pressing $=$ after each value.
- Press AC after inputting your last value.
- Clear the screen by selecting SHIFT and then STAT (the STAT button appears above the number 1 on most calculators).
- Select VAR from the sub menu that appears.
- To find the mean select $\bar{x}$ from the submenu that appears.
- Submenu: 1: n 2: $\bar{x}$ 3: σx 4: sx
- To find the standard deviation select σx followed by $=$ from the menu that appears.

TOPIC 9 Statistics: Regression and correlation

> **For grouped data**
> - Start by setting your calculator up to enter grouped data: [SHIFT] [SET UP].
> - In the submenu that appears, use the bevel to scroll down once.
> - In the submenu that appears, select [STAT] Switch Frequency ON.
> - To enter your data, use the same method you used for ungrouped data.
> - Use the midpoint of each interval as your *x*-values and enter the respective frequency for each interval into 'f' column.
> - Find the sum, mean and the standard deviation as you would for ungrouped data.

Solutions

1. Mean = $\frac{\sum x}{n} = \frac{6\,585}{11} \approx 598{,}64$

2. Standard deviation by calculator: $\sigma x \approx 86{,}95$

3. The median of 615 lies slightly above the mean of 598,64 which indicates that this distribution is slightly negatively skewed, i.e. it tails off a little to the left.

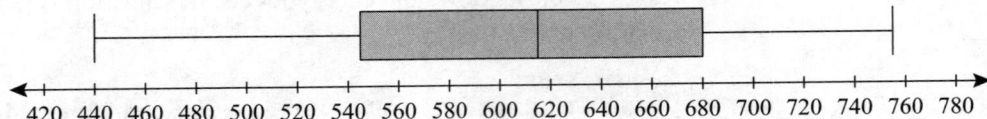

420 440 460 480 500 520 540 560 580 600 620 640 660 680 700 720 740 760 780

4. IQR = $Q_3 - Q_1$ = 680 − 545 = 135
   $1{,}5 \times 135 = 202{,}5$
   No outliers exist since 440 lies only 105 units away from the box and 755 lies only 75 units away from the box.

5.

	Mean	Standard deviation
Snack foods	598,64	86,95
Breakfast cereals	545,7	28

Snack foods have a greater variation. The standard deviation for snack foods is 86,95 kilocalories whilst the standard deviation for breakfast is 28 kilocalories. This means the energy levels for the cereals is clustered closer to the mean than those for the snack foods.

Worked examples

Mpho is employed as a human resources officer at a company. She collected data on the hourly earnings of non-salaried employees at her company and organised the data in the following table.

1. Calculate the mean for the hourly earnings of the men.

Hourly earnings (Rands)	Number of women	Number of men
$9{,}7 < x \le 9{,}9$	6	5
$9{,}9 < x \le 10{,}10$	31	16
$10{,}10 < x \le 10{,}30$	15	25
$10{,}30 < x \le 10{,}50$	29	30
$10{,}50 < x \le 10{,}70$	19	24

2. **Manually** calculate the standard deviation for the hourly earnings of the men and explain what this tells us about the 'spread' of the men's salaries.

3. Draw an ogive (cumulative frequency curve) and a box and whisker plot for the hourly earnings for the men.

4. Comment on the skewness of this distribution.

5. As part of the analysis Mpho also calculated the statistics for the women. They are: Mean: R10,25, Standard deviation: R0,25. Mpho reached the conclusion that there was little difference in the hourly earnings between men and women. Do you agree with Mpho? Explain.

Note
- Calculating the mean for grouped data is actually an estimate of the mean because we use the midpoint of each interval multiplied by the frequency to calculate the mean.
- You may be asked to work out the standard deviation without using your calculator for small data sets, i.e. by using a table of values and the definition.

Remember
To find the midpoint add the extremes and divide by 2.

Solutions

1.

Hourly earnings (Rands)	Midpoint of interval (x)	Frequency (f)	Total (fx)
$9,7 < x \leq 9,9$	9,80	5	49
$9,9 < x \leq 10,10$	10,00	16	160
$10,10 < x \leq 10,30$	10,20	25	255
$10,30 < x \leq 10,50$	10,40	30	312
$10,50 < x \leq 10,70$	10,60	24	254,4

Mean $= \frac{\sum(fx)}{n}$

$= \frac{1030,4}{100}$

$\approx R10,30$

2.

Hourly earnings (Rands)	Midpoint of interval (x)	Frequency (f)	$(x - \bar{x})$	$(x - \bar{x})^2$	$f(x - \bar{x})^2$
$9,7 < x \leq 9,9$	9,80	5	–0,5	0,25	1,25
$9,9 < x \leq 10,10$	10,00	16	– 0,3	0,09	1,44
$10,10 < x \leq 10,30$	10,20	25	– 0,1	0,01	0,25
$10,30 < x \leq 10,50$	10,40	30	0,1	0,01	0,3
$10,50 < x \leq 10,70$	10,60	24	0,3	0,09	2,16
Sum		100			5,4

Standard deviation $= \sqrt{\frac{\sum f(x - \bar{x})^2}{n}} = \sqrt{\frac{5,4}{100}} = 0,2323... \approx 0,23$ cents

The standard deviation is low, which means that the men's salaries are closely clustered about the mean.

Note
The formula for standard deviation is not given on your formula sheet.

Remember
When drawing an ogive (cumulative frequency curve), plot the cumulative frequency at the end of the interval.

3.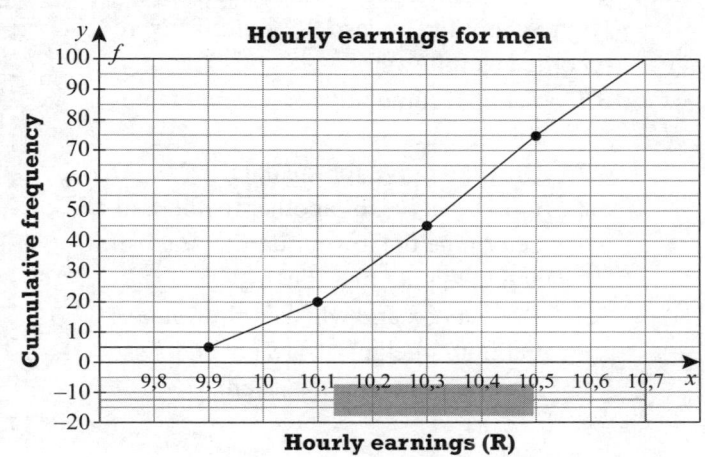

TOPIC 9 Statistics: Regression and correlation

> **Note**
> The five-point summary and the box and whisker plot can be determined directly from the ogive.

4. The distribution is asymmetrical, i.e. it is negatively skewed and tails off to the left. The median is higher than the mean.

5. Yes, she is correct. The difference in the mean between men and women is only 5 cents and the difference between the standard deviation is only 2 cents so the salaries for both the men and the women are closely clustered around the mean.

Exercise 1

1. The scores for Ms Mthethwa's Maths learners are given below:

| 72 | 83 | 84 | 83 | 79 | 78 | 86 | 92 | 95 | 88 |
| 87 | 84 | 75 | 77 | 71 | 81 | 77 | 82 | 84 | 91 |

   1.1 Calculate the mean and the standard deviation for this data set.
   1.2 What percentage of Ms Mthethwa's class lies within one standard deviation on either side of the mean?
   1.3 Use a stem-and-leaf diagram to rank these scores.
   1.4 Set up an accurate box and whisker plot.
   1.5 Use the box and whisker plot and any other relevant information to discuss the skewness of this data set.
   1.6 Which measure of dispersion would best be used to describe this data set: the mean or the median? Support your answer.

2. The distributions for the Grade 12 Maths marks for two different schools are shown in the diagram. Both Grade 12 groups have a mean of 68%. Group A has a standard deviation of 3,5 and Group B has a standard deviation of 7.

   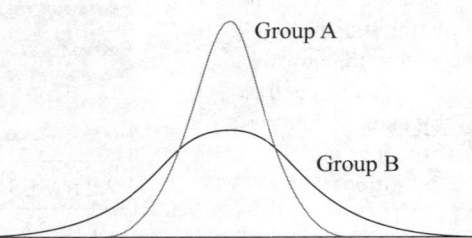

   It is given that both of these classes have normal distributions and that Group A has 136 learners and Group B 68 learners.
   2.1 Discuss the similarities and differences between these two distributions.
   2.2 How many learners in each class scored above 75%?
   2.3 Given that the results obtained by the learners in both of these classes is perfectly symmetrical, use the normal distribution to predict both the lowest and the highest scores for each of the classes.

3. The heights, h, of the learners at Nkosi High School in Grades 10, 11 and 12 were recorded as follows:
   3.1 Set up a cumulative frequency table for the data.
   3.2 Draw an ogive for the data.
   3.3 Use the ogive, or another method, to determine the lower quartile, median and the upper quartile.
   3.4 Draw a box and whisker plot for a minimum height of 118 cm and a maximum height of 178 cm.

Heights of learners in Grades 10, 11 and 12 (in cm)	Frequency
$118 \leq h < 127$	16
$127 \leq h < 136$	26
$136 \leq h < 145$	42
$145 \leq h < 154$	54
$154 \leq h < 163$	26
$163 \leq h < 172$	22
$172 \leq h < 181$	14

3.5 Comment on the symmetry of the distribution of the heights of the learners.

3.6 Approximately how many learners are between 138 cm and 158 cm tall? The heights for **only the Grade 12 learners** at Nkosi High school are given below. Use this information to answer the questions which follow.

Height of learners in Grade 12 (in cm)	Frequency
$118 \leq h < 127$	2
$127 \leq h < 136$	1
$136 \leq h < 145$	6
$145 \leq h < 154$	5
$154 \leq h < 163$	10
$163 \leq h < 172$	15
$172 \leq h < 181$	8

3.7 What is the modal height for Grade 12 learners?

3.8 Use your calculator to calculate an estimate of the mean height for the Grade 12 learners.

3.9 Set up a frequency ogive for the Grade 12 learners.

3.10 Use the ogive to set up a box and whisker plot.

3.11 By referring to the relationship between the mean and the median, state whether the distribution of the data is normal, positively skewed or negatively skewed.

4. Geoff, a driver of a courier motorcycle, recorded the distance he travelled (in kilometres) during 15 trips. The data is given below:

24	19	21	27	20	17	32	22
26	18	13	23	30	10	13	

4.1 What is the median for the above data?

4.2 Write down the upper and lower quartiles.

4.3 Draw a box and whisker diagram for the data of Geoff's travels

4.4 Another driver, Thabo, in the same company also completed 15 trips. The five number summary of his data (in kilometres) is: (12; 21; 25; 32; 34). The box and whisker diagram is shown below.

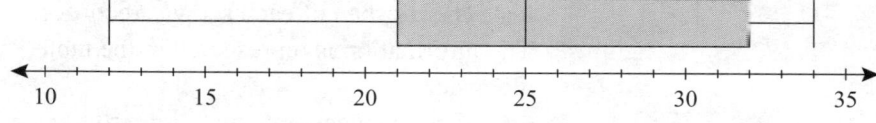

Carefully analyse the box and whisker diagrams of Geoff and Thabo's travels. Comment on the symmetry of the respective distributions and comment on the differences, if any, between the distances covered by each on the 15 trips.

5. A firm has 132 employees working in their Gauteng branch. The distance x in kilometres that they travel to work each day is summarised in the group frequency table on the next page:

5.1 Determine the median interval for this data.
5.2 Determine the estimated mean distance covered.
5.3 Determine the standard deviation for the data.
5.4 Draw an ogive (cumulative frequency curve) for this data.
5.5 Estimate the median distance using your graph.
5.6 By referring to the relationship between the mean and the median, state whether the distribution is normal, positively skewed or negatively skewed.

Interval	Frequency
$0 < x \leq 5$	12
$5 < x \leq 10$	29
$10 < x \leq 15$	13
$15 < x \leq 20$	63
$20 < x \leq 25$	12
$25 < x \leq 30$	3

6. The number of SMS messages sent by a group of teenagers was recorded over a period of a week. The data was found to be normally distributed with a mean of 140 messages and a standard deviation of 12 messages.

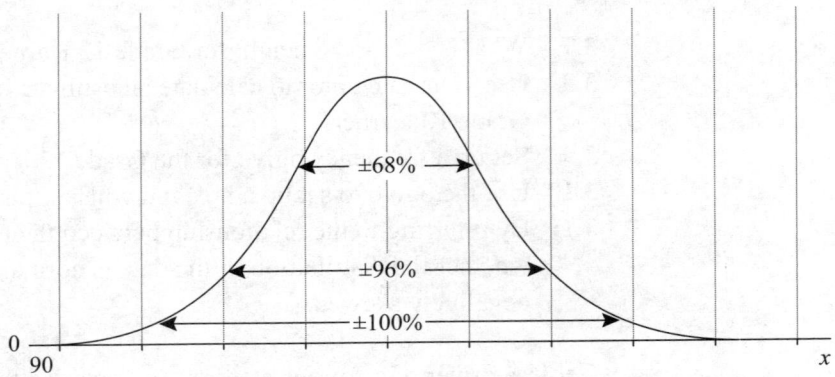

Answer the following questions with reference to the information provided in the graph:
6.1 What percentage of teenagers sent fewer than 128 messages?
6.2 What percentage of teenagers sent between 116 and 152 messages?
6.3 A local magazine reported that 96% of teenagers who communicate via SMS messages send between 464 and 656 messages every month. Is this statement justified by these research findings? Support your answer.

7. A manufacturer producing television sets decided to check the lifespan (in years) of its most popular model. The firm selected 50 of the most popular model at random for this test. The lifespan of each set was recorded. The information is represented in the table alongside.

Lifespan (in years)	Frequency
$4,95 \leq x \leq 5,65$	2
$5,65 \leq x \leq 6,35$	6
$6,35 \leq x \leq 7,05$	18
$7,05 \leq x \leq 7,75$	17
$7,75 \leq x \leq 8,45$	5
$8,45 \leq x \leq 9,15$	2

7.1 Set up an accurate histogram to represent this data.
7.2 Calculate the estimated average lifespan (the mean) of the most popular model of television set, correct to the nearest year.
7.3 The data representing the lifespan of this batch of television set is normally distributed. Calculate the standard deviation for this data set. Translate this number into months, rounded off to the nearest month.
7.4 Approximately 68% of this batch of television set lies within one standard deviation of the mean, approximately 96% of the data lies within

2 standard deviations of the mean, and approximately 100% lies within 3 standard deviations of the mean. Calculate the lifespan of the television set such that 84% of the lifespan of all the sets will exceed this value.

7.5 The firm wants to issue a five-year guarantee with this model of television set. What would you recommend? Justify your recommendation.

7.6 If you buy one of these TV sets, what is the chance that your TV set will last for 8,25 years or more?

Bivariate data: regression and correlation

Correlation

In Grades 10 and 11 you worked only with **univariate data**. These are data for *one* variable, for example, shoe size, height or age. But measuring one variable at a time means that data cannot be compared. **Bivariate data** is data that is gathered on two variables at the same time for the purposes of comparison and to see if there is a relationship between the two variables. For example, you may wish to see whether age and shoe size are related, or whether the amount of carbon dioxide pollution in the air affects the average world temperature.

When we collect bivariate data, we usually try to see if the data are **correlated**. Two variables are correlated when change in one variable has a predictable change in the other variable. One of the easiest ways of seeing whether two variables are correlated is to plot the data on a **scatter plot**.

- No correlation – there is no pattern formed in the scatter plot.

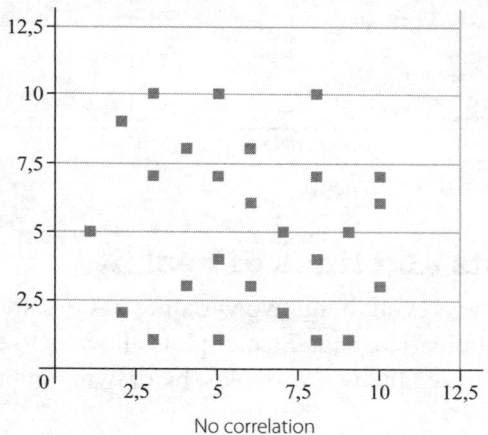

No correlation

- Perfect linear correlation – the points in the scatter plot fall in a perfect straight line.

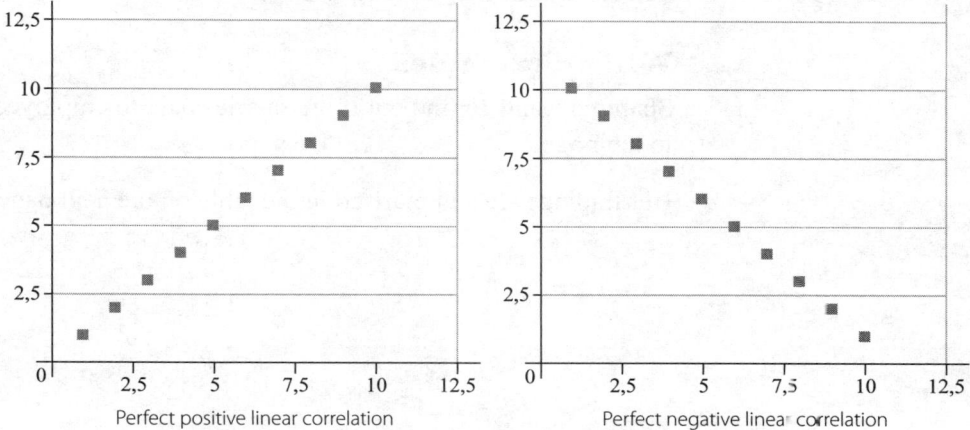

Perfect positive linear correlation   Perfect negative linear correlation

- Strong linear correlation – the points in the scatter plot follow a clear diagonal trend.

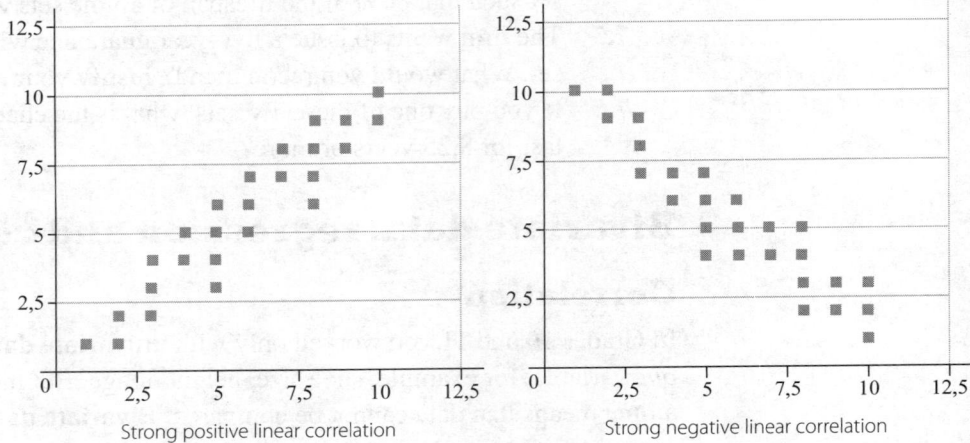

Strong positive linear correlation   Strong negative linear correlation

- Weak linear correlation – the points in the scatter plot form a diagonal pattern, but it is not very clear.

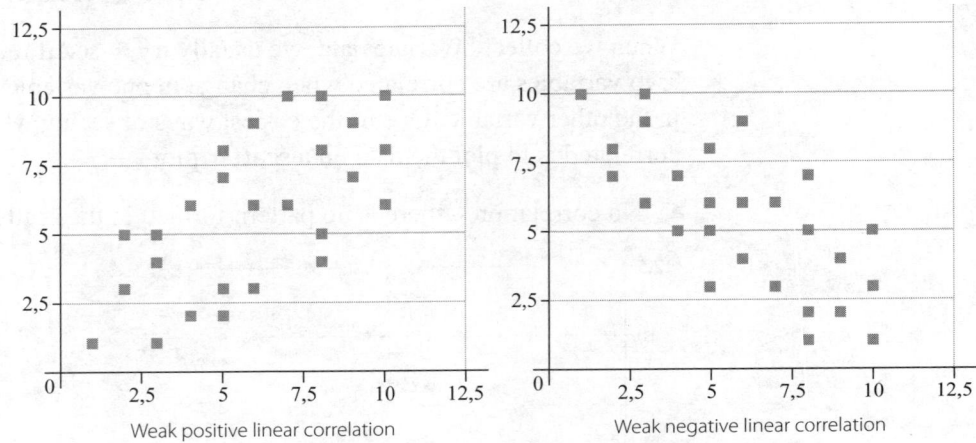

Weak positive linear correlation   Weak negative linear correlation

Scatter plots and lines of best fit

Bivariate data involves studying two variables at the same time. Scatter plots are used to represent bivariate data. Scatter plots allow us to establish whether there is a relationship between the two variables, by drawing in the regression line, or the line of best fit.

You will be required to use raw data to set up scatter plots and to draw in the line of best fit and to recognise whether the relationship is linear, exponential or parabolic.

Worked examples

Shahima wants to find out if the salaries paid to employees in her office are related to their age.

Her findings are summarised in the table on the next page.

1. Draw a scatter plot for this data.

2. Draw in the line of best fit.

3. Comment on the relationship between the two sets of data.

4. Use your scatter plot to estimate what a 50 year old can expect to earn.

5. Shahima asks for similar information from two other businesses. The relationship between age and salary for these two businesses is shown in the scatter plots below. Describe the relationship between age and salary for each of the businesses.

Age of employee	Monthly salary (in R1 000)
33	35
25	31
19	18
44	48
51	56
54	60
38	44
29	35
21	25
31	33
36	41
55	62
58	64
24	28
48	54

6. Use each of these scatter plots to estimate what a 50 year old can expect to earn in Business A and Business B.

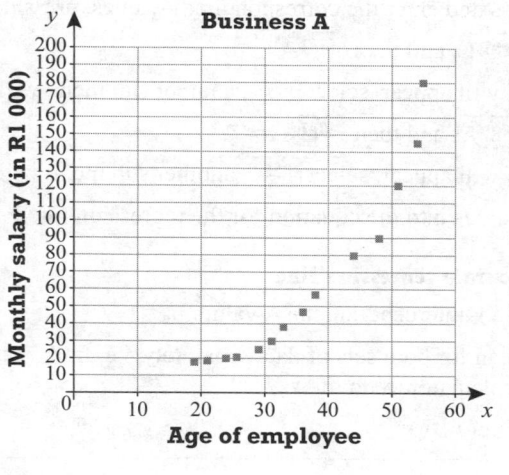
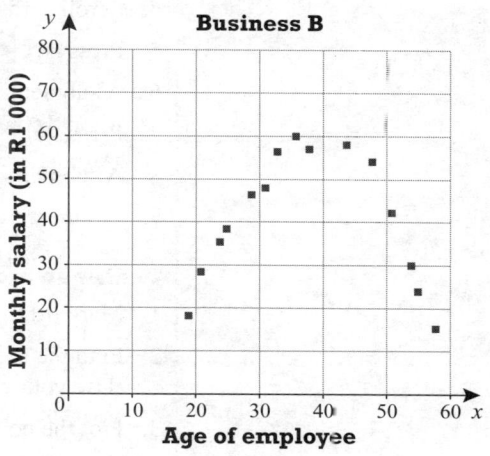

Note
When drawing in a line of best fit, try to get an equal number of data points on either side of the line. These lines are estimates of the line of best fit.

Solutions

1. and 2.

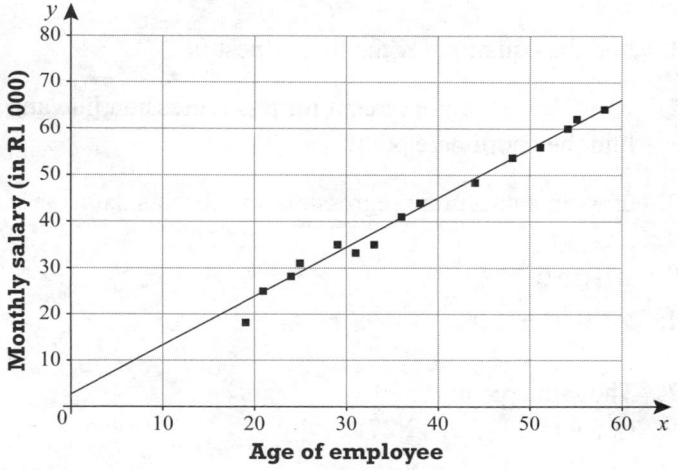

Note

You will be asked to estimate/predict values using a both interpolation and extrapolation.
- Interpolation is predicting or estimating between the given data points.
- Extrapolation is predicting or estimating values beyond the data set. **NB:** this is sometimes not possible depending on the nature of the data.

3. From this data, there seems to be a strong positive linear relationship between age and salary.

4. A 50 year old can expect to earn approximately R56 000 per month.

5. In the first graph the relationship is exponential, i.e. salary increases exponentially with age. In the second graph the relationship is parabolic. i.e. salary increases with age up to a maximum point after which it decreases with age.

6. In Business A a 50 year old can expect to earn around R105 000.
   In Business B a 50 year old can expect to earn around R45 000.

Using a calculator to calculate the linear regression line

Calculating an accurate regression line ensures that we draw in the most accurate line of best fit, which can then be used to make more accurate predictions. The regression line is an accurate equation for the line of best fit. The equation for the regression line is $y = A + Bx$ where A is the y-intercept and B is the gradient of the line.

How to use a calculator to find a regression line

1. Select the [STAT] mode on your calculator.
2. A sub menu will appear. Select the equation for a regression line: **A + Bx**
3. A table of values will appear. Enter all the x-values, pressing [=] after every entry.
4. Scroll across and enter the corresponding y-values, pressing [=] after every entry.
5. Press [AC], [SHIFT], and then [STAT].
6. A submenu will appear, select [REG], another sub menu will appear, select **A** [=].
7. Press [AC], [SHIFT], and then [STAT].
8. A submenu will appear, select [REG], another sub menu will appear, select **B** [=].
9. Fill these values into the equation for the regression line $y = A + Bx$.

To draw an accurate regression line

1. Mark off the y-intercept, i.e. the A value.
2. Find the mean for both sets of data separately, i.e. find $\bar{x}$ and $\bar{y}$. (Use your calculator to do this)
3. Plot the point $(\bar{x}; \bar{y})$.

Worked examples

Use the information Shahima summarised in the table in the previous worked example to:

1. find the equation for the line of best fit

2. write down the y-intercept for this regression line and use your calculator to find the coordinate point: $(\bar{x}; \bar{y})$

3. draw in an accurate regression line for this data.

Solutions

1. $y = 0{,}93 + 1{,}09x$

2. The y-intercept: $(0; 0{,}93)$
   $(\bar{x}; \bar{y}) = (37{,}73; 42{,}27)$

Note

The regression line is calculated manually by minimising the sum of the squares, and is therefore is often referred to as the 'least squares line'. Your calculator is programmed to perform this complex operation. You will not be asked to find the regression line without a calculator.

Remember

To draw an accurate regression line:
- Plot the y-intercept and the point $(\bar{x}; \bar{y})$.
- Join the points and extend.

3.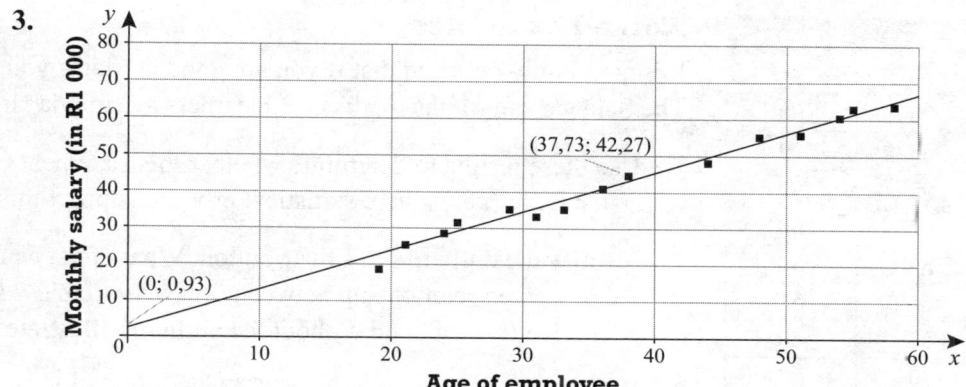

Calculating the correlation coefficient and making relevant deductions

You will be expected to use your calculator to find the correlation coefficient for a bivariate set of data and to comment on the strength of the correlation.

> **To find the correlation coefficient, r, using a calculator**
> 1. Select the [STAT] mode on your calculator.
> 2. A sub menu will appear. Select the equation for a regression line: **A + Bx**
> 3. A table of values will appear. Enter all the x-values, pressing [=] after every entry.
> 4. Scroll across and enter the corresponding y-values, pressing [=] after every entry.
> 5. Press [AC], [SHIFT], and then [STAT].
> 6. A submenu will appear. Select [REG], and then **r** [=].
>
> **Correlation can be seen as a continuum from perfectly positive to perfectly negative:**
>
> | Value | Description | Value | Description |
> |---|---|---|---|
> | +1 | Perfectly positive | −0,2 | Weak negative |
> | 0,9 | Very strong positive | −0,5 | Moderately negative |
> | 0,7 | Strong positive | −0,7 | Strong negative |
> | 0,5 | Moderately positive | −0,9 | Very strong negative |
> | 0,2 | Weak positive | −1 | Perfectly negative |
> | 0 | No correlation | | |

Worked example

Use the information Shahima summarised in the table in the previous worked example to find the correlation coefficient for this set of data. Use this value to comment on the strength of the correlation between age and salary.

Note

Use your calculator to find the value for r.

Solution

$r = 0,98$

The correlation is very strong positive.

Putting it all together

Questions involving bivariate data are seldom asked in isolation. Setting up scatter plots, working out the equations for regression lines, determining correlation and the effects of outliers will commonly all form part of the same question.

Maths	Science
80	85
90	90
85	79
95	90
40	30
50	50
65	55
60	60
80	20
90	90
95	85
100	95
62	75
48	52
75	69
85	80
90	95
80	90
78	75
82	82

Note
The correlation coefficient is used to establish the strength and the nature of the relationship between variables.

Remember
An outlier is a data point that is far removed from the general trend of the data set.

Note
The respective means, $\bar{x}$ and $\bar{y}$ can be calculated by selecting VAR on the submenu, so there is no need to calculate the means manually.

Worked examples

It is commonly believed that if you are good at Maths you will be good at Science. The Science and Maths marks of 20 learners at Mpinda High are given on the left.

1. Use these results to determine whether this statement can be validated statistically (i.e. is there statistical proof to support this common conception?).

2. Identify the outlier in this distribution. What effect can an outlier have on the perceived relationship between the two variables? Use the correlation coefficient(s), with and without the outlier to illustrate your point.

3. Work out the mean scores for both Maths and Science with and without the outlier.

4. Use the given information to set up a scatter plot.

5. Work out two regression lines, one with and one without the outlier, and draw them in. Summarise the effect of the outlier on the regression line.

6. Speculate and give two possible reasons for this outlier.

7. Choose the most suitable regression line to estimate what a learner who gets 48% for Maths will get for Science.

Solutions

1. The correlation coefficient for this data set is 0,73. This suggests that a fairly strong positive correlation exists between a learner's Maths and Science results, which lends credence to the common belief that if you are good at Maths you will be good at Science.

2. There is one outlier in this data set. The ninth data point in which the learner scored 80 for Maths and 20 for Science is an outlier. The outlier will result in a lower correlation coefficient, which will suggest that the correlation is weaker than it is without the outlier.
With the outlier the correlation coefficient is $r = 0,73$.
Without the outlier the correlation coefficient is $r = 0,93$.

3.

	With the outlier	Without the outlier
Mean score for Maths	76,5%	76,32%
Mean score for Science	72,35%	75,11%

4.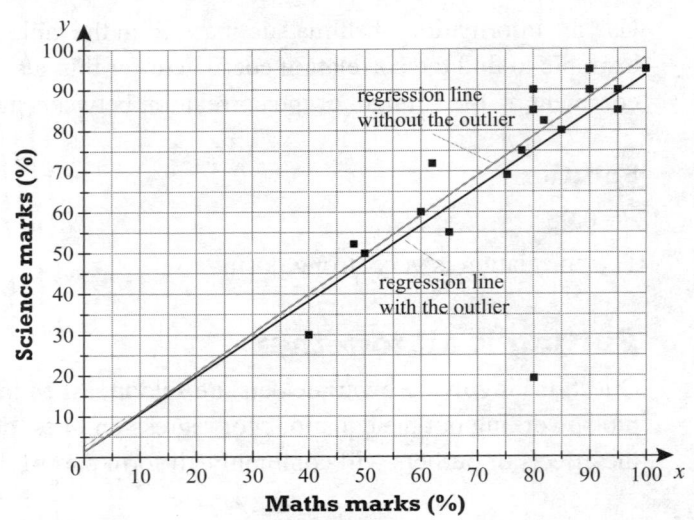

5. Regression line with outlier: $y = 1{,}404 + 0{,}927x$
   Regression line without outlier: $y = 1{,}461 + 0{,}964x$
   The regression line without the outlier will provide a more realistic picture of the relationship.
   The y-intercept is slightly higher and it has a steeper gradient.

6. It is possible that this learner was unprepared for the tests and exams that made up this Science mark, perhaps due to illness. This learner may not have completed all the assessment tasks that made up this mark, i.e. received zero for not handing in assessment pieces, which resulted in this poor mark.

7. Science $= 1{,}461 + 0{,}964x$
   $= 1{,}461 + 0{,}964(48)$
   $= 47{,}789$
   $\approx 48\%$

> **Note**
> This mark may also be read off directly from an accurately drawn regression line.

Using your calculator and a regression line to interpolate and/or extrapolate

Worked examples

The following table summarises the number of revolutions per minute, x, and the corresponding output (horse power), y, of a diesel engine:

x (rev/min)	400	500	600	700	800
y (horse power)	580	1 030	1 420	1 880	2 100

1. Calculate the correlation coefficient for this data set, and use this result to discuss the correlation between the variables x and y.

2. Find the least squares regression line $y = a + bx$.

3. Use this line to estimate the power output when the engine runs at 800 revolutions/min.

4. Roughly how fast is the engine running when it has an output of 1 200 horse power?

Solutions

1. A very strong positive correlation of $r = 0{,}9944$ exists between the number of revolutions and the output of a diesel engine.

   > **Note**
   > A regression line can be calculated between any two variables, but this can sometimes result in a nonsense correlation that is meaningless. For this reason you need to establish first whether the correlation is relevant, and only if it is should you find the regression line.

2. $y = -932 + 3{,}89x$

   > **Note**
   > Once the regression line has been found, you can substitute x-values into the regression equation to make other projections based on the regression line.

Note
Some inaccuracy will creep in due to rounding.
These calculations can also be done using your calculator:
- Press `AC` 800 `SHIFT` `STAT` select `REG`, then **y** `=`.
- Press `AC` 1200 `SHIFT` `STAT` select `REG`, then **x** `=`.

3. Substitute for $x = 800$ in $y = -932 + 3{,}89x$.
   $y = -932 + 3{,}89(800)$
   $ = 2\,180$

   Based on the regression line, the power output when an engine runs at 800 revolutions/min is 2 180 horse power.

4. Substitute $y = 1\,200$ in $y = -932 + 3{,}89x$.
   $1\,200 = -932 + 3{,}89x$
   $2\,132 = 3{,}89x$
   $x = 548{,}07$

   Based on the regression line, an engine runs at 548,07 revolutions/min when it has a horse power of 1 200.

Exercise 2

1. For each of the data sets given below:
   - set up an accurate scatter plot
   - draw in an approximate line of best fit
   - identify any outliers, if they exist
   • comment on the relationship between the variables for each set, stating whether the relationship is linear, quadratic or exponential.

1.1

x	0	0,5	1	1,5	2	2,5	3	3,5	4	4,5	5
y	2,1	1,4	2	3,7	5,9	9,3	48	19,5	25,1	35	48

1.2

x	1	2	3	4	5	6	7	8	9	10	11	12	13	14	15	16	17	18	19	20
y	10	9,7	9,3	9	9	8,8	8,5	8,1	7,5	7,6	7,3	7,2	6,8	6,7	6,3	6	5,8	5,3	5,3	5

1.3

x	1	2	3	4	5	6	7	8	9	10
y	88	77	66	63	53	46	42	35	29	23
x	11	12	13	14	15	16	17	18	19	20
y	22	20	16	13	12	10	9	7	8	6

1.4 From the graph for 1.1:
    1.4.1 predict the y-value if $x = 2{,}8$
    1.4.2 predict a y-value if $x = 10$

1.5 In the graph for 1.2:
    1.5.1 predict the y-value if $x = -5$
    1.5.2 predict a y-value if $x = 30$

1.6 If you were told that the graph for 1.3 was a representation of the depreciation of an asset over time:
    1.6.1 predict the y-value if $x = 4{,}5$
    1.6.2 predict a y-value if $x = 30$

2. Match the correlation coefficients given below to one of the graphs shown below:
   2.1 $r \approx 0{,}68$ **2.2** $r \approx -0{,}7$
   2.3 $r \approx -0{,}88$ **2.4** $r \approx 0{,}12$

   (a)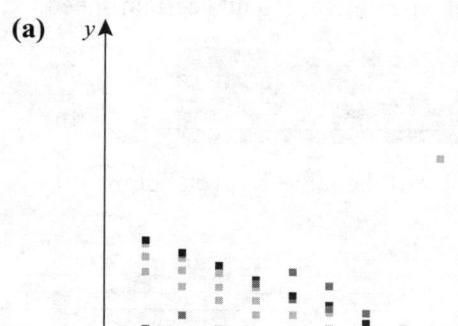
   (b)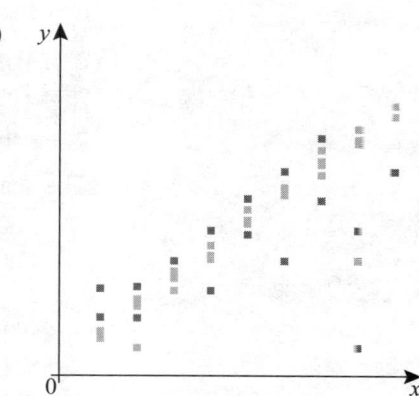
   (c)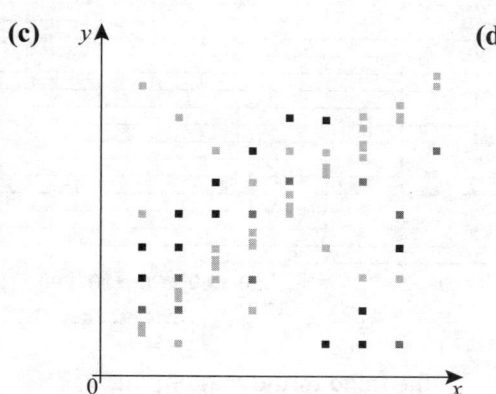
   (d)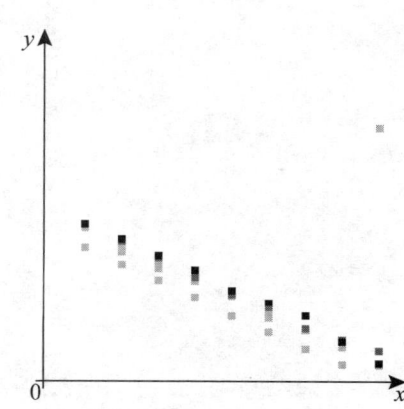

3. Data was collected to compare the length of time in months, x, that couples have been dating, to the amount of money in rands, y, that they spend when going out on a date. The equation of regression is determined to be $y = 165 - 6{,}3x$.
   3.1 What does the slope of the line tell us about the cost of an average date as the duration of the relationship increases?
   3.2 Can we use this line to predict the cost of a date in a three-year relationship?

4. The owner of Star Travel and Tours compiled the following data to illustrate the relationship between the annual profit of a business and its annual advertising expenditure (both in thousands of rands).

Annual advertising Expenditure (x)	12	14	17	21	25	30
Annual Profit (y)	60	70	90	100	100	120

   4.1 Draw a scatter plot for the data.
   4.2 Calculate the equation of the least squares line for the data.
   4.3 Draw the least squares line for the data.
   4.4 Predict the annual profit if the annual advertising expenditure is R25 000.
   4.5 Calculate the correlation coefficient.
   4.6 What conclusion can you reach about the strength of the relationship between annual profit and the annual advertising expenditure?

   > **Note**
   > You can use your calculator to carry out the least squares line operation.

5. 'Speed kills' is the slogan used by the Arrive Alive campaign in an effort to decrease the high death toll on South African roads. Insurance companies have proved statistically that people under the age of 25 are more likely to

drive above the speed limit, and the insurance premiums for this age group are therefore higher than for other age groups.

The table below indicates the distance in metres required by a vehicle to come to a standstill when travelling at a certain speed.

x speed km/h	20	40	60	80	100	120	140
y distance in m needed to stop	6	16	30	48	70	80	110

The scatter plot of the table is given below.

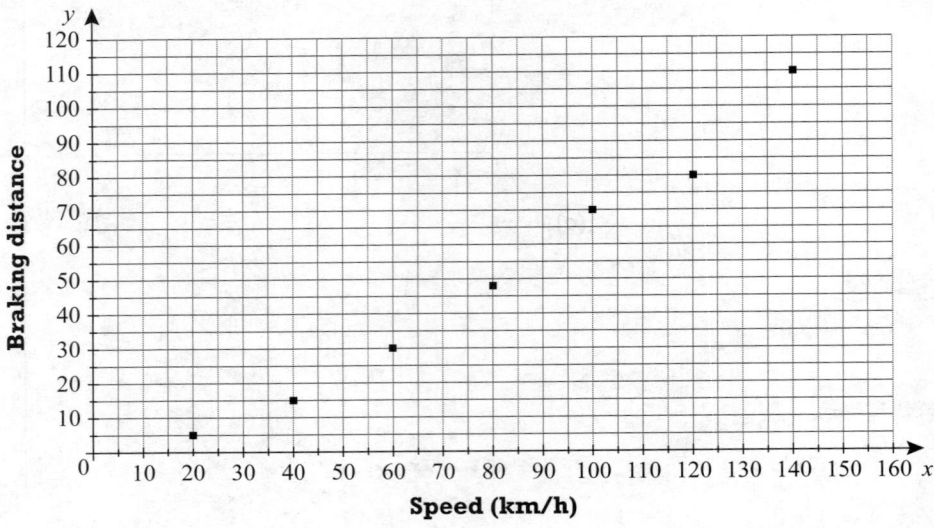

5.1 Discuss the trend of the scatter plot.
5.2 Determine the linear regression equation of the line of best fit.
5.3 Copy the scatter plot given above and draw in the line of best fit.
5.4 Determine the correlation coefficient that will indicate the correlation strength.
5.5 Discuss the strength of the correlation between the speed that a vehicle travels and the distance required to bring it to a standstill.

6. A learner conducts an experiment to investigate the relationship between age and resting heart rate (in beats per minute). He sought the assistance of the local clinic. The information for 12 people is shown below.

Age	59	32	42	50	22	39	21	20	27	40	29	47
Resting heart rate (beats per minute)	88	74	74	93	85	71	78	82	70	75	95	75

6.1 Represent the data in a scatter plot.
6.2 Determine the equation of the least squares line.
6.3 Draw the least squares line on the scatter plot.
6.4 Calculate the correlation coefficient for the data.
6.5 Use the correlation coefficient to comment on the relationship between age and the resting heart rate.
6.6 If a learner uses the least squares line to predict the resting heart rate of a 45-year-old person, will his answer be reliable? Motivate your answer.

7. A firm that rents out cars calculated the average cost per kilometre of maintaining a new car for different distances covered during the first year. The data gathered is given below.

Annual mileage in thousands of km	5	10	15	20	25	30
Cost per km in R	2,50	2,46	2,42	2,37	2,31	2,25

7.1 Draw a scatter plot for the data.
7.2 Decide which of the following graphs fit the data best: straight line, parabola or exponential.
7.3 Find the equation for the graph that best fits this data. Draw this graph onto your scatter plot.
7.4 Calculate the correlation coefficient for the data, and use it to comment on the relationship between the two variables.
7.5 Use your graph to estimate the total cost (i.e. for the entire year) that may be incurred to maintain a car that has 45 000 km on the clock for its first year.

Tests

The tests on regression and correlation are combined with the tests on counting and probability, and are provided at the end of Topic 10.

TOPIC 10 Counting and probability

In Grade 10 you studied the use of probability models to compare relative frequency (practical experimentation) of events with theoretical probability (where formulae are used). You also used Venn diagrams to solve probability problems, working with mutually exclusive events and complementary events.

In Grade 11 you learnt how to identify dependent and independent events and how to use the product rule for independent events. Your knowledge of Venn diagrams was extended to working with three events and calculating various probabilities of stated outcomes. You also learnt how to use tree diagrams to calculate various probabilities.

In Grade 12 you will revise all of the above and learn how to work with two-way contingency tables and to use and apply the fundamental counting principle.

Knowledge and skills for this topic

For the Grade 12 work in this Topic, you need a good grasp of the following knowledge and skills:
- understand the meaning of a ratio, percentage and decimal
- understand Venn diagrams and how to calculate various probabilities
- ability to use statistical terminology and apply the rules applicable to dependent, independent, mutually exclusive and complementary events, including:
  - the product rule for independent events: $P(A \text{ and } B) = P(A) \times P(B)$
  - the addition (sum) rule for mutually exclusive events:
    $P(A \text{ or } B) = P(A) + P(B) - P(A \text{ and } B)$, and B are mutually exclusive if $P(A \text{ and } B) = 0$
  - the complementary rule: $P(\text{not } A) = 1 - P(A)$
  - the identity $P(A \text{ or } B) = P(A) + P(B) - P(A \text{ and } B)$
- understand and work with the structure of tree diagrams.

Content of final exam
- Work with dependent and independent events.
- Apply the product rule for independent events.
- Apply the sum rule for mutually exclusive events, the sum rule for mutually exclusive events and the complementary rule.
- Solve probability problems (where events are not necessarily independent) using Venn diagrams, trees, two-way contingency tables and other techniques (like the fundamental counting principle).

Independent events

Independent events are events that do not affect the outcome of one another. Two events A and B are said to be independent if the probability of B occurring is not influenced by the probability of A occurring (e.g. random selection of an item with replacement). Therefore:

$$P(A \text{ and } B) = P(A) \times P(B)$$

- An event is a set of possible outcomes.
- The probability of an event occurring is the likelihood or chance of it happening.
- Probability = $\dfrac{\text{the number of successful outcomes}}{\text{the number of total possible outcomes}}$

A tree diagram can be used to represent independent events:

Tree diagram for independent events

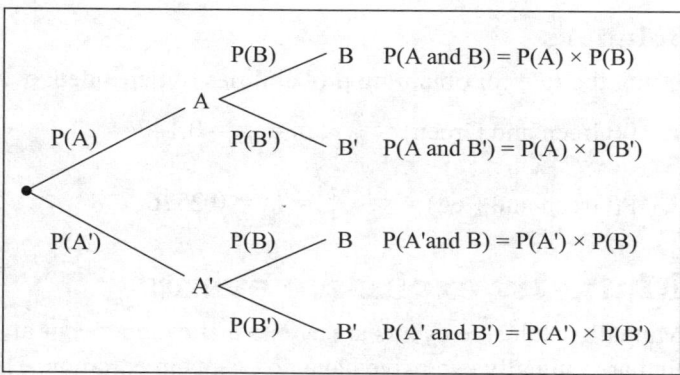

The sum of the resulting probabilities of all possible outcomes must be 1.

Worked example

If one coin is tossed twice, clearly indicate all possible outcomes on a tree diagram.

Solution

The probability of obtaining an event

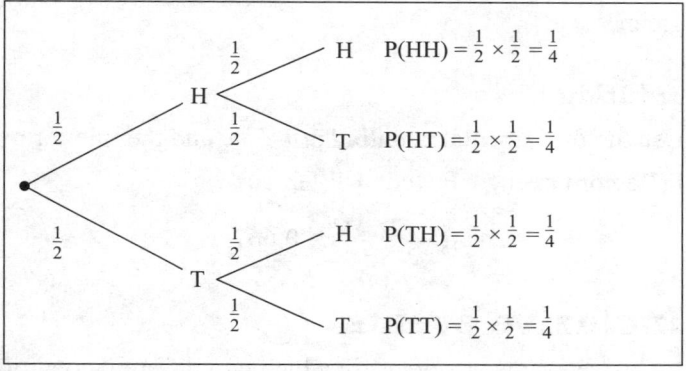

The sum of all the outcomes is 1: $\frac{1}{4} + \frac{1}{4} + \frac{1}{4} + \frac{1}{4} = 1$.

TOPIC 10 *Counting and probability*

Dependent events

Dependent events are events that affect the outcomes of one another. Two events A and B are said to be dependent if the probability of B occurring is influenced by the probability of A occurring. An adjustment must be made to event B that is dependent on the effect of event A's occurrence. An example of this is the random selection of an item without the replacement of that item, which has the effect of reducing the total number of outcomes by 1.

The rule for obtaining probabilities of dependent events is:

$$P(A \text{ and } B) = P(A) \times P(B \text{ following the effect of } A)$$

Worked examples

From a bag containing 12 red marbles and 8 green marbles, two marbles are removed without replacing the first marble. What is the probability of removing:

1. 2 green marbles
2. 1 green and one red?

Solutions

Using the rule for obtaining probabilities of dependent events.

1. $P(\text{Green and Green}) = \frac{8}{20} \times \frac{7}{19} = \frac{14}{95} = 0{,}1474$

2. $P(\text{Green and Red}) = \frac{8}{20} \times \frac{12}{19} = \frac{24}{95} = 0{,}2526$

Mutually exclusive events

Mutually exclusive events are events that cannot occur at the same time. Events that are mutually exclusive have no events in common. This means that if event A occurs then event B cannot occur and vice versa. The rule for obtaining probabilities of mutually exclusive events is:

$$P(A \text{ or } B) = P(A) + P(B)$$

Worked example

From a bag containing 5 red marbles, 6 blue marbles and 7 green marbles, a marble is selected at random. What is the probability that the marble removed is red or green?

Solution

Use the fundamental counting principle and the rule for mutually exclusive events:

$P(\text{Red or Green}) = P(\text{Red}) + P(\text{Green})$

$= \frac{5}{18} + \frac{7}{18} = \frac{12}{18} = 0{,}667$

Inclusive events

Inclusive events are events in which two different conditions occur in the same event. The rule/identity for obtaining probabilities of inclusive events is:

$$P(A \text{ or } B) = P(A) + P(B) - P(A \text{ and } B)$$

Worked example

The event is drawing a single card from a pack of 52 cards. What is the probability of drawing an ace or a black card?

Solution

Using the identity for inclusive events:

P(ace or black) = P(ace) + P(black) − P(ace and black)

P(ace or black) = $\frac{4}{52} + \frac{26}{52} - \frac{2}{52} = \frac{28}{52} = 0{,}5385$

Complementary rule

We can use the complementary rule when an event is either guaranteed to occur or not to occur. In this case it is often easier to find the probability of the complement of the event rather than the probability of the event itself.

This rule can be used when the Event (A) + the complement of the Event (A') = 1, which will give us the probability of the event occurring.

The complementary rule (or identity) is:

$$P(\text{not } A) = 1 - P(A)$$

Worked example

The numbers 1 to 20 inclusive (which means 1 and 20 are included) are written on pieces of paper and placed in a box for a draw. Three numbers are drawn at random and put back in the box (which we call 'with replacement'). What is the probability that at least one of the numbers is odd?

Solution

If the event (A) is that at least one is odd, then the complementary event (A') is that none are odd.

$P(A) = 1 - P(A')$ Use the complementary rule.

$P(A') = \frac{n(A')}{n(s)} = \frac{10 \times 10 \times 10}{20 \times 20 \times 20} = \frac{1}{8}$ where S is the sample space

$\therefore P(A) = 1 - \frac{1}{8} = \frac{7}{8}$

Exercise 1

Classify the following events as either independent, mutually exclusive or dependent events. In the case of mutually exclusive events, state whether the events are complementary or not complementary.

1. A black card is selected from a pack of 52 cards, and then replaced, and another card is selected.

2. The Ace of Hearts is selected from a pack of 52 playing cards. This card is not replaced and another card is selected.

3. A 6 is rolled on a die and then a tail is obtained on tossing a coin.

4. A die is rolled twice and both numbers are the same.

5. A sweet is selected from a packet containing 10 blue, 4 red and 6 green sweets. What is the probability the sweet is red or green.

Exercise 2

Use the product rule for independent events, the addition (sum) rule for mutually exclusive events or the complementary rule.

1. A bag contains 18 blue balls and 6 yellow balls. What is the probability of drawing one blue ball and one yellow ball (blue then yellow or yellow then blue), if:
   1.1 a first ball is drawn and replaced, and then a second ball is drawn
   1.2 a first ball is drawn and not replaced, and then a second ball drawn?

2. On rolling a die twice, calculate the probability of the following:
   2.1 the first number is even and the second number is less than 3
   2.2 the sum of the numbers on the faces landing face-up is greater than 5.

3. During winter in a certain city in South Africa the probability of a sunny day is $\frac{2}{5}$ and the probability of a rainy day is $\frac{3}{5}$.

   If it is a sunny day, the probability that Faranaaz cycles to work is $\frac{3}{4}$, the probability that she drives to work is $\frac{1}{5}$ and the probability that she takes the train to work is $\frac{1}{20}$.

   If it is a rainy day, then the probability that Faranaaz cycles to work is $\frac{1}{5}$, the probability that she drives to work is $\frac{5}{8}$ and the probability that she takes the train to work is $\frac{7}{40}$.

   3.1 Draw a tree diagram to represent the above information. Clearly indicate on your diagram the probabilities associated with each branch as well as all the outcomes.
   3.2 If a day is selected at random. What is the probability that:
      3.2.1 it is sunny and Faranaaz will drive to work
      3.2.2 Faranaaz will drive to work?
   3.3 If Faranaaz works 240 days in a year, on approximately how many occasions does she take the train to work?

4. The probability that it will rain in winter in Newlands, a suburb of Cape Town, is 65%. A toddler has a 12% chance of falling in dry weather and is three times more likely to fall in wet weather.
   4.1 Draw a tree diagram to represent all possible outcomes of the information provided.
   4.2 What is the probability that a child will not fall on a given day?
   4.3 What is the probability that a child will fall in dry weather?

Counting

The basic rule used for counting in statistics is the **fundamental counting principle**.

This rule can be stated as follows: If one operation can be performed in x ways and a second operation can be performed in y ways; then the total number of different ways in which both operations can be performed is $x \times y$ ways.

Worked examples

1. A new restaurant has the following choices for a fixed menu for a 3 course meal.

   Course 1: (Starters) – Fish, meat and vegetarian options.
   Course 2: (Mains) – Pasta, steak, chicken and vegetarian options.
   How many different meal orders can be made from these two courses?

2. How many different ways are there of predicting the outcomes of eight soccer matches? Each soccer match can result in a win, lose or draw.

Solutions

1. Number of different orders possible = $3 \times 4 = 12$

2. Number of possible predictions = $8 \times 3 = 24$

Exercise 3

1. For internet banking, clients are required to have personal codes of four digits. How many different possible personal codes are there under the following conditions?

   1.1 No restrictions are placed on the order of the digits and digits may be repeated.

   1.2 No restrictions are placed on the order of the digits, but digits may not be repeated.

2. How many four-character codes can be formed if the first two characters must be letters and the last two characters must be digits?

3. Using your answers from questions 1 and 2, which options are better to use when banks require as many different codes as possible?

Two-way contingency tables

When analysing data which consists of more than one variable, the data can be organised (or categorised) into a two-way contingency table.

The tables given in the worked example below show the relationship between two or more variables, using the data observed.

Worked example

Learners in Grades 9 and 10 at a certain high school were asked whether they preferred to watch an action movie on television or at a cinema.

A **two-way frequency table** categorising the learners by Grade and by choice of preference can be drawn up:

	Grade 9	Grade 10	Totals
Television	78	56	134
Cinema	42	74	116
Totals	120	130	250

If we have two variables, Grade 9 and Grade 10, and two levels of choice for viewing a movie (television or cinema), we have a 2×2 contingency table.

The grand total in bold at the bottom-right-hand corner indicates the total number of individuals in the survey. The other totals in the bottom row are known as marginal totals, and these totals give the total number of either Grade 9s or 10s in the survey. The totals on the right-hand side of the table give the total number of learners in both Grades who either watch a movie on television or at a cinema.

The first step is to convert all numbers to percentages, and change these to decimals, where the grand total becomes 1.

This table is now known as a two-way relative frequency table:

	Grade 9	Grade 10	Totals
Television	0,31	0,22	0,53
Cinema	0,17	0,30	0,47
Totals	0,48	0,52	1

The table of percentages now allows us to see at a glance the probability of an event.

1. What is the probability that a learner will choose to watch a movie at a cinema?

2. What is the probability that a Grade 9 learner will select to watch a movie at a cinema?

3. Are the events 'Grade 10' and 'watch a movie on television' mutually exclusive? Use the values in the table to justify your answer.

4. Are the events 'Grade 9' and 'watch at a cinema' independent? Show ALL calculations to support your answer.

Solutions

1. P(watch at cinema) = 0,47

2. P(Grade 9 watch at cinema) = 0,17

3. Number from the table P(Grade 10 and watch on television) = 0,22, which is greater than zero. Since the probability of the intersection of these two events is greater than zero, these events are not mutually exclusive.

4. P(Grade 9) = 0,48
   P(watching at cinema) = 0,47
   P(Grade 9) × P(watching at cinema) = 0,48 × 0,47
   $\qquad\qquad\qquad\qquad\qquad\quad$ = 0,2256
   P(Grade 9 and cinema) = 0,17
   So P(Grade 9) × P(cinema) ≠ P(Grade 9 and cinema)
   ∴ the event 'Grade 9' and 'watching at a cinema' are not independent.

Exercise 4

1. The data in the two-way contingency table indicates the number of undergraduates and postgraduates at a university who apply for loans to finance their university studies.

	Have taken loans	Have not taken loans	Total
Undergraduates	4 222	3 898	8 120
Postgraduates	1 879	731	2 610
Total	6 101	4 629	10 730

Determine the probability that a student selected at random will:
- **1.1** have not taken a loan
- **1.2** have taken a loan and is a postgraduate
- **1.3** have not taken a loan and is an undergraduate

2. Are the events 'being an undergraduate' and 'taken a loan' independent? Show all your working to support your answer.

Venn diagrams

Venn diagrams give an illustration of basic set theory and show simple set relationships in probability and logic. In drawing Venn diagrams we can work with mutually exclusive events or inclusive events.

Worked examples

In a Grade 10 class:
- 8 learners play soccer and do athletics
- 5 learners do not play soccer or do athletics
- 12 learners play soccer
- 17 learners do athletics.

1. Illustrate this information in a Venn diagram.
2. How many learners are in the class?
3. What is the probability that a randomly selected learner plays soccer and does athletics?
4. What is the probability that a randomly selected learner only plays soccer?

Solutions

1.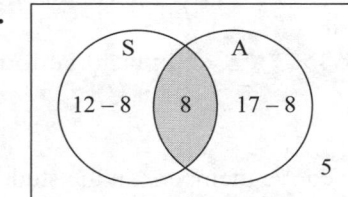

2. Total in class
   $= 5 + 9 + 8 + 4$
   $= 26$

3. P(plays soccer and does athletics)
   $= \frac{8}{26} = 0{,}308$

4. P(only plays soccer)
   $= \frac{4}{26} = 0{,}154$

Exercise 5

1. There are 120 learners in Grade 11 at a particular school. 54 learners do mathematics, while 40 of the learners do drama and 44 of the learners do neither mathematics nor drama.
   - **1.1** Represent this information in a Venn diagram.
     (*Hint:* let the number of learners studying mathematics and drama be *x*.)
   - **1.2** Determine the probability that a randomly selected learner is studying both mathematics and drama.
   - **1.3** Determine the probability that a randomly selected drama learner does not do mathematics.

1.4 Determine whether the events 'studying drama' and 'studying mathematics' are independent events. Show all your working to justify your answer.

2. Complaints about a restaurant fell into three main categories: the menu (M), the food (F) and the service (S). In total, 173 complaints were received in a certain month. The complaints were as follows:

- 110 complained about the menu
- 55 complained about the food
- 67 complained about the service
- 20 complained about the menu and the food, but not the service
- 11 complained about the menu and the service, but not the food
- 16 complained about the food and the service, but not the menu
- The number who complained about all three is unknown.

2.1 Draw a Venn diagram to illustrate the above information.
2.2 Determine the number of people who complained about ALL THREE categories.
2.3 Determine the probability that a complaint selected at random from those received, complained about AT LEAST TWO of the categories (that is menu, food and service).

Factorial notation and its uses

Factorial notation is an exclamation mark placed after a number, e.g. 5! It indicates that a series of descending positive integers must be multiplied by each other, for example $5! = 5 \times 4 \times 3 \times 2 \times 1$.

We use factorial notation to determine that there are $n!$ ways to arrange n objects. It can only be used for positive integers. $0! = 1$ is a special case, as there is only one way to arrange zero objects.

Worked examples

1. Express $8 \times 7 \times 6 \times 5 \times 4 \times 3 \times 2 \times 1$ in factorial form.

2. Give the value of 6!.

3. There are ten senior executive members on the student leadership council at a school. They sit in the front row at all assemblies in the school hall. If order does not matter, in how many different ways can these ten learners be seated?

Solutions

1. 8! 2. $6 \times 5 \times 4 \times 3 \times 2 \times 1 = 720$

3. $10 \times 9 \times 8 \times 7 \times 6 \times 5 \times 4 \times 3 \times 2 \times 1 = 3\ 628\ 800$ ways the learners can be seated.

Exercise 6

1. Express the following in factorial form:
   1.1 $5 \times 4 \times 3 \times 2 \times 1$
   1.2 $11 \times 10 \times 9 \times 8 \times 7 \times 6 \times 5 \times 4 \times 3 \times 2 \times 1$
   1.3 $4 \times 3 \times 2 \times 1$
   1.4 $10 \times 9 \times 8 \times 7 \times 6 \times 5$

2. Give the values of the following factorials:
   2.1 5! **2.2** 6! **2.3** 3!
   2.4 4! **2.5** $\frac{7!}{4!}$ **2.6** $\frac{6!}{4!}$

3. At a school prize-giving there are four senior members of staff and a guest speaker who will sit in the front row. In how many different ways can their seating positions be arranged?

4. Mrs Nxumalo offers to assist in transporting the learners in her daughter's class for a school outing. Four learners will be transported in her car. In how many different ways can she arrange their seating positions?

5. At an athletics event there are eight athletes running the 100 m race. In how many different ways can they be lined up for the start of the race?

Test A: Knowledge and routine procedures

Section A: Regression and correlation

1. On the beach you find ten shells and measure their lengths. These lengths are given in the table below.

Length (in cm)	$(x_i - \bar{x})$	$(x_i - \bar{x})^2$
3,2		
3,6		
5,0		
4,1		
4,3		
4,7		
3,4		
5,2		
4,6		
4,3		

  1.1 Calculate the mean length of these ten shells. (2)

  1.2 Set up an accurate box and whisker plot for the length of the sea shells. (5)

  1.3 Use the IQR and the characteristics of the box and whisker plot to comment on the nature of this distribution. (3)

  1.4 Use the table to calculate manually the standard deviation of the length of these ten shells. (4)

  1.5 You also measure the width of the ten shells. These widths are given in the table below. Set up an accurate scatter plot of this data.

Length (in cm)	3,2	3,6	5,0	4,1	4,3	4,7	3,4	5,2	4,6	4,3
Width (in cm)	2,1	2,0	3,1	2,6	2,7	2,1	2,1	3,2	2,8	2,1

(3)

  1.6 Calculate the correlation coefficient, r, for this data and use it to comment on the relationship between the length and the width of these ten sea shells. (2)

1.7 Use your calculator to find the equation of the regression line for this data set. Round your values off to two decimal places. (2)

1.8 Your friend says he found a large shell that had a length of 12 cm and a width of 10,5 cm. Does this fit your findings? Use your findings and the regression line to decide whether this is probably true or not. (4)

[25]

Section B: Counting and probability

2. From a packet of sweets containing 28 red sweets, 21 green sweets and 26 orange sweets, a sweet is selected at random.

   2.1 What is the probability that the sweet selected is red or orange? (3)

   2.2 What is the probability of that sweet not being orange? (3)

   2.3 What is the probability of selecting a green sweet and then a red sweet, without replacing the green sweet (correct to 3 decimal places)? (3)

   [9]

3. A survey of 80 learners at a local library indicated the reading preferences below:

   - 44 read the *National Geographic* magazine
   - 33 read the *Getaway* magazine
   - 39 read the *Leadership* magazine
   - 23 read both *National Geographic* and *Getaway*
   - 19 read both *Leadership* and *National Geographic*
   - 9 read all three magazines
   - 6 read at least one magazine.

   3.1 Let the number of learners who read *Leadership* and *Getaway*, but not *National Geographic*, be represented by x. Draw a Venn diagram to represent reading preferences. (5)

   3.2 What is the value of x? (3)

   3.3 How many learners did not read any magazine? (1)

   3.4 What is the probability, correct to THREE decimal places, that a learner selected at random will read at least two of the three magazines? (3)

   [12]

4. A smoke detector system in a large warehouse uses two devices, A and B. If smoke is present, the probability that it will be detected by device A is 0,95. The probability that it will be detected by device B is 0,98, and the probability that it will be detected by both devices simultaneously is 0,94.

   4.1 If smoke is present, what is the probability that it will be detected by device A or device B or both devices? (3)

   4.2 What is the probability that the smoke will not be detected? (1)

   [4]

Total: 50

Test B: Problem solving and complex procedures

Section A: Regression and correlation

1. Mr Zondi is a car salesman. Last year the selling price for the cars he sold approximated a normal distribution with a mean of R135 000 and a standard deviation of R28 000. Refer to the standard normal distribution given below to answer the questions that follow:

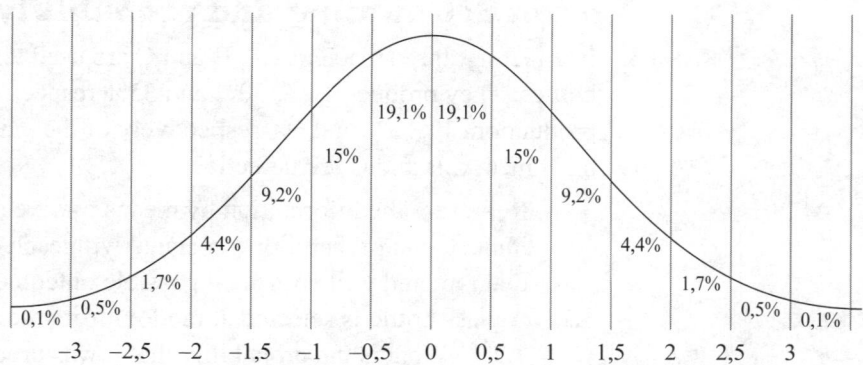

1.1 What is the percentile rank (to the nearest %) of a car that Mr Zondi sold for R163 000. (2)

1.2 Mr Zondi maintains that most of the cars he sold had a selling price of between R107 000 and R163 000. Explain why this is correct. (3)

1.3 Theoretically, how many cars would Mr Zondi have sold if he sold one car in the R220 000 to R250 000 price bracket? Support your answer fully. (3)

1.4 If Mr Zondi sold 200 cars in total, how many cars did he sell that cost less than R93 000? (4)

[12]

2. The scatter plot alongside compares the mass of the eggs and the mass of the new-born chicken for a number of chicken eggs.

Each of the lines can be used to predict the mass of a new-born chicken for a given egg mass.

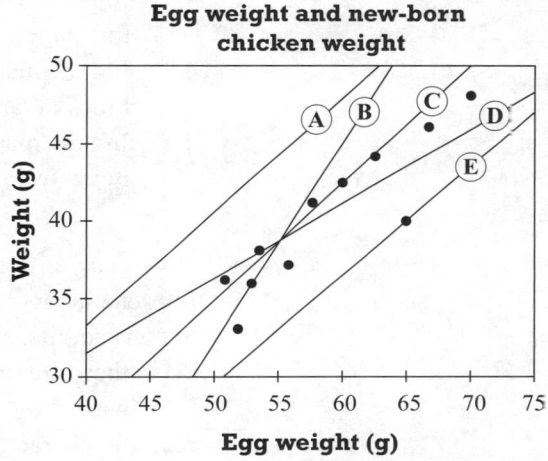

State which line does each of the following:

2.1 Predicts new-born chicken masses that are too high. How can you tell this from the plot? (2)

2.2 Predicts new-born chicken masses that are too low. (1)

2.3 Overestimates new-born chicken mass for lighter eggs. How can you tell this from the plot? (2)

2.4 Overestimates new-born chicken mass for heavier eggs. (1)

2.5 Which line tends to be the best predictor of new-born chicken mass. How can you tell this from the plot? (2)

2.6 Use the graph to find a reasonable estimate for the equation of regression line C. (2)

[10]

Section B: Counting and probability

3. In a factory, three machines A, B and C are used to manufacture glass bottles. They produce 15%, 50% and 35% respectively of the total production. 1%, 3% and 6% respectively of the glass bottles produced by machines A, B and C are defective.

   3.1 Represent the information by means of a tree diagram. Clearly indicate the probability associated with each branch of the tree diagram and write down all possible outcomes. (4)

   3.2 A glass bottle is selected at random from the total production.

   3.2.1 What is the probability that it was produced by machine B and it is not defective? (3)

   3.2.2 What is the probability that the bottle is defective? (3)

   [10]

4. The page layout of a magazine shows four different items from three different businesses, as indicated alongside. One item will be placed in each block.

A	B	C	D
E	F	G	H
I	J	K	L

   4.1 In how many different ways can all of these items be arranged on this page? (2)

   4.2 In how many different ways can the items be arranged if the centre blocks F and G are already prebooked (i.e. already specified)? (2)

   4.3 In how many different ways can the items be arranged on the page if items from the same business are grouped together? (3)

   [7]

5. How many different codes can be created if the password requires the first four characters must be alpha-numeric and the last two characters to be numeric digits, and if:

   5.1 there are no restrictions placed on repetition of any of the characters used (3)

   5.2 no character may be repeated. (3)

   [6]

6. People leaving a soccer match were asked if they supported Orlando Pirates or Kaizer Chiefs. They were also asked if they were happy with the outcome of the match. The table below gives the survey results.

	Orlando Pirates	Kaizer Chiefs	Totals
Not Happy	23	42	a
Happy	85	b	c
Totals	108	d	200

   6.1 Determine the values of a, b, c and d. (2)

   6.2 Determine the probability that people leaving a soccer match are happy. (1)

   6.3 Determine the probability of a Kaizer Chiefs supporter being unhappy for this match. (1)

6.4 Based on the probabilities in this table, which team do you think won the match? Validate your answer. (1)

[5]

Total: 50

Test C: Breakdown and content as per final exam

Section A: Regression and correlation

1. The percentages achieved by 10 learners studying Mathematics Core in Grade 11 were recorded. They then changed to Mathematical Literacy in Grade 12 and their results were recorded in the table below.

Candidate Number	Mathematics Core	Mathematical Literacy
1	17	72
2	19	74
3	32	79
4	39	84
5	35	83
6	27	68
7	26	78
8	29	82
9	37	60
10	40	90

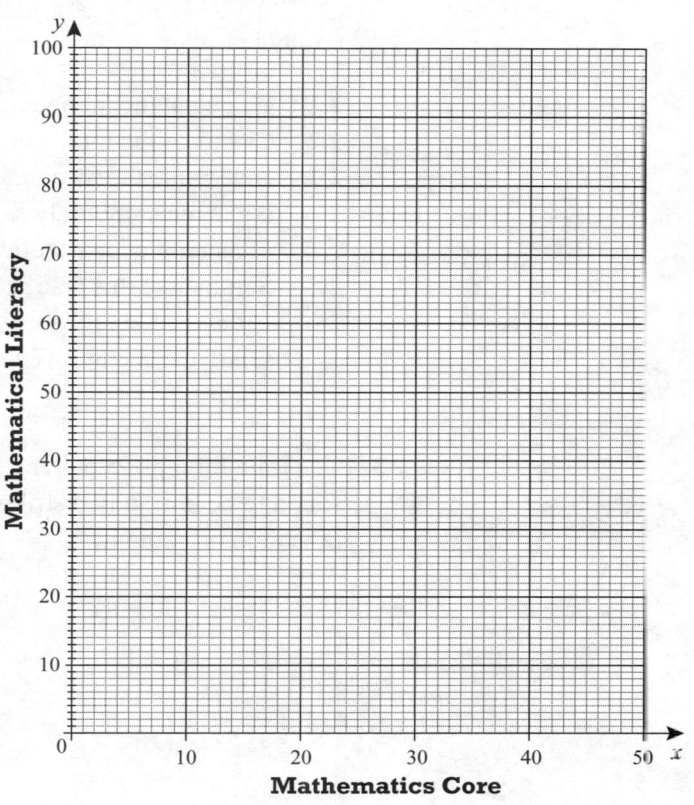

1.1 Copy the axes given and draw a scatter plot of the data on the axes given. (3)
1.2 Calculate the equation of the regression line of best fit. (2)
1.3 Calculate the correlation coefficient for the data. (1)
1.4 Describe the strength of the correlation. (2)
1.5 Which candidate appears to be an outlier? (1)
1.6 David wants to study a course at university that requires a score of 40% to 50% for Mathematics Core or a score of 80% to 100% for Mathematical Literacy. He is currently in Grade 11 and achieved 38% on his latest report. Would you advise him to continue with Mathematics Core? Motivate your answer. (3)

[12]

2. A large company employs several people. The table on the next page shows the number of people employed in each position and the monthly salary paid to each person in that position.

Position	Number employed in position	Monthly salary per person (in rands)
Managing director	1	150 000
Director	2	100 000
Manager	2	75 000
Foreman	5	15 000
Skilled Workers	30	10 000
Semi-skilled workers	40	7 500
Unskilled workers	65	6 000
Administration	5	5 000

2.1 Calculate the number of people employed by the company. (1)
2.2 Calculate the total amount needed to pay salaries in ONE month. (1)
2.3 Determine the mean monthly salary for an employee in this company. (2)
2.4 Is the mean monthly salary calculated in question 2.3 a good indicator of an employee's monthly salary? (2)
2.5 Summarise this data in a five-point summary. (2)
2.6 Is the median, the mean or the mode the best descriptor of the average salary of an employee in this company? (2)
[10]

3. The time for a pizza outlet to deliver to a customer is recorded. The data is found to be normally distributed with a mean time of 24 minutes and a standard deviation of 3 minutes.

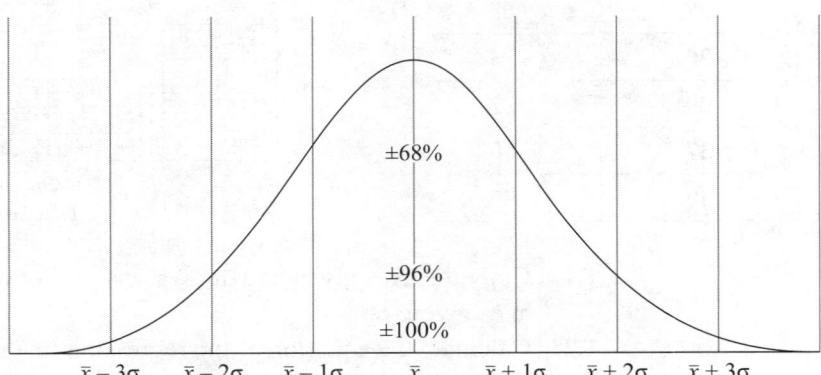

Answer the following questions with reference to the information provided in the graph.

3.1 What percentage of pizzas is delivered in between 21 and 24 minutes? (2)
3.2 What percentage of pizzas is delivered in between 15 and 27 minutes? (3)
3.3 The outlet advertises that they will not charge for a pizza that takes longer than a certain time to deliver. If they want to give away no more than 2% of all deliveries, how many minutes should they allow for delivery? (3)
[8]

Section B: Counting and probability

4. Figures obtained from a city's police department seem to incidicate that of all the motor vehicles reported stolen, 80% were stolen by syndicates to be sold off, and 20% were stolen by individual people for their own use.

   Of those vehicles presumed stolen by syndicates:
   - 24% were recovered within 48 hours
   - 16% were recovered after 48 hours
   - 60% were never recovered.
   - Of those vehicles presumed stolen by individuals:
   - 38% were recovered within 48 hours
   - 58% were recovered after 48 hours
   - 4% were never recovered.

   4.1 Draw a tree diagram for the information above. (5)
   4.2 Calculate the probability that if a vehicle were stolen in this city, it would be stolen by a syndicate and recovered within 48 hours. (2)
   4.3 Calculate the probability that a vehicle stolen in this city will not be recovered. (3)

   [10]

5. In a survey, 1 530 skydivers were asked if they had ever broken a limb as a result of skydiving. The results of the survey were as follows:

	Broken a limb	Not broken a limb	Total
Male	463	b	782
Female	a	c	d
Total	913	617	1 530

   5.1 Calculate the values of a, b, c and d. (4)
   5.2 Calculate the probability of choosing at random in the survey a female skydiver who has not broken a limb. (2)
   5.3 Are being a female skydiver and having broken a limb independent events? Use calculations, correct to TWO decimal places, to motivate your answer. (4)

   [10]

   Total: 50

SOLUTIONS

TOPIC 1   Patterns, sequences and series   (page 1)

Exercise 1   (page 5)

1.1 $a = 180$
$d = T_2 - T_1$
$\quad = 173 - 180$
$\quad = -7$

1.2 $T_{40} = 180 + (40 - 1)(-7) = 180 + 39(-7) = -93$

1.3 $33 = 180 + (n - 1)(-7)$
$33 = 180 - 7n + 7$
$33 = 187 - 7n$
$7n = 154$
$\quad n = 22$

1.4 $T_n = 180 + (n - 1)(-7)$
$\quad = 180 - 7n + 7$
$T_n = 187 - 7n$

2.1 $r = \dfrac{T_2}{T_1} = \dfrac{\frac{1}{4}}{\frac{1}{8}} = 2$

2.2 $T_9 = ar^{9-1} = \left(\tfrac{1}{8}\right)(2)^8 = 2^{-3}.2^8 = 2^5 = 32$

2.3 $T_n = 2$
$\therefore 2 = ar^{n-1} = \tfrac{1}{8}(2)^{n-1}$
$\therefore 2(8) = (2)^{n-1}$
$\therefore 2^4 = (2)^{n-1}$
$\therefore n - 1 = 4$
$\therefore n = 5$

2.4 $T_n = ar^{n-1} = \left(\tfrac{1}{8}\right)(2)^{n-1}$
$\quad = \left(\tfrac{1}{2^3}\right)(2)^{n-1}$
$T_n = 2^{n-4}$

3.1 $T_1 = \tfrac{3}{15} = \tfrac{1}{5}; \; T_2 = \tfrac{3^2}{15} = \tfrac{9}{15} = \tfrac{3}{5}; \; T_3 = \tfrac{3^3}{15} = \tfrac{27}{15} = \tfrac{9}{5}$
$\dfrac{T_2}{T_1} = \tfrac{3}{5} \div \tfrac{1}{5} = \tfrac{3}{5} \times \tfrac{5}{1} = 3$
$\dfrac{T_3}{T_2} = \tfrac{9}{5} \div \tfrac{3}{5} = \tfrac{9}{5} \times \tfrac{5}{3} = 3$
$\dfrac{T_2}{T_1} = \dfrac{T_3}{T_2} = 3$

The sequence is geometric because it has a common ratio of 3.

3.2 $T_n = \tfrac{729}{15}$
$\therefore ar^{n-1} = \tfrac{729}{15}$, with $a = \tfrac{1}{5}$ and $r = 3$
By substitution: $\tfrac{1}{5}(3)^{n-1} = \tfrac{729}{15}$
$\qquad\qquad (3)^{n-1} = \tfrac{729}{15} \times \tfrac{5}{1}$
$\qquad\qquad (3)^{n-1} = 243$
$\qquad\qquad (3)^{n-1} = 3^5$
$\qquad\qquad \therefore n = 6$

3.3 $T_n = ar^{n-1} = \tfrac{1}{5}(3)^{n-1} = \tfrac{3^{n-1}}{5}$
$T_{10} = 3\tfrac{9}{5} = 3\,936{,}6$

4. $9; -6; 4; \ldots$
$\dfrac{T_2}{T_1} = \tfrac{-6}{9} = -\tfrac{2}{3}$ and $\dfrac{T_3}{T_2} = \tfrac{4}{-6} = -\tfrac{2}{3}$
The sequence is geometric with $a = 9$ and $r = -\tfrac{2}{3}$.
$T_n = ar^{n-1} = 9\left(-\tfrac{2}{3}\right)^{n-1}$
$\quad = 3^2.(-2)^{n-1}.3^{1-n}$
$\quad = 3^{3-n}.(-2)^{n-1}$

5.1 $T_k = 2.3^{n+1}$
$T_1 = 2.3^{1+1} = 2.3^2 = 18$
$T_2 = 2.3^{2+1} = 2.3^3 = 54$
$T_3 = 2.3^{3+1} = 2.3^4 = 162$
The sequence is geometric with $r = \tfrac{54}{18} = \tfrac{162}{54} = 3$.
$T_8 = 2.3^{8+1} = 2.3^9 = 39\,366$

5.2 $T_k = 2(3n - 1)$
$T_1 = 2[3(1) - 1] = 2(2) = 4$
$T_2 = 2[3(2) - 1] = 2(5) = 10$
$T_3 = 2[3(3) - 1] = 2(8) = 16$
The sequence is arithmetic with $d = 10 - 4 = 16 - 10 = 6$.
$T_8 = 2[3(8) - 1] = 2(23) = 46$

5.3 $T_k = \frac{k}{k+2}$

$T_1 = \frac{1}{1+2} = \frac{1}{3}$

$T_2 = \frac{1}{2+2} = \frac{1}{4}$

$T_3 = \frac{1}{3+2} = \frac{1}{5}$

$T_2 - T_1 = \frac{1}{4} - \frac{1}{3} = -\frac{1}{12}$; $T_3 - T_2 = \frac{1}{5} - \frac{1}{4} = -\frac{1}{20}$

The sequence is not arithmetic because $T_2 - T_1 \neq T_3 - T_2$.

$\frac{T_2}{T_1} = \frac{1}{4} \div \frac{1}{3} = \frac{3}{4}$; $\frac{T_3}{T_2} = \frac{1}{5} \div \frac{1}{4} = \frac{4}{5}$

The sequence is not geometric because $\frac{T_2}{T_1} \neq \frac{T_3}{T_2}$.

$T_8 = \frac{8}{8+2} = \frac{8}{10} = \frac{4}{5}$

Exercise 2 (page 6)

1. The geometric mean is $p = \pm\sqrt{\frac{2}{3} \times \frac{27}{2}} = \pm\sqrt{9} = \pm3$.

2. AM $= \frac{4+6}{2} = 5$

GM $= \pm\sqrt{4 \times 6} = \pm\sqrt{24} = \pm2\sqrt{6}$

3.1 $p = \frac{7}{2} = 3{,}5$

3.2 $a = 2$ and $d = 3{,}5 - 2 = 1{,}5$

$T_{77} = a + 76d = 2 + 76 \times 1{,}5 = 116$

3.3 $77 = a + (n-1)d$

$77 = 2 + (n-1)1{,}5$

$77 = 2 + 1{,}5n - 1{,}5$

$\frac{153}{2} = 1{,}5n$

$\therefore n = 51$

4. $81; x; 4$

4.1 $x = \pm\sqrt{81 \times 4} = \pm 18$

But $x < 0$, $\therefore x = -18$ is the only value for x.

4.2 $a = 81$ and $r = -\frac{18}{81} = -\frac{2}{9}$

$T_{10} = ar^9 = 81\left(-\frac{2}{9}\right)^9$

$= -0{,}000107$

Exercise 3 (page 8)

1. $T_6 = 14$; $T_{14} = -2$

$14 = a + 5d$ [Equation 1]

$-2 = a + 13d$ [Equation 2]

$2 = -a - 13d$

$16 = -8d$

$\therefore d = -2$

Substitute for d in Equation 1: $14 = a + 5(-2)$:

$14 = a - 10$

$\therefore a = 24$

$T_{10} = a + 9d = 24 + 9(-2) = 6$

2. $T_4 = 54$ and $T_7 = -1\,458$

$\therefore 54 = ar^3$ ....①

and $-1\,458 = ar^6$ ....②

$\frac{ar^6}{ar^3} = \frac{-1\,458}{54}$

$r^3 = -27$

$\therefore r = -3$

Substitute for r in ①: $54 = a(-3)^3$:

$a = \frac{54}{-27} = -2$

3. $3; x; y; z; 19; \ldots$

$T_1 = 3 = a$; $T_5 = a + 4d = 19$

Substitute for a in $T_5 = a + 4d = 19$:

$3 + 4d = 19$

$4d = 16$

$d = 4$

$\therefore x = 3 + 4 = 7$

$\therefore y = 7 + 4 = 11$

$\therefore z = 11 + 4 = 15$

4. $T_2 = 6$ and $T_7 = 192$

$6 = ar$; $192 = ar^6$

$\frac{ar^6}{ar} = \frac{192}{6}$

$r^5 = 32$

$r^5 = 2^5$

$\therefore r = 2$

and $ar = 6$

$a(2) = 6$

$\therefore a = 3$

The sequence is $3; 6; 12; \ldots$

$T_{21} = ar^{20} = (3)(2)^{20} = 3\,145\,728$

5. $T_3 = x$; $T_7 = y$

$a + 2d = x$ ....①

$a + 6d = y$ ....②

Solving simultaneously:

①$-$②: $\quad a + 2d = x$

$\quad \underline{-a - 6d = -y}$

$\quad -4d = x - y$

$d = \frac{y-x}{4}$

①$\times 3 -$②: $3a + 6d = 3x$

$\underline{-a - 6d = -y}$

$\quad 2a = 3x - y$

$a = \frac{3x-y}{2}$

Substituting for x and y:

$T_{11} = a + 10d$

$\phantom{T_{11}} = \frac{3x - y}{2} + 10\left(\frac{y - x}{4}\right)$

$\phantom{T_{11}} = \frac{3x - y + 5y - 5x}{2}$

$\phantom{T_{11}} = \frac{4y - 2x}{2}$

$T_{11} = 2y - x$

6. Original terms: $T_1 = a$; $T_2 = ar$; $T_3 = ar^2$

   New terms: $a + 42 = ar + 32 = ar^2 + 2$

   $a + 42 = ar + 32$ and $ar + 32 = ar^2 + 2$

   $a - ar = -10$; $ar - ar^2 = -30$

   $a(1 - r) = -10$; $ar(1 - r) = -30$

   $(1 - r) = \frac{-10}{a}$; $(1 - r) = \frac{-30}{ar}$

   $\therefore \frac{-10}{a} = \frac{-30}{ar}$

   $\therefore -10ar = -30a$

   $\therefore r = \frac{-30a}{-10a} = 3$

   By substituting for r: $a + 42 = 3a + 32$

   $-2a = -10$

   $\therefore a = 5$

   Original terms: 5; 15; 45

Exercise 4 (page 11)

1. $\sum_{n=1}^{23} (5n - 1)$

   1.1 $T_1 = 5(1) - 1 = 4$

   1.2 $23_1 = 5(23) - 1 = 114$

   1.3 $S_{23} = \frac{23}{2}(4 + 114) = 1\ 357$

2.1 $T_n = 2.3^{n-1}$

   $T_1 = 2.3^{1-1} = 2$

   $T_2 = 2.3^{2-1} = 2.3 = 6$

   $T_3 = 2.3^{3-1} = 2.3^2 = 18$

   The sequence is 2; 6; 18; ...

2.2 $r = 3$; $S_7 = \frac{2(3^7 - 1)}{3 - 1} = 3^7 - 1 = 2\ 186$

2.3 The series is divergent because $r > 1$ and for convergence $-1 < r < 1$.

3. $\sum_{k=4}^{85} (5k + 2)$

   $T_1 = 5(4) + 2 = 22$

   $T_2 = 5(5) + 2 = 27$

   $T_3 = 5(6) + 2 = 32$

   This sequence is arithmetic: $a = 22$, $d = 5$ and $n = 85 - 4 + 1 = 82$

   $S_{82} = \frac{82}{2}[2(22) + 81(5)] = 18\ 409$

4. 3; –9; 27; ...   The sequence is geometric.

   $a = 3$ and $r = -3$

   4.1 $T_{11} = ar^{10} = 3(-3)^{10} = 177\ 147$

   4.2 $T_n = ar^{n-1} = 3(-3)^{n-1}$ $\therefore \sum_{n=1}^{11} 3(-3)^{n-1}$

   4.3 $S_{11} = \frac{3[(-3)^{11} - 1]}{-3 - 1} = 132\ 861$

5. $T_1 = \frac{4}{3}\left(\frac{3}{2}\right)^{1-1} = \frac{4}{3}\left(\frac{3}{2}\right)^0 = \frac{4}{3}$

   $T_2 = \frac{4}{3}\left(\frac{3}{2}\right)^{2-1} = \frac{4}{3}\left(\frac{3}{2}\right)^1 = 2$

   $T_3 = \frac{4}{3}\left(\frac{3}{2}\right)^{3-1} = \frac{4}{3}\left(\frac{3}{2}\right)^2 = 3$

   $r = \frac{T_2}{T_1} = \frac{3}{2}$

   $S_n = \frac{665}{24} = \frac{\frac{4}{3}\left[\left(\frac{3}{2}\right)^n - 1\right]}{\frac{3}{2} - 1}$

   $\frac{665}{24} = \frac{8}{3}\left[\left(\frac{3}{2}\right)^n - 1\right]$

   $\frac{1995}{192} = \left[\left(\frac{3}{2}\right)^n - 1\right]$

   $\frac{1995}{192} + 1 = \left(\frac{3}{2}\right)^n$

   $\frac{729}{64} = \left(\frac{3}{2}\right)^n$

   $\left(\frac{3}{2}\right)^6 = \left(\frac{3}{2}\right)^n$

   $\therefore n = 6$

6. $T_n = 5 - 6n$

   $T_1 = 5 - 6 = -1$

   $T_2 = 5 - 12 = -7$

   $T_3 = 5 - 18 = -13$

   The sequence is arithmetic with $a = -1$ and $d = -6$.

   $S_{43} = \frac{43}{2}[2(-1) + (43 - 1)(-6)] = -5\ 461$

7. 2; $3\frac{1}{2}$; 5; ... is arithmetic with $a = 2$ and $d = \frac{3}{2}$.

   $T_{12} = 2 + 11\left(\frac{3}{2}\right) = \frac{37}{2}$

   $S_{12} = \frac{12}{2}\left[2(2) + 11\left(\frac{3}{2}\right)\right] = 123$

8. 1; 2; 3; 4; ... $a = 1$ and $d = 1$

   8.1 $T_n = 1 + (n - 1)1 = n$, $\therefore \sum_{n=1}^{89} n$

   8.2 $S_{89} = \frac{89}{2}[2(1) + 88(1)] = 4\ 005$

9. 2; 4; 6; 8; ... is arithmetic with: $a = 2$ and $d = 2$.

   $S_{21} = \frac{21}{2}[2(2) + 20(2)] = 462$

10.1 $12{,}5 = a + (n-1)d$
$12{,}5 = 1{,}25 + 1{,}25n - 1{,}25$
$12{,}5 = 1{,}25n$
$n = 10$

10.2 $S_{10} = \frac{10}{2}[2(1{,}25) + 9(1{,}25)] = 68{,}75$

11. $\sum_{5}^{12}(2r-5)\sqrt{p} = 5\sqrt{p} + 7\sqrt{p} + 9\sqrt{p} + \ldots$

The sequence has $a = 5\sqrt{p}$ and $d = 2\sqrt{p}$.
$S_8 = \frac{8}{2}\left[2(5\sqrt{p}) + 7(2\sqrt{p})\right]$
$= 4\left[10\sqrt{p} + 14\sqrt{p}\right]$
$= 4\left[24\sqrt{p}\right]$
$= 96\sqrt{p}$

12. $8 - 3 + \frac{9}{8} - \ldots$ $a = 8$ and $r = \frac{-3}{8}$
$S_\infty = \frac{8}{1-\frac{-3}{8}} = \frac{64}{11}$

13. $\sum_{n=1}^{\infty} 8^{1-n}$

$T_1 = 8^{1-1} = 8^0 = 1$
$T_2 = 8^{1-2} = 8^{-1} = \frac{1}{8}$
$T_3 = 8^{1-3} = 8^{-2} = \frac{1}{64}$
$r = \frac{1}{8}$, $S_\infty = \frac{a}{1-r} = \frac{1}{1-\frac{1}{8}} = \frac{8}{7}$

14. $\sum_{n=1}^{\infty} 2r^{n-1} = 12$

$a = 2$, $T_2 = 2r$, $T_3 = 2r^2$
$r = r$
$S_\infty = \frac{a}{1-r}$
$\therefore 12 = \frac{2}{1-r}$
$\therefore 12(1-r) = 2$
$12 - 12r = 2$
$-12r = -10$
$r = \frac{-10}{-12} = \frac{5}{6}$

Exercise 5 (page 14)

1. 11; 16; 21; ...   The sequence is arithmetic.
$a = 11$ and $d = 5$

1.1 $T_n > 200$
$11 + (n-1)5 > 200$
$11 + 5n - 5 > 200$
$5n > 194$
$n > 38{,}8$
$\therefore n = 39$

1.2 $S_n = 1\,170$
$1\,170 = \frac{n}{2}[2(11) + (n-1)5]$
$1\,170 = \frac{n}{2}[17 + 5n]$
$2\,340 = 17n + 5n^2$
$0 = 5n^2 + 17n - 2\,340$
$n = \frac{-17 \pm \sqrt{17^2 - 4(5)(-2\,340)}}{2(5)}$
$n = \frac{-117}{5}$ or $n = 20$

n cannot be negative $\therefore n = 20$

1.3 $S_n > 1\,500$
$\frac{n}{2}[2(11) + (n-1)5] > 1\,500$
$n[5n + 17] > 3\,000$
$5n^2 + 17n - 3\,000 > 0$
$n = \frac{-17 \pm \sqrt{17^2 - 4(5)(-3\,000)}}{2(5)}$
$n \approx 22{,}85$ or $n \approx -26{,}25$
n cannot be negative and $n \in \mathbb{N}$ $\therefore n = 23$

2. $12 + 15 + 18 + \ldots$ with $S_n = 255$
The series is arithmetic, with $a = 12$ and $d = 3$.
$255 = \frac{n}{2}[2(12) + (n-1)3]$
$510 = n[21 + 3n]$
$0 = 3n^2 + 21n - 510$
$n = \frac{-21 \pm \sqrt{21^2 - 4(3)(-510)}}{2(3)}$
$n = 10$ or $n = -17$

n cannot be negative and $n \in \mathbb{N}$ $\therefore n = 10$
Ten terms must be added together to give a sum of 255.

3. $S_n > 200$, $a = 7$ and $d = 4$
$\frac{n}{2}[2(7) + (n-1)4] > 200$
$n[10 + 4n] > 400$
$4n^2 + 10n - 400 > 0$
$2n^2 + 5n - 200 > 0$
$n = \frac{-5 \pm \sqrt{5^2 - 4(2)(-200)}}{2(2)}$
$n = \approx 8{,}8$ or $n \approx -11{,}3$

n cannot be negative and $n \in \mathbb{N}$ $\therefore n = 9$
So nine terms must be added to give a sum larger than 200.

4.1 $S_n = n^2 + 3n$
      $S_1 = 1^2 + 3(1) = 4 = a$
      $S_2 = 2^2 + 3(2) = 10 = T_2 + T_1$
      $\therefore T_2 = 10 - 4 = 6$
      $a = 4$ and $d = 2$

4.2 $S_8 = n^8 + 3n = 64 + 24 = 88$

4.3 $T_8 = 4 + 7(2) = 18$

4.4 $S_p > 880$
      $\frac{p}{2}[2(4) + (p-1)2] > 880$
              $p(2p + 6) > 1\,760$
                   $0 < 2p^2 + 6p - 1\,760$
                   $0 < p^2 + 3p - 880$
      $p = \frac{-3 \pm \sqrt{3^2 - 4(1)(-880)}}{2(1)}$
      $p \approx 28{,}2$ or $p \approx -31{,}2$
      p cannot be negative and $p \in \mathbb{N}$ $\therefore p = 9$

5.   When $a = 3; T_3 = 6 + 3n$
                $a = 4; T_4 = 8 + 3n$
                $a = 5; T_5 = \underline{10 + 3n}$
    Add together: $24 + 9n = 51$
    $\therefore n = 3$

6. $T_1 = 22 - 4 = 18$
      $T_2 = 22 - 8 = 14$
      $a = 18$ and $d = -4$
      $\frac{p}{2}[2(18) + (p-1)(-4)] < -160$
               $p(40 - 4p) < -320$
                   $0 < 4p^2 - 40p - 320$
                   $0 < p^2 - 10p - 80$
      $p = \frac{10 \pm \sqrt{10^2 - 4(1)(-80)}}{2(1)}$
      $p = \approx 15{,}24$ or $p \approx -5{,}24$
      p cannot be negative and $p \in \mathbb{N}$ $\therefore p = 16$

Exercise 6   (page 18)

1.1 $\frac{T_2}{T_1} = \frac{T_3}{T_2}$
           $\frac{2k-6}{4(k-2)} = \frac{k-2}{2k-6}$
           $(2k-6)^2 = 4(k-2)^2$
      $4k^2 - 24k + 36 = 4k^2 - 16k + 16$
       $-24k + 16k = 16 - 36$
             $-8k = -20$
              $\therefore k = \frac{5}{2}$

1.2 $4(k-2); 2k-6; k-2 = 4\left(\frac{5}{2} - 2\right); 2\left(\frac{5}{2}\right) - 6;$
      $\frac{5}{2} - 2 = 2; -1; \frac{1}{2}; r = \frac{T_2}{T_1} = -\frac{1}{2}$
      $\therefore$ The sequence is convergent because
      $-1 < r < 1$

1.3 $S_\infty = \frac{a}{1-r} = \frac{2}{1-\left(-\frac{1}{2}\right)} = \frac{4}{3}$

2.   For $151 + 149 + 147 + \ldots + 101$,
      $a = 151, d = -2$
      $T_n = a + (n-1)d$
      $101 = 151 + (n-1)(-2)$
      $101 = 151 - 2n + 2$
      $2n = 52$
      $n = 26$
      $S_n = \frac{n}{2}(a + l)$
      $S_{26} = \frac{26}{2}(151 + 101) = 3\,276$
      For $99 + 97 + 95 + \ldots + 51$, $a = 99$ and $d = -2$
      $T_n = a + (n-1)d$
      $51 = 99 + (n-1)(-2)$
      $51 = 99 - 2n + 2$
      $2n = 50$
      $n = 25$
      $S_n = \frac{n}{2}(a + l)$
      $S_{25} = \frac{25}{2}(99 + 51) = 1\,875$
      $\frac{151 + 149 + 147 + \ldots + 101}{99 + 97 + 95 + \ldots + 51} = \frac{3\,276}{1\,875} = \frac{1\,092}{625}$

3. $S_4 = 4$
      $S_4 = a + (a+d) + (a+2d) + (a+3d)$
      $\therefore 4 = 4a + 6d$ $2 = 2a + 3d$ …①
      $T_3 = 6$ $6 = a + 2d$ ……②
      ① $2 = 2a + 3d$
      ② × –2: $\underline{-12 = -2a - 4d}$
                $-10 = -d$
      $\therefore d = 10$
      Substitute for d in ②: $6 = a + 2(10)$ …………②
      $a = 6 - 20 = -14$
      $S_6 = \frac{6}{2}[2(-14) + 5(10)] = 66$

4. $S_n = 760, T_1 = -5, T_n = 100$
      $\frac{n}{2}(a + l) = 760$
      $\frac{n}{2}(-5 + 100) = 760$
              $95n = 1\,520$
               $n = 16$
      $T_n = a + (n-1)d$
      $100 = -5 + 15d$
      $105 = 15d$
      $\therefore d = 7$

5. $T_2 - T_1 = 2x + 3 - (x^2 + 3x - 2)$
$= 2x + 3 - x^2 - 3x + 2$
$= -x^2 - x + 5$
$T_3 - T_2 = x^2 - 2x - 1 - (2x + 3)$
$= x^2 - 2x - 1 - 2x - 3$
$= x^2 - 4x - 4$
$= -x^2 - x + 5 = x^2 - 4x - 4$
$0 = 2x^2 - 3x - 9$
$0 = (2x + 3)(x - 3)$
$\therefore x = -\frac{3}{2}$ or $x = 3$

6. Given: $T_2 = -1$, $S_{10} = 130$, $S_n = 400$
$T_2 = a + d = -1$
$\therefore a = -1 - d$
$S_{10} = 130 = \frac{n}{2}[2a + (10 - 1)d]$
$130 = \frac{10}{2}[2(-1 - d) + 9d]$
$130 = 5(-2 - 2d + 9d)$
$130 = 5(-2 + 7d)$
$130 = -10 + 35d$
$35d = 140$
$d = 4$
$\therefore a = -5$
$S_n = 400 = \frac{n}{2}[2(-5) + (n - 1)4]$
$400 = \frac{n}{2}(-10 + 4n - 4)$
$800 = n(-14 + 4n)$
$800 = -14n + 4n^2$
$0 = 4n^2 - 14n - 800$
$0 = 2n^2 - 7n - 400$
$0 = (2n + 25)(n - 16)$
$n = -\frac{25}{2}$ or $n = 16$
n/a $\therefore n = 16$

7. $T_1 + T_3 = 2\frac{1}{20} (T_2)$
$a + ar^2 = \frac{41}{20}(ar)$
$a - \frac{41}{20}ar + ar^2 = 0$
$20a - 41ar + 20ar^2 = 0$
$a(20r^2 - 41r + 20) = 0$
$(4r - 5)(5r - 4) = 0$
$r = \frac{5}{4}$ or $r = \frac{4}{5}$

Alternative method:
$4 + 4r^2 = \frac{41}{20}(4r)$ ($T_1 = a = 4$)
$80 + 80r^2 = 164r$
$80r^2 - 164r + 80 = 0$
$20r^2 - 41r + 20 = 0$
$(4r - 5)(5r - 4) = 0$
$r = \frac{5}{4}$ or $r = \frac{4}{5}$

8. First 100 m: $100 + 150 + 200 + \ldots$ (100 terms)
$a = 100$, $d = 50$, $T_{100} = 100 + 99(50) = $ R5 050
$S_{100} = \frac{n}{2}(a + l) = \frac{100}{2}(100 + 5\ 050) = 257\ 500$
Thereafter: $5\ 150 + 5\ 250 + 5\ 350 + \ldots$
$= (307\ 450 - 257\ 5000) = 49\ 950$
$a = 5\ 150$, $d = 100$
$\therefore S_n = \frac{n}{2}[2a + (n - 1)d] = 49\ 950$
$\frac{n}{2}[2(5\ 150) + (n - 1)(100)] = 49\ 950$
$\frac{n}{2}(10\ 300 + 100n - 100) = 49\ 950$
$10\ 200n + 100n^2 = 99\ 900$
$100n^2 + 10\ 200n - 99\ 900 = 0$
$n^2 + 102n - 999 = 0$
$n = \frac{-102 \pm \sqrt{102^2 - 4(1)(-999)}}{2(1)}$
$n = 9$ or $n = -111$
$n = -111$ is inadmissible $\therefore n = 9$
The borehole is 109 m deep.

9. $a = 303$, $d = 3$, $l = 600 - 3 = 597$
$T_n = a + (n - 1)d = 303 + (n - 1)3$
$597 = 303 + 3n - 3$
$297 = 3n$
$\therefore n = 99$
$S_{99} = \frac{99}{2}(303 + 597) = 44\ 550$

10. $T_2 = 4 = ar$, $\therefore a = \frac{4}{r}$ ....①
$S_\infty = \frac{a}{1 - r} = 18$, $\therefore a = 18 - 18r$ ....②
① = ② = a, $\therefore \frac{4}{r} = 18 - 18r$
$4 = 18r - 18r^2$
$18r^2 - 18r + 4 = 0$
$9r^2 - 9r + 2 = 0$
$(3r - 2)(3r - 1) = 0$
$\therefore r = \frac{2}{3}$ or $r = \frac{1}{3}$

The first three terms are: 6; 4; $\frac{8}{3}$ or 12; 4; $\frac{4}{3}$

11. $a + ar + ar^2 = 31$ .... ①
    $a(ar)(ar^2) = 25$ .... ②
    $\therefore a^3r^3 = 125$
    $\therefore ar = 5$
    $\therefore a = \frac{5}{r}$
    $\frac{5}{r} + 5 + 5r = 31$ Substitute $\frac{5}{r}$ for a in ①
    $\therefore 5 + 5r + 5r^2 = 31r$
    $\therefore 5r^2 - 26r + 5 = 0$
    $\therefore (5r - 1)(r - 5) = 0$
    $a = \frac{5}{\frac{1}{5}} = 25$ OR $a = \frac{5}{5} = 1$

    $\therefore$ The first 3 terms are 25; 5; 1
    $\therefore$ The first 3 terms are 1; 5; 25

12.
	1st year	2nd Year	3rd year
Salary (R)	100 000	110 000	120 000
Expenses (R)	x	$x + 6000$	$x + 12000$
Savings (R)	$(100000 - x)$	$(104000 - x)$	$(108000 - x)$

    $S_n = 350\,000$, $a = (100\,000 - x)$,
    $d = 4\,000$, $n = 10$
    $350\,000 = \frac{10}{2}[2(100\,000 - x) + 9(4\,000)]$
    $350\,000 = 5(200\,000 - 2x + 36\,000)$
    $350\,000 = 1\,000\,000 - 10x + 180\,000$
    $10x = 830\,000$
    $x = 83\,000$

13. $S_\infty = \frac{a}{1-r} = \frac{3}{2}$ $3(1-r) = 2a$ ....①
    $S_3 = \frac{a(r^3-1)}{r-1} = \frac{14}{9}$ $14(r-1) = 9a(r^3-1)$ ...②
    $\frac{②}{①}$: $\frac{14(r-1)}{3(1-r)} = \frac{9a(r^3-1)}{2a}$
    $\frac{14(r-1)}{-3(r-1)} = \frac{9a(r^3-1)}{2a}$
    $\frac{14}{-3} = \frac{9(r^3-1)}{2}$
    $28 = -27(r^3 - 1)$
    $\frac{28}{-27} + 1 = r^3$
    $r^3 = \frac{-1}{27}$
    $r = -\frac{1}{3}$
    $\therefore S_\infty = \frac{a}{1+\frac{1}{3}} = \frac{3}{2}$
    $\therefore a = 2$

    The first three terms are $2; -\frac{2}{3}; \frac{2}{9}$

14. $-1 < \frac{x}{2x-1} < 1$
    $-1 < \frac{x}{2x-1}$ or $\frac{x}{2x-1} < 1$
    $\frac{x}{2x-1} > -1$ $\frac{x}{2x-1} - 1 < 0$
    $\frac{x+2x-1}{2x-1} > 0$ $\frac{x-(2x-1)}{2x-1} < 0$
    $\frac{3x-1}{2x-1} > 0$ $\frac{-x+1}{2x-1} < 0$

    $\underline{\quad + \quad 0 \quad - \quad\quad UD \quad +\quad}$ $\underline{\quad - \quad UD \quad +\quad\quad 0 \quad -\quad}$
    $\quad\quad\quad\frac{1}{3}\quad\quad\quad\quad\frac{1}{2}$ $\quad\quad\quad\frac{1}{2}\quad\quad\quad\quad 1$

    $x < \frac{1}{3}$ or $x > \frac{1}{2}$ $x < \frac{1}{2}$ or $x > 1$
    $\therefore x < \frac{1}{3}$ or $x > 1$

15. $0,34\dot{2} = 0,3 + \frac{42}{1000} + \frac{42}{100\,000} + \frac{42}{10\,000\,000} + \ldots$
    $= \frac{3}{10} + \frac{42}{1000} + \frac{42}{100\,000} + \frac{42}{10\,000\,000} + \ldots$
    $= \frac{3}{10} + S_\infty$ with $a = \frac{42}{1000}$ and $r = \frac{1}{100}$
    $= \frac{3}{10} + \frac{\frac{42}{1000}}{1 - \frac{1}{100}}$
    $= \frac{3}{10} + \frac{7}{165} = \frac{113}{330}$

16. Let the three consecutive terms be: $a - d$; a;
    $a + d$ and $S_3 = 27$
    $a - d + a + a + d = 27$
    $3a = 27$
    $\therefore a = 9$
    The product of the terms: $(a-d)(a)(a+d)$
    $= 585$
    Substituting for a: $(9-d)(9)(9+d) = 585$
    $(9)(81 - d^2) = 585$
    $(81 - d^2) = 65$
    $d^2 = 16$
    $d = \pm 4$
    If $a = 9$ and $d = 4$, then the three terms are: 5; 9; 13
    If $a = 9$ and $d = -4$, then the three terms are: 13; 9; 5

Test A (page 20)

1. Bookwork
   (see page 10 of this Study Guide) (5)

2.1 $\sqrt{12} - \sqrt{3} = \sqrt{27} - \sqrt{12} = \sqrt{3}$
    Remember: $\sqrt{12} = 2\sqrt{3}$; $\sqrt{27} = 3\sqrt{3}$
    The sequence is arithmetic with $d = \sqrt{3}$ (2)

2.2 $S_{10} = \frac{10}{2}(2\sqrt{3} + 9\sqrt{3}) = 55\sqrt{3}$ (2)

3.1 $T_1 = 2(-2)^{1-1} = 2(-2)^0 = 2$
$T_2 = 2(-2)^{2-1} = 2(-2)^1 = -4$
$T_3 = 2(-2)^{3-1} = 2(-2)^2 = 8$ (3)

3.2 The sequence is geometric because
$r = \frac{-4}{2} = \frac{8}{-4} = -2$ (2)

4. $T_n = -4 + (n-1)(3)$
$= -4 + 3n - 3$
$T_n = 3n - 7$
$T_n = 20 \therefore 20 = 3n - 7$
$27 = 3n$
$n = 9$
$\therefore -4 - 1 + 2 + 5 + \ldots + 20 = \sum_{n=1}^{9} (3n - 7)$ (4)

5.1 $T_5 = ar^4 = 2\left(\frac{3}{2}\right)^4 = \frac{81}{8}$ (2)

5.2 $S_{10} = \frac{a(r^n - 1)}{r - 1} = \frac{2[(\frac{3}{2})^{10} - 1]}{\frac{3}{2} - 1} = 226{,}66$ (2)

6.1 $x = \frac{4 + 32}{2} = 18$ (2)

6.2 $x = \pm\sqrt{4 \times 32} = \pm\sqrt{128} = \pm 8\sqrt{2}$ (2)

7. $r = \frac{T_2}{T_1} = \frac{-3}{8}$
The series is convergent because $-1 < r < 1$
$S_\infty = \frac{a}{1-r} = \frac{8}{1-(\frac{-3}{8})} = \frac{64}{11} \approx 5{,}81$
Sum to infinity is always < 6. (5)

8.1 $T_1 = 5 - 3 = 2$
$T_2 = 10 - 3 = 7$
$T_3 = 15 - 3 = 12$
$\therefore T_2 - T_1 = T_3 - T_2 = 5$
Therefore the sequence is arithmetic. (4)

8.2 $S_n = 2\,235$
$\therefore 2\,235 = \frac{n}{2}[2(2) + (n-1)(5)]$
$= \frac{n}{2}(4 + 5n - 5)$
$4\,470 = n(5n - 1)$
$4\,470 = 5n^2 - n$
$0 = 5n^2 - n - 4\,470$
$n = \frac{-b \pm \sqrt{b^2 - 4ac}}{2a}$
$n = \frac{-(-1) \pm \sqrt{(-1)^2 - 4(5)(-4\,470)}}{2(5)}$
$n = 30$ or $n \approx -29{,}8$
n cannot be negative, therefore $n = 30$ (6)

9. The series is geometric with:
$a = 4;\ r = \frac{1}{2};\ S_n = 7\frac{31}{32}$
$\frac{4[(\frac{1}{2})^n - 1]}{\frac{1}{2} - 1} = 7\frac{31}{32}$
$[(\frac{1}{2})^n - 1] = 7\frac{31}{32} \times \frac{-1}{2} \div 4$
$[(\frac{1}{2})^n - 1] = \frac{-255}{256}$
$(\frac{1}{2})^n = \frac{-255}{256} + 1$
$(\frac{1}{2})^n = \frac{1}{256}$
$\therefore n = 8$ (6)

10. The series is geometric with:
$a = \cos x;\ r = \frac{\cos^3 x}{\cos x} = \cos^2 x.$
$S_\infty = \frac{a}{1-r} = \frac{\cos x}{1 - \cos^2 x} = \frac{\cos x}{\sin^2 x}$ (3)

Total: 50

Test B (page 21)

1. $S_3 = 18$
$\therefore T_1 + T_2 + T_3 = 18$
$\therefore (a) + (a + d) + (a + 2d) = 18$
$\therefore 3a + 3d = 18$
$\therefore a + d = 6$ ①
$T_8 + T_9 + T_{10} = 81$
$\therefore (a + 7d) + (a + 8d) + (a + 9d) = 81$
$\therefore 3a + 24d = 81$
$\therefore a + 8d = 27$ ②
② − ① = $a + 8d = 27$
$-a - d = -6$
$\ \ \ 7d = 21$
$\ \ \ \ d = 3$
$\therefore a = 6 - 3 = 3$
$S_{10} = \frac{10}{2}[2(3) + 9(3)] = 165$ (8)

2.1 Perimeter of the first triangle
$= 3 \times 100 = 300$ cm
Perimeter of the second triangle
$= 3 \times 50 = 150$ cm
Perimeter of the third triangle
$= 3 \times 25 = 75$ cm
Infinite series has: $a = 300$ and $r = 0{,}5$
Sum of the perimeters $= S_\infty = \frac{300}{1 - 0{,}5}$
$= 600$ cm (4)

3.1 $-1 < (x^2 - 3) < 1$

$(x^2 - 3) > -1$ and $(x^2 - 3) < 1$

$x^2 - 2 > 0$ $\qquad x^2 - 4 < 0$

$(x - \sqrt{2})(x + \sqrt{2}) > 0 \qquad (x-2)(x+2) < 0$

$x < -\sqrt{2}$ or $x > \sqrt{2}$ and $-2 < x < 2$

$\therefore -2 < x < -\sqrt{2}$ or $\therefore \sqrt{2} < x < 2$ (6)

3.2 $a = 1$; $r = (1{,}5^2 - 3) = \frac{-3}{4}$

$S_\infty = \frac{1}{1 - \frac{-3}{4}} = \frac{4}{7}$ (3)

4.1 $a + (a + d) + (a + 2d) = 24$

$3a + 3d = 24$

$\therefore a + d = 8$ (2)

4.2 $a + d = 8$

$\therefore d = 8 - a$

The numbers in the arithmetic sequence are:
a; $a + d$; $a + 2d$

Substitute $8 - a$ for d:
a; $a + 8 - a$; $a + 2(8 - a)$
$= a$; 8; $16 - a$

$\therefore$ The new numbers are: $a - 1$; 6; $16 - a$

These numbers form a geometric sequence

$\therefore \frac{6}{a-1} = \frac{16-a}{6}$

$36 = (16 - a)(a - 1)$

$36 = 17a - a^2 - 16$

$a^2 - 17a + 52 = 0$

$(a - 4)(a - 13) = 0$

$\therefore a = 4$ or $a = 13$

The original numbers were:
4; 8; 12 or 13; 8; 3

The numbers in geometric sequence are:
3; 6; 12 or 12; 6; 3 (8)

5.1 3; 9; 15 is an arithmetic series with $a = 3$ and $d = 6$

The next term is $T_7 = 15 + 6 = 21$ (1)

3; 6; 12; … is a geometric series with $a = 3$ and $r = 2$

The next term is $T_8 = 12 \times 2 = 24$ (1)

5.2 T_{21} must be arithmetic:
$T_{21} = a + (n-1)d = 3 + (21-1)6 = 123$

T_{22} must be geometric:
$T_{22} = ar^{n-1} = 3.2^{21} = 6\,291\,456$

$\therefore T_{22} - T_{21} = 6\,291\,456 - 123$
$= 6\,291\,333$ (6)

5.3 For the arithmetic sequence:
$T_n = 3 + (n-1)6 = 6n - 3$

$T_n = 3(2n - 1)$, which will always be a multiple of 3 for all values of n.

For the geometric sequence: $T_n = 3.2^{n-1}$

$T_n = 3.2^{n-1}$ will always be a multiple of 3 for all values of n. (4)

6. $\sum_{p=1}^{n} \frac{2}{5}(2)^{2p-1} > 11\,000$

$T_1 = \frac{2}{5}(2)^{2-1} = \frac{4}{5}$

$T_2 = \frac{2}{5}(2)^{4-1} = \frac{16}{5}$

$T_3 = \frac{2}{5}(2)^{6-1} = \frac{64}{5}$

$\therefore a = \frac{4}{5}$; $r = 4$; $S_n > 11\,000$

$\frac{\frac{4}{5}(4^n - 1)}{4 - 1} > 11\,000$

$\frac{4}{15}(4^n - 1) > 11\,000$

$4^n > 41\,251$

$\log 4^n > \log 41\,251$

$n > \frac{\log 41\,251}{\log 4}$

$n > 7{,}66$

$n = 8$ (7)

Total: 50

Test C (page 22)

1. Bookwork
(see page 15 of this Study Guide) (5)

2. 3; $3\sqrt{3}$; 9 …

The sequence is geometric.
$a = 3$ and $r = \sqrt{3}$
$T_{11} = 3(\sqrt{3})^{10} = 729$ (3)

3.1 $\log x^1 + \log x^2 + \log x^3 + \ldots$ (1)

3.2 $\log x^1 + \log x^2 + \log x^3 + \ldots$
$= 1 \log x + 2 \log x + 3 \log x + \ldots$

$2 \log x - \log x = 3 \log x - 2 \log x$

$\therefore \log x = \log x$

$\therefore T_2 - T_1 = T_3 - T_2$

Therefore the series is arithmetic, with $d = \log x$ (2)

4. $S_n = \frac{n}{2}\left[2\left(\frac{-4}{5}\right) + (n-1)\left(\frac{1}{5}\right)\right]$

$= \frac{n}{2}\left(\frac{-8}{5} + \frac{n}{5} - \frac{1}{5}\right)$

$= \frac{-8n + n^2 - n}{10}$

$S_n = \frac{n^2 - 9n}{10} = \frac{n(n-9)}{10}$ (4)

5. $M = \sum_{k=3}^{11} 5^{k-4}$

$T_3 = 5^{3-4} = 5^{-1}$

$T_4 = 5^{4-4} = 5^0 = 1$

$T_5 = 5^{5-4} = 5^1 = 5$

The sequence is geometric with $a = 3$, $r = 5$

Then: $S_9 = \frac{5^{-1}(5^9 - 1)}{5-1} = \frac{390\,624,8}{4} \approx 97\,656,2$ (5)

6. $T_4 = -2 = a + 3d$

$\underline{T_8 = -18 = a + 7d}$

$16 = 0a - 4d$

$\therefore d = -4$

$a = -2 - (3 \times -4) = 10$

$S_n = -144 = \frac{n}{2}[2(10) + (n-1)(-4)]$

$-288 = n(20 - 4n + 4)$

$-288 = n(24 - 4n)$

$4n^2 - 24n - 288 = 0$

$n^2 - 6n - 72 = 0$

$(n+6)(n-12) = 0$

$n = 12$

$6 + p + 3\frac{3}{8} + \ldots$ and $S_\infty = 3\frac{3}{7}$ (8)

7. $\frac{24}{7} = \frac{6}{1-r}$

$\therefore 42 = 24 - 24r$

$\therefore 24r = -18$

$\therefore r = -\frac{3}{4}$

$\therefore p = T_2 = ar = 6\left(-\frac{3}{4}\right) = -\frac{9}{2}$ (5)

8.1 See solution at bottom of page.

8.2 $7 - x = 6$ OR $12 - (7-6) = 6$

$\therefore x = 1$ (the first difference) (2)

9.1 a; b; $\sqrt{3}$ is a geometric sequence $\therefore \frac{\sqrt{3}}{b} = \frac{b}{c}$

$\therefore b^2 = \sqrt{3}a$ (2)

9.2 $a^2 + b^2 = 3$ by Pythagoras (2)

9.3 From 9.1 and 9.2, $a^2 + \sqrt{3}a = 3$

$\therefore a^2 + \sqrt{3}a - 3 = 0$

Using $\frac{-b \pm \sqrt{b^2 - 4ac}}{2a}$:

$a = \frac{-\sqrt{3} \pm \sqrt{(\sqrt{3})^2 - 4(1)(-3)}}{2(1)}$

$a = \frac{-\sqrt{3} \pm \sqrt{3 + 12}}{2}$

$a = \frac{-\sqrt{3} + \sqrt{15}}{2}$

Only + is used because a is a length.

$a = \frac{\sqrt{3}(-1 + \sqrt{5})}{2}$

$a = \frac{\sqrt{3}(\sqrt{5} - 1)}{2}$ (6)

Total: 50

8.1

The sequence:	x		7		19		y		61
First difference:		$[7-x]$		$[12]$		$[y-19]$		$[61-y]$	
Second difference:					$[y-31]$		$[80-2y]$		

$y - 31 = 80 - 2y$

$3y = 111$

$y = 37$

Second difference: $80 - 2y = 80 - 2(37) = 6$ (5)

TOPIC 2   Functions and inverses   (page 23)

Exercise 1   (page 28)

1.1 $x < -1$
1.2 $x \in \mathbb{R}, x \neq 1$
1.3 $x > 0$
1.4 $x \in (0°; 90°)$ and $x \in (270°; 360°)$

2.1 $x > -4$
2.2 $x \in (-\infty; -2)$ and $x \in (-2; \infty)$
2.3 $x \in (-6; 3)$
2.4 $x < -2$ and $x \in (1; 2)$

Exercise 2   (page 31)

1. $f(x) = 2x - 3; x \in (-3; 4)$

   1.1 Domain: $-3 \leq x \leq 4$
   Range: When $x = -3$, $y = 2(-3) - 3 = -9$
   When $x = 4$, $y = 2(4) - 3 = 5$
   $-9 \leq y \leq 5$

   1.2 One-to-one mapping, because it is a linear function.

   1.3 $y = 2x - 3$
   $x = 2y - 3$
   $2y = x + 3$
   $y = \frac{1}{2}x + \frac{3}{2}$

   1.4 Yes, you can label it $f^{-1}(x)$ because it is also a function.

   1.5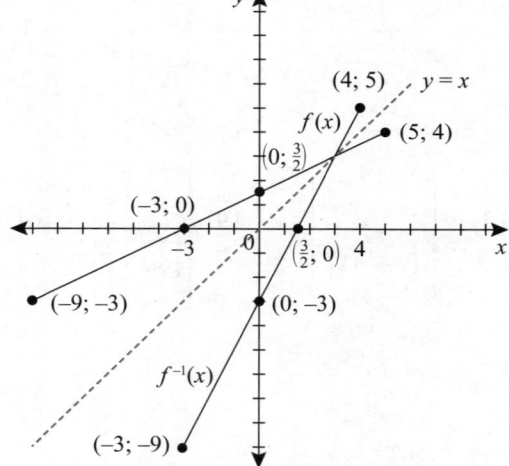

   The x intercept of $f(x)$ becomes the y intercept of $f^{-1}(x)$.
   The y intercept of $f(x)$ becomes the x intercept of $f^{-1}(x)$.

   1.6 $y = x$; draw on graph: the function and its inverse intersect.

   1.7 Increasing, because the gradient is positive.

2. $f(x) = x^2 - 1$

   2.1 Domain: $x \in \mathbb{R}$; Range: $y \geq -1$

   2.2 many-to-one (quadratic)

   2.3 $y = x^2 - 1$
   $x = y^2 - 1$
   $y^2 = x + 1$
   $y = \pm\sqrt{x + 1}$

   2.4 No, you cannot label it $f^{-1}(x)$, because every x-value has two y-values, and the inverse is therefore not a function.

   2.5 Restrictions of $f(x)$ should be such that $x \geq 0$ or $x \leq 0$.

   2.6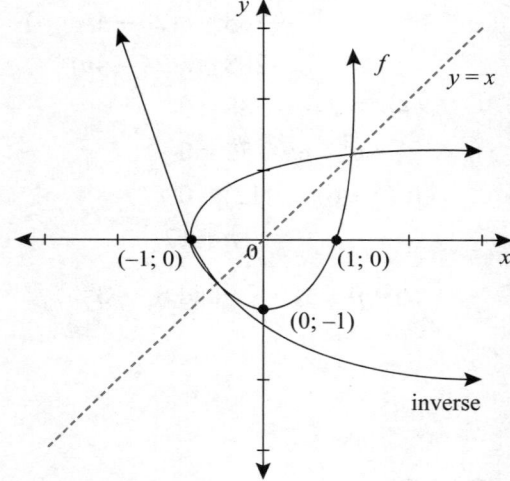

   2.7 The graph and its inverse intersect.

   2.8.1 Decreasing, because the gradient of the tangent to the curve is negative.

   2.8.2 Increasing, because the gradient of the tangent to the curve is positive.

Exercise 3   (page 33)

1. $f(x) = -x^2 + 2x + 3$

   1.1 $f(0) = -(0)^2 + 2(0) + 3 = 3$

   1.2 $f(3) = -(3)^2 + 2(3) + 3 = 0$

1.3 $f(x+1) = -(x+1)^2 + 2(x+1) + 3$
$= -(x^2 + 2x + 1) + 2x + 2 + 3$
$= -x^2 - 2x - 1 + 2x + 5$
$= -x^2 + 4$

1.4 $f(-1) = -(-1)^2 + 2(-1) + 3$
$= 0$

1.5 $f(x) = 0$
$-x^2 + 2x + 3 = 0$
$x^2 - 2x - 3 = 0$
$(x - 3)(x + 1) = 0$
$x = 3 \text{ or } -1$

1.6 The x-intercepts of the graph. They are calculated where $y = 0$.

2. $f(x) = x^2 - 4$

2.1 $f(3) = (3)^2 - 4 = 5$

2.2 $f(3 + h)$
$= (3 + h)^2 - 4$
$= 9 + 6h + h^2 - 4$
$= h^2 + 6h + 5$

2.3 $\dfrac{f(3+h) - f(h)}{h}$
$= \dfrac{h^2 + 6h + 5 - 5}{h}$
$= \dfrac{h^2 + 5h}{h}$
$= h + 6$

2.4 The y-value when $x = 3$.

2.5 Average gradient

3. $s(t) = 2t + t^2$

3.1 $s(0) = 0$
The speed is zero when the time is zero.

3.2 $s(5) = -2(5) + (5)^2$
$= 35$
After 5 second the speed is 35 m/s.

3.3 $s(1) = +2 + 1 = 3$ m/s
$s(8) = 2(8) + 8^2 = 80$ m/s
Average speed $= \dfrac{80 - 3}{8 - 1} = \dfrac{77}{7} = 11$ m/s

3.4 $s(5 + h)$
$= 2(5 + h) + (5 + h)^2$
$= 10 + 2h + 25 + 10h + h^2$
$= h^2 + 12h + 35$

3.5 $\dfrac{s(5+h) - s(5)}{h}$
$= \dfrac{h^2 + 12h + 35 - 35}{h}$
$= \dfrac{h^2 + 12h}{h}$
$= h + 12$

3.6 The average speed as t increases from 5 seconds to a greater number of seconds.

4. $p(x) = \dfrac{2}{x+3} - 1$

4.1 Domain p: $x \in (-\infty; -3)$ and $x \in (-3; \infty)$

4.2 $y = \dfrac{2}{x+3} - 1$
For p^{-1} swop x and y:
$x = \dfrac{2}{y+3} - 1$
Make y the subject:
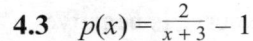
$(x + 1)(y + 3) = 2$
$y + 3 = \dfrac{2}{x+1}$
$y = \dfrac{2}{x+1} - 3$

4.3 $p(x) = \dfrac{2}{x+3} - 1$

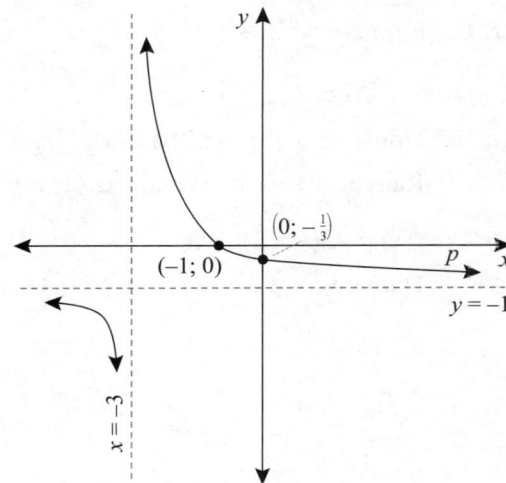

4.4 Perform a horizontal line test. If any horizontal line cuts the graph only once then p^{-1} is a function.

4.5 Domain p^{-1}: $x \in \mathbb{R}, x \neq -1$
Range p^{-1}: $y \in \mathbb{R}, y \neq -3$

4.6 Decreasing, because the gradient of the tangent to the curve is negative.

4.7 $p(0) = -\dfrac{1}{3}$
$p(2) = \dfrac{2}{5} - 1 = -\dfrac{3}{5}$
Average rate of change $= \dfrac{-\frac{3}{5} - (-\frac{1}{3})}{2 - 0}$
$= -\dfrac{2}{15}$

5. $g(x) = \sqrt{3-x}$

5.1 Domain$_g$: $3 - x \geq 0$
$-x \geq -3$
$x \leq 3$

5.2 Range$_g$ $y \geq 0$

5.3 $g(x): y = \sqrt{3-x}$
$g^{-1}: x = \sqrt{3-y}$
$x^2 = 3 - y$
$g^{-1}(x) = y = -x^2 + 3, x > 0$

5.4 Yes.
It is a parabola in the form $x = ax^2 + c$

5.5 Domain$_{g^{-1}}$: $x > 0$
Range$_{g^{-1}}$: $y \leq 3$

5.6 $g(-6) = \sqrt{3+5} = \sqrt{9} = 3$
$g(-1) = \sqrt{3+1} = \sqrt{4} = 2$
Average of change $= \frac{3-2}{-6-(-1)} = -\frac{1}{5}$

5.7 Decreasing, because the gradient of the tangent to the curve is negative.

6.1 $p(x) = \frac{6}{2-x} + 1$
$\therefore p(x) = \frac{-6}{x-2} + 1$
Domain$_p$: $x \in (-\infty; 2)$ and $x \in (2; \infty)$
Range$_p$: $y \in (-\infty; 1)$ and $y \in (1; \infty)$

6.2 $f(x) = -2(x+1)^2 + 3$
Domain$_f$: $x \in \mathbb{R}$

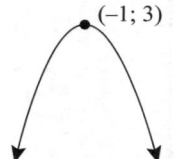
(−1; 3)

Range$_f$: $y \in (-\infty; 3]$

6.3 $t(x) = \sqrt{x^2 - 4}$
Domain$_t$: $x^2 - 4 \geq 0$
$(x-2)(x+2) \geq 0$

$\begin{array}{c|c|c|c|c} + & & - & & + \\ \hline & -2 & & 2 & \end{array}$

$x \leq -2$ or $x \geq 2$
Range$_t$: $y \geq 0$

7.1 $x \in (-2; 1)$

7.2 $x = 2$

7.3 $x = 3$

7.4 $x \in (-1; 0)$

8.1 $f(-1) = -5 - 2 = -7$
$f(4) = 5(4) - 2 = 18$
$y \in [-7; 18]$
$y = 5x - 2$
$x = 5y - 2$
$5y = x + 2$
$y = \frac{1}{5}x + \frac{2}{5}$
$f^{-1}(x) = \frac{1}{5}x + \frac{2}{5}, x \in [-7; 18]$

8.2 $h(x) = x^2 - 4$
$y = x^2 - 4$
$x = y^2 - 4$
$y^2 = x + 4$
$h^{-1}(x) = y = \sqrt{x+4}, y > 0$

8.3 $g(x) = \frac{3}{x-1}$
$y = \frac{3}{x-1}$
$x = \frac{3}{y-1}$
$x(y-1) = 3$
$y - 1 = \frac{3}{x}$
$y = \frac{3}{x} + 1$
$g^{-1}(x) = \frac{3}{x} + 1$

8.4 $p(x) = 3^x + 1$
$y = 3^x + 1$
$x = 3^y + 1$
$x - 1 = 3^y$
$p^{-1}(x) = y = \log_3(x-1)$

Exercise 4 (page 36)

1. $y = 3x + 6$

2. $y - 2 = x$
$y = x + 2$

3. $2y - 3x + 6 = 0$
y-intercept: $y = -3$
x-intercept: $x = 2$

4. $3 + y = 0$
$y = -3$

5. $x - 3 = 0$
$x = 3$

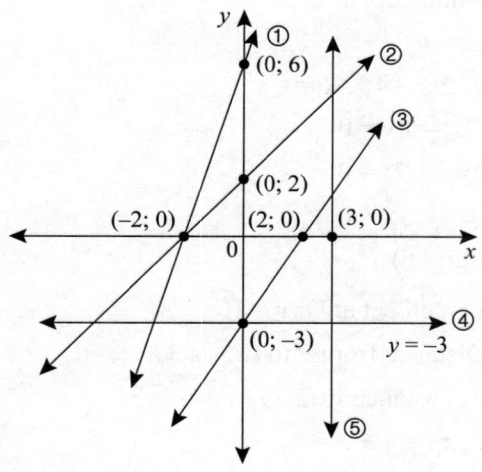

Exercise 5 (page 39)

1.1 S –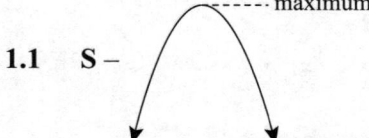

C – y-intercept: $y = 4$

R – roots: $x^2 - 3x - 4 = 0$
$(x - 4)(x + 1) = 0$
$x = 4$ or $x = -1$

A – A/S: $x = \frac{4-1}{2} = \frac{3}{2}$

M – Max:
$y = -\left(\frac{3}{2}\right)^2 + 3\left(\frac{3}{2}\right) + 4$
$= \frac{31}{4}$

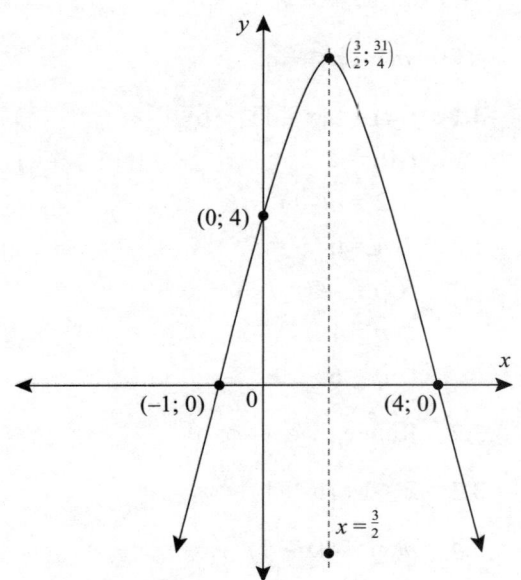

1.2 $x \in \left(-\infty; \frac{3}{2}\right)$

2.1 $y = 2x^2 + 4x - 6$

S – 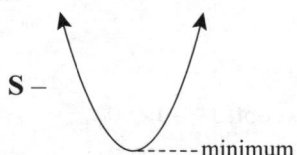 ---- minimum

C – y-intercept: $y = -6$

R – roots: $2x^2 + 4x - 6 = 0$
$x^2 + 2x - 3 = 0$
$(x + 3)(x - 1) = 0$
$x = -3$ or $x = 1$

A – A/S: $x = \frac{-3+1}{2} = -1$

M – Min: $y = 2(-1)^2 + 4(-1) - 6$
$y = -8$

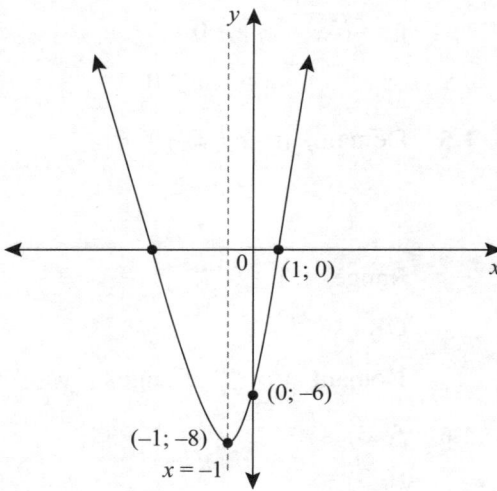

2.2 $x \in (-\infty; -1)$

Exercise 6 (page 39)

1. $f(x) = -x^2 + 1$, $x \in (-1; 1)$

1.1 $f(-1) = -(-1)^2 + 1 = 0$
$f(1) = -(1)^2 + 1 = 0$

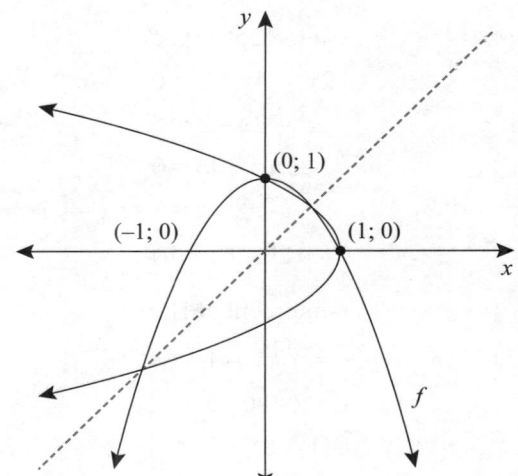

S – ⌢

C – y-intercept: $y = 1$

R – x-intercept: $x^2 - 1 = 0$
$$x = \pm 1$$

A – A/S: $x = 0$

M – Max: $y = 1$

1.2 Range: $y \in (-\infty; 1]$

1.3 Sketch

1.4 $y = -x^2 + 1$
$x = -y^2 + 1$
$y^2 = -x + 1$
$y = \sqrt{-x+1}, y \geq 0$
or $y = -\sqrt{-x+1}, y \leq 0$

1.5 Domain$_{f-1}$: $-x + 1 \geq 0$
$$-x \geq -1$$
$$x \leq 1$$

Range$_{f-1}$: $y \geq 0$

OR

Domain$_{f-1}$: $x \leq 1$; Range$_{f-1}$: $y \leq 0$

1.6 $f(-5) = -24$
$f(-3) = -8$
Average rate of change $= \frac{-24 - (-8)}{-5 - (-3)}$
$= \frac{-16}{-2} = 8$

1.7 Any two x-values greater than 1

2. $f(x) = 2x^2 - 4x - 6$

2.1 A(0; –6)

x-intercept at C & D:
$2x^2 - 4x - 6 = 0$
$x^2 - 2x - 3 = 0$
$(x - 3)(x + 1) = 0$
$x = 3$ or $x = -1$
C(–1; 0); D(3; 0)

x-intercept at B:
$x = \frac{-1 + 3}{2} = 1$
$y = 2 - 4 - 6 = -8$
B(1; –8)

x-intercept at E:
$y = -6$
$\therefore 2x^2 - 4x - 6 = -6$
$2x^2 - 4x = 0$
$2x(x - 2) = 0$
$x = 0$ or $x = 2$
E(2; –6)

x-intercept at Q: $y = 10$
Distance from P to A/S is 3
$\therefore$ Distance from Q to A/S is 3
$\therefore x_Q = 1 + 3 = 4$
Q(4; 10)

2.2 $g(x) = mx + c$
$y = mx - 6$
$m = \frac{y_D - y_A}{x_D - x_A} = \frac{0 - (-6)}{3 - 0}$
$= \frac{6}{3} = 2$
$g(x) = 2x - 6$

2.3 Domain$_f$: $x \in (-\infty; \infty)$ Range$_f$: $y \in [-8; \infty)$

2.4 $x \geq 1$ or $x \leq 1$

2.5.1 $2x^2 - 4x - 6 > 0$
$x \in (-\infty; -1)$ and $x \in (3; \infty)$

2.5.2 For equal roots the graph of f must touch the x-axis.
$f(x)$ is shifted 8 units up
$\therefore p = -6 + 8 = 2$

3. $f(x) = a(x - p)^2 + q$

3.1 $f(x) = a(x - 1)^2 + 6$
$f(0) = 2$
$2 = a(-1)^2 + 6$
$-4 = a$
$f(x) = -4(x - 1)^2 + 6$
$p = 1$
$q = 6$

3.2 Range$_f$: $y \in (-\infty; 6]$

3.3 $x \leq 1$ or $x \geq 1$

3.4 $h(x) = 4(x - 1)^2 - 6$

3.5 $f(x) - h(x)$ when $x = 0$
$= 2 - (-2)$
$= 4$

3.6 $f(x) > h(x)$

Need x-intercept; let $y = 0$:

$-4(x-1)^2 + 6 = 0$

$(x-1)^2 = \frac{+6}{+4}$

$x - 1 = \pm\frac{\sqrt{6}}{2}$

$x = 1 + \sqrt{\frac{6}{2}}$ or $1 - \sqrt{\frac{6}{2}}$

$x \in \left(1 - \frac{\sqrt{6}}{2}; 1 + \frac{\sqrt{6}}{2}\right)$

3.7 $f(x)$ must be shifted left one unit, downwards 6 units, and then reflected in the x-axis.

Exercise 7 (page 42)

1. $\left(\frac{27x^{-3}}{8\sqrt{x^4}}\right)^{-\frac{4}{3}}$

$= \left(\frac{8\sqrt{x^4}}{27x^{-3}}\right)^{\frac{4}{3}}$

$= \left(\frac{2^3 \cdot x^2 \cdot x^3}{3^3}\right)^{\frac{4}{3}}$

$= \frac{2^4 \cdot x^{\frac{8}{3}} \cdot x^4}{3}$

$= \frac{16 x^{\frac{20}{3}}}{3}$

2. $\frac{2^{2n+3} \cdot 3^{2n-1}}{6^{2n}}$

$= \frac{2^{2n+3} \cdot 3^{2n-1}}{3^{2n} \cdot 2^{2n}}$

$= 2^3 \cdot 3^{-1}$

$= \frac{8}{3}$

3. $\frac{5^{x+1} \cdot 125^{x-2}}{25^{2(x-1)}}$

$= \frac{5^{x+1} \cdot (5^3)^{x-2}}{5^{4(x-1)}}$

$= \frac{5^{x+1} \cdot 5^{3x-6}}{5^{4x-4}}$

$= \frac{5^{4x-5}}{5^{4x-4}}$

$= 5^{-5-(-4)}$

$= 5^{-1} = \frac{1}{5}$

4. $\frac{4^x \cdot 15^{x-2}}{6^{x+1} \cdot 10x}$

$= \frac{(2^2)^x \cdot (3 \cdot 5)^{x-2}}{2^{x+1} \cdot 3^{x+1} \cdot 2^x \cdot 5^x}$

$= \frac{2^{2x} \cdot 3^{x-2} \cdot 5^{x-2}}{2^{x+1} \cdot 3^{x+1} \cdot 5^x}$

$= \frac{2^{2x} \cdot 3^x \cdot 3^{-2} \cdot 5^x \cdot 5^{-2}}{2^{2x} \cdot 2^1 \cdot 3^x \cdot 3^1 \cdot 5^x}$

$= \frac{1}{2 \cdot 3 \cdot 3^2 \cdot 5^2}$

$= \frac{1}{1350}$

5. $\frac{50^{-n+1} \cdot 2^{n-1} \cdot 25^{-1}}{9^{n+2} \cdot (225)^{-n-1}}$

$= \frac{(2 \cdot 5^2)^{-n+1} \cdot 2^{n-1} \cdot (5^2)^{-1}}{(3^2)^{n+2} \cdot (5^2 \cdot 3^2)^{-n-1}}$

$= \frac{2^{-n+1} \cdot 5^{-2n+2} \cdot 2^{n-1} \cdot 5^{-2}}{3^{2n-4} \cdot 5^{-2n-2} \cdot 3^{-2n-2}}$

$= \frac{2^0 \cdot 5^{-2n}}{3^2 \cdot 5^{-2n-2}}$

$= \frac{1 \cdot 5^{-2n}}{9 \cdot 5^{-2n} \cdot 5^{-2}}$

$= \frac{25}{9}$

Exercise 8 (page 43)

1. $\frac{3^{n+2} - 3^{n+1}}{3^n + 3^{n+2}}$

$= \frac{3^n(3^2 - 3^1)}{3^n(1 + 3^2)}$

$= \frac{9 - 3}{1 + 9}$

$= \frac{6}{10}$

$= \frac{3}{5}$

2. $\frac{2^{n+4} - 6 \cdot 2^{n+1}}{2^{n+2}}$

$= \frac{2^{n+1}(2^3 - 6)}{2^{n+2}}$

$= \frac{2^n \cdot 2(8-6)}{2^n \cdot 2^2}$

$= \frac{2 \cdot 2}{2^2}$

$= 1$

3. $\frac{2 \cdot 3^x - 9 \cdot 3^{x-2}}{3^x - 2 \cdot 3^{x-1}}$

$= \frac{2 \cdot 3^x - 3^2 \cdot 3^x \cdot 3^{-2}}{3^x - 2 \cdot 3^x \cdot 3^{-1}}$

$= \frac{3^x(2 - 3^2 \cdot 3^{-2})}{3^x(1 - 2 \cdot 3^{-1})}$

$= \frac{2 - 3^0}{1 - \frac{2}{3}}$

$= \frac{2 - 1}{\frac{1}{3}}$

$= \frac{1}{\frac{1}{3}}$

$= 3$

Exercise 9 (page 43)

1. $x - 8x^{\frac{1}{2}} + 15$

$= \left(x^{\frac{1}{2}} - 5\right)\left(x^{\frac{1}{2}} - 3\right)$

2. $3^{2x} + 3 \cdot 3^x - 10$

$= (3^x)^2 + 3 \cdot 3^x - 10$

let $k = 3^x$
$k^2 + 3k - 10$
$= (k + 5)(k - 2)$
$\therefore (3^x + 5)(3^x - 2)$

3. $2^{2x+1} - 2^x - 3$
$= 2 \cdot 2^{2x} - 2^x - 3$
let $k = 2^x$
$2 \cdot k^2 - k - 3$
$= (2k - 3)(k + 1)$
$= (2 \cdot 2^x - 3)(2^x + 1)$

Exercise 10 (page 45)

1.1 $f(x) = a^x$
$8 = a^3$
$\therefore a = 2$
$f(x) = 2^x$

1.2 $y = a^x$
$\frac{27}{8} = a^3$
$\left(\frac{3}{2}\right)^3 = a^3$
$a = \frac{3}{2}$
$f(x) = \left(\frac{3}{2}\right)^x$

2. $y = 2^x + 1$

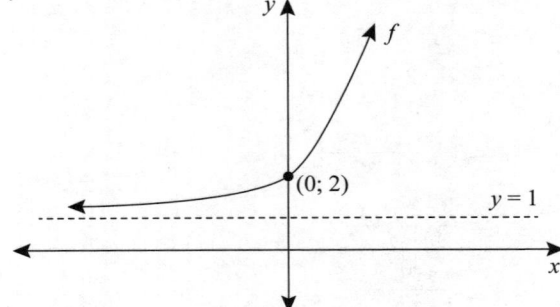

2.1 $f(-3) = 2^{-3} + 1$
$= \frac{1}{8} + 1 = \frac{9}{8}$
$f(1) = 2^1 + 1 = 3$

2.2 $f(x) = 17$
$2^x + 1 = 17$
$2^x = 16$
$2^x = 2^4$
$x = 4$

2.3 Domain$_f$: $x \in \mathbb{R}$; Range$_f$: $y > 1$, $y \in \mathbb{R}$

2.4 Increasing, because the gradient of tangent lines to the curve are positive.

2.5.1 $f(x)$ is reflected in the y-axis
$\therefore$ change the sign of x in the equation:
$g(x) = 2^{-x} + 1$
OR $g(x) = \left(\frac{1}{2}\right)^x + 1$

2.5.2 $f(x)$ is reflected in the x-axis
$\therefore$ change the sign of y in the equation:
$p(x) = -2^x - 1$

Exercise 11 (page 46)

1.1 $\log_5 25 = 2$
1.2 $\log_7 40 = 2$
1.3 $\log_2 32 = 5$
1.4 $\log_6 1 = 0$
1.5 $\log_9 3 = \frac{1}{2}$
1.6 $\log_{64} 16 = \frac{2}{3}$

2.1 $3^4 = 81$
2.2 $4^3 = 64$
2.3 $5^4 = 625$
2.4 $8^{\frac{2}{3}} = 4$
2.5 $3^1 = 3$
2.6 $9^{\frac{5}{2}} = 243$

Exercise 12 (page 46)

1. $\log_8 32 = \log_{2^3} 2^5$
$= \frac{5}{3}$

2. $\log_9 27 = \log_{3^2} 3^3$
$= \frac{3}{2}$

3. $\log_{125} 25 = \log_{5^3} 5^2$
$= \frac{2}{3}$

4. $\log_{16} 64 = \log_{2^4} 2^6$
$= \frac{6}{4} = \frac{3}{2}$

5. $\log_{49} 7 = \log_{7^2} 7^1$
$= \frac{1}{2}$

6. $\log_{\frac{1}{2}} 4 = \log_{2^{-1}} 2^2$
$= \frac{2}{-1}$
$= -2$

Exercise 13 (page 49)

$f(x) = \log_a x, a > 0, a \neq 1$

1. $y = \log_a x$ (81; 4)
   $a^y = x$
   $a^4 = 81$
   $a = 3$

2. $f(x)\ y = \log_3 x$
   $x = \log_3 y$
   $f^{-1}(x) = y = 3^x$

3. Domain$_f$: $x \in (0; \infty)$; Range$_f$: $y \in (-\infty; \infty)$
   Domain$_{f^{-1}}$: $x \in (-\infty; \infty)$
   Range$_{f^{-1}}$: $y \in (0; \infty)$

4.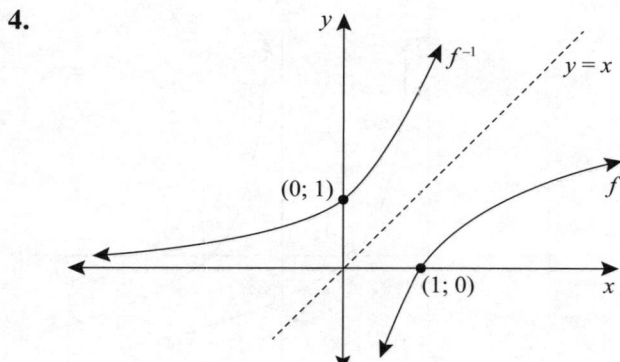

5. Perform a vertical line test – only cuts f once. Perform a horizontal line test – only cuts once, therefore one-to-one relation.

Exercise 14 (page 51)

1. $f(x) = \log_2 x$

   1.1 $x = \log_2 y$
   $f^{-1}(x) = y = 2^x$

   1.2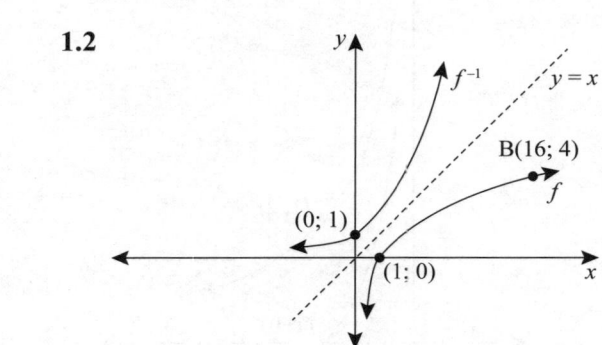

   1.3 $x < 0$

   1.4 $x \in (0; 16)$

2.1 Reflect in the y-axis – change the sign of x:
$f(x) = \log_2 x$
$h(x) = \log_2(-x), x < 0$

2.2 Reflect in the x-axis – change the sign of y:
$f(x) = \log_2 x$
$p(x) = -\log_2 x$
$\quad\quad = \log_2 x^{-1}$
$\quad\quad = \log_2 \frac{1}{x}$

2.3 $f(x) = \log_2 x$
$k(x) = \log_2(x - 2)$

2.4 $q(x) = \log_2 x - 1$

3.1

Domain$_h$: $x < 0$; Range$_h$: $y \in \mathbb{R}$

3.2

Domain$_p$: $x > 0$; Range$_p$: $y \in \mathbb{R}$

3.3

Domain$_k$: $x > 2$; Range$_k$: $y \in \mathbb{R}$

3.4

Domain$_q$: $x > 0$; Range$_q$: $y \in \mathbb{R}$

4. $g(x) = \log_{\frac{1}{2}} x$ C(4; –2)

4.1 $g: y = \log_{\frac{1}{2}} x$

$g^{-1}: x = \log_{\frac{1}{2}} y$

$y = \left(\frac{1}{2}\right)^x = 2^{-x}$

$g^{-1}(x) = 2^{-x}$

4.2

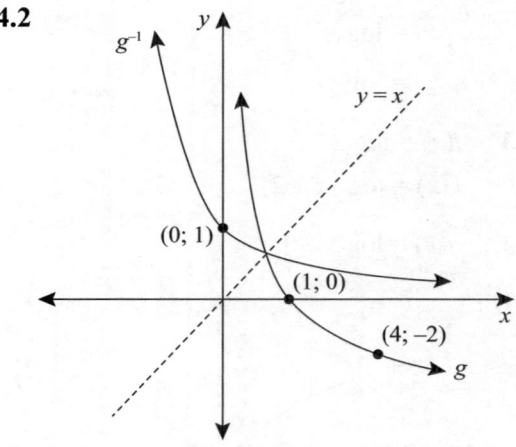

4.3 $x > 0$

4.4 $x \in (0; 4)$

5.1 Reflect in y-axis so change sign of x:
$h(x) = \log_{\frac{1}{2}}(-x), x < 0$

5.2 Reflect in the x-axis so change the sign of y:
$p(x) = -\log_{\frac{1}{2}} x$
$= \log_2 x$

5.3 $g(x) = \log_{\frac{1}{2}} x$
$k(x) = \log_{\frac{1}{2}}(x + 2)$

5.4 $q(x) = 1 + \log_{\frac{1}{2}} x$

6.1

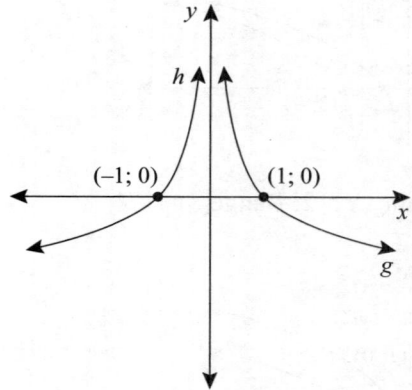

Domain$_h$: $x < 0$

Range$_h$: $y \in \mathbb{R}$

6.2

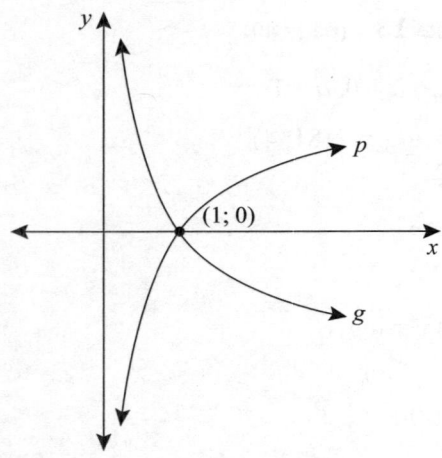

Domain$_p$: $x > 0$

Range$_p$: $y \in \mathbb{R}$

6.3

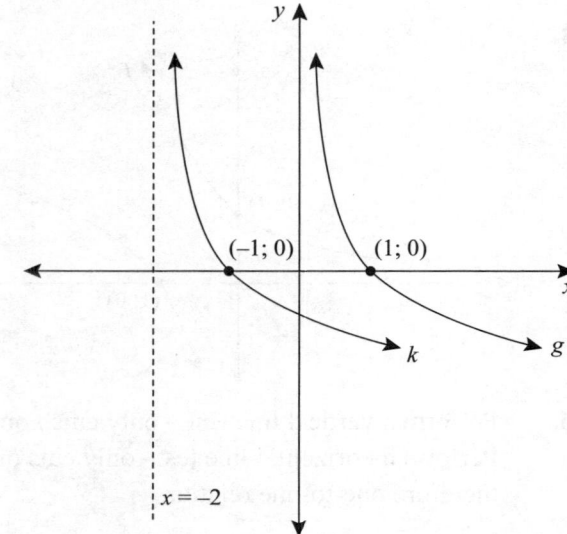

Domain$_k$: $x > -2$

Range$_k$: $y \in \mathbb{R}$

6.4

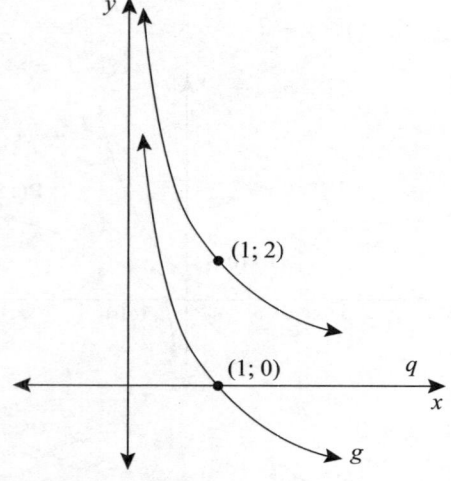

Domain$_q$: $x > 0$

Range$_q$: $y \in \mathbb{R}$

Exercise 15 (page 52)

1. $1{,}05^n = 5{,}6$
$\log 1{,}05^n = \log 5{,}6$
$n \log 1{,}05 = \log 5{,}6$
$n = \frac{\log 5{,}5}{\log 1{,}05}$
$n \approx 35{,}3$

2. $\left(1 + \frac{0{,}12}{4}\right)^n = 1{,}026$
$\log\left(1 + \frac{0{,}12}{4}\right)^n = \log 1{,}026$
$n \log\left(1 + \frac{0{,}12}{4}\right) = \log 1{,}026$
$n = \frac{\log 1{,}026}{\log\left(1 + \frac{0{,}12}{4}\right)}$
$n \approx 0{,}868$

3. $250(1{,}075)^{n+1} = 5\,076$
$(1{,}075)^{n+1} = \frac{5\,076}{250}$
$\log(1{,}075)^{n+1} = \log 20{,}304$
$(n+1)\log 1{,}075 = \log 20{,}304$
$n + 1 = \frac{\log 20{,}304}{\log 1{,}075}$
$n = 41{,}63\ldots - 1$
$n \approx 40{,}63$

4. $10\,000\left(1 + \frac{0{,}08}{12}\right)^{n-1} = 15\,000$
$\left(1 + \frac{0{,}08}{12}\right)^{n-1} = 1{,}5$
$\log\left(1 + \frac{0{,}08}{12}\right)^{n-1} = \log 1{,}5$
$(n-1)\log\left(1 + \frac{0{,}08}{12}\right) = \log 1{,}5$
$n - 1 = \frac{\log 1{,}5}{\log\left(1 + \frac{0{,}08}{12}\right)}$
$n - 1 = 61{,}028\ldots$
$n \approx 62{,}03$

5. $85(1{,}05)^{n-2} = 400$
$(1{,}05)^{n-2} = \frac{400}{85}$
$\log(1{,}05)^{n-2} = \log \frac{400}{85}$
$(n-2)\log 1{,}05 = \log \frac{400}{85}$
$n - 2 = \frac{\log \frac{400}{85}}{\log 1{,}05}$
$n - 2 = 31{,}74\ldots$
$n \approx 33{,}74$

Test A (page 53)

1. $P^m = x$
$\log_P x = m$ \hfill (1)

2.1 $3^4 = 81$
$\log_3 81 = 4$

2.2 $\left(\frac{1}{2}\right)^3 = \frac{1}{8}$
$\log_{\frac{1}{2}} \frac{1}{8} = 3$ \hfill (2 × 2)

2.3 $\log_{10} 100 = 2$
$10^2 = 100$

2.4 $\log_2 64 = 6$
$2^6 = 64$

2.5 $\log_a b = k$
$a^k = b$ \hfill (3 × 2)

3. Let $\log_{25} 125 = x$
$\therefore 25^x = 125$
$5^{2x} = 5^3$
$\therefore 2x = 3$
$x = \frac{3}{2}$ \hfill (2)

4.1 $f(1) = -(1)^2 + 2(1) + 3$
$= 4$ \hfill (1)

4.2.1 $f(x) = 0$
$\therefore f(x) = -x^2 + 2x + 3 = 0$
$x^2 - 2x - 3 = 0$
$(x - 3)(x + 1) = 0$
$\therefore x - 3 = 0$ or $x + 1 = 0$
$\therefore x = 3$ or $x = -1$ \hfill (3)

4.2.2 $f(x) = 4$
$\therefore f(x) = -x^2 + 2x + 3 = 4$
$\therefore -x^2 + 2x - 1 = 0$
$x^2 - 2x + 1 = 0$
$(x - 1)^2 = 0$
$x - 1 = 0$
$\therefore x = 1$ \hfill (3)

4.3 Axis of symmetry:
$\frac{x_1 + x_2}{x}$
$= \frac{3 + (-1)}{2}$
$= 1$
OR $x = \frac{-b}{2a}$
$= \frac{-2}{2(-1)} = 1$

$f(1) = -(1)^2 + 2(1) + 3$
$\quad\quad\ = 4$
$\therefore$ T.P. (turning point) is at $(1; 4)$ (1)

4.4 $y \in (-\infty; 4]$ (1)

4.5 $\because$ (because) $(1; 4)$ is the turning point
$\therefore y = a(x - 1)^2 + 4$
$\because (3; 0)$ is a point on the graph $f(x)$
$\therefore 0 = a(3 - 1)^2 + 4$
$\quad\ 0 = a(2)^2 + 4$
$\ -4 = 4a$
$\ \ a = -1$
$\therefore y = -(x - 1)^2 + 4$ (3)

5.1 $f(x) = a(x - P)^2 + Q$
$\because$ T.P. $= B\left(-1\tfrac{1}{2}; 6\tfrac{1}{4}\right)$
$\therefore f(x) = a\left(x + 1\tfrac{1}{2}\right)^2 + 6\tfrac{1}{4}$
$\because C(0; 4)$ is a point on the graph $f(x)$
$\therefore 4 = a\left(0 + 1\tfrac{1}{2}\right)^2 + 6\tfrac{1}{4}$
$\quad\ 4 = \tfrac{a}{4}a + \tfrac{25}{4}$
$\ -\tfrac{a}{4} = \tfrac{a}{4}a$
$\therefore a = -1$
$\therefore f(x) = -\left(x + 1\tfrac{1}{2}\right)^2 + 6\tfrac{1}{4}$
$\therefore a = -1, P = 1\tfrac{1}{2}, Q = 6\tfrac{1}{4}$ (4)

5.2.1 $f(x)$ is a maximum valued curve (1)

5.2.2 $f(x) = 6\tfrac{1}{4}$ (1)

5.3 Range: $y \in \left(-\infty; 6\tfrac{1}{4}\right]$; Domain: $x \in (-\infty; \infty)$ (2)

5.4.1 $C(0; 4), D(1; 0)$
$M_{CD} = \dfrac{y_D - y_C}{x_D - x_C}$
$\quad\quad = \dfrac{0 - 4}{1 - 0}$
$\quad\quad = -\dfrac{4}{1}$
$\quad\quad = -4$ (3)

5.4.2 $A(-4; 0), B(-1,5; 6,25)$
$M_{AB} = \dfrac{y_B - y_A}{x_B - x_A}$
$\quad\quad = \dfrac{6,25 - 0}{-1,5 - (-4)}$
$\quad\quad = \dfrac{6,25}{2,5}$
$\quad\quad = 2,5$ (2)

5.5.1 many-to-one (1)
5.5.2 one-to-one (1)

5.6 $C(0; 4), A(-4; 0)$
$g(x) = mx + c$
Substitute $C(0; 4)$ and $A(-4; 0)$ into $g(x)$:
$\quad 4 = 0m + c$
$\therefore c = 4$
$\quad 0 = -4m + c$
$\quad\ \ = -4m + 4$
$\therefore m = 1$
$\therefore g(x) = x + 4$ (2)

5.7 $x = y + 4$
$y = x - 4$
$g^{-1}(x) = x - 4$ (3)

5.8.1

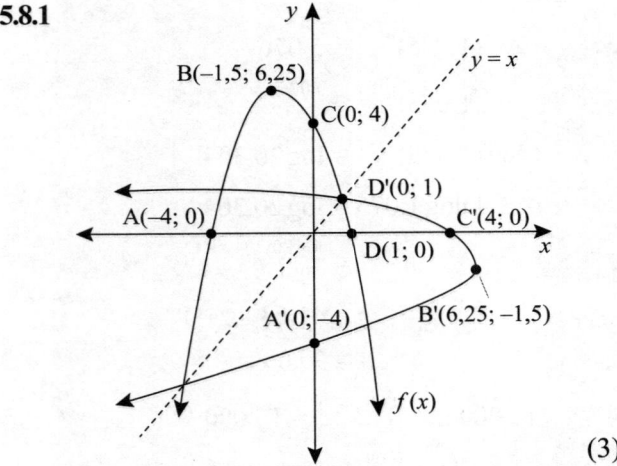

(3)

5.8.2 $x \geq -1,5$ or $x \leq -1,5$ (2)

Total: 50

Test B (page 54)

1. $f(x) = \left(\tfrac{1}{3}\right)^x$

1.1 y-intercept: $(0; 1)$
(or any other valid point) (2)

1.2 $f(x) = y = \left(\tfrac{1}{3}\right)^x$

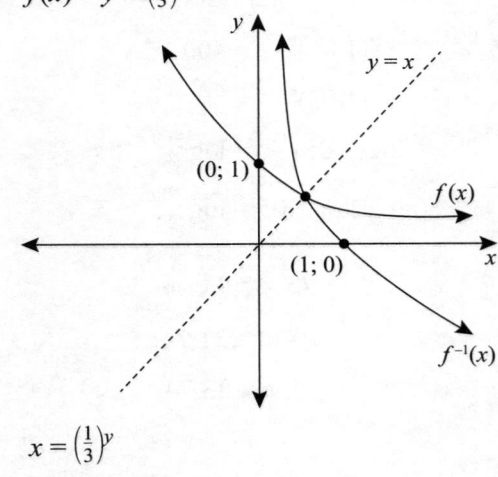

$x = \left(\tfrac{1}{3}\right)^y$
$f^{-1}(x) = y = \log_{\tfrac{1}{3}} x$ (3)

1.3 $x \in (0; 1)$ (1)

1.4 $\left(\frac{1}{3}\right)^x = 27$
$3^{-x} = 3^3$
$x = -3$
$x \in (-3; \infty)$ (2)

1.5 $f(x) = \left(\frac{1}{3}\right)x = 3^{-x}$
$g(x)$ is $f(x)$ reflected in the y-axis
$g(x) = y = 3^x$ (2)

1.6.1 $x = 0$ $y = 1$
$x = 2$ $y = \left(\frac{1}{3}\right)^2 = \frac{1}{9}$
Average gradient $= \frac{1-\frac{1}{9}}{0-3} = -\frac{8}{27}$ (4)

1.6.2 Decreasing (1)

1.6.3 Decreasing (1)

2.1 $x - 2 > 0$
$x > 2$ (2)

2.2 $f(x)$ will be moved 2 units to the left. (2)

2.3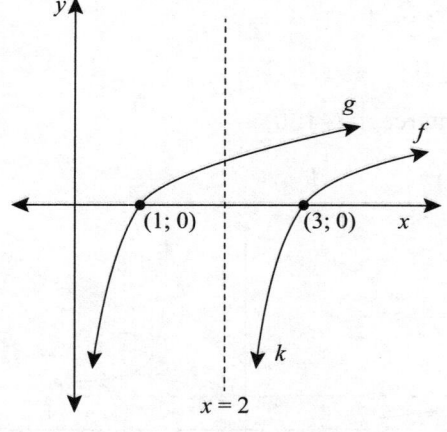

$x \in (2; 3)$
$y = \log_3(x - 2)$

Vertical asymptote: $x = 2$
x-intercept: $0 = \log_3(x - 2)$
$3^0 = x - 2$
$1 = x - 2$
$x = 3$ (3)

2.4 $g(x): y = \log_3 x$
$g^{-1}(x): x = \log_3 y$
$y = 3^x$ (3)

2.5 $f(x) = \log_3(x - 2)$
$h(x)$ is $f(x)$ reflected in the x-axis
$h(x) = -\log_3(x - 2) = \log_{\frac{1}{3}}(x - 2)$ (3)

3.1 $x : y = 1\,000\,000\,000 : 1\,000\,000 = 1\,000$ 1.
This indicates that an earthquake of magnitude 9 releases 1 000 times more energy than an earthquake of magnitude 6 on the Richter scale. (4)

3.2 $T_n = 6 \cdot 5^n = 38\,7000$
$5^n = 63\,000$
$n = \log_5 63\,000$
$n = 6{,}866304$
$\therefore n = 7$ (4)

4.1 R(1; 0) (1)

4.2 Yes. Using the vertical and horizontal line tests the lines only cut $f(x)$ once. (2)

4.3 At P(a; -1): $y = \log_{\frac{1}{2}} x$
$-1 = \log_{\frac{1}{2}} x$
$x = \left(\frac{1}{2}\right)^{-1} = 2$
$a = 2$ (1)

4.4 At Q(4; b): $y = \log_{\frac{1}{2}} x$
$y = \log_{\frac{1}{2}} 4$
$y = \log_{2^{-1}} 2^2$
$y = \frac{2}{-1} = -2$
$b = -2$ (1)

4.5 Average gradient: $= \frac{y_Q - y_P}{x_Q - x_P}$
$= \frac{-2 - (-1)}{4 - 2}$
$= -\frac{1}{2}$ (2)

4.6 $x \in (0; 2]$ and $x \in [4; \infty)$ (2)

4.7 $h(x) = -\log_{\frac{1}{2}} x$
$h(x) = \log_2 x$ (2)

4.8 $k(x) = \log_{\frac{1}{2}}(x - 1)$ (2)

Total: 50

Test C (page 55)

1.1

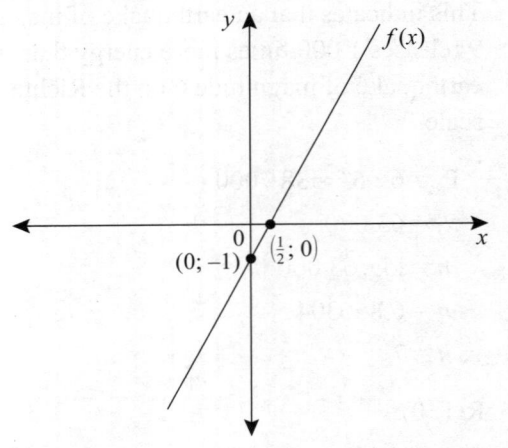

(1)

1.2.1 $x = 2y - 1$
$2y = x + 1$
$f^{-1}(x) = y = \tfrac{1}{2}x + \tfrac{1}{2}$

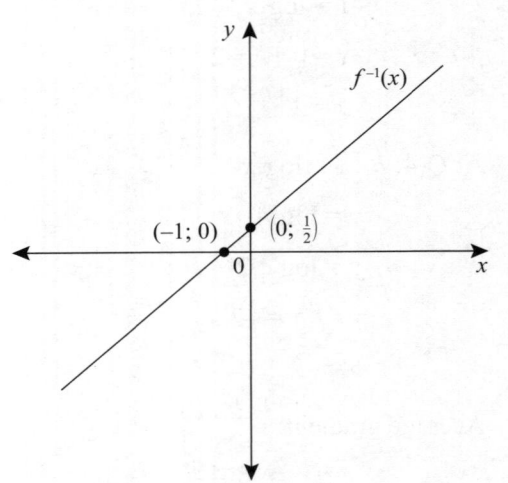

(3)

1.2.2 $h(x) = \dfrac{1}{2x - 1}$

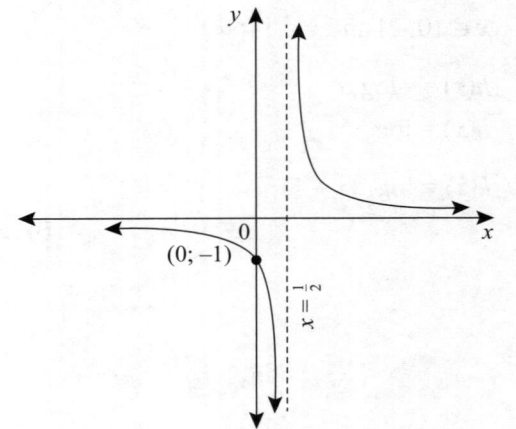

(3)

1.2.3 $g(x) = 2\left(\tfrac{1}{x}\right) - 1$
$g(x) = \tfrac{2}{x} - 1$

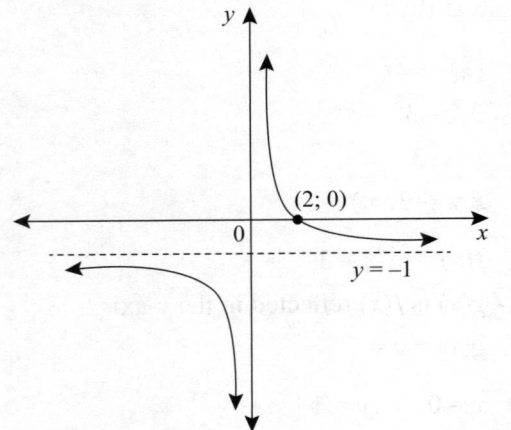

(3)

2.1 $x = 2$ and $y = 1$ (2)

2.2 Let $x = 0$:
$y = \dfrac{3}{0-2} + 1 = -\tfrac{1}{2}$
y-intercept: $\left(0; -\tfrac{1}{2}\right)$

Let $y = 0$:
$\dfrac{3}{x-2} + 1 = 0$
$\dfrac{3}{x-2} = -1$
$x - 2 = -3$
$x = -1$
x-intercept: $(-1; 0)$ (4)

2.3 $h(x) = \dfrac{3}{x-2} + 1$

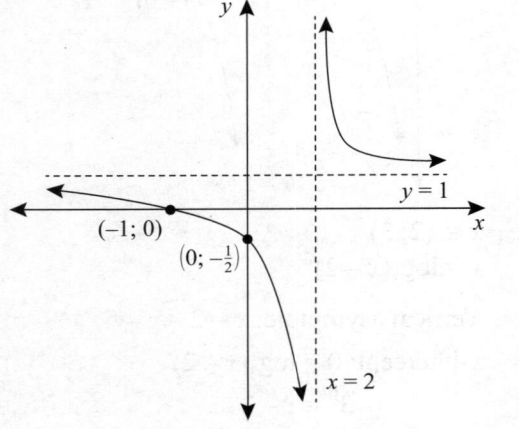

(4)

2.4.1 P$(a; -2)$
$-2 = \dfrac{3}{x-2} + 1$
$-3 = \dfrac{3}{x-2}$
$-3x + 6 = 3$
$\therefore -3x = -3$
$\therefore x = 1 \therefore a = 1$ (1)

2.4.2 $Q(-1; b)$

$b = \frac{3}{-1-2} + 1$

$= -1 + 1$

$= 0$

This can be read from the graph. (1)

2.4.3 Average gradient $= \frac{y_Q + y_P}{x_Q - x_P}$

$= \frac{0 - (-2)}{-1 - (1)}$

$= \frac{2}{-2}$

$= -1$ (2)

2.4.4 Decreasing (1)

2.5 2 units left, 1 unit up (2)

3.1 At B, the x-intercept of $f(x)$ is:

$3^x - 9 = 0$

$3^x = 9$

$x = 2$

B(2; 0)

At C, the y-intercept of $f(x)$ is:

Let $x = 0$

$y = 3^0 - 9 = -8$

C(0; -8) (4)

3.2 $y = -9$ (1)

3.3 $g(x) = f(2x) + 6$

$= 3^{2x} - 9 + 6$

$= 3^{2x} - 3$ (2)

3.4 $y = 3^{2x} - 3$

$x = 3^{2y} - 3$

$3^{2y} = x + 3$

$\log_3(x + 3) = 2y$

$g^{-1}(x) = y = \frac{1}{2}\log_3(x + 3)$ (2)

3.5 $f(x) = 3^x - 9$

$p(x) = -(3^x - 9) = -3^x + 9$ (2)

3.6 $x + 3 > 0$

$x > -3$ (2)

4.1 $(\sqrt{3x^2} - 1)^2 + \sqrt{12x^2}$

$= 3x^2 - 2\sqrt{3x^2} + 1 + 2\sqrt{3x^2}$

$= 3x^2 + 1$ (3)

4.2 $\frac{x^2 - 1}{x + 1} = \frac{(x-1)(x+1)}{(x+1)}$

$= x - 1$

$= 1\ 000\ 000\ 000\ 000$ (3)

4.3 $2\ 013^2 - 2\ 011 \times 2\ 015 + 2\ 010 \times 2\ 016 - 2\ 008 \times 2\ 018$

Let $x = 2\ 013$

$\therefore x^2 - (x - 2)(x + 2) + (x - 3)(x + 3) - (x - 5)(x + 5)$

$= x^2 - (x^2 - 4) + (x^2 - 9) - (x^2 - 25)$

$= 4 - 9 + 25$

$= 20$ (4)

Total: 50

TOPIC 3   Finance: Growth and decay   (page 57)

Exercise 1   (page 59)

1.1 interest per period = $\frac{0,09}{4}$ = 0,0225 per quarter

1.2 interest per period = $\frac{0,084}{12}$ = 0,007 per month

1.3 interest per period = $\frac{0,078}{365}$ = 0,000214 per day

1.4 interest per period = $\frac{0,08}{2}$ = 0,04 per 6 months

1.5 interest per period = 0,092 × 2 = 0,184 bi-annual

1.6 interest per period = $\frac{0,085}{52}$ = 0,0016 weekly

2.1 $1 + i_{eff} = \left(1 + \frac{i_{nom}}{n}\right)^n$ *n* represents number of periods per year

$1 + i_{eff} = \left(1 + \frac{0,09}{4}\right)^4$

$i_{eff} = 0,0931$ ∴ rate = 9,31% p.a.

2.2 $(1 + i_{eff}) = \left(1 + \frac{i_{nom}}{n}\right)^n$

$1 + i_{eff} = \left(1 + \frac{0,084}{12}\right)^{12}$

$i_{eff} = 0,0873$ ∴ rate = 8,73% p.a

2.3 $(1 + i_{eff}) = \left(1 + \frac{i_{nom}}{n}\right)^n$

$1 + i_{eff} = \left(1 + \frac{0,078}{365}\right)^{365}$

$i_{eff} = 0,081113$ ∴ rate = 8,11% p.a

2.4 $1 + i_{eff} = \left(1 + \frac{i_{nom}}{n}\right)^n$

$1 + i_{eff} = \left(1 + \frac{0,08}{2}\right)^2$

$i_{eff} = 0,0816$ ∴ rate = 8,16% p.a

2.5 $1 + i_{eff} = \left(1 + \frac{i_{nom}}{n}\right)^n$

$i_{eff} = \left(1 + \frac{0,092}{\frac{1}{2}}\right)^{\frac{1}{2}} - 1$

$i_{eff} = 0,088117$ ∴ r = 8,81% p.a

2.6 $1 + i_{eff} = \left(1 + \frac{i_{nom}}{n}\right)^n$

$i_{eff} = \left(1 + \frac{0,085}{52}\right)^{52} - 1$

= 0,08864 ∴ r = 8,86% p.a

Exercise 2   (page 59)

1.1 A: $1 + i_{eff} = \left(1 + \frac{i_{nom}}{n}\right)^n$

$i_{eff} = \left(1 + \frac{0,084}{365}\right)^{365} - 1$

= 0,08762 ∴ r = 8,76% p.a

B: $1 + i_{eff} = \left(1 + \frac{i_{nom}}{n}\right)^n$

$i_{eff} = \left(1 + \frac{0,085}{52}\right)^{52} - 1$

= 0,08864 ∴ r = 8,86% p.a

B is the better investment.

1.2 C: $1 + i_{eff} = \left(1 + \frac{i_{nom}}{n}\right)^n$

$i_{eff} = \left(1 + \frac{0,0825}{12}\right)^{12} - 1$

= 0,08569 ∴ r = 8,57% p.a

D: $1 + i_{eff} = \left(1 + \frac{i_{nom}}{n}\right)^n$

$i_{eff} = \left(1 + \frac{0,083}{4}\right)^4 - 1$

= 0,08562 ∴ r = 8,56% p.a

C is the better investment.

2. period – 6 years

Option A: $F = P(1 + i)^n$

$= x(1 + 0,079)^6 = 1,5781x$

Option B: $F = P(1 + i)^n$

$= x\left(1 + \frac{0,078}{12}\right)^{6 \times 12} = 1,5944x$

Option C: $F = P(1 + i)^n$

$= x\left(1 + \frac{0,0775}{52}\right)^{52 \times 6} = 1,5915x$

He should select option B.

Exercise 3   (page 59)

1.1 $F = P\left(1 + \frac{i}{12}\right)^{12 \times 5}$

$= 56\,700\left(1 + \frac{0,075}{12}\right)^{60}$

= R82 401,79

1.2 $1 + i_{eff} = \left(1 + \frac{i_{nom}}{12}\right)^{12}$

$i_{eff} = \left(1 + \frac{0,075}{12}\right)^{12} - 1$

= 0,07763

r = 7,76% p.a.

1.3

T_0 ———— $T_{2 \times 12}$ ←— $n = 3 \times 12$ —→ $T_{5 \times 12}$

56 700   10 000   F

$i = \frac{0,075}{12}$

$F = 56\,700\left(1 + \frac{0,075}{12}\right)^{5 \times 12} + 10\,000\left(1 + \frac{0,075}{12}\right)^{36}$

= R94 916,25

2.

```
T₀          T₂ₓ₁₂    T₃ₓ₁₂              T₅ₓ₁₂
├───────────┼────────┼──────────────────┤
12 000      7 500    5 000              F
                                        i = 0,078/12
```

We will use the formula $F = P(1 + i)^n$ on all 3 amounts deposited to find the future value of the money at $T_{5 \times 12}$.

$F = 12\,000\left(1 + \frac{0{,}078}{12}\right)^{5 \times 12} + 7\,500\left(1 + \frac{0{,}078}{12}\right)^{3 \times 12}$
$\quad + 5\,000\left(1 + \frac{0{,}078}{12}\right)^2$
$= R33\,012{,}76$

3.1 $1 + i_{\text{eff}} = \left(1 + \frac{i_{\text{nom}}}{12}\right)^{12}$

$i_{\text{eff}} = \left(1 + \frac{0{,}105}{12}\right)^{12} - 1 = 0{,}110203$

rate $= r = 11{,}02\%$ p.a.

3.2 $1 + i_{\text{eff}} = \left(1 + \frac{i_{\text{nom}}}{52}\right)^{52}$

$i_{\text{eff}} = \left(1 + \frac{0{,}093}{52}\right)^{52} - 1 = 0{,}09737$

rate $= r = 9{,}74\%$ p.a.

3.3 $1 + i_{\text{eff}} = \left(1 + \frac{i_{\text{nom}}}{4}\right)^4$

$i_{\text{eff}} = \left(1 + \frac{0{,}087}{4}\right)^4 - 1 = 0{,}089879$

rate $= r = 8{,}99\%$ p.a.

3.4 $1 + i_{\text{eff}} = \left(1 + \frac{i_{\text{nom}}}{2}\right)^2$

$i_{\text{eff}} = \left(1 + \frac{0{,}075}{2}\right)^2 - 1 = 0{,}07641$

rate $= r = 7{,}64\%$ p.a.

4. $\quad 1 + i_{\text{eff}} = \left(1 + \frac{i_{\text{nom}}}{12}\right)^{12}$

$1 + 0{,}09 = \left(1 + \frac{i_{\text{nom}}}{12}\right)^{12}$

$\sqrt[12]{1{,}09} = \left(1 + \frac{i_{\text{nom}}}{12}\right)$

$12\left(\sqrt[12]{1{,}09} - 1\right) = i_{\text{nom}} = 0{,}086487$

Nominal rate of interest is 8,65% p.a. compounded monthly.

5.

```
T₀             T₂ₓ₁₂  T₃ₓ₁₂                  T₆ₓ₁₂
├──────────────┼──────┼──────────────────────┤
300 000        -158 000 +35 000
                                              i = 0,0875/12
```

We need to calculate the future value of the money at $T_{6 \times 12}$. Use the formula $F = P(1 + i)^n$ on all three amounts.

$F_{6 \times 12} = 300\,000\left(1 + \frac{0{,}0875}{12}\right)^{6 \times 12}$
$\quad - 158\,000\left(1 + \frac{0{,}0875}{12}\right)^{(6-2) \times 12}$
$\quad + 35\,000\left(1 + \frac{0{,}0875}{12}\right)^{(6-3) \times 12}$
$= R327\,707{,}30$

```
T₀         T₁ₓ₄       T₂ₓ₄        T₃ₓ₄
├──────────┼──────────┼───────────┤
x          x          x           65 000
                                  i = 0,078/4
```

6. $F = P(1 + i)^n$ for all 3 amounts separately:

$= x\left(1 + \frac{0{,}078}{4}\right)^{12} + x\left(1 + \frac{0{,}078}{4}\right)^8 + x\left(1 + \frac{0{,}078}{4}\right)^4$

$65\,000 = x\left[\left(1 + \frac{0{,}078}{4}\right)^{12} + \left(1 + \frac{0{,}078}{4}\right)^8 + \left(1 + \frac{0{,}078}{4}\right)^4\right]$

$x = \frac{65\,000}{\left(1 + \frac{0{,}078}{4}\right)^{12} + \left(1 + \frac{0{,}078}{4}\right)^8 + \left(1 + \frac{0{,}078}{4}\right)^4}$

$= R18\,528{,}10$

7.1 $F = P(1 + i)^n$
$= 125\,000(1 + 0{,}055)^5 = R163\,370{,}00$

7.2.1 $F = P(1 - i)^n$
$= 125\,000(1 - 0{,}12)^5 = R65\,966{,}49$

7.2.2 $F = P(1 - in)$
$= 125\,000(1 - 0{,}12 \times 5) = R50\,000$

7.3 Amount to pay $= 163\,370 - 65\,966{,}49$
$\qquad\qquad\qquad = R97\,403{,}51$

8. $F = P(1 + i)^n$
$P = \frac{F}{(1+i)^n} = F(1+i)^{-n}$
$= 200\,000(1 + 0{,}105)^{-4}$
$= R134\,146{,}97$

9.1 $\quad F = P(1+i)^n \qquad n$ is minutes
$6\,000 = 2\,000(1+i)^{20}$
$i = \sqrt[20]{\frac{6}{2}} - 1$
$= 0{,}056467\ldots$ /min

rate per minute $= 5{,}65\%$

9.2 After 1 hour
$F = P(1+i)^{60}$
$= 2\,000(1 + 0{,}056467\ldots)^{60}$
$= 54\,000$ bacteria

10.1 $\qquad F = P(1+i)^n$
$51{,}7 = 44{,}8(1+i)^{10}$
$\sqrt[10]{\frac{51{,}7}{44{,}8}} - 1 = i = 0{,}014428\ldots$
$r = 1{,}44\%$ p.a.

10.2 $F = P(1 + i)^n$
$= 51,7(1 + 0,014428\ldots)^{10}$
$= 59,7$ million

Exercise 4 (page 62)

1.1 $F = x\left[\dfrac{(1+i)^n - 1}{i}\right]$

$= 500\left[\dfrac{\left(1 + \frac{0,085}{12}\right)^{36} - 1}{\frac{0,085}{12}}\right] = $ R20 421,33

1.2 $F = 800\left[\dfrac{\left(1 + \frac{0,085}{12}\right)^{36} - 1}{\frac{0,085}{12}}\right] = $ R32 674,13

1.3 $F = 1\,000\left[\dfrac{\left(1 + \frac{0,085}{12}\right)^{36} - 1}{\frac{0,085}{12}}\right] = $ R40 842,66

1.4 $F = 1\,200\left[\dfrac{\left(1 + \frac{0,085}{12}\right)^{36} - 1}{\frac{0,085}{12}}\right] = $ R49 011,19

1.5 $F = 1\,500\left[\dfrac{\left(1 + \frac{0,085}{12}\right)^{36} - 1}{\frac{0,085}{12}}\right] = $ R61 263,99

2. $T_0 \qquad\qquad\qquad T_{20}$

$\qquad\qquad\qquad\qquad F = 85\,000$

2.1 $i = \dfrac{0,085}{4}$

$n = 20$

$F = x\left[\dfrac{(1+i)^n - 1}{i}\right]$

$x = \dfrac{F}{\frac{(1+i)^n - 1}{i}} = \dfrac{85\,000}{\left[\frac{\left(1 + \frac{0,085}{4}\right)^{20} - 1}{\frac{0,085}{4}}\right]} = $ R3 454,99

2.2 $x = \dfrac{85\,000}{\left[\frac{\left(1 + \frac{0,0875}{4}\right)^{20} - 1}{\frac{0,0875}{4}}\right]} = $ R3 433,48

2.3 $x = \dfrac{85\,000}{\left[\frac{\left(1 + \frac{0,09}{4}\right)^{20} - 1}{\frac{0,09}{4}}\right]} = $ R3 412,08

3. $F = x\left[\dfrac{(1+i)^n - 1}{i}\right]$

$x = 1\,200$

$n = 6 \times 4$

$i = \dfrac{0,082}{4}$

$= 1\,200\left[\dfrac{\left(1 + \frac{0,082}{4}\right)^{24} - 1}{\frac{0,082}{4}}\right]$

$= $ R36 729,78

4. $F = x\left[\dfrac{(1+i)^n - 1}{i}\right]$

$x = 890$

$n = 48$

$i_{\text{nom}} = $ to be calculated

The periods for compounding (annually) are not the same as the periods when deposits are made (monthly). Convert effective to nominal.

$1 + i_{\text{eff}} = \left(1 + \dfrac{i_{\text{nom}}}{12}\right)^{12}$

$1 + 0,077 = \left(1 + \dfrac{i_{\text{nom}}}{12}\right)^{12}$

$\left(\sqrt[12]{1,077} - 1\right)12 = i_{\text{nom}}$

$= 0,0744\ldots$

Note: Do not approximate, place into memory.

$F = 890\left[\dfrac{\left(1 + \frac{i_{\text{nom}}}{12}\right)^{48} - 1}{\frac{i_{\text{nom}}}{12}}\right]$

$= $ R49 580,58

5. $F = x\left[\dfrac{(1+i)^n - 1}{i}\right]$

$x = \dfrac{F}{\frac{(1+i)^n - 1}{i}}$

$= \dfrac{220\,000}{\left[\frac{\left(1 + \frac{0,092}{12}\right)^{3 \times 12} - 1}{\frac{0,092}{12}}\right]} = $ R5 329,77

6. $T_0 \qquad\qquad\qquad T_{25 \times 12}$

$30 \qquad\qquad\qquad 55$

$i = \dfrac{0,09}{12}$

$n = 25 \times 12$

$F = 2\,000\,000$

$x = \dfrac{F}{\left[\frac{(1+i)^n - 1}{i}\right]} = \dfrac{2\,000\,000}{\left[\frac{\left(1 + \frac{0,09}{12}\right)^{25 \times 2} - 1}{\frac{0,09}{12}}\right]}$

$= $ R1 783,93

7. The periods for compounding (annually) are not the same as the period when deposits are made (monthly). Convert effective to nominal.

$1 + i_{\text{eff}} = \left(1 + \dfrac{i_{\text{nom}}}{12}\right)^{12}$

$1 + 0,0785 = \left(1 + \dfrac{i_{\text{nom}}}{12}\right)^{12}$

$F = x\left[\dfrac{(1+i)^n - 1}{i}\right]$

$\left(\sqrt[12]{1,0785} - 1\right)12 = i_{\text{nom}} = 0,0758096\ldots$

Note: Place in memory. Do not approximate here.

$F = 1\,200\left[\dfrac{\left(1 + \frac{i_{\text{nom}}}{12}\right)^{10 \times 12} - 1}{\frac{i_{\text{nom}}}{12}}\right]$

$= $ R214 476,98

8.

T_0 T_1 T_{16}
5   2 500

                                    21
                                    $i = 0,083$
                                    $n = 16$

$$F = x\left[\frac{(1+i)^n - 1}{i}\right]$$

$$= 2\,500\left[\frac{(1+0,083)^{16} - 1}{0,083}\right] = R77\,753,63$$

9.

T_0 T_5

                                1 000 000
                                $i = 0,22$ p.a.
                                compounding
                                annually

$$1 + i_{\text{eff}} = \left(1 + \frac{i_{\text{nom}}}{12}\right)^{12}$$

$$12\left(\sqrt[12]{1,22} - 1\right) = i_{\text{nom}}$$

$$= 0,200507\ldots \quad \text{Place in memory}$$

$$x = \frac{F}{\left[\frac{\left(1 + \frac{i_{\text{nom}}}{12}\right)^n - 1}{\frac{i_{\text{nom}}}{12}}\right]}$$

$F = 1\,000\,000$

$n = 5 \times 12 = 60$

$i = \frac{i_{\text{nom}}}{12}$

$$= \frac{1\,000\,000}{\left[\frac{\left(1 + \frac{i_{\text{nom}}}{12}\right)^{60} - 1}{\frac{i_{\text{nom}}}{12}}\right]}$$

$= R9\,813,17$

10. $F = x\left[\frac{(1+i)^n - 1}{i}\right]$

$x = \frac{157\,531,28}{\left[\frac{\left(1 + \frac{0,088}{12}\right)^{48} - 1}{\frac{0,088}{12}}\right]} = R2\,750,00$

Exercise 5 (page 63)

1.1

T_0 $T_{10 \times 12}$ $T_{42 \times 12}$

2 000
18   28   60
monthly   compound growth $i = \frac{0,085}{12}$
payments   on lump sum

$x = 2\,000$

Payments start immediately:
$n = (10 \times 12) + 1 = 121$

for Fv of lump sum: $n = (60 - 28) \times 12 = 384$

Total in her account at $T_{42} \times 12$

Future value of 121 monthly payments $\times (1 + i)$

$$= x\left[\frac{(1+i)^n - 1}{i}\right](1+i)^n$$

$$= 2\,000\left[\frac{\left(1 + \frac{0,085}{12}\right)^{121} - 1}{\frac{0,085}{12}}\right]\left(1 + \frac{0,085}{12}\right)^{384}$$

$= R5\,727\,643,01$

1.2

T_0 $T_{35 \times 12}$

2 000
25   60
                                    $i = \frac{0,085}{12}$

$x = 2\,000$

Payments start immediately: $n = (35 \times 12) + 1$
$\qquad\qquad\qquad\qquad\qquad\quad = 421$

$$F = x\left[\frac{(1+i)^n - 1}{i}\right]$$

$$= 2\,000\left[\frac{\left(1 + \frac{0,085}{12}\right)^{421} - 1}{\frac{0,085}{12}}\right]$$

$= R5\,229\,903,04$

1.3.1 Interest earned
$= 5\,727\,643,01 -$ number of payments
$\quad \times$ value of payments
$= 5\,727\,643,01 - (121)(2\,000)$
$= R5\,485\,643,01$

1.3.2 Interest earned
$= 5\,229\,903,04 - 421(2\,000)$
$= R4\,387\,903,04$

2.

T_0 T_1 T_{12} $T_{10 \times 12}$

      2 500   2 500
                 $i = \frac{0,09}{12}$ $\rightarrow$ memory
                 10 000

Joseph is running two annuities. For the annuity in which he deposits annually, the nominal interest rate of 9% p.a compounded monthly must be converted to an effective interest rate, which is used to calculate the future value of the annual payments he makes.

$$1 + i_{\text{eff}} = \left(1 + \frac{0,09}{12}\right)^{12}$$

$i_{\text{eff}} = 0,0938\ldots$ Keep in memory

$F = $ Fv of monthly payments for 10 years
$\quad +$ Fv of annual payments

$$= 2\,500\left[\frac{\left(1 + \frac{0,09}{12}\right)^{120} - 1}{\frac{0,09}{12}}\right] + 10\,000\left[\frac{(1 + i_{\text{eff}})^{10} - 1}{i_{\text{eff}}}\right]$$

$= R638\,503,21$

3.1 $F = P(1 + i)^n$
$= 17\,500(1 + 0{,}048)^3 = R20\,142{,}90$

3.2.1 Alex

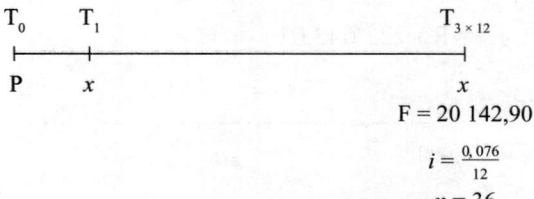

$F = x\left[\dfrac{(1+i)^n - 1}{i}\right]$

$x = \dfrac{20\,142{,}90}{\left[\dfrac{\left(1+\frac{0,076}{12}\right)^{36}-1}{\frac{0,076}{12}}\right]} = R499{,}93$

3.2.2 Kayla

$F = x\left[\dfrac{(1+i)^n - 1}{i}\right]$

$= 3\,000\left[\dfrac{\left(1+\frac{0,082}{2}\right)^{6}-1}{\frac{0,082}{2}}\right] = R19\,949{,}01$

No, she will not have enough money.

3.2.3 Anne-marie

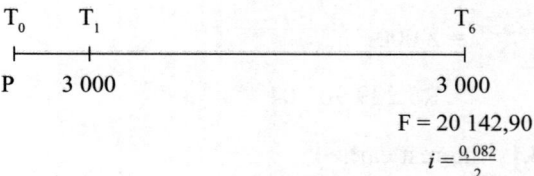

$F = P(1 + i)^n$
$P = F(1 + i)^{-n}$
$= 20\,142{,}90\left(1 + \dfrac{0,082}{4}\right)^{-12}$
$= R15\,789{,}41$

Exercise 6 (page 66)

1.

1.1 $F = P(1 + i)^n$
$= 180\,000(1 + 0{,}045)^3 = R205\,409{,}90$

1.2 $F = x\left[\dfrac{(1+i)^n - 1}{i}\right]$

$x = \dfrac{205\,409{,}90}{\left[\dfrac{\left(1+\frac{0,075}{4}\right)^{12}-1}{\frac{0,075}{4}}\right]}$
$= R15\,423{,}24$

2. $x = \dfrac{F}{\left[\frac{(1+i)^n-1}{i}\right]}$, $F = 60\,000$, $i = \dfrac{0,075}{12}$, $n = 5 \times 12$

$= \dfrac{60\,000}{\left[\dfrac{\left(1+\frac{0,075}{12}\right)^{60}-1}{\frac{0,075}{12}}\right]}$
$= R827{,}28$

3.1 $F = P(1 - i)^n$
$= 250\,000(1 - 0{,}15)^{10}$
$= R49\,218{,}60$

3.2 Cost of new bus:
$F = P(1 + i)^n$
$= 250\,000(1 + 0{,}05)^{10}$
$= R407\,223{,}66$

3.3 Money needed
$= 407\,223{,}66 - 49\,218{,}60$
$= R358\,005{,}06$

3.4 $x = \dfrac{F}{\left[\frac{(1+i)^n-1}{i}\right]} = \dfrac{358\,005{,}06}{\left[\dfrac{\left(1+\frac{0,08}{12}\right)^{10\times12}-1}{\frac{0,08}{12}}\right]}$
$= R1\,956{,}89$

4. $x = \dfrac{F}{\left[\frac{(1+i)^n-1}{i}\right]}$
$F = 150\,000$, $i = \dfrac{0,085}{12}$, $n = 60$
$= \dfrac{150\,000}{\left[\dfrac{\left(1+\frac{0,085}{12}\right)^{60}-1}{\frac{0,085}{12}}\right]}$
$= R2\,014{,}98$

5.1 $F = P(1 + i)^n$
$= 45\,000(1 + 0{,}12)^7 = R161\,243{,}14$

5.2 $F = P(1 - i)^n$
$= 45\,000(1 - 0{,}12)^7 = R18\,390{,}40$

5.3

3 months $i = 0{,}08$

Compounding period ≠ interest compoundings
∴ calculate the nominal interest required.

$$\left(1 + \tfrac{i_4}{4}\right)^4 = 1 + i_{\text{eff}}$$

$$\left(1 + \tfrac{i_4}{4}\right)^4 = 1,08$$

$$i_{\text{nom}} = \left(\sqrt[4]{1,08} - 1\right)4 = 0,077706$$

$$x = \frac{F}{\left[\frac{\left(1+\frac{i_4}{4}\right)^n - 1}{\frac{i_4}{4}}\right]} = \frac{161\,243,14 - 18\,390,40}{\left[\frac{\left(1+\frac{0,0777\ldots}{4}\right)^{28}-1}{\frac{0,0777\ldots}{4}}\right]}$$

$$= R3\,887,70$$

Exercise 7 (page 68)

1. Formula: $P = x\left[\frac{1-(1+i)^{-n}}{i}\right]$, $x = 750$, $n = 20$

1.1 $i = \frac{0,08}{12}$, $n = 20$

$$P = 750\left[\frac{1-\left(1+\frac{0,08}{12}\right)^{-20}}{\frac{0,08}{12}}\right] = R13\,999,43$$

1.2 $i = \frac{0,078}{12}$, $n = 20$

$$P = 750\left[\frac{1-\left(1+\frac{0,078}{12}\right)^{-20}}{\frac{0,078}{12}}\right] = R14\,023,28$$

1.3 $i = \frac{0,082}{12}$, $n = 20$

$$P = 750\left[\frac{1-\left(1+\frac{0,082}{12}\right)^{-20}}{\frac{0,082}{12}}\right] = R13\,975,63$$

1.4 $i = \frac{0,086}{12}$, $n = 20$

$$P = 750\left[\frac{1-\left(1+\frac{0,086}{12}\right)^{-20}}{\frac{0,086}{12}}\right] = R13\,928,21$$

1.5 $i = \frac{0,098}{12}$, $n = 20$

$$P = 750\left[\frac{1-\left(1+\frac{0,098}{12}\right)^{-20}}{\frac{0,098}{12}}\right] = R13\,787,30$$

1.6 $i = \frac{0,165}{12}$, $n = 20$

$$P = 750\left[\frac{1-\left(1+\frac{0,165}{12}\right)^{-20}}{\frac{0,165}{12}}\right] = R13\,036,55$$

2.

```
T₀    T₁                              T₁₆
-30 000  x                              x
```

Formula: $x = \frac{P}{\left[\frac{1-(1+i)^{-n}}{i}\right]}$

2.1 $i = \frac{0,083}{4}$

$$x = \frac{30\,000}{\left[\frac{1-\left(1+\frac{0,083}{4}\right)^{-16}}{\frac{0,083}{4}}\right]}$$

$$= R2\,222,65$$

2.2 $i = \frac{0,095}{4}$

$$x = \frac{30\,000}{\left[\frac{1-\left(1+\frac{0,095}{4}\right)^{-16}}{\frac{0,095}{4}}\right]}$$

$$= R2\,275,68$$

2.3 $i = \frac{0,112}{4}$

$$x = \frac{30\,000}{\left[\frac{1-\left(1+\frac{0,112}{4}\right)^{-16}}{\frac{0,112}{4}}\right]}$$

$$= R2\,351,96$$

2.4 $i = \frac{0,14}{4}$

$$x = \frac{30\,000}{\left[\frac{1-\left(1+\frac{0,14}{4}\right)^{-16}}{\frac{0,14}{4}}\right]}$$

$$= R2\,480,54$$

2.5 $i = \frac{0,142}{4}$

$$x = \frac{30\,000}{\left[\frac{1-\left(1+\frac{0,142}{4}\right)^{-16}}{\frac{0,142}{4}}\right]}$$

$$= R2\,489,87$$

2.6 $i = \frac{0,17}{4}$

$$x = \frac{30\,000}{\left[\frac{1-\left(1+\frac{0,17}{4}\right)^{-16}}{\frac{0,17}{4}}\right]}$$

$$= R2\,622,31$$

Exercise 8 (page 68)

1. $P = x\left[\frac{1-(1+i)^{-n}}{i}\right]$

$x = 800$, $n = 20$, $i = \frac{0,09}{12}$

$$= 800\left[\frac{1-\left(1+\frac{0,09}{12}\right)^{-20}}{\frac{0,09}{12}}\right] = R14\,806,42$$

2. $P = x\left[\frac{1-(1+i)^{-n}}{i}\right]$

$$x = \frac{P}{\left[\frac{1-(1+i)^{-n}}{i}\right]}a$$

$P = 165\,000$

$i = \frac{0,175}{12}$

$n = 5 \times 12$

$$= \frac{165\,000}{\left[\frac{1-\left(1+\frac{0,175}{12}\right)^{-60}}{\frac{0,175}{12}}\right]}$$

$$= R4\,145,17$$

3. T_0 T_1 $\qquad\qquad T_{25\times 12}$

   1 350 $\qquad\qquad i = \frac{0,085}{12}$

   $P = x\left[\frac{1-(1+i)^{-n}}{i}\right]$

   $= 1\,350\left[\frac{1-\left(1+\frac{0,085}{12}\right)^{-25\times 12}}{\frac{0,085}{12}}\right]$

   $= R167\,654,57$

4. T_0 T_1 $\qquad\qquad T_{6\times 12}$

   1 650 $\qquad\qquad$ 1 650

   $\qquad\qquad i = \frac{0,078}{12}$

   $P = x\left[\frac{1-(1+i)^{-n}}{i}\right]$

   $= 1\,650\left[\frac{1-\left(1+\frac{0,078}{12}\right)^{-72}}{\frac{0,078}{12}}\right]$

   $= R94\,633,17$

5.1 Deposit $= \frac{40}{100} \times 2\,200\,000 = R880\,000$

5.2 $x = \frac{P}{\left[\frac{1-(1+i)^{-n}}{i}\right]}$

   $P = 1\,320\,000$

   $i = \frac{0,082}{12}$

   $n = 15 \times 12$

   $= \frac{1\,320\,000}{\left[\frac{1-\left(1+\frac{0,082}{12}\right)^{-15\times 12}}{\frac{0,082}{12}}\right]}$

   $= R12\,767,49$

Exercise 9 (page 70)

1. $1,075^n = 2,865$ exponent form
   $n = \log_{1,075} 2,865$ log form
   $= \frac{\log 2,865}{\log 1,075}$
   $= 14,55$

2. $30\,000(1,082)^n = 38\,000$
   $(1,082)^n = \frac{38\,000}{30\,000} = \frac{19}{15}$
   $n = \log_{1,082} \frac{19}{15}$
   $= 2,999$
   $= 3,00$

3. $15\,000(1,085)^{-n} = 12\,000$
   $(1,085)^{-n} = \frac{12\,000}{15\,000} = \frac{4}{5}$
   $-n = \log_{1,085} \frac{4}{5}$
   $= -2,74$
   $n = 2,74$

4. $5\,670\left(\frac{1,07^n - 1}{0,07}\right) = 120\,000$

   $\frac{1,07^n - 1}{0,07} = \frac{120\,000}{5\,670}$

   $1,07^n = \frac{120\,000 \times 0,07}{5\,670} + 1$

   $n = \log_{1,07}\left(\frac{120\,000 \times 0,07}{5\,670} + 1\right)$

   $= 13,43$

   The number of annual payments of R5 670 paid into an account earning 7% p.a. to obtain an investment value of R120 000:

   T_0 T_1 $\qquad\qquad T_{13}$ T_{14}

   5 670 $\qquad\qquad$ 5 670   <5 670

   $\qquad\qquad F = 120\,000$

   $\qquad\qquad i = 0,07$

Exercise 10 (page 70)

1.1 $F = P(1 + i)^n$, $i = 0,08$
   $2P = P(1 + 0,08)^n$
   $2 = 1,08^n$
   $n = \log_{1,08} 2 = 9,00646$
   $n = 10$ years

1.2 $4P = P(1,08)^n$
   $4 = 1,08^n$
   $n = \log_{1,08} 4 = 18,01$
   $n = 19$ years

2. $F = P(1 + i)^n$
   $18,38 = 9,19(1 + 0,117)^n$
   $2 = 1,117^n$
   $n = \log_{1,117} 2$
   $= 6,26$
   7 years

3. $F = x\left[\frac{(1+i)^n - 1}{i}\right]$
   $x = 1\,500$
   $F = 100\,000$
   $i = \frac{0,09}{12}$

   $100\,000 = 1\,500\left[\frac{\left(1+\frac{0,09}{12}\right)^n - 1}{\frac{0,09}{12}}\right]$

   $\left(\frac{100\,000}{1\,500} \times \frac{0,09}{12} + 1\right) = 1,0075^n$

   $n = \log_{1,0075}\left(\frac{1000}{15} \times \frac{0,09}{12} + 1\right)$

   $= 54,26$

   It will take 54 years and 97 days.

4. $P = x\left[\dfrac{1-(1+i)^{-n}}{i}\right]$

$P = 14\,000$, $x = 800$, $i = \dfrac{0,09}{12}$

$14\,000 = 800\left[\dfrac{1-\left(1+\frac{0,09}{12}\right)^{-n}}{\frac{0,09}{12}}\right]$

$\left(\dfrac{14\,000}{800} \times \dfrac{0,09}{12}\right) = 1 - \left(1+\dfrac{0,09}{12}\right)^{-n}$

$(1,0075)^{-n} = 1 - \dfrac{21}{160} = \dfrac{139}{160}$

$-n = \log_{1,0075}\dfrac{139}{160}$

$= -18,83$

$n = 18$ payments of R800 and 1 payment of less than R800

5.1 $P = x\left[\dfrac{1-(1+i)^{-n}}{i}\right]$

$P = 800\,000$, $i = \dfrac{0,085}{12}$, $n = 20 \times 12$

$x = \dfrac{800\,000}{\left[\dfrac{1-\left(1+\frac{0,085}{12}\right)^{-20\times 12}}{\frac{0,085}{12}}\right]}$

$= R6\,942,59$

5.2 $800\,000 = 7\,500\left[\dfrac{1-\left(1+\frac{0,085}{12}\right)^{-n}}{\frac{0,085}{12}}\right]$

$\dfrac{800\,000}{7\,500} \times \dfrac{0,085}{12} = 1 - \left(\dfrac{2\,417}{2\,400}\right)^{-n}$

$\left(\dfrac{2\,417}{2\,400}\right)^{-n} = 1 - \dfrac{34}{45} = \dfrac{11}{45}$

$-n = \log_{\frac{2\,417}{2\,400}}\dfrac{11}{45}$, $n = 199,59$

200 payments

5.3 Extra payment = $7\,500 - 6\,942,59 = R557,41$

5.4 Original period of loan = $20 \times 12 = 240$ months. So she settled the loan 40 months earlier.

Exercise 11 (page 71)

1.1 $P = x\left[\dfrac{1-(1+i)^{-n}}{i}\right]$

$x = 3\,500$, $i = \dfrac{0,09}{12}$, $n = 20 \times 12$

$= 3\,500\left[\dfrac{1-\left(1+\frac{0,09}{12}\right)^{-20\times 12}}{\frac{0,09}{12}}\right]$

$= R389\,007,34$

$T_0 \quad T_1 \qquad T_{4\times 12} \qquad\qquad T_{20\times 12}$

3 500 .... 3 500

$-389\,007,34$

1.2.1 Payments still to be made = $(20 - 4) \times 12 = n$

At $T_{4\times 12}$ outstanding balance

= Pi of 16×12 payments of R3 500

$= x\left[\dfrac{1-(1+i)^{-n}}{i}\right]$

$i = \dfrac{0,09}{12}$

$= 3\,500\left[\dfrac{1-\left(1+\frac{0,09}{12}\right)^{-16\times 12}}{\frac{0,09}{12}}\right]$

$= R355\,504,69$

1.2.2 Outstanding balance at $T_{8\times 12}$

$= x\left[\dfrac{1-(1+i)^{-(20-8)\times 12}}{i}\right]$

$= R307\,548,82$

1.2.3 Outstanding balance at $T_{12\times 12}$

$= x\left[\dfrac{1-(1+i)^{-8\times 12}}{i}\right]$

$= R238\,904,53$

1.2.4 Outstanding balance at $T_{16\times 12}$

$= x\left[\dfrac{1-(1+i)^{-4\times 12}}{i}\right]$

$= R140\,646,74$

1.2.5 Outstanding balance at $T_{20\times 12} = 0$

1.3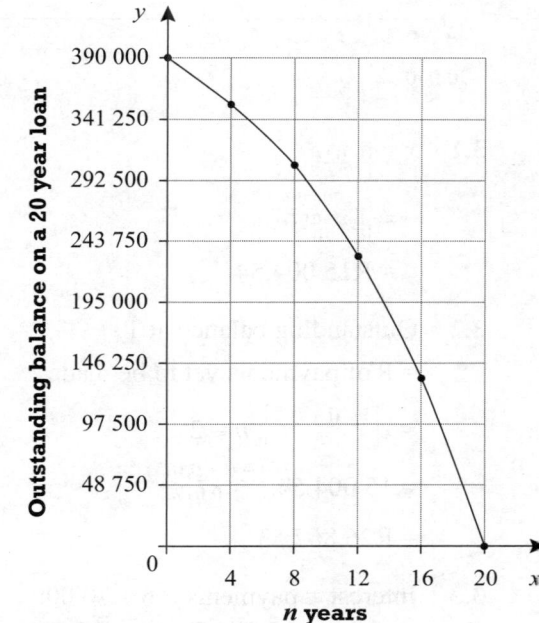

1.4 1st quarter

2.1 $P = x\left[\dfrac{1-(1+i)^{-n}}{i}\right]$

$P = 220\,000$

$i = \dfrac{0{,}095}{12}$

$n = 5 \times 12$

$x = \dfrac{220\,000}{\left[\dfrac{1-\left(1+\frac{0{,}095}{12}\right)^{-60}}{\frac{0{,}095}{12}}\right]}$

$= R4\,620{,}41$

2.2 Outstanding balance after 3 years.
Number of outstanding payments
$= (5 - 3) \times 12 = 24$

$P = x\left[\dfrac{1-(1+i)^{-n}}{i}\right]$

$n = 24$

$= 4\,620{,}41\left[\dfrac{1-\left(1+\frac{0{,}095}{12}\right)^{-24}}{\frac{0{,}095}{12}}\right]$

$= R100\,630{,}74$

2.3 Interest paid
$=$ monthly payments $\times\, 60 - 220\,000$
$= 4\,620{,}41 \times 60 - 220\,000$
$= R57\,224{,}57$

3. $T_0 \quad T_1 \qquad\qquad\qquad T_6$

$\qquad\quad x \qquad\qquad\qquad\quad x$

$-70\,000 \qquad\qquad\qquad i = 0{,}077$

3.1 $x = \dfrac{P}{\left[\frac{1-(1+i)^{-n}}{i}\right]}$

$= \dfrac{70\,000}{\left[\frac{1-(1+0{,}077)^{-6}}{0{,}077}\right]}$

$= R15\,004{,}54$

3.2 Outstanding balance at T_4
$=$ P of payments yet to be made
$= x\left[\dfrac{1-(1+i)^{-n}}{i}\right], n = 2$

$= 15\,004{,}54\left[\dfrac{1-(1+0{,}077)^{-2}}{0{,}077}\right]$

$= R26\,867{,}53$

3.3 Interest $=$ payments $\times\, 6 - 70\,000$
$= 15\,004{,}54 \times 6 - 70\,000$
$= R20\,027{,}24$

4.1 $T_0 \qquad\qquad\qquad\qquad T_6$

$8\,000 \qquad\qquad\qquad\qquad i = 0{,}04$

$P = x\left[\dfrac{1-(1+i)^{-n}}{i}\right]$

$x = \dfrac{8\,000}{\left[\frac{1-(1+0{,}04)^{-6}}{0{,}04}\right]} = R1\,526{,}10$

4.2 Balance on loan
$=$ P of payments still to be made
$= x\left[\dfrac{1-(1+i)^{-n}}{i}\right]$

$= 1\,526{,}09\left[\dfrac{1-(1+0{,}04)^{-3}}{0{,}04}\right]$

$= R4\,235{,}05$

4.3 Interest paid $=$ monthly payments $\times\, 6 - 8\,000$
$= 1\,526{,}10 \times 6 - 8\,000$
$= R1\,156{,}57$

5.1 $T_0 \qquad\qquad T_{10\times12} \longleftarrow i = \dfrac{0{,}08}{12} \longrightarrow T_{30\times12}$

$-1\,200\,000 \qquad\qquad\qquad\qquad\qquad i = \dfrac{0{,}086}{12}$

$P = 1\,200\,000 \quad i = \dfrac{0{,}086}{12} \quad n = 30 \times 12$

income $= R5\,000$

$x = \dfrac{P}{\left[\frac{1-(1+i)^{-n}}{i}\right]}$

$= \dfrac{1\,200\,000}{\left[\frac{1-\left(1+\frac{0{,}086}{12}\right)^{-360}}{\frac{0{,}086}{12}}\right]}$

$= R9\,312{,}14$ monthly payments

They receive R5 000 per month for rental.
They pay $9\,312{,}14 - 5\,000$
$= R4\,312{,}14$

5.2 $n = (30 - 10) \times 12 = 240$
Outstanding balance $= P$

$= x\left[\dfrac{1-(1+i)^{-n}}{i}\right]$

$= 9\,312{,}14\left[\dfrac{1-\left(1+\frac{0{,}086}{12}\right)^{-240}}{\frac{0{,}086}{12}}\right]$

$= R1\,065\,263{,}94$

5.3 $i = \dfrac{0{,}08}{12}$, $P = R1\,065\,263{,}94$

$x = \dfrac{P}{\left[\frac{1-(1+i)^{-240}}{i}\right]}$

$= R8\,910{,}29$

5.4 $1\,065\,263{,}94 = 9\,312{,}14\left[\dfrac{1-\left(1+\frac{0{,}08}{12}\right)^{-n}}{\frac{0{,}08}{12}}\right]$

$1 - \dfrac{1\,065\,263{,}94}{9\,312{,}14} \times \dfrac{0{,}08}{12} = \left(\dfrac{151}{150}\right)^{-n}$

Change to log form:
$n = 217$
$\quad = 18$ years 1 month
$\therefore$ new period $= 28$ years 1 month

Test A (page 73)

1.1 R900 000(0,1) = R90 000 is the deposit.
R900 000 − R90 000 = R810 000 is
the loan. (2)

1.2 $(1 + ie) = \left(1 + \frac{im}{m}\right)^m$

$ie = \left(1 + \frac{0,08}{12}\right)^{12} - 1$

$ie = 0,0829...$

Interest rate ≈ 8,3%

Yes, her calculation is correct. (4)

1.3 T_0 T_1 $T_{20 \times 12}$

 x x
810 000

$i = \frac{0,08}{12}$
$n = 20 \times 12$

$Pv = x\left(\frac{1 - (1+i)^{-n}}{i}\right)$

$810\ 000 = x\left[\frac{1 - \left(1 + \frac{0,08}{12}\right)^{-20 \times 12}}{\frac{0,08}{12}}\right]$

x = R6 775,16 which is her monthly instalment. (4)

1.4 $Pv = x\left[\frac{1 - (1+i)^{-n}}{i}\right]$

$810\ 000 = 10\ 000\left[\frac{1 - \left(1 + \frac{0,08}{12}\right)^{-n}}{\frac{0,08}{12}}\right]$

$\frac{810\ 000}{10\ 000} \times \frac{0,08}{12} = 1 - \left(1 + \frac{0,08}{12}\right)^{-n}$

$\left(1 + \frac{0,08}{12}\right)^{-n} = 1 - 81 \times \frac{0,08}{12}$

$-n = \log_{\left(1 + \frac{0,08}{12}\right)}\left(1 - 81 \times \frac{0,08}{12}\right)$

$n = 116,87$

It will take 117 months. She will make 116 payments of R10 000 and 1 payment which is less than R10 000. (4)

2. $Fv = Pv(1-i)^n$

$\frac{1}{4}x = x(1 - 0,05)^n$

$\frac{1}{4} = 0,95^n$

$n = \log_{0,95} \frac{1}{4}$

$n = 27,026$

$n ≈ 28$ years (4)

3. Ditiro: $Fv = Pv(i + in) + Pv(0,025)$
   $= 800\ 000[1 + (0,095)(5)]$
   $+ 800\ 000(0,025)$
   $= R1\ 200\ 000$

Khumo: $Fv = Pv(1+i)^n$
   $= 800\ 000\left(1 + \frac{0,09}{4}\right)^{5 \times 4}$
   $= R1\ 248\ 407,36$

Khumo's version is better, as its future value is greater. (6)

4.1 T_0 T_1 T_{36}

5 000 x x
1/5/13 31/5/13

$i = \frac{0,075}{12}$

$x = 600$

Fv of loan at T_{36}

$= Pv(1+i)^n + x\left(\frac{(1+i)^n - 1}{i}\right)$

$= 5000\left(1 + \frac{0,075}{12}\right)^{36} + 600\left[\frac{\left(1 + \frac{0,075}{12}\right)^{36} - 1}{\frac{0,075}{12}}\right]$

$= R30\ 396,059...$

Interest = ≈ R30 396,06 (6)

4.2 R30 396,059... − 5 000 − 600(36)
$= R3796,059...$
$≈ R3796,06$ (3)

5. $Fv = Pv(1+i)^n$

$12\ 755,35 = 7\ 565\left(1 + \frac{i}{12}\right)^{30}$

$\left(\sqrt[30]{\frac{12\ 755,35}{7\ 565}} - 1\right)12 = i$

$i = 0,21079...$

Interest rate ≈ 21,08% p.a. compounded monthly. (4)

6.1 Linear (1)

6.2
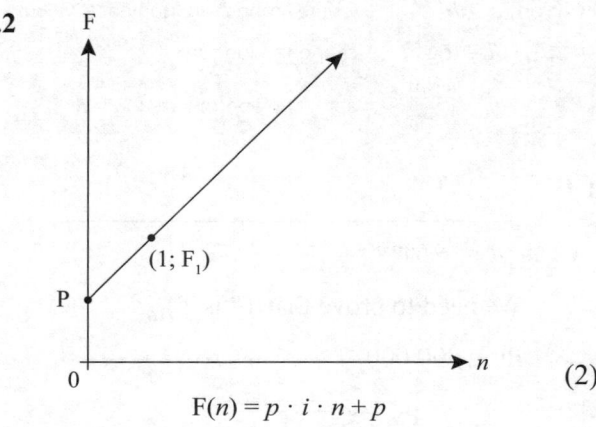

$F(n) = p \cdot i \cdot n + p$ (2)

6.3.1 Exponential (1)

6.3.2

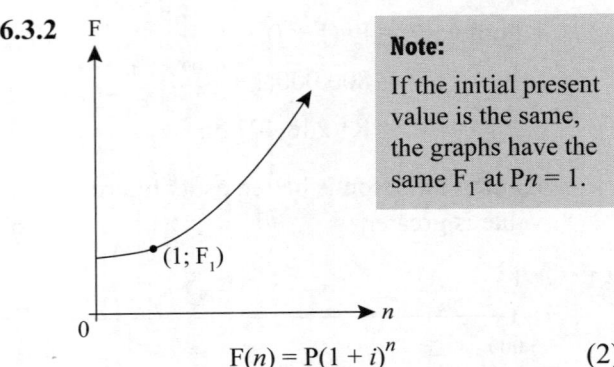

Note:
If the initial present value is the same, the graphs have the same F_1 at $Pn = 1$.

$F(n) = P(1 + i)^n$ (2)

7.

T_0 T_1 $T_{(55-21) \times 12 = 408}$

1 200 x

$i = \frac{0,084}{12}$

$Fv = x\left[\frac{(1+i)^n - 1}{i}\right]$

$= 1\,200\left[\frac{\left(1 + \frac{0,084}{12}\right)^{408} - 1}{\frac{0,084}{12}}\right]$

$= R2\,780\,509{,}158\ldots$

$\approx R2\,780\,509{,}16$ (4)

8. $Fv = x\left[\frac{(1+i)^n - 1}{i}\right]$ $\quad n = 60, i = \frac{0,075}{12}$

$60\,000 = x\left[\frac{\left(1 + \frac{0,075}{12}\right)^{60} - 1}{\frac{0,075}{12}}\right]$

$x = \frac{60\,000}{\left[\frac{\left(1 + \frac{0,075}{12}\right)^{60} - 1}{\frac{0,075}{12}}\right]}$

$= R827{,}28$ (3)

Total: 50

Test B (page 74)

Remember that when solving for a variable that is an exponent, we use the following log law:

Given: $a = b^n$ where a and b are numerical values
$n = \log_b a$ change to log form
$n = \frac{\log a}{\log b}$ apply the appropriate log law

1.1

T_0 T_1 $T_?$

$x = 9\,000$ x

We need to prove that $T_?$ is T_{216}.

$Pv = 900\,000 \qquad i = \frac{0,1}{12} \quad n = ?$

$Pv = x\left[\frac{1 - (1+i)^{-n}}{i}\right]$

$900\,000 = 9\,000\left[\frac{1 - \left(1 + \frac{0,1}{12}\right)^{-n}}{\frac{0,1}{12}}\right]$

$\left(\frac{900\,000}{9\,000}\right)\left(\frac{0,1}{12}\right) = 1 - \left(1 + \frac{0,1}{12}\right)^{-n}$

$\left(1 + \frac{0,1}{12}\right)^{-n} = 1 - (100)\left(\frac{0,1}{12}\right)$

$-n = \log_{\left(1 + \frac{0,1}{12}\right)}\left[1 - (100)\left(\frac{0,1}{12}\right)\right]$

$-n = \frac{\log\left[1 - (100)\left(\frac{0,1}{12}\right)\right]}{\log\left(1 + \frac{0,1}{12}\right)}$

$-n = -215{,}905\ldots$

$n \approx 216$

They will make 215 payments of R9 000 and one payment of less than R9 000, rather than making 240 (12 × 20) payments of smaller amounts. (4)

1.2

T_0 T_1 T_{99} T_{100} T_{101} T_{102} T_{103} T_{216}

         9 000   9 000 x x x y ... y

$-900\,000$

F

$i = \frac{0,1}{12}$ Ⓐ Store i in memory.

Balance outstanding at T_{99}:

Fv of loan at T_{99} − Fv of monthly payments at T_{99}

Outstanding balance

$= Pv(1 + i)^n - \left[\frac{(1+i)^n - 1}{i}\right]$

$= 900\,000\left(1 + \frac{0,1}{12}\right)^{99} - 9\,000\left[\frac{\left(1 + \frac{0,1}{12}\right)^{99} - 1}{\frac{0,1}{12}}\right]$

$= R670\,663{,}1834$ Ⓑ Store BO in memory.

The outstanding balance becomes the present value of the loan at T_{99}, and you must now calculate the future value at T_{102}. (The rest is an annuity starting at T_{102} as first new payment at T_{103}.)

Fv of loan at T_{102}:

$Fv = 670\,663{,}1834\ldots\left(1 + \frac{0,1}{12}\right)^3$

$= R687\,569{,}87\ldots$ Ⓒ Store in memory.

$= Pv$ at T_{103} for new annuity

T_{102} T_{103} T_{216}

Ⓒ x x

T_0 is at 102, $n = 216 - 102$
T_1 is at 103

$$Pv = x\left[\frac{1-(1+i)^{-n}}{i}\right]$$

$$© = x\left[\frac{1-\left(1+\frac{0,1}{12}\right)^{-114}}{\frac{0,1}{12}}\right]$$

$$x = \frac{©}{\left[\frac{1-\left(1+\frac{0,1}{12}\right)^{-114}}{\frac{0,1}{12}}\right]}$$

$$x = R9\,366{,}41 \quad (7)$$

2.1 In this question timelines are important.

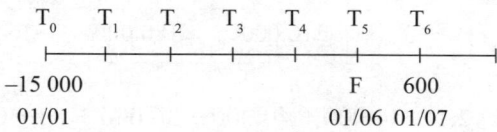

T_0 T_1 T_2 T_3 T_4 T_5 T_6
−15 000   F   600
01/01   01/06 01/07

$i = \frac{0,09}{12}$ Ⓐ Store i in memory.

Fv at $T_5 = P(1+i)^n$

$= 15\,000\left(1+\frac{0,09}{12}\right)^5$

$= R15\,571{,}00$ Ⓑ Store in memory. (2)

2.2 The future value of the loan at T_5 becomes the present value of the loan (annuity) at T_0. This may become confusing, so draw a new timeline as T_5 on the old line becomes T_0 for the loan.

T_0 T_1 T_2 ... T_n
01/06 01/07 01/08
−15 571 600   600

R15 571 is the present value of the loan with monthly payments of R600. Always write down the formula you will use first, and then fill in the variables.

$$Pv = x\left[\frac{1-(1+i)^{-n}}{i}\right]$$

Ⓑ from 2.1 $= 600\left[\frac{1-(1+Ⓐ\text{ from 2.1})^{-n}}{Ⓐ}\right]$

$\left(\frac{15\,571}{600} \times Ⓐ\right) = 1 - (1+Ⓐ)^{-n}$

$(1+Ⓐ)^{-n} = \left(1 - \frac{15\,571}{600} \times Ⓐ\right)$

$-n = \log_{(1+Ⓐ)}\left(1 - \frac{15\,571}{600} \times Ⓐ\right)$

$n = 28{,}9688...$

$n \approx 29$ months (4)

2.3 Outstanding balance = Fv of loan − Fv of monthly payments

For $n = 20$

Outstanding balance

$= P(1+i)^n - x\left[\frac{(1+i)^n-1}{i}\right]$

$= 15\,571(1+Ⓐ)^{20} - 600\left[\frac{(1+Ⓐ)^{20}-1}{Ⓐ}\right]$

$= R5\,186{,}07$ (3)

3. T_0 $T_{4 \times 12}$
       −75 000 $n = 48$

Option 1: $i = 0{,}105$

3.1 $F = P(1 + in)$
$= 7\,500(1 + 0{,}105 \times 4)$
$= R106\,500$

Monthly instalment $= \frac{106\,500}{48}$

$= R2\,218{,}75$ (4)

3.2 Option 2: $i = \frac{0{,}11}{12}$ memory Ⓐ

$$P = x\left[\frac{1-(1+i)^{-n}}{i}\right]$$

$$x = \frac{75\,000}{\left[\frac{1-\left(1+\frac{0{,}11}{12}\right)^{-48}}{\frac{0{,}11}{12}}\right]}$$

$= R1\,938{,}41...$ Ⓑ (6)

3.3 Option 2 is the better option. (2)

3.4 Future value for option 1
$= 1\,938{,}41 \times 48$
$= R93\,043{,}88...$ ©

$F = P(1 + in)$

$930\,433{,}88 = 75\,000(1 + 4i)$

$\frac{93\,043{,}88}{75\,000} = 1 + 4i$

$i = \frac{\left(\frac{93\,043{,}88...}{75\,000}\right) - 1}{4}$

$i = 0{,}0601...$

Interest rate would be 6,01% p.a. (3)

4. Balance at $T_6 = P(1+i)^n - x\left[\frac{(1+i)^n - 1}{i}\right]$

$i = \frac{0{,}09}{4}$ ....Ⓐ

$= 20\,000(1+i)^6 - 2\,500\left[\frac{(1+i)^6-1}{i}\right]$

$= R\,6\,987{,}015...$

$\approx R6\,987{,}02$ (10)

5.

```
T₀      T₂     T₅        T₁₀   T₁₂
|-------|------|---------|-----|
4 000   x    4 000      2x   50 000
                              F₇
                              i = 0,09
```

$F = 50\,000 = 4\,000(1 + i)^{12} + x(1 + i)^{10}$
$\qquad + 4\,000(1 + i)^{7} + 2x(1 + i)^{2}$

$50\,000 - 4\,000(1 + i)^{12} - 4\,000(1 + i)^{7}$
$= x[(1 + i)^{10} + 2(1 + i)^{2}]$

$x = \dfrac{50\,000 - 4\,000(1 + i)^{12} - 4\,000(1 + i)^{7}}{(1 + i)^{10} + 2(1 + i)^{2}}$

> **Remember** the value of i is in memory Ⓐ.

$x = R6\,627{,}334752$

$\approx R6\,627{,}33$ \hfill (5)

\hfill **Total: 50**

Test C (page 75)

1.1
```
T₀                          Tₙ
|---------------------------|
60 000                   20 000
```

$i = 0{,}16$ reducing balance.

$F = P(1 - i)^{n}$

$20\,000 = 60\,000(1 - 0{,}16)^{n}$

$\dfrac{20\,000}{60\,000} = 0{,}84^{n}$

$\dfrac{1}{3} = 0{,}84^{n}$

$n = \log_{0{,}84} \dfrac{1}{3}$

$ = 6{,}301\ldots$

The equipment will be worth R20 000 after 6 years and 4 months. (4)

1.2
```
T₀       T₁        T₂        T₃       Tₙ
|--------|---------|---------|--------|
P = 120 000 [–30 000] [–30 000] [–30 000]  [<30 000]
                                            i = 0,09
```

$P = x\left(\dfrac{1 - (1 + i)^{-n}}{i}\right)$

$120\,000 = 30\,000\left[\dfrac{1 - (1 + 0{,}090)^{-n}}{0{,}09}\right]$

$\dfrac{\cancel{120\,000}}{\cancel{30\,000}} \times 0{,}09 = 1 - (1{,}09)^{-n}$

$1{,}09^{-n} = 1 - 4 \times 0{,}09$

$-n = 0{,}64$

$-n = \log_{1{,}09} 0{,}64$

$-n = 0{,}64$

$n = 5{,}178\ldots$

The investment will finance her studies for 5 full years. (4)

2. Placing this information in a table makes interpretation quick and easy.

Time in years	Income	Expenses	Savings
1	180 000	136 000	44 000
2	198 000	158 000	40 000
3	216 000	180 000	36 000

2.1 $44\,000 + 40\,000 + 36\,000 + \ldots + 0$ (4)

2.2 Savings = income – expenses

Income in year n
$= 180\,000 + 18\,000(n - 1)$

Expenses in year n
$= 136\,000 + 22\,000(n - 1)$

Income = expenses, so there are no savings.

$180\,000 + 18\,000(n - 1)$
$= 136\,000 + 22\,000(n - 1)$

$44\,000 = 4\,000(n - 1)$
$44\,000 = 4\,000n - 4\,000$
$48\,000 = 4\,000n$
$n = 12$

He will have nothing left to save after 12 years. (3)

2.3 $180\,000 + 18\,000(25 - 1) = 136\,000 + x(25 - 1)$

$x = R19\,833{,}33$ (2)

3.1
```
T₀                              T₅
|-------------------------------|
350 000
                         dep i = 0,15
                         inc i = 0,06
```

$Fv = Pv(1 - i)^{n}$
$= 350\,000(1 - 0{,}15)^{5}$
$= R155\,296{,}8594\ldots$
$\approx R155\,296{,}86$ (3)

3.2 $Fv = Pv(1 + i)^{n}$
$= 350\,000(1 - 0{,}06)^{5}$
$= R468\,378{,}95$ (3)

3.3 Money needed = R468 378,95 − R155 296,86
= R313 082,09 (1)

3.4 $T_0 \quad T_1 \quad T_2 \qquad\qquad\qquad T_{5\times12}$

$\quad x \quad x \qquad\qquad\qquad\qquad x$

$\qquad\qquad\qquad\qquad\qquad\qquad 313\,082,09$

$\qquad\qquad\qquad\qquad\qquad\qquad i = \tfrac{0,075}{12}$ Ⓐ

$\qquad\qquad\qquad\qquad\qquad\qquad n = 60$

$$Fv = x\left(\frac{(1+i)^n - 1}{i}\right)$$

$$313\,082,09 = x\left[\frac{(1+\tfrac{0,075}{12})^{60} - 1}{\tfrac{0,075}{12}}\right]$$

$$x = R4\,316,76 \qquad (6)$$

3.5 $T_0 \quad T_1 \qquad T_6 \qquad T_{12} \qquad\qquad T_{60}$

$\quad 4\,316,76 \quad [-3\,000] \quad [-3\,000] \qquad 313\,082,09$

> **Remember** these amounts are withdrawn every **6 months** while the interest is 7,5% p.a. compounded **monthly**.

$\left(1 + \tfrac{i_2}{2}\right)^2 = \quad \left(1 + \tfrac{i_{12}}{12}\right)^{12} = \quad 1 + i$

$\quad\downarrow \qquad\qquad \downarrow \qquad\qquad \downarrow$

6 monthly $\qquad$ monthly $\qquad$ annual effective

$$\left(1 + \tfrac{i_2}{2}\right)^2 = \left(1 + \tfrac{0,075}{12}\right)^{12}$$

$$i_2 = \left[\sqrt[2]{\left(1 + \tfrac{0,075}{12}\right)^{12}} - 1\right]2$$

$$= 0,076\,18\ldots \qquad\qquad Ⓑ$$

Future value at T_{60} for maintenance total:

$$F = x\left(\frac{(1+i)^n - 1}{i}\right)$$

$$= 3\,000\left(\frac{\left(1 + \tfrac{Ⓑ}{2}\right)^{10} - 1}{\tfrac{Ⓑ}{2}}\right) = R35\,701,05352 \quad Ⓒ$$

Total amount needed at T_{60}
= 313 082,09 + 35 701,05
= R348 783,14

$$F = x\left[\frac{\left(1 + \tfrac{i_{12}}{12}\right)^n - 1}{\tfrac{i_{12}}{12}}\right]$$

$$x = \frac{348\,783,14}{\left[\frac{\left(1 + \tfrac{0,075}{12}\right)^{60} - 1}{\tfrac{0,075}{12}}\right]}$$

= R4 809,00 (4)

4.1 $T_0 \quad T_1 \quad T_2 \quad T_3 \leftarrow\text{60 payments}\rightarrow T$

$-150\,000 \qquad\qquad x \qquad\qquad i = \tfrac{0,10}{12}$ Ⓐ

F at $T_2 = P(1+i)^n$ or $P(1+Ⓐ)^n$
$= 150\,000\left(1 + \tfrac{0,10}{12}\right)^2$
$= R152\,510,4167$ ....Ⓑ
$\approx R152\,510,42$ (3)

4.2.1 The future value of the loan at T_2 now becomes the present value of an annuity of 60 equal payments.

$$P = x\left[\frac{1 - (1+i)^{-n}}{i}\right]$$

$$Ⓑ = x\left[\frac{1 - (1+Ⓐ)^{-60}}{Ⓐ}\right]$$

$$x = \frac{Ⓑ}{\frac{1-(1+Ⓐ)^{-60}}{Ⓐ}} \text{ OR } \frac{152\,510,4167}{\left[\frac{1-\left(1+\tfrac{0,10}{12}\right)^{-60}}{\tfrac{0,10}{12}}\right]}$$

= R3 240,395642 ....Ⓒ
$\approx R3\,240,40$ (3)

4.2.2 Total of payments
= 3 240,40 × 60
= R194 423,7385
$\approx R194\,423,74$ (1)

4.2.3 Interest paid = total of payment − loan
= 194 423,74 − 150 000
= R44 423,74 (2)

4.3 $T_0 \quad T_1 \qquad\qquad\qquad T_{60}$

$-150\,000 \quad x \qquad\qquad\qquad$

$\qquad\qquad\qquad\qquad\qquad i = \tfrac{0,10}{12}$ Ⓐ

4.3.1 $P = x\left[\frac{1-(1+i)^{-n}}{i}\right]$

$$x = \frac{150\,000}{\left[\frac{1-\left(1+\tfrac{0,10}{12}\right)^{-60}}{\tfrac{0,10}{12}}\right]}$$

= R3 187,056707 ....Ⓑ
$\approx R3\,187,06$ (3)

4.3.2 Total of payments
= Ⓑ × 60
= R191 223,40 ....Ⓒ (1)

4.3.3 Interest paid = total of payments − loan
= 191 223,40 − 150 000
= R41 223,40 (2)

4.4 Xholani paid 44 423,74 − 41 223,40 more interest.
Difference = R3 200,34 (1)

Total: 50

TOPIC 4   Trigonometry   (page 77)

Exercise 1   (page 83)

1.1 $\cos(x - 20°) = \cos x \cos 20° + \sin x \sin 20°$

1.2 $\sin(A + 45°) = \sin A \cos 45° + \cos A \sin 45°$
$= \sin A\left(\frac{1}{\sqrt{2}}\right) + \cos A\left(\frac{1}{\sqrt{2}}\right)$
$= \left(\frac{\sqrt{2}}{2}\right)(\sin A + \cos A)$

1.3 $\cos(2A + 30°)$
$= \cos 2A \cos 30° - \sin 2A \sin 30°$
$= \cos 2A\left(\frac{\sqrt{3}}{2}\right) - \sin 2A\left(\frac{1}{2}\right)$
$= \frac{1}{2}(\sqrt{3}\cos 2A - \sin 2A)$
$= \frac{1}{2}(\sqrt{3}(\cos^2 A - \sin^2 A) - 2\sin A \cos A)$
$= \frac{\sqrt{3}}{2}\cos^2 A - \frac{\sqrt{3}}{2}\sin^2 A - \sin A \cos A$

1.4 $\sin(2A - 45°)$
$= \sin 2A \cos 45° - \cos 2A \sin 45°$
$= \sin 2A\left(\frac{1}{\sqrt{2}}\right) - \cos 2A\left(\frac{1}{\sqrt{2}}\right)$
$= \frac{\sqrt{2}}{2}(\sin 2A - \cos 2A)$
$= \frac{\sqrt{2}}{1}(2\sin A \cos A - \cos^2 A + \sin^2 A)$

2.1 $\sin 35° \cos 25° + \cos 35° \sin 25°$
$= \sin(35° + 25°)$
$= \sin 60°$
$= \frac{\sqrt{3}}{2}$

2.2 $\cos 22{,}5° \cos 37{,}5° - \sin 22{,}5° \sin 37{,}5°$
$= \cos(22{,}5 + 37{,}5°)$
$= \cos 60°$
$= \frac{1}{2}$

2.3 $\cos 20° \cos 40° - \sin 20° \sin 40°$
$= \cos(20° + 40°)$
$= \cos(60°)$
$= \frac{1}{2}$

2.4 $\cos 170° \cos 50° + \sin 170° \sin 50°$
$= \cos(170° - 50°)$
$= \cos 120°$
$= -\cos 60°$
$= -\frac{1}{2}$

2.5 $\sin(A + 45°)\cos(15° + A) - \cos(A + 45°)\sin(15° + A)$
$= \sin[(A + 45°) - (15° + A)]$
$= \sin 30°$
$= \frac{1}{2}$

3. $\sin 75° = \sin(45° + 30°)$
$= \sin 45° \cos 30° + \cos 45° \sin 30°$
$= \left(\frac{1}{\sqrt{2}}\right)\left(\frac{\sqrt{3}}{2}\right) + \left(\frac{1}{\sqrt{2}}\right)\left(\frac{1}{2}\right)$
$= \frac{\sqrt{3}}{2\sqrt{2}} \cdot \frac{\sqrt{2}}{\sqrt{2}} + \frac{1}{2\sqrt{2}} \cdot \frac{\sqrt{2}}{\sqrt{2}}$
$= \frac{\sqrt{3} \cdot \sqrt{2} \cdot 1\sqrt{2}}{4}$
$= \frac{\sqrt{2}(\sqrt{3} + 1)}{4}$

4. $\sin 23° = p \therefore y = p, r = 1, x = \sqrt{1 - p^2}$

4.1 $\cos 23° = \frac{\sqrt{1 - p^2}}{1}$
$= \sqrt{1 - p^2}$

4.2 $\sin 46°$
$= \sin 2(23°)$
$= 2 \sin 23° \cos 23°$
$= 2(p)\left(\sqrt{1 - p^2}\right)$
$= 2p\sqrt{1 - p^2}$

5. $\frac{\tan(-60°)\cos(-156°)\cos 294°}{\sin 492°}$
$= \frac{-\tan 60° \cos 204°}{\sin 132°}$
$= \frac{-\tan 60°(-\cos 24°)\cos 66°}{\sin 48°}$
$= \frac{-\tan 60°(-\cos 24°)\sin 24°}{2\sin 24° \cos 24°}$
$= \frac{\tan 60°}{2}$
$= \frac{\sqrt{3}}{2}$

6.1 $\sin \alpha = \frac{8}{17}$ where $90° \leq \alpha \leq 270°$
α lies in quad 2
$\therefore y = 8, r = 17, x = -15$
$\therefore \cos \alpha = \frac{-15}{17}$

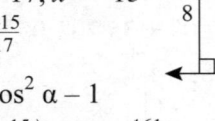

6.2 $\cos 2\alpha = 2\cos^2 \alpha - 1$
$\cos 2\alpha = 2\left(\frac{-15}{17}\right)^2 - 1 = \frac{161}{289}$

7. $\sin 33° = \sqrt{a}$
By definition: $y = \sqrt{a}, r = 1$
By Pythagoras: $x = \sqrt{1 - a}$
$\cos 48° \cos 15° + \sin 48° \sin 15°$
$= \cos(48° - 15°)$
$= \cos 33°$
$= \sqrt{1 - a}$

Exercise 2 (page 83)

1. $\cos x = 2 \sin y \cos y$
$\cos x = \sin 2y$
$\cos x = \cos(90° - 2y)$
$\therefore x = 90° - 2y$
$\therefore x + 2y = 90°$

2.

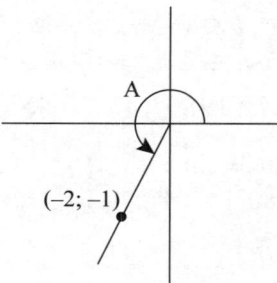

$\tan A = 0{,}5$ and $\cos A < 0$
A is in quad 3
$\therefore y = -1, x = -2, r = \sqrt{(-2)^2 + (-1)^2} = \sqrt{5}$
$2 \sin \frac{A}{2} \cos \frac{A}{2} = \sin 2\left(\frac{A}{2}\right) = -\frac{1}{\sqrt{5}} = -\frac{\sqrt{5}}{5}$

3.1 $\sin(45° + \theta)\sin(45° - \theta)$
$= (\sin 45° \cos \theta + \cos 45° \sin \theta)(\sin 45° \cos \theta - \cos 45° \sin \theta)$
$= \left(\frac{1}{\sqrt{2}}\cos\theta + \frac{1}{\sqrt{2}}\sin\theta\right)\left(\frac{1}{\sqrt{2}}\cos\theta - \frac{1}{\sqrt{2}}\sin\theta\right)$
$= \left(\frac{1}{\sqrt{2}}\right)(\cos\theta + \sin\theta)\left(\frac{1}{\sqrt{2}}\right)(\cos\theta - \sin\theta)$

> Could use difference of two squares:
> $= \frac{1}{2}\cos^2\theta - \frac{1}{2}\sin^2\theta$
> OR
> $= \left(\frac{1}{\sqrt{2}}\right)^2(\cos\theta + \sin\theta)(\cos\theta - \sin\theta)$

$= \frac{1}{2}(\cos^2\theta - \sin^2\theta)$
$= \frac{1}{2}\cos 2\theta$

3.2 $\sin 75° \sin 15°$
$= \sin(45° + 30°)\sin(45° - 30°)$
$= \frac{1}{2}\cos 2(30°)$ (from answer to 3.1)
$= \left(\frac{1}{2}\right)\left(\frac{1}{2}\right) = \frac{1}{4}$

4. $\cos 165° = \cos(120° + 45°)$
$= \cos 120° \cos 45° - \sin 120° \sin 45°$
$= -\cos 60° \cos 45° - \sin 60° \sin 45°$
$= -\left(\frac{1}{2}\right)\left(\frac{1}{\sqrt{2}}\right) - \left(\frac{\sqrt{3}}{2}\right)\left(\frac{1}{\sqrt{2}}\right)$
$= -\frac{\sqrt{2}}{4} - \sqrt{2}\left(\frac{\sqrt{3}}{4}\right)$
$= -\frac{\sqrt{2}}{4}(1 + \sqrt{3})$

5. $2\cos^2(x - 45°) - \sin 2x = 1$
LHS $= 2\cos^2(x - 45°) - \sin 2x$
$= 2[\cos(x - 45°)\cos(x - 45°)] - 2\sin x \cos x$
$= 2(\cos x \cos 45° + \sin x \sin 45°)^2 - 2\sin x \cos x$
$= 2\left[\cos x\left(\frac{1}{\sqrt{2}}\right) + \sin x\left(\frac{1}{\sqrt{2}}\right)\right]^2 - 2\sin x \cos x$
$= 2\left[\cos^2 x\left(\frac{1}{2}\right) + 2\sin x \cos x\left(\frac{1}{2}\right) + \sin^2 x\left(\frac{1}{2}\right)\right] - 2\sin x \cos x$
$= 2\cdot\frac{1}{2}(\cos^2 x + 2\sin x \cos x + \sin^2 x) - 2\sin x \cos x$
$= 1 + 2\sin x \cos x - 2\sin x \cos x$
(because $\sin^2 x + \cos^2 x = 1$)
$= 1$
$\therefore$ LHS = RHS
Hence: $\cos^2(-15°) = \frac{1}{2}\left(1 + \frac{\sqrt{3}}{2}\right)$
Using the identity: $2\cos^2(x - 45°) - \sin 2x = 1$
Let $x = 30°$:
$2\cos^2(30° - 45°) - \sin 2(30°) = 1$
$2\cos^2(-15°) - \sin 60° = 1$
$\cos^2(-15°) = \frac{1 + \sin 60°}{2}$
$\cos^2(-15°) = \frac{1}{2}\left(1 + \frac{\sqrt{3}}{2}\right)$

Exercise 3 (page 86)

1. $\sin 2x + 2\sin x + \cos^2 x + \cos x = 0$
$2\sin x \cos x + 2\sin x + \cos^2 x + \cos x = 0$
$2\sin x(\cos x + 1) + \cos x(\cos x + 1) = 0$
$(\cos x + 1)(2\sin x + \cos x) = 0$
$\cos x + 1 = 0$ OR $2\sin x + \cos x = 0$
$\cos x = -1$ $\qquad 2\sin x = -\cos x$
$\qquad\qquad\qquad\therefore \frac{\sin x}{\cos x} = -\frac{1}{2}$
$\qquad\qquad\qquad\therefore \tan = -0{,}5$
$x = 180° + n360°$ OR $x = 153{,}4° + n180°, n \in \mathbb{Z}$

2. $\cos 2x = 1 - 3\cos x$
$\cos 2x + 3\cos x - 1 = 0$
$2\cos^2 x - 1 + 3\cos x - 1 = 0$
$2\cos^2 x + 3\cos x - 2 = 0$
$(2\cos x - 1)(\cos x + 2) = 0$
$2\cos x - 1 = 0$ OR $\cos x + 2 = 0$
$\cos x = \frac{1}{2}$ $\qquad\qquad \cos x = -2$
$x = 60° + n360°$ OR $x = -60° + n360°$
$\qquad\qquad\qquad\therefore$ No solution

3. $\sin 2x = \sin x - \cos x + 2\sin^2 x$
and $-90° \le x < 90°$

$-2\sin^2 x + 2\sin x \cos x - \sin x + \cos x = 0$
$2\sin^2 x - 2\sin x \cos x + \sin x - \cos x = 0$
$2\sin x(\sin x - \cos x) + (\sin x - \cos x) = 0$
$(\sin x - \cos x)(2\sin x + 1) = 0$

$\sin x - \cos x = 0$ OR $2\sin x + 1 = 0$
$\sin x = \cos x$ $\qquad 2\sin x = -1$
$\tan x = 1 \quad \sin x = -\frac{1}{2}$

$x = 45° + n180°$ OR $x = 210° + n360°$
OR $x = 330° + n360°$

$x = 45°; -30°$

4. $\sin^2 \beta + 2\sin\beta\cos\beta - \sin^2\beta - \cos^2\beta = 0$
$2\sin\beta\cos\beta - \cos^2\beta = 0$
$\cos\beta(2\sin\beta - \cos\beta) = 0$
$\cos\beta = 0$ OR $(2\sin\beta - \cos\beta) = 0$

$\beta = 90° + n180° \qquad 2\sin\beta = \cos\beta$

∴ No solution

$\frac{\sin\beta}{\cos\beta} = \frac{1}{2}$

$\tan\beta = 0{,}5$
$\beta = 26{,}6° + n180°, n \in \mathbb{Z}$

5.1 $\sin x = \cos 2x - 1$
$\sin x = 1 - 2\sin^2 x - 1$
$\sin x = -2\sin^2 x$
$2\sin^2 x + \sin x = 0$

5.2 $\sin x = \cos 2x - 1$
$2\sin^2 x + \sin x = 0$
$\sin x(2\sin x + 1) = 0$

$\sin x = 0$ OR $2\sin x + 1 = 0$
$x = 0° + n180°, n \in \mathbb{Z}$ $\qquad \sin x = -\frac{1}{2}$
$x = 210° + n360°, n \in \mathbb{Z}$
$x = 330° + n360°, n \in \mathbb{Z}$

6. $\tan x = \sin 2x$
$\frac{\sin x}{\cos x} = 2\sin x \cos x$
$2\sin x \cos^2 x - \sin x = 0$
$\sin x(2\cos^2 x - 1) = 0$

$\sin x = 0$ OR $(2\cos^2 x - 1) = 0$
$x = 0° + n180°, n \in \mathbb{Z}$ OR $\cos x = \pm\frac{1}{\sqrt{2}}$
$x = 45° + n180°, n \in \mathbb{Z}$
$x = -45°; 0°; 45°; 135°; 180°$

7. $6\sin^2 x + 2\sin 2x = 1$ for $x \in [-180°; 200°]$
$6\sin^2 x + 4\sin x \cos x - \sin^2 x - \cos^2 x = 0$
$5\sin^2 x + 4\sin x \cos x - \cos^2 x = 0$
$(5\sin x - \cos x)(\sin x + \cos x) = 0$
$5\sin x = \cos x$ OR $\sin x = -\cos x$
$\tan x = \frac{1}{5}$ $\qquad \tan x = -1$

$x = 11{,}3° + n180°, n \in \mathbb{Z}$
$x = 135° + n180°, n \in \mathbb{Z}$
$x = 11{,}3°; -168{,}7°; 191{,}3°; 135°; -45°$

8. $\cos 3x \cos x + \sin 3x \sin x = -\frac{1}{\sqrt{2}}$
for $x \in [-90°; 180°]$
$\cos(3x - x) = -\frac{1}{\sqrt{2}}$
$\cos 2x = -\frac{1}{\sqrt{2}}$

$2x = 135° + n360°, n \in \mathbb{Z}$
OR $2x = 225° + n360°, n \in \mathbb{Z}$
$x = 67{,}5° + n180°, n \in \mathbb{Z}$
OR $x = 112{,}5° + n180°, n \in \mathbb{Z}$
$x = 67{,}5°; 112{,}5°; -67{,}5°$

Exercise 4 (page 88)

1. $\frac{1 - \cos 2x - \sin x}{\sin 2x - \cos x}$

$= \frac{1 - (1 - 2\sin^2 x) - \sin x}{2\sin x \cos x - \cos x}$

$= \frac{2\sin^2 x - \sin x}{2\sin x \cos x - \cos x}$

$= \frac{\sin x(2\sin x - 1)}{\cos x(2\sin x - 1)}$

$= \frac{\sin x}{\cos x}$

$= \tan x$

2. LHS $= \frac{\sin 2\beta - \sin\beta}{\cos 2\beta + \cos\beta}$

$= \frac{2\sin\beta\cos\beta - \sin\beta}{2\cos^2\beta - 1 + \cos\beta}$

$= \frac{\sin\beta(2\cos\beta - 1)}{(2\cos\beta - 1)(\cos\beta + 1)}$

$= \frac{\sin\beta}{(\cos\beta + 1)}$

∴ LHS = RHS

3.1 $\sin 3A = 3\sin A - 4\sin^3 A$
LHS $= \sin 3A = \sin(2A + A)$
$= \sin 2A \cos A + \cos 2A \sin A$
$= 2\sin A \cos A \cos A + (1 - 2\sin^2 A)\sin A$
$= 2\sin A \cos^2 A + \sin A - 2\sin^3 A$
$= 2\sin A(1 - \sin^2 A) + \sin A - \sin^3 A$
$= 2\sin A - 2\sin^3 A + \sin A - 2\sin^3 A$
$= 3\sin A - 4\sin^3 A$

∴ LHS = RHS

3.2 Minimum value for $\frac{\sin 3A}{\sin A} = 3 - 4\sin^2 A$.
Therefore the minimum value $= 3 - 4(1) = -1$.

4.1 LHS $= (\sin x + \cos x)^2$
$= \sin^2 x + 2\sin x \cos x + \cos^2 x$
$= 1 + 2\sin x \cos x$
$= 1 + \sin 2x$
$\therefore$ LHS = RHS

4.2 $(\sin x + \cos x)^2 = \sin 2x + 1$ Proved above
$\therefore \sin x + \cos x = \sqrt{\sin 2x + 1}$
$= \sqrt{1 + 1}$ Max value of $\sin 2x$ is 1
$\therefore$ Maximum value of $\sin x + \cos x = \sqrt{2}$

5.

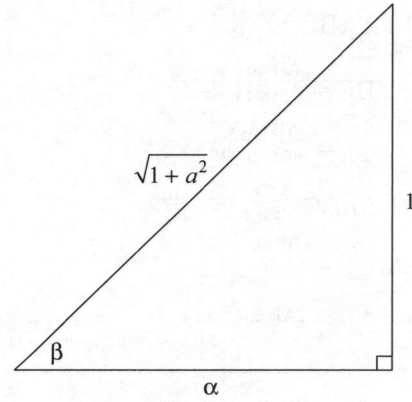

$\tan \beta = \frac{1}{a}$, $y = 1$ and $x = a$

LHS $= a \cos 2\beta + \sin 2\beta$
$= a(\cos^2 \beta - \sin^2 \beta) + 2\sin\beta\cos\beta$
$= a\left[\left(\frac{a}{\sqrt{1+a^2}}\right)^2 - \left(\frac{1}{\sqrt{1+a^2}}\right)^2\right]$
$\quad + 2\left(\frac{1}{\sqrt{1+a^2}}\right)\left(\frac{a}{\sqrt{1+a^2}}\right)$
$= a\left(\frac{a^2 - 1}{1+a^2}\right) + 2\left(\frac{a}{1+a^2}\right)$
$= \frac{a^3 - a + 2a}{1+a^2}$
$= \frac{a^3 + a}{1+a^2}$
$= \frac{a(a^2+1)}{(1+a^2)}$
$= a$
$\therefore$ LHS = RHS

Exercise 5 (page 90)

1.

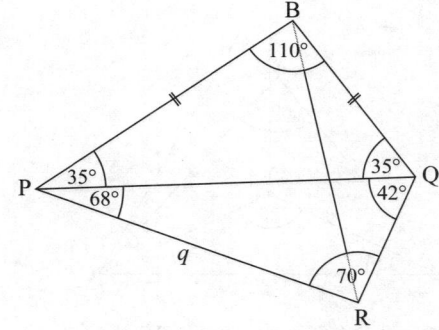

1.1 $B\hat{Q}P = B\hat{P}Q = 35°$ In $\triangle BPQ$, BP = BQ
$P\hat{B}Q = 110°$ Interior angles of $\triangle BPQ$
$P\hat{R}Q = 70°$ Interior angles of $\triangle PRQ$
$\frac{PQ}{\sin 70°} = \frac{q}{\sin 42°}$ In $\triangle PRQ$
$\therefore PQ = \frac{q \sin 70°}{\sin 42°}$ ....①
$\frac{PB}{\sin 35°} = \frac{PQ}{\sin 110°}$ In $\triangle PBQ$
$\therefore PB = \frac{PQ \sin 35°}{\sin 110°}$
$= \frac{q \sin 70° \sin 35°}{\sin 42° \sin 110°}$ Replace PQ with expression in ①
$= \frac{q \sin 35°}{\sin 42°}$ $\sin 110° = \sin 70°$

1.2 $q = \frac{PB \sin 42°}{\sin 35°} = \frac{54,5 \sin 42°}{\sin 35°}$
$= 63,6$ m

2.

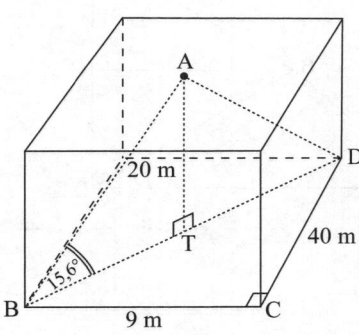

2.1 In $\triangle ABT$: $\sin 15,6° = \frac{AT}{20}$
$\therefore AT = 5,4$ m

2.2 $BD^2 = 9^2 + 40^2$ Pythagoras $\triangle BCD$
$= 1\,681$
$BD = 41$ m
$AD^2 = BA^2 + BD^2 - 2\,BA \cdot BD \cos 15,6°$
$= 501,413\ldots$
$AD = 22,4$ m

3.

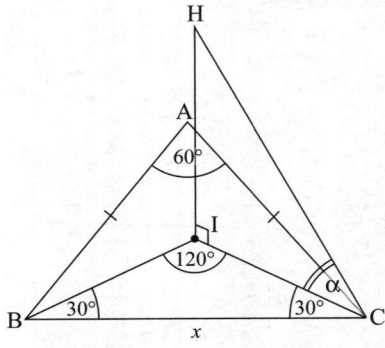

3.1 △BAC is equilateral

$B\hat{C}I = C\hat{B}I = 30°$ BI and IC are bisectors

In △BIC: $\frac{IC}{\sin 30°} = \frac{x}{\sin 120°}$

$$\therefore IC = \frac{x \sin 30°}{\sin 60°}$$

$$= \frac{x \sin 30°}{\cos 30°}$$

$$= x \tan 30° \quad \text{①}$$

In △HIC: $\tan \alpha = \frac{HI}{IC}$

$\therefore HI = x \tan 30° \tan \alpha$ Replace IC with ①

3.2 $HI = 25{,}6 \tan 30° \tan 70{,}6°$

$= 42{,}0$ m

4.

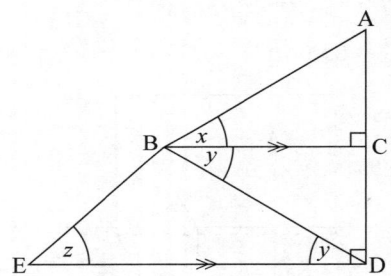

Note
BC ∥ ED

In △BDE:

$\frac{BD}{\sin z} = \frac{BE}{\sin y}$ $B\hat{D}E = y = $ alt. $C\hat{B}D$; BC ∥ ED

$\therefore BD = \frac{BE \sin z}{\sin y}$ .... ①

In △ABD:

$\frac{AD}{\sin(x+y)} = \frac{BD}{\sin(90°-x)}$ $\hat{A} = (90° - x)$; three angles of △ABC

$\therefore AD = \frac{BD \sin(x+y)}{\cos x}$ $\sin(90° - x) = \cos x$

$= \frac{BD \sin z \sin(x+y)}{\cos x \sin y}$ Replace BD with expression in ①

5.

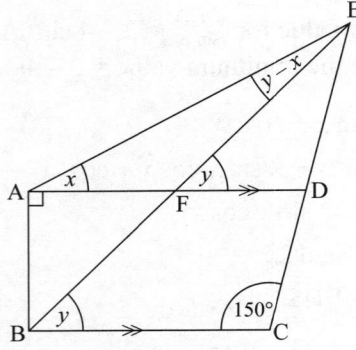

5.1 $E\hat{F}D$ = corresponding $F\hat{B}C$

$= y$ AD ∥ BC

$E\hat{F}D = x + A\hat{E}F$ Exterior angle of △AEF

$A\hat{E}F = y - x$

In △ABE: $\frac{\sin A\hat{E}B}{AB} = \frac{\sin E\hat{A}B}{BE}$

$\therefore BE = \frac{AB \sin(90° + x)}{\sin(y - x)}$

$= \frac{AB \cos x}{\sin(y - x)}$

5.2 In △EBC: $\frac{CE}{\sin y} = \frac{BE}{\sin 150°}$

$\therefore CE = \frac{BE \sin y}{\frac{1}{2}}$

$= \frac{2 AB \cos x \sin y}{\sin(y - x)}$ $BE = \frac{AB \cos x}{\sin(y - x)}$

6.

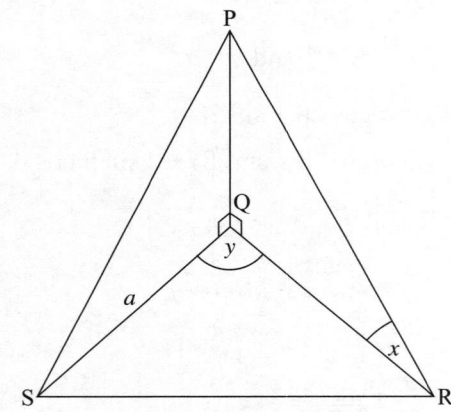

6.1 In △RQS: Area △RQS = $\frac{1}{2}$ SQ · RQ sin y

$\therefore A = \frac{1}{2} a \cdot RQ \sin y$

$\therefore \frac{2A}{a \sin y} = RQ$

In △PQR: $\tan x = \frac{PQ}{QR}$

$\therefore PQ = QR \tan x$

$= \frac{2A \tan x}{a \sin y}$

6.2 $PQ = \dfrac{2A \tan x}{a \sin y}$

$\therefore 77 = \dfrac{2(1\,480)\tan 46,5°}{89 \sin y}$

$\therefore \sin y = 0,45515\ldots$

$y = 27,1°$ or $y = 180° - 27,1°$

$\quad = 27,1°$ or $y = 152,9°$

7.

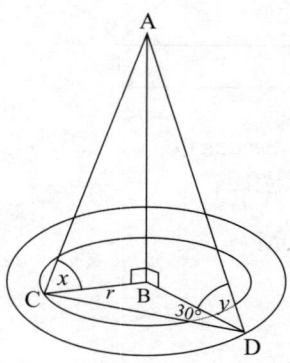

7.1 In $\triangle ABC$: $\tan x = \dfrac{AB}{r}$

$\therefore AB = r \tan x$ .... ①

In $\triangle ABD$: $\tan y = \dfrac{AB}{BD}$

$\therefore BD = \dfrac{AB}{\tan y}$

$\quad = \dfrac{r \tan x}{\tan y}$ Replace AB with ①

7.2 $\dfrac{\sin B\hat{C}D}{BD} = \dfrac{\sin 30°}{r}$

$\therefore \sin B\hat{C}D = \dfrac{\tan x \sin 30°}{\tan y} = \dfrac{\tan x}{2 \tan y}$

7.3 $\sin B\hat{C}D = \dfrac{\tan 45°}{2 \tan 30°} = \dfrac{1}{2}(1)\dfrac{\sqrt{3}}{1} = \dfrac{\sqrt{3}}{2}$

$\therefore B\hat{C}D = 60°$

$\therefore C\hat{B}D = 90°$

8.

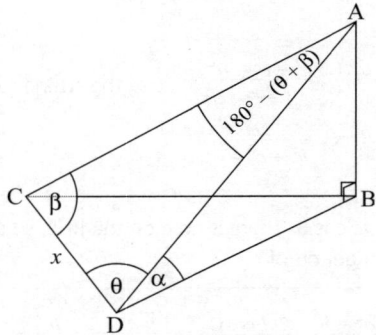

8.1 $C\hat{A}D = 180° - (\beta + \theta)$ Angles of $\triangle CAD$

$\therefore \dfrac{AD}{\sin \beta} = \dfrac{x}{\sin[180° - (\beta + \theta)]}$

$\therefore AD = \dfrac{x \sin \beta}{\sin(\beta + \theta)}$ .... ①

8.2 $\sin \alpha = \dfrac{AB}{AD}$

$\therefore AB = AD \cdot \sin \alpha$

$\quad = \dfrac{x \sin \beta \sin \alpha}{\sin(\beta + \theta)}$ Replace AD with ①

$\quad = \dfrac{50 \sin 63° \sin 42°}{\sin(63° + 54°)}$

$\quad = 33,5 \text{ m}$

9.

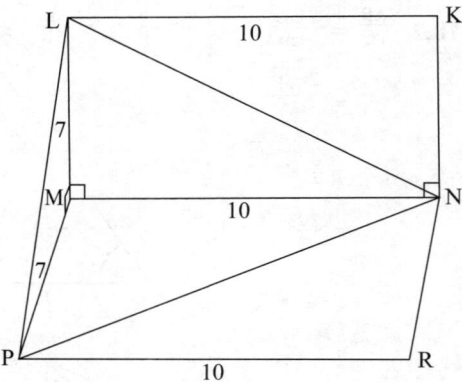

$LN^2 = PN^2$ Pythagoras: $\triangle PMN$

$\quad = 7^2 + 10^2$

$\quad = 149$

$LP^2 = 7^2 + 7^2$ Pythagoras: $\triangle LMP$

$\quad = 98$

In $\triangle LPN$:

$LP^2 = LN^2 + PN^2 - 2LN \cdot PN \cos L\hat{N}P$

$\therefore 98 = 149 + 149 - 2\sqrt{149} \cdot \sqrt{149} \cos L\hat{N}P$

$\therefore \cos L\hat{N}P = 0,671\ldots$

$\therefore L\hat{N}P = 47,8°$

10.

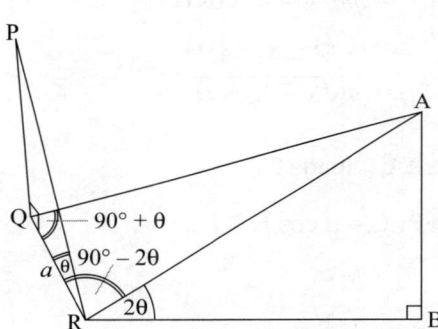

10.1 $R\hat{A}Q = 180° - (90° + \theta) - (90° - 2\theta)$

$\quad = \theta$

In $\triangle RAQ$: $\dfrac{AR}{\sin(90° + \theta)} = \dfrac{a}{\sin \theta}$

$\therefore AR = \dfrac{a \cos \theta}{\sin \theta}$ .... ①

In $\triangle ARB$: $\sin 2\theta = \dfrac{AB}{AR}$

$\therefore AB = \dfrac{a \cos \theta}{\sin \theta} \sin 2\theta$ Replace AR with ①

$\quad = \dfrac{a \cos \theta \, 2 \sin \theta \cos \theta}{\sin \theta}$

$\quad = 2a \cos^2 \theta$

In $\triangle PQR$: $\tan \theta = \dfrac{PQ}{a}$

$\therefore PQ = a \tan \theta$

$\therefore \dfrac{AB}{PQ} = \dfrac{2\cancel{a} \cos^2 \theta}{\cancel{a} \tan \theta}$

$\quad = \dfrac{2 \cos^2 \theta}{\tan \theta}$

10.2 $\dfrac{AB}{PQ} = \dfrac{2\cos^2 30°}{\tan 30°}$

$= \dfrac{2\left(\frac{\sqrt{3}}{2}\right)^2}{\frac{1}{\sqrt{3}}}$

$= \dfrac{3}{2} \times \dfrac{\sqrt{3}}{1}$

$= \dfrac{3\sqrt{3}}{2}$

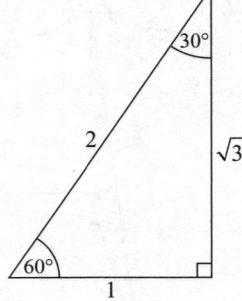

11.

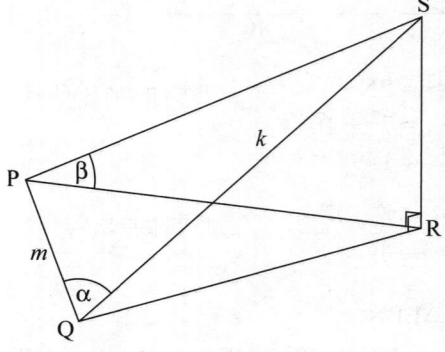

In $\triangle PQS$:

$PS^2 = m^2 + k^2 - 2mk\cos\alpha$

$= m^2 + 4m^2 - 2m(2m)\cos\alpha$

$= 5m^2 - 4m^2\cos\alpha$

$= m^2(5 - 4\cos\alpha)$

$\therefore PS = m\sqrt{5 - 4\cos\alpha}$

Exercise 6 (page 93)

1. **RTP:** $C = a\cos B + b\cos A$

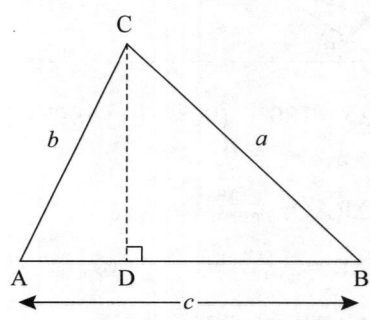

RHS $= a\cos B + b\cos A$

$= a\left(\dfrac{DB}{a}\right) + b\left(\dfrac{AD}{b}\right)$

$= DB + AD$

$= C$

$\therefore$ RHS = LHS

2. **RTP:** $q\cos R + r\cos Q = p$

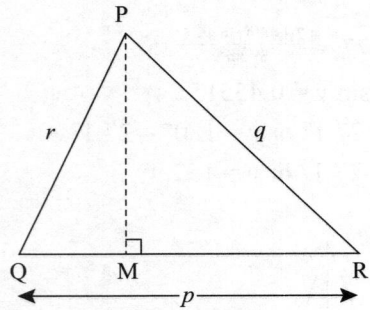

LHS $= q\cos R + r\cos Q$

$= q\left(\dfrac{MR}{q}\right) + r\left(\dfrac{QM}{r}\right)$

$= MR + QM$

$= QR$

$= P$

$\therefore$ LHS = RHS

Exercise 7 (page 94)

1.1 **RTP:** $\dfrac{\cos B}{\cos A} = \dfrac{a - b\cos C}{b - a\cos C}$, $\hat{A} \neq 90°$

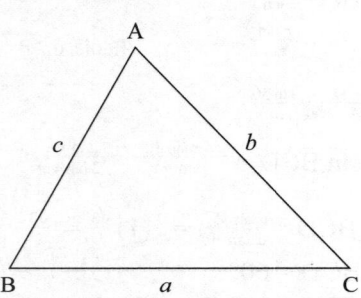

LHS $= \dfrac{\cos B}{\cos A}$

$= \dfrac{a^2 + c^2 - b^2}{2ac} \div \dfrac{b^2 + c^2 - a^2}{2bc}$ Use the cosine rule.

$= \dfrac{a^2 + c^2 - b^2}{2ac} \times \dfrac{2bc}{b^2 + c^2 - a^2}$

> $b^2 = a^2 + c^2 - 2ac\cos B$. There is no c on the RHS, so use the cosine rule to get rid of c.

$= \dfrac{a^2 - b^2 + a^2 + b^2 - 2ab\cos C}{a} \times \dfrac{b}{b^2 - a^2 + a^2 + b^2 - 2ab\cos C}$

$= \dfrac{2a^2 - 2ab\cos C}{a} \times \dfrac{b}{2b^2 - 2ab\cos C}$

$= \dfrac{2a(a - b\cos C)}{a} \times \dfrac{b}{2b(b - a\cos C)}$

$= \dfrac{a - b\cos C}{b - a\cos C}$

$\therefore$ LHS = RHS

1.2 RTP: $\dfrac{\cos A}{\cos C} = \dfrac{C - a\cos B}{a - c\cos B}$, $\hat{C} \neq 90°$

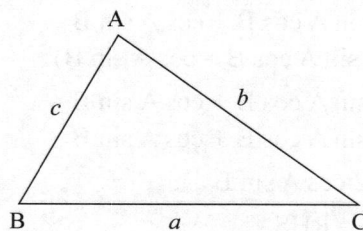

LHS $= \dfrac{\cos A}{\cos C}$

$= \dfrac{b^2 + c^2 - a^2}{2bc} \div \dfrac{a^2 + b^2 - c^2}{2ab}$

$= \dfrac{c^2 - a^2 + a^2 + c^2 - 2ac\cos B}{2bc} \times \dfrac{2ab}{a^2 - c^2 + a^2 + c^2 - 2ac\cos B}$

$= \dfrac{2c^2 - 2ac\cos B}{c} \times \dfrac{a}{2a^2 - 2ac\cos B}$

$= \dfrac{2c(c - a\cos B)}{c} \times \dfrac{a}{2a(a - c\cos B)}$

$= \dfrac{c - a\cos B}{a - c\cos B}$

∴ LHS = RHS

2. RTP: $\dfrac{\cos P}{\cos R} = \dfrac{r - P\cos Q}{P - r\cos Q}$, $\hat{R} \neq 90°$

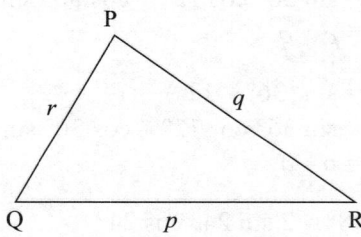

LHS $= \dfrac{\cos P}{\cos R}$

$= \dfrac{q^2 + r^2 - p^2}{2qr} \times \dfrac{2pq}{p^2 + q^2 - r^2}$

$= \dfrac{r^2 - p^2 + r^2 + p^2 - 2rp\cos Q}{r} \times \dfrac{p}{p^2 - r^2 + p^2 + r^2 - 2pr\cos Q}$

$= \dfrac{2r^2 - 2rp\cos Q}{r} \times \dfrac{p}{2p^2 - 2pr\cos Q}$

$= \dfrac{2r(r - p\cos Q)}{r} \times \dfrac{p}{2p(p - r\cos Q)}$

$= \dfrac{r - p\cos Q}{p - r\cos Q}$

∴ LHS = RHS

Exercise 8 (page 95)

1. RTP: In △ABC, prove that $\tan B = \dfrac{b\sin C}{a - b\cos C}$

LHS $= \tan B = \dfrac{\sin B}{\cos B}$ $\dfrac{\sin B}{b} = \dfrac{\sin C}{c}$

$= \dfrac{b\sin C}{c} \div \dfrac{a^2 + c^2 - b^2}{2ac}$

∴ $\sin B = \dfrac{b\sin C}{c}$

$= \dfrac{b\sin C}{c} \times \dfrac{2ac}{a^2 - b^2 + a^2 + b^2 - 2ab\cos C}$

$= \dfrac{b\sin c}{1} \times \dfrac{2a}{2a(a - b\cos C)}$

$= \dfrac{b\sin c}{a - b\cos C}$

∴ LHS = RHS

Test A (page 96)

1. $\dfrac{\cos(60° - A) + \cos(60° + A)}{\cos A}$

$= \dfrac{\cos 60° \cos A + \sin 60° \sin A + \cos 60° \cos A - \sin 60° \sin A}{\cos A}$

$= \dfrac{2\cos 60° \cos A}{\cos A}$

$= 2\cos 60°$

$= 2\left(\dfrac{1}{2}\right) = 1$ (4)

2.1 $\cos^2 12° - \sin^2 12° = m$

$\cos 2(12°) = m$

$\cos 24° = m$ (1)

2.2 $\dfrac{\sqrt{3}}{2}\cos 6° + \dfrac{1}{2}\sin 6°$

$= \cos 30° \cos 6° + \sin 30° \sin 6°$

$= \cos(30° - 6°)$

$= \cos 24° = m$ (4)

3. $\dfrac{1}{2}\sin(\theta + 10°) = \sin\theta\cos\theta$

$\sin(\theta + 10°) = 2\sin\theta\cos\theta$

$\sin(\theta + 10°) = \sin 2\theta$

$(\theta + 10°) = 2\theta + n360°$

OR $(\theta + 10°) = (180° - 2\theta) + n360°$

$-\theta = -10° + n360°$ OR $3\theta = 170° + n360°$

$\theta = 10° + n360°$ OR $\theta = \dfrac{170°}{3} + n120°$, $n \in \mathbb{Z}$ (7)

4.1 $\dfrac{1 - \cos 2\theta}{\sin 2\theta} = \tan\theta$

LHS $= \dfrac{1 - \cos 2\theta}{\sin 2\theta}$

$= \dfrac{1 - \cos^2\theta + \sin^2\theta}{2\sin\theta\cos\theta}$

$= \dfrac{\cos^2\theta + \sin^2\theta - \cos^2\theta + \sin^2\theta}{2\sin\theta\cos\theta}$

$= \dfrac{2\sin^2\theta}{2\sin\theta\cos\theta}$

$= \dfrac{\sin\theta}{\cos\theta}$

$= \tan\theta$

∴ LHS = RHS   (5)

4.2 $\tan\theta = \dfrac{1-\cos 2\theta}{\sin 2\theta}$

$\therefore \tan 22,5° = \dfrac{1-\cos 2(22,5°)}{\sin 2(22,5°)}$

$= \dfrac{1-\cos 45°}{\sin 45°}$

$\therefore \tan 22,5° = \dfrac{1-\frac{1}{\sqrt{2}}}{\frac{1}{\sqrt{2}}} = \sqrt{2}-1$ (4)

5.1

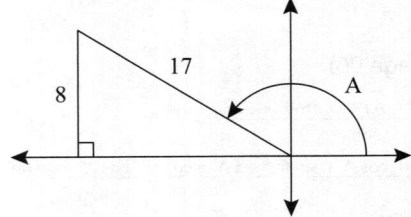

$\sin A = \dfrac{8}{17}$ and $90° < A < 180°$

$y = 8, r = 17,$

$x = -\sqrt{17^2 - 8^2} = -15$

$\cos A = \dfrac{-15}{17}$ (3)

5.2

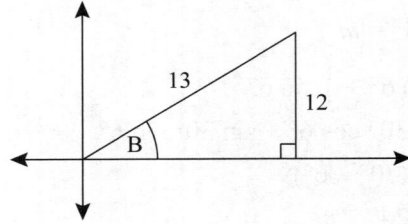

$\sin B = \dfrac{12}{13}$

$y = 12, r = 13, x = \sqrt{13^2 - 12^2} = 5$

$\tan(720° + A + B) = \tan(A + B)$

$= \dfrac{\sin(A+B)}{\cos(A+B)}$

$= \dfrac{\sin A \cos B + \cos A \sin B}{\cos A \cos B - \sin A \sin B}$

$= \dfrac{\left(\frac{8}{17}\right)\left(\frac{5}{13}\right) + \left(\frac{-15}{17}\right)\left(\frac{12}{13}\right)}{\left(\frac{-15}{17}\right)\left(\frac{5}{13}\right) - \left(\frac{8}{17}\right)\left(\frac{12}{13}\right)}$

$= \dfrac{\frac{-140}{221}}{\frac{-171}{221}}$

$= \dfrac{140}{171}$ (4)

6. $\cos(A + B) = \cos[A - (-B)]$
$= \cos A \cos(-B) - \sin A \sin(-B)$
$= \cos A \cos B - \sin A(-\sin B)$
$= \cos A \cos B + \sin A \sin B$ (4)

7. $\sin 2P = \sin(P + P)$
$= \sin P \cos P + \cos P \sin P$
$= 2 \sin P \cos P$ (2)

8.1 $\sin(A + B) - \sin(A - B) = 2\cos A \sin B$
LHS $= \sin(A + B) - \sin(A - B)$
$= \sin A \cos B + \cos A \sin B -$
$\quad (\sin A \cos B - \cos A \sin B)$
$= \sin A \cos B + \cos A \sin B -$
$\quad \sin A \cos B + \cos A \sin B$
$= 2 \cos A \sin B$
$\therefore$ LHS = RHS (3)

8.2 $\sin(3x + 2x) - \sin(3x - 2x)$
$= 2 \cos 3x \sin 2x$ (4)

8.3 $2 \cos 3x \sin 2x = 0$

$\cos 3x = 0$ OR $\sin 2x = 0$

$3x = \pm 90° + n180°$ $\quad 2x = 0° + n180°$

$x = \pm 30° + n60°, n \in \mathbb{Z}$ $\quad x = n90°, n \in \mathbb{Z}$ (5)

Total: 50

Test B (page 97)

1.1 $\sin 48° = \sin(36° + 12°)$
$= \sin 36° \cos 12° + \cos 36° \sin 12°$
$= p + q$ (3)

1.2 $\sin 24° = \sin(36° - 12°)$
$= \sin 36° \cos 12° - \cos 36° \sin 12°$
$= p - q$ (3)

1.3 $\sin 48° = 2 \sin 24° \cos 24°$

$\therefore p + q = 2(p - q) \cos 24°$

$\therefore \cos 24° = \dfrac{p+q}{2(p-q)}$ (3)

2.1 $4 \tan \theta = 3$
and $180° < \theta < 360°$
$\tan \theta = \dfrac{3}{4}$
θ lies in quad 3
$\therefore y = -3, x = -4,$
$r = -\sqrt{(-3)^2 + (-4)^2}$
$= \sqrt{25} = 5$

$\sin \theta + \cos \theta = \dfrac{-3}{5} + \dfrac{-4}{5} = -\dfrac{7}{5}$ (4)

2.2 $\tan 2\theta = \dfrac{\sin 2\theta}{\cos 2\theta}$

$= \dfrac{2 \sin \theta \cos \theta}{2 \cos^2 \theta - 1}$

$= \dfrac{2\left(\frac{-3}{5}\right)\left(\frac{-4}{5}\right)}{2\left(\frac{-4}{5}\right) - 1}$

$= \dfrac{24}{25} \div \dfrac{7}{25} = \dfrac{24}{7}$ (5)

3. $\sin 2\beta = 1 - 4\cos^2\beta$
$\sin 2\beta - 1 + 4\cos^2\beta = 0$
$2\sin\beta\cos\beta - \sin^2\beta - \cos^2\beta + 4\cos^2\beta = 0$
$3\cos^2\beta + 2\sin\beta\cos\beta - \sin^2\beta = 0$
$(3\cos\beta - \sin\beta)(\cos\beta + \sin\beta) = 0$

$(3\cos\beta - \sin\beta) = 0$ OR $(\cos\beta + \sin\beta) = 0$
$3\cos\beta = \sin\beta$ $\qquad \cos\beta = -\sin\beta$
$\tan\beta = 3$ $\qquad\qquad \tan\beta = -1$
$\beta = 71{,}6° + n180°$ $\qquad \beta = 135° + n180°$
(6)

4. LHS $= \sin^2 20° + \sin^2 40° + \sin^2 80°$

$= \sin^2 20° + [\sin(60° - 20°)]^2 +$
$\quad [\sin(60° + 20°)]^2$

$= \sin^2 20° + (\sin 60° \cos 20° - \cos 60° \sin 20°)^2$
$\quad + (\sin 60° \cos 20° + \cos 60° \sin 20°)^2$

$= \sin^2 20° + \left(\tfrac{\sqrt{3}}{2}\cos 20° - \tfrac{1}{2}\sin 20°\right)^2$
$\quad + \left(\tfrac{\sqrt{3}}{2}\cos 20° + \tfrac{1}{2}\sin 20°\right)^2$

$= \sin^2 20° + \tfrac{3}{4}\cos^2 20° - \tfrac{\sqrt{3}}{2}\cos 20°\sin 20°$
$\quad + \tfrac{1}{4}\sin^2 20° + \tfrac{3}{4}\cos^2 20°$
$\quad + \tfrac{\sqrt{3}}{2}\cos 20°\sin 20° + \tfrac{1}{4}\sin^2 20°$

$= \sin^2 20° + \tfrac{3}{2}\cos^2 20° + \tfrac{1}{2}\sin^2 20°$

$= \tfrac{3}{2}(\sin^2 20° + \cos^2 20°)$

$= \tfrac{3}{2}$

∴ LHS = RHS (7)

5. In △MEF:
$\tan\beta = \dfrac{h}{EF}$
$EF = \dfrac{h}{\tan\beta}$

In △DEF
$D\hat{E}F = 180° - (\theta + \alpha)$

$\dfrac{DF}{\sin(\theta+\alpha)} = \dfrac{EF}{\sin\theta}$

$DF = \dfrac{EF\sin(\theta+\alpha)}{\sin\theta}$

$= \dfrac{h}{\tan\beta} \cdot \dfrac{\sin(\theta+\alpha)}{\sin\theta\tan\alpha}$

$= \dfrac{h\sin(\theta+\alpha)}{\sin\theta\tan\alpha}$ (4)

6.1 $2x + 2\sin x = \dfrac{2\sin x(2\cos x - 1)(\cos x + 1)}{\cos 2x}$

LHS $= \tan 2x + 2\sin x$

$= \dfrac{\sin 2x}{\cos 2x} + 2\sin x$

$= \dfrac{2\sin x\cos x + 2\sin x(\cos^2 x - \sin^2 x)}{\cos^2 x - \sin^2 x}$

$= \dfrac{2\sin x\cos x + 2\sin x(\cos^2 x - \sin^2 x)}{\cos^2 x - \sin^2 x}$

$= \dfrac{2\sin x[\cos x + \cos^2 x(1 - \cos^2 x)]}{\cos 2x}$

$= \dfrac{2\sin x(\cos x + \cos^2 x - 1 - \cos^2 x)}{\cos 2x}$

$= \dfrac{2\sin x(2\cos^2 x + \cos x - 1)}{\cos 2x}$

$= \dfrac{2\sin x(2\cos x - 1)(\cos x + 1)}{\cos 2x}$

∴ LHS = RHS (6)

6.2 $\tan 2x + 2\sin x = \dfrac{2\sin x(2\cos x - 1)(\cos x + 1)}{\cos 2x}$

$0 = \dfrac{2\sin x(2\cos x - 1)(\cos x + 1)}{\cos 2x}$

$0(\cos 2x) = 2\sin x(2\cos x - 1)(\cos x + 1)$
$0 = 2\sin x(2\cos x - 1)(\cos x + 1)$

$2\sin x = 0$ OR $(2\cos x - 1) = 0$
$\sin x = 0$ $\qquad \cos x = \tfrac{1}{2}$
$x = 0°$ $\qquad\qquad x = 0°$ or $x = 300°$

OR $(\cos x + 1) = 0$
$\cos x = -1$
$x = 180°$ (6)

6.3 Undefined when $\cos 2x = 0$
$2x = 90° + n180°$
$x = 45° + n90°, n \in \mathbb{Z}$
$x = 45°; 135°; 225°; 315°$ (3)

Total: 50

Test C (page 98)

1. $\dfrac{\sin(180° - 2x)\tan(-45°)}{\cos(-90° - x)}$

$= \dfrac{\sin 2x - \tan 45°}{\sin x}$

$= \dfrac{2\sin x\cos x(-\tan 45°)}{\sin x}$

$= \dfrac{2\sin x\cos x(-1)}{\sin x}$

$= -2\cos x$ (4)

2.1 $\sin 34° = \sin(22° + 12°)$
$= \sin 22°\cos 12° + \cos 22°\sin 12°$
$= a + b$ (2)

2.2 $\cos 10° = \cos(22° - 12°)$
$= \cos 22° \cos 12° + \sin 22° \sin 12°$
$= c + d$ (2)

3.1

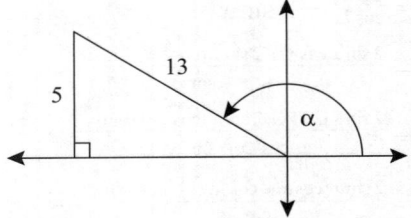

$13 \sin \alpha - 5 = 0$ where $\alpha \in [90°; 270°]$
$\sin \alpha = \frac{5}{13}$, α lies in quad 2
$\therefore y = 5, r = 13, x = -12$
$\therefore \cos \alpha = \frac{-12}{13}$ (3)

3.2

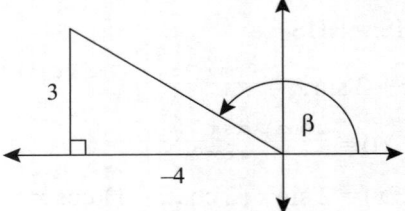

$\tan \beta = -\frac{3}{4}$ where $\beta \in [90; 270°]$
$\tan \beta = -\frac{3}{4}$, β lies in quad 2
$\therefore y = 3, x = -4, r = 5$
$\cos(\alpha + \beta) = \cos \alpha \cos \beta - \sin \alpha \sin \beta$
$= \left(\frac{-12}{13}\right)\left(\frac{-4}{5}\right) - \left(\frac{5}{13}\right)\left(\frac{3}{5}\right)$
$= \frac{48 - 15}{65} = \frac{33}{65}$ (5)

4. $b\sqrt{1-a^2} - a\sqrt{1-b^2}$
$= \cos 32° \sqrt{1 - \sin^2 28°}$
$\quad - \sin 28° \sqrt{1 - \cos^2 32°}$
$= \cos 32° \cos 28° - \sin 28° \sin 32°$
$= \cos(32° + 28°)$
$= \cos 60°$
$= \frac{1}{2}$ (4)

5. $\sin\left(\frac{\beta}{2} + 45°\right) \cos\left(\frac{\beta}{2} + 45°\right)$
$= \frac{1}{2} \sin 2\left(\frac{\beta}{2} + 45°\right)$

> **Hint**
> $2 \sin A \cos A = \sin 2A$
> $\therefore \sin \frac{A}{2} \cos \frac{A}{2} = \frac{1}{2} \sin 2\left(\frac{A}{2}\right) = \frac{1}{2} \sin A$

$= \frac{1}{2} \sin(\beta + 90°)$
$= \frac{1}{2} \cos \beta$
$= \frac{1}{2} m$ (4)

6. $\frac{\cos 2\theta}{\sin 4\theta} = 1$

$\frac{\cos 2\theta}{2 \sin 2\theta \cos 2\theta} = 1$

$\frac{1}{2 \sin 2\theta} = 1$

$2 \sin 2\theta = 1$

$\sin 2\theta = \frac{1}{2}$

$2\theta = 30° + n360°$ OR $2\theta = 150° + n360°$
$\theta = 15° + n180°$ OR $\theta = 75° + n180°, n \in \mathbb{Z}$
$\therefore \theta = 15°; 75°$ (8)

7. $\tan 2A + \frac{1}{\cos 2A} = \frac{\sin A + \cos A}{\cos A - \sin A}$

LHS $= \tan 2A + \frac{1}{\cos 2A}$

$= \frac{\sin 2A}{\cos 2A} + \frac{1}{\cos 2A}$

$= \frac{\sin 2A + 1}{\cos 2A}$

$= \frac{2 \sin A \cos A + 1}{\cos^2 A - \sin^2 A}$

$= \frac{2 \sin A \cos A + \sin^2 A + \cos^2 A}{\cos^2 A - \sin^2 A}$

$= \frac{(\sin A + \cos A)(\sin A + \cos A)}{(\cos A - \sin A)(\sin A + \cos A)}$

$= \frac{\sin A + \cos A}{\cos A - \sin A}$

$\therefore$ LHS = RHS (9)

8.1 $\frac{AB}{10} = \sin \alpha$
$AB = 10 \sin \alpha$ (2)

8.2 $\frac{BC}{\sin(90° + \alpha)} = \frac{AB}{\sin 2\alpha}$

$BC = \frac{AB \sin(90° + \alpha)}{\sin 2\alpha}$

$= \frac{10 \sin \alpha}{2 \sin \alpha \cos \alpha}$

$= 5$ (2)

8.3 $A\hat{B}C = 180° - (90° + \alpha) - 2\alpha$
$= 90° - \alpha - 2\alpha$
$= 90° - 3\alpha$

$\frac{AC}{\sin 90° - 3\alpha} = \frac{5}{\sin(90° + \alpha)}$

$= \frac{5 \cos 3\alpha}{\cos \alpha}$ (5)

Total: 50

TOPIC 5 Polynomial functions (page 99)

Exercise 1 (page 103)

1. Let $f(x) = x^3 + 4x^2 - x + 3$, if $2x + 1$ is a factor:

   $\text{Rem} = f\left(-\frac{1}{2}\right)$
   $= \left(-\frac{1}{2}\right)^3 + 4\left(-\frac{1}{2}\right)^2 - \left(-\frac{1}{2}\right) + 3$
   $= -\frac{1}{8} + 1 + \frac{1}{2} + 3$
   $= 4\frac{3}{8}$

2. > You can use the table mode on your calculator to find x-values for which $y = 0$ or all three factors can be found by taking intervals of $\frac{1}{2}$.

   $f(x) = 2x^3 + x^2 - 5x + 2$
   $f(1) = 2 + 1 - 5 + 2$
   $\quad\quad = 0$
   $\therefore (x - 1)$ is a factor
   $\therefore f(x) = (x - 1)(2x^2 + 3x - 2)$
   $\quad\quad = (x - 1)(2x - 1)(x + 2)$

3. $f(x) = 2x^3 + ax^2 + ax - 2$
   $\text{Rem} = f\left(-\frac{1}{2}\right) = b$
   $\therefore 2\left(-\frac{1}{2}\right)^3 + a\left(-\frac{1}{2}\right)^2 + a\left(-\frac{1}{2}\right) - 2 = b$
   $\therefore -\frac{1}{4} + \frac{1}{4}a - \frac{1}{2}a - 2 = b$
   $\therefore -1 + a - 2a - 8 = 4b$
   $\therefore -a = 4b + 9$
   $\therefore a = -4b - 9$

4. $g(x) = x^3 + max^2 + na^2x + 8a^3, a \neq 0$
   $g(a) = 0$ \hfill $(x - a)$ is a factor
   $\therefore a^3 + ma^3 + na^3 + 8a^3 = 0$
   $\therefore 1 + m + n + 8 = 0$ \hfill $\div a^3, a \neq 0$
   $\therefore m + n = -9$ ....①

   $g(-2a) = 0$ \hfill $(x + 2a)$ is a factor
   $\therefore (-2a)^3 + ma(-2a)^2 + na^2(-2a) + 8a^3 = 0$
   $\therefore -8a^3 + 4a^3m - 2a^3n + 8a^3 = 0$
   $\therefore 4a^3m - 2a^3n = 0$ \hfill $\div 2a^3, a \neq 0$
   $\therefore 2m - n = 0$ ....②

   ① + ②: $3m = -9$
   $\therefore m = -3$
   $\therefore n = -6$

5. Let $g(x) = x^3 - 2x + 3yx^2 - 6y$
   $g(-3) = (-3)^3 - 2(-3) + 3y(-3)^2 - 6y$
   $\quad\quad = 0$
   $\therefore (x + 3)$ is a factor of $g(x)$

6. Let $p(x) = x^3 + m^2x^2 - 11x - 15m$
   $(x - 3)$ is a factor of $p(x) \therefore p(3) = 0$
   $\therefore (3)^3 + m^2(3)^2 - 11(3) - 15m = 0$
   $\therefore 27 + 9m^2 - 33 - 15m = 0$
   $\therefore 9m^2 - 15m - 6 = 0$
   $\therefore 3m^2 - 5m - 2 = 0$
   $\therefore (3m + 1)(m - 2) = 0$
   $\therefore m = -\frac{1}{3}$ or $m = 2$

7. Let $f(p) = p^4 - ap^3 - 5p^2 + 8p - b$

   > If $p^2 + p - 2 = (p + 2)(p - 1)$, then $(p + 2)$ and $(p - 1)$ will be factors.

   $\therefore f(-2) = 0$ \hfill $(p + 2)$ is a factor.
   $\therefore 16 + 8a - 20 - 16 - b = 0$
   $\therefore 8a - b = 20$ ....①

   $f(1) = 0$ \hfill $(p - 1)$ is a factor
   $\therefore 1 - a - 5 + 8 - b = 0$
   $\therefore -a - b = -4$ ....②

   ① − ②: $9a = 24$
   $\therefore a = 2\frac{2}{3}$
   $\therefore b = 1\frac{1}{3}$

8.1 Let $f(x) = 2x^3 + m^2x + 81$
   $(x - m)$ is a factor of $f(x) \therefore f(m) = 0$
   $\therefore 2m^3 + m^3 + 81 = 0$
   $\therefore 3m^3 = -81$
   $\therefore m^3 = -27$
   $\therefore m = -3$

8.2 $2x^3 + 9x + 81$ \hfill $m^2 = (-3)^2$
   $= (x + 3)(2x^2 - 6x + 27)$

   > Remember that $(x - m)$ is a factor. $(2x^2 - 6x + 27)$ has no rational factors.

9.1 $f(m) = m^3 - 3m + 2$

$f(1) = 0 \therefore m - 1$ is a factor

$$m^3 - 3m + 2 = (m-1)(m^2 + m - 2)$$
$$= (m - 1)(m + 2)(m - 1)$$
$$= (m - 1)^2(m + 2)$$

9.2 $(3x - 4)^3 - 3(2x - 5) - (3x + 1) = 0$

> Let $m = 3x - 4$ and take away what you had to add in this manner.

$(3x - 4)^3 - 3(3x - 4) + 3x + 3 - 3x - 1 = 0$

$(3x - 4)^3 - 3(3x - 4) + 2 = 0$

$\therefore (3x - 4) = 1$ or $3x - 4 = -2$

$x = \frac{5}{3}$ or $x = \frac{2}{3}$ From the factors in 9.1.

Exercise 2 (page 104)

1. $x^3 + x^2 - 4x - 4 = 0$ The ratio of the coefficients is the same, so factorise.

$x^2(x + 1) - 4(x + 1) = 0$
$(x + 1)(x^2 - 4) = 0$
$(x + 1)(x - 2)(x + 2) = 0$
$x = -1$ or ± 2

2. $2x^3 - 3x^2 - 2x + 3 = 0$
$x^2(2x - 3) - (2x - 3) = 0$
$(2x - 3)(x^2 - 1) = 0$
$(2x - 3)(x - 1)(x + 1) = 0$
$x = \frac{3}{2}$ or ± 1

3. $3x^3 - x^2 + 3x - 1 = 0$
$x^2(3x - 1) + (3x - 1) = 0$
$(3x - 1)(x^2 + 1) = 0$
$x = \frac{1}{3}$

OR $x^2 + 1 = 0$
$\therefore x^2 = -1$
$\therefore$ no real roots (no real solution for x)

Exercise 3 (page 106)

2.1 $f(x) = 2x^3 + 3x^2 - 3x - 2$

$f(-2) = 0$

$\therefore x + 2$ is a factor

$2x^3 + 3x^2 - 3x - 2 = 0$
$2x^2(x + 2) - x^2 - 3x - 2 = 0$
$2x^2(x + 2) - x(x + 2) - x - 2 = 0$
$2x^2(x + 2) - x(x + 2) - (x + 2) = 0$
$(x + 2)(2x^2 - x - 1) = 0$
$(x + 2)(2x + 1)(x - 1) = 0$
$x = -2$ or $-\frac{1}{2}$ or 1

y-intercept is $y = -2$

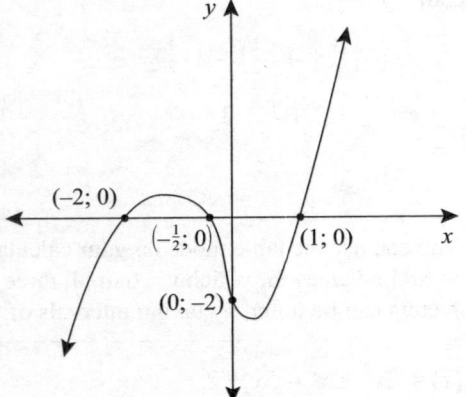

2.2 $f(x) = 2x^3 - 3x^2 - 11x + 6$

$f(3) = 0$

$\therefore x - 3$ is a factor

$2x^3 - 3x^2 - 11x + 6 = 0$
$2x^2(x - 3) + 3x^2 - 11x + 6 = 0$
$2x^2(x - 3) + 3x(x - 3) - 2x + 6 = 0$
$2x^2(x - 3) + 3x(x - 3) - 2(x - 3) = 0$
$(x - 3)(2x^2 + 3x - 2) = 0$
$(x - 3)(2x - 1)(x + 2) = 0$
$x = 3$ or $\frac{1}{2}$ or -2

y-intercept is $y = 6$

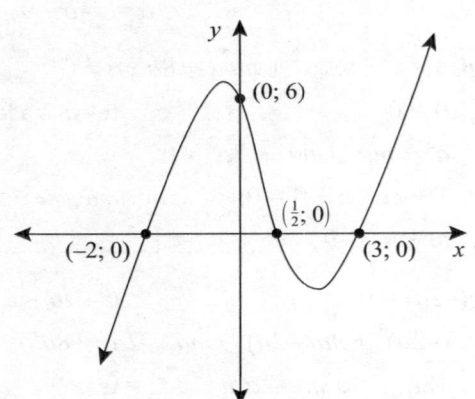

2.3 $f(x) = 2x^3 - x^2 - 18x + 9$ The ratio of the coefficients is the same, so factorise.

$$2x^3 - x^2 - 18x + 9 = 0$$
$$x^2(2x - 1) - 9(2x - 1) = 0$$
$$(2x - 1)(x^2 - 9) = 0$$
$$(2x - 1)(x - 3)(x + 3) = 0$$
$$x = \tfrac{1}{2} \text{ or } 3 \text{ or } -3$$

y-intercept is $y = 9$

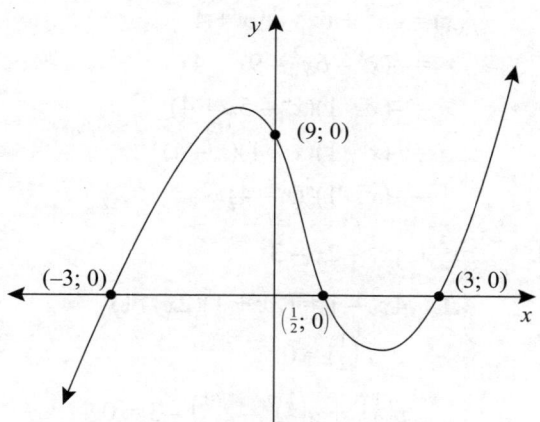

2.4 $f(x) = 3x^3 + 8x^2 + 3x - 2$
$f(-1) = 0$
$\therefore x + 1$ is a factor

$$3x^3 + 8x^2 + 3x - 2 = 0$$
$$3x^2(x + 1) + 5x^2 + 3x - 2 = 0$$
$$3x^2(x + 1) + 5x(x + 1) - 2x - 2 = 0$$
$$3x^2(x + 1) + 5x(x + 1) - 2(x + 1) = 0$$
$$(x + 1)(3x^2 + 5x - 2) = 0$$
$$(x + 1)(x + 2)(3x - 1) = 0$$
$$x = -1 \text{ or } -2 \text{ or } \tfrac{1}{3}$$

y-intercept is $y = -2$

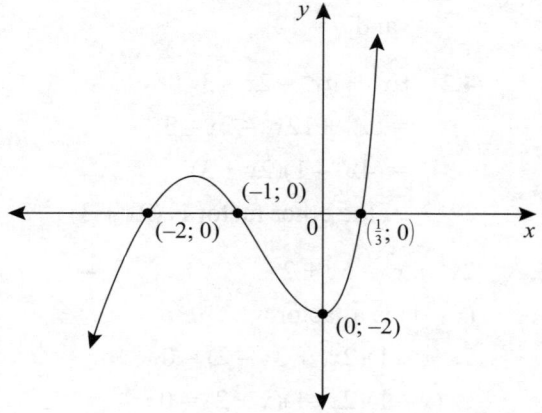

2.5 $f(x) = 2x^3 + 9x^2 - 8x - 15$
$f(-1) = 0$
$x + 1$ is a factor

$$2x^3 + 9x^2 - 8x - 15 = 0$$
$$(x + 1)(2x^2 + 7x - 15) = 0$$
$$(x + 1)(x + 5)(2x - 3) = 0$$
$$x = -1 \text{ or } -5 \text{ or } \tfrac{3}{2}$$

y-intercept is $y = -15$

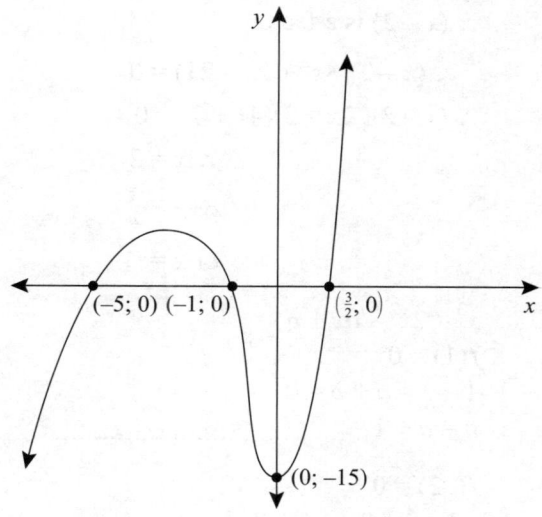

Test A (page 107)

1. $f(x) = x^3 + 3x^2 - 2x - 4$

1.1 $f(-1) = (-1)^3 + 3(-1)^2 - 2(-1) - 4$
$= -1 + 3 + 2 - 4 = 0$ (2)

1.2 $\therefore (x + 1)$ is a factor of $f(x)$, because $f(-1) = 0$
$\therefore x^3 + 3x^2 - 2x - 4 = 0$
$\therefore (x + 1)(x^2 + 2x - 4) = 0$ the trinomial cannot be factorised
$\therefore x = -1$ OR $\left[\frac{-2 \pm \sqrt{4 + 16}}{2}\right]$ use quadratic formula to solve trinomial
$x = -1 \pm \sqrt{5}$ (5)

2. $f(x) = 2x^3 - 26x^2 - 24$

2.1 $f(-3) = 2(-3)^3 - 26(-3)^2 - 24$
$= -54 + 78 - 24 = 0$
$\therefore (x + 3)$ is a factor of $f(x)$ (3)

2.2 $(x + 3)(2x^2 - 6x^2 - 8)$
$= 2(x + 3)(x + 1)(x - 4)$ (4)

3.1 $x^3 - x^2 - 8x + 12 = 0$

$f(2) = 8 - 4 - 16 + 12 = 0$

$\therefore (x - 2)$ is a factor

$\therefore (x - 2)(x^2 + x - 6) = 0$

$\therefore (x - 2)(x - 2)(x + 3) = 0$

$\therefore x = 2$ or $x = 3$ (6)

3.2 $8x^3 - 14x^2 - 25x + 42 = 0$

$f(2) = 8(2)^3 - 14(2)^2 - 25(2) + 42 = 0$

$\therefore (x - 2)$ is a factor

$\therefore (x - 2)(8x^2 + 2x - 21) = 0$

$\therefore (x - 2)(2x - 3)(4x + 7) = 0$

$\therefore x = 2$

or $x = \frac{3}{2}$

or $x = \frac{-7}{4}$ (8)

4. $x^3 - 2x^2 - ax + b$

$f(1) = 0$

$1 - 2 - a + b = 0$

$b = a + 1$ ....①

$f(-2) = 0$

$-8 - 8 + 2a + b = 0$

$b = 16 - 2a$ ....②

$\therefore a + 1 = 16 - 2a$ from ① and ②

$3a = 15$

$\therefore a = 5$ and $b = 6$

$\therefore x^3 - 2x^2 - ax + b = (x^2 + x - 2)(x - 3)$

$\therefore$ the other factor is $x - 3$ (7)

Total: 35

Test B (page 107)

1. $f(x) = x^3 - 3x^2 + 2$

1.1 $f(1) = 1 - 3 + 2 = 0$

$\therefore (x - 1)$ is a factor

$\therefore (x - 1)(x^2 + x - 2)$

$= (x - 1)(x - 1)(x + 2)$ (4)

1.2 $(x - 1)^2(x + 2) \leq 0$ $(x - 1)^2$ is always positive

$\therefore x \leq -2$, but also $x = 1$ (3)

> You could draw a sketch graph to confirm these solutions.

2. $3x^3 + 4x^2 - 5x + 2$

$f(3) = 3(3)^3 + 4(3)^2 - 5(3) + 2$

$= 81 + 36 - 15 + 2 = 104$

$\therefore -104$ must be added for the expression to be divisible by $(x - 3)$. (3)

3. $f(x) = -x^3 + 6x^2 - 9x + 4$

$f(-1) = -(-1)^3 + 6(-1)^2 - 9(-1) + 4$

$\therefore (x - 1)$ is a factor

$f(x) = -x^3 + 6x^2 - 9x + 4$

$= -(x^3 - 6x^2 - 9x - 4)$

$= -(x - 1)(x^2 - 5x + 4)$

$= -(x - 1)(x - 1)(x - 4)$

$= -(x - 1)^2(x - 4)$ (6)

4. $px^3 + qx^2 - 2x - 3$

4.1 $4x^2 - 1 = (2x + 1)(2x - 1)$

$\therefore f\left(\frac{1}{2}\right) = 0$

$p\left(\frac{1}{2}\right)^3 + q\left(\frac{1}{2}\right)^2 - 2\left(\frac{1}{2}\right) - 3 = 0$

$\frac{p}{8} + \frac{q}{4} = 4$

$p + 2q = 32$

$2q = 32 - p$ ....①

and $f\left(-\frac{1}{2}\right) = 0$

$p\left(-\frac{1}{2}\right)^3 + q\left(-\frac{1}{2}\right)^2 - 2\left(-\frac{1}{2}\right) - 3 = 0$

$\frac{-p}{8} + \frac{q}{4} = 2$

$-p + 2q = 16$

$2q = 32 - p$

$2q = 16 + p$ ....②

$16 + p = 32 - p$ (both $= 2q$)

$\therefore 2p = 16$

$\therefore p = 8$

and $q = 12$ (9)

4.2 $px^3 + qx^2 - 2x - 3$

$= 8x^3 + 12x^2 - 2x - 3$

$= (4x^2 - 1)(2x + 3)$

$\therefore$ the other factor is $(2x + 3)$ (2)

5. $2x^3 + x^2 - 5x + 2$

$(x - 1)$ is a factor

$\therefore (x - 1)(2x^2 + 3x - 2) = 0$

$\therefore (x - 1)(2x - 1)(x + 2) = 0$

$\therefore$ the other roots are $x = \frac{1}{2}$ and $x = -2$ (6)

6. $f(x) = x^3 + mx^2 - nx + 8$

6.1 $\quad f(1) = 0$
$\therefore 1 + m - n + 8 = 0$
$\therefore m = n - 9$ ....①

and $f(-4) = 0$
$\therefore (-4)^3 + m(-4)^2 - n(-4) + 8 = 0$
$\therefore -64 + 16m + 4n + 8 = 0$
$\therefore 16m + 4n - 56 = 0$ ....②

$\therefore 16(n - 9) + 4n - 56 = 0$ ① into ②
$\therefore 20n = 200$
$\therefore n = 10$
and $m = 1$ (8)

6.2 $\quad x^3 + x^2 - 10x + 8$
$x - 1(x^2 + 2x - 8) = 0$
$\therefore (x - 1)(x - 2)(x + 4) = 0$
$\therefore x = 1$
or $x = 2$
or $x = -4$ (4)

Total: 45

Test C (page 108)

1.1 If a polynomial $f(x)$ is divided by $(x - a)$ and $(x - a)$ is a factor, then $f(a) = 0$. (2)

1.2 If a polynomial $f(x)$ is divided by $(x - a)$ until the remainder is independent of x, then $f(a) = \mathbb{R}$. (2)

1.3 $f(x) = 5 - 2x^2$
$f(-k) = 5 - 2k^2 = 9k$
$0 = 2k^2 + 9k - 5$
$= (2k - 1)(k + 5)$
$k = \frac{1}{2}$ or $k = -5$ (5)

1.4 $f(x) = x^3 + 3x^2 - 4$

1.4.1 $f(1) = 1^3 + 3(1)^2 - 4 = 0$ (2)

1.4.2 $x^3 + 3x^2 - 4 = 0$
$x - 1$ is a factor because $f(1) = 0$.
$\therefore (x - 1)(x^2 + 4x + 4) = 0$
$\therefore (x - 1)(x + 2)^2 = 0$
$\therefore x = 1$
or $x = -2$ (5)

1.4.3

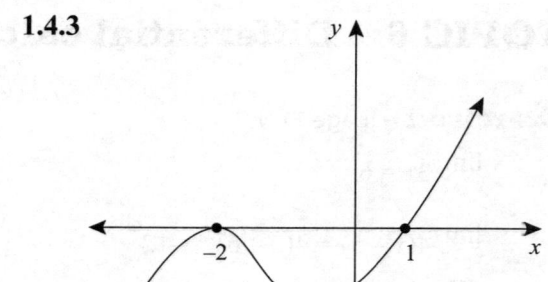

From the sketch:
$x \geq 1$ or $x = -2$
$x \in [1; \infty)$ or $x = -2$ (2)

2.1 $g(5) = 3 \therefore$ remainder $= 3$ (2)

2.2 1 (1)

2.3 For no real roots $\triangle < 0$
$\triangle = b^2 - 4ac \qquad a = 1, b = 3, c = 5$
$= (3)^2 - 4(5)$
$= -11$
$\therefore$ no real roots (3)

3. $f(x) = -(2x^3 + 7x^2 + x - 10)$

3.1 If $x + 2$ is a factor, then $x = -2$ is a root.
$f(-2) = -[2(-2^3) + 7(-2^2) + (-2) - 10]$
$= 0$
$\therefore x + 2$ is a factor. (2)

If $x - 1$ is a factor, then $x = 1$ is a root.
$f(1) = -(2 + 7 + 1 - 10)$
$= 0$
$\therefore x - 1$ is a factor (2)

3.2 Quadratic factor is:
$(x + 2)(x - 1)$
$= x^2 + x - 2$
$\therefore -(2x^3 + 7x^2 + x - 10)$
$= -(x^2 + x - 2)(2x + 5)$
$\therefore$ factor is $2x + 5$ (3)

3.3 $A(-2\frac{1}{2}; 0)$, $B(1; 0)$ (2)

3.4 Increasing, because as x increases, y increases. (2)

3.5 $-2\frac{1}{2} \leq x \leq -2$ and $x \geq 1$
(or you can write $x \in \left[-2\frac{1}{2}; -2\right]$
and $x \in [1; \infty)$ (2)

Total: 37

TOPIC 6 Differential calculus (page 109)

Exercise 1 (page 111)

1. $\lim_{x \to 2} 3x = 6$

2. $\lim_{x \to 2} 4(x - 5) = 4(2 - 5) = -12$

3. $\lim_{x \to -4} \frac{2x^2 + 9x - 5}{2x - 1} = \lim_{x \to -4} \frac{(2x - 1)(x + 5)}{2x - 1}$
   $= \lim_{x \to -4} x + 5 = 1$

4. $\lim_{x \to 1} \frac{x^3 + 64}{x + 4} = \lim_{x \to 1} \frac{(x + 4)(x^2 - 4x + 16)}{x + 4}$
   $= \lim_{x \to 1} x^2 - 4x + 16$
   $= 1 - 4 + 16 = 13$

5. $\lim_{x \to 1\frac{1}{2}} \frac{8x^2 - 8x - 6}{2x - 3} = \lim_{x \to 1\frac{1}{2}} \frac{2(2x - 3)(2x + 1)}{(2x - 3)}$
   $= \lim_{x \to 1\frac{1}{2}} 2(2x + 1)$
   $= 2\left[2\left(1\frac{1}{2}\right) + 1\right] = 8$

6. $\lim_{x \to 3} \frac{x^3 + 3x^2 + x + 3}{x + 3} = \lim_{x \to 3} \frac{(x + 3)(x^2 + 1)}{(x + 3)}$
   $= \lim_{x \to 3} x^2 + 1$
   $= (-3)^2 + 1 = 10$

Exercise 2 (page 115)

1. $f(1) = 4(1)^2 - 3 = 1$
   $f(3) = 4(3)^2 - 3 = 33$

   Method 1: (You can use either method)
   Average gradient $= \frac{f(x + h) - f(x)}{h}$
   $= \frac{33 - 1}{2} = \frac{32}{2} = 16$

   Method 2:
   Average gradient $= \frac{y_2 - y_1}{x_2 - x_1}$
   $= \frac{33 - 1}{3 - 1} = \frac{32}{2} = 16$

2. $f(x + h) = 4(x + h)^2 - 3$
   $= 4(x^2 + 2xh + h^2) - 3$
   $= 4x^2 + 8xh + 4h^2 - 3$

   Average gradient $= \frac{f(x + h) - f(x)}{h}$
   $= \frac{4x^2 + 8xh + 4h^2 - 3 - 4x^2 + 3}{h}$
   $= \frac{8xh + 4h^2}{h}$
   $= \frac{h(8x + 4h)}{h}$
   $= 8x + 4h$

3. $f(-1) = -(-1)^2 - 1 = -2$
   $f(0) = -(0)^2 - 1 = -1$

   Method 1:
   Average gradient $= \frac{f(x + h) - f(x)}{h}$
   $= \frac{-2 - (-1)}{-1 - 0} = \frac{-1}{-1} = 1$

   Method 2:
   Average gradient $= \frac{y_2 - y_1}{x_2 - x_1}$
   $= \frac{-2 - (-1)}{-1 - 0} = \frac{-1}{-1} = 1$

4. $f(x + h) = 2(x + h)^2 + 3$
   $= 2(x^2 + 2xh + h^2) + 3$
   $= 2x^2 + 4xh + 2h^2 + 3$

   Average gradient $= \frac{f(x + h) - f(x)}{h}$
   $= \frac{2x^2 + 4xh + 2h^2 + 3 - 2x^2 - 3}{h}$
   $= \frac{4xh + 2h^2}{h}$
   $= \frac{h(4x + 2h)}{h}$

   Gradient function $= 4x + h$

   Gradient at a point $= \lim_{h \to 0} \frac{f(x + h) - f(x)}{h}$
   $= \lim_{h \to 0} 4x + h$

   Gradient when $x = -3$: $\lim_{h \to 0} 4(-3) + h$
   $= -12$

   Gradient when $x = 9$: $\lim_{h \to 0} 4(9) + h = 36$

Exercise 3 (page 116)

1. $f(x) = 3x^2$
   $f(x + h) = 3(x + h)^2$
   $= 3(x^2 + 2xh + h^2)$
   $f'(x) = \lim_{h \to 0} \frac{f(x + h) - f(x)}{h}$
   $= \lim_{h \to 0} \frac{3x^2 + 6xh + 3h^2 - 3x^2}{h}$
   $= \lim_{h \to 0} \frac{h(6x + 3h)}{h}$
   $= \lim_{h \to 0} 6x + 3h = 6x$

2. $f(x) = 5x - 3$
   $f(x + h) = 5(x + h) - 3 = 5x + 5h - 3$
   $f'(x) = \lim_{h \to 0} \frac{f(x + h) - f(x)}{h}$
   $= \lim_{h \to 0} \frac{5x + 5h - 3 - 5x + 3}{h}$
   $= \lim_{h \to 0} \frac{5h}{h} = 5$

3. $f(x) = -x^2 + 3$
    $f(x+h) = -(x+h)^2 + 3$
    $\qquad = -(x^2 + 2xh + h^2) + 3$
    $f'(x) = \lim_{h \to 0} \frac{f(x+h) - f(x)}{h}$
    $\qquad = \lim_{h \to 0} \frac{-x^2 - 2xh - h^2 + 3 + x^2 - 3}{h}$
    $\qquad = \lim_{h \to 0} \frac{-2xh - h^2}{h}$
    $\qquad = \lim_{h \to 0} \frac{h(-2x - h)}{h}$
    $\qquad = \lim_{h \to 0} -2x - h = -2x$

4. $f(x) = 3x^2 + 3x$
    $f(x+h) = 3(x+h)^2 + 3(x+h)$
    $\qquad = 3(x^2 + 2xh + h^2) + 3(x+h)$
    $\qquad = 3x^2 + 6xh + 3h^2 + 3x + 3h$
    $f'(x) = \lim_{h \to 0} \frac{f(x+h) - f(x)}{h}$
    $\qquad = \lim_{h \to 0} \frac{3x^2 + 6xh + 3h^2 + 3x + 3h - 3x^2 - 3x}{h}$
    $\qquad = \lim_{h \to 0} \frac{6xh + 3h^2 + 3h}{h}$
    $\qquad = \lim_{h \to 0} \frac{h(6x + 3h + 3)}{h}$
    $\qquad = \lim_{h \to 0} 6x + 3h + 3 = 6x + 3$

5. $f'(x) = \lim_{h \to 0} \frac{f(x+h) - f(x)}{h}$
    $\qquad = \lim_{h \to 0} \frac{m(x+h) + c - (mx + c)}{h}$
    $\qquad = \lim_{h \to 0} \frac{mx + mh + c - mx - c}{h}$
    $\qquad = \lim_{h \to 0} \frac{mh}{h} = m$

Exercise 4 (page 117)

1.1 $\frac{d}{dx} = -12x$

1.2 $\frac{-6}{x^3} = -6x^{-3}, \frac{d}{dx} = \frac{18}{x^4}$

1.3 $-6^3\sqrt{x^5} = -6x^{\frac{5}{3}}, \frac{d}{dx} = -10x^{\frac{2}{3}}$

1.4 $\frac{-6x^5 + 3x^2}{x^2} = -6x^3 + 3$
    $\frac{d}{dx} = -18x^2$

1.5 $\frac{2x^2 - 7x + 3}{2x - 1} = \frac{(2x - 1)(x - 3)}{(2x - 1)} = x - 3$
    $\frac{d}{dx} = 1$

2.1 $f(x) = (2x - 5)^2 = 4x^2 - 20x + 25$
    $f'(x) = 8x - 20$

2.2 $f(x) = \frac{x^4 - 3x^2 + 1}{x^2} = x^2 - 3 + x^{-2}$
    $f'(x) = 2x - \frac{2}{x^3}$

3.1 $D_x\left(2\sqrt{x} - \frac{5}{\sqrt{x}}\right) = D_x\left(2x^{\frac{1}{2}} - 5x^{-\frac{1}{2}}\right)$
    $\qquad = x^{-\frac{1}{2}} + \frac{5x^{-\frac{3}{2}}}{2}$
    $\qquad = \frac{1}{x^{\frac{1}{2}}} + \frac{5}{2x^{\frac{3}{2}}}$

3.2 $y = \frac{9 - 5t + 3t^{\frac{1}{2}}}{t} = 9t^{-1} - 5 + 3t^{-\frac{1}{2}}$
    $\frac{dy}{dt} = -9t^{-2} - \frac{3}{2}t^{-\frac{3}{2}}$
    $\qquad = -\frac{9}{t^2} - \frac{3}{2t^{\frac{3}{2}}}$

3.3 $3xy = 3x - 9x^2 + 6$
    $y = \frac{3x - 9x^2 + 6}{3x}$
    $y = 1 - 3x + 2x^{-1}$
    $\frac{dy}{dx} = -3 - 2x^{-2}$
    $\qquad = -3 - \frac{2}{x^2}$

4. $f(x) = \left(6x^2 - \frac{2}{x^2}\right)^2 = 36x^4 - 24 + 4x^{-4}$
    $\frac{df(x)}{dx} = 144x^3 - 16x^{-5}$
    $\qquad = 144x^3 - \frac{16}{x^5}$

5. $y = \frac{4x^2 + 5}{3x^3} = \frac{4x^{-1}}{3} + \frac{5x^{-3}}{3}$
    $\frac{dy}{dx} = -\frac{4}{3}x^{-2} - 5x^{-4}$
    $\qquad = -\frac{4}{3x^2} - \frac{5}{x^4}$

Exercise 5 (page 119)

1. $f(x) = x^2$
    $f'(x) = 2x$
    $f'(-3) = 2(-3) = -6 = m_{\text{tangent}}$
    The point of contact: $(-3; f(-3)) = (-3; 9)$

    The equation of the tangent is:
    $y - y_1 = m(x - x_1)$
    $y - 9 = -6(x + 3)$
    $y - 9 = -6x - 18$
    $\therefore y = -6x - 9$

2. $g(x) = (x - 2)^2 = x^2 - 4x + 4$
    $g(x)$ meets the y-axis at 4.
    Point of contact: $(0; 4)$
    $g'(x) = 2x - 4$

$g'(0) = 2(0) - 4 = -4 = m_{tangent}$

The equation of the tangent is:
$y - y_1 = m(x - x_1)$
$y - 4 = -4(x - 0)$
$y = -4x + 4$

3. $x + y = 3 \therefore y = 3 - x, m_{tangent} = -1$
$h(x) = -2x^2 - x + 4$
$h'(x) = -4x$
$-1 = -4x$
$\therefore x = \frac{1}{4}$
$h\left(\frac{1}{4}\right) = -2\left(\frac{1}{4}\right)^2 - \left(\frac{1}{4}\right) + 4 = \frac{29}{8} = 3\frac{5}{8}$
Point of contact: $\left(\frac{1}{4}; 3\frac{5}{8}\right)$

4. $y = \frac{6}{x} = 6x^{-1}$
$\frac{dy}{dx} = -6x^{-2} = \frac{-6}{x^2}$
$m_{tangent} = \frac{-6}{(-2)^2} = -\frac{3}{2}$
Point of contact: $(-2; -3)$
Equation of tangent: $y - y_1 = m(x - x_1)$
$y - (-3) = -\frac{3}{2}(x - (-2))$
$y + 3 = -\frac{3}{2}x - 3$
$y = -\frac{3}{2}x - 6$

Equation of normal at $(-2; -3)$
$m_{tangent} = \frac{2}{3}$
$y - (-3) = \frac{2}{3}[x - (-2)]$
$y + 3 = \frac{2}{3}x + \frac{4}{3}$
$y = \frac{2}{3}x - \frac{5}{3}$

5.1 $f(x + h) = -(-2 + h)^2 + 1$
$= -(4 - 4h + h^2) + 1$
$= -4 + 4h - h^2 + 1$
$= -3 + 4h - h^2$

$f(-2) = -(-2)^2 + 1 = -3$
Average gradient $= \frac{f(x+h) - f(x)}{h}$
$= \frac{-3 + 4h - h^2 - (-3)}{h}$
$= \frac{4h - h^2}{h}$
$= \frac{h(4 - h)}{h}$
$= 4 - h$

5.2 Gradient at a point $= \lim_{h \to 0} 4 - h = 4$
The gradient of the tangent at the given point $= 4$.
Using $y - y_1 = m(x - x_1): y - (-3) = 4(x - (-2))$
$y + 3 = 4x + 2$
$y = 4x + 5$

5.3 $f(x) = -x^2 + 1$
$f'(x) = -2x$
$-2x = 10 \therefore x = -5$

6. $y = -2x^3 + 4x^2 + 3$
$\frac{dy}{dx} = -6x^2 + 8x$
Gradient at $x = 2$: $m = -6(2)^2 + 8(2) = -8$
Point of contact: $(2; 3)$
Equation: $y - 3 = -8(x - 2)$
$\therefore y = -8x + 19$

7. $y = x^2 + x$
$\frac{dy}{dx} = 2x + 1$
Gradient at $x = -\frac{1}{2}$: $m = 2\left(-\frac{1}{2}\right) + 1 = 0$
Point of contact: $\left(-\frac{1}{2}; -\frac{1}{4}\right)$
Equation: $y = -\frac{1}{4}$ because $m = 0$, so the line is horizontal

8. $y - 3 = x$
$y = x + 3 \therefore m_{tangent} = 1$
$\frac{dy}{dx} = -2x + 6 = 1$
$\therefore -2x = -5$
$x = -\frac{5}{2}$
At $x = -\frac{5}{2}, y = -\left(\frac{5}{2}\right)^2 + 6\left(\frac{5}{2}\right) = \frac{35}{4}$
Using $y - y_1 = m(x - x_1)$
$y - \frac{35}{4} = 1\left(x - \frac{5}{2}\right)$
$y = x + \frac{25}{4}$

Exercise 6 (page 120)

1. $\lim_{h \to 0} \frac{(5-h)^2 - 25}{h} = \lim_{h \to 0} \frac{25 - 10h + h^2 - 25}{h}$
$= \lim_{h \to 0} \frac{h(-10 + h)}{h}$
$= \lim_{h \to 0} -10 + h = -10$

2.1 $D_x(4x^{-3}) = -12x^{-4} = -\frac{12}{x^4}$

2.2 $D_x\left(\frac{x^2 - 3}{3x}\right) = D_x\left(\frac{x^2}{3x} - \frac{3}{3x}\right) = D_x\left(\frac{x}{3} - \frac{1}{x}\right) = \frac{1}{3} + \frac{1}{x^2}$

3.1 $\lim\limits_{h\to 0} \dfrac{f(x+h)-f(x)}{h} = \lim\limits_{h\to 0} \dfrac{5(x^2+2xh+h^2)-5x^2}{h}$

$= \lim\limits_{h\to 0} \dfrac{5x^2+10xh+5h^2-5x^2}{h}$

$= \lim\limits_{h\to 0} \dfrac{h(10x+5h)}{h}$

$= \lim\limits_{h\to 0} 10x+5h = 10x$

3.2 $f(x+h)-f(x)$ is the resulting value in terms of x and h when the given function is subtracted from the function that has been increased by h.

3.3 $\lim\limits_{h\to 0} \dfrac{f(-2+h)-f(-2)}{h} = \lim\limits_{h\to 0} \dfrac{5(-2+h)^2-5(-2)^2}{h}$

$= \lim\limits_{h\to 0} \dfrac{5(4-4h+h^2)-5(4)}{h}$

$= \lim\limits_{h\to 0} \dfrac{20-20h+5h^2-20}{h}$

$= \lim\limits_{h\to 0} \dfrac{h(-20+5h)}{h}$

$= \lim\limits_{h\to 0} -20+5h = -20$

3.4 Point of contact: $(-2; 5(-2)^2) = (-2; 20)$

Gradient at $x = -2$ is -20.

Equation of tangent: $y - y_1 = m(x - x_1)$

$y - 20 = -20[x-(-2)]$

$y - 20 = -20x - 40$

$y = -20x - 20$

4.1 Gradient $= \dfrac{y_2 - y_1}{x_2 - x_1}$

$= \dfrac{3(1+h)^2 - 1 - 2}{1+h-1}$

$= \dfrac{3 + 6h + 3h^2 - 3}{1+h-1}$

$= \dfrac{6h + 3h^2}{h}$

$= \dfrac{h(6+3h)}{h}$

Gradient $= 6 + 3h$

4.2 Gradient of AB when $h = 3$:

$= 6 + 3h = 6 + 3(3) = 15$

5.1 $\dfrac{dy}{dx} = \lim\limits_{h\to 0} \dfrac{-3(x+h)^2 - (-3x^2)}{h}$

$= \lim\limits_{h\to 0} \dfrac{-3(x^2+2xh+h^2) + 3x^2}{h}$

$= \lim\limits_{h\to 0} \dfrac{-3x^2 - 6xh - 3h^2 + 3x^2}{h}$

$= \lim\limits_{h\to 0} \dfrac{h(-6x-3h)}{h}$

$= -6x$

5.2 The gradient function is given as $-6x$. Therefore the gradient at $x = -\frac{1}{6}$.

$m = -6\left(-\frac{1}{6}\right) = 1$

5.3 Point of contact: $\left(-\frac{1}{6}; -3\left[-\frac{1}{6}\right]^2\right) = \left(-\frac{1}{6}; -\frac{1}{12}\right)$

Equation of tangent: $y - y_1 = m(x - x_1)$

$y - \left(-\frac{1}{12}\right) = 1\left[x - \left(-\frac{1}{6}\right)\right]$

$y + \frac{1}{12} = x + \frac{1}{6}$

$y = x + \frac{1}{12}$

6.1 $f(x) = (x+1)(x^2 - 3)$

$= x^3 + x^2 - 3x - 3$

$f'(x) = 3x^2 + 2x - 3$

6.2 $f(x) = \dfrac{x^2 - x - 6}{x+2}$

$= \dfrac{(x-3)(x+2)}{(x+2)}$

$= x - 3$

$f'(x) = 1$

6.3 $f(x) = \dfrac{3}{x} = 3x^{-1}$

$f'(x) = -3x^{-2} = -\dfrac{3}{x^2}$

7.1 $f(3) = (3)^2 - 2 = 7$

$f(1) = (1)^2 - 2 = -1$

$\therefore \dfrac{f(3) - f(1)}{2} = \dfrac{7-(-1)}{2} = 4$

7.2 The answer above represents the average gradient of the curve between the x-values of 3 and 1.

7.3 $f(x+h) = (x+h)^2 - 2 = x^2 + 2xh + h^2 - 2$

$f'(x) = \lim\limits_{h\to 0} \dfrac{f(x+h) - f(x)}{h}$

$= \lim\limits_{h\to 0} \dfrac{x^2 + 2xh + h^2 - 2 - x^2 + 2}{h}$

$= \lim\limits_{h\to 0} \dfrac{2xh + h^2}{h}$

$= \lim\limits_{h\to 0} \dfrac{h(2x+h)}{h}$

$= \lim\limits_{h\to 0} 2x + h = 2x$

7.4 $f'(x) = 2x = 4$

$\therefore x = 2$

$f(x) = x^2 - 2$

$\therefore f(2) = (2)^2 - 2 = 2$

$\therefore M(2; 2)$

Exercise 7 (page 123)

1. $f(x+h) = 2(x+h)^3$

$= 2(x^3 + 3x^2h + 3xh^2 + h^3)$

$= 2x^3 + 6x^2h + 6xh^2 + 2h^3$

$$f'(x) = \lim_{h \to 0} \frac{f(x+h) - f(x)}{h}$$
$$= \lim_{h \to 0} \frac{2x^3 + 6x^2h + 6xh^2 + 2h^3 - 2x^3}{h}$$
$$= \lim_{h \to 0} \frac{h(6x^2 + 6xh + 2h^2)}{h}$$
$$= \lim_{h \to 0} 6x^2 + 6xh + 3h^2$$
$$= 6x^2$$

2. $f(x + h) = a(x + h)^2 + b(x + h) + c$
    $= ax^2 + 2axh + ah^2 + bx + bh + c$

    $$f'(x) = \lim_{h \to 0} \frac{f(x+h) - f(x)}{h}$$
    $$= \lim_{h \to 0} \frac{ax^2 + 2axh + ah^2 + bx + bh + c - ax^2 - bx - c}{h}$$
    $$= \lim_{h \to 0} \frac{2axh + ah^2 + bh}{h}$$
    $$= \lim_{h \to 0} \frac{h(2ax + ah + b)}{h}$$
    $$= \lim_{h \to 0} 2ax + ah + b$$
    $$= 2ax + b$$

3.1 $f(x) = \frac{(x+2)^3}{\sqrt{x}}$
    $= \frac{x^3 + 6x^2 + 12x + 8}{x^{\frac{1}{2}}}$
    $= x^{\frac{5}{2}} + 6x^{\frac{3}{2}} + 12x^{\frac{1}{2}} + 8x^{-\frac{1}{2}}$

    $f'(x) = \frac{5}{2}x^{\frac{3}{2}} + 9x^{\frac{1}{2}} + 6x^{-\frac{1}{2}} - 4x^{-\frac{3}{2}}$
    $= \frac{5}{2}x^{\frac{3}{2}} + 9x^{\frac{1}{2}} + \frac{6}{x^{\frac{1}{2}}} - \frac{4}{x^{\frac{3}{2}}}$

3.2 $f(\beta) = (\beta^{\frac{3}{2}} - 3\beta^{\frac{1}{2}})^2 = \beta^3 - 6\beta + 9\beta^{-1}$
    $f'(\beta) = 3\beta^2 - 6 - 9\beta^{-2}$
    $= 3\beta^2 - 6 - \frac{9}{\beta^2}$

4.1 $\frac{dy}{dx} = -5$

4.2 To find $\frac{dy}{dx}$, rewrite the equation with x as the subject of the formula:
    $5x = 6 - y$
    $x = \frac{6-y}{5}$
    $\therefore \frac{dx}{dy} = -\frac{1}{5}$

4.3 $-5 = 1 \div -\frac{1}{5}$
    $= 1 \times -5 = -5$

5.1 $f(\beta) = \beta - \beta^{\sqrt{3}} + \beta^{-2\sqrt{3}}$
    $f'(\beta) = 1 - \sqrt{3}\beta^{\sqrt{3}-1} - 2\sqrt{3}\beta^{-2\sqrt{3}-1}$
    $= 1 - \sqrt{3}\beta^{\sqrt{3}}\beta^{-1} - 2\sqrt{3}\beta^{-2\sqrt{3}}\beta^{-1}$
    $= 1 - \frac{3\beta^{\sqrt{3}}}{\beta} - \frac{2\sqrt{3}}{\beta^{2\sqrt{3}+1}}$

5.2 $\frac{d}{dx}\left(\frac{dy}{dx}\right)$ if $y = -3x^4 + 4x^3 + 6x^2 - 22$
    $\frac{dy}{dx} = -12x^3 + 12x^2 + 12x$
    $\frac{d}{dx} = -36x^2 + 24x + 12$

    Note: This is called the second derivative.

6. $f(t) = (2t - 1)^2(\sqrt{t} - 1)$
    $= 4t^{\frac{5}{2}} - 4t^2 - 4t^{\frac{3}{2}} + 4t + t^{\frac{1}{2}} - 1$
    $f'(t) = 10t^{\frac{3}{2}} - 8t - 6t^{\frac{1}{2}} + 4 + \frac{1}{2t^{\frac{1}{2}}}$
    $f'(2) = 10(2)^{\frac{3}{2}} - 8(2) - 6(2)^{\frac{1}{2}} + 4 + \frac{1}{2(2)^{\frac{1}{2}}} \approx 8{,}15$

7. $D_t\left(\frac{t^2 - 3t - 2}{2\sqrt{t^3}}\right) = D_t\left(\frac{t^{\frac{1}{2}}}{2} - \frac{3t^{-\frac{7}{2}}}{2}\right)$
    $= \frac{1}{4t^{\frac{1}{2}}} + \frac{21}{4t^{\frac{9}{2}}}$

Exercise 8 (page 127)

1.1 $f(1) = 1^3 - 1^2 - 1 + 1 = 0$
    $\therefore (x - 1)$ is a factor of $f(x)$
    $f(x) = (x - 1)(x^2 - 1)$
    $= (x - 1)^2(x + 1)$
    $\therefore x = 1$ or $x = -1$

1.2 $f'(x) = 3x^2 - 2x - 1$
    $0 = (3x + 1)(x - 1)$
    $x = -\frac{1}{3}$ or $x = 1$
    $f\left(-\frac{1}{3}\right) = \left(-\frac{1}{3}\right)^3 - \left(-\frac{1}{3}\right)^2 - \left(-\frac{1}{3}\right) + 1 = \frac{32}{27}$
    $f(1) = 1^3 - 1^2 - 1 + 1 = 0$

    Shape: $a > 0$ $\therefore$

    $\therefore \left(-\frac{1}{3}; \frac{32}{27}\right)$ is a local maximum and $(1; 0)$ the local minimum

1.3 Note that when a factor of is $f(x)$ is $(x \pm p)^2$, the graph will have a turning point at p on the x-axis.

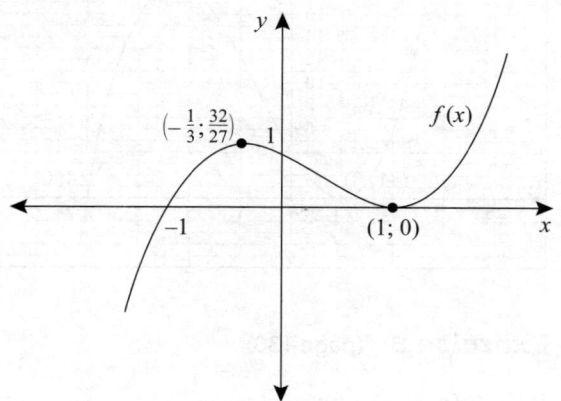

1.4 $f(x) > 0$ where $x > -1$, $x \neq 1$

1.5 $f'(x) > 0$ where $x < -\frac{1}{3}$ or $x > 1$

1.6 $f'(-2) = 3(-2)^2 - 2(-2) - 1 = 15$
∴ $m_{tangent} = 15$

$f(-2) = (-2)3 - (-2)2 - (-2) + 1 = -9$
∴ Point of contact: $(-2; -9)$

Equation of tangent:
Using $y - y_1 = m(x - x_1)$:
$y + 9 = 15(x + 2)$
$y = 15x + 21$

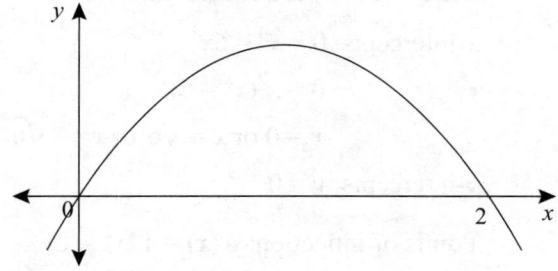

2. $y = x^3 + 3x^2 - 9x - 27$

2.1 Shape: $a > 0$ ∴

y-intercept: $y = -27$
x-intercepts: $x^3 + 3x^2 - 9x - 27 = 0$
$f(3) = 0$ ∴ $(x - 3)(x^2 + 6x + 9) = 0$
∴ $(x - 3)(x + 3)(x + 3) = 0$
∴ $x = 3$ or $x = -3$

Local maximum and minimum points:
$f'(x) = 3x^2 + 6x - 9$
$0 = (x + 3)(x - 1)$
$x = -3$ or $x = 1$

$f(-3) = (-3)^3 + 3(-3)^2 - 9(-3) - 27 = 0$
$f(1) = 1^3 + 3(1)^2 - 9(1) - 27 = -32$
Turning points: $(-3; 0)$ and $(1; -32)$

Point of inflection:
$f'(x) = 3x^2 + 6x - 9$
$f''(x) = 6x + 6$
$0 = 6x + 6$
$x = -1$
$f(-1) = (-1)^3 + 3(-1)^2 - 9(-1) - 27$
$= -16$

Point of inflection: $(-1; -16)$
$f''(-3) = -12$, so $f'(-3) < 0$
∴ f is concave down at $x = -3$
$f''(1) = 12$, so $f''(1) > 0$
∴ f is concave up at $x = 1$

Local maximum: $(-3; 0)$ and local minimum: $(1; -32)$

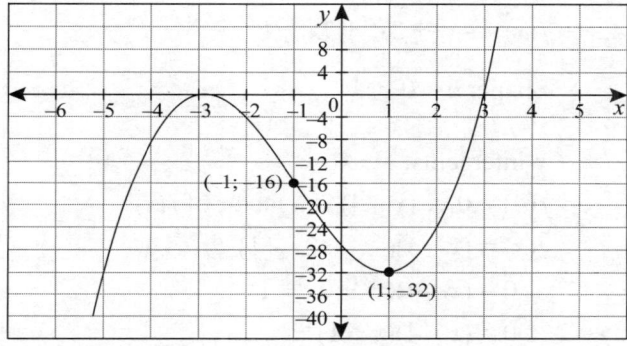

2.2 This graph is increasing for $x \in (-\infty, -3)$ or $x \in (1; \infty)$

2.3 $f(x) < 0$ for $x < 3$, $x \neq -3$

3. $f(x) = 5 + 3x^2 - x^3$
$f'(x) = 6x - 3x^2$
$0 = 3x(2 - x)$
$x = 0$ or $x = 2$ (x-values of turning point)

$f''(x) = 6 - 6x$
$0 = 6 - 6x$, $x = 1$
$f(1) = 5 + 3(1)^2 - (1)^3 = 7$
$(1; 7)$ is a point of inflection.

$f''(0) = 6$ ∴ $f''(x) > 0$ at $x = 0$
∴ f is concave up at $x = 0$
$f(0) = 5$ ∴ $(0; 5)$ is a local minimum

$f''(2) = -6 \therefore f''(x) < 0$ at $x = 2$

$\therefore f$ is concave down at $x = 2$

$f(2) = 5 + 3(2)^2 - (2)^3 = 9$

$\therefore (2; 9)$ is a local maximum

Function is increasing where $f'(x) > 0$.

$6x - 3x^2 > 0$

$3x(2 - x) > 0$

$0 < x < 2$

Function is decreasing where $f'(x) < 0$

$3x(2 - x) < 0$

$x < 0$ or $x > 2$

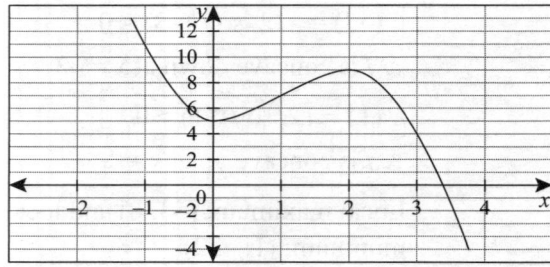

4. $f(x) = -x^3 + 2x^2 + 7x + 4$

Shape: $a < 0$ ∴

x-intercepts:

$f(4) = 0 \therefore (x - 4)$ is a factor of $f(x)$

$f(x) = (x - 4)(-x^2 - 2x - 1)$

$0 = (x - 4)(x^2 + 2x + 1)$

$0 = (x - 4)(x + 1)^2$

$x = 4$ or $x = -1$

y-intercept = 4

Turning points:

$f'(x) = -3x^2 + 4x + 7$

$0 = -3x^2 + 4x + 7$

$0 = 3x^2 - 4x - 7$

$0 = 3x^2 - 4x - 7$

$0 = (x + 1)(3x - 7)$

$x = -1$ or $x = \frac{7}{3}$

$f(-1) = -(-1)^3 + 2(-1)^2 + 7(-1) + 4 = 0$

$f\left(\frac{7}{3}\right) = -\left(\frac{7}{3}\right)^3 + 2\left(\frac{7}{3}\right)^2 + 7\left(\frac{7}{3}\right) + 4 \approx 18{,}5$

Local minimum: $(-1; 0)$

Local maximum: $\left(\frac{7}{3}; 18{,}5\right)$

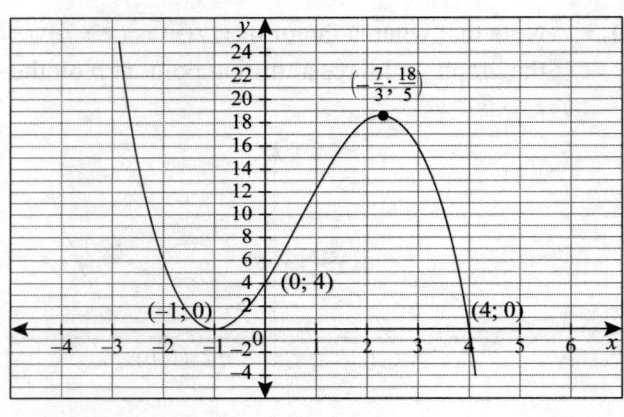

Exercise 9 (page 130)

1. $g(x) = x^4 - 6x^2$

$g'(x) = 4x^3 - 12x$

$4x^3 - 12x = 0$

$4x(x^2 - 3) = 0$

$x = 0$ or $x = \sqrt{3}$ or $x = -\sqrt{3}$

$g''(x) = 12x^2 - 12$

$g''(\sqrt{3}) = 24 \therefore g$ is concave up at $x = \sqrt{3}$, and $(\sqrt{3}; -9)$ is a local minimum

$g''(0) = -12 \therefore g$ is concave down at $x = 0$, and $(0; 0)$ is a local maximum

$g''(-\sqrt{3}) = 24 \therefore g$ is concave up at $x = -\sqrt{3}$, and $(-\sqrt{3}; -9)$ is a local minimum

x-intercepts: $0 = x^4 - 6x^2$

$0 = x^2(x^2 - 6)$

$x = 0$ or $x = \sqrt{6}$ or $x = -\sqrt{6}$

y-intercepts: $y = 0$

Points of inflection: $g'(x) = 12x^2 - 12$

$0 = 12(x^2 - 1)$

$x = 1$ or $x = -1$

$g(1) = g(-1) = 1 - 6 = 5$

$(1; 5)$ and $(-1; 5)$

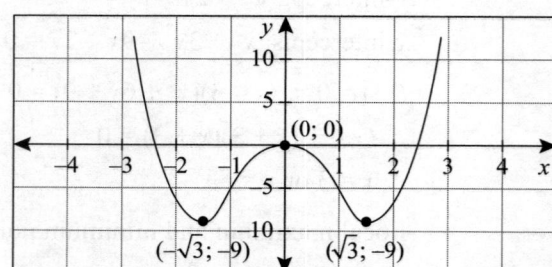

2. $g(x) = x + 4x^{-1}$

$g'(x) = 1 - \frac{4}{x^2}$

$0 = 1 - \frac{4}{x^2}$

$0 = x^2 - 4$

$x = 2$ or $x = -2$

$g''(x) = 8x^{-3}$

$g''(2) = 8(2)^{-3} = 1$

At $x = 2$, $g''(x) > 0$

$\therefore g$ is concave up at $x = 2$

$g''(-2) = 8(-2)^{-3} = -1$

At $x = -2$, $g''(x) < 0$

$\therefore g$ is concave down at $x = -2$

3. $f(x) = x^3 - 3x^2 + 3x + 2$

3.1 y-intercept $y = 2$

x-intercept $x \approx -0{,}44$

$f''(x) = 6x - 6$

$0 = 6x - 6$

$\therefore x = 1, y = 3$

Point of inflection: (1; 3)

3.2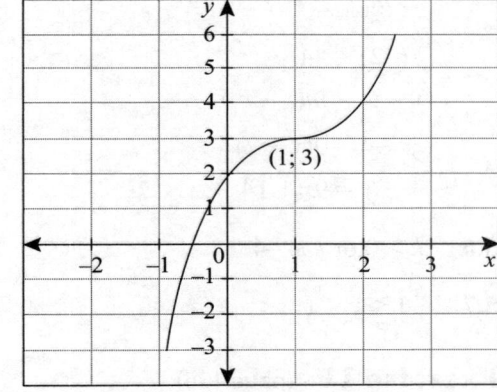

3.3 $x < -0{,}44$

3.4 For all values of $x \in$ R, $x \neq 1$.
Gradient is neither positive or negative at point of inflection.

4. $f(x) = ax^3 + bx^2 + cx + d$

4.1 $f(1) = f(4) = 0$ x-intercepts

$f(0) = f(3) = 4$ points (0; 4) and (3; 4) lie on the graph

$f'(1) = f'(3) = 0$ x-values of the turning points

$f'(x) > 0$ for $1 < x < 3$ graph is increasing in this interval

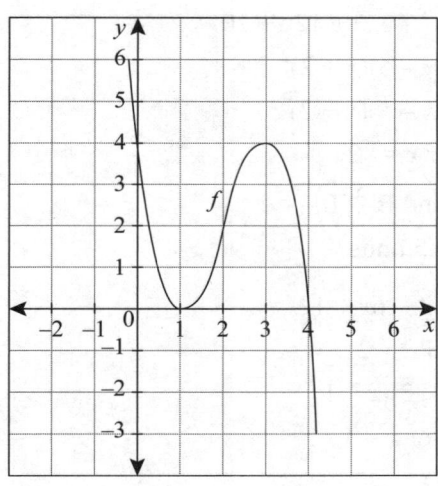

Exercise 10 (page 133)

1. $f(x) = a(x + 2)(x + 1)(x - 1)$

From the graph: $f(0) = 2$

$\therefore f(0) = a(0 + 2)(0 + 1)(0 - 1)$

$2 = a(2)(1)(-1)$

$2 = -2a$

$\therefore a = -1$

$\therefore f(x) = -1(x + 2)(x^2 - 1)$

$= -x^3 - 2x^2 + x + 2$

2. $f(x) = a(x + 3)(x - 1)(x - 1)$

From the graph: $f(0) = 3$

$\therefore f(0) = a(0 + 3)(0 - 1)(0 - 1)$

$3 = a(3)(-1)(-1)$

$3a = 3$

$\therefore a = 1$

$\therefore f(x) = 1(x + 3)(x - 1)^2$

$= 1(x + 3)(x^2 - 2x + 1)$

$= x^3 + x^2 - 5x + 3$

3. $f(x) = x^3 + ax^2 + bx - 4$

$f'(x) = 3x^2 + 2ax + b$

$f'(1) = 3(1)^2 + 2a(1) + b$

$0 = 3 + 2a + b$

$\therefore b = -3 - 2a$ ....①

$f'(3) = 3(3)^2 + 2a(3) + b$

$0 = 27 + 6a + b$

$\therefore b = -27 - 6a$ ....②

Putting ① = ②: $-2a - 3 = -6a - 27$

$4a = -24$

$a = -6$

$b = -2(-6) - 3$

$b = 9$

4.1 $g(x) = -2x^3 - 3x^2 + 12x + 20$
$g(x) = -(2x - 5)(x + 2)^2$
$0 = -(2x - 5)(x + 2)^2$
$\therefore x = \frac{5}{2}$ or $x = -2$
A(-2; 0) and B$\left(\frac{5}{2}; 0\right)$
$\therefore$ AB = 4,5 units

4.2 $g'(x) = -6x^2 - 6x + 12$
$0 = x^2 + x - 2$
$0 = (x + 2)(x - 1)$
$\therefore x = -2$ or $x = 1$
$\therefore$ T(1; 27)

4.3 $g'(-3) = -6(-3)^2 - 6(-3) + 12 = -24$
$\therefore m_{tangent} = -24$
$y - y_1 = m(x - x_1)$
$y - 11 = -24(x + 3)$
$y = -24x - 61$

4.4 $0 < k < 27$

4.5 $g''(x) = -12x - 6$
$0 = -2x - 1$
$2x = -1$
$x = -\frac{1}{2}$
$g\left(-\frac{1}{2}\right) = -2\left(-\frac{1}{2}\right)^3 - 3\left(-\frac{1}{2}\right)^2 + 12\left(-\frac{1}{2}\right) + 20$
$g\left(-\frac{1}{2}\right) = \frac{27}{2}$
Point of inflection: $\left(-\frac{1}{2}; \frac{27}{2}\right)$

4.6 $x > \frac{5}{2}$

4.7 $x < -2$ or $x > 1, x \in \mathbb{R}$
OR can be written $(-\infty; -2) \cup (1; \infty)$

5.1 $x = 2 \therefore$ A(2; 0)   from $g(x)$

5.2 $f(x) = ax^3 - cx - 2$
$0 = a(-1)^3 - c(-1) - 2$
$2 = c - a$ .... ①
$0 = a(2)^3 - c(2) - 2$
$1 = -c + 4a$ .... ②
① + ②: $2 = c - a$ .... ①
           $1 = -c + 4a$ .... ②
           $3 = 3a$
$a = 1$

$\therefore 2 = c - 1$ .... ①
$\therefore c = 3$

5.3 $f(x) = x^3 - 3x - 2$
$f'(x) = 3x^2 - 3$
$0 = x^2 - 1$
$x = 1$ or $x = -1$
$f(1) = (1)^3 - 3(1) - 2 = -4$
B(1; -4)

5.4 $x^3 - 3x - 2 = x - 2$
$x^3 - 4x = 0$
$x(x^2 - 4) = 0$
$x(x - 2)(x + 2) = 0$
$x = 0$ or $x = -2$ or $x = 2$
$\therefore$ C(-2; -4), B(1; -4)
$m_{BC} = \frac{-4 - (-4)}{1 - (-2)} = \frac{0}{3} = 0$
The gradient of the x-axis is also = 0
$\therefore$ BC $\parallel$ x-axis

5.5 $f'(x) = 3x^2 - 3$
$f'(-2) = 3(-2)^2 - 3 = 9$
$\therefore m_{tangent} = 9$
$f(-2) = -4$
$y - y_1 = m(x - x_1)$
$y + 4 = 9(x + 2)$
$y = 9x + 14$

5.6 $k > 0$ or $k < -4$

5.7 $-1 < x < 1$

Exercise 11   (page 136)

1.1 Gradient = -4 $g'(x)$ is a parabola

1.2 $x < 3$

1.3 Minimum value because the curve goes from a negative to a positive gradient.

2. $g(x) = x^3 + 3x^2 - 4$
$g'(x) = 3x^2 + 6x$
$0 = 3x(x + 2)$
$g(x)$ is increasing where $g'(x) > 0$
$3x(x + 2) > 0$
$x < -2$ or $x > 0$

3.1 $h(x) = 2x^3 + x^2 + x - 4$
$h'(x) = 6x^2 + 2x + 1$
$0 = 6x^2 + 2x + 1$
$\Delta = b^2 - 4ac = 2^2 - 4(6)(1) = -20$
∴ roots are non-real
∴ no x-values exist for $h'(x) = 0$
∴ no maximum or minimum points exist for $h(x)$

3.2 $h''(x) = 12x + 2$
$0 = 12x + 2$
$x = -\frac{1}{6}, y = 2(-\frac{1}{6})^3 + (-\frac{1}{6})^2 + (-\frac{1}{6}) - 4 = -\frac{112}{27}$
Coordinates: $(-\frac{1}{6}; -\frac{112}{27})$

4.1 $(-\infty; 4)$

4.2 $(1; 3)$

4.3 $(1; 2)$

4.4 $x \leq 1$ and $3 \leq x \leq 4$
OR can be written $(-\infty; 1] \cup [3; 4]$

5. $f(x) = ax^3 + bx^2 + cx + 2$
$f'(x) = 3ax^2 + 2bx + c$
Turning point = point of inflection: (0; 2)
$f'(0) = 3a(0)^2 + 2b(0) + c$
$f'(0) = c$
$c = 0$
$f''(x) = 6ax + 2b$
$f''(0) = 2b$
$2b = 0$
∴ $b = 0$
Substitute for point (1; 0), c and b.
$f(x) = ax^3 + bx^2 + cx + 2$
$0 = a + b + c + 2$
$0 = a + 2$
∴ $a = -2$
Equation ∴ $f(x) = -2x^3 + 2$

6. $f'(x) = -5x^2 - 7x + 6$

6.1 $f(x)$ is decreasing where $f'(x) < 0$
$-5x^2 - 7x + 6 < 0$
$5x^2 + 7x - 6 > 0$
$(5x - 3)(x + 2) > 0$
$x < -2$ or $x > \frac{3}{5}$

6.2 $f(0) = 2$ ∴ the y-intercept is 2
$f'(x) = -5x^2 - 7x + 6$
$f(x) = -\frac{5}{3}x^3 - \frac{7}{2}x^2 + 6x + 2$

Exercise 12 (page 142)

1. $2(x + l) = \frac{1}{6}$
$x + l = 53$
∴ $l = 53 - x$
$A(x) = x(53 - x)$
$A(x) = 53x - x^2$
$A'(x) = 53 - 2x$
$0 = 53 - 2x$
$x = 26,5$ cm
∴ $l = 26,5$ cm
The maximum area of the rectangle is 702,25 cm².

2.1 $\frac{dh}{dt} = 25 - 10t$

2.2 At $t = 1,5$: velocity = $25 - 10(1,5) = 10$ m/s

2.3 Average velocity = $\frac{31,25 - 20}{2,5 - 1} = 7,5$ m/s

2.4 $0 = 25 - 10t$
$t = 2,5$ seconds
$h = 25(2,5) - 5(2,5)^2 = 31,25$ m
The stone reaches its maximum height of 31,25 m after 2,5 seconds. Its speed at this point is 0 m/s, as it is a stationary point where $f'(x) = 0$.

3.1 $f(x) = x^3 - 8x^2 + 5x + 50$
$= (-x + 5)(-x^2 + 3x + 10)$
∴ $A(x) = (-x^2 + 3x + 10)$ area = lbh

3.2 $A'(x) = -2x + 3$
$0 = -2x + 3$
$x = \frac{3}{2}$

4.1 $36 - x$

4.2 $l = x - 4, b = 36 - x - 4 = 32 - x$

4.3 $A(x) = (x - 4)(32 - x)$
$A(x) = -x^2 + 36x - 128$

4.4 $A'(x) = -2x + 36$
$x = 18$ cm
Dimensions of mirror: 18 cm × 18 cm

5.1 $\text{Vol} = \pi r^2 h$

$200 = \pi r^2 h$

$h = \dfrac{200}{\pi r^2}$

5.2 $S(r) = \pi r^2 + 2\pi rh$

$S(r) = \pi r^2 + 2\pi r\left(\dfrac{200}{\pi r^2}\right)$

$S(r) = \pi r^2 + \dfrac{400}{r}$

5.3 $S'(r) = 2\pi r + 400r^{-2}$

$0 = 2\pi r^3 - 400$

$r = \sqrt[3]{\dfrac{400}{2\pi}} \approx 3{,}99$

6.1 $s = 6(9) - 24\sqrt{9} + 30 = 12$ mm

6.2 $s(t) = 6t - 24t^{\frac{1}{2}} + 30$

$s'(t) = 6 - 12t^{-\frac{1}{2}}$

$0 = 6 - 12t^{-\frac{1}{2}}$

$12t^{-\frac{1}{2}} = 6$

$t^{-\frac{1}{2}} = \dfrac{1}{2}$

$\left(t^{-\frac{1}{2}}\right)^{-2} = (2^{-1})^{-2}$

$t = 4$ seconds

Exercise 13 (page 144)

1. $y = x^3 + 2x^2 + 9x + 8$

$\dfrac{dy}{dx} = 3x^2 + 4x + 9$

$0 = 3x^2 + 4x + 9$

$x = \dfrac{-4 \pm \sqrt{(4)^2 - 4(3)(9)}}{2(3)}$

$\therefore x = \dfrac{-4 \pm \sqrt{-92}}{6}$

This equation cannot be factorised and has no real values for x. Therefore there are no maximum of minimum values for this curve.

2.1 $y = x^2 \sin 60° - 8x \cos 60°$

$= x^2\left(\dfrac{\sqrt{3}}{2}\right) - 8x\left(\dfrac{1}{2}\right)$

$= \dfrac{\sqrt{3}}{2}x^2 - 4x$

$\dfrac{dy}{dx} = 2\left(\dfrac{\sqrt{3}}{2}\right)x - 4$

$= \sqrt{3}x - 4$

$0 = \sqrt{3}x - 4$

$x = \dfrac{4}{\sqrt{3}} = 2{,}309401$ km$\ldots \approx 2\,309$ m

Maximum height this projectile can reach is 2 309 m.

2.2 $y = \dfrac{\sqrt{3}}{2}x^2 - 4x$ from 2.1

$0 = \dfrac{\sqrt{3}}{2}x^2 - 4x$ vertical height = 0 at ground level

$0 = x\left(\dfrac{\sqrt{3}}{2}x - 4\right)$

$x = 0$ km or $x = \dfrac{8}{\sqrt{3}} = 4{,}618802\ldots \approx 5$ km

2.3 Gradient at origin: $\dfrac{dy}{dx} = \sqrt{3}x - 4$

$0 = \sqrt{3}x - 4$

$x = \dfrac{4}{\sqrt{3}}$

$\tan\theta = \dfrac{4}{\sqrt{3}}$ angle of inclination formula

$\theta = 66{,}58\ldots \approx 69°$

Launch angle $\approx 69°$

3.1 Length of wire for perimeter of the square $= 4 - x$

One side of the square $= \dfrac{4-x}{4}$

Area of square $= \left(\dfrac{4-x}{4}\right)^2 = \dfrac{16 - 8x + x^2}{16}$

Circumference of the circle: $2\pi r = x \therefore r = \dfrac{x}{2\pi}$

Area of circle $= \pi r^2 = \pi\left(\dfrac{x^2}{4\pi^2}\right) = \dfrac{x^2}{4\pi}$

Combined area $= \dfrac{16 - 8x + x^2}{16} + \dfrac{x^2}{4\pi}$

$\therefore f(x) = 1 - \dfrac{1}{2}x + \dfrac{1}{16}x^2 - \dfrac{1}{4\pi}x^2$

3.2 $f'(x) = -\dfrac{1}{2} + \dfrac{1}{8}x + \dfrac{1}{2\pi}x$

$\therefore 0 = -\dfrac{1}{2} + \dfrac{1}{8}x + \dfrac{1}{2\pi}x$ LCD: 8π

$0 = -4\pi + \pi x + 4x$

$4\pi = x(\pi + 4)$

$x = \dfrac{4\pi}{\pi + 4} \approx 1{,}759 \approx 1{,}76$ m

4.1 $r^2 = (5\sqrt{3})^2 - x^2$ Pythagoras

$r^2 = 75 - x^2$

Volume of a cylinder $= \pi r^2 h = \pi(75 - x^2)2x$

$V(x) = 150\pi x - 2\pi x^3$

4.2 $V'(x) = 150\pi - 6\pi x^2$

$0 = 150\pi - 6\pi x^2$

$0 = 6\pi(25 - x^2)$

$x = 5$ or $x = -5$

$x > 0 \therefore x = 5$

Height of cylinder $= 2 \times 5 = 10$ cm

5.1 Vol of cone $= \frac{1}{3}\pi r^2 h = 90$

$\therefore h = \frac{90 \times 3}{\pi r^2}$

But height of cone $= h - 3$

$\therefore h - 3 = \frac{270}{\pi r^2}$

$h = \frac{270}{\pi r^2} + 3$

$h = \frac{270 + 3\pi r^2}{\pi r^2}$

5.2 Total surface area without base: $= \pi rs + 2\pi rh$

$S(r) = \pi r(7) + 2\pi r\left(\frac{270 + 3\pi r^2}{\pi r^2}\right)$

$S(r) = 7\pi r + 540 r^{-1} + 6\pi r$

$S(r) = 13\pi r + 540 r^{-1}$

$S'(r) = 13\pi - 540 r^{-2}$

$0 = 13\pi r^2 - 540$

$r = \sqrt{\frac{540}{13\pi}} \approx 3{,}64 \text{ cm}$

$S(3{,}64) = 13\pi(3{,}64) + 540(3{,}64)^{-1}$

$\approx 297{,}01 \text{ cm}^2$

Maximum total surface area to the nearest square cm $= 297 \text{ cm}^2$.

Test A (page 146)

1.1 $f(x) = x^3 \cdot f(x+h) = (x+h)^3$

$= x^3 + 3x^2 h + 3xh^2 + h^3$

$f'(x) = \lim_{h \to 0} \frac{f(x+h) - f(x)}{h}$

$= \lim_{h \to 0} \frac{x^3 + 3x^2 h + 3xh^2 + h^3 - x^3}{h}$

$= \lim_{h \to 0} \frac{h(3x^2 + 3xh + h^2)}{h}$

$= \lim_{h \to 0} 3x^2 + 3xh + h^2$

$= 3x^2$ (5)

1.2 Average gradient $= \frac{f(x+h) - f(x)}{h}$

$= \frac{f(1) - f(-3)}{4}$

$= \frac{1 + 27}{4} = 7$ (3)

2.1 $y = \frac{2}{3\sqrt{x}} - \sqrt[5]{x}$

$= \frac{2}{3}x^{-\frac{1}{2}} - x^{\frac{1}{5}}$

$\frac{dy}{dx} = -\frac{1}{3}x^{-\frac{3}{2}} - \frac{1}{5}x^{-\frac{4}{5}}$

$= \frac{-\frac{1}{3}}{x^{\frac{3}{2}}} - \frac{\frac{1}{5}}{x^{\frac{4}{5}}}$ (4)

2.2 $y = \frac{x^4 + 3x^2 - 5}{x}$

$y = x^3 + 3x - 5x^{-1}$

$\frac{dy}{dx} = 3x^2 + 3 + 5x^{-2}$

$= 3x^2 + 3 + \frac{5}{x^2}$ (4)

3. $f(x) = x^3 + x^2 - 5x + 3$

3.1 $f(1) = 1^3 + 1^2 - 5 + 3 = 0$

$\therefore (x - 1)$ is a factor of $f(x)$

$f(x) = (x - 1)(x^2 + 2x - 3)$

$= (x - 1)(x - 1)(x + 3)$

x-intercepts: $x = 1$ or $x = -3$

y-intercept: $y = 3$ (5)

3.2 $f'(x) = 3x^2 + 2x - 5$

$0 = (3x + 5)(x - 1)$

$x = 1$ or $x = -\frac{5}{3}$

$f\left(-\frac{5}{3}\right) = \left(-\frac{5}{3}\right)^3 + \left(-\frac{5}{3}\right)^2 - 5\left(-\frac{5}{3}\right) + 3$

$= \frac{256}{27} \approx 9{,}48$

Turning points: $(1; 0)$ and $\left(-\frac{5}{3}; \frac{256}{27}\right)$ (5)

3.3 $f''(x) = 6x + 2$

$0 = 6x + 2$

$x = -\frac{1}{3}$

$\therefore f\left(-\frac{1}{3}\right) = \left(-\frac{1}{3}\right)^3 + \left(-\frac{1}{3}\right)^2 - 5\left(-\frac{1}{3}\right) + 3$

$= \frac{128}{27}$

Point of inflection: $\left(-\frac{1}{3}; \frac{128}{27}\right)$ (3)

3.4

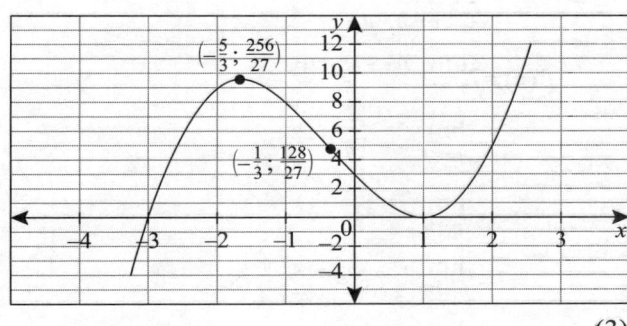

(3)

3.5 $f'(2) = 3(2)^2 + 2(2) - 5 = 11$

$m_{\text{tangent}} = 11$

$f(2) = 2^3 + 2^2 - 5(2) + 3 = 5$

Point of contact: (2; 5)
$$y - y_1 = m(x - x_1)$$
$$y - 5 = 11(x - 2)$$
$$y = 11x - 17 \quad (3)$$

3.6 $x = 2$ or $x = -\frac{2}{3}$ (2)

4. $f(x) = a(x - 1)^2(x - 4)$
Substitute for (0; 4):
$$4 = a(-1)^2(-4)$$
$$4 = -4a$$
$$a = -1$$
$$f(x) = -1(x - 1)^2(x - 4)$$
$$= -x^3 + 6x^2 - 9x + 4 \quad (6)$$

5.1 Area $= \frac{bh}{2} = \frac{(x+2)(3-x)}{2}$
$$A(x) = \frac{-x^2 + x + 6}{2}$$
$$A(x) = \frac{-x^2}{2} + \frac{x}{2} + 3 \quad (2)$$

5.2 $A'(x) = -x + \frac{1}{2}$
$$0 = -x + \frac{1}{2}$$
$$x = \frac{1}{2} \quad (3)$$

5.3 $A\left(\frac{1}{2}\right) = -\frac{\left(\frac{1}{2}\right)^2}{2} + \frac{\left(\frac{1}{2}\right)^2}{2} + 3 = \frac{25}{8} \approx 3{,}125$ units^2 (2)

Total: 50

Test B (page 147)

1. $f(x) = \frac{1}{x^2}$
$$f(x) = \frac{1}{(x+h)^2}$$
$$= \frac{1}{(x^2 + 2xh + h^2)}$$
$$f'(x) = \lim_{h \to 0} \frac{f(x+h) - f(x)}{h}$$
$$= \lim_{h \to 0} \frac{\frac{1}{x^2 + 2xh + h^2} - \frac{1}{x^2}}{h}$$
$$= \lim_{h \to 0} \frac{\frac{x^2 - (x^2 + 2xh + h^2)}{x^2(x^2 + 2xh + h^2)}}{h}$$
$$= \lim_{h \to 0} \frac{x^2 - x^2 - 2xh - h^2}{x^2(x^2 + 2xh + h^2)} \times \frac{1}{h}$$
$$= \lim_{h \to 0} \frac{-2xh - h^2}{x^2(x^2 + 2xh + h^2)} \times \frac{1}{h}$$
$$= \lim_{h \to 0} \frac{h(-2x - h)}{x^2(x^2 + 2xh + h^2)} \times \frac{1}{h}$$
$$= \lim_{h \to 0} \frac{(-2x - h)}{x^2(x^2 + 2xh + h^2)}$$
$$= \frac{-2x - 0}{x^2[x^2 + 2x(0) + 0^2]} = \frac{-2x}{x^4} = \frac{-2}{x^3} \quad (5)$$

2. $f'(x) = 21x^2 - 3$
$$0 = 3(7x^2 - 1)$$
$$x = \pm\sqrt{\frac{1}{7}}$$
$$f''(x) = 42x$$
$$f''\left(\sqrt{\frac{1}{7}}\right) = 42\left(\sqrt{\frac{1}{7}}\right) = \frac{42}{\sqrt{7}}$$
$$f''(x) > 0 \text{ at } x = \sqrt{\frac{1}{7}}$$
$\therefore f(x)$ is concave up at this point.
$$f''\left(-\sqrt{\frac{1}{7}}\right) = 42\left(-\sqrt{\frac{1}{7}}\right) = -\frac{42}{\sqrt{7}}$$
$$f''(x) < 0 \text{ at } x = -\sqrt{\frac{1}{7}}$$
$\therefore f(x)$ is concave down at this point. (6)

3. $f(x) = \frac{25x^2 - 70x + 49}{x - \frac{7}{5}}$
$$f(x) = \frac{(5x - 7)^2}{\frac{(5x-7)}{5}} = 5(5x - 7) = 25x - 35$$
$$f'(x) = 25 \quad (5)$$

4. $y = x^3 - 2x^2 + 3x - 4$

4.1 $\frac{dy}{dx} = 3x^2 - 4x + 3$
$$3x^2 - 4x + 3 = 2$$
$$3x^2 - 4x + 1 = 0$$
$$(3x - 1)(x - 1) = 0$$
$$\therefore x = \frac{1}{3} \text{ or } x = 1$$
Points of contact: $\left(\frac{1}{3}; \frac{86}{27}\right)$ and $(1; -2)$ (5)

4.2 Equations of the respective tangents:
$$y - y_1 = m(x - x_1)$$
$$y + \frac{86}{27} = 2\left(x - \frac{1}{3}\right) \quad \text{①}$$
$$y = 2x - \frac{104}{27}$$
$$y + 2 = 2(x - 1) \quad \text{②}$$
$$y = 2x - 4 \quad (5)$$

5.1 $\frac{h}{r} = \tan 40°$
$$\therefore h = \frac{r}{\tan 40°}$$
Volume $= \frac{1}{3}\pi r^2 h$
$$= \frac{1}{3}\pi r^2 \left(\frac{r}{\tan 40°}\right)$$
$$= \frac{\pi r^3}{3\tan 40°} \quad (3)$$

5.2 $\frac{\pi r^3}{3\tan 40°} = 72\,000$
$$\therefore r^3 = \frac{72\,000 \cdot 3 \cdot \tan 40°}{\pi}$$
$$\therefore r \approx 39 \text{ m} \quad (3)$$

5.3 $V(r) = \frac{\pi r^3}{3\tan 40°}$

$V'(r) = \frac{3\pi r^2}{3\tan 40°} = \frac{\pi r^2}{\tan 40°}$

$V'(39) = \frac{\pi(39)^2}{\tan 40°} \approx 5\,694{,}63 \text{ m}^3$ (4)

6. $f(x) = ax^2 - 6$

$f'(x) = 2ax$

$\therefore f'(4) = 8a$ .... ①

Inverse function: $x = ay^2 - 6$

$ay^2 = x + 6$

$y^2 = \frac{x+6}{a}$

$y = \sqrt{\frac{x+6}{a}}$ (given restriction $y > 0$)

$\therefore f^{-1}(2) = \sqrt{\frac{8}{a}}$ .... ②

Putting ① = ②: $8a = \sqrt{\frac{8}{a}}$

Squaring both sides: $64a^2 = \frac{8}{a}$

$a^3 = \frac{1}{8}$

$a = \frac{1}{2}$ (8)

7.1 $f'(x) = -2x - 4$ (2)

7.2 $f(x) = ax^2 + bx + c$

$f'(x) = 2ax + b$

$\therefore a = -1$

And $b = -4$

$f(x) = -x^2 - 4x + c$

Roots are equal $\therefore$ the trinomial must be a perfect square, i.e. $-(x+2)^2$

$\therefore f(x) = -x^2 - 4x - 4$

$\therefore a = -1,\ b = -4,\ c = -4$ (4)

Total: 50

Test C (page 148)

1.1 $f(x) = \frac{x^3}{3}$

$f(x+h) = \frac{(x+h)^3}{3} = \frac{x^3 + 3x^2h + 3xh^2 + h^3}{3}$

$f'(x) = \lim_{h \to 0} \frac{f(x+h) - f(x)}{h}$

$= \lim_{h \to 0} \frac{\frac{x^3 + 3x^2h + 3xh^2 + h^3}{3} - \frac{x^3}{3}}{h}$

$= \lim_{h \to 0} \frac{h(3x^2 + 3xh + h^2)}{3} \times \frac{1}{h}$

$= \lim_{h \to 0} \frac{3x^2 + 3xh + h^2}{3}$

$= \frac{3x^2}{3} = x^2$ (5)

1.2 $f'(x) = x^2$

$f''(x) = 2x$

$0 = 2x$

$\therefore x = 0$

Point of inflection: $(0;\ 0)$ (2)

1.3 Not possible, because $f(x) = \frac{x^3}{3}$ is increasing for all values of x, so the gradient at all points is positive. (2)

2. $\lim_{x \to 5} \frac{3x^2 - 13x - 10}{2x^2 - 9x - 5} = \frac{(3x+2)(x-5)}{(2x+1)(x-5)}$

$= \lim_{x \to 5} \frac{(3x+2)}{(2x+1)}$

$= \frac{17}{11}$ (3)

3.1 $y = (x^3 + 1)(x^2 - 2) = x^5 - 2x^3 + x^2 - 2$

$\frac{dy}{dx} = 5x^4 - 6x^2 + 2x$ (4)

3.2 $y = \frac{\sqrt{x-4}}{\sqrt{x}} = 1 - 4x^{-\frac{1}{2}}$

$\frac{dy}{dx} = 2x^{-\frac{3}{2}} = \frac{2}{x^{\frac{3}{2}}}$ (4)

4.1 Vol = $x^2 h$

$500 = x^2 h$

$h = \frac{500}{x^2}$ (2)

4.2 Total surface area with no lid = $x^2 + 4hx$

$S(x) = x^2 + 4x\left(\frac{500}{x^2}\right)$

$S(x) = x^2 + \frac{2\,000}{x}$ (2)

4.3 $S'(x) = 2x - 2\,000x^{-2}$

$0 = 2x^3 - 2\,000$

$x = 10,\ h = \frac{500}{100} = 50$

To minimise costs, the base must be 10 m × 10 m and the height must be 50 m. (4)

4.4 Minimum cost: total surface area × cost:

$= (x^2 + 4hx) \times R120$

$= [(10)^2 + 4(50)(10)] \times R120$

$= R252\,000$ (2)

5.1 $f(x) = x(x^2 - 9x + 24)$

$x = 0$, or $x^2 - 9x + 24 = 0$

$\Delta = b^2 - 4ac$

$\Delta = (-9)^2 - 4(1)(24) = -15$

Roots are imaginary/non real, therefore only one solution exists. (4)

5.2 $f(x) = x^3 - 9x^2 + 24x$

$f'(x) = 3x^2 - 18x + 24$

$0 = x^2 - 6x + 8$

$0 = (x - 2)(x - 4)$

$x = 2$ or $x = 4$

$f(2) = 20$

$f(4) = 16$

Turning points: $(2; 20)$ and $(4; 16)$

$f''(x) = 6x - 18$

$0 = x - 3$

$x = 3$

$f(3) = 18$

Point of inflection: $(3; 18)$ (5)

5.3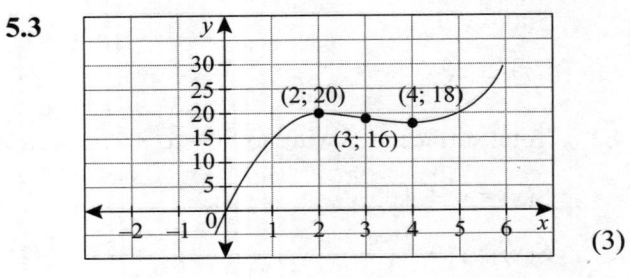
(3)

5.4 $k = 18$ or $k = 20$ (2)

6. $f(x) = ax^2 + bx$ and $y - x - 4 = 0$ ∴ $y = x + 4$

so the gradient of the tangent = 1

$f'(x) = 2ax + b = 1$

Substitute -1 for x in $f'(x)$ and $f(x)$:

$f'(-1) = 2a(-1) + b$

∴ $-2a + b = 1$ ....①

Substitute $(-1; 3)$ into $f(x)$:

$f(-1) = a(-1)^2 + b(-1)$

$3 = a - b$

∴ $a = 3 + b$ ....②

By substitution: $-2(3 + b) + b = 1$

$-6 - 2b + b = 1$

$-6 - b = 1$

$b = -7$

and $a = 3 - 7 = -4$ (6)

Total: 50

TOPIC 7 Analytical geometry (page 149)

Exercise 1 (page 156)

1.1 $x^2 + y^2 = (\sqrt{3})^2$
       $x^2 + y^2 = 3$

1.2 $(-5)^2 + (6)^2 = r^2$
       $x^2 + y^2 = 61$

1.3 $2x + y = 5, \therefore y = -2x + 5$
       $\therefore m_{tangent} = -2$
       $\therefore m_{radius} = \frac{1}{2}$

       Equation of radius: $y = \frac{x}{2}$

       Point of contact: $\frac{x}{2} = -2x + 5$
                          $\therefore x = 2, y = 1$

       Equation of circle: $(2)^2 + (1)^2 = r^2$
                               $x^2 + y^2 = 5$

2. $2y - x = 5$
      $y = \frac{x+5}{2}$ ....①
      $x^2 + y^2 = 10$ ....②

      Substitute for y in ②: $x^2 + \left(\frac{x+5}{2}\right)^2 = 10$
                         $x^2 + \left(\frac{x^2 + 10x + 25}{4}\right) = 10$
                         $4x^2 + x^2 + 10x + 25 = 40$
                         $5x^2 + 10x - 15 = 0$
                         $x^2 + 2x - 3 = 0$
                         $(x + 3)(x - 1) = 0$

      $x = -3$ or $x = 1$
      $y = \frac{-3+5}{2}$ or $y = \frac{1+5}{2}$
      $y = 1$ or $y = 3$
      Points of intersection: $(-3; 1), (1; 3)$

3. $5y = -x + 13$
      $x = 13 - 5y$
      $x^2 + y^2 = 13$ ....②

      Substitute for x in ②: $(13 - 5y)^2 + y^2 = 13$
                        $169 - 130y + 25y^2 + y^2 = 13$
                        $26y^2 - 130y + 156 = 0$
                              $y^2 - 5y + 6 = 0$
                              $(y - 2)(y - 3) = 0$

      $y = 2$ or $y = 3$
      $x = 3$ or $x = -2$

Points of intersection: C(3; 2), D(–2; 3)

$CD = \sqrt{(x_C - x_D)^2 + (y_C - y_D)^2}$
      $= \sqrt{[3 - (-2)]^2 + (2 - 3)^2} = \sqrt{26}$

4. $m_{radius} = -\frac{4}{3} \therefore m_{tangent} = \frac{3}{4}$

      Equation of tangent: $y - 4 = \frac{3}{4}[x - (-3)]$
                              $y - 4 = \frac{3}{4}x + \frac{9}{4}$
                                   $y = \frac{3}{4}x + \frac{25}{4}$

5. $[x - (-3)]^2 + (y - 4)^2 = 2^2$
      $(x + 3)^2 + (y - 4)^2 = 4$

6.1 $x^2 + y^2 - 2x + 4y + 1 = 0$
       $x^2 - 2x + \left(\frac{2}{2}\right)^2 + y^2 + 4y + \left(\frac{4}{2}\right)^2 = -1 + \left(\frac{2}{2}\right)^2 + \left(\frac{4}{2}\right)^2$
                         $(x - 1)^2 + (y + 2)^2 = 4$

       Centre: $(1; -2)$, radius: $\sqrt{4} = 2$

6.2 $x^2 + y^2 + 6x - 8y = 11$
       $x^2 + 6x + \left(\frac{6}{2}\right)^2 + y^2 - 8y + \left(\frac{8}{2}\right)^2 = 11 + \left(\frac{6}{2}\right)^2 + \left(\frac{8}{2}\right)^2$
                       $(x + 3)^2 + (y - 4)^2 = 36$

       Centre: $(-3; 4)$, radius: 6

7.   Equation of the circle:
      $(x + 1)^2 + (y - 0{,}5)^2 = 2{,}5^2$ ....①
      $y + 1 = 0 \therefore y = -1$ ....②

      Substitute for y in ①:
      $(x + 1)^2 + (-1 - 0{,}5)^2 = 2{,}5^2$
      $x^2 + 2x + 1 + \frac{9}{4} - \frac{25}{4} = 0$
              $x^2 + 2x - 3 = 0$
           $(x + 3)(x - 1) = 0$
                    $x = -3$ or $x = 1$

      Points of intersection: $(-3; -1)$ and $(1; -1)$

8. $x^2 - 2x + 1^2 + y^2 + 2y + 1^2 = 11 + 2$
             $(x - 1)^2 + (y + 1)^2 = 13$

      Centre: $(1; -1)$

      $m_{radius} = \frac{1 - (-1)}{-2 - 1} = -\frac{2}{3} \therefore m_{tangent} = \frac{3}{2}$

      Equation of tangent: $y - 1 = \frac{3}{2}[x - (-2)]$
                               $y = \frac{3}{2}x + 4$

Exercise 2 (page 163)

1. A(3; –8); B(9; 10); Q(9; 4)

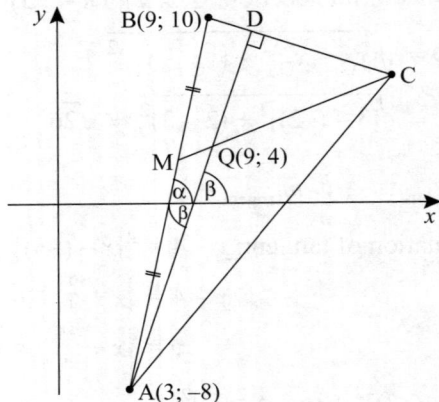

1.1 $m_{AQ} = \frac{12}{6} = 2$

1.2 $m_{BC} = -\frac{1}{2}$ through B(9; 10)   AD ⊥ BC

$\therefore \frac{y-10}{x-9} = -\frac{1}{2}$

$\therefore 2y - 20 = -x + 9$

$\therefore 2y = -x + 29$

$\therefore y = -\frac{1}{2}x + 14\frac{1}{2}$

1.3 M(6; 1)

$m_{QM} = \frac{3}{3} = 1$ through Q(9; 4)

$\therefore \frac{y-4}{x-9} = 1$

$\therefore y = x - 5$

1.4 $\tan \alpha = m_{AB} = \frac{18}{6} = 3$

$\therefore \alpha = 71{,}6°$

$\tan \beta = m_{AQ} = 2$

$\therefore \beta = 63{,}4°$

BÂQ = 71,6° – 63,4°   Exterior angle of triangle

= 8,2°

2. AB: $y = 5x - 17$

BC: $y = 13 - x$

$\therefore 5x - 17 = 13 - x$ Point of intersection B

$\therefore 6x = 30$

$\therefore x = 5$

$\therefore y = 8$ $\therefore$ B(5; 8)

D(6; 4)

$m_{BD} = -\frac{4}{1} = -4$ through B(5; 8)

$\therefore \frac{y-8}{x-5} = -4$

$\therefore y - 8 = -4x + 20$

$\therefore y + 4x = 28$

$\therefore y = -4x + 28$

3.

3.1 $x^2 + y^2 - 6x - 2y + 1 = 0$

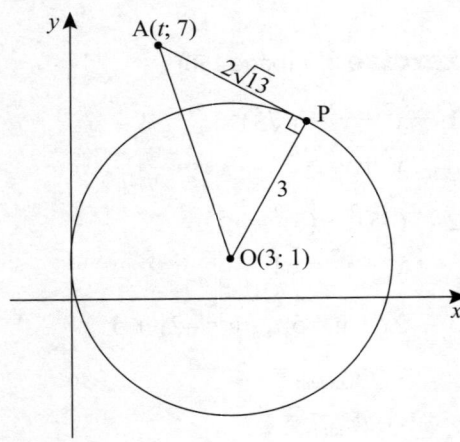

$\therefore x^2 - 6x + 9 + y^2 - 2y + 1 = 9$

$(x-3)^2 + (y-1)^2 = 9$

$\therefore$ Centre (3; 1)

Radius: 3

3.2 AP̂O = 90°   Tangent ⊥ radius

OP = 3

$\therefore AO^2 = 4(13) + 9$ Pythagoras △AOP

= 61

$AO^2 = (t-3)^2 + 36 = 61$ Distance formula

$\therefore (t-3)^2 = 25$

$\therefore t - 3 = \pm 5$

$\therefore t = 8$ or $t = -2$

4.

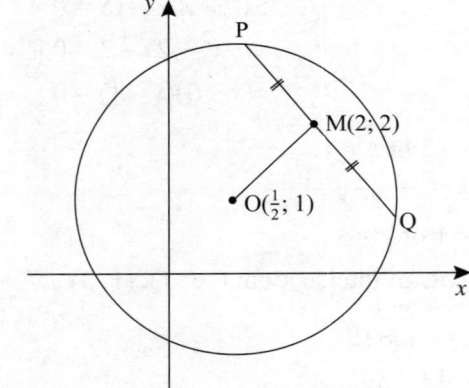

4.1 $x^2 + y^2 - x - 2y - 5 = 0$

$\therefore x^2 - x + \frac{1}{4} + y^2 - 2y + 1 = 5 + 1 + \frac{1}{4}$

$\therefore \left(x - \frac{1}{2}\right)^2 + (y-1)^2 = 6\frac{1}{4}$

Centre $O\left(\frac{1}{2}; 1\right)$

Radius: $\sqrt{6\frac{1}{4}} = \sqrt{\frac{25}{4}} = \frac{5}{2}$

4.2 $O\hat{M}P = 90°$ PM = MQ
$m_{OM} = \frac{1}{1\frac{1}{2}} = \frac{2}{3}$
$\therefore m_{PQ} = -\frac{3}{2}$ through M(2; 2)
$\therefore \frac{y-2}{x-2} = -\frac{3}{2}$
$\therefore 2y - 4 = -3x + 6$
$\therefore 2y - 3x = 10$
$\therefore y = -\frac{3}{2}x + 5$

5.

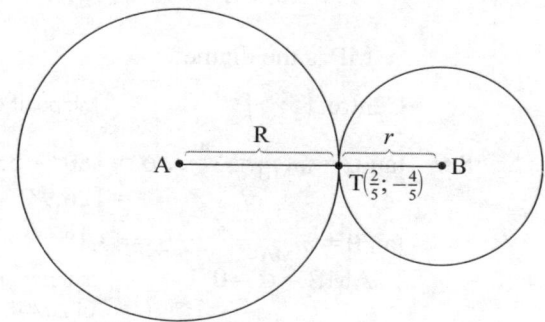

5.1 $x^2 + y^2 + 4x - 2y + k = 0$
$x^2 + 4x + 4 + y^2 - 2y + 1 = -k + 4 + 1$
$(x+2)^2 + (y-1)^2 = -k + 5$

Radius B: $\sqrt{5-k}$
Centre B(−2; 1)
Centre A(2; −2)

5.2 AB = $\sqrt{16 + 9}$ Distance formula
= 5

Length AB = R + r
$\therefore 5 = 2 + \sqrt{5-k}$
$3 = \sqrt{5-k}$
$9 = 5 - k$
$\therefore -4 = k$

5.3 $m_{AT} = \frac{-1\frac{1}{5}}{1\frac{3}{5}}$
$= -\frac{6}{8} = -\frac{3}{4}$

$m_{tangent}: \frac{4}{3}$ through T$\left(\frac{2}{5}; -\frac{4}{5}\right)$

$\therefore \frac{y + \frac{4}{5}}{x - \frac{2}{5}} \times \frac{\times 5}{\times 5} = \frac{4}{3}$

$\therefore \frac{5y + 4}{5x - 2} = \frac{4}{3}$

$\therefore 15y + 12 = 20x - 8$
$\therefore 15y = 20x - 20$
$\therefore 20x - 15y - 20 = 0$

6.

6.1 $B\hat{A}C = 90°$ Radius ⊥ tangent
BC = 25
$\therefore$ AB = 15   Pythagoras 3 : 4 : 5
$\therefore$ Radius: 15

6.2 $(x+1)^2 + (y-1)^2 = 225$
$x^2 + 2x + y^2 - 2y = 223$

6.3 $m_{CR} = \tan \theta$ $C\hat{R}O$
$= \frac{20}{15}$ In △ABC
$= \frac{4}{3}$ Through C(−1; 26)
$\therefore \frac{y - 26}{x + 1} = \frac{4}{3}$
$\therefore 3y - 78 = 4x + 4$
$\therefore 3y = 4x + 82$

Equation$_{CR}$: $y = \frac{4}{3}x + 27\frac{1}{3}$

6.4 $m_{AB} = -\frac{3}{4}$ AB ⊥ CR
$\therefore \frac{y-1}{x+1} = -\frac{3}{4}$
$\therefore 4y - 4 = -3x - 3$
$\therefore 4y + 3x = 1$
$\therefore$ Equation$_{AB}$: $y = -\frac{3}{4}x + \frac{1}{4}$

6.5 Let AB = CR: $\frac{4}{3}x + 27\frac{1}{3} = -\frac{3}{4}x + \frac{1}{4}$
$16x + 328 = -9x + 3$ Multiply by 12
$\therefore 25x = -325$
$\therefore x = -13$
$\therefore y = 10$
$\therefore$ A(−13; 10)

7.

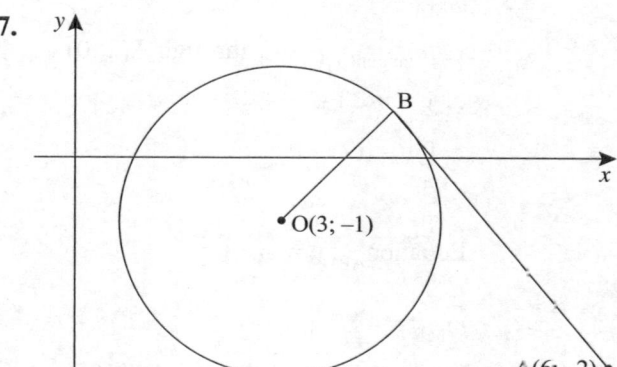

$x^2 + y^2 - 6x + 2y + 8 = 0$
$\therefore x^2 - 6x + 9 + y^2 + 2y + 1 = -8 + 1 + 9$
$\therefore (x - 3)^2 + (y + 1)^2 = 2$
$\therefore$ Centre: (3; −1)
$\therefore$ Radius: $\sqrt{2}$

AO = √(9+1) = √10   Distance formula
BO = √2   Radius of circle
∴ AB² = 10 − 2   Pythagoras
  OB̂A = 90°; radius/tangent
  = 8
∴ AB = √8
  = 2,83 rounded to two decimals

8.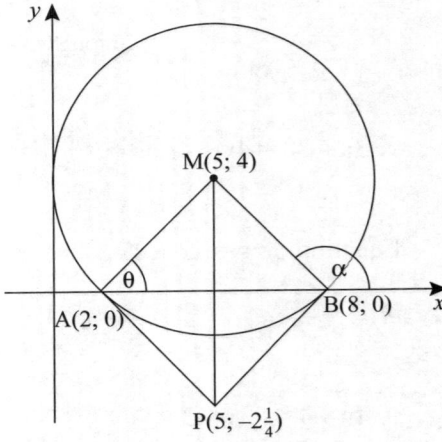

8.1 $(x-5)^2 + (y-4)^2 = 25$

8.2 For A and B: Let $y = 0$:
∴ $(x-5)^2 + 16 = 25$
∴ $(x-5)^2 = 9$
∴ $x - 5 = \pm 3$
∴ $x = 8$ or $x = 2$
∴ A(2; 0) and B(8; 0)

8.3 $m_{MA} = \frac{4}{3}$
∴ $m_{\text{tangent PA}} = -\frac{3}{4}$ through A(2; 0)
∴ $y = mx + c$
∴ $0 = -\frac{3}{4}(2) + c$
∴ $\frac{3}{2} = c$
Equation$_{AP}$: $y = -\frac{3}{4}x + \frac{3}{2}$

$m_{MB} = -\frac{4}{3}$
∴ $m_{\text{tangent PB}} = \frac{3}{4}$ through B(8; 0)
∴ $y = mx + c$
∴ $0 = \frac{3}{4}(8) + c$
∴ $-6 = c$
Equation$_{PB}$: $y = \frac{3}{4}x - 6$

8.4 P: $\frac{3}{4}x - 6 = -\frac{3}{4}x + \frac{3}{2}$
$3x - 24 = -3x + 6$ Multiply by 4
∴ $6x = 30$
∴ $x = 5$
∴ $y = -2\frac{1}{4}$
∴ P$(5; -2\frac{1}{4})$

8.5 MÂP = MB̂P = 90°   Radius/tangent
∴ MAPB is a cyclic quad   Opposite angles are supplementary
∴ MP is the diameter
Centre: $(5; \frac{7}{8})$ Midpoint of MP

8.6 $\tan \alpha = m_{MB} = -\frac{4}{3}$ ∴ $\alpha = 180° - 53,1°$
  = 126,9°
$\tan \theta = m_{MA} = \frac{4}{3}$ ∴ $\theta = 53,1°$
∴ AM̂B = $\alpha - \theta$ Exterior angle of △MAB
  = 73,8°

9.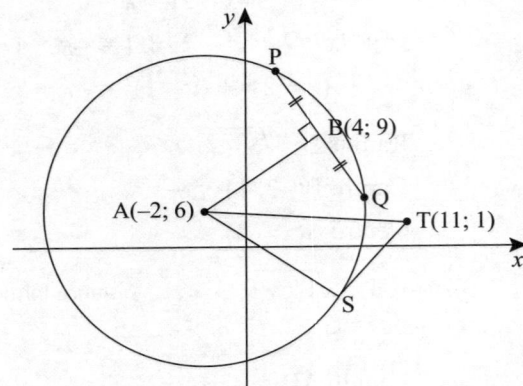

9.1 $(x + 2)^2 + (y - 6)^2 = 50$ ..... ①
∴ $x^2 + 4x + 4 + y^2 - 12y + 36 = 50$
∴ $x^2 + y^2 + 4x - 12y - 10 = 0$

9.2 $m_{AB} = \frac{3}{6} = \frac{1}{2}$
$m_{PQ} = -2$ through B(4; 9)   AB ⊥ PQ; PB = BQ
∴ $\frac{y-9}{x-4} = -2$
∴ $y - 9 = -2x + 8$
∴ $y + 2x = 17$

9.3 Substitute $y = -2x + 17$ into ①
∴ $(x+2)^2 + (-2x + 17 - 6)^2 = 50$
∴ $x^2 + 4x + 4 + 4x^2 - 44x + 121 = 50$
∴ $5x^2 - 40x + 75 = 0$
∴ $x^2 - 8x + 15 = 0$
∴ $(x - 5)(x - 3) = 0$
∴ $x = 5$ or $x = 3$
∴ $y = 7$ or $y = 11$
∴ P(3; 11) and Q(5; 7)

9.4 $AT = \sqrt{13^2 + 25}$ Distance formula
      $= \sqrt{194}$
      $\therefore AT >$ radius
      $\therefore T$ lies outside the circle.

9.5 $TS^2 = AT^2 - AS^2$ Pythagoras $A\hat{S}T = 90°$
      $= 194 - 50$
      $= 144$
      $\therefore TS = 12$

10.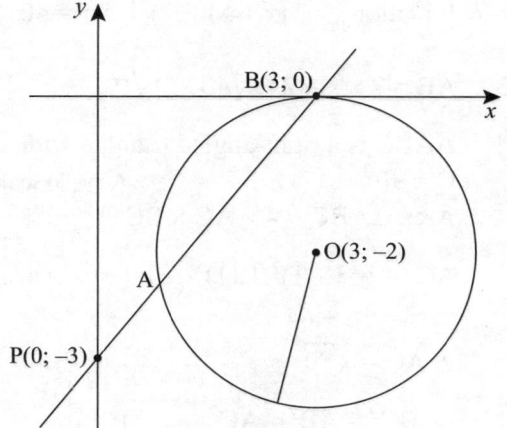

10.1 $x^2 + y^2 - 6x + 4y = -9$ ....①
      $\therefore x^2 - 6x + 9 + y^2 + 4y + 4 = -9 + 9 + 4$
      $(x - 3)^2 + (y + 2)^2 = 4$
      Centre: $(3; -2)$
      Radius: 2

10.2 $y = x - 3$

10.3 Substitute $y = x - 3$ into ①
      $\therefore x^2 + (x - 3)^2 - 6x + 4(x - 3) = -9$
      $\therefore x^2 + x^2 - 6x + 9 - 6x + 4x - 12 = -9$
      $2x^2 - 8x + 6 = 0$
      $x^2 - 4x + 3 = 0$
      $(x - 3)(x - 1) = 0$
      $x = 1$ or $x = 3$
      $y = -2$ or $y = 0$
      $\therefore A(1; -2), B(3; 0)$

10.4 $AB = \sqrt{4 + 4}$ Distance formula
      $= \sqrt{8}$

Test A   (page 165)

1. $x^2 + 6x + 9 + y^2 - 4y + 4 = 23 + 9 + 4$
    $\therefore (x + 3)^2 + (y - 2)^2 = 36$
    Radius: 6 units
    Midpoint: $(-3; 2)$ (6)

2.1 $M(2; 3)$ therefore gradient of $AM = \frac{3-5}{2+1} = -\frac{2}{3}$
    $\therefore m_{tangent} = \frac{3}{2}$ Radius $\perp$ tangent
    Equation$_{tangent}$: $y - 5 = \frac{3}{2}(x + 1)$
    $\therefore y = \frac{3}{2}x + \frac{3}{2} + 5$
    $\therefore y = \frac{3}{2}x + \frac{13}{2}$ or $2y = 3x + 13$ (5)

2.2 $3y - 2x - 5 = 0 \therefore x = \frac{3y - 5}{2}$
    $(x - 2)^2 + (y - 3)^2 = 13$
    $\therefore \left(\frac{3y - 5 - 4}{2}\right)^2 + y^2 - 6y + 9 = 13$ Replace x and multiply by 4
    $\therefore 9y^2 - 54y + 81 + 4y^2 - 24y + 36 - 52 = 0$
                                   Add like terms and $\div 13$
    $\therefore y^2 - 6y + 5 = 0$
    $\therefore (y - 1)(y - 5) = 0$
    $\therefore y = 1$ or $y = 5$
    then $x = -1$ and $x = 5$
    $\therefore B(-1; 1)$ and $C(5; 5)$ (8)

2.3 Substitute $M(2; 3)$ in BC: $3y - 2x - 5 = 0$
    LHS $= 3(3) - 2(2) - 5 = 0$
         $=$ RHS
    Therefore M, the centre, lies on BC
    BC is a diameter of the circle.   (3)

3. Substitute $x = 3y - 10$ in $x^2 + y^2 = 10$
    $\therefore (3y - 10)^2 + y^2 = 10$
    $\therefore 9y^2 - 60y + 100 + y^2 - 10 = 0$
    $\therefore y^2 - 6y + 9 = 0$
    $\therefore (y - 3)(y - 3) = 0$
    $\therefore y = 3$
    and $x = -1$
    There is only one y-value; therefore the line is a tangent to the circle and the point of contact is $(-1; 3)$.   (5)

4.1 $\tan C\hat{T}X = \frac{1}{3}$
    $\therefore C\hat{T}X = 18,43°$ (2)

4.2 $\tan A\hat{K}X = m_{BA}$

$\qquad = \frac{12-4}{4-0}$

$\qquad = 2$

$\therefore A\hat{K}X = 63,43°$

$\quad T\hat{A}K = 63,43° - 18,43°$

$\qquad = 45°$

$\therefore B\hat{A}C = 45°$ Vertically opposite to T$\hat{A}$K   (5)

5.1 $QR = \sqrt{(9-1)^2 + (-5+1)^2}$

$\qquad = \sqrt{64+16}$

$\qquad = 4\sqrt{5}$ (2)

5.2 $y + 1 = \frac{-5+1}{9-1}(x-1)$

$y + 1 = -\frac{4}{8}(x-1)$

$y + 1 = -\frac{1}{2}x + \frac{1}{2}$

$y = -\frac{1}{2}x - \frac{1}{2}$ (4)

5.3 PW ⊥ QR

$m_{QR} = -\frac{1}{2} \therefore m_{PW} = 2$

PW: $y - 2 = 2(x-5)$

$\qquad y = 2x - 8$ (3)

5.4 $2x - 8 = -\frac{1}{2}x - \frac{1}{2}$

$4x - 16 = -x - 1$

$5x = 15$

$x = 3$

$\therefore y = -2$

$\therefore W(3; -2)$ (3)

5.5 Area $\triangle PQR = \frac{1}{2} \times QR \times PW$

$\qquad = \frac{4\sqrt{5} \times 2\sqrt{5}}{2}$ $PW = \sqrt{(5-3)^2 + (2+2)^2}$

$\qquad\qquad\qquad\qquad\qquad = 2\sqrt{5}$

$\qquad = 20$ units²   (4)

Total: 50

Test B (page 166)

1.1 $m_{AC} = \frac{3-11}{1+3} = -2$, therefore gradient of perpendicular bisector $= \frac{1}{2}$

Midpoint$_{AC} = \left(\frac{-3+1}{2}; \frac{11+3}{2}\right) = (-1; 7)$

Equation of perpendicular bisector of AC:

$y - 7 = \frac{1}{2}(x+1)$

$y = \frac{1}{2}x + 7\frac{1}{2}$ (6)

1.2 The perpendicular bisector of a chord will pass through the centre of the circle. The line from the centre of the circle, bisecting the chord, is perpendicular to the chord.

Determine the centre of the circle by finding the intersection of the perpendicular bisector and AB:

$6x + 40 = x + 15$

$\therefore x = -5$ and $y = 5$

$r^2 = (-3+5)^2 + (11-5)^2 = 40$

Equation$_{circle}$: $(x+5)^2 + (y-5)^2 = 40$ (6)

1.3 $AB = 2 \times r = 2 \times \sqrt{40} = 4\sqrt{10}$ (2)

1.4 $\triangle ABC$ is a right-angled triangle with

$\hat{C} = 90°$ Angle in semicircle

Area $\triangle ABC = \frac{1}{2} \times AC \times BC$

$AC^2 = (-3-1)^2 + (11-3)^2$ Distance formula

$\qquad = 16 + 64$

$\therefore AC = \sqrt{80}$

$BC^2 = AB^2 - AC^2$ Pythagoras

$\therefore BC^2 = 160 - 80$

$\therefore BC = \sqrt{80}$

$\therefore$ Area $= 40$ units²   (4)

2.1 $y = -2x - 4$

$(m; n) \rightarrow n = -2m - 4$ ....①

PQ: $r^2 = m^2$

Radius ⊥ tangent, which is y-axis, $\therefore Q(0; n)$

PR:

$r^2 = (m+1)^2 + (n+1)^2$ Distance formula

$m^2 = m^2 + 2m + 1 + n^2 + 2n + 1$

$0 = 2m + 1 + n^2 + 2n + 1$ ....②

$2m + 1 + (-2m-4)^2 + 2(-2m-4) + 1 = 0$

                   Substitute ① → ②

$\therefore 2m^2 + 7m + 5 = 0$

$\therefore (2m+5)(m+1) = 0$

$\therefore m = -2\frac{1}{2}$ or $m = -1$

$n = 1$ or $n = -2$

$\therefore P(-2\frac{1}{2}; 1)$ or $P(-1; -2)$ (10)

2.2 Radius in each case is distance PR:

$\left(x + 2\frac{1}{2}\right)^2 + (y-1)^2 = 6\frac{1}{4}$ or $(x+1)^2 + (y+2)^2 = 1$ (4)

3.1 $\hat{ABO} = 90°$ Angle in semicircle
∴ AB ⊥ OB
x-coordinate of B is the same as
x-coordinate of A   (2)

3.2 $P\left(\frac{3}{2}; 1\right)$ Midpoint of OA

Length of radius $= \sqrt{\left(3 - \frac{3}{2}\right)^2 + (2-1)^2} = \frac{\sqrt{13}}{2}$

Equation of circle: $\left(x - \frac{3}{2}\right)^2 + (y-1)^2 = \frac{13}{4}$ (4)

3.3 Gradient OA = gradient of parallel line through B = $\frac{2}{3}$

$y - 0 = \frac{2}{3}(x - 3)$

∴ $y = \frac{2}{3}x - 2$ (3)

3.4 $\tan \beta = \frac{2}{3}$

∴ $\beta = 33,69°$

∴ $\theta = 56,31°$

∴ $P\hat{A}B = 56,31°$ Lines parallel, alternate angles

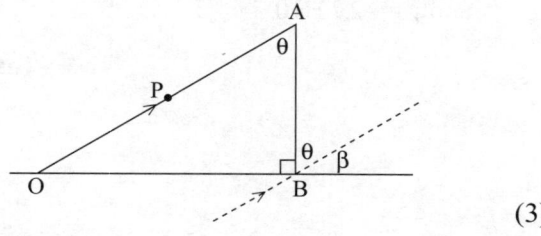

(3)

3.5 B'(0; 3)   (2)

3.6 B' lies outside the circle on the y-axis.   (2)

3.7 $(x-3)^2 + y^2 = 4$ (2)

Total: 50

Test C (page 167)

1.1 $m_{AB} = \frac{-3-3}{-3-(-2)} = \frac{-6}{-1} = 6$

$\tan \theta = m_{AB} = 6$

$\theta = 80,54° \approx 80,5°$ (3)

1.2 Midpoint of AC: $M\left(\frac{-2+4}{2}; \frac{3+0}{2}\right) = \left(1; \frac{3}{2}\right)$ (2)

1.3 $AB = \sqrt{[-2-(-3)]^2 + [3-(-3)]^2} = \sqrt{37}$

$BC = \sqrt{(-3-4)^2 + (3-0)^2} = \sqrt{58}$

$CA = \sqrt{[4-(-2)]^2 + (0-3)^2} = \sqrt{45}$

Perimeter = AB + BC + CA
$= \sqrt{37} + \sqrt{58} + \sqrt{45}$
$= 20,406 \approx 20$ units   (7)

1.4 $y - y_1 = m(x - x_1)$

$y - \frac{3}{2} = 6(x - 1)$

$y = 6x - 6 + \frac{3}{2}$

$y = 6x - \frac{9}{2}$

$2y - 12x = -9$ (4)

1.5 $m_{AB} = 6$

∴ m_{BD} must also = 6 for the points to be collinear.

∴ $m_{BD} = \frac{-3-t}{-3-(-1)} = \frac{-3-t}{-2}$

∴ $\frac{-3-t}{-2} = 6$

$-3 - t = -12$

∴ $t = 9$ (2)

2.1 Substitute point (2; −9):

$x^2 + y^2 - 8x + 6y = 15$

$(2)^2 + (-9)^2 - 8(2) + 6(-9) = 15$

$4 + 81 - 16 - 54 = 15$

$15 = 15$

∴ Point (2; −9) lies on the circumference of the given circle.   (2)

2.2 $x^2 + y^2 - 8x + 6y = 15$

$x^2 - 8x + \left(\frac{8}{2}\right)^2 + y^2 + 6y + \left(\frac{6}{2}\right)^2 = 15 + \left(\frac{8}{2}\right)^2 + \left(\frac{6}{2}\right)^2$

$(x-4)^2 + (y+3)^2 = 40$

Circle has centre: (4; −3)

Gradient of radius to point of contact:

$m_{radius} = \frac{-3-(-9)}{4-2} = \frac{6}{2} = 3$

$m_{tangent} = -\frac{1}{3}$

Equation of tangent: $y - y_1 = m(x - x_1)$

$y - (-9) = -\frac{1}{3}(x - 2)$

$y + 9 = -\frac{1}{3}x + \frac{2}{3}$

$y = -\frac{1}{3}x - \frac{25}{3}$ (7)

3.

Let the circle centre for $(x-3)^2 + (y+1)^2 = 10$ be D.

Then D(3; –1) and DB = $\sqrt{10}$

AD = $\sqrt{(3-6)^2 + (-1-4)^2} = \sqrt{34}$

AB = $\sqrt{(\sqrt{34})^2 - (\sqrt{10})^2}$ Pythagoras

AB = $\sqrt{34-10} = \sqrt{24} = 4{,}898 \approx 4{,}9$ (5)

4.1 $(0-3)^2 + (y+2)^2 = 25$

$9 + y^2 + 4y + 4 = 25$

$y^2 + 4y - 12 = 0$

$(y+6)(y-2) = 0$

$\therefore y = -6$ or $y = 2$

$\therefore$ B(0; 2) (4)

4.2 $\left(x - \frac{9}{2}\right)^2 + (y+3)^2 = \left(\frac{15}{2}\right)^2$ (3)

4.3.1 A(3; –2) and B(12; 10)

AB = $\sqrt{(3-12)^2 + (-2-10)^2}$

$= \sqrt{225} = 15$ (2)

4.3.2 Radius of circle with centre A + radius of circle with centre B = 5 + 10 = 15, $\therefore$ these two circles have only one point of contact. (2)

5. $y = -2x + 4$ .... ①

$x^2 + y^2 = 20$ .... ②

$\therefore$ Equation of tangents: $y = -2x + c$

Substitute for $y = -2x + c$ in ②:

$x^2 + (-2x + c)^2 = 20$

$x^2 + 4x^2 - 4xc + c^2 - 20 = 0$

$5x^2 - 4xc + c^2 - 20 = 0$

Since the lines are tangents to the circle, the roots of this equation must be = 0.

$\therefore b^2 - 4ac = 0$

Substituting: $a = 5$, $b = -4c$, and $c = (c^2 - 20)$:

$(-4c)^2 - 4(5)(c^2 - 20) = 0$

$16c^2 - 20c^2 + 400 = 0$

$-4c^2 + 400 = 0$

$-4(c^2 - 100) = 0$

$\therefore c = 10$ or $c = -10$

Equations of the tangents: $y = -2x - 10$ and $y = -2x + 10$ (7)

Total: 50

TOPIC 8   Euclidean geometry and measurement (page 168)

Test A (page 175)

1. $\frac{a+1}{3} = \frac{4}{a}$ NP ∥ LM
    $\therefore a^2 + a = 12$
    $a^2 + a - 12 = 0$
    $(a+4)(a-3) = 0$
    $a = \cancel{-4}$ or 3
    $a = 3$ (5)

2. $\frac{b}{3} = \frac{4}{2}$ FG ∥ DE
    $\therefore b = 6$
    $\frac{c}{12} = \frac{4}{6}$ △CFG ∣∣∣ △CDE
    $6c = 48$
    $c = 8$ (5)

3. $\frac{d}{d+4} = \frac{8}{12}$ △DFG ∣∣∣ △DCE
    $12d = 8d + 32$
    $4d = 32$
    $d = 8$
    $\frac{6}{e} = \frac{8}{4}$ FG ∥ CE
    $\therefore e = 3$ (5)

4. $\frac{f}{6} = \frac{6}{4}$ VU ∥ RS
    $\therefore 4f = 36$
    $f = 9$
    and $\frac{8}{g} = \frac{6}{10}$ △TUV ∣∣∣ △TRS
    $\therefore 6g = 80$
    $\therefore g = 13,3$ (5)

5. $\frac{3}{h} = \frac{5}{8}$ △DGH ∣∣∣ △DEF
    $\therefore 5h = 24$
    $h = 4,8$
    and $\frac{i}{2} = \frac{8}{3}$ GH ∥ EF
    $\therefore 3i = 16$
    $i = 5,3$ (5)

6. $\frac{j}{6} = \frac{6}{3}$ △RST ∣∣∣ △UVW
    $\therefore j = 12$
    and $\frac{k}{3} = \frac{16}{6}$ △RST ∣∣∣ △UVW
    $\therefore 6k = 48$
    $k = 8$ (5)

7. $\frac{l}{2} = \frac{5}{4}$ △DEF ∣∣∣ △PQR
    $\therefore 4l = 10$
    $l = 2,5$
    and $\frac{2}{m} = \frac{4}{6}$ △DEF ∣∣∣ △PQR
    $\therefore 4m = 12$
    $m = 3$ (5)

8. $\frac{8}{p} = \frac{12}{15}$ △LMN ∣∣∣ △UVW
    $\therefore 12p = 120$
    $p = 10$
    and $\frac{n}{8} = \frac{6}{12}$
    $\therefore n = 4$ (5)

9. △KLM ∣∣∣ △NLK
    $\therefore \frac{KL}{LM} = \frac{NL}{LK}$
    $\therefore \frac{4}{2} = \frac{q+2}{4}$
    $\therefore q + 2 = 8$
    $q = 6$ (5)

10. △LQP ∣∣∣ △LMN
    $\therefore \frac{LQ}{LM} = \frac{LP}{LN}$
    $\therefore \frac{2}{4+r} = \frac{4}{10}$
    $\therefore 16 + 4r = 20$
    $4r = 4$
    $r = 1$ (5)

    Total: 50

Test B (page 176)

1. $\frac{TR}{12} = \frac{22}{24}$ VT ∥ PS
    $\therefore TR = 11$ cm
    $\frac{SR}{QR} = \frac{22}{46}$ VS ∥ PQ
    $\therefore \frac{23}{QR} = \frac{22}{46}$
    $\therefore QR = 48,1$ cm   (4)

2. $\frac{OC}{OR} = \frac{2}{5}$ QO ∥ BC

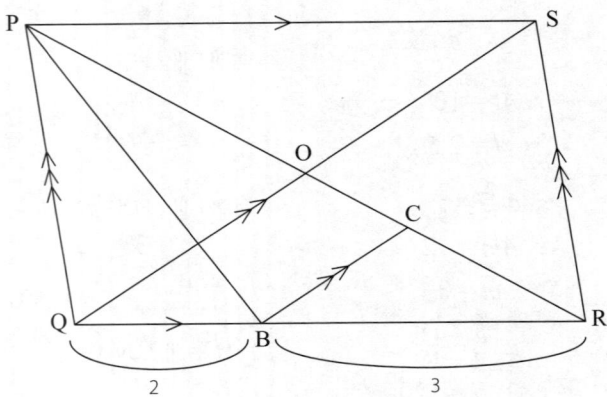

PO = OR diagonals of a parallelogram

∴ $\frac{PO}{OC} = \frac{5}{2}$ (3)

3.1 In △s ABC and ADB

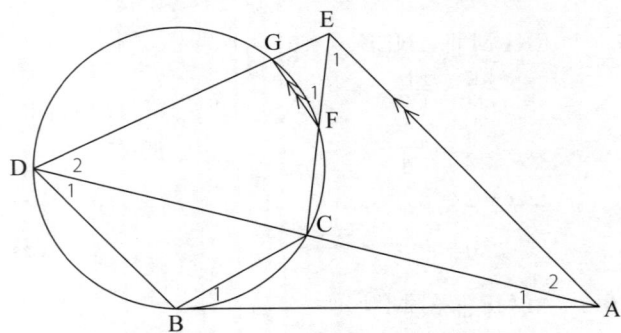

   1. $\hat{A}_1$ is common
   2. $\hat{B}_1 = \hat{D}$ Tangent : AB;
                             Chord : BC

      ∴ △ABC ||| △ADB   ∠, ∠   (2)

3.2   ∴ $\frac{AB}{AD} = \frac{AC}{AB}$

      ∴ $AB^2 = AC \cdot AD$ (2)

3.3 In △s ACE and AED:
   1. $\hat{A}_2$ is common
   2. $\hat{E}_1 = \hat{F}_1$ Alt. ∠s, AE ∥ GF
          = $\hat{D}_2$ Ext. ∠: cyclic quad GDCF

      ∴ △ACE ||| △AED   ∠, ∠   (4)

3.4 $\frac{AE}{AD} = \frac{AC}{AE}$ △ACE ||| △AED;
                        proved in 3.3

      ∴ $AE^2 = AC \cdot AD$
        $AB^2 = AC \cdot AD$ Proved in 3.2

      ∴ AE = AB   (4)

4.   Produce BS to T.
      ∴ BT is a median   S: centroid
      ∴ AT = TC

$\frac{AQ}{QT} = \frac{AF}{FB} = \frac{1}{1}$ FQ ∥ BT

∴ AQ = QT

∴ AQ = $\frac{1}{4}$AC   (5)

5.

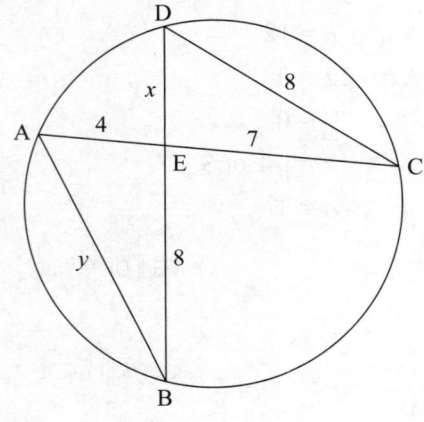

$\hat{A} = \hat{D}$ ∠ in same seg
$\hat{B} = \hat{C}$ ∠ in same seg
$A\hat{E}B = D\hat{E}C$ Vert. opp. ∠s

△DEC ||| △AEB   ∠∠∠

$\frac{DE}{AE} = \frac{EC}{EB} = \frac{DC}{AB}$ Sides in proportion

Let AC = 11

$\frac{x}{4} = \frac{7}{8}$

$x = \frac{28}{8}$

$x = 3{,}5$

$\frac{y}{8} = \frac{8}{7}$ Sides in proportion

$y = \frac{64}{7} = 9{,}14$ (6)

6.1 $M\hat{E}C = 90°$ Tan ⊥ rad
       $M\hat{D}C = 90°$ Line from cent bisects ch
       $M\hat{E}C + M\hat{D}C = 180°$

      ∴ MDCE is a cyclic quad   Opp. ∠s of quad
                                        supplementary

OR

       $M\hat{E}C = 90°$ Tan ⊥ rad
       $M\hat{D}A = 90°$ Line from cent bisects ch
       $M\hat{E}C = M\hat{D}A$

      ∴ MDCE a cyclic quad   Ext. ∠ quad = int. opp. ∠
                                                (3)

6.2 $MD^2 = MB^2 - DB^2$ Pythagoras △MBD
       $MC^2 = MD^2 + DC^2$ Pythagoras △MDC

      ∴ $MC^2 = MB^2 - DB^2 + DC^2$ (3)

6.3 DB = 30   Given
  MB = 40   Radii
  $MC^2 = (40)^2 + (50)^2 - (30)^2$
  $ = 3\,200$
  $MC = 40\sqrt{2} = 56{,}57$
  $MC^2 = ME^2 + CE^2$ Pythagoras
  $CE^2 = 3\,200 - 1\,600$
  $CE = 40$ mm

  OR

  $MC^2 = CE^2 + ME^2 - 2CE \cdot ME \cdot \cos M\hat{E}C$
  $3\,200 = CE^2 + (40)^2 - 2CE(40)\cos 90°$
  $ = CE^2 + 1\,600$
  $CE^2 = 3\,200 - 1\,600$
  $CE^2 = 1\,600$
  $CE = 40$ mm   (4)

  Total: 40

Test C (page 178)

1.1 FM : MC = 2 : 1   M is the centroid   (1)

1.2 GE ∥ AD   In △FDA, FG = GA and FE = ED
  FK = KC   In △FDC, FE = ED and EK = DC
  ∴ FK : KC = 1 : 1   (5)

1.3 $FK = \frac{1}{2}FC$ FK = KC, proved
  $MC = \frac{1}{3}FC$ FM : MC = 2 : 1, proved
  ∴ $KM = \left(1 - \frac{1}{2} - \frac{1}{3}\right)FC$
  ∴ $FK : KM = \frac{1}{2} : \frac{1}{6}$
  $= 3 : 1$ (4)

1.4 In △GKM and △DCM:
  1. $G\hat{M}K = D\hat{M}C$ Vertically opp. ∠s
  2. $K\hat{G}M$ = alternate $M\hat{D}C$ GE ∥ AD
  ∴ △GKM ||| △DCM   ∠, ∠
  ∴ $\frac{GM}{DM} = \frac{KM}{CM} = \frac{1}{2}$ 1.3

  $\frac{\text{Area } \triangle GKM}{\text{Area } \triangle DCM} = \frac{\frac{1}{2} GM \cdot KM \sin G\hat{M}K}{\frac{1}{2} MD \cdot MC \sin C\hat{M}D}$

  $= \frac{GM \cdot KM}{DM \cdot MC} = \frac{1}{2} \cdot \frac{1}{2}$ $G\hat{M}K = C\hat{M}D$; proved

  $= \frac{1}{4}$ (6)

2.1 In △s KZS and SRP:

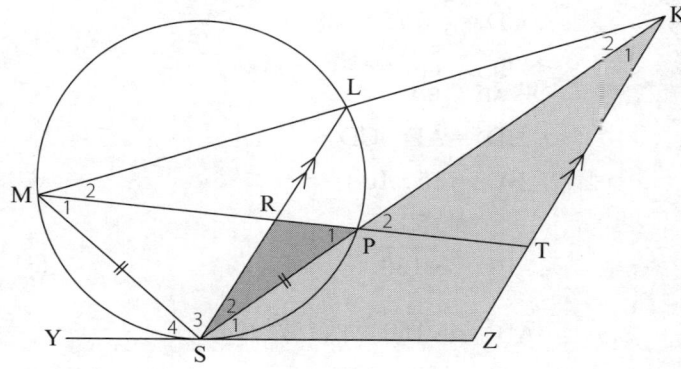

  $\hat{K}_1 = \hat{S}_2$ Alt. ∠s, RS ∥ KZ
  $\hat{S}_1 = \hat{M}_1$ Tangent ZS, chord PS
  $= \hat{P}_1$ SM = SP
  ∴ △KZS ||| △SRP   ∠, ∠   (4)

2.2 In △s KPT and KSZ:
  $\hat{K}_1$ common
  $\hat{P}_2 = \hat{P}_1$ Vert. opp. ∠s
  $= \hat{S}_1$ Proved in 2.1
  ∴ △KPT ||| △KSZ   ∠, ∠
  ∴ $\frac{PK}{KS} = \frac{KT}{KZ}$
  ∴ KT · KS = KP · KZ

  OR

  $\hat{S}_1 = \hat{P}_1$ Proved in 2.1
  ∴ PT ∥ SZ   Alt. ∠s equal
  ∴ $\frac{KP}{KS} = \frac{KT}{KZ}$ PT ∥ SZ
  ∴ KT · KS = KP · KZ   (4)

2.3 $\hat{K}_1 = \hat{S}_2$ Alt. ∠s KZ ∥ LS
  $= \hat{M}_2$ Chord LP
  ∴ $\hat{K}_1 = \hat{M}_2$
  ∴ TK is tangent to circle KMP   (4)

2.4 △TKP ||| △TMK   ∠, ∠
  ∴ $\frac{TK}{TM} = \frac{TP}{TK}$
  ∴ $TK^2 = TM \cdot TP$
  ∴ $TK = \sqrt{TM \cdot TP}$ (4)

3.1 In △BDA and △CDB
  $B\hat{D}A = C\hat{D}B = 90°$
  $\hat{B}_1 = \hat{C}$ Both = x
  $\hat{A} = \hat{B}_2$ Remaining angles
  △BDA ||| △CDB   equiangular   (3)

3.2 AD : DC = 3 : 2

$\therefore$ CD = $\frac{2}{3} \times 15 = 10$

But $\frac{BD}{AD} = \frac{CD}{BD}$

$\therefore$ BD^2 = AD $\cdot$ CD

BD^2 = 15 $\cdot$ 10

= 150

$\therefore$ BD = $\sqrt{150}$ (3)

3.3 AB^2 = $(\sqrt{150})^2 + (15)^2$ Pythagoras

= 150 + 225

= 375

$\therefore$ AB = $\sqrt{375}$

$\hat{E}$ = A$\hat{B}$C = 90°

$\therefore$ BC ∥ DE   Corr. ∠s

$\frac{AE}{AB} = \frac{AD}{AC}$ Proportion theorem

$\frac{AE}{\sqrt{375}} = \frac{15}{25}$

AE = $\frac{15 \times \sqrt{375}}{25} = \sqrt{135} = 3\sqrt{15}$ (6)

4.1 $\hat{Q}_3 = \hat{R}_1 = \hat{R}_2 = x$ Ext. ∠ of cyclic quad and RA bisects $\hat{R}$

$\hat{R}_2 = \hat{Q}_2 = x$ ∠s in the same segment

$\therefore \hat{Q}_2 = \hat{Q}_3$

OR

$\hat{Q}_2 + \hat{Q}_3 = \hat{R}_1 + \hat{R}_2$ Ext. ∠ of cyclic quad.

but $\hat{Q}_2 = \hat{R}_2 = \hat{R}_1$ ∠s in the same segment, RA bisects $\hat{R}$

$\therefore \hat{Q}_3 = \hat{Q}_2$

OR

$\hat{Q}_2 + \hat{Q}_2 = \hat{R}_1 + \hat{R}_2$ Ext. ∠ cyclic quad.

but $\hat{Q}_2 = \hat{R}_2$ ∠s in the same segment

$\therefore \hat{Q}_3 = \hat{R}_1$

but $\hat{R}_1 = \hat{R}_2 = \hat{Q}_1$ Given

$\therefore \hat{Q}_3 = \hat{Q}_2$

$\therefore$ AQ bisects P$\hat{Q}$B   (3)

4.2 $\hat{Q}_3 = \hat{B} = x$ ∠s opp equals sides. AQ = AB

$\hat{R}_1 = \hat{B} = x$ From 4.1

$\therefore$ TR = TB   Sides opp. equal ∠s   (2)

4.3 $\hat{P} = \hat{A}_1$ ∠ in same segment

$\hat{A}_1 = \hat{Q}_3 + \hat{B}$ Ext. ∠ △ABC = sum int. opp. ∠s

$\hat{Q}_3 + \hat{B} = 2\hat{Q}_3$ $\hat{Q}_3 = \hat{B}$ ∠s opp equal sides

$2\hat{Q}_3 = 2\hat{R}_1$ From 4.1

$2\hat{R}_1 = P\hat{R}T$ Given

OR

T$\hat{R}$P = 2x from above

$\hat{A}_1 = \hat{Q}_3 + \hat{B} = 2x$ Exterior ∠ of triangle

And $\hat{P} = \hat{A}_1 = 2x$ ∠s in the same segment

= T$\hat{R}$P   (3)

Total: 52

TOPIC 9 Statistics: Regression and correlation (page 180)

Exercise 1 (page 188)

1.1 Mean = $\frac{1649}{20}$ = 82,45, s = 6,3

1.2 Boundaries for one standard deviation on either side of the mean
82,45 – 6,3 to 82,45 + 6,3 = 76,15 to 88,75

14 learners lie within 1 standard deviation: $\frac{14}{20} \times 100 = 70\%$

70% of Ms Mthethwa's learners lie within one standard deviation of the mean.

1.3

7	1	2	5	7	7	8	9	
8	1	2	3	3	4	4	4	6	7	8
9	1	2	5					

1.4 Five-point summary:
- Lowest Score: 71
- Q_1: 77
- Q_2: 83
- Q_3: 87
- Highest Score: 95

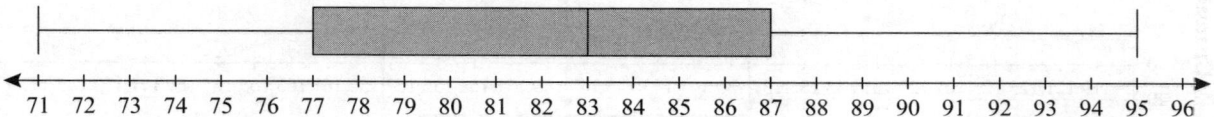

1.5 The mean is slightly lower than the median which means that the distribution is slightly negatively skewed.

1.6 The median is a more reliable measure of dispersion when a distribution is heavily skewed, and it also negates the effect of outliers. This distribution is only slightly skewed, and has no significant outliers, so it would be better to use the mean because it takes into account all the scores.

2.1 The learner results in group A are tightly clustered around the mean while the results in group B are loosely clustered around the mean. The range of results for group B is greater than those for group A, which means that the learners in group A all have a similar Maths ability while the abilities of the learners in group B range from poor results to brilliant results.

2.2 **Group A:** 68% + 2(3,5)% = 75%
In group A a score of 75% is two standard deviations above the mean, therefore only 2% of these learners will score higher than 75%. 2% of 136 = 2,72, which means that 2 or 3 learners will score above 75%.

Group B: 68% + 7% = 75%
In group B a score of 75% is one standard deviation above the mean, therefore 14% + 2% of these learners will score higher than 75%. 16% of 68 = 10,88, which means that 10 or 11 learners will score above 75%.

2.3

	Lowest score	Highest score
Group A	68 – 3(3,5) = 57,5%	68 + 3(3,5) = 78,5%
Group B	68 – 3(7) = 47%	68 + 3(7) = 89%

3.1

Height (in cm)	Frequency	Cumulative frequency
$118 \leq h < 127$	16	16
$127 \leq h < 136$	26	42
$136 \leq h < 145$	42	84
$145 \leq h < 154$	54	138
$154 \leq h < 163$	26	164
$163 \leq h < 172$	22	186
$172 \leq h < 181$	14	200

3.2, 3.3 and 3.4

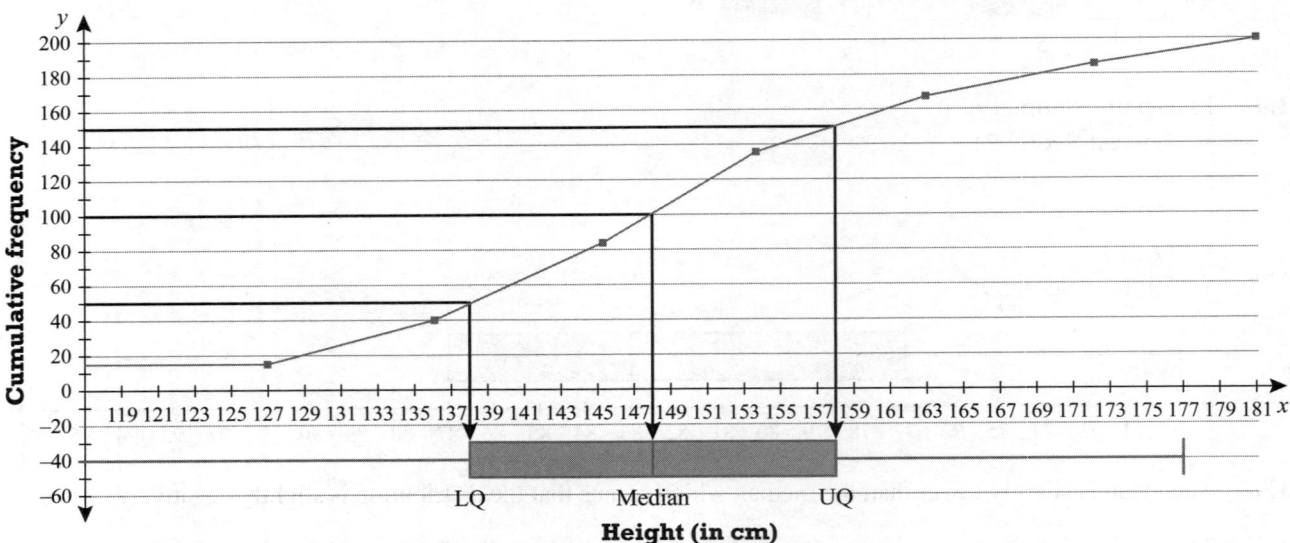

LQ ≈ 138 cm, Median ≈ 148 cm, UQ ≈ 158 cm

3.5 The heights of the learners are spread fairly evenly, i.e. it is fairly symmetrical and it approximates a normal distribution, because the distribution is not skewed to the left or the right.

3.6 The number of learners between 138 cm and 158 cm is read off directly from the ogive as shown below, i.e. there are 100 learners between 138 cm and 158 cm.

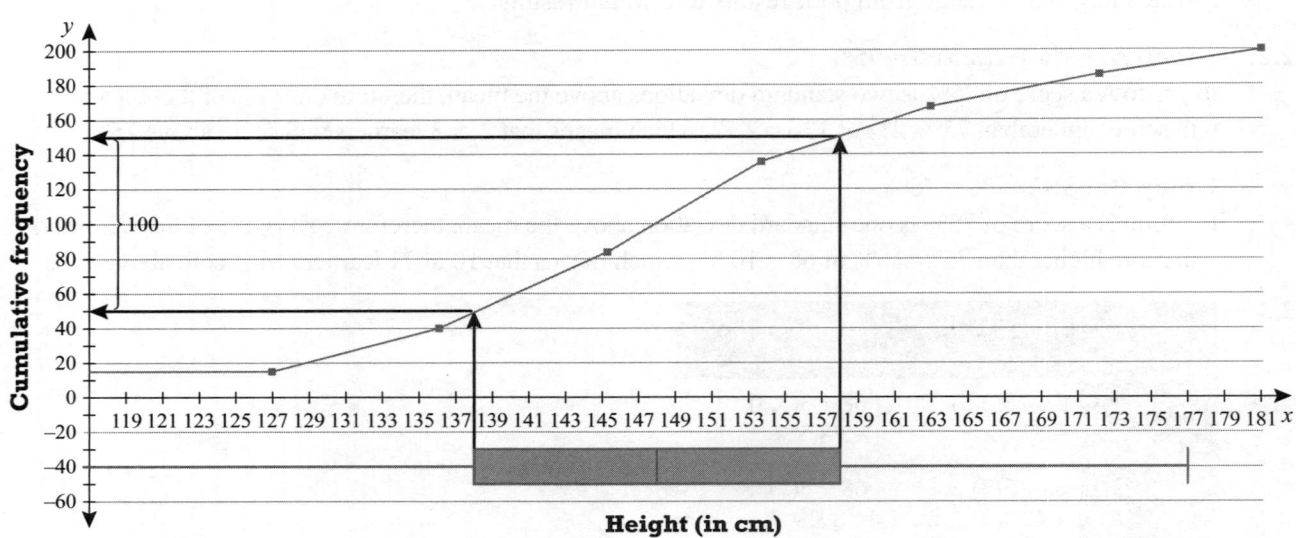

3.7 Modal height: $163 \leq h \leq 172$; median height (interval): $154 \leq h \leq 163$

3.8 **Note:** When using your calculator to find an estimate of the mean, use the midpoint of each interval as the x value.

Mean = 159,07

Height (in cm)	Frequency f	Midpoint x
$118 \leq h < 127$	2	122,5
$127 \leq h < 136$	1	131,5
$136 \leq h < 145$	6	140,5
$145 \leq h < 154$	5	149,5
$154 \leq h < 163$	10	158,5
$163 \leq h < 172$	15	167,5
$172 \leq h < 181$	8	176,5

3.9 and **3.10**

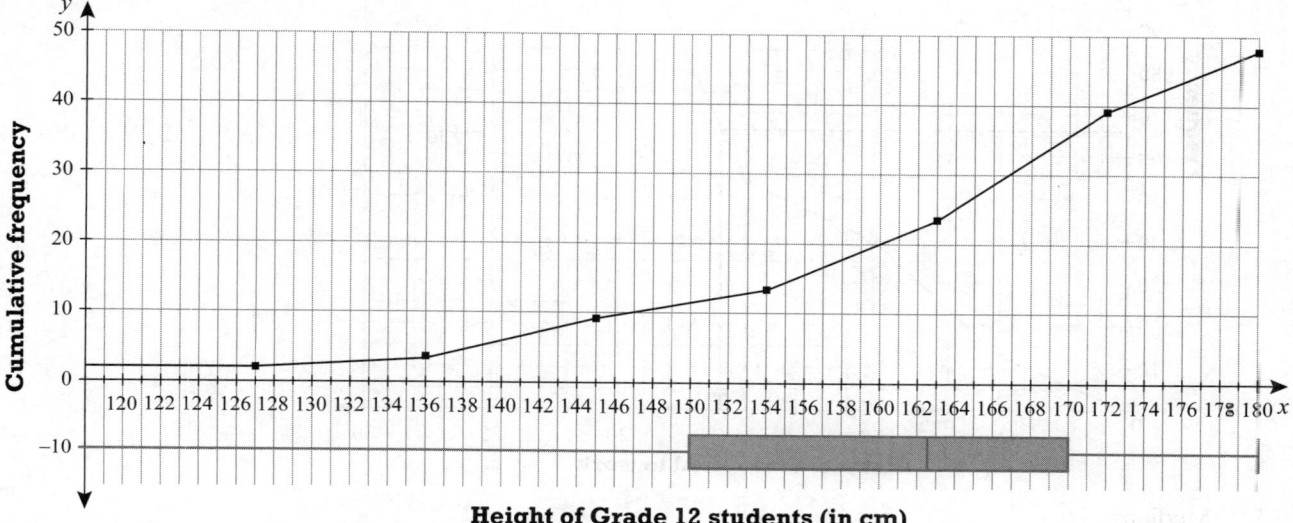

3.11 The mean score of 159,07 is lower than the median score of 162,5. This distribution is not symmetrical. It is negatively skewed and tails off to the left.

4.1 Median = 21 (Reorder from lowest to highest and find the middle most score.)

4.2 Upper quartile: 26, Lower quartile: 17.

4.3

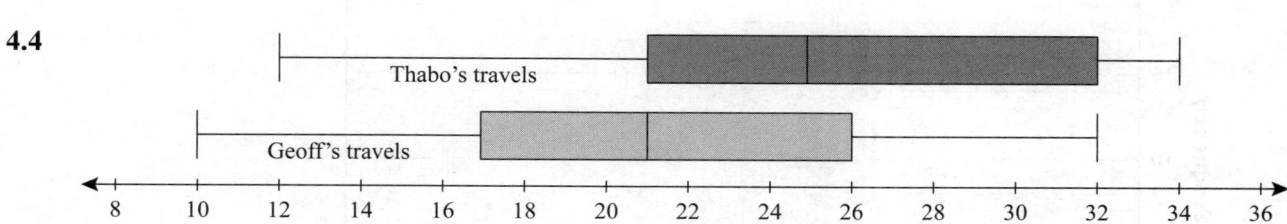

4.4

The range of the distances that Thabo and Geoff travelled is the same. (In other words the range for both sets = 22.) The IQR is slightly different. The IQR for Thabo's travels is larger than Geoff's IQR. (Thabo: 32 − 21 = 11. Geoff: 26 − 17 = 9)

Thabo's summary is heavily skewed to the left while Geoff's summary is more evenly distributed.

This suggests that Thabo has travelled greater distances than Geoff. This is supported by the fact that Thabo's median (25) is larger than Geoff's median (21) and the fact that 75% of Thabo's travels are greater than 21 km, while only 50% of Geoff's travels are above 21 km.

5.1 Median interval: $15 < x \leq 20$

5.2 Mean distance covered = 14,13

5.3 Standard deviation = 4,57

5.4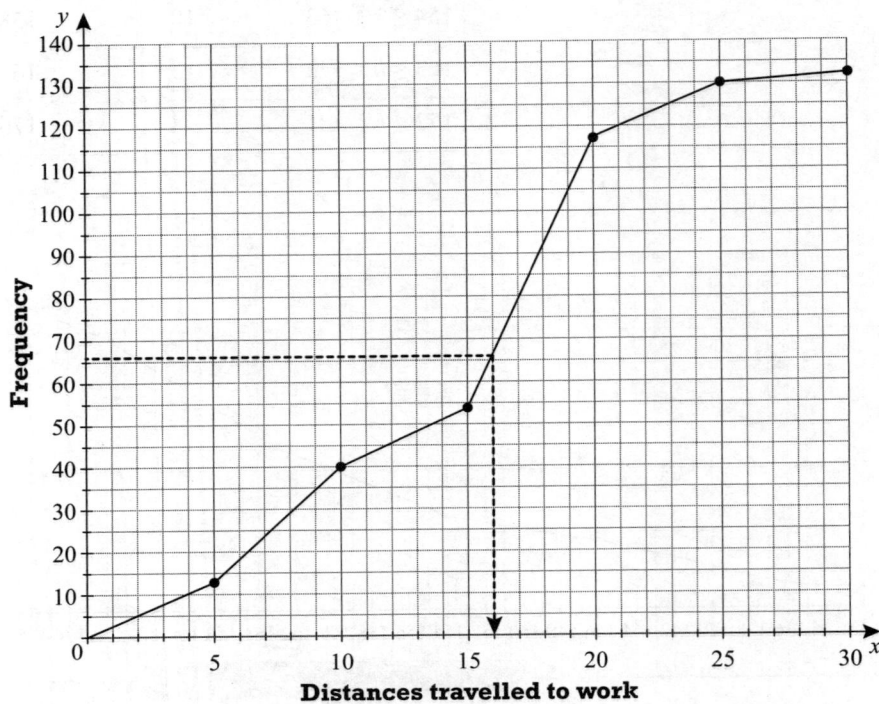

5.5 Median = 16

5.6 The median, 16, is much higher than the mean, therefore the distribution is negatively skewed.

6.1 128 lie 1 standard deviation to the left of the mean, so 16% of the teenagers sent fewer than 128 messages.

6.2 116 lies 2 standard deviations to the left of the mean and 152 one standard deviation to the right of the mean, therefore 14% plus 68% = 82% of the teenagers sent between 116 and 152 messages.

6.3 This statement is justified, because 96% of the teenagers send between 116 and 164 SMS messages per week, which is equal to 464 to 656 per month.

7.1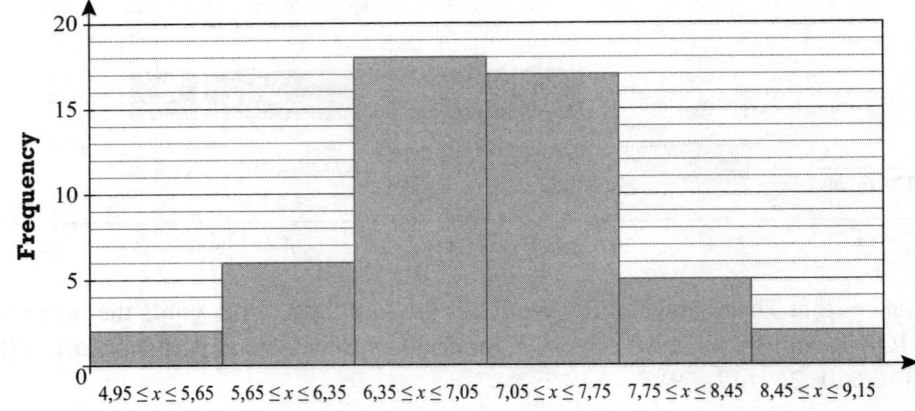

7.2 Mean: (estimated lifespan) = 7 years

7.3 s = 0,7566 years ≈ 9 months.

7.4 84% of the population are found below the first standard deviation to the right of the mean. 7 years and 9 months is the lifespan of a TV set at one standard deviation above the mean.

7.5 A guarantee of 5 years is not 100% safe because the lifespan of a TV set 3 standard deviations to left of the mean is 4 years and 9 months. If this guarantee is given the company may have to replace up to 2% of these TV sets that will not last for 5 years.

7.6 The chance of one of these TV sets lasting for $8\frac{1}{4}$ years (which is 8 years and 3 months) is only 2% because 8 years 3 months lies on the 2nd standard deviation above the mean of 7 years.

Exercise 2 (page 198)

1.1 Outlier (3; 48), relationship is strong and parabolic.

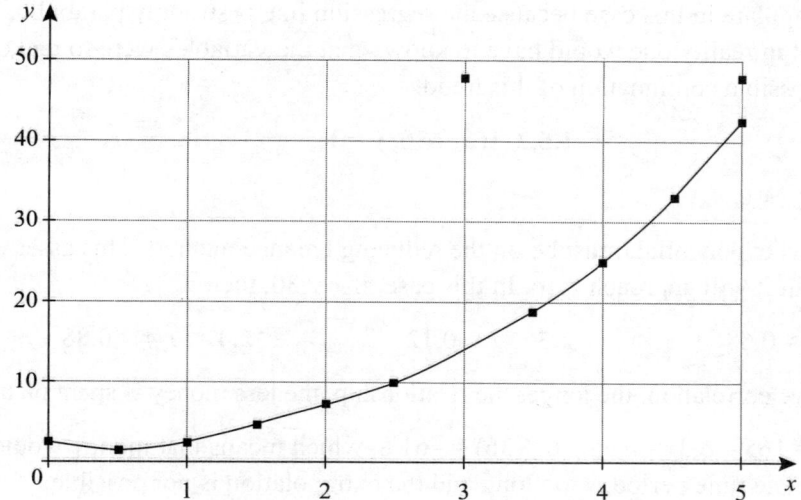

1.2 No outliers, strong, negative, linear relationship.

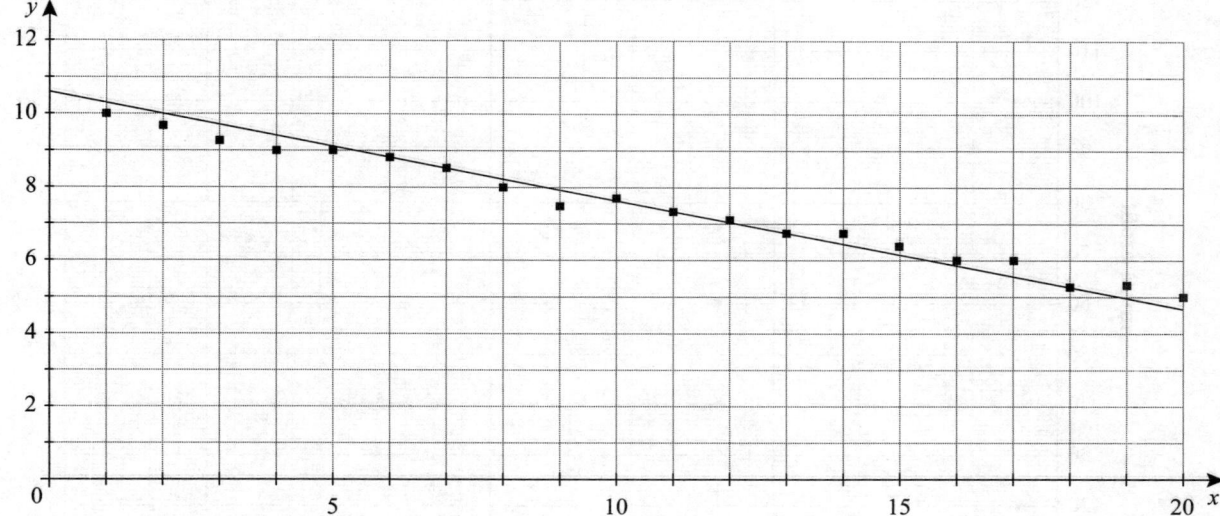

1.3 No outliers, relationship is negatively exponential.

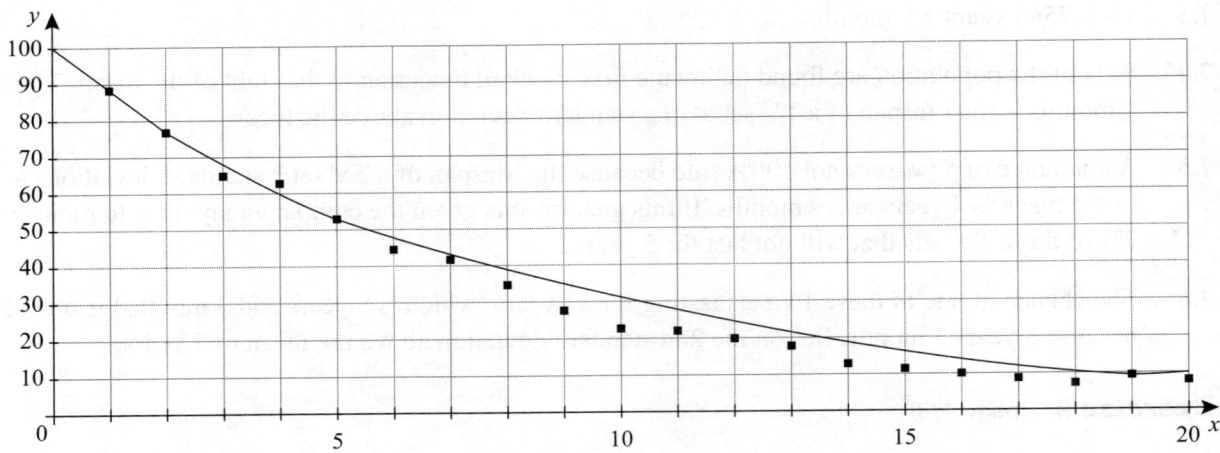

1.4.1 If $x = 2,8$, then $y = 12$

1.4.2 Mathematically one can extrapolate in this case because the regression line is strongly parabolic, so if $x = 10$, then $y = 180$. But in reality one would have to know what the variables were to make a decision with regard to the possible continuation of this trend.

1.5.1 If $x = -5$, $y = 12$ **1.5.2** If $x = 30$, $y = 1,5$

1.6.1 $y = 56$

1.6.2 Yes, depreciation, because it is exponential, must be on the reducing balance method. This asset will never have a value of zero, but it will approach zero. In this case, if $x = 30$, then $y = 2$.

2.1 $r \approx -0,7$ **2.2** $r \approx 0,68$ **2.3** $r \approx 0,12$ **2.4** $r \approx -0,88$

3.1 This relationship has a negative correlation: the longer the relationship, the less money is spent on a date.

3.2 No, if $x = 36$ months then $y = 165 - 6,3x = 165 - 6,3(36) = -61,8$, which means that money would be paid to them to go on a date. The time period is too long and the extrapolation is not possible.

4.1

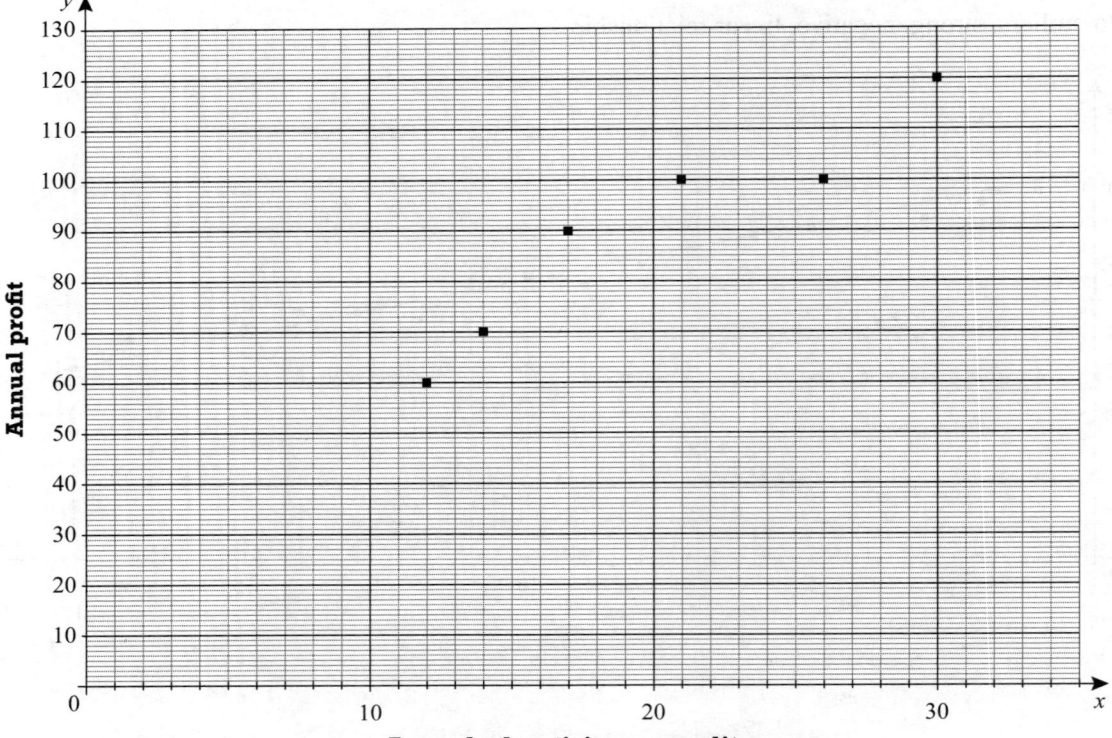

4.2 A = 30,65, B = 2,97
∴ $y = 30,65 + 2,97x$

4.3
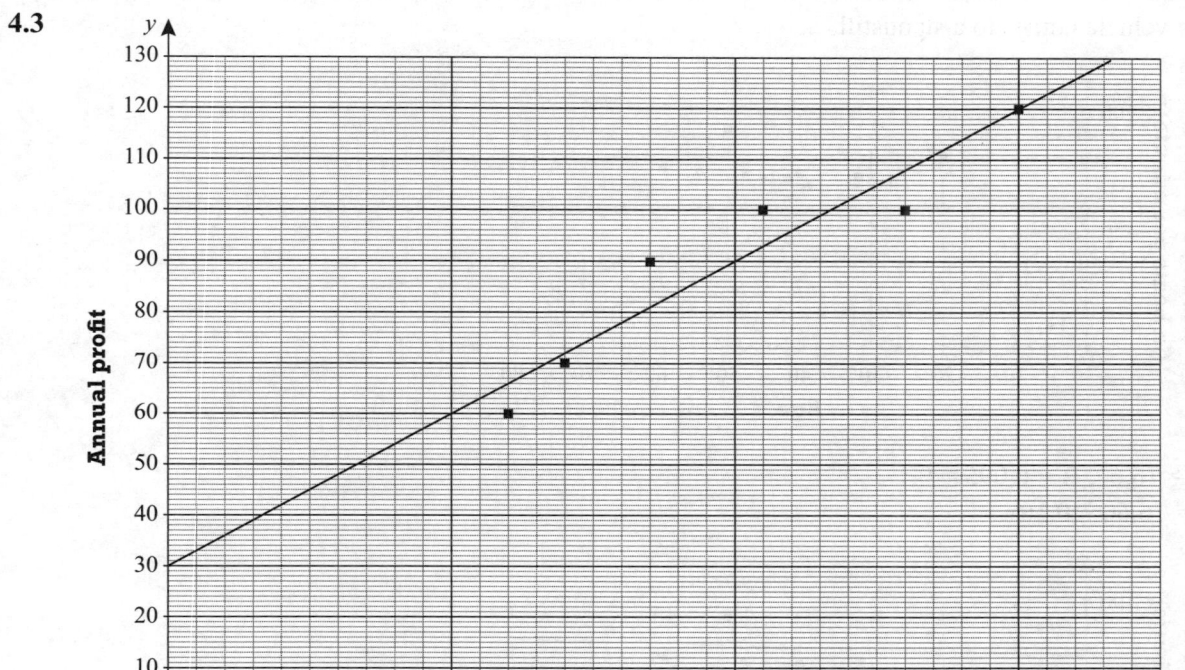

4.4 Profit = 30,65 + 2,97(25 000) = R74 280,65

4.5 $r = 0,95$

4.6 A strong positive relationship exists between annual profit and annual advertising expenditure, because the correlation coefficient is 0,95, with 1,00 being the strongest possible positive correlation.

5.1 A strong linear positive correlation.

5.2 A = −17,14, B = 0,86
$y = -17,14 + 0,86x$

5.3
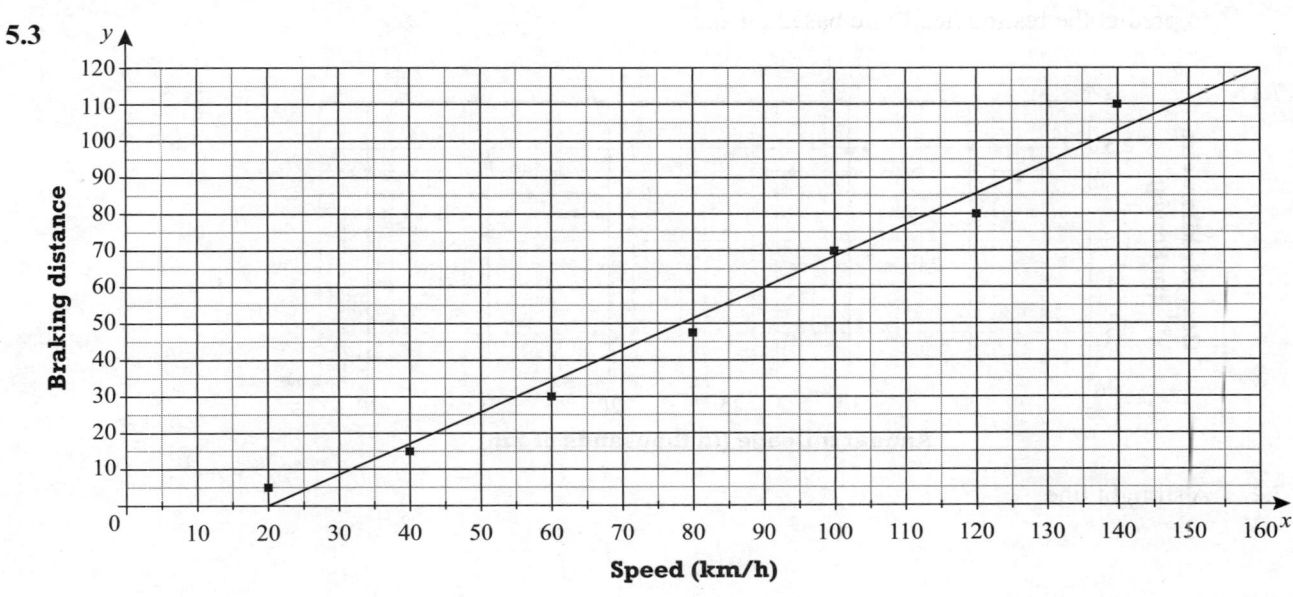

5.4 $r = 0,99$

5.5 There is a very high positive correlation. The faster you travel, the greater the braking distance before the vehicle comes to a standstill.

6.1
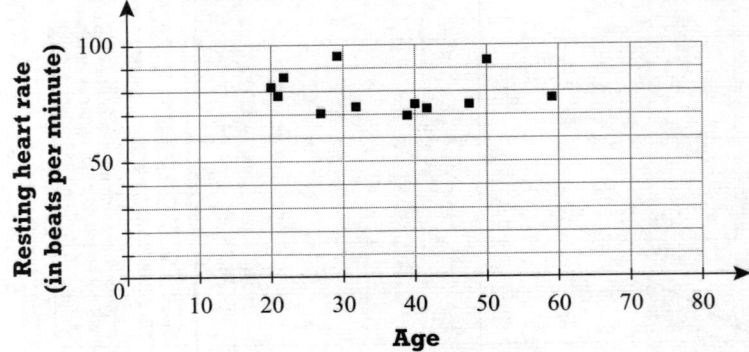

6.2 A = 76,60, B = 0,095 = 0,1
$y = 76,60 + 0,10x$.

6.3
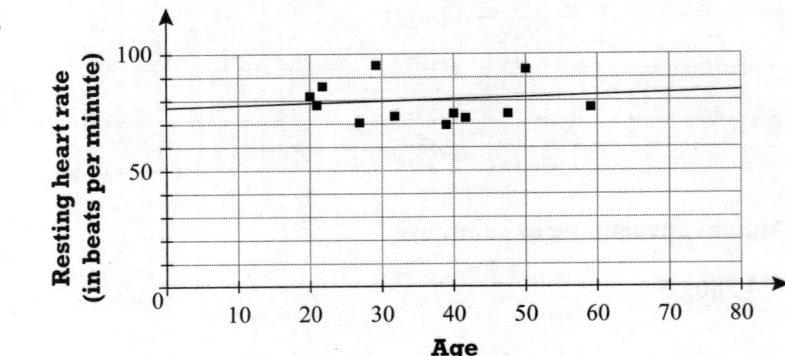

6.4 $r = 0,14$

6.5 A weak positive correlation exists between age and resting heart rate, because the correlation coefficient is positive but close to zero. This suggests that there is an insignificant relationship between age and resting heart rate.

6.6 No. The value of the correlation coefficient is so close to zero that it is unreliable and cannot be used to predict the resting heart rate based on age.

7.1
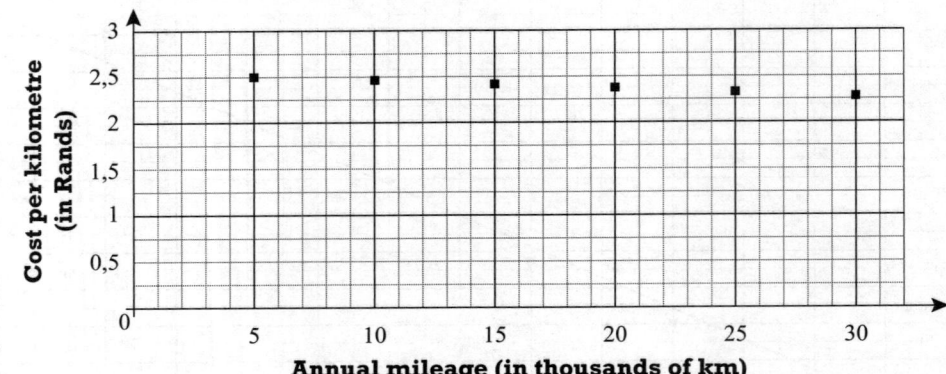

7.2 A straight line.

7.3 Line of best fit: $y = 2{,}56 - 0{,}01x$

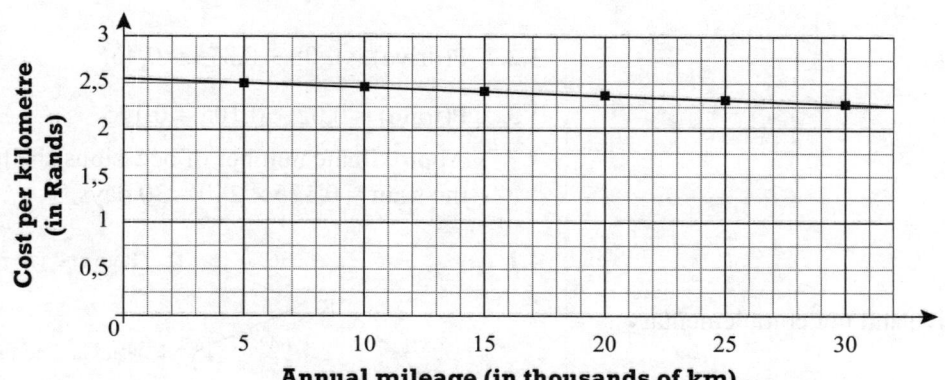

7.4 $r = -0{,}995$. A strong negative correlation exists between these two sets of data. This means that there is a strong inverse relationship between the mileage of the new car and the cost to maintain it, i.e. as the mileage increases, the cost to maintain the car decreases.

7.5 Cost per km for a car with 45 000 on the clock: $y = 2{,}56 - 0{,}01(45) = R2{,}11$

Total cost: $45\,000 \times R2{,}11 = \approx R94\,950{,}00$

TOPIC 10 Counting and probability (page 202)

Exercise 1 (page 205)

1. independent
2. dependent
3. independent
4. independent
5. mutually exclusive and not complementary

Exercise 2 (page 206)

1.1 P(Blue and Yellow) = $\frac{18}{24} \times \frac{6}{24} = \frac{3}{16} = 0{,}1875$

1.2 P(Blue and Yellow) without replacement
$= \frac{18}{24} \times \frac{6}{23}$
$= \frac{9}{46} = 0{,}1957$

2.1 P(even and less than 3) = $\frac{3}{6} \times \frac{2}{6} = \frac{1}{6}$

2.2 P(sum of numbers is greater than 5) = $\frac{26}{36} = \frac{13}{18}$

Draw a diagram:

	1	2	3	4	5	6	Die 1
1	2	3	4	5	6	7	
2	3	4	5	6	7	8	
3	4	5	6	7	8	9	
4	5	6	7	8	9	10	
5	6	7	8	9	10	11	
6	7	8	9	10	11	12	
Die 2							

3.1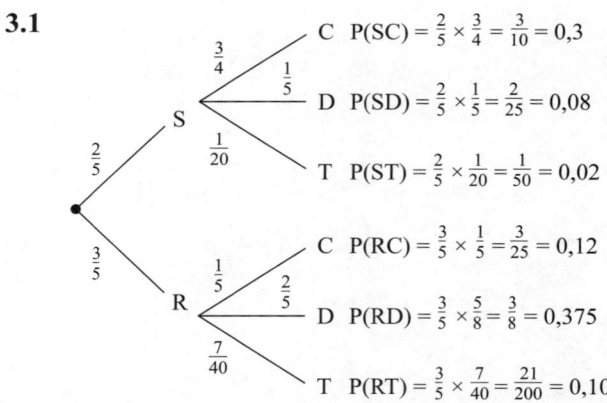

C P(SC) = $\frac{2}{5} \times \frac{3}{4} = \frac{3}{10} = 0{,}3$

D P(SD) = $\frac{2}{5} \times \frac{1}{5} = \frac{2}{25} = 0{,}08$

T P(ST) = $\frac{2}{5} \times \frac{1}{20} = \frac{1}{50} = 0{,}02$

C P(RC) = $\frac{3}{5} \times \frac{1}{5} = \frac{3}{25} = 0{,}12$

D P(RD) = $\frac{3}{5} \times \frac{5}{8} = \frac{3}{8} = 0{,}375$

T P(RT) = $\frac{3}{5} \times \frac{7}{40} = \frac{21}{200} = 0{,}105$

3.2.1 P(SD) = 0,08

3.2.2 P(drive) = 0,08 + 0,375 = 0,455

3.3 P(train) = 0,02 + 0,105 = 0,125

Approximate number of occasions she takes the train = 0,125 × 240 = 30 days.

4.1

```
            36%   F   Rain and fall
      R
65%      64%   NF  Rain and no fall

         12%   F   No rain and fall
35%  NR
         88%   NF  No rain and no fall
```

4.2 P(no fall) = $\left(\frac{65}{100} \times \frac{64}{100}\right) + \left(\frac{35}{100} \times \frac{88}{100}\right) = \frac{181}{250}$

4.3 P(fall and no rain) = $\frac{35}{100} \times \frac{12}{100} = \frac{21}{500} = 0{,}042$

Exercise 3 (page 207)

1.1 $10 \times 10 \times 10 \times 10 = 10\,000$

1.2 $10 \times 9 \times 8 \times 7 = 5\,040$

2. $26 \times 26 \times 10 \times 10 = 67\,600$

3. The option where four-character codes are formed by using two letters and two digits gives the most possible combinations or codes.

Exercise 4 (page 208)

1.1 P(not taken a loan) = $\frac{4\,629}{10\,730} = 0{,}43$

1.2 P(taken a loan and a postgraduate) = $\frac{1\,879}{10\,370}$
$= 0{,}18$

1.3 P(not taken a loan and undergraduate) = $\frac{3\,898}{10\,730}$
$= 0{,}36$

2. Let the event UG represent an undergraduate and L represent taking a loan.

P(UG and L) = $\frac{4\,222}{10\,730}$
$= 0{,}39$

P(UG) × P(L) = $\frac{8\,120}{10\,730} \times \frac{6\,101}{10\,730}$
$= 0{,}43$

The event 'being an undergraduate' and 'has taken a loan' are NOT independent because P(UG and L) ≠ P(UG) × P(L).

Exercise 5 (page 209)

1.1

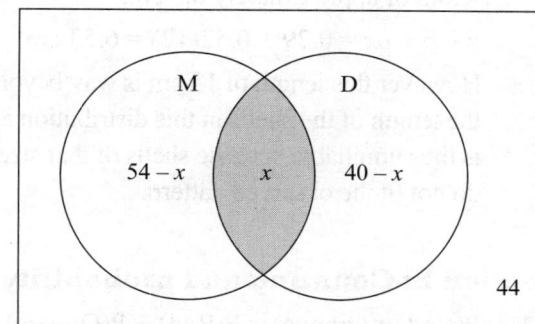

1.2 Total number of learners is 120.
$120 = 54 - x + x + 40 - x + 44$
$120 = 138 - x$
$x = 138 - 120$
$= 18$
P(mathematics and drama) $= \frac{18}{120} = 0{,}15$

1.3 P(no maths by drama learners) $= \frac{40-18}{40} = 0{,}55$

1.4 For independent events:
P(maths) × P(drama) = P(maths and drama)
P(maths) $= \frac{54}{120} = \frac{9}{20}$
P(drama) $= \frac{40}{120} = \frac{1}{3}$
P(maths and drama) $= \frac{18}{120} = \frac{3}{20}$
P(maths) × P(drama) $= \frac{9}{20} \times \frac{1}{3} = \frac{3}{20}$
$=$ P(maths and drama)
∴ The events are independent.

2.1

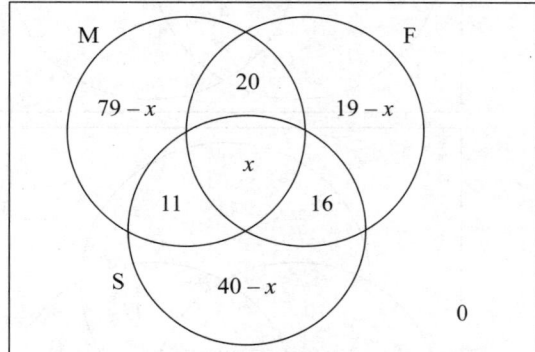

2.2 $79 - x + 20 + x + 11 + 19 - x + 16 + 40 - x = 173$
$185 - 2x = 173$
$x = 6$

OR

232 complaints and 173 people in total
94 complaints from 47 people
138 complaints from remaining 126 people

For the two to be equal:
$126 - x = 138 - 3x$
$2x = 12$
$x = 6$

OR

$110 + 55 + 67 = 232$
$2x + 20 + 11 + 16 = 232 - 173$
$2x + 47 = 59$
$2x = 12$
$x = 6$

2.3 P(at least two complaints)
$= \frac{11 + 20 + 6 + 16}{173}$
$= \frac{53}{173}$
$= 0{,}31 \ (0{,}30635838)$

OR 30,64 %

Exercise 6 (page 210)

1.1 5!   **1.2** 11!   **1.3** 4!   **1.4** 2!

2.1 $5 \times 4 \times 3 \times 2 \times 1 = 120$

2.2 $6 \times 5! = 6 \times 120 = 720$

2.3 $3 \times 2 \times 1 = 6$

2.4 $4 \times 3! = 4 \times 6 = 24$

2.5 $\frac{7!}{4!} = \frac{7 \times 6 \times 5 \times 4 \times 3 \times 2 \times 1}{4 \times 3 \times 2 \times 1} = 7 \times 6 \times 5 = 210$

2.6 $\frac{6!}{4!} = 6 \times 5 = 30$

3. $5 \times 4 \times 3 \times 2 \times 1 = 120$ ways

4. $4 \times 3 \times 2 \times 1 = 24$ ways

5. $8 \times 7 \times 6 \times 5 \times 4 \times 3 \times 2 \times 1 = 40\ 320$ ways

Test A (page 211)
Section A: Regression and correlation

1.1 Mean $= \frac{42{,}4}{10} = 4{,}24$ cm   (2)

1.2 Five-point summary: Lowest score: 3,2
First quartile: 3,6
Median: 4,3
Upper quartile: 4,7
Highest score: 5,2   (5)

Box and whisker plot:

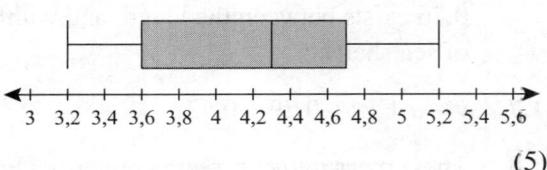

(5)

1.3 The distribution is asymmetrical and is negatively skewed, i.e. it tails off to the left. The median is higher than the mean. (4,24 < 4,3)
The IQR of 1,1 shows us that the distribution is fairly spread out around the median, i.e. it is not tightly clustered. There are no outliers. (3)

1.4

Length (in cm)	$(x_i - \bar{x})$	$(x_i - \bar{x})^2$
3,2	–1,04	1,0816
3,6	–0,64	0,4096
5,0	0,76	0,5776
4,1	–0,14	0,0196
4,3	0,06	0,0036
4,7	0,46	0,2116
3,4	–0,84	0,7056
5,2	0,96	0,9216
4,6	0,36	0,1296
4,3	0,06	0,0036
		4,064

Standard deviation $= \sqrt{\dfrac{\sum f(x - \bar{x})^2}{n}}$

$= \sqrt{\dfrac{4,064}{10}}$

$= 0,6374 \ldots$ (4)

1.5

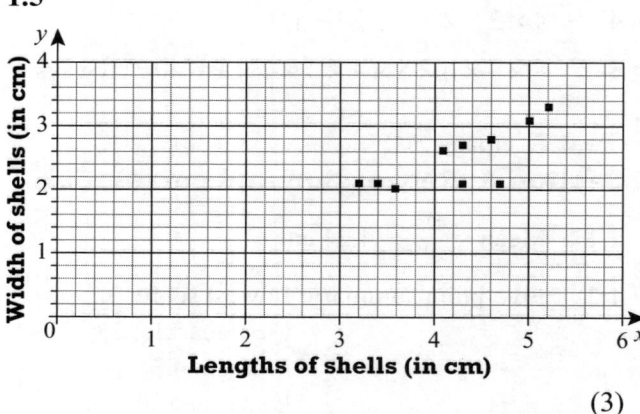

(3)

1.6 The correlation coefficient is $r = 0,76$. A relatively strong positive correlation of 0,76 exists between the length and width of sea shells. (2)

1.7 $y = a + bx = 0,29 + 0,52x$ (2)

1.8 These measurements seem unrealistic. From extrapolation, according to the regression line, a shell with a length of 12 cm should have a width of approximately 6,5 cm.
$y = a + bx = 0,29 + 0,52(12) = 6,53$ cm
However this length of 12 cm is way beyond the length of the shells in this distribution and is thus unreliable because shells of that size do not fit the observed pattern. (4)

[25]

Section B: Counting and probability

2.1 P(Red or Orange) = P(Red) + P(Orange)
$= \dfrac{28}{75} + \dfrac{26}{75} = 0,72$ (3)

2.2 P(not Orange) = 1 – P(Orange)
$= 1 - \dfrac{26}{75} = 0,653$ (3)

2.3 P(green then red without replacement)
$= \dfrac{21}{75} \times \dfrac{28}{74} = 0,106$ (3)

[9]

3.1 Let N represent learners reading the *National Geographic* magazine, G represents learners reading the *Getaway* magazine and L represents learners reading the *Leadership* magazine.

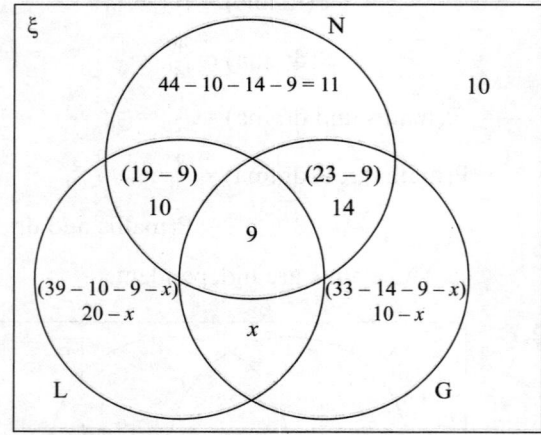

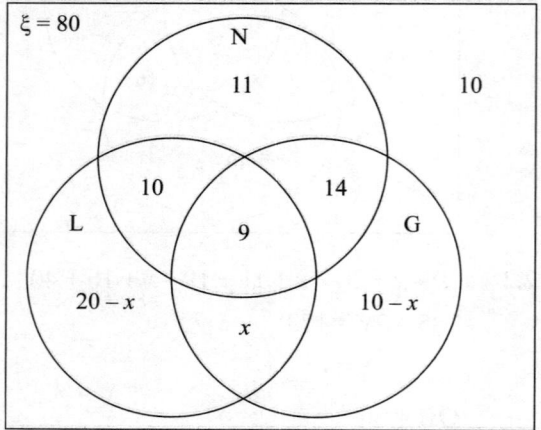

(5)

3.2 6 read at least one magazine (given):
x in the equations in either L or G could

be solved to give an answer of 6. If the equation in L is solved, it gives $x = 14$; but that will result in a negative answer in G. Therefore the equation in G should be solved:
$33 - 14 - 9 - x = 6$
$x = 4$ (3)

3.3 $80 - (11 + 10 + 9 + 14 + 16 + 4 + 6) = 10$
10 learners did not read any magazine. (1)

3.4 P(learner reads at least two magazines)
$= \frac{4 + 14 + 10 + 9}{80} = 0{,}463$ (3)
[12]

4.1 P(smoke detected by device A or device B)
= P(smoke detected by A)
+ P(smoke detected by B)
− P(smoke detected by both)
= 0,95 + 0,98 − 0,94
= 0,99 (3)

4.2 P(smoke not detected) = 1 − 0,99 = 0,01 (1)
[4]
Total: 50

Test B (page 212)
Section A: Regression and correlation

1.1 A car with a price of R163 000 lies one standard deviation above the mean:
R135 000 + R28 000 = R163 000

This selling price lies on the 69th percentile, because 0,1% + 0,5% + 1,7% + 4,4% + 9,2% + 15% + 19,1% + 19,1% = 69,1% (2)

1.2 R107 000 and R163 000 lie on the respective boundaries of one deviation on either side of the mean:
R135 000 − R28 000 = R107 000,
and R135 000 + R28 000 = R163 000.

The percentage of all sales that lie between −1 and +1 standard deviation = 2(15% + 19,1%) = 68,2%. Therefore 68,2% of Mr Zondi's sales lie in the R107 000 to R163 000 price bracket. This statement is correct because close to 70% of all of his sales lie in this price bracket. (3)

1.3 R220 000 lies just above the 3rd standard deviation above the mean of R135 000. Only 0,1% of all of Mr Zondi's sales lie above R219 000.
0,1% represents a 1 in 1 000 chance, therefore, theoretically he would have to sell 1000 cars to have sold one car in this price bracket. (3)

1.4 R135 000 − 28 000 − 14 000 = R93 000.
R93 000 lies −1,5 standard deviations below the mean.
0,1% + 0,5% + 1,7% + 4,4% = 6,7%. 6,7% of 200 = 13,4. Mr Zondi sold 13 cars in this price bracket. (4)
[12]

2.1 A. The line is above all points. (2)

2.2 E. (1)

2.3 D. The line goes above the points for the lighter eggs and below the point for the heavier eggs. (2)

2.4 B. (1)

2.5 C. The line goes through the majority of the points. (2)

2.6 These values are approximate:
Gradient $= \frac{8}{16} \approx 0{,}5$, y intercept ≈ 32
$\therefore y = 32 + 0{,}5x$ (2)
[10]

Section B: Counting and probability

3.1

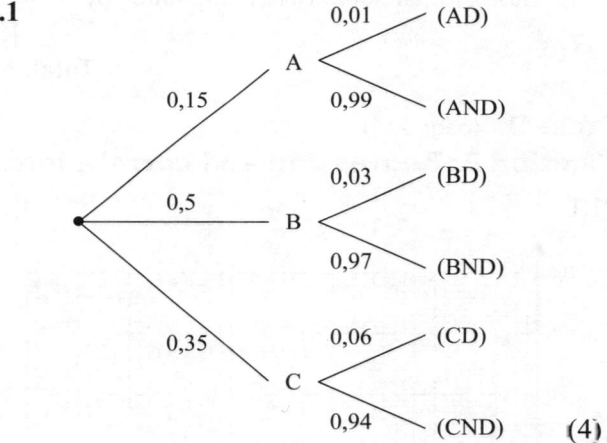

3.2.1 P(BND) = 0,5 × 0,97 = 0,485 (3)

3.2.2 P(D)
= 0,15 × 0,01 + 0,5 × 0,03 + 0,35 × 0,06
= 0,0375 (3)
[10]

4.1 12 × 11 × 10 × 9 × 8 × 7 × 6 × 5 × 4 × 3 × 2 × 1
= 12!
= 479 001 600 different ways. (2)

> **Remember**
> 12! means 12 factorial, which means 12 × 11 × 10 …, as given above.

4.2 $10 \times 9 \times 8 \times 7 \times 6 \times 5 \times 4 \times 3 \times 2 \times 1$
$= 10! = 3\,628\,800$. (2)

4.3 The articles from each company can be arranged in 4! ways.
The companies can be arranged in 3! ways.
So the articles can be arranged in
$4! \cdot 3!$ ways $= 24 \times 6 = 144$ ways. (3)
[7]

5.1 Number of codes
$= 26 \times 26 \times 26 \times 26 \times 10 \times 10 = 45\,697\,600$ (3)

5.2 Number of codes
$= 26 \times 25 \times 24 \times 23 \times 10 \times 9 = 32\,292\,000$ (3)
[6]

6.1 $a = 65$, $b = 50$, $c = 135$ and $d = 92$. (2)

6.2 P(Happy) $= \frac{135}{200} = 0{,}675$ (1)

6.3 P(Kaizer Chiefs supporter and Unhappy)
$= \frac{42}{200} = 0{,}21$ (1)

6.4 Orlando Pirates – Any valid answer where the emphasis is placed on more of their supporters being happy after a match and less of their supporters being unhappy. (1)
[5]
Total: 50

Test C (page 215)
Section A: Regression and correlation

1.1

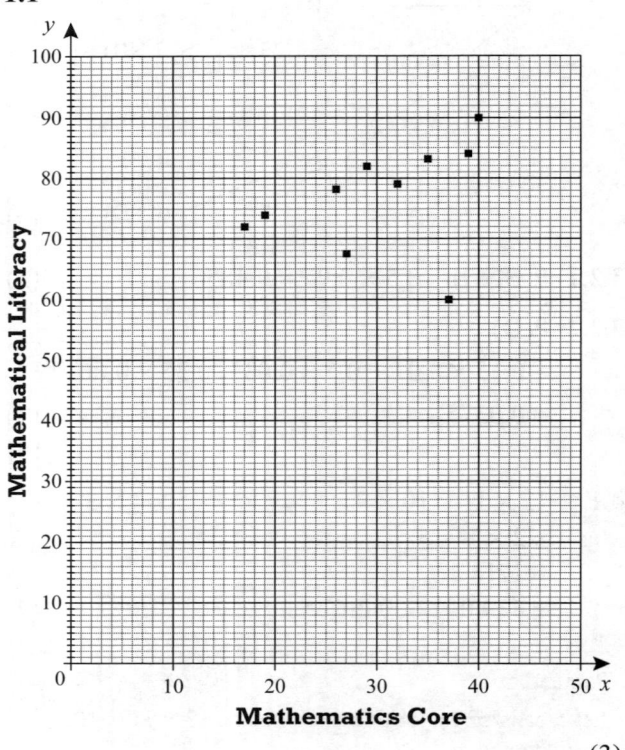

(3)

1.2 A = 65,27, B = 0,39
$\therefore y = 65{,}27 + 0{,}39x$ (2)

1.3 $r = 0{,}3561 \approx 0{,}36$ (1)

1.4 Moderately strong with a low positive r value. (2)

1.5 As can be seen from the scatter plot, candidate 9 is the possible outlier. (1)

1.6 Using the regression equation we can predict that David will score approximately 80% on Maths Literacy.
$y = 65{,}27 + 0{,}39(38) = 80{,}09\%$
Advise him to change because he is likely to make the 80% which is the minimum requirement.
On the other hand we can advise him to stay on Core Maths and work harder, because he is only 2% from the required minimum. (3)
[12]

2.1 150 (1)

2.2 Total amount needed: R1 590 000 (1)

2.3 Mean salary = R10 600 (2)

2.4 No. The distribution is heavily skewed. Only 10 employees in this company earn more than the mean salary of R10 600. The majority, 140 of the employees, earn below this amount. It is therefore not a good indicator of the average monthly salary earned by an employee. (2)

2.5 Five-point summary:
Lowest: R5 000
First quartile: R6 000
Median: R7 500
Third quartile: R10 000
Highest score: R150 000
Or 110 of the employees earn R7 500 or less. (2)

2.6 The median is a better descriptor than the mean because 50% of the employees earn R7 500 or less. But in this case the mode of R6 000 is actually the best descriptor of the average salary earned because 43% of these employees earn R6 000. (2)
[10]

3.1 21 minutes is 1 standard deviation away from the mean (to the left). Therefore 34% of the pizzas are delivered in between 21 and 24 minutes. (2)

3.2 15 minutes is the 3rd standard deviation to the left of the mean. 27 minutes is 1 standard deviation to the right of the mean, therefore 50% + 34% = 84% of the pizzas are delivered in between 15 and 27 minutes. (3)

3.3 The required 2% is the area found to the right of the 2nd standard deviation on the right hand side of the mean. Maximum time allowed for delivery should be:
24 + 2(3) = 30 minutes. (3)

[8]

Section B: Counting and probability

4.1

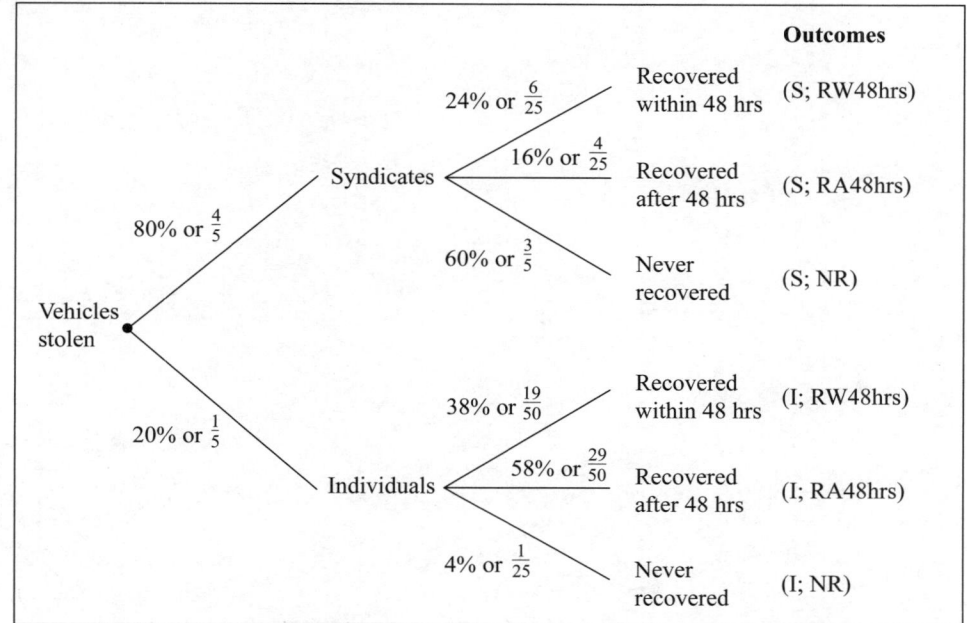

(5)

4.2 P(S; RW48hrs) = $\frac{80}{100} \times \frac{24}{100} = \frac{1920}{10\,000}$
= 0,192
= 19,2% (0,19)

OR

P(S; RW48hrs) = $\frac{4}{5} \times \frac{6}{25} = \frac{24}{125}$ (2)

4.3 P(stolen and not recovered):
= $\left(\frac{80}{100} \times \frac{60}{100}\right) + \left(\frac{20}{100} \times \frac{4}{100}\right)$
= 0,488 = 48,8% (0,49)

OR

P(stolen and not recovered):
= $\left(\frac{4}{5} \times \frac{3}{5}\right) + \left(\frac{1}{5} \times \frac{1}{25}\right) = \frac{12}{25} + \frac{1}{125} = \frac{61}{125}$ (3)

[10]

5.1 $a = 450$, $b = 319$, $c = 298$, $d = 748$ (4)

5.2 P(Female who has not broken a limb)
= $\frac{298}{1530}$
= $\frac{149}{765} = 0,19$ (2)

5.3 P(Female and broken a limb)
= $\frac{450}{1530}$
= $\frac{5}{17}$
= 0,2941176471…
= 0,29

P(Female) × P(Broken a limb)
= $\frac{748}{1530} \times \frac{913}{1530}$
= 0,29

The events of being female and having broken a limb are independent. (4)

[10]

Total: 50